THE PAPERS OF

FREDERICK LAW OLMSTED

CHARLES CAPEN McLAUGHLIN

Editor in Chief

THE PAPERS OF

FREDERICK LAW OLMSTED

VOLUME I

THE FORMATIVE YEARS

1822 to 1852

CHARLES CAPEN McLAUGHLIN

Editor

CHARLES E. BEVERIDGE

Associate Editor

THE JOHNS HOPKINS UNIVERSITY PRESS
Baltimore and London

Originally published, 1977
Second printing, 1983

The Johns Hopkins University Press, Baltimore, Maryland 21218
The Johns Hopkins Press Ltd., London

Library of Congress Cataloging in Publication Data

Olmsted, Frederick Law, 1822–1903.
  The formative years, 1822 to 1852.

  (The Papers of Frederick Law Olmsted; v. 1)
  Includes index.
  1. Olmsted, Frederick Law, 1822–1903.
  2. Landscape, architects—United States—
Correspondence. 3. Landscape architects—United
States—Biography. I. Title.
SB470.05A2 1977 vol. 1 712′.08s [712′.08] 76–47378
ISBN 0–8018–1798–6

CONTENTS

ILLUSTRATIONS

ACKNOWLEDGMENTS

A LARGE EDITORIAL PROJECT depends upon the collaborative efforts of scores of people and institutions. I want to thank all those who have helped me to shape this multi-volume edition of the Frederick Law Olmsted Papers. I am grateful, initially, to the late John Merriman Gaus of Harvard, who generously shared his wide range of insights on American civilization and encouraged my interest in Olmsted when few other scholars understood his importance. In the spring of 1950, his advice led me to write my senior essay at Yale on Olmsted; there my advisers, the late David M. Potter and Howard A. Lamar, urged me on with generous enthusiasm. Christopher Tunnard and Jacqueline Tyrwhitt gave me timely support and further insight into Olmsted's importance in nineteenth-century city planning. I had the good fortune to meet Frederick Law Olmsted, Jr., on his last day at the Olmsted Associates' office in Brookline, Massachusetts. In addition to pointing me toward significant Olmsted reports, he let me use the papers there, where I had the obliging help of the firm's secretary, Stella D. Obst. Katherine MacNamara, of the Landscape Architecture Library at Harvard, guided me through those extensive collections of Olmsted's professional reports.

I shall always be deeply grateful to Laura Wood Roper, whom I met in the summer of 1950 as she was beginning her own work on Olmsted. Besides granting me access to the Olmsted Papers at the Library of Congress, she generously answered all my questions, saving me much time and effort. Ever since, she has freely shared the insights derived from her years of painstaking research.

In February 1951 I had my first look at the Olmsted Papers in the Manuscript Division of the Library of Congress and began then my reliance on the patiehce and thoroughness of the staff, who have continued to help me over the last twenty-four years. In the reading room I had the expert assistance of John De Porry, C. Percy Powell, and Katherine Brand. David C. Mearns, then Chief of the Division, went out of his way to encourage and facilitate my work on the papers as he has done ever since.

Laura Roper proposed in 1956 that I edit the Olmsted Papers for publication. The Committee on the History of American Civilization at Harvard let me start the work as a dissertation. My stepfather, Kenneth Ballard Murdock, gave uniquely practical and imaginative advice on how to proceed. He suggested that I consult Lyman H. Butterfield, editor of the Adams Papers, who gave me the wisest and most helpful advice I could possibly have had about the craft of historical editing. Now on the advisory board, he has continued to aid and encourage the project in innumerable ways.

The members of my dissertation committee understood that a pilot edition of thirty-five letters could be just as demanding an intellectual task as a conventional thesis. John M. Gaus urged me to look beyond the welter of detail and see Olmsted's broad significance. Perry G. E. Miller did his best to impart his Olympian standards of scholarship and writing. Kenneth S. Lynn assumed a role he continues on our advisory board, that of gently encouraging the editor to keep at his task and see it through.

Outside of the committee, Thomas H. Johnson, then at work on the Emily Dickinson Manuscripts, gave me much valuable advice on research problems. Lewis Mumford gave me imaginative suggestions about some particulars of Olmsted's career and helped me to understand Olmsted's contribution to city planning. I had the strong encouragement of the late Arthur M. Schlesinger, Sr., who had long been interested in Olmsted's role as a commentator on the ante-bellum South. Barbara Perkins volunteered to help me with the seemingly endless puzzles of identification and chronology, and proofread all my transcriptions for the thesis. My wife, Ann, made the first card catalog of Olmsted's writings and letters for our use. Her accurate and thorough work has been invaluable ever since. She also labored over my gnarled prose and often was able to discover what I was trying to say. As the work expanded I could count on her penetrating good sense when I was perplexed by the problems inevitable in a growing project.

I surveyed the papers in the Bancroft Library at the University of California, where the staff was most helpful. I am grateful to Helen E. Worden of the General Library, who pointed out the relevant correspondence in the University Archives. Arthur B. Waugh, Head of the Environmental Design Libraries, gave me much help with Olmsted's California work. Professor Mellior G. Scott shared his own thoughts on Olmsted and introduced me to his student, Diane Kostial McGuire, who was one of the first to point out how brilliantly Olmsted had adapted his picturesque aesthetic to the requirements of semiarid California.

While in the Bay Area I met Olmsted's descendants in Palo Alto: Charlotte Kursh, his granddaughter, and her children, Sarah Gill Bridges and

Stephen Gill. They let me see the documents, books, and pictures remaining in the family and gave permission for me to use the Olmsted letters in the files of the McLean Hospital in Waverly, Massachusetts, where Olmsted died. There, Dr. Willis H. Bower, Curator of Medical Records, let me see them and helped me to interpret the medical record.

I continued my work in Cambridge, more and more grateful to the great resources of the Widener and Houghton libraries and their courteous and obliging staffs. During my final summer, John Conway, then Master of Leverett House, generously set aside a room for my work. I finished the thesis at Stanford University, where I had my first teaching job. There I depended on the libraries of Stanford and Berkeley. The late Professor Joseph S. Davis kindly gave me the use of his study.

In the spring of 1960 Thomas J. Wilson, then of the Harvard University Press, suggested that I start work on a multi-volume edition. Florie Berger of Menlo Park organized my card index, and Theodore Marmor, one of my former Harvard students, gave me energetic research assistance for a summer. Happily, I again had the benefit of David Potter's probing counsel when he moved to Stanford from Yale. Julius P. Barclay, head of Stanford University's Division of Special Collections, greatly facilitated my search for Olmsted correspondence outside the repositories I already knew. Using the guides he made available, I was able to locate seven hundred Olmsted letters in archives throughout the country.

A year later I was able to follow up my leads on material in both public and private holdings. The late William Quentin Maxwell shared the voluminous notes he had accumulated in writing *Lincoln's Fifth Wheel*, his book on the United States Sanitary Commission, giving me the whereabouts of four hundred more letters.

Robert W. Hill, Keeper of Manuscripts at the New York Public Library, made it possible for me to make effective use of the collections with the most obliging help of his staff. Thompson M. Little, at the Microfilm Collection of the Columbia University Library, went out of his way to be of service to me. Chester M. Lewis, Archivist of the *New York Times*, granted me access to the *Times* collections and supplied me with valuable information. James J. Heslin, Director of the New-York Historical Society, aided me greatly, as did Clifford K. Shipton, Custodian of the Harvard University Archives, and W. H. Bond, Curator of Manuscripts at the Houghton Library of the Harvard College Library. My own letter searching was greatly facilitated by the tireless labors of H. Bruce Fant of the staff of the National Historical Publications and Records Commission. At the National Archives, Theodore R. Schellenberg, Assistant Archivist of the United States, Victor Gondos, Chief, Civil War Branch, and his assistant, Francis J. Heppner, helped me find many letters. I also had the aid of Stephen T. Riley, Director of the Massachusetts Historical Society, and his staff in searching their collections.

Harriet Baldwin Bryan surveyed the Smithsonian Institution's papers for me, and Wilcomb Washburn kindly arranged for me to have copies made of the correspondence that was found. Joseph Hudak and Artemus Richardson, Olmsted Associates' partners, let me explore the firm's enormous files. Their secretary, Mary Tynan, on this occasion and ever since, has been tireless and resourceful in meeting my many requests. In 1967 and 1971 the Olmsted Associates generously gave their manuscript files to the Library of Congress.

In addition to the Olmsted family, many others have aided the search for papers. The Brace family and their relatives have helped the project immensely. Gerald Warner Brace of Belmont, Massachusetts, let me copy his collection. Mrs. Hale F. Shirley lent me her Brace pictures and allowed me to copy some other materials. Mrs. Julia Barnet, Eleanor Brace, and C. Loring Brace have aided in the hunt for further letters. Mrs. Ludlow S. Bull of Litchfield, Connecticut, permitted me to copy several pertinent Kingsbury letters and suggested a look at the Mattatuck Historical Society, where we found Frederick John Kingsbury's journal, an invaluable editing tool for the project. The society allowed me to copy this journal as well.

The Olmsted project found a home at the Library of Congress when I moved to Washington to teach at The American University. Dudley Ball, chief of the Stack and Reader Division, and his assistant, Herbert Davis, made me welcome in the fall of 1964 and have continued to do so ever since. At the Manuscript Division I came to rely on John J. McDonough's expert knowledge of the library's nineteenth-century manuscript collections. Joseph D. Sullivan and Caroline F. Sung processed the later acquisitions to the Olmsted papers and helped me find my way through the new material. Mary Wolfskill, who prepared the Olmsted papers for microfilming, always accommodated my inconvenient editorial needs. I am also grateful for the many courtesies extended by Roy P. Basler, then chief of the Manuscript Division, and his successor, John Broderick, who has always offered help and counsel to the project. In the Reference Division I have saved much time and difficulty by following the prompt and well-informed suggestions of Eileen Donahue, Barbara Burkey Walsh, and Mrs. Jeffie Smith when trying to solve annotation problems.

I am grateful to the many American University students who have worked from time to time on the Olmsted Papers. Susan McDonald was the first, in the spring of 1965. She set a high standard for those to come and picked her successor, Ray E. Wilson, who replaced her that summer. From the beginning his tactful and adept assistance has spared me perplexity and saved me time. With a few interruptions, he toiled on the project until the first volume went to press, and he took on many of the administrative details as the work expanded. Jane Davidson Winer next added her editorial and research skills to the edition. She was in large part responsible for the research on Olmsted's China voyage of 1843. Later she rejoined the project and regularized the footnote form for the early chapters of Volume I, handling all the complications with aplomb.

Richard N. Wright, Director of the Onondaga Historical Association, supplied valuable information about the George Geddes family and their farm near Syracuse, New York. Eulalie Fenhagen and her son, James, did research for the first volume in Hartford, Connecticut. Patti L. Mesner did some Hartford research and also surveyed ship's records for me at Old Mystic Seaport. In the summer of 1974, E. Scott Creedy helped me annotate Olmsted's letter about Olmsted Hall in Cambridgeshire, England. The present owners, Mr. and Mrs. W. S. Kiddy, and their daughter, Mrs. K. Robert Nott, were most hospitable and gave me valuable information about the house.

Other American University students have lent their aid. Duane Ball quickly showed a talent for historical detective work. Mark Sandler cleared up questions on some of Olmsted's southern itinerary. Kenneth Ayres took on some identification problems of the 1850s. William Morrison worked at the card file. William Sweeney indexed John Olmsted's journal. Gary Weaver did lengthy transcriptions of Olmsted's newspaper letters. Richard Norment systematized the bibliographical references. David Schuyler devoted a summer helping with the final stages of Volume I, and he has added his substantial skills as a researcher and historian to the project for two years.

Pamela Hoes Cohen, who joined the project in 1966, has given the longest continuous service. She did most of the family and genealogical research used in the first volume and proved herself adept at solving identification problems that have baffled the rest of us. She also has located private collections of letters and papers. Her cheer and resourcefulness have kept the project moving even when spirits and funds were low.

Many busy historians and friends have set aside time to consult with me on questions ranging from handwriting deciphering to plans for the edition. Roy Ohrn of Governor Dummer Academy in Massachusetts cleared up some handwriting mysteries. Fred Shelley of the National Historical Publications and Records Commission gave advice on the use of microfilming and indexing. Edward C. Papenfuse of the Maryland State Archives was particularly helpful in discussing new developments in indexing. Three of my fellow editors in Washington have shared their wealth of experience with me. Stuart B. Kaufman, editor of the Samuel Gompers Papers, has enriched my understanding of the various approaches to editing. Louis R. Harlan, editor of the Booker T. Washington Papers, has freely shared his wide range of editorial experience with me. Nathan Reingold, editor of the Joseph Henry Papers, gave me a convincing demonstration of the computer's value in an editing project. Oliver W. Holmes, former Executive Director of the National Historical Publications and Records Commision, and his successors E. Berkeley Tompkins and Frank Burke, have always let me benefit from their wide acquaintance with editorial projects throughout the United States.

As the scope and significance of the edition became clearer, I found I sorely needed the services of a professional historian as associate editor. I had been in correspondence with Charles Eliot Beveridge in 1962 and had read his excellent dissertation, "Frederick Law Olmsted: The Formative Years, 1822–1865," done in 1966 at the University of Wisconsin. His skills as a social and cultural historian of the nineteenth century and his unique understanding of Olmsted's achievement as a landscape architect made him especially valuable to me. He joined the project in 1973. In addition to assuming responsibility for later volumes, he has made a substantial contribution to the first. He has reviewed and strengthened the annotation, often adding new material and pruning the old of irrelevancies. He has helped me draft and revise all the biographical sketches and chapter headnotes.

I came to know Victoria Post Ranney in 1968 when we conferred on her work concerning Olmsted's California years. I learned of her great interest in putting together the manuscript fragments Olmsted left of a book on civilization in the United States. In 1971 she agreed to join the project and become editor of the fourth volume, on Olmsted's California years. While working on the texts and annotation for it she has given me the benefit of her considerable editorial skill by reviewing all the typescript of the first volume, consulting on editorial procedures and on the general plan of the whole edition.

The project took a quantum leap forward when Frederick A. Gutheim, as chairman of the Olmsted Sesquicentennial Committee in the fall of 1971, saw the edition's scholarly significance and came to grips with its financial problems. His persistent and timely efforts meant that the editing of the Olmsted papers could move ahead as a collaborative project.

In the fall of 1971 The Johns Hopkins University Press accepted the edition for publication when, on very short notice, Howard Mumford Jones, David Levin, Roger H. Brown, Kenneth S. Lynn, and Daniel Aaron reviewed my lengthy draft of first volume materials and my plans for the succeeding series. I am most grateful that they were able to see the possible merits of the project and its potential significance in the tentative materials I gave them to read. I have depended upon these friends' encouragement and help for a long time.

During Olmsted's sesquicentennial year (1972) I renewed my acquaintance with many scholars working on Olmsted and met others for the first time. William Alex pointed up for me Olmsted's urgent relevance for present-day cities, and his sesquicentennial Olmsted exhibit at the Whitney Museum in New York brought the message home to a wider audience than ever before. Elizabeth Barlow shared her insights about New York's park planning and helped me to seek support for the project. David W. Scott of the National Gallery gave me generous encouragement when he was busy setting up the fine Olmsted exhibit. J. L. Sibley Jennings, Jr., of the Fine Arts

Commission in Washington, D. C., helped me locate papers and find support. Eleanor McPeck gave me discerning scholarly advice and helped me grapple with funding problems. I had a chance to compare notes with Albert Fein, upon whom I have always depended for encouragement and stimulating insights. Dana F. White of Atlanta and Emory universities, who has done much collaborative work on Olmsted's southern writings and post–Civil War landscaping in Atlanta, sustained me with his discerning appreciation for Olmsted's varied accomplishments. Leonard H. Gerson shared with me his writings on Olmsted's Buffalo park work. I also came to value the careful scholarship of Cynthia Zaitzevsky.

Joan Ansheles Leach, first, and then her sister, Carole J. Ansheles, helped me handle my increasingly heavy correspondence as I sought project funding and answered scholarly request. Their cheerful efficiency greatly eased my labors.

In the first year of our full-time operation on a collaborative basis, Lyman H. Butterfield, Editor Emeritus of the Adams Papers, and professors Neil Harris, Jon L. Wakelyn, and Kenneth S. Lynn agreed to form the project's advisory board. At their first meeting in the summer of 1973 they helped me formulate editorial procedures. Since then they have reviewed the work in progress, saving me from pitfalls I had not anticipated and reminding me of the needs of both scholars and a wider audience that might want to use the volumes.

As the mass of annotation and texts assumed the shape of a first volume I depended heavily on Virginia Rapport to carry on the work of ensuring the stylistic consistency of footnotes and text, smoothing out my prose, and helping with the index. Stephen Kraft provided the maps, which clarify the details of Olmsted's journeys in the 1840s and 1850s.

The staff of The Johns Hopkins University Press were always available for advice. Kenneth Arnold and Nancy Romoser helped to plan the format of the volumes. Their successors, Henry Y. K. Tom, Theresa A. Czajkowska, and JoAnn Gutin, brought the first volume through the editing process to its final form.

Nancy Goodell accomplished the enormous task of checking all the references to the first volume with great efficiency and dispatch. Judith Mc-Callum cheerfully carried out the onerous task of proofreading all the letter texts. There would have been no texts or annotations at all if I had not had skilled typists from the beginning. Helen Kmetovic of Palo Alto, California, typed my Ph.D. thesis—the nucleus of the whole project. Anne Hesse Nuss of the Garden Library at Dumbarton Oaks did early drafts of Volume I. Carol Davis and Cathy Gilbert did the first complete version of the letter texts. Dorothy Machan typed the front matter for the advisory board's review. Martha Murphy assumed the huge burden of typing the last two drafts of Volume I, working rapidly and accurately despite many last-minute changes.

ACKNOWLEDGMENTS

When I began my search for Olmsted correspondence I had the generous support of the American Philosophical Society. Later I had grants from the Faculty Development Fund of the American University to support research and provide clerical help. I also had a faculty fellowship at the Washington Center for Metropolitan Studies, followed by a year's junior fellowship in landscape architecture at the Garden Library of Dumbarton Oaks. I received further research assistance from the National Historical Publications and Records Commission, which has continued to support the project in a generous and timely fashion. Starting in 1972, major support for the project has come from the National Endowment for the Humanities with matching funds supplied by the Queene Ferry Coonley Foundation, William H. Greer, Jr., William S. Payson, the Sulzberger Foundation, Inc., the Gaylord Donnelley Foundation, Robert G. Olmsted, the D. M. Ferry Trustee Corporation, Mr. and Mrs. George A. Ranney, Sr., the George and Margarita Delacorte Foundation, the Palisades Foundation, Inc., and the Forest Fund. The Rockefeller Foundation has also supplied the project with timely and generous support.

I am deeply grateful to the officials, faculty and staff of The American University, which is the sponsoring institution of the Frederick Law Olmsted Papers. The officials of the university have taken on the complicated burdens of administering the project, helping with funding proposals, and keeping the paperwork up-to-date. I also want to thank my understanding and patient colleagues in the departments of History and American Studies, whom I have repeatedly called upon to juggle my schedules and teaching loads to accommodate the vagaries of my unpredictable needs as an editor. They have also given me valuable advice throughout the years the edition has been in preparation.

Finally I would like to acknowledge the understanding and steady support I have had from my family. My parents, Donald H. McLaughlin and Eleanor E. Murdock, have tactfully furthered the venture ever since it began. My wife, Ann, has not only worked with me but has calmed the domestic seas so that I have always had time and space for work. My children, John and Ellen, have known about Olmsted ever since they could talk and have patiently encouraged the mysterious enterprise from the beginning.

FREDERICK LAW OLMSTED

HIS LIFE AND WORK

FREDERICK LAW OLMSTED

HIS LIFE AND WORK

I N   T H E   C E N T E R   O F   N E W   Y O R K   C I T Y   lies Central Park, the eye of an
urban hurricane, green, sunny, and tranquil. So it has remained for over one
hundred years, the gray storm around it spiraling out many miles into the
once-quiet farming country surrounding Manhattan Island. Twenty other cities in the United States and Canada have set aside similar parks, all of them
monuments to the tenacity, vision, and artistic skill of Frederick Law Olmsted, who also laid out the Fenway in Boston, presented the first plan for the
Berkeley campus of the University of California, and designed the grounds
and suggested the great terrace of the United States Capitol. His accomplishments seem so worthwhile and far-sighted today that it is hard to imagine
they were once stigmatized as impractical dreams.

Olmsted left another monument: his personal and professional papers comprise some 60,000 separate items which cover the span of years
from 1838 to 1903.[1] His well-known books on the South in the 1850s gained
him a lasting reputation as an acute and perceptive observer, but these repre-
sent the writings of a few years. The major part of his writing was for a
private, or at least a limited public, audience. Olmsted's best and most representative letters and papers are printed here for the first time and contain
accurate and shrewd observations of nineteenth-century American life from
one who witnessed and participated in the major events of his day. In his
various roles as park planner, gentleman farmer, or newspaper correspondent, he was always looking to the future, even to anticipate the needs of
the freed slave in adjusting to independent citizenship. Just as his designed
parks were intended to enhance the lives of future generations living in
greatly expanded cities, his planned suburbs were to be part of a metropolitan
area far beyond the imagining of the real-estate speculator of his day.

3

Frederick Law Olmsted, the first child of John Olmsted and Charlotte Hull, was born on April 26, 1822. Fortunately, his father, a well-established dry-goods merchant in Hartford, Connecticut, was able to support his growing family comfortably, so that he could travel with them on extensive vacation trips, send the children to the best private schools, even abroad for further education. But John Olmsted's first wife died shortly after the birth of another son, and he did not trust his own generous instincts in the rearing of their first-born. He thought the village ministers of Connecticut could do a better job than he, both in providing a daily example of piety and moral probity and in teaching the child how to read, write, and calculate.[2]

Frederick Olmsted had already tried several schools in Hartford by the time he was seven, when he was sent to live with the Reverend Zolva Whitmore, a Congregational minister of North Guilford who enjoyed gardening and flowers.[3] Much later in his life Olmsted was to look back on this stay as a rural idyll. His lessons at the village school and duties on Whitmore's farm were not so onerous that he could not listen to the talk at the village store in the evening, go on his own exploring expeditions in the woods and fields, or satisfy his curiosity about such rural activities as beekeeping and the drilling of the local militia.[4]

The free and pleasant life at North Guilford came suddenly to an end,[5] perhaps because the elder Olmsted thought his son should have a more rigorous education. Unfortunately, in his attempt to find the ideal tutor, John Olmsted moved his son twelve times before his elementary and high school education were considered complete in 1840.[6]

If the first of these experiments was the happiest, the longest and loneliest was his five years at Newington, Connecticut, in a drafty clapboard building that the minister, Joab Brace,[7] had set up in his farmyard to house four pupils. Brace, who was stern and awesome, kept the little boys under his care busy from before dawn until bedtime. When he was not occupied by his lessons, Olmsted was set to hours of wood-chopping. Joab Brace did not take time to conduct Olmsted's scripture lessons. He delegated those to some bigger boys and girls of the village, whom Olmsted thought ignorant, bullying, and conceited.[8]

At vacation times Olmsted returned home to several half-brothers and -sisters much younger than he, and to a brother, John Hull Olmsted, who came to share more and more in his life. John must have provided the sympathy, ready ear, and sense of humor that Olmsted's busy father and stepmother apparently could not give this energetic, independent, and perhaps somewhat obstreperous young man. Another person who had the patience and time to devote to young Olmsted was his scholarly uncle, Jonathan Law, a friend of John Greenleaf Whittier, who read Latin poetry to his nephew, shared his library with him, and gave him a plot in his garden for experiments in horticulture.[9]

The senior Olmsteds were fond of taking long family trips, sometimes by public coach or canal boat, and often in the family carriage, to the White Mountains, the Maine coast, and into upper New York State. They stayed at the local inns along the way and searched out the picturesque views described in the travel books of such writers as Timothy Dwight and Benjamin Silliman. Although they themselves were inarticulate about such matters, the elder Olmsteds were eager for their children to appreciate the beauties of landscape in which they found evidence of the goodness of God. When we consider the tastes of his family and their interest in travel, it seems no accident that the boy who was to become a great landscape architect had read such eighteenth-century English writers on the picturesque as Uvedale Price and William Gilpin. They instructed the British gentry on how to lay out their country estates and how to appreciate scenery on their travels.[10]

Olmsted's wide, indiscriminate reading and his vacation trips with his family meant much more to him than the tedious memorizing and catechizing that the village schools and country parsons demanded. He had hoped to go on to Yale, but his formal education was cut short when he was fifteen by a case of sumac poisoning that spread to his eyes and threatened him with blindness. A New York doctor advised him to forgo college and spend as much time as possible outdoors until his eyes were better.[11] His father sent him off to study civil engineering with Frederick Augustus Barton, then teaching in Phillips Academy at Andover, Massachusetts.[12]

The regime of Professor Barton for the next three years turned out to be much to Olmsted's liking. He learned some of the rudiments of surveying, but spent most of his time fishing, hunting, or collecting rocks and plants. He also amused himself by drawing plans of hypothetical towns and cities. It was a period of his life which he enjoyed recalling later, maintaining that the instruction in surveying, the town planning, and the outdoor life were unwitting preparation for his later career as a landscape architect.[13]

John Olmsted, though, could not have foreseen a connection between this boyhood idyll and his son's future professional life. He decided that the boy should next learn French and see how he liked business. He arranged that his son start clerking at the store of James Benkard and Benjamin H. Hutton, importers of French silks on Beaver Street in New York. Olmsted missed his carefree life at Barton's and did not find the attractions of his job or the city enough to keep him in New York much more than a year and a half.[14]

After a period back in Hartford enjoying the whirl of parties there and making visits to New Haven to see his brother and other friends at Yale College, Olmsted suddenly decided to go to sea. On April 24, 1843, he left New York on the bark *Ronaldson* under Captain Warren Fox as an apprentice seaman bound for Canton, China. The voyage around the Cape of Good Hope and on to Hong Kong lasted until September.[15] Olmsted was sick and miserable much of the time. To the end of his life, he remembered the wretched conditions of life on board the *Ronaldson* and the rain and spray dripping down on his bunk in the forecastle.[16]

The *Ronaldson* had to wait until December to load a cargo of tea, cassia, and raw silk, because another Gordon and Talbot ship had to be filled first and shipment of tea from the interior of China was delayed. Sickness and duties on the ship kept Olmsted from seeing much of Canton in spite of the weeks the ship lay at anchor in Whampoa Reach. The voyage home, starting on December 30, was made wretched by scurvy and overwork which drove the crew close to mutiny. Olmsted's nearly disastrous adventure ended on April 15, 1844, when the *Ronaldson* docked in New York.[17]

Home again, the twenty-two-year-old Olmsted decided that, instead of becoming a civil engineer, a merchant, or a ship captain, he would be a scientific farmer. This seemed the best and most useful life both for himself and to serve his countrymen, the majority of whom were farmers too.[18] As a start, Olmsted visited his uncle David Brooks's nearby farm in Cheshire, Connecticut, for a few months in late 1844 and early 1845. During May, after looking for another place near Boston or Northampton, he settled at Joseph Welton's farm, close to Waterbury, Connecticut, with which he was very pleased. Welton made a great impression on Olmsted. Much later he recalled that he had hardly ever known so good a man: not one of his teachers had been more conscientious or led a more simple, healthy, moral life.[19]

He took time off from the practical study of agriculture to visit his brother, John, then starting his sophomore term at Yale in the fall of 1845. Although Olmsted was not an enrolled student, he probably had a chance to hear some of Benjamin Silliman's lectures on chemistry and scientific agriculture. He joined John and some of his friends in experiments in Silliman's laboratory, and they included him in their discussions and social life.[20]

The months spent in New Haven seem to have been a turning point in Olmsted's early life. Until he had made the decision to become a scientific farmer, he had been following the advice of his father and his family. Now, on his own, he had found a career that would benefit his fellow countrymen, coincide with the noblest aims of science, and happily fulfill his own love of outdoor life. At the same time, the romantic tastes that he had gained earlier through an acquaintance with the writings of Benjamin Silliman, Timothy Dwight, William Gilpin, and Uvedale Price were supported by his Yale friends, among them Governor Roger Sherman Baldwin's pretty daughter

Elizabeth. By introducing him to the writings of Emerson and Lowell, who seemed to think the way he did, she convinced him that the ideas he had come upon in his random and informal education were quite respectable and worthy of pursuit.[21] Other friends, such as Frederick Kingsbury and Charles Loring Brace, probably also urged him to read widely. In the summer he wrote Kingsbury that he was reading Richard Whately's *Elements of Logic*, James Mill's *History of British India*, the *Federalist Papers*, and some poetry, fiction, and ecclesiastical literature.[22]

After spending the following spring and summer with George Geddes near Syracuse, New York, where he had a chance to observe the methods used on a prize-winning farm, Olmsted decided that he was ready to start his career as a scientific agriculturalist at Sachem's Head, Connecticut. The farm that his father bought him there was close enough to New Haven for Olmsted to keep up with the debates and social activities of his brother's class at Yale, but was too rocky and infertile to be a commercial success. Accordingly, in the spring of 1848, he moved to a much better farm which his father bought him on Staten Island.[23]

Dr. Cyrus Perkins, one of Olmsted's neighbors, advised him to put his farm into top condition right away. Despite protests from his more economical father, Olmsted eagerly applied his neighbor's advice. He spent thirty-four dollars an acre to prepare a field for wheat planting. This investment, he explained to his father, would reap a profit in about eight years, but then it would be time to redo the ground. To Olmsted's surprise, the application of Dr. Perkins's seductive theory never made the farm profitable.[24]

In the management of his new farm, though, the twenty-six-year-old Olmsted showed the administrative ability that became one of his most striking traits in later life. He shrewdly made use of the old and run-down buildings and equipment, had his hired men do their chores on an hourly schedule, and required his foreman to give him a report on the day's work every evening before supper. Olmsted recalled later that his crops of wheat and turnips won prizes for him at the Richmond County agricultural fairs. He won a silver spoon for his pears in 1852.[25]

Olmsted did more than tend his own garden; he became secretary of the Richmond County Agricultural Society, founded to persuade the local farmers to refine their tastes in architecture and landscapes, to make their houses more convenient, their roads better, and their tools and farming methods up-to-date. In a few years, Olmsted also started one of the earliest cylindrical drainage tile works in America, so that the local farmers could practice the latest English method of removing excess water from the soil by laying a network of tile pipes under their fields. He was a strong advocate of a plank road for Staten Island to lower transportation costs for his neighbors. Another of his projects dealt with the planting of imported fruit trees to improve the types grown in America.[26]

7

But as Olmsted learned by reading the agricultural journals of the day, farming was much more than a way to produce food. It could be the most healthy, virtuous, and happy way of life of all if the farmer learned to cultivate not only turnips but his rural taste as well. To please himself and to set an example for his farming neighbors, Olmsted transformed his Staten Island farm from a dirty and somewhat disagreeable spot into a gentleman's country seat. He moved the barns to a new location behind a knoll and changed the driveway so it approached the house in a graceful curve. A small pond behind the house was just a mudhole until he shored its edges with stones and plantings and protected it from contamination. The cost of Olmsted's improvements to his property was small, and was, according to Frederick Kingsbury, as successful as anything he was ever to do later as a landscape architect. His neighbors were impressed with his accomplishment, and one, William Henry Vanderbilt, who became a successful railroad promoter and manager like his father, asked Olmsted to make similar improvements to his farm at New Dorp, Staten Island.[27]

Andrew Jackson Downing, the nationally prominent landscape gardener of Newburgh, New York, influenced Olmsted's approach to farming and his taste in landscape design and architecture. Olmsted had met him and read both his books and the magazine he edited, the *Horticulturist*, in which he urged his readers to practice scientific farming, improve their livestock breeds, and grow better strains of fruits and vegetables. Olmsted imported French pear trees for himself and others. He also took to heart Downing's plea that his fellow citizens should tastefully arrange and embellish their dwellings and property for both convenience and beauty. He sold shade trees and evergreens and gained a modest reputation among his neighbors for "some special knowledge, inventiveness, and judgment" in landscaping and the placing of buildings.[28]

The life of a gentleman farmer, even with the addition of the nursery, did not satisfy Olmsted completely. His interest in the outside world was stimulated by frequent visits from his brother, John, then studying medicine in Dr. Willard Parker's office in New York, and other Yale friends such as Charles Loring Brace, now a student at the Union Theological Seminary. When these two proposed to go to England and the Continent on a walking tour in early 1850, Olmsted was beside himself with envy. John was going because his health had broken down from incipient tuberculosis. Brace, depressed by the death of his twenty-one-year-old sister, Emma, agreed to join him. Brace, like Olmsted, had found that his purely theological interests were waning and hoped that his travels would help him to prepare for a career of Christian service in social work. Olmsted tried to persuade his father that he should accompany the two because both his ailing brother and the impractical Brace could use his help. He argued further that he would learn much more about farming by traveling abroad than by staying at home. Olmsted's father agreed to let him go along. His brother was delighted to have him but hoped that the farm would be left in good hands while he was gone and wondered if others would understand Olmsted's sudden decision to leave it.[29]

The enthusiastic and detailed letters home showed Olmsted's delight in travel and in writing about everything he encountered along the way. He was beginning a pattern which he would follow the rest of his life whatever his occupation: the combination of frequent trips away from home with detailed observation and reporting.

On April 30, Olmsted joined his brother and Charles Loring Brace aboard the *Henry Clay* to sail to Liverpool. Their walking trip through England, France, Belgium, Holland, Germany, Ireland, and Scotland kept such a leisurely pace that the Olmsteds did not embark for home until October. Charles stayed on almost another year.[30]

The only comprehensive record of the walking tour is contained in the two volumes that George Palmer Putnam, the New York publisher, invited Olmsted to make out of his journals and letters upon his return. Unfortunately, the books tell nothing of the adventures in Europe, but only of the walk through the English countryside. Perhaps this is because the pace of the book reflects that of the original journey. The first volume of Olmsted's *Walks and Talks of an American Farmer in England* hardly gets the reader more than sixty miles from Liverpool after a detailed account of the voyage across the Atlantic from New York.[31]

When he came upon Birkenhead and its impressive new stone docks along the Mersey River across from Liverpool, Olmsted was greatly excited. Starting in 1836, the Edinburgh architect Gillespie Graham had laid out the streets around Hamilton Square with buildings in a Doric style, and Olmsted remarked that it was the only town he had ever seen built with the advanced technology, taste, and enterprise that supposedly characterized the nineteenth century.[32] He was delighted with Birkenhead's public park, which Edward Kemp had completed in 1847 from preliminary plans of the Crystal Palace designer, Joseph Paxton: "Five minutes of admiration, and a few more spent in studying the manner in which art had been employed to obtain from nature so much beauty, and I was ready to admit that in democratic America there was nothing to be thought of as comparable to this People's Garden."[33] Olmsted's strong approval of Birkenhead and its park showed that he had already formed the ideals that would dominate his later landscape career in America.

The travelers found England "green, dripping, glistening, gorgeous,"[34] but were critical when they found things they did not like. Olmsted could admire English agricultural methods and at the same time deplore the condition of the farm laborer. Although he respected the generations of good taste that went into the furnishing of a nobleman's house, he nevertheless concluded that such was not the proper nursery for a nineteenth-century statesman.[35]

The great private estates and parks of the English nobility, although hardly appropriate for a democratic society, gave Olmsted examples of the way landscape architects could mediate between man and nature to achieve beauty. He wrote:

> Probably there is no object of art that Americans of cultivated taste generally more long to see in Europe, than an English Park. What artist, so noble, has often been my thought, as he who, with far-reaching conception of beauty and designing power, sketches the outline, writes the colours, and directs the shadows of a picture so great that Nature shall be employed upon it for generations, before the work he has arranged for her shall realize his intentions.[36]

He admired Eaton Park, outside of Chester, unaware that the famous eighteenth-century landscape gardener, Lancelot "Capability" Brown, may have designed some of it. He found the formal gardening around Eaton Hall, a style reintroduced by W. E. Nesfield in the nineteenth century, curious but not disagreeable.[37] He was unreservedly delighted by the deer park bathed in late-afternoon sunlight. He and his companions settled down under a tree to take it all in, gazing across

> a gracefully, irregular, gently undulating surface of close-cropped pasture land, . . . trees scattered singly and in groups—so far apart as to throw long unbroken shadows across broad openings of light, and leave the view in several directions unobstructed for a long distance. Herds of fallow-deer, fawns, cattle, sheep, and lambs quietly feeding near us, and moving slowly in masses at a distance. . . .[38]

Olmsted, John, and Charles Brace arrived in London on June 21 after spending nearly a month walking from Liverpool into Wales and thence down into the south of England and the Isle of Wight. The nineteen days in London were filled "running from one fine thing to another." They visited the ragged schools and model lodgings for the poor, Kew Gardens, the picture galleries, the House of Commons, and they attended a Fourth of July dinner for the United States Ambassador to Great Britain, Abbott Lawrence.[39] The group then went on to Paris and the Continent for a month. This portion of the trip was not recorded in Olmsted's subsequent book or in letters home. They spent several weeks in France and Germany before returning to London on August 5. The remainder of their tour included a bit more of England, "dirty, wretched, hospitable" Ireland, and then some time in Scotland, from whence they sailed for New York on October 5, leaving Charles Loring Brace to study theology in Berlin and to travel in Europe for another year.[40]

Back at the Staten Island farm in late October, Olmsted wrote Brace in November urging him to stay abroad as long as he could afford to. He recalled that while they were traveling, "they were all living a great deal more—loving oftener, hating oftener—and reaching a great many more milestones." Everybody at home seemed frivolous and materialistic. He found his own farm shabby in comparison with what he had seen in Scotland. Happily, he was soon absorbed in farming, and he branched out into the nursery business. He also started making a book out of his letters and journals of the English trip.[41]

In February 1851 Olmsted revived a high-minded correspondence he had begun two years before with Emily Perkins of Hartford, the daughter of a prominent lawyer. His occasional visits to Hartford strengthened their friendship and admiration for each other. Apparently, he overcame her reluctance to consider marriage. By August they were unofficially engaged, but Emily Perkins did not want to make it public because of the fuss of congratulations. Olmsted, too, displayed some doubts. He wrote a friend that he did not want to get married until late November, after he had sold the sixty thousand cabbages he was growing for the New York market.[42]

In her last letter to Olmsted, Emily Perkins complained about the bother of buying carpets and furniture but said that she was about to announce their engagement publicly, which she did. Olmsted, apparently cheerful about his prospects, was then stunned by a letter from Emily's mother reporting that her daughter had had a change of heart and wanted to break off the engagement.

Emily's mother also asked Olmsted to meet her in New Haven to discuss the matter. It is not clear what happened next, except that Olmsted released Emily Perkins from the engagement toward the end of August. She went off to visit relatives, regain her composure, and let the gossip at home die down. In Worcester, Massachusetts, she met her future husband, Edward Everett Hale, who was rapidly becoming a leading Unitarian minister. In October Olmsted's father was puzzled by Olmsted's reaction to the breakup with Emily Perkins. He wrote a friend: "Pray tell me what it is makes Fred so happy since his *disappointment*, as it is called. He seems like a man who has thrown off a tremendous weight. Can it be that he brought it about purposely?"[43]

Olmsted may have felt under particularly intense pressure to get married. One of his close friends, Frederick Kingsbury, had married in April. Another friend who was close to the family, Sophia Stevens, had married in August. His brother, John, despite severe doubts about his health, suddenly decided to marry their Staten Island neighbor, Mary Cleveland Bryant Perkins, in October.[44]

After his engagement fell through, Olmsted, already busy as a farmer, took up again his project of writing a book about the trip through England. On the basis of his first chapters, George Palmer Putnam, the New York publisher, urged him to go ahead with a book of about 250 pages. The book, *Walks and Talks of an American Farmer in England*, appeared in 1852.[45]

The charm of *Walks and Talks* brought Olmsted a modest literary reputation. One of the most appealing qualities of the book was its reflection of the author's abundant and intelligent curiosity. His descriptions evoked everything he saw, from drab Liverpool slums to hedgerow scenery. With a good ear for dialect, he set down his conversations with farmers, innkeepers, and servants to illustrate a wide range of British opinion and character. He was to use the same technique later in his books on the ante-bellum South. In the dialogues Olmsted revealed himself to be a good talker with a gift for both humor and wry comment.[46]

In his book Olmsted recorded his observations on English character and countryside and his feelings as an American visitor. He felt a strong love for the land of his ancestors and found the British friendly and sympathetic, even to the point of celebrating the Fourth of July with their American friends. But the existence of Negro slavery in the United States spoiled the close rapport Olmsted felt he otherwise had with ardently democratic Englishmen. He wrote that there was "a hundred times more hard feeling in England towards America from this cause, than from all others. . . ." The English, he found, scolded him—unjustly, he thought—for his part in allowing slavery to exist, as if all Americans, except for a few martyrs called abolitionists, were equally responsible and condemnable for it. He wished that southerners would send lecturers to England to explain why northerners had nothing to do with slavery and could not be expected to defend it.[47]

Upon his return Olmsted found that the passage of the Fugitive Slave Act by Congress in September 1850 had brought the federal enforcement of slavery to his very doorstep. The Act provided for federal commissioners to pursue and recapture escaped slaves for their owners anywhere in the country. Northerners could no longer aid fugitive slaves without punishment from their own government. It was becoming harder to remain uninvolved with slavery. Olmsted decided that if called upon, he would take in an escaped slave and shoot anyone who came after him. He exchanged letters on the subject with Charles Loring Brace, still in Europe. Brace, a red-hot abolitionist, came home in the fall of 1851 eager to get his friends to adopt his position; but despite his best efforts, bolstered by a visit each from Theodore Parker and William Lloyd Garrison to the Staten Island farm, he could not turn Olmsted into a whole-hearted abolitionist. Olmsted thought that slaves, like children, needed to be helped towards the exercise of intelligent judgment before they could be given the duties and rights of freedom.[48]

Soon Olmsted had a chance to see slavery first hand. In 1852, Henry J. Raymond, the editor of the one-year-old *New-York Daily Times* (as it was called until 1857), was looking for someone to send South as a roving reporter. He told Brace, who sent Olmsted to see him. Raymond did not

12

inquire into Olmsted's views on slavery, nor did he ask him to follow the editorial position of the *Times*. All he expected of Olmsted was that he confine his letters to firsthand observation.[49] It was a satisfactory arrangement for both.

On December 11, 1852, Olmsted took the train for Washington to start on a four months' journey through the slave states. He traveled through the South by train, stagecoach, and steamboat, and made side trips on horseback. First he went through the eastern slave states as far south as Savannah, then pushed westward through central Georgia and Alabama to Mobile. By late February he had reached New Orleans. After an unsuccessful attempt to explore eastern Texas, he started for home on a route that took him through the interior of the slaveholding South, going from New Orleans to Vicksburg. Heavy rains and flooding prevented Olmsted from seeing the Yazoo cotton lands north of Vicksburg, so he postponed that important investigation until a later trip and took a steamer from Vicksburg to Memphis. From there, he journeyed along the eastern base of the Appalachians, returning to Staten Island on April 6, 1853.[50]

Olmsted's descriptions, day by day, of his travels through the seaboard South appeared first in the *New-York Daily Times* and later in his book *A Journey in the Seaboard Slave States*. He relentlessly built up an image of southern life as being as wretched and violent as that on any frontier, with the important difference that life in the West—under a free labor system—was usually changing for the better; it was increasing in civilized comfort, safety, and opportunity. Olmsted undercut the myth that southern chivalry and hospitality were so benign and creative that they justified the institution of slavery. Instead, he pictured a stagnant, even retrogressive, society that, at its best—on the James River in Virginia—was little better than it had been one hundred years before.[51]

Fortunately for his readers, Olmsted was not so bent upon showing the South's backwardness that he told of nothing but the vexations and discomforts of a traveler used to English roads and inns. In one of his happiest bits of writing he described getting lost in eastern Virginia while riding a sprightly mare named Jane Gillin; elsewhere he describes the removal of underwater cypress stumps from a swamp as a form of titanic dentistry.[52]

Olmsted's brother went with him on his second trip through the South and wrote up the Texas portion from Olmsted's notes and letters.[53] The book, *A Journey through Texas; or, A Saddle-Trip on the South-western Frontier*, mentions only briefly their rail and steamboat trip from Baltimore to New Orleans. Of special note to the reader would have been their two- or three-day visit in Nashville with Samuel P. Allison, a Yale classmate of John's, who nearly persuaded both Olmsteds that the aristocratic society in the South was superior to any equivalent in the North.[54]

The horseback trip across Texas from Natchitoches, Louisiana, made in late December and early January, facing into the cold northwest winds, sleet, and rain, was almost unrelieved misery. It was made no better by a monotonous diet of fried pork, corn bread, and muddy coffee, and drafty sleeping quarters, which were all the slave-owning Texans could provide for travelers. The Olmsteds had high praise, however, for the Texas General Assembly at Austin, comparing it favorably with both British Houses of Parliament, but they had little else good to say for Texas society until they came to the German settlement of New Braunfels, near San Antonio.[55] Here one could see the Olmsteds' ideal: the magic of free labor creating an oasis of civilization in the midst of the ignorance and barbarism fostered by a slave economy.

At New Braunfels the jaded travelers experienced "a sudden and complete transfer of associations." The little inn at which they stopped was exactly like the ones they had encountered on their walking tour of the Rhine three years before. The meal they had, too, was nothing more or less than they would have had along the Rhine: soup, two courses of meat, vegetables, salad, fruit, "coffee with milk, wheat bread from the loaf, and beautiful and sweet butter. . . ." The neat little town with smiling schoolchildren and cheerful and cultivated inhabitants must have overwhelmed the Olmsteds. Although it is not mentioned in *Journey through Texas*, John Hull Olmsted, who had taken the saddle trip to improve his health, for a time was strongly tempted to send for his family and settle near the town.[56]

After their arrival in San Antonio the Olmsteds' western adventures began. The brothers spent several weeks camping beside streams on the live oak prairies; these, they discovered, were inexpressibly beautiful in the early spring when the burnt-over prairie grass returned, bright green and studded with wild flowers. The landscape was the best pastoral scenery the Olmsteds had ever observed; the low massing of the picturesque live oaks set in smooth, rolling greensward as fine, they thought, as that of any English park. After a few adventures, such as battling a prairie fire they had inadvertently set, the travelers returned to San Antonio to prepare for a journey into Mexico.[57]

They had planned to go on to California, but the route westward was blocked by a tribe of Lipan Indians on the warpath. A week or so before hostilities began, the Olmsted brothers had seen enough of these Indians to convince them that the legend of the noble savage was a humbug—their camps were filthy and disgusting, and the best expression that an Indian could summon up was "either a silly leer or stupid indifference."[58] Prevented from going to California, they headed for Mexico with John Woodland, a remarkably virtuous and perspicacious Texas Ranger, as their guide. He had been born in London, but had grown up in America and spoke Mexican and Indian tongues perfectly. His knowledge and preparations probably saved the party from attack by bandits and Indians.[59]

14

John Hull Olmsted described their short jaunt into northern Mexico with a fine eye for the beauties of the countryside, architecture, and the Mexican women. Their official greeting upon crossing the border set the tone for the whole excursion: five Mexicans wrapped in serapes, sitting immobile, rose like an opera chorus and saluted them gracefully as they approached. The trip must have been truly enjoyable, because the stern remarks that appear at the end of the story about the fixed stagnancy and slow national decay caused by the religious enslavement of the Mexican mind seem a conscientious Yankee afterthought. There is little in the earlier descriptions to warrant such a condemnation.[60]

The last weeks of the journey through Texas were spent traveling along the almost impassable muddy and swampy roads of the Gulf Coast back to the Mississippi River. In the *Journey through Texas* John confessed that the 2000 miles of exposure, abominable diet, and fatigue of the last stage of the trip through the wet country were debilitating and depressing to him. His tuberculosis must have flared up, especially with the "hot, soggy breath of the approaching summer," for at one point, lagging behind his brother, he became so weak that he fell from the saddle and lay for half an hour alone, hardly breathing and unable to speak.[61]

John Hull Olmsted took the steamer from New Orleans to New York, but the persistent Frederick set off alone on horseback to make a late spring and early summer's trek through the infrequently visited southern hill country. Starting in lower Mississippi, he went through the mountains of Alabama, Georgia, Tennessee, and North Carolina. When he reached Richmond, Virginia, he returned to New York by steamer. Olmsted found the farmers in the hill country who had no slaves were more amiable and prosperous than their slave-owning neighbors. One man he talked to considered slavery unprofitable on small holdings, but even if it were profitable he and other farmers he knew would not own slaves because those who did became passionate, proud, and ugly. Slavery, he thought, was a curse on the country. Slaveholders should be reimbursed for their property, but he agreed with those who thought slaves should be sent off to Liberia.[62]

After arriving home in August 1854 Olmsted apparently was convinced that the South might abandon slavery if free farmers were given a chance to compete with slave-owners. To strengthen the antislavery sentiment among the Germans of West Texas, he secretly gathered funds to support Adolf Douai's German newspaper, the *San Antonio Zeitung*. He began working with the New England Emigrant Aid Society, which was building up a colony of free farmers in Lawrence, Kansas. He helped them raise money to buy a howitzer to protect New Englanders and other free farmers emigrating to Kansas against the attacks of slave-owning southerners. He hoped he could gain support of the New England Emigrant Aid Society for the German colonies in West Texas, but the fortunes of these free farmers grew worse

15

under the harassment of the pro-slavery Texans. The Emigrant Aid Society concentrated on the more hopeful prospects of Kansas.[63]

Olmsted's final attempt to put his Free Soil theory to the test was made in the summer of 1857, when he asked the assistance of the Cotton Supply Associations of Manchester and Liverpool, England, to send free laborers into West Texas to join the Germans in growing what he still maintained would be cheaper and better cotton than that which could be purchased from the slave plantations. He had to give up this plan because the German Free Soil faction under Douai were forced to sell their newspaper due to pressure from the Texans and conservative Germans, and the English were reluctant to meddle in the affairs of the United States in this matter.[64]

Even though Olmsted was unable to convince all the intelligent and enlightened slave owners that it would be to their interest to change to a free labor system, his articles and the books that followed wrung from them some reluctant praise and won him a great many favorable reviews from northerners and from the English. Even such abolitionists as Theodore Parker and William Lloyd Garrison, who disliked his conciliatory and gradualist tone, praised his picture of southern society. Although Horace Greeley had sent correspondents down South, and many others, from Harriet Beecher Stowe to Charles Dickens, wrote descriptive articles and books, Olmsted's writings received special praise from readers such as Charles Darwin for being particularly informative. Most southern papers and magazines declared that Olmsted was grossly unfair, but the *New Orleans Delta* found him manly and honest. A "Native Southerner" wrote in the *New-York Daily Times* that although it was clear that he was looking at things through "a pair of sharp Northern eyes," Olmsted's candor and intelligence were remarkable.[65]

In the spring of 1855, Joshua A. Dix, a young friend of Charles Loring Brace, asked Olmsted to become a partner in Dix and Edwards, a firm which published the American edition of Charles Dickens's magazine, *Household Words*, and *Putnam's Monthly Magazine*. The twenty-four-year-old Dix probably wanted Olmsted for the capital he could bring into the partnership. His other partner, Arthur Edwards, agreed to contribute $500, but Olmsted was to put up $5,000, which he persuaded his father to lend him. He was allowed to draw $1,500 a year from the firm's account to support himself.[66] In return, Olmsted saw that his connection with *Putnam's Monthly* would give him influence in cultivated circles. The prospect of a salary appealed to him, because it looked unlikely that the Staten Island farm would ever support him unless he gave it his full attention, something he had not been willing to do for almost five years. Leaving his Staten Island farm in the hands of his reluctant brother, he embarked upon his career as a New York publisher with enthusiasm.

Putnam's list of contributors was impressive. James Russell Lowell, Nathaniel Hawthorne, and the elder Henry James had written for it. Olmsted had long thought that this "great country and cursedly little people" needed the democratic and spiritual uplift that a well-edited magazine could supply. He had hoped for a journal which was a cross between the *Westminster Review* and the *New York Daily Tribune*. It looked as if he could help make *Putnam's* fit the formula.[67]

Olmsted left the major editorial decisions to George William Curtis, the writer and lecturer, who became another partner. He also had the experienced advice of Charles A. Dana, writer for the *New York Daily Tribune*, and Parke Godwin of the *New York Evening Post*. They all contributed articles and reviews as well. Although Olmsted spent most of his time answering correspondence and dealing with rejected authors, he did make some last-minute revisions for Henry David Thoreau on his Cape Cod manuscript and persuaded the magazine to publish Herman Melville's story, "Benito Cereno."[68]

Olmsted's association with *Putnam's Monthly* was perhaps the happiest part of his work for Dix and Edwards. It gave him an opportunity to meet such contributors as Ralph Waldo Emerson, Henry W. Longfellow, Asa Gray, and Harriet Beecher Stowe. He must have enjoyed the literary parties of Anne Charlotte Lynch, who, since 1845, had entertained a circle of writers including Edgar Allan Poe, Horace Greeley, and Margaret Fuller. His own place in the literary world allowed him to give a breakfast for James Russell Lowell and to attend a dinner at the Press Club for William Thackeray.[69]

Olmsted's most important project as a partner of Dix and Edwards was his trip to England to persuade publishers and authors there to consign their books to his firm in return for a guarantee of royalty payments from the sales in the United States. Without an enforceable international copyright law, however, Olmsted's months in London trying to make consignments were a waste of time, because other American publishers could pirate an English work and undersell the legitimate edition. After encouraging Olmsted to commit the firm to foreign royalty payments in return for the right to publish overseas authors in the United States, Dix and Edwards failed to honor the commitments he had made, because of declining sales and financial mismanagement.[70]

When Olmsted returned to New York in the fall of 1856 empty-handed, Dix and Edwards was close to failure. The firm managed to bring out Olmsted's *Journey through Texas* in January 1857, but went bankrupt before getting a chance to publish his last volume of southern travels, *A Journey in the Back Country*. Fortunately, Mason Brothers in New York and Sampson Low, Son and Company of London issued it in 1860. Although the demise of his publishing business was assured, Olmsted still hoped to continue writing books and articles on social questions that interested him. Henry Raymond of the *New-York Daily Times* wished to send his former correspondent to Kansas to report on the warfare between the free-soil and slavery factions.

Charles Dana of the *New York Daily Tribune* wanted him to go to Utah to write about the Mormon settlement. Olmsted, himself, was tempted to sail for Jamaica to see at first hand the results of Negro emancipation on the sugar plantations.[71]

None of these projects materialized. Prospects of a literary life faded for Olmsted as *Putnam's Monthly* and the successor firm to Dix and Edwards tottered toward failure, which eventually came in August 1857. Olmsted had already begun to seek other ways to support himself and pay off his debts to his father left over from the failure of Dix and Edwards. He had long since abandoned farming. The Staten Island farm could not be made profitable. The ailing John had tried in vain to sell it before he left in January 1857, with his family, to seek a more healthy climate.[72] In late June, Olmsted wrote Dr. Samuel Cabot, Jr., of the New England Emigrant Aid Society that he wanted to throw his heart and soul into a project of encouraging British farmers and others to settle West Texas and raise cotton for the textile mills at home. His hopes faded when he learned that English politicians and manufacturers refused to meddle in internal American affairs and that fear of angry proslavery Americans would deter emigration.[73]

Meanwhile an entirely unexpected opportunity was in the making. The movement to build a great central park for New York, which the journalist and poet, William Cullen Bryant, and the influential landscape gardener, Andrew Jackson Downing, had championed for years, was on the brink of success.[74] Soon the park work would provide Olmsted with a job and start him on an unanticipated career in landscape design. For the next forty years, except for an interruption during the Civil War, Olmsted's considerable administrative and artistic skills would be employed throughout the country building landscape parks and suburbs.

The New York State Legislature had just appointed eleven commissioners to take over the immense landscaping project in the middle of Manhattan. The commissioners, who were trying to keep some of the patronage of the park away from the city Democrats, were looking for an unpolitical man of Republican sympathies to manage both the labor force building the park and the park police. He would have to work under the incumbent Democratic engineer-in-chief, Egbert Viele, a holdover from the earlier Central Park Commission appointed by the mayor.[75] Word of the job opening came to Olmsted in August when he was at work on the proofs of his book, *A Journey in the Back Country*, at a seaside inn outside New Haven.

By chance, Charles Wyllys Elliott, one of the commissioners and an admirer of Olmsted's, encountered him at the inn. He urged him to apply for the job, and Olmsted decided to try. He hurried to New York to collect signatures from the most notable men he could find for his petition to the Central Park Commission. He hoped that his grasp of the problems of agricultural labor as a scientific farmer, as shown in his books on England and the South, would persuade people to sign.[76] Probably his reputation as an author and his connection with *Putnam's Monthly* helped to secure the signatures of William Cullen Bryant, George Palmer Putnam, and most important of all, Washington Irving. Asa Gray, the Harvard botanist and cousin of Charles Brace, sent a warm endorsement. With these signatures and the names of Peter Cooper, August Belmont, and David Dudley Field on his petition, he overcame the competition of John W. Audubon, son of the great ornithologist, and of Joel B. Nott, whose father, Eliphalet Nott, was a well-known preacher and inventor, and was president of Union College.[77] The Republican commissioners, a minority on the Board, wanted a Republican superintendent. The Democrats agreed to concede, but only if the new man were not "practical," that is, someone who would use the job to gain political power. Olmsted was literary and "unpractical," making him acceptable to the Democrats but not politically useful to the Republicans.[78]

When Olmsted took up his new duties, only the most vague and dispirited beginnings were being made in the effort to improve the 770 rocky and treeless acres of Central Park, following the topographical survey and unimaginative plan which Egbert Viele had made for the park at his own expense. The land cried out for much improving. It was either rocky and barren or malodorous swamp. At best, it was adorned with a few scrubby bushes. The only touches of civilization were those provided by the local squatters living in shacks and engaged in slaughtering cows and pigs, bone boiling, and goat farming.[79]

From the beginning, Egbert Viele resented the Republican underling forced upon him by the park commissioners. When Olmsted presented himself in the dignified dress of a young gentleman, Viele sent him with a deputy for an embarrassing tour of the park, which was in many places knee-deep in mud. To add to Olmsted's burdens of a difficult job and a resentful superior, he was under pressure day and night from New York City politicians and their unemployed constituents to give every man who presented himself a position regardless of his qualifications. The Panic of 1857 made Central Park the only likely employer for thousands of jobless. The new superintendent did manage to put more than 900 men to work, but he took pride in the fact that they worked efficiently and he would not be forced to take on more, even when besieged far into the night by mobs waving banners demanding "Bread or Blood."[80]

In the fall of 1857, Olmsted needed all the distractions that his new job could provide him. He had accepted it, although the salary was but $1,500 a year, because it gave him the only chance he could see to support himself without his father's help. He had been bitterly humiliated by the financial failure and disappointments of his literary and publishing career, which he had hoped would make him influential and financially independent, as gentleman farming had not. Instead, he was more in debt to his father than ever. Added to these woes was the sorrow he felt because his brother, always his friend and confidant, was dying of tuberculosis in Europe, where he had gone to seek a climate that would prolong his life. In a way, Olmsted's youthful high spirits died with John in 1857; he sought to escape his troubles and sorrows by plunging deeper and deeper into his new job. Compulsive overwork became a habit that would last a lifetime.[81]

Olmsted's first great opportunity as a landscape designer came in October 1857, when Calvert Vaux invited him to collaborate on a new design for Central Park. Vaux was a young English architect who had been Downing's partner and who had taken over the landscape practice when Downing died in 1852. Vaux decided to enter the competition for a new Central Park that the design commissioners had instituted when they decided to discard Egbert Viele's plan. At first Olmsted hesitated, fearing to wound his superior's feelings, but he concluded that nothing could soothe Viele's injured pride.[82]

He was fortunate to have the chance to work with the charming, enthusiastic, and intelligent Vaux, who had had seven years of experience as a landscape designer in the United States when he met Olmsted. Vaux's first two years as an assistant to Downing must have been especially valuable because Downing, at the height of his fame, had just been commissioned by President Fillmore to create a "national park" on the Mall between the Capitol and the Washington Monument with a cross axis to the White House. This project, Olmsted wrote later, was the first great public undertaking in landscape architecture carried through by the government.[83]

Designing Central Park with Calvert Vaux was Olmsted's apprenticeship in landscape architecture. As he later admitted, he would have been at a loss to know what to do without the professional help Vaux provided. The two men worked together at night or whenever Olmsted could get away from his superintending duties and the swarm of job seekers who plagued his office and home. Their plan, entitled "Greensward," won the competition when they submitted it in the spring of 1858.[84]

The Greensward design followed the English precedents of park planning as they had been transmitted through Humphry Repton and his American disciple, Andrew Jackson Downing. The most important compositions were pastoral, made up of massed foliage framing vistas of meadow or greensward. The designers reasoned that horizontal passages of scenery were most appropriate for a large urban park, because the intent of its landscape should be to soothe rather than excite the spirits of the city dweller agitated and wearied by the jarring sights and sounds of the crowded streets.[85]

Olmsted and Vaux wanted the users of the park to have a respite from not only the sights but the dangers of lower Broadway. Olmsted and Vaux designed Central Park so that the footpaths, bridle paths, and carriage roads were separate from each other and never crossed except at over- and underpasses. The pedestrian never had to fear being run down. The horseman could have his canter and the carriage owner his drive without accident while moving through the refreshing and beautiful landscape.[86]

The man out for a holiday stroll in Central Park might want to see others in a gregarious mood as well as view the scenery. Accordingly, Vaux and Olmsted planned a mall, which offered promenaders a wide walk and benches sheltered by an arch of American elms, and a terrace with a fountain overlooking Central Park Lake. Here people of all ages and occupations, freed from the bustle of a city sidewalk, could mingle in a common enjoyment of fine weather and lovely scenery. The designers hoped that their mall, like public promenades they had seen in England and Europe, would be a democratic institution where park frequenters could meet without being hindered by artificial social distinctions.[87]

Central Park, located in the middle of Manhattan, formed an enormous barrier two and one-half miles long and half a mile wide to any traffic going east and west across the island from above 59th Street to 106th Street. The Commissioners required that plans submitted for the competition have east-west roads running across the park to accommodate future crosstown traffic. Olmsted and Vaux did not want this noisy and dangerous city traffic streaming across the park in full view of those who wanted to enjoy rural scenery, so they designed four transverse roads sunken below the landscape, screened by careful planting, and crossed by park roadways and paths on wide bridges. The sunken transverse roads and the ingenious separation of the rest of the traffic paths and carriage ways were features unique to their design. The transverse roads could accommodate crosstown traffic even at night, when Olmsted and Vaux suggested that the park should be closed. In no other plans submitted for the competition were such provisions made to integrate the park with the city plan.[88]

Impressed by Olmsted's work as superintendent and his part with Vaux in winning the design competition, the Board of Commissioners of Central Park made Olmsted architect-in-chief in May 1858 and raised his salary to $2,500 a year. They abolished the office of chief engineer, a move which must have permanently estranged Egbert Viele from Olmsted. Even with Viele off the scene Olmsted had to contend with persistent and noisy opposition to his work from politicians and members of the Park Commission. Robert J. Dillon, for instance, one of the commissioners who had voted against the Greensward Plan, came forward with his own ideas for the park, getting editorial support in the *Tribune* and notice in the *Times* and *Herald*. In place of the scenic emphasis of the Vaux and Olmsted plan, Dillon wanted the main feature of Central Park to be a grand avenue, like the Champs Elysées in Paris, starting from the middle of the south end of the park and extending in a straight line to the old reservoir, crossing Central Park Lake on an impressive wire suspension bridge.[89] As a way to reply to Dillon's proposals, Olmsted invited his friends Henry J. Raymond of the *Times* and Charles A. Dana of the *Tribune* to have breakfast with him one morning on a large boulder overlooking the southern end of Central Park. When the gentlemen were at their cigars, he pointed out to them the line of Dillon's proposed gigantic boulevard and all the irreplaceable landscape effects which would be destroyed in its construction. After this breakfast party Dillon lost two supporters and even admitted himself that his scheme was impractical.[90]

At the same time that Olmsted was learning to practice his new profession and deal with newspapers, he quite suddenly took on the cares of a large family. His dying brother had written him a farewell note in which he said, "Don't let Mary suffer while you are alive." Olmsted carried out the request by marrying John's widow in June 1859, thereupon assuming the support of three small children.[91]

It would be impossible to say in what proportions love and duty were compounded in this marriage. Olmsted had not taken particular notice of the pert little Mary Perkins when they first met at her grandfather's house in 1848, but he did express his delight when she and John became engaged in 1850. Following the summer of 1851, when his own fiancée, Emily Perkins of Hartford, had broken off her engagement to him after a little more than a month, Olmsted made no effort to find himself a wife.[92] The one he "inherited" from his brother on June 13, 1859, was ambitious, strong-willed, energetic, and demanding. She could not have been relaxing company for the high-strung Olmsted, but must have gained his respect because of her intelligence and wide range of interests. Thus, within two years, Olmsted had embarked upon what was to become his lifetime profession and had suddenly become the head of a family of five.[93]

These heavy professional and family commitments, acquired so close together in time, must often have conflicted with each other. Not only did Olmsted have to meet the demands of his young family; he also sometimes had to direct the labors of as many as 4000 men on the park. He had driven himself so hard by late summer in 1859 that his health gave way and he became subject to intermittent fevers. The Park Board granted him a leave of absence from the end of September until early December. He used the time to travel abroad by himself to study park design and management on the Continent and in England.[94]

In Paris he had the good fortune to meet Jean Alphand, a civil engineer who had, since 1854, been in charge of laying out the beautiful great public parks of Paris at the Bois de Boulogne and the Bois de Vincennes. He must have learned from him about the uses of pampas grass and large-leafed, hardy, subtropical trees and bushes that added much to the luxuriance of the Paris parks and seen, too, how the new boulevards spread parklike greenery throughout the city.[95] In London he visited Sir Richard Mayne, the commanding officer of the London Metropolitan Police, who could tell him about the problems of policing the West End parks, information which enabled Olmsted to set up an excellent police force in Central Park.[96]

Upon his return, Olmsted and Vaux extended their collaboration beyond the limits of Central Park. They landscaped an estate in New Rochelle and in the spring started work on plans for the grounds of the Hartford Retreat for the Insane. More importantly, the commissioners in charge of laying out Manhattan north of 155th Street appointed them landscape architects and designers for the project. This was the first time that Olmsted had had a chance to make suggestions about the future growth of a large city area. He and Vaux thought that the upper part of Manhattan should remain suburban. To keep the area from losing its charm as had Jones's Woods and Clifton on Staten Island, he advocated an elaborate street system that would discourage direct traffic, recommended that areas be specifically set off for shops and services, and suggested public green spaces to protect the district from urban encroachments.[97]

Just before Olmsted left for Europe in late 1859, the Central Park Board appointed one of the commissioners, Andrew Haswell Green, to be their comptroller. When he returned, Olmsted sensed that Green was usurping the designers' authority to carry out their Central Park plan. The comptroller looked with the suspicion of an economical and conscientious administrator on all suggestions Vaux and Olmsted made. Green must have been difficult in the way that only the self-righteous can be. He took a great deal of pride in his part in the building of Central Park, but Olmsted felt so obstructed and harassed by the dominating comptroller that he threatened to resign in late January 1861 unless he regained complete control over his park work and did not have to get the comptroller's approval for every dime he spent. The park commissioners persuaded him to withdraw his resignation by admitting that his complaints were justified and by pointing out that his resigning would jeopardize the passage of a bill before the New York State Legislature to extend the park from 106th street to 110th.[98] The committee that introduced the bill had just vindicated every aspect of Central Park's management from hostile criticism.

Even after he had taken his first job on Central Park, Olmsted continued writing commentary on the South. He thought that he had done too much work on his *Journey in the Back Country* not to finish it, and was able to get it published by Mason Brothers of New York in 1860. The English edition of *Back Country* sold so well that the London publishers, Sampson Low, Son and Company, asked Olmsted to prepare for British readers a condensed version of all three of his books about the slave states. Mason Brothers offered to publish it in America using the English plates. The public demand for accounts of southern society, increasing with the sectional tensions that would soon tear the country apart, justified the new undertaking. Olmsted explained to the publishers that his duties on Central Park were too pressing to allow him time to do the volume alone. They permitted him to get Daniel R. Goodloe, editor of the abolitionist *National Era* in Washington, D.C., to help him prepare the book, to be called *The Cotton Kingdom*.[99]

Goodloe accepted the job eagerly but had to be restrained from including his own thoughts and inferences and from writing a "copious introduction" which would assert that, contrary to Olmsted's thesis, it was not the basic inefficiency of slave labor that was keeping the South poor. Rather, Goodloe felt, it was the one-crop system, which was wrecking the soil and absorbing all the capital and labor of the South. Olmsted's contention that inefficient and unmotivated slave labor was preventing the South from becoming a prosperous and civilized section of the country remained the principal conclusion one could draw from the generous selections from Olmsted's other books that Goodloe assembled in *The Cotton Kingdom*.[100]

The Cotton Kingdom was published in England shortly after the Civil War broke out, and it sold well both in Britain and in the United States, even though it showed signs of being a rather hasty compilation and was longer than any one of the previous volumes. Olmsted had added new comments about the southern attempts to secede from the Union: the South, he stated, could not become an independent people because there was no natural boundary to divide us as a nation. We were united by mountain ranges, valleys, and the great waters of America. The South had to share in our free institutions or our American republic would fail as we submitted to the yoke of a slave society.[101]

With the Confederate attack on Fort Sumter on April 12, 1861, Olmsted decided to leave the Central Park job. He was disqualified from the fighting because he had badly injured his leg in a carriage accident the summer before. Instead, he thought of joining the Navy or of getting a job managing escaped slaves as free laborers,[102] but an opportunity for him to serve the Union cause came from a different quarter. It was created by the vast medical needs of the newly recruited army; the wants of the new forces were on a scale far greater than those which the Army Medical Bureau, crippled by peacetime neglect and an aging staff, was capable of answering, even when bolstered by the scattered efforts of the volunteer relief organizations.

A committee of prominent New Yorkers with the Unitarian minister Henry Whitney Bellows at their head sought to remedy the lack and to focus volunteer efforts with an overall organization modeled on the British Sanitary Commission, which had accomplished vital services in the Crimean War. By June 13, 1861, the members of this group had persuaded President Lincoln to sign an executive order establishing a "Commission of Inquiry and Advice in respect of the Sanitary Interests of the United States Forces."[103]

Seven days after Lincoln signed the order for a Sanitary Commission, Henry Bellows asked Olmsted to be its general secretary. Olmsted was granted a three-month leave of absence from Central Park[104] so that he could go to Washington, D.C., to direct the stream of supplies from relief societies where they were needed, act as intermediary between the Sanitary Commission and the War Department, and appoint and supervise all the subordinate agents to carry out the great task. Leaving Calvert Vaux and Ignaz Pilat (an Austrian landscape gardener who supervised the planting) to go on with the park work, which continued throughout the war, Olmsted arrived in Washington in late June to set up his office.[105] And so began what Olmsted later considered his greatest single public service.

Olmsted's new job demanded that he apply the most advanced practices of the public health movement of his day to protect the health of the Union army. An unanticipated result was that after the war he became one of the leaders in the struggle to control and prevent disease in our great cities by providing parks, pure water supply, adequate sewage systems, and the careful siting of dwellings for sunlight and air. More immediately, his letters of the time show that he had an unusual chance to serve the Union cause and observe at first hand the common soldiers and their leaders in the great battles of the Civil War.

Olmsted soon impressed the commission with his remarkable organizing powers and captured the devotion of his well-chosen subordinates. As Henry Bellows realized, he was capable of planning far ahead. He anticipated that the war might last two or three years and cost the government as much as six hundred million dollars—a shrewd guess, compared to the naive optimism of the day.[106]

The disastrous battle of Bull Run on July 12, 1861, demonstrated at once to Olmsted the impossibility of fighting a war with an undisciplined mob of volunteers who were wretchedly clothed, shod, fed, and sheltered. Most of the wounded had been left behind on the battlefield, unattended in the retreat. Olmsted's *Report on the Demoralization of the Volunteers*, written within a week of Bull Run, was such a damning indictment of government and army policies that the Sanitary Commission decided to postpone its publication until the public's confidence in the war effort had returned.[107]

The officials of the Army Medical Bureau ignored the Sanitary Commission's recommendations as long as they could—even the advice that they follow army regulations was distasteful to them. In the early days of its battle against the Commission, the Medical Bureau gained some curious allies. Besides Henry J. Raymond, editor of the *New-York Daily Times*, who was on their side because he was a personal friend of Surgeon General Finley, they had the unhappily married editor's admiring friend, Elizabeth Powell, who was a voluntary superintendent of nurses at a hospital near Washington. She insisted that the Surgeon General was a beneficent, godlike creature and that Olmsted, though a "man of consummate abilities," worshiped power "and the handling of millions" and was in conspiracy to raid the public funds. Her praises of the martyred Finley and censure of the diabolical Olmsted appeared in the *Times* articles signed by "Truth."[108]

Mrs. Raymond's outrage and the publication of a masterful *Report to the Secretary of War* by the Sanitary Commission, which Olmsted had written, forced the editor of the *Times* to abandon his attack and end his "silly platonic friendship" with Miss Powell. The *Report* won praise in this country and in Europe as a convincing discussion of the various causes that affected the army's morale and efficiency. It even persuaded Raymond that the Sanitary Commission's purpose was to see that the health of the volunteer army was fully protected under all conditions.[109]

The Army Medical Bureau ignored the *Report* and continued for a time to resist the efforts of the Sanitary Commission to improve the sanitation and medical care of the Union armies. During McClellan's costly and futile Peninsula campaign in the spring and early summer of 1862, Olmsted wrote his superiors that the Sanitary Commission had had to supply the army with nearly all its medical aid and supplies. His devoted assistants toiled night and day in the field and on the river steamers which the army had lent them for conversion into hospital transports. One of his aides, Frederick N. Knapp, was sent home afterward worn out and almost deranged. The highly intelligent and adoring Katharine Prescott Wormeley, who later went on to a distinguished career as a literary translator, found working at Olmsted's side to have been the major experience of her life. His ability to bring order out of great confusion and provide medical care to an army despite great difficulties impressed her deeply.[110]

Before the end of the Peninsula campaign, the Army Medical Bureau began to cooperate with the U.S. Sanitary Commission because William A. Hammond, the Sanitary Commission's favorite candidate, replaced Finley as surgeon general. He carried out many of Olmsted's suggestions for reforming the Medical Bureau and took further aid and advice from the commission in a constructive spirit. Gradually, the Medical Bureau was able to supply more and more of the relief needed by troops on the battlefield and in hospitals. A year after Hammond became surgeon general, Olmsted reported that the bureau was now supplying nine-tenths of the medical care of the army.[111]

While the enormous organization of the Sanitary Commission worked more and more smoothly, sending relief agents and stores to camps, battlefields, and hospitals, and coordinating the efforts of 7,000 aid societies in northern cities and towns, Olmsted was growing more and more restive in a subordinate's role. As early as February 1862 he had been thinking about other jobs that he might be doing, such as the management of contraband slaves freed by the Union army.[112] As time went on, the commissioners thought he was trying to pick quarrels with them. The group of men who were his superiors were disposed to be sympathetic and admiring, but there seemed to be no way to soothe his feelings. George Templeton Strong, a wealthy lawyer whose diary has proved a remarkably informative record of his times, was one of Olmsted's superiors. Strong found him the most extraordinary man he had ever known, with rare talent and energy, absolute purity and disinterestedness. After two years, though, he sensed that Olmsted wanted complete control over the Sanitary Commission's activities. Strong confided to his diary that he detected in the general secretary a monomania for elaborately thought-out and generally impractical paper schemes and that his appetite for power was turning him into "a lay-Hildebrand." Two months after Strong had visited Washington to find Olmsted working feverishly day and night in five-day stretches, he was reconciled to the idea that the Sanitary Commission needed a new general secretary.[113]

Olmsted's last services to the commission were in the spring and early summer of 1863. He went west to Cincinnati, Chicago, and St. Louis, and down the Mississippi to Grant's encampment before Vicksburg, on a trip which was supposed to bring the western branches of the Sanitary Commission under the tighter control of the national organization. General Grant gave the U.S. Sanitary Commission the exclusive use of a steamer to bring in medical supplies to his army and forbade the competing state sanitary commissions to operate within the area under his command. Olmsted, though, was not successful in his efforts to persuade the branch sanitary commission officers to submit fully to national control or even to cooperate with one another. To make matters worse, Olmsted found that the Executive Committee to which he reported was disposed to be more lenient toward the western branches than he was.[114] In July he directed the great stream of supplies and relief to the battlefield at Gettysburg; and in August he resigned from the Sanitary Commission because he thought the commissioners had not supported his efforts to run the organization in a unified and efficient manner.[115]

The difficulties which Olmsted had come to find unendurable arose not only because of the independence of the western commissions and the obstructive attitude of the Executive Committee but also because officials in the federal government, such as Secretary of War Edwin M. Stanton, were consistently suspicious and hostile toward the Sanitary Commission throughout the war. Stanton viewed the appointment of the strong-willed and competent William Hammond as surgeon general as a threat to his own authority, partly because Hammond was friendly to the Sanitary Commission and, once in office, adopted some of their suggested reforms for the Army Medical Bureau. Stanton refused to cooperate with him and finally had the personal satisfaction of discharging him in August 1864 because of an unfounded accusation that he had been responsible for irregularities in the letting of contracts for hospital supplies.[116]

When Olmsted left, the Sanitary Commission lost some of its direction and purpose. It never again had an executive secretary who tried so conscientiously to give unified management to all of its far-flung activities.[117] Olmsted, himself, was at a loss as to what to do next. Because of political pressure, Vaux and Olmsted had been forced to resign from the Central Park job in the middle of May. Olmsted had hoped to become associated with Edwin L. Godkin, a rising young journalist, in publishing a weekly newspaper that would strengthen interest in national public policy, support the war effort, the arts and literature, and promote loyalty to the Union. Despite the best efforts of fund-raisers like George Templeton Strong, Olmsted could not commit himself to the project because it had not yet attracted enough money. Olmsted needed a well-paying job to support his family and pay off the $12,000 debt to the creditors of Dix and Edwards that he had incurred with the failure of the firm in 1857.[118]

There was such a job available, but it was in California. The position of resident manager of a gold mining property in the Sierra Nevada foothills could be his at $10,000 a year in gold, plus $10,000 of the company's stock per year. To take the job would mean that he would have to leave his friends, give up any part in the Central Park project, and abandon the possibility of serving his country in the Civil War. Yet the California episode, which ended in 1865 when the mines failed, was a turning point in Olmsted's life. Thereafter he was no longer dependent upon his father's generosity. The isolation of the mining frontier gave him a chance to ponder the tendencies of American life and history, and when Governor Low asked him to report on the future use of Yosemite Valley for the state of California, he took advantage of the opportunity to outline a national policy for preserving natural scenery.

In August of 1863, a group of New York investors, including George Opdyke and Morris Ketchum, bought the Mariposa Estate in California, which had been owned at one time by John C. Fremont. They paid $10,000,000 to Trenor Park, a San Francisco lawyer who was in possession as its resident manager. The group needed a resident manager of its own to run the property, upon which there were seven gold mines. From his work for Central Park and the Sanitary Commission, Olmsted had acquired a reputation for being a brilliant administrator. The investors must have realized that his exhausting war duties had left him in poor mental and physical health, but they decided to take the chance that he would recover in California. The New Yorkers, who called themselves the Mariposa Company, promised Olmsted "complete, entire control of the whole operation."[119]

Olmsted accepted the job after seeking the advice of his father, his friend George Templeton Strong, and David Dudley Field, the prominent New York legal reformer and lawyer who was one of the new owners of the Mariposa Company. Olmsted must have hoped that the California climate would improve his frail health and that the excellent salary would at last allow him both to pay off his publishing debts and support his family. His

28

salary as architect-in-chief of Central Park had not been enough, and he had only accepted half of the $4,000 that had been offered by the Sanitary Commission.[120] For Olmsted there had to be a higher justification for his leaving the East in the midst of a civil war than money or health. Embarrassed by the fact that he seemed to be accepting a call to a richer parish, he tried to justify his decision by arguing that he would be grasping his only definite opportunity to advance civilization. His presence on the mining frontier of California would be an "influence favorable to religion, good order and civilization."[121]

The friends who had hoped that Olmsted would help them gather funds to start a weekly newspaper loyal to the Union cause were rudely surprised by his sudden departure. It is probable that neither Edwin L. Godkin, the scholarly journalist, nor Professor Charles Eliot Norton of Harvard —the two most interested in the project—knew the extent of Olmsted's financial burdens.[122]

In September 1863 Olmsted sailed alone from New York for California via the Isthmus of Panama. His family was to follow in the early spring. The major experience of the trip was discovering in the dense and luxuriant jungle of Panama a "sense of the superabundant creative power, infinite resource, and liberality of Nature—the childish playfulness and profuse careless utterance of Nature."[123] After this sight of tropical luxuriance, his arrival in California in the midst of one of its worst droughts was depressing. To get to Bear Valley, where he was to live on the forty-five-thousand-acre Mariposa Estate, he had to spend a long day traveling by carriage from Stockton through the hot and dusty Central Valley. The climate of the foothills of the Sierra Nevada was cooler and the scenery more attractive than in the Central Valley, but he was appalled by the dryness and the stunted vegetation.[124]

Olmsted immediately set about getting the best information about the future prospects of the seven gold mines on the Mariposa Estate. These, together with the mills, workshops, warehouses, wagon roads, railroads, and water system, made up the greatest single mining property in California, save for the New Almaden quicksilver mines.[125] Josiah Dwight Whitney, head of the California State Geological Survey, lent him the services of two geologists, the French-trained William Ashburner and the brilliant twenty-two-year-old Clarence King, who later became head of the United States Geological Survey. Even with such expert assistance, the unhappy truth about the Mariposa mines (which Trenor Park already knew) came to light very slowly.[126]

In 1847 John Charles Fremont had acquired the Mariposa Estate in the foothills of the Sierra Nevada from the Mexican governor of California, Juan B. Alvarado. Gold was discovered there in 1849. The mining operations had looked promising during the early 1850s, and Fremont must have made some money at the start, but it was not long before the estate was in debt. Mining within its limits had to be suspended entirely on several occasions. The basic and unremediable difficulty with the mines was that they were on the wrong end of the mother lode. The enticingly rich quartz outcroppings that Fremont's men had discovered in the southern mother lode district decreased abruptly in value when they were followed down to a moderate depth.[127] To make matters worse, some of the gold occurred in sulphide ores and could be extracted only by following the newly imported chlorination process. This method was known in California, but because the needed machines were lacking and the process was only efficient in treating large amounts of sulphide ore, the use of it did not spread from Grass Valley and Nevada City, profitable mother lode mines to the north, for more than six years.[128]

Until Olmsted appeared in the fall of 1863, the Fremont Estate had been successfully exploited by the only method possible: trading on the supposed future value of the property. This is exactly what Trenor Park had done when he acquired a one-eighth interest in the estate as one of Fremont's creditors and gained control of the property as resident manager in June 1860.[129]

When he had made a fortune advancing large sums on the security of the estate, Park decided to sell the mines. By exploiting only the richest veins and neglecting any development work he made the mines produce $100,000 worth of gold a month, which persuaded the New York buyers to pay him $10,000,000 for the property. He gave possession when accounts were cleared for $1,400,000. Park had a large part in forming the Mariposa Company, which bought the Estate; then the shorn lambs chose Olmsted, as it turned out, to disillusion them.[130]

Not realizing the poor prospects of the mines, Olmsted took the advice of another member of the San Francisco law firm that had defended Fremont's claims, Frederick Billings, later the president of the Northern Pacific Railroad. Billings told the new manager soon after his arrival that his success with the enterprise would depend upon "radical and expensive" operations.[131] Olmsted made demands for funds from New York, which the company had never expected would be necessary, in order to build a fifty-five-stamp mill, continue the development of other surface installations, divert water from the Merced River to the estate, and improve the housing and living standards for employees and staff.[132] Olmsted could not get the money necessary for all of his projects because the company was more heavily in debt than he realized. Even at its height, production of gold could not always keep up with the expenses, let alone pay off the debts. Geologist Benjamin Silliman's optimistic report of May 1864 and two short-lived bonanzas helped to obscure the truth about the mines until January 1865.[133]

Happily, Olmsted did not have to be trapped in the wreckage of the

Mariposa Company. While in California he took advantage of more promising financial and professional opportunities. Starting in 1864, he invested part of his salary and a loan from his father in California stocks which eventually would augment his income handsomely. Thanks to his reputation as a designer of New York's Central Park, several clients consulted him on California projects. The directors of Mountain View Cemetery had him design their grounds at Oakland and, in early 1865, he gave advice for the design of two estates south of San Francisco. That spring he agreed to make a preliminary plan for a campus, village, and park for the College of California.[134]

Frederick F. Low, governor of California, appointed Olmsted in September 1864 to a board of eight commissioners to take over the Yosemite Valley and the adjoining Big Tree Grove, which the United States had withdrawn from the public lands and ceded to California to preserve for the public. Olmsted was, in effect, head of the commission. The governor stipulated that Olmsted was to review all propositions for the improvement of the grant and all applications for leases. Also, Low asked Olmsted to prepare a preliminary report for the California Legislature on the uses appropriate for the Yosemite grant and how best to provide for them.[135]

Before state funds were made available, Olmsted advanced $500 of his own money to pay Clarence King and his friend on the California State Geological Survey, James T. Gardiner, to make a topographical map of the Yosemite Valley.[136] Olmsted himself had visited the Yosemite, which was close to the Estate. His family had spent part of the summer of 1864 there, and in the last week in August Professor William Brewer of Yale, another State Survey geologist, joined Olmsted and his stepson John for a pack trip through the High Sierra adjacent to the grant.[137]

Olmsted was far more aware of the national importance of the Yosemite as a scenic reserve than most Californians were. In his report to the state legislature he pointed out that this magnificent scenery was so valuable a resource for the health of everyone that it should belong to all the people and never be parceled out to private owners. Setting aside and caring for large public reservations of natural scenery was one way, he suggested, that the government could protect the pursuit of happiness of all against the selfish aims of a few.

The report he wrote was not directly influential, because it was suppressed. It anticipated, however, the argument used later in establishing Yellowstone Park in 1872 and in the National Park Act of 1916: the federal government has a duty to set aside natural areas of extraordinary beauty and significance and manage them for the benefit and free use of the people.

At the time he delivered his report to the Yosemite commissioners, Olmsted was fortunate in having the encouragement of some distinguished visitors to the Yosemite Valley, among them Samuel Bowles, editor of the *Springfield* (Mass.) *Republican*, and the speaker of the United States House

31

of Representatives, Schuyler Colfax. Bowles, who struck up a friendship with Olmsted, was so impressed with his ideas that in his book about the trip he proposed that the admirable example of the Yosemite park be followed throughout the Union at such places as Niagara Falls and the Adirondacks.[138]

Several difficulties with the grant prevented prompt and effective steps to establish a permanent Yosemite State Reservation based on Olmsted's recommendations. The grant of the United States public lands to California provided no federal funds with which to reimburse those who would have to relinquish property within the reservation. As a result, more than a decade of litigation over the holdings of J. M. Hutchings and others who held lands in the valley hampered the public use of the area. Some of the eight commissioners chosen by Governor Low had divided loyalties. William Ashburner and Josiah D. Whitney were leading members of the California State Geological Survey, which had to battle continually for funds from the legislature to carry on its scientific work because the legislators doubted its practical utility. Whitney—the head of the survey—fought the diversion of the scanty public funds to any other enterprise, worthy or not. He tried to prevent the legislature from contributing to the College of California; and it seems highly likely that Ashburner and Whitney, taking advantage of their position as commissioners, prevented Olmsted's Yosemite report—which they knew asked for $37,000—from ever reaching the legislature.[139]

More important than the fact that the Yosemite Commission received only a tardy and meager appropriation of $12,000 (compared to $30,000 for the survey), the legislators, who never saw Olmsted's report, were unable by themselves to formulate a well-defined policy for administering the reservation. Perhaps if they had had the benefit of the Olmsted report they would have realized the national significance of the Yosemite, the necessity of protecting it from private exploitation and of making it accessible to the general public without spoiling its beauty. As it was, the state floundered so badly in its administration of the grant that the valley and the Big Trees were returned to federal care in 1905.[140]

Olmsted's first opportunity to do independent landscape designing came during the fall of 1864, when the trustees of the new Mountain View Cemetery in Oakland, California, asked him to plan their cemetery. He began work in December. The assignment must have been especially satisfying to him because, unlike his work on Central Park, the Sanitary Commission, and the Yosemite Commission, he had a free hand to do exactly what he thought was best, with the assurance that his designs would be faithfully carried out.[141]

Olmsted's plan was a bold departure from what he had done in the East: the planting was specifically appropriate to a semiarid country and to a cemetery. He made no attempt to create broad vistas of turf framed by luxuriant trees. Instead, the effects he thought suitable for the native oaks and cedars were much more formal. Rather than turning to the English picturesque tradition of landscape, he made use of what he remembered of the Mediterranean villa gardens he had seen on his trip to Rome in the spring of 1856.

The cemetery has a broad central avenue with regularly spaced trees on either side. At the farthest end there is a formal, terraced circle and fountain. The paths and roads which lead off this to the cemetery lots are curved to follow the topography rather than a geometrical plan, but the planting of drought- and wind-resistant ground cover, low bushes, and small trees indigenous to the region make an effect completely different from the pastoral Central Park. Little if any watering is necessary to maintain the planting through the dry season.[142]

The trustees of the College of California asked Olmsted in March of 1864 to suppy them with a plan for a village and a college campus on land which they held a few miles north of the town of Oakland, across the bay from San Francisco. In this design, he decided that the village should have a plan similar to that of Llewellyn Park, which Eugene A. Baumann and Alexander Jackson Davis had laid out in 1857 on a rugged and picturesque hillside in the Orange Mountains of New Jersey. The streets and avenues of Olmsted's town followed the topography rather than an unyielding rectangular grid. The campus and residence area were to be close together in the center of the plan, because he thought that an academic community should not be too separated from everyday life—though an ordinary, dusty, noisy, commercial town, in his opinion, was a distracting place for a scholar. In the plan he provided a road around the outskirts of the village to divert any future north and south traffic away from the center of town.[143]

Olmsted was careful to provide for the wants of the residents of his proposed village. He planned a small park secluded from the rest of the village for mothers and young children. Each house was to have two to five acres of land around it and be well set back from the road. He hoped that the architecture of the houses would not be ostentatious and would harmonize with their grounds, encouraging the out-of-door living that is so much easier in California than elsewhere. Although the Mountain View Cemetery plan was carried out, only a few parts of Olmsted's California College plan remain: the original line of Piedmont Avenue in Berkeley and parts of Strawberry Creek. Olmsted's idea of planting trees and bushes and ground cover that could survive the dry season without watering has been discarded in California. Almost everywhere on the Berkeley campus are lawns and flowers that require sprinkling from April to October during the dry season.[144]

In 1865, with the collapse of the Mariposa Company only a matter of time, Olmsted had to worry again about his future occupation. He thought he might turn back to writing and gathered notes for "a heavy sort of book" about the social tendencies of American civilization in the past fifty years, which, after his stay in California, he considered were generally for the good. Since the project for a weekly newspaper with E. L. Godkin did not yet have enough financial support, Olmsted tried to buy the San Francisco newspaper, the *Daily Alta California*, and persuade his friend Godkin to come out from New York to help him edit it. The *Daily Alta*, however, was not for sale. He thought, too, of becoming the president of a railroad or of an insurance company, only to discover that one had to have access to a large amount of capital to move into such a position.[145]

By August 1865 Olmsted had decided to leave California. Godkin had written him that at last he had gathered enough money to publish the first number of the *Nation*, as the new weekly was called, and wanted Olmsted's help on further issues. Calvert Vaux wanted to know whether to accept for Olmsted and himself their re-appointment as landscape architects of Central Park and take on the designing of Prospect Park in Brooklyn. Olmsted wrote back to Vaux and Godkin that he would accept the proffered jobs and re-signed from the Mariposa Company in September.[146]

During his last few months on the Pacific coast, Olmsted joined a campaign to provide a park for San Francisco. As a result, the Municipal Board asked him to suggest a location and prepare plans for a park. Although his design was not carried out, being considered too elaborate and expensive, the report he wrote is one of his most interesting because it goes far beyond the immediate project of a park to discuss city planning.[147]

The appropriate street plan for a city built upon extraordinarily steep hills like San Francisco, Olmsted advised the board, was not a rectangular grid of streets, because the grades resulting from carrying streets directly up and down the hills would be practically impossible for horse-drawn vehicles and for pedestrians. To save effort, annoyance, and danger, he recommended that the city lay out the streets to climb the hills with easy grades by having them follow winding courses (presumably of a spiral or switchback pattern). The other problem San Francisco faced was the extreme danger of fire in the windy dry season. To prevent fires from spreading out of control throughout the city, Olmsted planned a sunken parkway to form a firebreak, dividing the city in two. It also was to be a pleasant thoroughfare, better protected from the cold winds off the Pacific than were ordinary San Francisco streets.

The Municipal Board followed neither of Olmsted's suggestions. If they had respected the handsome shapes of the hills when they laid out the streets, the city might have become more beautiful and convenient than it is today; and Olmsted's boulevard might have confined the great fire of 1906 to only half the city. But, as Josiah Royce said of San Francisco when there was no longer any choice, its citizens had not yet learned that most civilized of arts—to enhance rather than destroy nature in the building of cities.[148]

The opportunity to work with Calvert Vaux on Prospect and Central parks and with E. L. Godkin on the newly founded *Nation* beckoned Olmsted and his family home. On October 13, 1865, Olmsted sailed from San Francisco to New York, bringing with him plans for Mountain View Cemetery and the California College grounds to be finished and engraved in the Olmsted, Vaux and Company office. The forty-one-day trip back by steamer down the Pacific coast, across the Isthmus via the Nicaraguan land route, and thence to New York on another steamer was miserable but well worthwhile, since Olmsted's greatest professional opportunities lay ahead of him in the East.[149]

Two days after Olmsted's arrival back in New York in November, George Templeton Strong took him to dinner at Delmonico's. He found the man who had become so difficult in his last days with the Sanitary Commission looking well, "as bright as ever," and full of talk about his California experiences.[150] Olmsted was in much better health than when he had left New York two years before; and thanks to his good salary and the comfortable returns he was getting on his California investments, he could pay off his publishing debts and no longer had to turn to his father for money.[151] He was sure that he had a profession to follow. The opportunities for a landscape architect that he had found in California, and the renewal of his work with Vaux in New York, must have showed him that his services were needed in this new field and that he could support himself and his family by practicing the art.

The landscape architects of Prospect Park returned to the Arcadian ideal of landscape beauty they had first tried to pursue in their design of Central Park in New York. The rolling and well-wooded site of the Brooklyn park made their task much easier than it had been on the rocky spine of Manhattan Island. When both Central Park and Prospect Park were within a few years of completion, George Templeton Strong weighed the merits of the Brooklyn park against his favorite:

> This park beats Central Park ten to one in trees. Its wealth of forest is most enviable. I think we cannot match its softly undulating lawns. But we beat it in rock and the boxes of landscape. Prospect Park's attempts at rock are pitiable, most palpable piles of boulders. We beat it also in water and bridges and other like structures. But it beats us in views and is a most lovely pleasance. . . .[152]

As in the San Francisco and College of California reports, Olmsted and Vaux's recommendations for Prospect Park contain many thoughts on city planning. They instructed the Brooklyn commissioners in the history of street systems from the Middle Ages onward. They made the point that a park would be of no use to Brooklyn unless it were accessible. The means of access, they argued, should make a pleasurable transition from city to country scenes. Furthermore, they advised that as more scattered parks came under the jurisdiction of the commission, these should be connected to each other by shaded drives like the new boulevards in Paris.[153]

They designed two boulevards or parkways based on the plan of the Avenue de l'Impératrice (now Foch) in Paris, having a central pleasure drive for carriages flanked on either side by pedestrian paths which, in turn, were bordered by service roads for delivery and local traffic with sidewalks for pedestrians along their outside edges. Each road or pathway was made separate from its neighbor by a strip of turf and a line of trees. The Eastern and Ocean parkways were built to provide pleasant greenbelts around the city which would enhance the value of the adjacent land for villa sites.[154]

Until July 1866 the arduous and apparently unpaid work Olmsted did for E. L. Godkin as an associate editor of the newly founded magazine, the *Nation*, distracted him from his budding career as a landscape architect. He shared editorial duties with Godkin, and after the first issue appeared in the summer of 1865, he tried to placate the disappointment of Major George L. Stearns, wartime recruiter of black troops for the Union army, who had raised money for the magazine expecting it to give substantial support to the rights of freed slaves. Despite Olmsted's efforts, Stearns and others withdrew their support from the venture.[155] Olmsted stood by Godkin. He had made a heavy investment of his time and energy in the *Nation*, which was the kind of magazine he had envisioned in 1852 and had tried to make *Putnam's* into in 1855. The *Nation* often took editorial positions with which Olmsted could agree. He, too, advocated an international copyright law and the protection of merchant seamen from arbitrary ship's officers, and he was angered by California's cession of parts of the Yosemite Valley to squatters. It may have been his suggestion to have a correspondent for the *Nation* travel through the postwar South to report what he saw and heard, leaving the public to draw its own inferences.[156]

In 1867, Vaux and Olmsted continued to expand their joint practice of landscape architecture. In addition to their heavy responsibilities connected with Central Park and Prospect Park, they took on park work at New Britain, Connecticut and Newark, New Jersey; and they began to design other parks in Brooklyn. Over the next five years they also wrote reports for the park commissions of Fall River, Providence, Albany, Philadelphia, and Hartford.[157]

One of their most important commissions came in 1868, when Emery E. Childs asked them to lay out a model suburban village to be called Riverside, nine miles west of the center of Chicago on David A. Gage's 1,600-acre farm overlooking the Des Plaines River. The designers now had their first great opportunity to replace the real estate speculator, the politician, and the surveyor in town planning when the Riverside trustees voted to adopt their plan.[158]

A month after visiting the site, Vaux and Olmsted had drawn up a preliminary plan and drafted a financial agreement with the trustees of the village. At the outset, they made it clear that their plan was not going to be a landscaped park with houses placed in it. The purpose of the Riverside plan was different from that of a park. Instead of helping to create the illusion of uninterrupted countryside stretching away as far as one could see, the suburban landscape was to suggest domesticity, seclusion, and community.[159]

The landscapers carefully brought all the elements of their plan into keeping with an overriding theme of "rural effect and domestic seclusion." Rather than placing shade trees at regular intervals along the streets as was the custom in Chicago, the designers planted maples, elms, and horse chestnut trees irregularly so as to display foliage along the curving streets in great and varied masses. To keep the visual tone of the village muted and tranquil, undisturbed by any architectural whimsies, each property owner had to plant one or two trees between his house and the roadway.[160]

Riverside was to be a fortunate combination of rural scenery and civilized comfort. The roadways, unlike most country highways, were built for dust-free and mud-free travel all year round. The Riverside Company piped gas and pure water to every house. Vaux and Olmsted sincerely believed that suburbs like Riverside, which were appearing throughout the country, represented "the best application of the arts of civilization to which mankind has yet attained." They tried to make Riverside a place which could foster the "harmonious cooperation of men in a community, and the intimate relationship and constant intercourse, and interdependence between families." To this end, they provided for greens like those of country villages, croquet grounds, ball fields, boat landings, skating facilities, and vine-draped pavilions.[161]

Like most of Olmsted and Vaux's plans, the one for Riverside went further than its apparent purpose. Olmsted and Vaux wanted to make the suburban village serve the interests of the people of Chicago. The designers proposed that a six-mile parkway should be built from Riverside to the outskirts of Chicago to allow businessmen to commute on horseback; it would also provide pleasant, tree-shaded riding paths, walks, and a carriage road for families who wished to come out from Chicago to the parks and picnic grounds of Riverside for holiday recreation and rural fetes.[162]

The trustees adopted the expensive and elaborate Olmsted, Vaux and Company plan after a lengthy, soul-searching debate.[163] The landscape architects asked $15,000 for their plan and a 7 percent commission upon gross expenditures, which would have brought them, if the estimates were correct, $112,500.[164] In spite of the financial depression after the Chicago fire, the village of Riverside was laid out substantially following the Vaux and Olmsted design, except for the proposed parkway, which fell victim to lack of funds and opposition from the landowners of Cicero and Chicago. The plan eventually became a very prosperous investment for the trustees in spite of the initial expense, but during the financial crisis the trustees defaulted on their payments to Olmsted, Vaux and Company, and the lots that they were given in lieu of payment sold for very little.[165]

In the middle 1870s, Olmsted collaborated in an even more comprehensive, original, and far-seeing city planning project than the design of Riverside. This was the plan the New York Department of Public Parks asked him to prepare for the Twenty-third and Twenty-fourth wards of New York, consisting of the recently annexed area of the Bronx between the Harlem river and Yonkers. His collaborator in this plan was not Calvert Vaux but an experienced civil engineer who had worked for the Croton Water Board, John James Robertson Croes.[166]

The Public Park Department wanted the two to design a rapid transit system and a network of streets for the area. Olmsted and Croes divided the work between them: Croes did the preliminary topographical survey, the design for the rapid transit system, and the plan for the main road pattern; and Olmsted did the secondary roads for the residential sections. The scheme Olmsted and Croes developed for the wards was a marriage of railroad engineering and picturesque park planning, and as a result, it was the first important departure after Central Park from the New York Street Commissioners' rectangular block system of 1811.[167]

The topography of the area was the determining consideration for every detail of the plan; this was both good railroad practice and orthodox late-eighteenth-century landscape design. Croes first determined the site of a loop of tracks which would encircle the wards and a connecting line which cut through the middle. This had to be done before anything else, because the proposed steam rapid-transit lines had to be as straight and as level as possible, and also because the designers wanted to apply the principle of grade separation which Olmsted and Vaux had first used in Central Park. At no place were the tracks to be crossed on a level by any of the roadways. Croes's proposed steam rapid-transit lines were far cheaper to build, less ugly, and much quieter than the new elevated railways being built at that time over the streets of Manhattan, and they were far safer and faster than the horse and cable cars already running in the streets of many American cities.[168]

Once the site of the railroad lines and main roads had been settled for the plan, Olmsted proposed that a curving secondary road system be established that would follow closely the contour lines of the varied topography. Such a scheme, he argued, would be less expensive and more appropriate for a suburban district than a straight street system. These roads would, like the primary thoroughfares, cross the railway lines only at over or underpasses.[169]

The remarkable proposal was drawn up by Croes and Olmsted during a short period in the affairs of the city of New York when the Department of Public Parks was under the control of a reform group who had broken the hold of the Tweed ring. When the time came to carry out the Olmsted and Croes ideas, though, the reform politicians had been thrown out of office by a reconstituted Tammany Hall group of Democrats who had found a way to get back into power under the Self-Government Charter granted New York City by the state legislature in 1873. Olmsted's health broke down under systematic harassment from the Tammany politicians and their friends in office. Just after he requested and received a leave of absence from his job as landscape architect to the Department of Public Parks, the Office of Design and Superintendence of the New York Parks was abolished and all salaried officials discharged.[170]

The fate of the Twenty-third and Twenty-fourth ward plans was not sealed when Olmsted left for Europe with his stepson John. Croes remained to defend the plans in an unequal battle with entrenched politicians, real estate speculators, and the Gilbert and New York Elevated Railway Companies, who were eager to obtain franchises from the city to build iron bridges down the streets of the annexed districts now that the Sixth Avenue extended almost the length of Manhattan Island. They were so proud of their structures that they even suggested that an elevated line would be a picturesque addition to Central Park.[171]

The opportunity to create a handsome suburban district was a victim of the power struggles, cupidity, and narrow vision of the age. The chance to have an inexpensive and rational rapid transit system, perhaps better than any ever built in America, was lost. Later citizens of New York were asked to pay for the subway system after millions had already been spent on the ill-advised elevated lines.[172]

Olmsted's experiences with the interference of politicians made him consider leaving New York when he returned from his European trip. His ties to the city had been gradually loosening for more than a decade. He had given up his partnership with Calvert Vaux in 1872 for "reasons of mutual convenience" and perhaps because he no longer really needed his help. In the meantime, too, his practice of landscape architecture was hardly confined to New York. Many of his clients were ranged around Boston, and he had already started work on the Boston parks and others in cities such as Montreal.[173]

An important reason for Olmsted's decision to leave New York must have been his growing friendship and professional association with the architect Henry Hobson Richardson, who had moved from New York to live in Brookline, Massachusetts, in 1874. He probably knew Richardson as early as 1867, when they both lived on Staten Island. The architect, then just beginning his career, had charm, gaiety, exuberant energy, and eager sympathy, which must have been a great comfort to Olmsted when conducting the obstinate affairs of Central Park[174] and business with his demanding private and public clients elsewhere. Also, Richardson's informal architectural style, combining craftsmanship and integrity, must have attracted him more than Vaux's fussy and staccato Victorian Gothic.

In 1871 Olmsted and Richardson had worked together on the Staten Island Improvement Commission, a remarkable example of what nineteenth century cooperative planning could produce. It integrated the knowledge of geologists, public health doctors, and sanitary engineers with the aesthetic and social theories of Olmsted and Richardson to create a comprehensive plan for the island, taking into account both the natural ecology and the future needs of its inhabitants for housing, transportation, water supply, and open space.

Even though an important impulse for the report was a mistaken attempt to rid the island of malaria by preventing the creation of miasmas from undrained and stagnant bodies of water, the thoughts expressed in the report accorded so well with a rational, far-seeing development of Staten Island that the community missed a great opportunity to plan for the future when the commission did not adopt the report.[175] Olmsted and H. H. Richardson also collaborated on the buildings and grounds for the State Hospital at Buffalo, New York.[176]

Richardson urged the Olmsteds to move to Brookline, even offering to sell them some land he owned and build a house there for them. They did come in 1882, although Olmsted kept his New York office open until 1883. Olmsted was greatly relieved to be away from the frustrations and strains of life in New York during the Gilded Age. He confessed to his friend, Charles Loring Brace, that he now felt he was living again "after several years of real despair." He told Brace that he enjoyed suburban life beyond description and thought of Brookline as one of the best governed and most civilized places in America.[177]

After his move to Brookline, Olmsted was no longer in a subordinate's role. Even when he worked on the Boston parks, the commissioners, unlike those in New York, showed him the respect due a professional. His private clients, the Appletons, Hunnewells, and Charles Eliot Norton, must have been far more sympathetic to his aims than the wealthier and more ostentatious patrons he could have had in New York. He heartily disliked the latter's lavish displays, and so did his Boston neighbors.[178]

Olmsted had the pleasure of collaborating with the Falstaffian Richardson on several of his projects in New England. Richardson designed a bridge of Roxbury puddingstone for the Fenway. The simple, undecorated arch of rough-faced stone over the Muddy River was so perfectly in keeping with Olmsted's landscape that it served as a model for many other park bridges, including those in Franklin Park. Olmsted landscaped several of Richardson's suburban railroad stations on the Boston to Albany line.[179] In his book on Richardson, Henry-Russell Hitchcock concedes that Olmsted's contribution in one of their joint projects was probably more distinguished than the architect's. Richardson's town hall at North Easton, an awkward building with abrupt shifts of scale, style, and construction, could at best be considered, he writes, only as a successful part of Olmsted's splendid, naturalistic treatment of the rocky hillside site and the great stairs rising up through the ledges.[180]

The Olmsted firm took on an impressive number of clients from all over the country. One of Olmsted's stepsons, the methodical and hardworking John, became a partner in 1884 and had a large part in keeping the stream of work moving through the office smoothly. During this time, the firm designed great public parks for many cities, including Bridgeport, Buffalo, Boston, Detroit, and Rochester, and for the Niagara Falls Reservation. Its members also designed various subdivisions, among them that of the Newport Land Trust in Rhode Island and Chestnut Hill in Brookline, Massachusetts.[181]

Olmsted, characteristically, took a long-range and comprehensive view of any project about which he was consulted. When asked to propose a plan for the United States Capitol grounds in 1874, he discussed the Capitol's relationship to the Mall and to the White House. His plan of Riverside, Illinois, included a proposed parkway to downtown Chicago, six miles away. He saw Prospect Park as a part of a system of public open spaces linked by parkways throughout the greater New York area. His plans for Boston were equally comprehensive.[182]

In 1878, the commissioners of the Boston Park System wanted to abate the peril and stench of the polluted, stagnant water gathering behind the city in the Back Bay by draining it into the Charles River. They also wanted to provide more access from Boston to the surrounding towns. Olmsted suggested that they could meet both objectives and extend the Boston park system if they built the necessary causeways, bridges, roads, interceptor sewers, basins, tidal gates, and dams so as to form a green necklace of pleasure drives, parks, and ponds around the city. His proposed Arborway and Fenway would give access to the western suburbs and link Franklin Park and the Arnold Arboretum to the Charles River and to the tree-lined Commonwealth Avenue which ran downtown to the Public Garden and the Common. The brilliant scheme, completed in the early 1890s, provided a precedent for the extension of the Boston park system to include the Blue Hills Reservation and Middlesex Fells and the damming of the Charles River in 1910.[183]

Although Olmsted encompassed the Boston region in his plan, he also remained sensitive to the unique qualities of the Franklin Park site in West Roxbury. The stony 500 acres, partly wooded and partly pasture, were, he thought, a good site for a country park. He wrote that there was not within or near the city "any other equal extent of ground of as simple, and pleas-

41

ingly simple, rural aspect." It could be favorably compared with other parks, such as Fontainebleau, outside Paris. "The woods of Fontainebleau," he wrote, "that have been the models of a thousand painted landscapes, being mostly of artificially planted trees, grown stiffly for the timber market, and not for natural beauty, are no more art-educative than the woods that may be had on Franklin Park. And though the region to which the name Fontainebleau is applied is so much larger, it offers the student no better examples of landscape distance, intricacy, obscurity, and mystery than may be had in Franklin Park." He presented this landscape to the public by means of six miles of driveways, thirteen miles of walks, and two miles of bridle path.[184]

Olmsted displayed his architectural acumen as well as his landscaping abilities when commissioned to design the United States Capitol grounds in 1874. He wanted to keep the Capitol the dominant feature in his plan yet provide grounds which would be attractive and cool in Washington's sticky summer heat. To do this, he shaded the walks and carriageways with low, thickly branching trees which shut out the sun but allowed a good view of the building.[185]

William Thornton's design for the U.S. Capitol (approved in 1793) provided Olmsted with his major problem. The architect had designed the main façade to face east, mistakenly assuming the major growth of Washington would be in that direction instead of to the west. Olmsted proposed to give the neglected west side, which was most often seen, appropriate grandeur. The western slope of Capitol Hill being too steep for a grand avenue, Olmsted suggested a great terrace below the building with steps down to more level ground. This handsome foundation would make the Capitol look larger than it was. The idea seemed so unusual and radical to the Congress that the legislators took ten years to approve it; they feared that the vast structure would hide rather than enhance the Capitol. The success of the terrace on the western front and the enormous plaza on the eastern side demonstrate that Olmsted could design for monumentality as well as natural beauty.[186]

Olmsted faced another challenge when Senator Leland Stanford asked him for advice about his plans for a university in California he planned to found in memory of his son, who had died in 1884. Olmsted went to the West Coast in the fall of 1886 with his son Frederick and junior partner, Harry Codman, to select a site for the proposed university on Stanford's 7000 acres thirty miles south of San Francisco. Olmsted suggested that it would be best to have the main group of college buildings on a commanding site in the coastal range foothills west of Palo Alto, which were covered with the remains of a forest of firs, pines, oaks, and redwoods. Stanford, however, wanted the campus on the large, flat, meadowlike portion of the property, where his son had spent hours riding horseback.[187]

Olmsted acceded gracefully to Stanford's desire about the site but stood firm when it was suggested that the new university be a re-creation of a New England college with brick Georgian architecture, broad stretches of turf, and wine-glass elms.[188] He explained to Stanford that the planting and the building should be appropriate to the semiarid climate of California. It would be far better to model the campus on the gardens and buildings of the Mediterranean countries than to imitate Harvard or Amherst. To achieve this Mediterranean effect, which he deemed appropriate to Stanford, Olmsted took great pains to select plant materials from Spain and the North African coast which would thrive in Palo Alto's warm, dry climate.[189]

The firm of Shepley, Rutan, and Coolidge, which succeeded to the practice of H. H. Richardson when he died in 1886, designed the college in a Mediterranean-Romanesque style. The one- or two-story buildings were arranged to form arcaded quadrangles, and they embodied the Richardsonian motifs: short columns with decorated capitals, the hemisphere arch, and heavy stone walls. All buildings had pitched roofs of tile supported by wooden trusses. Instead of sodding the quadrangles, Olmsted had them paved with stone blocks and planted with ornamental palms.[190] No watering would be necessary to maintain his plantings through the dry season.

The architecture and landscaping of Stanford University was a departure from the usual American academic style. Olmsted's quadrangles surrounded by low, arcaded buildings created a less pretentious though more formal effect than that found on most other college campuses. Evolving a landscape style for a Mediterranean climate in the United States was a new idea for transplanted easterners in California, but the Stanford campus was later copied all over California in mission-style school and college buildings. The group of buildings is undeniably handsome, but perhaps if it had been situated on a hillside, as Olmsted had first suggested, it would have made an even more striking pattern in the California landscape.[191]

The vast difference in appearance between Central Park and the Stanford University grounds should not surprise anyone acquainted with Olmsted's flexible and non-doctrinaire approach to design. For instance, he saw no more conflict between informal and formal schools of design than he did between the work of the shoemaker and the hatter. The approach used in any design should be that which provided best for fullness of life by meeting the client's requirements within the possibilities of the local climate. The formal architectural design advocated by many of Olmsted's opponents would not have been right, he argued, for Central Park, which was supposed to provide relief from city sights and sounds. In the temperate and wet climate of New York, it was possible to provide scenes similar to those of the great English parks.[192] At Stanford, on the other hand, the picturesque landscape of England or New England was out of place: luxuriant foliage and sweeping vistas of greensward should not be expected in a warm, dry climate. Here, the necessary shade should be provided by formal arcades, as in Mediterranean countries, and the grounds embellished with native and foreign plants that did not need constant watering.[193]

In his last years in the profession Olmsted had to work with a group of men who insisted that the formal architecture and landscape of the Renaissance was appropriate at all times and places. It was right, they claimed, not only for a town house or a government building but for a seaside villa, a mountain retreat, or a world's fair. The leader of the architectural generation that followed Richardson's was the dominating and persuasive Richard Morris Hunt. He confirmed the desire of Richardson's former assistants, Charles F. McKim, Stanford White, and William R. Mead, to abandon Richardson's heavy, Romanesque style for public buildings and churches and his informal, wooden shingle style for houses, saying these styles were barbaric and undisciplined.[194]

Hunt worked with Olmsted on several estates for the Vanderbilts and Twomblys, and on the Vanderbilt mausoleum,[195] but there must have been some strain in the compromise between these two opinionated gentlemen. In the twenty years before their collaboration Hunt had lost two aesthetic struggles with Olmsted and his friends. In 1866, the park commissioners refused to carry out his grandiose gateway designs for Central Park, which they had approved three years before. Public protest and Olmsted and Vaux's complaint that the architectural designs were out of keeping with a rural park had changed their minds. In 1876 Hunt lost a heated battle against Olmsted, Leopold Eidlitz, and H. H. Richardson over whether the design for the New York State capitol at Albany should be Renaissance or Romanesque in style.[196] To plan George W. Vanderbilt's estate, "Biltmore," with Richard Morris Hunt, and the Chicago World's Fair with Hunt and McKim, Mead, and White, the sixty-seven-year-old Olmsted had to utilize all his gifts of compromise.

Happily, on Vanderbilt's vast mountain estate, covering many square miles near Asheville, North Carolina, there was room for both Olmsted's English deer park and Hunt's proposed mansion, a late Gothic French chateau. Olmsted confessed to a friend that the plan had cost him more worry than anything else he had done. Yet the two schools of thought blended magnificently—the formal grounds immediately around the castle and the rolling pastoral landscape of meadow and forest stretching off to the mountains beyond. The beautiful, winding drive into the estate was a triumph of picturesque unexpectedness and surprise, bursting upon Hunt's chateau and its sweeping view only at the end.[197]

It is ironic that at the New York dinner given for the artists and architects of the Chicago World's Fair, Daniel Burnham, who had directed their efforts, should have hailed Olmsted as the best adviser and chief planner of the exposition.[198] The landscape architect's concept of what the exposition should be like had differed completely from that of most of the architects who decided its final appearance. Instead of dazzling Americans with a vision of architectural magnificence which looked like a permanent white city, Olmsted had hoped for a frankly temporary bit of colorful pageantry.[199] The architects and artists of the fair, like Burnham, must have sensed Olmsted's disgruntlement and may have thought to show him their respect and friendship by the gesture.[200]

After the fair, Olmsted continued to concern himself with the immense number of projects his firm took on, such as the park designs for Louisville, Milwaukee, and Buffalo, and gave particular attention to Biltmore. He also had a part in the firm's design of the Charles River dam and their embankment scheme for Boston and the perimeter parks and parkways of the Metropolitan District Commission. These imaginative and far-seeing plans transformed the appearance of Boston and its expanding suburbs by preserving and enhancing the remaining natural scenery.[201]

By 1895, though, Olmsted realized that his memory was becoming unreliable and that his energies were declining. He told his partners that he could no longer be counted upon to play an important part in the firm's complicated and wide-ranging practice.[202] By this time, the office in Brookline was firmly in the hands of his stepson, John C. Olmsted, his son, Frederick Law Olmsted, Jr., and Charles Eliot, the son of the president of Harvard. Ambitious European tours and enforced rest with his worried family could no longer bring back Olmsted's health and enthusiasm. Plagued with insomnia and fits of anxiety and anger, he lapsed into senility. His family committed him to McLean Hospital outside of Boston in 1898, where he died in 1903.[203]

Olmsted left behind him an enormous amount of work accomplished: twenty great city parks, many college campuses, private estates, and institutional grounds. (Ironically, he had designed the grounds of McLean Hospital, where he spent his last years.) Despite the natural appearance of their great landscaped parks, citizens of such places as Louisville, Buffalo, and Montreal have come to realize that Olmsted did more for them than add a few benches and paths to previously existing scenery. Often the park site had been desolate and unpromising or hardly fit for public use. Perhaps, though, it is just as well for the repose of park frequenters that the artificial landscape they enjoy does not memorialize Olmsted's many struggles with real estate speculators, politicians, and budget trimmers.

As the scion of a generous, well-to-do family, Olmsted had the painful luxury of being able to take his time in choosing a career. From the beginning, he sought an occupation which would help to advance civilization: as a gentleman farmer, he tried to educate his neighbors both in methods and in taste, and as a writer, he attempted to reveal the effect of slavery on the civilization of the southern states. *Putnam's Monthly* and Dix and Edwards, partly under his management in the 1850s, were intended to raise the level of literary taste and information nationally, by publishing only the best wherever it might be found.

He began his work on Central Park, embittered by his publishing failure and in deep sorrow over his brother's death, as "a forlorn hope" to enhance civilized values in New York, and achieved astonishing success. When the existence of American civilization was threatened by the outbreak of the Civil War, Olmsted, as executive secretary of the Sanitary Commission, took the lead in providing for the medical and sanitary needs of the Union armies defending it. Exhausted by this service in the summer of 1863, he left to run a gold mine in California. He viewed even this endeavor, by which he recouped his publishing losses, as a chance to improve the society of the frontier. While there he seized the opportunity to plan Yosemite Park and design a campus and village for the College of California.

Olmsted's subsequent career as a landscape architect was built on the observation that the majority of American people would soon be living in or around cities. He had long since given up the notion of his scientific farming days that the quality of American life would be determined by the farmer. His bias was not anti-urban; rather, he looked toward the creation of a new kind of city, centralized at the core and dispersed at the periphery.[204] Partly because of the boss-ridden politics of his day, Olmsted had little part in the social, economic, and architectural planning of the center city, but his designs for parks, suburbs, and estates were intended to bring city comforts and natural beauty together into a life-giving and civilized amalgam, and create a happy environment for future generations of Americans.

Olmsted's great work was done at a time when the landscape architect and the sanitary engineer combined forces to plan for our cities. He lived into the period when architects like Daniel Burnham assumed the major role in comprehensive planning and put great emphasis on designing an unabashedly formal and monumental downtown. But Olmsted's legacy of open space and suburban planning combined well with what was to come and has remained an important corrective influence. We can still look to his work for guidance in controlling suburban sprawl, in giving access to open space within the city, and in preserving such examples of sublimity in our landscape as Niagara Falls and the Yosemite Valley. As farmer, author, administrator, and park planner, Olmsted fought selfish and short-sighted thinking with imaginative proposals to enhance the life of his own times and that of future generations.

Charles Capen McLaughlin

1. In 1947 and 1948 Frederick Law Olmsted, Jr., gave approximately twenty-four thousand items to the Library of Congress, most of which were from the period 1836 to 1903. In 1967, ninety containers of Olmsted Associates, Inc., records arrived, and

in 1971, four hundred additional containers with material dating from as late as 1954 were deposited. Although the majority of these later accessions do not contain items from the papers of Frederick Law Olmsted, Sr., they do contain important additional correspondence. (*Frederick Law Olmsted: A Register of His Papers in the Library of Congress*, Washington, D.C., 1963; "Olmsted Associates, Inc.," Manuscript Division, Library of Congress, Mimeographed Shelf List, AC 13,837.)

2. *Olmsted Genealogy*, pp. 60, 106–8; autobiographical fragments, entitled "Passages in the Life of an Unpractical Man," in Frederick Law Olmsted Papers, Library of Congress, hereafter cited as Olmsted Papers.
3. See Autobiographical Fragment A, note 10, below.
4. Autobiographical Fragment A.
5. JO Journal, Sept. 27, 1830.
6. *Forty Years*, 1:3–4.
7. See Autobiographical Fragment A, note 25, below.
8. Autobiographical Fragment A.
9. See Autobiographical Fragment B, note 6, below.
10. Autobiographical Fragment A; unititled manuscript reproduced as Autobiographical Fragment B; FLO to Elizabeth Baldwin Whitney, Dec. 16, 1890; Russell Noyes, *Wordsworth and the Art of Landscape* (Bloomington, Indiana, 1968), pp. 23–24, 32–34, 40–45.
11. JO Journal, June 14, 17, 1837; FLO to Elizabeth Baldwin Whitney, Dec. 16, 1890; FLO to Mariana Griswold Van Rensselaer, June 11, 1893; Autobiographical Fragment B.
12. See Autobiographical Fragment B, note 10, below.
13. Mariana Griswold Van Rensselaer, "Frederick Law Olmsted," *Century Illustrated Monthly Magazine* 46, no. 6 (Oct. 1893):860–67; Autobiographical Fragment B.
14. *Rode's New York City Directory for 1850–1851* (New York, 1850), pp. 43, 260: see Spear 990; JO Journal, Aug. 18, 1840, March 11, 1842; FLO to Mary Bull Olmsted, March 20, 1841.
15. FLO to JHO, April 8, 1843; JO Journal, April 23, 1843; FLO to Parents, Sept. 5, 1843.
16. FLO to Family, March 10, [1900], McLean Hospital Medical Records, McLean Hospital, Waverly, Mass.
17. FLO to JHO, Sept. 28, Dec. 10, 1843; JO Journal, April 15, 1844; [Frederick Law Olmsted], "A Voice from the Sea," *American Whig Review* 14 (Dec. 1851): 526–29; FLO to William James, July 8, 1891, typed copy in Olmsted Papers.
18. FLO to CLB, June 22, 1845.
19. JO Journal, Oct. 30, 1844, March 1, 21, 1845; FLO to FJK, May 18, 1894; FLO to JHO, May 27, 1845.
20. FJK Sketch of CLB; FLO to CLB, July 30, 1846.
21. FLO to JHO, June 23, 1845; FLO to Elizabeth Baldwin Whitney, December 16, 1890.
22. *Forty Years*, 1: 71; FLO to FJK, July 14, 1846.
23. JHO to Clinton Collins, May 11, 1847 (typed copy in Olmsted Papers, original in possession of Ruth Allen Wolkowska, East Hampton, Long Island, New York); *Forty Years*, 1: 78.
24. FLO to JO, Sept. 25, 1848; JHO to JO, March 19, 1855.
25. Autobiographical Fragment B; *Forty Years*, 1: 79–80. A silver spoon given Olmsted as "First Prize for Pears, October 1852," is now in possession of Charles C. McLaughlin.
26. Autobiographical Fragment B; *Forty Years*, 1: 79–81; FLO to FJK, Dec. 21, 1850. The owner of Olmsted's farm one hundred years later plowed up some of the drainage tile (information supplied by Laura Wood Roper).
27. *Forty Years*, 1: 63, 85–86; FLO to FJK, Oct. 14, 1848; Margaret Boyle-Cullen, "The Woods of Arden House," Part 3, *Staten Island Historian* 15, no. 2 (April–June 1954): 14; *DAB*, s.v. "Vanderbilt, William Henry."
28. *DAB*, s.v. "Downing, Andrew Jackson"; *Forty Years*, 1: 80–82, 88–93; Autobiographical Fragment B; FLO to JO, March 14, 1850, Nov. 6, 1851.

29. *Life of Brace*, pp. 58–63, 76–78; [Frederick Law Olmsted], *Walks and Talks of an American Farmer in England*, 2 vols. (New York, 1852), 1: 1–2; FLO to JO, [March 1], 1850; JHO to FJK, March 16, 1850.
30. JO Journal, April 30, Oct. 24, 1850; *Life of Brace*, pp. 89–114.
31. [F. L. Olmsted], *Walks and Talks*, 1: 14–49.
32. Ibid., 1: 78–83; *The Strangers' Guide Through Birkenhead* (Birkenhead, 1847), pp. 12–13; Charles Grey Mott, *Reminiscences of Birkenhead* (Liverpool, 1900), p. 11.
33. [F. L. Olmsted], *Walks and Talks*, 1: 79; *Strangers' Guide Through Birkenhead*, pp. 34–37; George F. Chadwick, *The Park and the Town: Public Landscape in the 19th and 20th Centuries* (New York, 1966), pp. 68–72, 89–91.
34. [F. L. Olmsted], *Walks and Talks*, 1: 87.
35. Ibid., 1: 213–14; 2: 99–109.
36. Ibid., 1: 133.
37. *The Eaton Tourists: or, A "Colloquial description" of the Hall, Grounds, Gardens &c. at Eaton . . .* (Chester, 1824), p. 88; Dorothy Stroud, *Capability Brown* (London, 1975), p. 224; *Gardens Old and New: The Country House & Its Garden Environment*, 3 vols. (London, 1900–1908), vol. 2, ed. John Leyland, pp. 204–6.
38. [F. L. Olmsted], *Walks and Talks*, 1: 135.
39. JHO to Mary Olmsted, July 4, 5, 1850; [F. L. Olmsted], *Walks and Talks*, 1 and 2, passim.
40. [F. L. Olmsted), *Walks and Talks*, 1 and 2, passim; JHO to Mary Olmsted, July 4, 5, 1850; FLO to Andrew Jackson Downing, Nov. 23, 1850; FLO to JO, Aug. 11, 1850; *Life of Brace*, pp. 101–2; JHO to FJK, Jan. 28, 1851.
41. FLO to CLB, Nov. 12, 1850; FLO to FJK, Dec. 21, 1850.
42. JHO to FJK, Sept. 12, 1851; FLO to CLB, May 27, 1851; FLO to FJK, Aug. 5, 1851.
43. JHO to FJK, Sept. 12, 1851; Elizabeth Baldwin to Henrietta Baldwin Foster, Aug. 29, 1851, Baldwin Family Papers, Historical Manuscripts Collection, Yale University Library, New Haven, Conn.; Elizabeth Baldwin to Roger Sherman Baldwin, Nov. 7, 1851, Baldwin Family Papers; JO to Sophie Hitchcock, Oct. 28, 1851, Letters of Mrs. Page, Archives of American Art, microfilm, National Collection of Fine Arts, Washington, D.C.
44. JHO to FJK, April 27, 1851; FLO to FJK, Aug. 5, 1851; JHO to FJK, Oct. 12, 1851.
45. FLO to FJK, Dec. 21, 1850; FLO to George Palmer Putnam, Nov. 6, 1851, Putnam Collection, New York Public Library; FLO to JO, fragment, n.d.; FLO to JO, Feb. 24, 1852.
46. FLO to JO, Feb. 24, 1852; "Reviews," *Horticulturist* 7, no. 3 (March 1852): 135–41.
47. [F. L. Olmsted], *Walks and Talks*, 1: 221.
48. *Life of Brace*, p. 182; FLO to Letitia Brace, Jan. 22, 1892, typed copy; *New-York Daily Times*, April 15, May 3, June 9, 1852; [F. L. Olmsted], *Walks and Talks*, 2: 105–6.
49. FLO to Letitia Brace, Jan. 22, 1892, typed copy; *New-York Daily Times*, Feb. 13, 1853.
50. Frederick Law Olmsted, *A Journey in the Seaboard Slave States, with Remarks on Their Economy* (New York, 1856), pp. 1, 16, 307–9, 546, 568, 602–7, 620; FLO to FJK, Feb. 26, 1853; "Yeoman" [Frederick Law Olmsted], "The South: Letters on the Production, Industry, and Resources of the Slave States; Number Forty-Four," *New-York Daily Times*, Nov. 21, 1853, p. 2; JO Journal, April 8, 1853.
51. Information supplied by Stella McGehee Landis; F. L. Olmsted, *Seaboard Slave States*, 1856 ed., p. 249.
52. F. L. Olmsted, *Seaboard Slave States*, 1856 ed., pp. 59–91, 352–55.
53. John Hull Olmsted prepared the text from Olmsted's journal of the trip "with free scope of expression and personality" (Frederick Law Olmsted, *A Journey through Texas; or, a Saddle-Trip on the Southwestern Frontier* [New York: Dix, Edwards and Co., 1857], preface, unpaged).

54. FLO to CLB and Charles Wyllys Elliott, Dec. 1, 1853.
55. F. L. Olmsted, *A Journey through Texas*, pp. 113, 142.
56. Ibid., pp. 140–45; FLO to [Alfred Field], March 12, 1854.
57. FLO to [Alfred Field], March 12, 1854; F. L. Olmsted, *A Journey through Texas*, pp. 219–20.
58. JO Journal, Oct. 1853; F. L. Olmsted, *A Journey through Texas*, pp. 294–95; M. G. Van Rensselaer, "Frederick Law Olmsted," p. 862.
59. F. L. Olmsted, *A Journey through Texas*, pp. 303–5.
60. Ibid., pp. 320–55.
61. Ibid., p. 380.
62. Frederick Law Olmsted, *A Journey in the Back Country* (New York, 1863), pp. 263–72.
63. Laura Wood Roper, "Frederick Law Olmsted and the Western Texas Free Soil Movement," *American Historical Review* 56 (Oct. 1950): 58–64, hereafter cited as L. W. Roper, "Texas"; Adolph Douai to JHO, Sept. 4, 1854; Adolph Douai to FLO, Oct. 28, 1854; JHO to JO, June 13, 1854; FLO to JO, Nov. 7, 1854; FLO to JO, Dec. 31, 1854; "A Few Dollars Wanted to Help the Cause of Future Freedom in Texas," manuscript in Olmsted Papers; FLO to Edward Everett Hale, Aug. 23, Oct. 23, 1855, Jan. 17, Feb. 4, 1856, New England Emigrant Aid Company Papers, Kansas State Historical Society, Topeka, Kansas; "The Abbott Howitzer—Its History," Kansas Historical Society *Collections*, 17 vols. (Topeka, 1881–1928), 1 and 2: 221–26.
64. Percy W. Bidwell, ed., "The New England Emigrant Aid Company and the English Cotton Supply Association: Letters of Frederick Law Olmsted, 1857," *American Historical Review* 23 (1917–1918): 114–17; L. W. Roper, "Texas," p. 61.
65. For detailed discussions of contemporary reactions to Olmsted's writings about the ante-bellum South, see: Frederick Law Olmsted, *The Cotton Kingdom: A Traveller's Observations on Cotton and Slavery in the American Slave States*, ed. Arthur M. Schlesinger (New York, 1953), pp. xxvi, xxvi n, xxvii, xxxiv–xxxvi, xlvi, xlvi n; Frederick Law Olmsted, *The Slave States, Before the Civil War*, ed. Harvey Wish (New York, 1959), pp. 7–35; Laura Wood Roper, "Frederick Law Olmsted in the 'Literary Republic,'" *Mississippi Valley Historical Review* 39, no. 3 (Dec. 1952): 459–82.
66. Memorandum of Agreement between Dix & Edwards and Olmsted, April 2, 1855; JHO to JO, March 19, 1855.
67. JHO to Bertha Olmsted, May 6, 1855; Laura Wood Roper, "'Mr. Law,' and *Putnam's Monthly Magazine*: A Note on a Phase in the Career of Frederick Law Olmsted," *American Literature* 26 (March 1954): 89–90; FLO to Charles Loring Brace and Charles Wyllys Elliott, Dec. 1, 1853.
68. L. W. Roper, "Mr. Law," pp. 88–93; Perry G. E. Miller, *The Raven and the Whale: The War of Words and Wit in the Era of Poe and Melville* (New York, 1956), p. 336.
69. FLO to JO, Nov. 23, 1855; FLO to FLO, Jr., Aug. 15, 1891; *DAB*, s.v. "Botta, Anne Charlotte Lynch"; FLO to JO, July 7, 1855.
70. FLO to Joshua Augustus Dix, Aug. 3, 1856, Dix and Edwards Papers, Houghton Library, Harvard University, Cambridge, Mass.; George Haven Putnam, *A Memoir of George Palmer Putnam*, 2 vols. (New York, 1903), 1:278–81; JHO to FLO, July 27, 28, 1856; FLO to Joshua Augustus Dix, Sept. 4–5, 1856, Dix and Edwards Papers.
71. L. W. Roper, "Frederick Law Olmsted in the 'Literary Republic,'" p. 474.
72. JHO to JO, Jan. 23, 1856; JHO to JO, July 20, 1856; FLO to Owen Pitkin Olmsted, Jan. 3, 1857; JHO to Owen Pitkin Olmsted, Jan. 6, 1857; FLO to JO, Feb. 7–17, 1857; George William Curtis to FLO, Aug. 6, 1857.
73. FLO to Samuel Cabot, Jr., June 29, 1857, Samuel Cabot, Jr., Papers, Mugar Library, Boston University, Boston, Mass.; L. W. Roper, "Texas," pp. 61–64.
74. *Forty Years*, 2: 22–29.
75. Ibid., pp. 30–33.

76. *NCAB*, 13: 465; Wilimena H. Emerson, Ellsworth Eliot, and George E. Eliot, comps. *Genealogy of the Descendants of John Eliot, "Apostle to the Indians," 1598–1905* (New Haven, 1905), pp. 159–61; FLO to JHO, Sept. 11, 1857; *Forty Years*, 2: 34–35; Frederick Law Olmsted, Jr., "Biographical Sketch," in Frederick Law Olmsted, *A Journey in the Seaboard Slave States in the Years 1853–1854* . . . , 2 vols. (New York, 1904), 1: xv–xvi.
77. FLO to JHO, Sept. 11, 1857; Sophie S. Rogers, Elizabeth S. Lane, and Edwin van Deusen Selden, *Selden Ancestry: A Family History* (Oil City, Penna., 1931), pp. 140, 168–69; *Forty Years*, 2: 37–38; Board of Commissioners of the Central Park, *Minutes of the Central Park Board Ending April 28, 1858*, pp. 33 ff.
78. *Forty Years*, 1: 120; 2: 31–36.
79. Ibid., 2: 33, 39–40.
80. Ibid., 2: 36, 38–40; FLO to CLB, Dec. 8, 1860.
81. FLO to Mariana Griswold Van Rensselaer, June 11, 1893; JHO to Owen Pitkin Olmsted, May 6, 1857; FLO to JHO, Sept. 11, 1857; JHO to FLO, Nov. 13, 1857.
82. *Forty Years*, 2: 32, 41–44.
83. Andrew Jackson Downing, *Rural Essays, edited, with a Memoir of the Author, by George William Curtis* . . . (New York, 1853), pp. xlvii, xlix; [Frederick Law Olmsted], "Appendix" to the *Annual Report of the Architect of the United States Capitol for the Fiscal Year Ending June 30, 1882* . . . , reproduced in U.S., Congress, House, *Documentary History of the Construction and Development of the United States Capitol Building and Grounds*, 58th Cong., 2d sess., 1903, H. rpt. 646 (Washington, D.C.: G.P.O., 1904), pp. 1184–96.
84. FLO to Mariana Griswold Van Rensselaer, June 11, 1893; *Forty Years*, 2: 42–44.
85. *Forty Years*, 2: 45–48, 188.
86. Ibid., pp. 217–19.
87. Ibid., p. 197; [F. L. Olmsted], *Walks and Talks*, 1: 67, 75–84; 2: 258–59.
88. *Forty Years*, 2: 47, 237, 560.
89. Ibid., pp. 49–50, 238, 554–62.
90. FLO to William Augustus Stiles, March 10, 1895; *Forty Years*, 2: 238–39.
91. JHO to FLO, Nov. 13, 1857; *Olmsted Genealogy*, pp. 106, 109.
92. JHO to FJK, Aug. 11, 1851; Elizabeth Baldwin to Henrietta Baldwin Foster, Aug. 29, 1851, Baldwin Family Papers; JHO to FJK, Sept. 12, 1851; *DAB*, s.v. "Hale, Edward Everett"; FLO to JO, March 10, 1850.
93. Information supplied by Charlotte Olmsted Kursh; *Olmsted Genealogy*, p. 106.
94. *Forty Years*, 1: 7; 2: 51–52, 55, 534.
95. Sigfried Giedion, *Space, Time, and Architecture: The Growth of a New Tradition* (Cambridge, Mass., 1949), pp. 544–52; *Forty Years*, 2: 56.
96. *Forty Years*, 2: 57, 60–61.
97. Ibid., 1: 8; FLO to Henry Hill Elliott, [Sept. 1860].
98. *DAB*, s.v. "Green, Andrew Haswell"; *Forty Years*, 2: 65, 70–73; FLO to JO, March 22, 1861; *Forty Years*, 2: 534.
99. F. L. Olmsted, *The Cotton Kingdom*, ed. A. M. Schlesinger, pp. xxiv–xxix, 3–5.
100. Ibid., pp. xxix–xxx.
101. Ibid., pp. xxxiv, 3–4.
102. FLO to JO, March 22, 1861; William Quentin Maxwell, *Lincoln's Fifth Wheel: The Political History of the United States Sanitary Commission* (New York, 1956), pp. 338–41; FLO to JO, April 17, 1861.
103. W. Q. Maxwell, *Lincoln's Fifth Wheel*, pp. 1–8.
104. FLO to JHO, June 26, 1861; George Templeton Strong, *The Diary of George Templeton Strong*, ed. Allan Nevins and Milton Halsey Thomas, 4 vols. (New York, 1952), 3: 159–60, 160 n.
105. FLO to Mary Perkins Olmsted, June 28, 1861.
106. W. Q. Maxwell, *Lincoln's Fifth Wheel*, p. 339; Alfred Field to Charlotte Field, July 9, 1861, typed copy.
107. W. Q. Maxwell, *Lincoln's Fifth Wheel*, pp. 20–23.
108. Ibid., pp. 109–10; G. T. Strong, *Diary*, 3: 197.
109. W. Q. Maxwell, *Lincoln's Fifth Wheel*, pp. 113–15; G. T. Strong, *Diary*, 3: 226.

110. W. Q. Maxwell, *Lincoln's Fifth Wheel*, pp. 339, 341, 349–50; Katharine Prescott Wormeley, *The Other Side of the War: With the Army of the Potomac* (Boston, 1889), pp. 63–64; [Frederick Law Olmsted, comp.], *Hospital Transports. A Memoir of the Embarkation of the Sick and Wounded from the Peninsula of Virginia in the Summer of 1862* (Boston, 1863), pp. 23, 139–42.
111. W. Q. Maxwell, *Lincoln's Fifth Wheel*, pp. 238–47; [F. L. Olmsted], *Hospital Transports*, appendix A.
112. Gordon Milne, *George William Curtis & the Genteel Tradition* (Bloomington, Ind., 1956), pp. 112–13; George W. Curtis to Salmon P. Chase, Feb. 24, 1862; Laura Wood Roper, "Frederick Law Olmsted and the Port Royal Experiment," *Journal of Southern History* 31 (Aug. 1965): 272–84.
113. G. T. Strong, *Diary*, 3: 291, 304–5.
114. Charles Eliot Beveridge, "Frederick Law Olmsted: The Formative Years, 1822–1865" (Ph.D. diss., University of Wisconsin, 1966), pp. 404–7; FLO to Mary Perkins Olmsted, July 7, 1863; FLO to Henry Whitney Bellows, May 20, 1863, private letterpress book, p. 271.
115. FLO to Mary Perkins Olmsted, July 7, 1863; FLO to Henry Whitney Bellows, July 28, 1863, Bellows Papers, Massachusetts Historical Society, Boston, Mass.; Henry Whitney Bellows to FLO, Aug. 18, 1863; FLO to Henry Whitney Bellows, Aug. 19, 1863, Bellows Papers; W. Q. Maxwell, *Lincoln's Fifth Wheel*, p. 220.
116. W. Q. Maxwell, *Lincoln's Fifth Wheel*, pp. 234–47; G. T. Strong, *Diary*, 3: 476.
117. W. Q. Maxwell, *Lincoln's Fifth Wheel*, p. 221.
118. *Forty Years*, 2: 72–76; FLO to Edwin Lawrence Godkin, Aug. 2, 1863, Edwin Lawrence Godkin Papers, Houghton Library, Harvard University, Cambridge, Mass.; M. G. Van Rensselaer, "Frederick Law Olmsted," pp. 860–67; FLO to Mary Perkins Olmsted, June 29, 1863; G. T. Strong, *Diary*, 3: 325, 325 n.
119. FLO to Mary Perkins Olmsted, Aug. 10, 1863; *DAB*, s.v. "Park, Trenor William"; FLO to JO, Aug. 20, 1863; Charles A. Dana to FLO, Aug. 7, 1863; FLO to JO, Aug. 13, 1863.
120. M. G. Van Rensselaer, "Frederick Law Olmsted," pp. 860–67; FLO to Mary Perkins Olmsted, Aug. 12, 1863.
121. FLO to Mary Perkins Olmsted, Aug. 11, 12, 1863; FLO to JO, Aug. 13, 1863; FLO to Henry Whitney Bellows, Aug. 13, 1863.
122. Charles Eliot Norton, *Letters of Charles Eliot Norton, With Biographical Comment by His Daughter Sara Norton and M. A. DeWolfe Howe . . .* 2 vols. (Boston and New York, 1913), 1: 264; Rollo Ogden, ed., *Life and Letters of Edwin Lawrence Godkin*, 2 vols. (New York, 1907), 1: 226.
123. *Forty Years*, 1: 10; 2: 343–49; FLO to Ignaz Pilat, Sept. 26, 1863.
124. FLO to Mary Perkins Olmsted, Oct. 15, Nov. 20, 1863.
125. Rodman W. Paul, *California Gold: The Beginning of Mining in the Far West* (Cambridge, Mass., 1947), pp. 288–89.
126. *DAB*, s.v. "Park, Trenor William"; Thurman Wilkins, *Clarence King, A Biography* (New York, 1958), pp. 60–62; *Boston Evening Transcript*, April 22, 1887, p. 53.
127. Allan Nevins, *Fremont, Pathmarker of the West* (New York, 1939), pp. 371, 394–96, 461–65, 583–87; Adolph Knopf, "The Mother Lode System of California," United States Geological Survey, Professional Paper No. 157 (Washington, D.C., 1929), pp. 83–84.
128. R. W. Paul, *California Gold*, p. 292.
129. *DAB*, s.v. "Park, Trenor William."
130. Ibid.
131. FLO to Mary Perkins Olmsted, Oct. 13, 1863; *DAB*, s.v. "Billings, Frederick William."
132. Newell D. Chamberlain, *The Call of Gold: True Tales on the Gold Road to Yosemite* (Mariposa, Calif., 1936), p. 114.
133. Morris Ketchum to FLO, Dec. 5, 13, 1863; FLO to James Hoy, Oct. 24, 1864, Mariposa letterpress book, p. 243; FLO to G. W. Farlee, Oct. 31, 1864, Mariposa letterpress book, pp. 247–51; FLO to James Hoy, Oct. 31, 1864, private letterbook; Benjamin Silliman, Jr., *A Report on the Examination of the Mariposa Estate in*

California Made in May 1864 (New York, 1864), p. 33; FLO to Morris Ketchum, Dec. 10, 1863, Mariposa letterpress book, p. 121; FLO to William Ashburner, Nov. 4, 1864, Mariposa letterpress book, p. 304; FLO to Edwin Lawrence Godkin, Jan. 10, 1865, Godkin Papers.

134. FLO to William Ashburner, Jan. 3, 1864, private letter book, p. 24; William Ashburner to Mary Perkins Olmsted, Oct. 11, 1865; *Forty Years*, 1: 10–12.

135. Laura Wood Roper, "The Preliminary Report on the Yosemite and the Big Trees by Frederick Law Olmsted," *Landscape Architecture* 43, no. 1 (Oct. 1952): 13, 25.

136. Mary Perkins Olmsted, "Notes," Olmsted Papers.

137. William Henry Brewer, *Up and Down California in 1860–1864*, ed. Francis P. Farquhar (Berkeley, Calif., 1966), p. 547.

138. L. W. Roper, "Report on the Yosemite by F. L. Olmsted," pp. 12–13; Hans Huth, *Nature and the American: Three Centuries of Changing Attitudes* (Berkeley, Calif., 1957), pp. 148–50, 150 n.

139. Samuel Bowles to FLO, July 8, 1866; William Deering to FLO, Jan. 4, 1867; J. D. Whitney to William Brewer, April 10, 1864, William Henry Brewer Papers, Bancroft Library, University of California, Berkeley, Calif.; William Brewer, J. D. Whitney, and I. W. Raymond to Governor Frederick G. Low, Nov. 29, 1865, California State Archives, Sacramento, Calif.; L. W. Roper, "Report on Yosemite by F. L. Olmsted," p. 25.

140. J. D. Whitney to William Brewer, March 29, 1866, Brewer Papers; H. Huth, *Nature and the American*, p. 155.

141. Diana Kostial McGuire, "Frederick Law Olmsted in California: An Analysis of His Contributions to Landscape Architecture and City Planning," (M.S. thesis, University of California at Berkeley, 1956), pp. 42, 113–14.

142. Frederick Law Olmsted, *Report to the Trustees of the Mountain View Cemetery* (n.p., n.d.), copy in Olmsted Papers; D. K. McGuire, "Olmsted in California," pp. 42–51; FLO to Calvert Vaux, March 12, 1865, Calvert Vaux Collection, New York Public Library.

143. FLO to JO, Feb. 11, 1865; Olmsted, Vaux and Co., *The Berkeley Neighborhood; Report on the Projected Improvement of the Estate of the College of California* (San Francisco: Towne and Bacon, 1866), pp. 3–26; Henry Winthrop Sargent, "Historical Notices," appendix to Andrew Jackson Downing, *A Treatise on the Theory and Practice of Landscape Gardening, Adapted to North America*, 7th ed. (New York, 1859), pp. 569–72.

144. D. K. McGuire, "Olmsted in California," pp. 52–73.

145. FLO to Edwin Lawrence Godkin, Feb. 10, March 12, [13], April 4, 1865, Godkin Papers; FLO to Mary Perkins Olmsted, Feb. 24, 1865; *Forty Years*, 1: 12; FLO to Mary Perkins Olmsted, Jan. 16, 1865.

146. Edwin Lawrence Godkin to FLO, July 23, 1865, quoted in R. Ogden, *Godkin*, 1: 239–40; Calvert Vaux to FLO, May 30, July 21, 1865; FLO to JO, Aug.. 31, 1865; FLO to Calvert Vaux, Sept. 19, 28, 1865, Calvert Vaux Collection; FLO to Edward Dugdale, Sept. 29, 1865, Mariposa letterpress book, p. 310.

147. "Rusticus in Urbe" [Frederick Law Olmsted], "The Project for a Great Park for San Francisco," *San Francisco Bulletin*, Aug. 4, 1865; D. K. McGuire, "Olmsted in California," pp. 74–78, 115–16; H. P. Coon et al. to FLO, Nov. 17, 1865; *Municipal Reports of the City of San Francisco, 1865/1866* (San Francisco, 1866), pp. 365–95, 403.

148. D. K. McGuire, "Olmsted in California," pp. 74–86; Olmsted, Vaux and Co., *Preliminary Report in Regard to a Plan of Public Pleasure Grounds for the City of San Francisco* (New York, 1866), pp. 19–23; Josiah Royce, *California from the Conquest to the Second Vigilance Committee in San Francisco: A Study of American Character* (Boston, 1886), pp. 215–19.

149. FLO to Henry Perkins, Oct. 23, 1865; *New York Daily Times*, Nov. 23, 1865; FLO to Calvert Vaux, Sept. 28, 1865, Calvert Vaux Collection.

150. G. T. Strong, *Diary*, 4: 52.

151. FLO to JO, Sept. 28, 1865; William Ashburner to Mary Perkins Olmsted, Oct. 11, 1865; Duncan, Sherman and Co. to FLO, April 21, 1866.

152. G. T. Strong, *Diary*, 4: 374.
153. Olmsted, Vaux and Co. "Report of the Landscape Architects and Superintendents" in *Eighth Annual Report of the Commissioners of Prospect Park* (Brooklyn, New York, 1868), pp. 173–202.
154. Ibid., pp. 7–21.
155. FLO to Charles Eliot Norton, Jan. 30, 1866, Charles Eliot Norton Papers, Houghton Library, Harvard University, Cambridge, Mass.; R. Ogden, *Godkin*, 1: 235–36, 242; Gustav Pollak, *Fifty Years of American Idealism: The New York Nation, 1865–1915* (Boston, 1915), pp. 9–10; *DAB*, s.v. "McKim, James Miller"; *NCAB*, 8: 231.
156. R. Ogden, *Godkin*, 1: 241–44; *Nation* 4 (June 1867): 520–22; 3 (August 1866): 498; 2 (March 1866): 30.
157. *Forty Years*, 1: 13–17.
158. Everett Chamberlin, *Chicago and Its Suburbs* (Chicago, 1874), pp. 414–16.
159. Olmsted, Vaux and Co., *Preliminary Report Upon the Proposed Suburban Village at Riverside, Near Chicago* (New York, 1868), p. 29; Frederick Law Olmsted, "Draft on Riverside," in "Riverside, Illinois; Selections from the Papers of Frederick Law Olmsted, Sr.," *Landscape Architecture* 21 no. 4 (July 1931): 278–79; Olmsted, Vaux and Co., *Preliminary Report Upon Riverside*, pp. 26–28.
160. Howard K. Menhinick, "Riverside Sixty Years Later," *Landscape Architecture* 22, no. 2 (Jan. 1932): 109–17; Olmsted, Vaux and Co., *Preliminary Report Upon Riverside*, pp. 24–25.
161. Olmsted, Vaux and Co., *Preliminary Report Upon Riverside*, pp. 20–24; E. Chamberlin, *Chicago and Its Suburbs*, p. 416; Olmsted, Vaux and Co., *Preliminary Report Upon Riverside*, pp. 7, 27–28.
162. Olmsted, Vaux and Co., *Preliminary Report Upon Riverside*, pp. 8–14.
163. E. Chamberlin, *Chicago and Its Suburbs*, p. 415.
164. F. L. Olmsted, "Draft on Riverside," pp. 278–79.
165. H. K. Menhinick, "Riverside Sixty Years Later," pp. 109–17; Calvert Vaux to FLO, June 18, 1869, n.d. (c. Oct. 1869), April 11, 1870; C. H. Hueller to FLO, Nov. 25, 1871; FLO to E. B. McCagg, Jan. 26, 1877.
166. William Irwin, Secretary to the Park Board, to FLO, Nov. 5, 1875; *Who Was Who in America: Historical Volume 1, 1897–1942* (Chicago, 1943), s.v. "Croes, John James Robertson."
167. John Charles Olmsted to Frederick Law Olmsted, Jr., received Oct. 8, 1913.
168. Frederick Law Olmsted and J. James R. Croes, *Preliminary Report of the Landscape Architect and the Civil and Topographical Engineer, upon the Laying Out of the Twenty-third and Twenty-fourth Wards, and the Report of the Landscape Architect and the Civil and Topographical Engineer, Accompanying a Plan for Laying out That Part of the Twenty-fourth Ward, Lying West of the Riverdale Road* ([New York], Board of the Department of Public Parks, Dec. 20, 1876), document 72; Frederick Law Olmsted and J. James R. Croes, *Report of the Civil and Topographical Engineer and the Landscape Architect, Accompanying a Plan for Local Steam Transit Routes in the Twenty-third and Twenty-fourth Wards* ([New York], Board of the Department of Public Parks, March 21, 1877), document 75. Both remarkable reports have been reprinted in Frederick Law Olmsted, *Landscape into Cityscape, Frederick Law Olmsted's Plans for a Greater New York City*, ed. Albert Fein (Ithaca, New York, 1968), map opposite p. 340, pp. 349–82; Arthur M. Schlesinger, *The Rise of the City, 1878–1898* (New York, 1933), pp. 90–93; John Charles Olmsted to FLO, Jr., received Oct. 8, 1913.
169. *Forty Years*, 2: 378 and fig. opposite; A. Fein, ed. *Landscape into Cityscape*, pp. 367–73.
170. *Forty Years*, 2: 110–12; A. M. Schlesinger, *Rise of the City*, p. 91.
171. J. James R. Croes to FLO, March 24, 1878.
172. John Charles Olmsted to FLO, Jr., received Oct. 8, 1913.
173. *Forty Years*, 1: 16–24.
174. *DAB*, s.v. "Richardson, Henry Hobson"; Mariana Griswold Van Rensselaer,

Henry Hobson Richardson and His Works (Boston and New York, 1888), pp. 23, 40.

175. A. Fein, ed., *Landscape into Cityscape*, pp. 168–69; 173–300; Jon Alvah Peterson, "The Origins of the Comprehensive City Planning Ideal in the United States, 1840–1911" (Ph.D. diss., Harvard University, 1967), pp. 111–16.

176. Henry-Russell Hitchcock, *The Architecture of H. H. Richardson and His Times* (New York, 1936), p. 119; John Charles Olmsted to Robert Underwood Johnson, Aug. 1909, Robert U. Johnson Papers, Bancroft Library, University of California at Berkeley; *Report of the Commissioners of the State Reservation at Niagara*, Albany, New York, Feb. 17, 1885, state of New York, in Senate No. 35, pp. 1–4.

177. Henry Hobson Richardson to FLO, February 6, 1883; FLO to CLB, March 7, 1882; *Forty Years*, 2: 24–26.

178. FLO to Charles Eliot Norton, September 19, 1878, Norton Papers; FLO to Frederick Newman Knapp, June 20, 1870; FLO to CLB, April 21, 1871; Richard Hofstader, *The Age of Reform: From Bryan to F.D.R.* (New York, 1955), p. 139, 139 n.

179. H. R. Hitchcock, *H. H. Richardson*, pp. 213–14; *Forty Years*, 1: 26.

180. H. R. Hitchcock, *H. H. Richardson*, pp. 197–98; 199 n.

181. FLO to CLB, Jan. 18, 1890; *DAB*, s.v. "Olmsted, John Charles"; *Forty Years*, 1: 24–32.

182. FLO to William Hammond Hall, March 28, 1874; Olmsted, Vaux and Co., *Preliminary Report Upon Riverside*, p. 13; A. Fein, ed., *Landscape into Cityscape*, pp. 157–64; H. R. Hitchcock, *H. H. Richardson*, pp. 213–14.

183. M. G. Van Rensselaer, "Frederick Law Olmsted," p. 865; E. W. Howe, "The Back Bay Park," pp. 126–33 (paper read at the Boston Society of Civil Engineers annual meeting, March 16, 1881, in Olmsted Papers); Sylvester Baxter, *Boston Park Guide Including the Municipal and Metropolitan Systems of Greater Boston* (Boston, 1896); Walter Muir Whitehill, *Boston: A Topographical History* (Cambridge, Mass., 1959), pp. 182, 188–89.

184. Boston, Department of Parks, [Frederick Law Olmsted], "Notes on the Plan of Franklin Park and Related Matters" (Boston, 1886), pp. 40, 65 n., 114; John Nolen, "Frederick Law Olmsted and His Work, IV, Franklin Park, Boston, Massachusetts," *House and Garden* 10, no. 1 (July 1906): 3–11.

185. Frederick Law Olmsted, "Appendix" to the *Annual Report of the Architect of the United States Capitol . . . 1882*"; John Nolen, "The Work of Frederick Law Olmsted, II, The Design of the United States Capitol Grounds," *House and Garden* 9, no. 3 (March 1906): 117–18.

186. Charles C. McLaughlin, "The Capitol in Peril? The West Front Controversy from Walter to Stewart," *Records of the Columbia Historical Society of Washington, D.C., 1969–1970* (Washington, D.C., 1971), pp. 241–46.

187. FLO to John Charles Olmsted, Sept. 29, 1886; FLO to John Charles Olmsted, Sept. 24, 1886; Diane Kostial McGuire, "Early Site Planning on the West Coast: Frederick Law Olmsted's Plan for Stanford University," *Landscape Architecture* 47, no. 2 (Jan. 1957): 345.

188. FLO to Charles Eliot, July 20, 1886.

189. D. K. McGuire, "Stanford," pp. 437–49; *Forty Years*, 1: 110.

190. D. K. McGuire, "Stanford," pp. 346–47.

191. Ibid.

192. *Forty Years*, 2; 255–56.

193. D. K. McGuire, "Stanford," p. 346.

194. *DAB*, s.v. "Hunt, William Morris," "McKim, Charles Follen."

195. *Forty Years*, 1: 28, 32; Wayne Andrews, *Architecture, Ambition, and Americans* (New York, 1955), p. 182.

196. *Forty Years*, 2: 75, 392; Russell Sturgis, "The Central Park Gateways," *Nation* 1 (September 1865): 186, 410; 3 (September 1866): 255; FLO to Charles Eliot Norton, April 2, 1876, Norton Papers; H. R. Hitchcock, *H. H. Richardson*, pp. 167–69.

197. FLO to John Charles Olmsted, Feb. 25, 1894; FLO to William Augustus Stiles,

March 10, 1885; John Nolen, "The Work of Frederick Law Olmsted, v, Biltmore and Biltmore Village," *House and Garden* 11, no. 4 (Dec. 1906); FLO to George W. Vanderbilt, July 12, 1889, draft.

198. *Forty Years*, 1: 37; Charles Moore, *Daniel Hudson Burnham, Architect, Planner of Cities*, 2 vols. (Boston and New York, 1921), 1: 78–79.

199. FLO to Partners, April 24, 1892.

200. One such letter would be FLO to Daniel H. Burnham, Dec. 28, 1894.

201. FLO to Charles Eliot, Dec. 11, 1894; W. M. Whitehill, *Boston: A Topographical History*, pp. 180–82, 188–89.

202. FLO to John C. Olmsted, May 10, 1895.

203. *Forty Years*, 1: 38–40; FLO to Charles Eliot, Dec. 11, 1894; *DAB*, s.v. "Eliot, Charles"; FLO, Jr., to Charles Eliot Norton, Sept. 5, 1903, Norton Papers.

204. FLO to Senator Francis G. Newlands, n.d., draft; [Frederick Law Olmsted], "The Future of New-York: Views of Frederick Law Olmsted," *New York Daily Tribune*, Dec. 28, 1879, p. 5.

THE PAPERS OF
FREDERICK LAW OLMSTED

EDITORIAL POLICY

THE PURPOSE of the Frederick Law Olmsted editorial project is to make generally available, in fully-annotated form, the best of Olmsted's letters, unpublished writings, and newspaper and periodical articles. The letterpress edition, as presently planned, will consist of seven volumes of selected documents arranged in chronological order and one volume containing Olmsted's general writings on landscape design. In order to make Olmsted's voluminous correspondence available to scholars in a less expensive form and at an earlier date than would be possible with a complete letterpress edition, the editors hope to produce a complete microfilm edition of all his extant correspondence and other writings.

Although the process of letter selection is partly a subjective matter, the editors have sought to make sure that every document published meets at least one of three criteria: first, that it gives the reader insight into Olmsted's character; second, that it presents valuable commentary on his times; and third, that it contains an important statement on landscape design. Letters have not been selected simply because they provide chronological continuity. As a result, some lean periods in Olmsted's correspondence go unrepresented while a number of excellent letters written within a short span of time are occasionally included. Volume I, for instance, contains all extant letters that Olmsted wrote during his China voyage of 1843–44.

The editors feel that it is their responsibility to make clear the context within which Olmsted wrote the documents selected, to identify persons, places, and events mentioned, and to clarify his relationship to them. The annotation is fuller in this edition that it would be in a complete edition of Olmsted's papers, where the greater number of documents would help to annotate one another. To supply background information and provide continuity, the editors make use of volume introductions, biographical directories, and chapter headnotes.

In transcribing the documents for publication, the editors have sought to present complete texts that clearly convey Olmsted's meaning. Instead of attempting to reproduce in print the appearance of the original manuscript, they have regularized the text and removed vagaries of spelling and punctuation that could distract the modern reader from the substance of what Olmsted had to say.

The complete existing text of each letter is presented. Drafts of letters and other writings appear in what is considered to be their final form. All legible words that Olmsted wrote are included, except those he inadvertently repeated. Words that Olmsted crossed out are omitted unless of particular interest. If included, they are accompanied by an explanatory footnote. The treatment of illegible and missing words is as follows:

1. [. . .] indicates illegible words or words missing because of mutilation of the manuscript.
2. [*italic*] indicates the editor's reading of partially missing words.
3. [roman] indicates a word supplied by the editor.

Olmsted's erratic spelling—he consistently misspelled words with double consonants, such as "dissapoint"—has been silently corrected unless it is clear he deliberately misspelled for humorous effect or to convey dialect. English variants of standard American spellings are left as he wrote them. Contractions and abbreviations are silently expanded except for some that are in common use, like "etc." Punctuation is altered as needed to provide greater clarity, and Olmsted's omnipresent dash is rendered as a comma or a period where appropriate. Paragraphing is supplied for long unparagraphed sections dealing with a series of subjects.

Olmsted's marginal additions that have no clear place in the text are printed at the end of the document with an explanatory note. Notes or jottings by other persons on the documents are not presented, but if informative, they are given in a note. Olmsted's rare footnotes are presented at the bottom of the page of text on which they occur.

Dates for documents are given as they appear in the original. If that information is partial, incorrect, or missing, the probable date or time-period is supplied in brackets, with an explanatory footnote if needed. Addresses on the letters are given whenever they occur.

The documents are presented in chronological order, except for occasional pieces like the autobiographical fragments and "The Real China," which are reminiscences written at a later time. They are presented with the letters of the period they describe.

A full bibliographical reference is given at the first use of a source in each chapter, except for the following sources, which are cited only in the short form indicated below. A full listing of sources for information on individuals is given at the time of their first mention in the volume. In subsequent references, sources are given only for additional information supplied. Birth and death dates of persons mentioned in the text of the letters are given in the first note identifying them and, for selected persons, in the index.

All manuscript material referred to, unless otherwise indicated, is in the Frederick Law Olmsted Papers, Library of Congress, Washington, D.C.

SHORT TITLES
USED IN CITATIONS

1. Correspondents' Names
   CLB   Charles Loring Brace
   FLO   Frederick Law Olmsted
   FJK   Frederick John Kingsbury
   JHO   John Hull Olmsted
   JO   John Olmsted

2. Standard References
   BDAC   *Biographical Directory of the American Congress, 1774–1971*
   DAB   *Dictionary of American Biography*
   DNB   *Dictionary of National Biography*
   EB   *Encyclopaedia Britannica*, 14th edition
   NCAB   *National Cyclopaedia of American Biography*
   OED   *Oxford English Dictionary*

3. Other Published Works

   Appleton's Cyc. Am. Biog. *Appleton's Cyclopedia of American Biography*, ed. James G. Wilson and John Fiske (New York, 1887–1889).

   Eleventh Reunion *The Eleventh Reunion of the Olmsted Family Held at Ridgefield, Connecticut, September 17, 1932* (privately printed, n:d.). Copy in possession of Charles C. McLaughlin.

   Forty Years Frederick Law Olmsted, Jr., and Theodora Kimball, eds., *Frederick Law Olmsted, Landscape Architect, 1822–1903* (*Forty Years of Landscape Architecture*), 2 vols. (New York, 1922, 1928).

   Geer's Directory for 18— [Elihu Geer], *Geer's Hartford City Directory for 18—* (Hartford, 18—).

   Hartford County James Hammond Trumbull, ed., *The Memorial History of Hartford County, Connecticut, 1633–1884*, 2 vols. (Boston, 1886).

Homes of Cheshire   Edwin R. Brown, comp., *Old Historic Homes of Cheshire, Connecticut, with an Account of the Early Settlement of the Town, Description of its Churches, Academy, and Old Town Cemetery, Places of Interest—Roaring Brook, Scott's Rock, Barytes and Copper Mines, Ancient Trees, etc.* (New Haven, 1895).

Horticulturist   *The Horticulturist and Journal of Rural Art and Rural Taste. Devoted to Horticulture, Landscape Gardening, Rural Architecture, Botany, Pomology, Entomology, Rural Economy, &c.*, ed. A. J. Downing (Albany, New York, 1846–1852).

Kingsbury Autobiography   *The Autobiography of Frederick J. Kingsbury*, Mattatuck Historical Society (Waterbury, Connecticut) *Occasional Publications*, n.s., no. 10 (1946), no. 11 (1947), no. 12 (1947), and no. 13 (October 1947). Cited as Part ɪ, Part ɪɪ, Part ɪɪɪ, and Part ɪᴠ, respectively. These volumes are not paginated.

Life of Brace   Charles Loring Brace, *The Life of Charles Loring Brace, Chiefly Told in His Own Letters*, ed. Emma Brace (New York, 1894).

Notable American Women   *Notable American Women, 1607–1950: A Biographical Dictionary*, ed. Edward T. James, 3 vols. (Cambridge, Mass., 1971).

Olmsted Genealogy   Henry K. Olmsted and George K. Ward, comps., *Genealogy of the Olmsted Family in America Embracing the Descendants of James and Richard Olmsted and Covering a Period of Nearly Three Centuries 1632–1912* (New York, 1912).

Perkins Genealogy   George A. Perkins, comp., *The Family of John Perkins of Ipswich, Massachusetts*, 3 pts. in 1 vol. (Salem, Mass., 1889).

Schaff-Herzog Encyc.   *The New Schaff-Herzog Encyclopedia of Religious Knowledge, Embracing Biblical, Historical, Doctrinal, and Practical Theology and Biblical, Theological, and Ecclesiastical Biography from the Earliest Times to the Present Day, Based on the Third Edition of the Realencyclopädie Founded by J. J. Herzog, and Edited by Albert Hauck, Prepared by More Than Six Hundred Scholars and Specialists Under the Supervision of Samuel Macauley Jackson . . . (Editor-in-Chief) With the Assistance of Charles Colebrook Sherman and George William Gilmore . . . (Associate Editors) and [Others]*, 13 vols. (New York, [1908–c. 1914]).

See Spear _____   Designates the number assigned to a city directory in the microfiche edition of Dorothea N. Spear, *Bibliography of American Directories through 1860* (Worcester, Mass., 1961).

Union List of Newspapers   Winifred Gregory, ed., *American Newspapers, 1821–1936: A Union List of Files Available in the United States and Canada* (New York, 1937).

Union List of Serials   Edna Brown Titus, ed., *Union List of Serials in Libraries of the United States and Canada*, 3d ed. (New York, 1965).

Yale Obit. Rec.   Yale University, *Obituary Record of Graduates of Yale University* (New Haven, [1860–]).

4. Unpublished Public Records

Headstone Inscriptions   Connecticut Headstone Inscriptions, in the Charles R. Hale Collection, Connecticut State Library, Hartford.

Vital Records   Connecticut Vital Records, in the Barbour Collection, Connecticut State Library, Hartford. In citations, name of city or town is given first (i.e., Guilford Vital Records, 2: 375).

5. Manuscript Sources

FLO Pocket Journal   A manuscript journal kept by Frederick Law Olmsted from March 1 to March 26, 1843, together with the "Log of the 'Lovely Abbey' of Lyme," the record of a cruise on Long Island Sound from August 22 to August 30, 1844. In the Frederick Law Olmsted Papers, Library of Congress.

FJK Journal   A manuscript journal kept by Frederick John Kingsbury between 1844 and 1847. In the Mattatuck Historical Society, Waterbury, Connecticut.

FJK Sketch of CLB   A five-page manuscript by Frederick Kingsbury, describing Brace's character and activities during his college years and identifying a number of the young men and women who were his friends while he was at Yale. In the possession of Charles Loring Brace's grandson Gerald Brace, in Belmont, Massachusetts.

FJK Sketch of FLO   A series of complete and excerpted letters from Frederick Law Olmsted to Frederick Kingsbury with accompanying reminiscences and editorial comment by Kingsbury, which he prepared and sent to Frederick Law Olmsted, Jr., in 1903, after Olmsted's death. The sketch is approximately sixty-five pages long. The pagination is erratic and therefore not cited in footnotes in this volume, but the letters are presented in chronological order. In the Frederick Law Olmsted Papers in the Library of Congress, as are a number of the original letters quoted in it.

JO Journal   A manuscript journal and domestic account book kept by John Olmsted from 1836 to 1873 and continued until 1888 by his widow, Mary Ann Bull Olmsted. Three volumes, in the Frederick Law Olmsted Papers, Library of Congress.

BIOGRAPHICAL
DIRECTORY

ELIZABETH WOOSTER BALDWIN (1824–1912) made the strongest impression on Olmsted of any of the girls he knew in his youth. Her social qualifications alone were impressive. She was a great-granddaughter of Roger Sherman, and her father, Roger Sherman Baldwin, was governor of Connecticut during the period of 1845–46 when Olmsted met and fell in love with her. Frederick Kingsbury later judged that she "had perhaps more social power or at all events more practical social initiative than any other young lady in New Haven."[1] Her parents gave her a good education, including attendance at the classes held in New Haven by the innovative educator and eccentric Shakespearean scholar Delia Bacon. Moreover, the Baldwin family was at the center of the intellectual and social life of New Haven.

In addition to her impressive social position, "Miss B.," as Olmsted and his friends respectfully called her, enjoyed a high reputation among them as a serious thinker. She combined her obvious intelligence with a prettiness and warmth that made Olmsted most responsive to the attention she showed him.

During his brief stay in New Haven in the fall of 1845, Olmsted met her and attended several literary evenings at her family's house. Then, while he was recuperating in Hartford in early 1846, she visited there and gave him an opportunity to continue their friendship. He saw her at several social functions and had a long carriage ride and a "*thick* talk" with her, during which he found to his delight that she had a "strong inclination for rural pleasures."[2] During the month after her visit he became increasingly sure that he was in love with her, but she dashed his hopes by saying that it was "neither right nor best" that she grant him the favor of a correspondence. This left him "right smack & square on dead in love with her, beached & broken backed."[3]

Her influence on him was not at an end, however. During the early months of 1846, Miss B. played an important part in a revival of religious concern among Olmsted's young friends in New Haven. In early April he hurried there to partake of the revival spirit and felt that he benefited greatly by talking with his friends, especially with her. He still had hopes of winning her affection and eagerly anticipated a visit from her when he was at George Geddes's farm in the summer of 1846. But the visit did not occur, and he saw her seldom thereafter.

Although their active friendship was over by mid-1846, Olmsted occasionally confessed his lingering admiration for her. Five years later, for instance, in the spring of 1851, Emily Perkins learned of his feelings just as she and Olmsted were about to become engaged. ". . . I was surprised to see how much he really loved you," Emily wrote her. "I don't think you ever felt any gratitude for his faithful regard for you. At least not half as much as it was deserved. I doubt if you have more than one or two friends in the world who have so much real attachment to you."[4]

Elizabeth Baldwin might well have seemed heartless to her cousin Emily. Not only had she neglected Olmsted, but in 1848 she had refused the marriage offer of a rich Boston merchant named Howe. Before the end of 1851, though, she had fallen in love with Clinton Camp, a promising Yale graduate student five years her junior. Much against her parents' wishes, she became engaged to him before he left for graduate study in Germany. Two years later he died of tuberculosis while still abroad. In 1856 she married a young scholar, William Dwight Whitney, a philologist and professor of Sanskrit at Yale who had been a friend of Camp's when they were fellow students in Germany. Whitney became an eminent lexicographer and Orientalist.

Despite Elizabeth's marriage and his own and the passage of many years, Olmsted's feeling for her persisted. It surfaced again in 1890 when he scribbled a letter to her on a piece of wrapping paper while under the influence of a heroic dose of whiskey, opium, calomel, and quinine that a local doctor gave him when he fell sick at the Biltmore Estate in North Carolina. After he recovered from the illness—and the medicine—Olmsted was relieved and flattered to receive a friendly reply from her.

He then wrote a letter of explanation and reminiscence in which he gave her much of the credit for what he had become. He recalled how he had first met her in New Haven soon after his return from China: "You lifted me a good deal out of my constitutional shyness," he wrote, "and helped more than you can think to rouse a sort of scatter-brained pride and to make me realize that my secluded life, country breeding and mis-education were not such bars to an 'intellectual life' as I was in the habit of supposing." He told her that partly through her influence he acquired his lifelong enthusiasm for Ralph Waldo Emerson, James Russell Lowell, John Ruskin, and "other real prophets." "And these," he declared, "gave me the needed respect for my own constitutional tastes and an inclination to poetical refinement in the cultivation of them that afterwards determined my profession."[5]

While this assessment, so many years after the fact, may have been exaggerated, it was an accurate reflection of the persistence of her image in his mind and of the role that young women had played in his intellectual development. They were for him the arbiters of the spheres of music, literature, and art. And in those readings and discussions, Elizabeth Baldwin, Emily Perkins, and Sophie Stevens did the most to encourage his interests in literature and the arts.

1. Manuscript autobiography of FJK, Mattatuck Historical Society, Waterbury, Conn.
2. FLO to JHO, Feb. 3, 1846.
3. FLO to JHO, Friday P.M., n.d. [March 27, 1846].
4. Emily Perkins to Elizabeth Baldwin, n.d. [spring 1851], Baldwin Family Papers, Historical Manuscripts Collection, Yale University Library, New Haven, Conn.
5. FLO to Elizabeth Baldwin Whitney, Dec. 16, 1890.

Additional Sources

DAB, s.v. "Baldwin, Roger Sherman" and "Baldwin, Simeon."
Jackson, Frederick H., *Simeon Eben Baldwin; Lawyer, Social Scientist, Statesman.* New York, 1955.
Sherman, Thomas Townsend. *Sherman Genealogy . . .* New York, 1920.

CHARLES LORING BRACE (1826–1890) was one of Olmsted's closest friends and a lifelong correspondent. Like Olmsted, he was descended from Puritan ancestors who settled Hartford in the seventeenth century and was a member of the seventh generation of the family in Connecticut. His grandfather James was the writing-master at the school of his wife's sister, Miss Sarah Pierce, in Litchfield, Connecticut, one of the first in the state to provide education for young women beyond that offered by the common schools.

Brace's father, John Pierce Brace, followed James's choice of a career. Educated by his aunts, Sarah and Mary Pierce, he became the head teacher in their school, adding scientific courses to the curriculum. With an encyclopedic knowledge of many subjects and a passion for passing it on to others, he made the school a leader in women's education and gained a considerable reputation for his learning and culture. One of his students, Harriet Beecher Stowe, described him as "one of the most stimulating and inspiring instructors I ever knew."[1] In 1832, when Charles was six, the family moved to Hartford, where John Pierce Brace became head of the Hartford

Female Seminary. In 1849 he became editor of the *Hartford Daily Courant*, a post he held until 1863.

Charles Brace's mother, Lucy Porter Brace, came from an important Maine family and was a descendant of Rufus King, the powerful Federalist politician. Her sister was the first wife of Lyman Beecher, and the two families lived near each other in Litchfield for six years. She died when Charles was fourteen and played little part in his upbringing, devoting her attention instead to his sickly younger brother.

It was Charles's father who played the crucial role in his development. John Brace eagerly supplied his son from his vast store of learning, and by the time the young man entered Yale College in 1842 he was well-read in the classics and European literature and had some knowledge of five languages. Olmsted and his friends recognized that Charles was unusually fortunate in the guidance and fellowship he had from his father.

Brace had come to know the Olmsted brothers sometime in the decade between his family's move to Hartford and the beginning of his college years, and John Hull Olmsted was his roommate during his freshman year at Yale. Living in such close quarters, Brace became more aware of the difference in their backgrounds than he had been before. Coming from a well-to-do family, John Hull Olmsted willingly shared the small luxuries he had always enjoyed, while Brace, accustomed to the frugal life of a teacher's family, felt uneasy at such generosity. He was reluctant to use John's fencing foils and boxing gloves and accept his special treats of food from home until he realized that they were an expression of friendship, not an attempt to make him subservient. When Olmsted visited Yale in the fall of 1842 and again in 1845, he too made Brace one of his closest friends.

The special contribution that Brace made to the group at Yale was energy and enthusiasm. He pitched into all activities with vigor: that quality, Olmsted later recalled, was his strong point. Likewise, Frederick Kingsbury later wrote that he first saw Brace in the midst of a boxing match with John Hull Olmsted and perceived "something . . . in the intense earnestness with which he went into the boxing that impressed me at once, and it was a true index of his character."[2] The Olmsted brothers relished his company in outdoor hikes and games, and their mutual enjoyment of vigorous debate about everything from aesthetics and religion to politics cemented a friendship that lasted the rest of their lives.

Like their contemporaries, Brace and Olmsted sought a strong religious faith and some assurance of their salvation. Brace helped introduce the Olmsted brothers to Horace Bushnell's doctrines, which they often read and discussed. The height of their religious concerns came during the religious revival at Yale in the spring of 1846, during which both Olmsteds and Brace experienced conversion to what they thought was a saving faith.

After graduating from Yale in 1846, Brace studied for the ministry.

He spent a year at the Yale Divinity School and then studied further at Union Theological Seminary in New York. This training led him to emphasize the importance of reaching decisions on points of doctrine, while Olmsted began to stress good works. "Throw your light on the path in Politics and Social Improvement and encourage me to put my foot down and *forwards*," Olmsted urged his friend. "There's a great *work* wants doing in this our generation, Charley, let us off jacket and go about it."[3]

Brace in effect took Olmsted's advice, swallowed his repugnance for the world of misery and sin, and in 1848 began ministering to New York's social derelicts on Blackwell's Island. In the meantime he completed his theological training and in the spring of 1850 left New York for two years of travel and study abroad.

He spent the first six months with Olmsted and his brother John, on a walking tour of the British Isles and the Continent, during which he learned how philanthropists there tried to help the poor. He also met his future wife, Letitia Neill, in Belfast when he and the Olmsteds were visiting her father, Robert Neill, a reformer and friend of American antislavery leaders. Because Brace could not afford the trip unless he traveled cheaply, the Olmsteds agreed to take second-class accommodations for the crossing and do much of their traveling on foot. Although Olmsted later regretted some of the penny-pinching, it meant that they saw more of the common life of the countries they visited than they would otherwise have done.

Brace supported himself during his remaining months abroad by writing travel letters for American newspapers. His time went smoothly until the spring of 1851, when, despite warnings, he insisted on visiting Hungary, where the Austrian government was still searching out those involved in the unsuccessful revolution of 1848. While the sympathetic Brace was enjoying Hungarian hospitality, an Austrian gendarme arrested him as an emissary from the Hungarian revolutionaries who had escaped to England. He spent five weeks in a miserable prison before the American ambassador could arrange for his release. The episode outraged Brace and alarmed his American friends. When he returned to New York he published an account of the Hungarian adventure, *Hungary in 1851: with an Experience of the Austrian Police.*

The following year he wrote a description of his six-month visit to Germany, entitled *Home-Life in Germany.* The book gave an enthusiastic picture of German family life, "whose affection and cheerfulness make the outside world as nothing in comparison."[4] He came to the conclusion, as had Horace Bushnell, that a revival of home life in silent and stern New England households would do more for Christianity than the traditional revivals. His views outraged some of his readers in Connecticut, one of whom concluded that the author would be at his happiest drinking himself under the table with boon companions.

69

Having published his first books, Brace turned his attention to the poor children of New York who had no home life at all. He became head of the newly formed Children's Aid Society, a post he held for the rest of his life. Under his direction the society fed, housed, and gave religious instruction to homeless children of the streets and sent over 90,000 of them out to grow up with farm families in upstate New York and the Midwest, far away from city temptations and poverty. Despite the heavy demands that directing the Children's Aid Society put on him, Brace found time to write seven books during the thirty-seven years he spent with that organization. They included works on philanthropy, travel accounts of Scandinavia and California, and studies of race and religion, with such varied titles as *The Races of the Old World: A Manual of Ethnology*, *The Dangerous Classes of New York, and Twenty Years' Work Among Them*, and *Gesta Christi: Or, A History of Humane Progress Under Christianity*.

From the beginning of their friendship, Brace gave Olmsted the benefit of his growing circle of acquaintances in the world of letters and philanthropy. He arranged for Olmsted to meet Henry Raymond, the editor of the *New-York Daily Times*, with the result that Olmsted undertook to travel through the South as a correspondent. In 1855 Brace's friend Joshua A. Dix enabled Olmsted to enter further into the "literary republic" of New York by offering him a partnership in the publishing firm of Dix & Edwards. In that capacity he worked with George W. Curtis and Parke Godwin editing *Putnam's Monthly Magazine* and made the acquaintance of many American writers. When Dix & Edwards went bankrupt in 1857, Olmsted received important advice from another of Brace's friends, Charles W. Elliott. He was a commissioner of Central Park in New York and urged Olmsted to apply to be superintendent of the park's construction. Among the prominent men whose letters of recommendation helped Olmsted to secure the post was Brace's uncle, the botanist Asa Gray.

Olmsted and Brace were close friends throughout their lives and carried on a remarkable correspondence. While Brace continued to argue theology with others, his exchanges with Olmsted in later years centered on the great social and political issues of the times. Throughout their lives they maintained a fondness and deep respect for one another. Six years before Brace died, Olmsted wrote him: "You decidedly have had the best & most worthily successful life of all whom I have known."[5] The Children's Aid Society, he assured his friend, was "the most satisfactory of all the benevolent works of our time."

1. *Life of Brace*, p. 3.
2. FJK Sketch of CLB.
3. FLO to CLB, July 26, 1847.

4. Charles Loring Brace, *Home Life in Germany* (New York, 1853).
5. FLO to CLB, Nov. 1, 1884.

Additional Sources

Brace, John Sherman. *Brace Lineage* . . . 2d ed. Bloomsburg, Pa., 1927.
Kingsbury, Frederick J. "Charles Loring Brace." *Journal of Social Science* 27 (Oct. 1890), pp. l–lii.
DAB, s.v. "Brace, Charles Loring," "Brace, John Pierce."
Notable American Women, s.v. "Pierce, Sarah."

EMMA BRACE (1828–1850), the youngest sister of Charles Loring Brace, showed a special affection for Olmsted as they were growing up in Hartford. This chagrined Olmsted's brother, John, who complained in 1845 that he had been trying since he was five years old to make her smile on him, "but never got anything more than 'respects' or 'compliments' for all my bouquets and walking home from parties and meetings with her."[1] Olmsted confessed to John at that time that "I really love her, love her dearly, but I've no intention of marrying her, and she knows it, and moreover I know that she's no intention of marrying me, whatever I may wish."[2]

In 1845 she graduated from the Hartford Female Seminary and went South the next spring to start a school in Garrettsburg, Kentucky. With this show of independence—and, perhaps, of ambition—she made herself no longer a burden on her father's slender means.

During her absence from Connecticut, Olmsted continued to feel his old affection for her. Others must have perceived this, since when she returned to Hartford for a vacation in 1847 she heard that they were "certainly engaged." "Do you believe it?" she asked his brother; "Please congratulate Fred and tell him he ought to tell me his secrets."[3] Her sojourn in Kentucky, followed by a period of teaching in Georgia, kept Emma and Olmsted apart, and when she returned to New England in 1849 she was fatally ill with tuberculosis. In February 1850, she died at the home of her uncle Asa Gray in Cambridge, Massachusetts.

1. Clinton Collins and JHO to FJK, May 23, 1845.
2. FLO to JHO, Sept. 30, 1845.
3. Emma Brace to JHO, Aug. 26, 1847.

Additional Sources

Life of Brace

HORACE BUSHNELL (1802–1876), the Congregational theologian, was an important figure in the Hartford of Olmsted's youth. Several of his social and religious views strongly influenced Olmsted and appeared—sometimes acknowledged and sometimes not—in his writing.

The Olmsted and Bushnell families were next-door neighbors on Ann Street from 1836 to 1841, when Bushnell moved and John Olmsted bought his house. Although the Olmsted family attended the church of Bushnell's rival and frequent antagonist Joel Hawes until 1849, Olmsted had ample opportunity to learn about Bushnell's ideas. He frequently heard Bushnell preach in Hartford, both in his youth and during visits there in later years.

After 1845 he often discussed Bushnell's doctrines with Charles Loring Brace, who later said that a sermon Bushnell gave in 1842 on "unconscious influence" had affected his whole life. Olmsted had at least one occasion to talk over his religious doubts with Bushnell, following a sail they had together in the late summer of 1847 from New Haven to Sachem's Head. Soon after, Bushnell sent him a copy of his newly published work, *Views of Christian Nurture.*

At this time Bushnell was turning toward a Christ-centered theology after experiencing a mystical vision of the gospel. His book *God in Christ,* published in 1848, seemed too close to Unitarianism for many orthodox Congregationalists, including the Olmsteds' minister, Joel Hawes. With other ministers in the Hartford area, Hawes tried to have Bushnell condemned for heresy.

One reason Bushnell quarreled with his more conservative fellow Congregationalists was that he thought they laid too much stress on adult conversion and neglected the child's early development. He taught that the parents should provide a domestic setting where children would grow up as Christians without ever thinking of themselves otherwise. "Christian nurture," as he called it, would enable others to forgo the years of anguish that he endured before experiencing, at the age of forty-six, an intense mystical experience.

Too strong an emphasis on adult conversion, he argued, had made American Christianity hard and rude and lacking in domesticity of character, showing "a want of sensibility to things that do not lie in action."[1] This thought was related to his earlier concept of "unconscious influence." Bushnell taught that the most constant and potent influence people exerted on each other was not verbal, but rather an unconscious emanation of their real character that showed in their habitual conduct.

These ideas were easily transferred to the secular world. They became the basis of Bushnell's critique of slavery and his view that the frontier produced barbarism. To reform the evils of slavery and the frontier, one had to strengthen the three institutions basic to civilized society: the family, the

HORACE BUSHNELL

church, and the school. His approach, while not original, was the clearest and most compelling restatement of long-standing Connecticut social views available to the young Olmsted. It is not surprising therefore, that Olmsted's approach to social issues strongly resembled Bushnell's.

In his writings on the South, Olmsted echoed the minister's observation that the slave grew up and worked under conditions that failed to prepare him for productive life as a free man. Like Bushnell, he concluded that the southern planter must be convinced that it was in his own interest and his Christian duty to protect the family life of his slaves, encourage Christian worship, and teach them to read and write.

From his own observation of the California mining frontier in 1863 Olmsted confirmed Bushnell's prediction that the individual on the frontier would lapse into barbarism when deprived, like the slave, of a good domestic life and the institutions of a civilized community. His writings on the subject echo Bushnell's 1847 sermon "Barbarism the First Danger."

Bushnell's influence, while obvious in Olmsted's younger days, may have also formed a part of the social and aesthetic rationale of Olmsted's landscape design in later years. Bushnell's distinction between "taste" and "fashion," expressed in an 1843 sermon, anticipated some of Olmsted's aesthetic views. Olmsted not only incorporated Bushnell's idea of "unconscious influence" into his thoughts on social reform but also made it the basis for his theory of the effect of landscape design. In addition, he used it in his autobiographical writings to show why his youthful wanderings through rural scenery had prepared him to be a landscape architect. Bushnell's concern for the civilizing value of domesticity appeared in Olmsted's landscape designs for private clients and in his plans and reports for suburban communities.

As a prominent theologian and commentator on his time, Bushnell expressed nineteenth-century Connecticut religious and social values that combined the old Puritan emphasis on religion and community with more recent concerns for sensibility and taste. Although he later abandoned the intense religious speculation of his youth, Olmsted continued for the rest of his life to promote many of the aesthetic and social values so well expressed by Bushnell.

1. Horace Bushnell, *Views of Christian Nurture, and of Subjects Adjacent Thereto* (Hartford, Conn., 1847), pp. 6, 8.

Additional Sources

Bushnell, Horace. *Sermons for the New Life.* New York, 1858.
———. "Taste and Fashion." *The New Englander* 1, no. 1 (April 1843): 153–68.
———. *Work and Play: Or, Literary Varieties.* New York, 1881.
Cheney, Mary A. (Bushnell), ed. *Life and Letters of Horace Bushnell.* New York, 1880.
Cross, Barbara M. *Horace Bushnell: Minister to a Changing America.* Chicago, 1958.

ANDREW JACKSON DOWNING (1815–1852), the horticulturist and landscape gardener, did more than any other man to shape Olmsted's concept of taste and of the role that landscape gardening could play in transforming and civilizing American society. Downing grew up in Newburgh, New York, finished school at age sixteen, and joined his brother Charles in managing the family nursery business. In 1841, after a decade of study and writing, he published *A Treatise on the Theory and Practice of Landscape Gardening, Adapted to North America,* a work that established Downing as the leading

American authority in that field. The next year he published *Cottage Residences*, a series of designs for picturesque houses and their grounds, and in 1845 completed the encyclopedic *Fruits and Fruit Trees of America*.

In 1846 Downing had become editor of *The Horticulturist and Journal of Rural Art and Rural Taste*. Olmsted first met Downing at this time, when he visited Luther Tucker, proprietor of the *Horticulturist* and the *Albany Cultivator*. During the next six years the two men frequently exchanged information on horticultural subjects, and Downing published several pieces by Olmsted in his magazine. When Olmsted went to England in 1850, Downing provided him with letters of introduction. When he returned, he wrote Downing about his experiences and contributed an essay on the suburban town of Birkenhead, near Liverpool, to the *Horticulturist*. In the fall of 1851, Downing favorably reviewed the first volume of Olmsted's *Walks and Talks of an American Farmer in England*, declaring it "extremely fresh and honest."[1] Downing died in a steamboat disaster in 1852, and Olmsted dedicated the second volume of *Walks and Talks* to his memory, giving him credit for "whatever of good, true, and pleasant thought" it contained. Indeed, the book echoed many of Downing's views on scientific farming, landscape design, and domestic architecture. This was also true of the "Appeal to the Citizens of Staten Island," which Olmsted wrote to promote the agricultural society there. The society would not only help to increase crop productivity, he assured the citizens, but would contribute to the improvement of taste and domestic surroundings.

One essay of Downing's that particularly impressed Olmsted was "The New-York Park," which appeared in the *Horticulturist* three months after his own enthusiastic description of the "People's Park" at Birkenhead. In this piece Downing advocated the creation of a large public park in New York as one of a series of public institutions that would meet the needs of people of all classes and ages "in the higher realms of art, letters, science, social recreation, and enjoyments." These institutions, he hoped, would break down social barriers as they spread taste and enlightenment. Olmsted adopted this program of popular education and social reform and urged it on his friends. When he and Calvert Vaux were seeking funds to erect a bust of Downing in Central Park, they proposed to inscribe the pedestal with a passage from "The New-York Park" that read in part:

> The higher social and artistic elements of every man's nature lie dormant within him, and every laborer is a possible gentleman, not by the possession of money or fine clothes, but through the refining influence of intellectual and moral culture. Open wide, therefore, the doors of your libraries and picture galleries, all ye true republicans! Build halls where knowledge shall be freely diffused among men, and not shut up within the narrow walls of narrower institutions. Plant spacious parks in your cities, and unloose their gates as wide as the gates of morning to the whole people. . . .[2]

75

ANDREW JACKSON DOWNING

In his own writings on landscape architecture, Olmsted made few references to Downing's work. He did, however, praise the 1851 plan for the grounds of the Smithsonian Institution, Downing's only important public work, as "the only essay, strictly speaking, yet made by our government in landscape gardening."[3] Using terms that characterize his own work as well, Olmsted praised the tendency he saw in all Downing's works, "namely to educate men to consult each his own wants, his own special taste, his own peculiar habits, and to be able to form or reform a homestead in a manner suitable thereto, and expressive thereof." But Olmsted had strong reservations about many of the plans for buildings and grounds that Downing offered in his books. He found them "far less excellent with reference to their ostensible ends, than they were with reference to the purpose of stimulating the exercise of judgment and taste in the audience addressed." These latter views Olmsted presented in a draft introduction to a new edition of *Cottage Residences*, written at the request of Downing's widow, but never published.[4]

Downing was important to Olmsted not only for the aesthetic taste and ideas he espoused during his brief lifetime but for the opportunities he left behind at his death. There was no one to replace him as the national authority on landscape gardening, and when in 1857 the city of New York needed a plan for Central Park, the park commissioners sponsored a general competition. Olmsted was co-author of the winning design with Calvert Vaux, the English architect Downing had brought to this country in 1850 as his partner. Vaux carried on Downing's practice after 1852 and brought to the Central Park plan all he had learned during their two years of close association. For the next fifteen years Olmsted and Vaux continued as partners in landscape design. They evolved a style that differed from Downing's, but they owed a substantial debt to his ideas.

Their final gesture to Downing's memory came in 1887, when Olmsted and Vaux collaborated, after fifteen years of independent work, on a plan for the Andrew Jackson Downing Memorial Park in Newburgh.

1. "Reviews," *Horticulturist* 7, no. 3 (March 1852): 135.
2. Andrew Jackson Downing, "The New-York Park," *Horticulturist* 6, no. 8 (Aug. 1851): 345–49, reprinted in Andrew Jackson Downing, *Rural Essays* . . . (New York, 1853), pp. 147–53; *Forty Years*, 1: 92–93.
3. Frederick Law Olmsted, "Appendix" to the *Annual Report of the Architect of the United States Capitol for the Fiscal Year Ending June 30, 1882* . . . reproduced in U.S., Congress, House, *Documentary History of the Construction and Development of the United States Capitol Building and Grounds*, 58th Cong., 2d sess., H. rpt. 646 (Washington, D.C., 1904), p. 1187.
4. Manuscript draft introduction to Downing's *Cottage Residences*, Olmsted Papers.

Additional Sources

Tatum, George Bishop. "Andrew Jackson Downing: Arbiter of American Taste, 1815–1852." Ph.D. dissertation, Princeton University, 1950.

GEORGE GEDDES (1809–1883) was a gentleman farmer, agricultural reformer, civil engineer, and politician at whose farm, "Fairmount," in Camillus, New York, Olmsted stayed during the summer of 1846. Olmsted found that in many ways the versatile and successful Geddes was a model of the man he himself wished to be. He respected Geddes's judgment, and their friendship lasted for many years.

Geddes had inherited "Fairmount" from his father James Geddes, who surveyed the routes of several major canals, including the Erie Canal, and served as construction engineer of the western section of the Erie. Although he first studied law, George Geddes became an engineer and turned his attention to railroad construction, the opening of coal mines, and the drainage of marshes in the Syracuse area. While Olmsted stayed with him, he was supervising the construction near Syracuse of one of the first plank roads in the United States.

After inheriting "Fairmount," Geddes devoted much effort to improving it. In 1845, at the age of thirty-six, he won the New York State Agricultural Society's prize for the best-cultivated farm in the state. Olmsted found that Geddes practiced a style of farming seldom seen in Connecticut. The soil was fertile and free of rocks, so that only ten of the three hundred acres were not fit for cultivation. Geddes carried on agricultural experiments, employed irrigation, and was building up a large flock of Merino sheep. In addition to helping run the farm, Olmsted assisted Geddes in his public role as an agricultural reformer. At the Onondaga County Fair in the fall, Geddes made him a member of the committee for judging farming utensils, and Olmsted wrote the committee's report.

Olmsted also enjoyed the civilized luxuries that Geddes could afford. The farm produced a variety of excellent fruits and vegetables for the table, and the Geddes tradition of afternoon tea and the use of "silver forks every day" were amenities rare among farmers. The conversational fare was similarly unusual and pleasing. Frederick Kingsbury recalled years later that Geddes was "an intelligent man, a good talker, positive, somewhat opinionated but withal breezy and interesting."[1]

A leading layman in the Methodist church, Geddes gave Olmsted an opportunity to discuss the religious questions that beset him. He and Olmsted also debated whether it was right for a Christian to go to war, particularly the war with Mexico going on that summer. Geddes had become a pacifist, perhaps in reaction to attending a military academy in his youth, and favored the disbanding of all armies and navies. As an advocate of world peace, he probably introduced Olmsted to Elihu Burritt's peace-reform journal, which Olmsted found to be a "capital good paper" with "striking and original" articles "worth a whole mail car of common namby pamby editorials."[2] Perhaps through Geddes's influence, too, Olmsted came to admire the Kentuckian Cassius Clay's antislavery newspaper, True American.

Although Geddes urged Olmsted to buy a farm near him, Olmsted was sure he would never feel at home outside Connecticut. He wanted a seaside farm and set out in the fall of 1846 to find one on the Connecticut coast. Geddes helped him to decide on a place at Sachem's Head near Guilford. In the years thereafter he saw Geddes only occasionally, but continued to value his advice and friendship.

GEORGE GEDDES

Like Geddes, Olmsted became actively involved in the affairs of his local agricultural society, and when he moved to a Staten Island farm he emulated Geddes by agitating for a plank road. In 1852 he dedicated to Geddes the first volume of his first book, *Walks and Talks of an American Farmer in England*. Many years later their paths crossed again. In 1879 the seventy-year-old Geddes, a member of the New York State Survey Commission, approved the report by Olmsted and James Gardiner calling for protection of Niagara Falls from commercial exploitation and its preservation for public use.

1. FJK Sketch of FLO.
2. FLO to JO, Aug. 12, 1846; FLO to FJK, May 15, 1846.

Additional Sources

NCAB, 10: 170–71; DAB, s.v. "Geddes, James."
"Farm Statements," *The Cultivator*, n.s. 3, no. 7 (July 1846): 204–6.
New York Times, October 9, 1883, p. 2, obituary notice.
Leavenworth, Elias W., comp. *A Genealogy of the Leavenworth Family in the United States.* . . . Syracuse, N.Y., 1873, pp. 264–67.

FREDERICK JOHN KINGSBURY (1823–1910) was a classmate and friend of John Hull Olmsted's at Yale and through him became one of Olmsted's closest friends. While Olmsted turned to Charles Loring Brace to discuss religious questions, he debated his political theories with Kingsbury, whose skepticism provided him, he said, with much-needed discipline of mind. After Kingsbury graduated from Yale, Olmsted was eager to continue their relationship. "You are just the right sort of man to arrive at correct conclusions," he wrote his friend, "& you ought, it seems to me, to be using a little more of your influence on the populace. At any rate with me."[1]

Like Olmsted and Brace, Kingsbury traced his ancestry in New England back to the early days of Puritan settlement. The original immigrant, Henry Kingsbury, came to the Massachusetts Bay Colony with John Winthrop in 1630, and his grandson removed to Connecticut in 1708. Kingsbury's grandfather John Kingsbury studied law at Tapping Reeve's law school in Litchfield, Connecticut, and then settled in Waterbury. There he became perennial judge of the County Court, held other judicial posts, and frequently represented the town in the state legislature. He passed on large landholdings near Waterbury to his son, Charles Denison Kingsbury, who was Frederick's father. After engaging for several years in trade and manufacturing, Charles Kingsbury retired at the age of forty-three and spent the next fifty-three years farming, looking after his lands, and holding offices in local governmental, educational, and charitable organizations.

Young Frederick received intermittent schooling during his youth, spent much of his time with his grandfathers, and learned various skills from local artisans. From 1837 to 1840 he lived with his uncle Abner Leavenworth in Virginia, and then decided to go to college. He quickly prepared himself to enter Yale and made up for his inadequate background by hard study as a freshman. Although he worked only moderately hard thereafter, he gained enough social and academic standing for his classmates to elect him to deliver the valedictory oration in their senior year. Olmsted was impressed by his intelligence and expected him to have a notable career in politics and the law.

After graduating from Yale, Kingsbury studied for a year at the Yale Law School and then went to Boston to prepare for the Massachusetts bar. He worked in the office of Charles Greely Loring, a prominent lawyer and uncle of Charles Loring Brace. Loring found Kingsbury so useful that he did not charge him the usual study fee. After passing the bar examination in 1848, Kingsbury seemed ready for a distinguished legal career in Boston. He gave it up, however, to return to Waterbury and care for his ailing mother and seventeen-year-old sister.

This sacrifice is hard to explain. Although his mother was to die of her illness four years later, there was no apparent need for Kingsbury to give up his career to come home to support her. His father, prosperous enough to be retired from business, was in vigorous health and lived until 1890. Kingsbury had decided to narrow his opportunities at a time when his friends Brace and Olmsted were moving away from home and widening their experience of the world.

They still remained close to Kingsbury, however, and kept up their correspondence. John Hull Olmsted, in particular, faced many poignant decisions when he learned he was dying of tuberculosis, and sought Kingsbury's advice as to whether he should marry and pursue his medical career in the short time left to him. When Olmsted traveled South as a correspondent for the *New York Times* in 1852, Kingsbury gave him a useful introduction to his uncle, Abner Leavenworth, a school principal in Virginia.

In 1848 Kingsbury prepared himself for a Waterbury law practice with a few months at the office of the Hartford lawyer Thomas Clap Perkins, father of Olmsted's friend and future fiancée, Emily Perkins. Once he opened an office in Waterbury, though, Kingsbury found that he disliked the combative role successful attorneys had to assume. In 1850 he was elected for the first of several terms to the state legislature and while there secured a charter for a savings bank in Waterbury. When he became secretary of the bank he began a business career that would eventually free him from the uncongenial practice of law.

Kingsbury had always shown managerial abilities. He had helped to run a newspaper in Petersburg, Virginia, before he entered college, and he took over a local business in Waterbury to settle an estate in his early years as a lawyer. Still, Olmsted was puzzled by his gradual immersion in the business and civic life of Waterbury, then a town of only five thousand. Olmsted sensed that Kingsbury was drawing apart from his old friends and slowing down—doing a great deal for others good but not much for himself. Olmsted's first impressions of Kingsbury's future wife, Alathea Scovill, were disappointing. She was, he reported to Brace, "nothing but an old fashioned sub half man. . . . Good enough for a wife or a servant—no equal friend."[2]

Almost as if he had known his friend's doubts in 1851, Kingsbury wrote forty years later that Alathea Scovill excelled the much-admired Hartford and New Haven girls both in refinement and cultivation. To be sure, her wealthy father, William H. Scovill, had been able to give her a good education. Perhaps Olmsted's reaction was prompted by the regret he felt that he and Kingsbury could no longer be on such close terms as they had once been.

There were practical advantages to the marriage. Kingsbury's father-in-law, William H. Scovill, was a partner in the Scovill Manufacturing Company, a brass manufacturing firm, and was one of the richest men in Waterbury. His wealth and connections must have been useful to Kingsbury when he and Abram Ives, a broker, raised $100,000 in capital to start the Citizen's Savings Bank in 1853. After opening the bank, Kingsbury gave up his law practice. In 1857 he was elected director of the Scovill Manufacturing Company. By this time his father-in-law and J.M.L. Scovill, a partner, had died. In 1868 Kingsbury became president of the company, a post he held for the next thirty-two years.

After his marriage, Kingsbury entered the Scovills' social and religious world, and joined the local Episcopal church that his wife's grandfather had founded. The Scovills were so closely identified with this church that it was known as "St. Scovill's." Kingsbury took pride in the fact that his children were the descendants of all the ministers in Waterbury during its first century of existence. He rose in the lay circles of the church, becoming treasurer of the diocese of Connecticut. Like his public-spirited father before him, he took an interest in local charities and schools, sometimes taking on their financial problems as treasurer. He also involved himself in the affairs of Yale College. From 1881 to 1899 he was an alumni member of the Yale Corporation.

In later years Charles Loring Brace upbraided Kingsbury for not being a literary man. He had shown definite promise both as a writer and a speaker while at Yale and had been tempted to embark on a literary career. Kingsbury's business commitments did, however, allow him time to indulge a taste for genealogy and local history. In the 1860s, like Olmsted and Brace, he joined the newly founded American Social Science Association, dedicated to the investigation of American social and economic problems. He tried his hand at articles on contemporary issues for the association's *Journal of Social Science*. These and his other writings reflected his conservative, skeptical approach and his taste for homely illustrations and turns of phrase.

He showed some capacity for historical perspective and synthesis and transcended his earlier provincial and antiquarian interests, particularly in one of the addresses he delivered as president of the American Social Science Association in the 1890s. It was entitled "The Tendency of Men to Live in Cities." Perhaps, though, his more characteristic contribution to the association was his serving successively as the organization's treasurer, director, president, and vice president from 1880 until its dissolution in 1908.

Kingsbury's life diverged sharply from that of his closest friends of the 1840s. Unlike them, he became heavily involved in business interests and rooted to small town life in Connecticut. A decade after they had first known each other, Olmsted and he had less and less opportunity to see one another and exchange views. Occasionally their correspondence revived the fire of their college debates, but Olmsted found that he had moved far from Kingsbury's conservative religious and political opinions, which remained much as he had first known them.

Kingsbury, from first to last, remained a considerate and admiring friend. He kept up a correspondence with all his early friends, including Emily Perkins and Elizabeth Baldwin, after both had married. He saved his lengthy correspondence with Olmsted, which included thoughtful letters in the later years. Using his collection of Olmsted's letters, he wrote a perceptive memoir of his friend after Olmsted's death.

1. FLO to FJK, Sept. 23, 1847, in FJK Sketch of FLO.
2. FLO to CLB, Nov. 12, 1850.

Additional Sources

Kingsbury Autobiography
Kingsbury, Frederick J. "What Did I Learn at College?" *Yale Alumni Weekly* 19, no. 19 (Jan. 28, 1910): 465–66, and no. 20 (Feb. 4, 1910): 487–88.
Kingsbury, Frederick John, and Talcott, Mary Kingsbury, eds. *The Genealogy of the Descendants of Henry Kingsbury, of Ipswich and Haverhill, Mass.* [Hartford, Conn.], 1905.
NCAB, 12: 208–9.
Yale Obit. Rec., 6th ser., no. 1 [June 1911]: 8–10.

JOHN OLMSTED (1791–1873), Olmsted's father, was a prosperous dry-goods merchant in Hartford, Connecticut. His successful business enabled him to provide many small luxuries for his children, give them a good education, finance the farming and publishing ventures of his eldest son, and still leave his heirs an estate of over $130,000.

John Olmsted's strong aesthetic sense directed much of his use of leisure and wealth. He took great care, for instance, in furnishing the Ann Street house where the family lived during Olmsted's childhood. The house impressed Frederick Kingsbury when he saw it in the mid-1840s as "better, in its way, than anything I had then seen, and, if I mistake not, better than anything then in Hartford." He thought that in taste and mental culture John Olmsted was "much in advance of the men of that time."[1]

Although John Olmsted inherited no wealth from his father and had

JOHN OLMSTED

to make his way with only a common school education, his family name stood him in good stead in Hartford. He was a member of the seventh generation of the family to live in the area. The first immigrant to New England, James, was one of the original proprietors of Hartford, having joined the band led by Thomas Hooker that founded it in 1636. Many of his descendants stayed in the vicinity for nearly two centuries, intermarrying with the other original families. As a consequence, many of John Olmsted's customers were his relatives as well.

His first wife, Charlotte Hull (1800–1826), was the daughter of a farmer in nearby Cheshire, Connecticut. While still a girl she went to live with an older sister whose husband, Jonathan Law, was the postmaster of Hartford. She married John Olmsted in 1821 and in the next four years gave birth to Olmsted and his brother John. In 1826 she died, allegedly from an overdose of laudanum that she mistook for other pain-killing medicine while suffering from a toothache.[2] In 1827 the widower married his late wife's friend, Mary Ann Bull (1801–1894). In the next fifteen years she bore him six children, of whom three lived to maturity. She was an earnest woman, anxious for the spiritual welfare of her children and sure of the correctness of her views. One acquaintance described her as "a Puritan, a model of order and system, most efficient as an organizer and full of interest in Nature and Man."[3] She shared her husband's love of scenic beauty and tried to foster it in their children.

John Olmsted may have been unaware of the extent of his own influence in this regard on his eldest son. Although he seldom expressed his pleasure in words, he imparted to the boy his unusual sensitivity to the beauty of nature. One of the most poignant of these moments came when Olmsted was still a young child. One evening he and his father were riding together across a meadow: "I soon noticed that he was inattentive to my prattle," Olmsted later recalled, "and looking in his face saw in it something unusual. Following the direction of his eyes, I said: 'Oh! there's a star.' Then he said something of Infinite Love with a tone and manner which really moved me, chick that I was, so much that it has ever since remained in my heart."[4]

As Olmsted grew older he took part in the family's annual "tours in search of the picturesque" through New England, New York, and the St. Lawrence valley. He believed that his father "gave more time and thought to the pursuit of this means of enjoyment than to all other luxuries, and more than any man I have known who could not and would not talk about it or in any way make a market of it."[5]

While taciturn John Olmsted succeeded in giving his children his love of natural scenery, he did not feel that he could transmit to them the active Christian faith that he craved for himself but could not attain. He therefore sent his son to live with various ministers in small Connecticut towns so that he might receive religious instruction with his schooling. The scheme failed, since the ministers left that instruction to incompetent Sunday school teachers.

John Olmsted bowed to the authority of his wife in religion, but was always a most generous and indulgent father to all his children. His letters do show an affectionate streak of sarcasm, but he did little else to keep his independent children in line. His journals are full of details about the weather, his finances, and activities of his children, but they display no personal emotions, except, perhaps, in his faithful recording of the first appearance of bluebirds every spring.

1. FJK to FLO, Jan. 31, 1873.
2. Mary Perkins Olmsted, manuscript fragment, Olmsted Papers.
3. Reminiscence by Mary Perkins Olmsted, quoted in *Forty Years*, 1: 80.
4. Autobiographical Fragment A, below.
5. Ibid.

Additional Sources

Olmsted Genealogy, p. 60.

JOHN HULL OLMSTED (1825–1857) was Olmsted's younger brother, the second child of John Olmsted and Charlotte Law Hull Olmsted. From boyhood on, the dark-eyed and handsome John, with his ready sympathy and easy manner, was an ideal confidant for his intense older brother. After their mother's death they drew closer together, as their strong-willed stepmother, increasingly occupied with her own children, took charge of running the Olmsted household. The bond between the two brothers was strong, although they seldom lived under the same roof, or even in the same town. Olmsted went away to school in the fall of 1829, when his brother was only four, and they spent only two school years together after that. Still, there were short holidays and summer vacations when they saw each other, and these opportunities increased as they grew older. The longest period they lived together was from June 1853 to April 1855, when John and his wife Mary lived with Olmsted on his Staten Island farm.

The earliest descriptions of John come from his friends at Yale, which he entered in 1842. Frederick Kingsbury remembered him as somewhat shy, but with an attractive personality, a delicate sense of humor, and well-formed aesthetic tastes. Charles Loring Brace found him very generous, treating his friends to food and the use of his sporting equipment. He was also impressionable, likely to be influenced in his conduct by that of his friends. John made warm friendships at Yale, and during his short stay there in the fall of 1845 Olmsted made his brother's circle of friends his own.

John worked hard and conscientiously at college but neglected exercise and fresh air. As a result, he was forced to leave Yale halfway through his sophomore year with weak eyes and infected lungs. In early 1843 he went to Jamaica for his health. He returned to Yale by summer, but had to enter the class below his, that of 1847.

Although his health was still frail, John determined to become a doctor, and in the fall of 1848 he went to study at the College of Physicians and Surgeons in New York City. He now saw more of his brother, visiting his Staten Island farm frequently on weekends and holidays. During those visits he met Olmsted's neighbors, the Perkins family, and their orphaned granddaughter, Mary Cleveland Bryant Perkins. She was attractive and witty, and Olmsted had found her "superior as a thinker" to Elizabeth Baldwin—high praise indeed.[1] John read Ruskin's *Modern Painters* with her, and they fell in love. They became engaged early in 1850, shortly before John left for Europe with Olmsted and Brace on a trip that was supposed to improve his health. Any improvement he experienced was short-lived, and by the summer of 1851 his condition had deteriorated dramatically. In August he began to bleed from his lungs, making it evident that he had tuberculosis and could not hope to live many more years.

That summer, John faced his situation and decided to continue his personal and professional life. He went on with his medical studies, and in

JOHN HULL OLMSTED

October 1851, he married Mary Perkins. Then the couple left for a year of travel in Europe, in an attempt to improve his health. Their first child, John Charles Olmsted, was born in Switzerland in September 1852. They returned to America the following June and settled with Olmsted on his Staten Island farm.

Aware of how little time was left to them, the two brothers shared many experiences during the next two years. They traveled South together in December 1853, on Olmsted's second journey there, and spent four months on a saddle trip across Texas to Mexico and back to New Orleans. John hoped to find a healthful climate and was tempted to settle among the Germans near San Antonio, but the return trip along the coast in the oppressive heat of late spring weakened him and forced him to abandon such plans.

Instead, he continued to live at the Staten Island farm and assist his brother in the activities that stemmed from their trip. He helped Olmsted raise money to support Adolph Douai and his antislavery *San Antonio Zeitung*, and while Olmsted was in England in 1856 he wrote most of *A Journey Through Texas* from his brother's notes. His style was freer and lighter than Olmsted's, although he remained faithful to the ideas they both shared.

In the meantime John's health deteriorated as his family and financial cares increased. When Olmsted moved to New York in April 1855, to become a partner in the publishing firm of Dix & Edwards, he left responsibility for the farm on John's shoulders. John's second child, Charlotte, had been born a month before, and he felt deserted. As he complained to his father, "I regret being left in the lurch."[2] Whatever his feelings, he took title to the farm at the end of April, borrowed money from his father, and dipped into his wife's small income in an effort to make it support his family.

John's attempt to run the farm lasted less than two years. His tuberculosis was so far advanced that he had once again to seek a more favorable climate. In January 1857, he took leave of his brother for what was to prove the last time. After a brief stay in Cuba he and his family went on to Europe. His third child, Owen Frederick, was born in August 1857 at Geneva, Switzerland, and soon afterward the family moved to Nice for the winter.

John's strength failed rapidly and on November 24 he died. In his last letter to his brother, John said a painful farewell. "I never have known a better friendship than ours has been & there can't be a greater happiness than to think of that," he wrote. "How dear we have been & how long we have held out such tenderness." In the last sentence of the letter he said, "Don't let Mary suffer while you are alive."[3]

John's death was a heavy blow to Olmsted. As his father said, "In his death I have lost not only a son, but a very dear friend. You almost your only friend."[4] Olmsted was just beginning his work as superintendent of Central Park and he immersed himself in the work. When Mary and her children returned to Staten Island he helped look after their needs, and in 1859 he married his brother's widow and took upon himself the care of his brother's children.

1. FLO to FJK, July 16, 1848, in FJK Sketch of FLO.
2. JHO to JO, March 20, 1855.
3. JHO to FLO, Nov. 13, 1857.
4. JO to FLO, Nov. 28, 1857.

Additional Sources

> *Kingsbury Autobiography*
> *Life of Brace*
> *Olmsted Genealogy*, p. 60.
> Yale University, *Biographical Notices of Graduates of Yale College* . . . (New Haven, 1913), p. 373.

EMILY BALDWIN PERKINS (1829–1914) was the granddaughter of Lyman Beecher and the niece of his equally famous children, Henry Ward Beecher and Harriet Beecher Stowe. Her father was Thomas Clap Perkins, a Hartford lawyer and politician, with whom Frederick Kingsbury studied law. Olmsted became particularly attracted to Emily during a visit to Hartford in the winter of 1849, when he joined a literary group of which she was a member. The petite and pretty Emily let him walk her home from the meetings and accepted his invitations to go sleigh-riding.

Olmsted already knew others of her family. He enjoyed talking to her mother, Mary Foote Beecher Perkins, whom he considered "a very intelligent woman."[1] Three years earlier he had taught her brother Frederick to ride over jumps on horseback. He had known some of Emily's other relatives as well, including her first cousin, Elizabeth Baldwin, and her young clergyman uncle, Thomas Kinnicut Beecher.

Although Olmsted's romance with Emily began in early 1849, he saw her only occasionally during the next two years. His duties on the Staten Island farm and his trip to Europe with his brother and Charles Loring Brace kept him away from Hartford. They had to resort to letters, and as John Hull Olmsted remarked, "they kept at work at one another for near three years, off & on, with a very vigorous & noble correspondence, (wh. I can't refrain from hoping may one day be given to the world for its benefit!)."[2] When the two finally did have some time together in the spring of 1851, Olmsted discovered that what he had thought of as an important religious difference could be resolved. To his surprise, Emily readily agreed with his views on the inspiration of the Bible. The response delighted him, since he had been moving toward a more and more rationalistic view of the Scriptures. Although he was not quite ready to admit that he was in love with Emily, he could characterize her as a "union of Faith and Courage, Religion & Freedom," and the noblest and most sensible woman he had ever known.[3] By mid-summer they were engaged.

Olmsted was cautious about setting a wedding date, however. He wrote Charles Brace that the marriage could not take place until after Thanksgiving, when he would have marketed his 60,000 cabbages. Emily, for her part, complained about the bother of receiving congratulations and worrying about furniture and carpets. After making a public announcement of the engagement in August, she suddenly changed her mind, and her mother wrote Olmsted saying that Emily wished to break it off. The stunned Olmsted released her. Some months later his father was puzzled that Olmsted seemed relieved, as if a great weight had been lifted from him. Perhaps he was putting up a brave front, because not until he married his brother's widow in 1859 was he willing to take a wife.

After breaking off the engagement, Emily left Hartford with Elizabeth Baldwin to visit relatives in Connecticut and Massachusetts until the

89

EMILY BALDWIN PERKINS

gossip at home quieted down. While visiting in Worcester, Massachusetts, she attracted the attention of several young men, including the young Unitarian clergyman Edward Everett Hale. Elizabeth Baldwin was distressed that Emily "was so much fascinated by a man of so much more surface than substance,"[4] but such doubts never troubled Emily, and she married Hale on October 17, 1852. Hale came to know Olmsted in connection with the New England Emigrant Aid Society in the 1850s and thirty years later he was a strong supporter of Olmsted's plans for the Boston park system.

After 1881, the Olmsteds and Hales lived only a few miles apart in the Boston suburbs, but they never exchanged visits. Apparently Emily Hale hesitated to call on the family because she feared Mary Olmsted would be jealous of the woman who had once been engaged to her husband. In 1899, when Olmsted was hopelessly senile, she wrote Frederick Kingsbury, saying, "I have always been sorry to see nothing of them, since they have lived in Brookline, but you know what Mary is, and I felt afraid of giving her an opportunity of being rude to me."[5]

1. FLO to CLB, Feb. 5, 1846.
2. JHO to FJK, Sept. 12, 1851.
3. FLO to CLB, May 27, 1851.
4. Elizabeth Baldwin to Roger Sherman Baldwin, Nov. 7, 1851, Baldwin Family Papers.
5. Emily Hale to FJK, Feb. 19, 1899, in possession of Mrs. Katherine Bull, Litchfield, Conn.

Additional Sources

   Perkins Family Genealogy, Part 3, pp. 80–81.

SOPHIA CANDACE STEVENS (1826–1892) became a warm friend of the Olmsteds when she lived with them in Hartford from 1848 to 1851, while teaching at the Hartford High School. She was born in Barnet, Vermont, where her father was a farmer, postmaster, innkeeper and mill-owner. He was also a book collector and antiquarian, and founded the Vermont Historical Society. Two of her brothers, Benjamin Franklin and Henry, continued their father's interest in books and became important book collectors and bibliographers.

Sophia was one of the young women who served Olmsted as a guide and companion in his exploration of art and literature, and was one of the few people with whom he could "talk esthetically."[1] During a visit to Hartford in 1849 he took great satisfaction in their reading John Ruskin's *Modern Painters* together. "The Modern Painters improves on acquaintance," he wrote his brother, John, "and Miss Stevens forms an amalgam with it in my heart. She is just the thing to read it or to have it read to one by. She is very sensitive to beauty, thoughtful, penetrating, enthusiastic."[2]

Olmsted lost her companionship in 1851 when Sophia married Stephen W. Hitchcock (1827?–1852), a teacher at the Female Seminary in Burlington, Vermont. Her husband died of tuberculosis the next year and the Olmsteds came to her aid. They helped her start a new life in Paris and in 1854 sent Bertha Olmsted to stay with her there and study French and music. She supported herself in part by writing a series of letters for the *New York Daily Tribune* entitled "An American Woman in Paris." Olmsted liked her work and offered to place her material in *Putnam's Monthly Magazine* and *Harper's Monthly*. Instead of continuing her literary career, however, the

SOPHIA CANDACE STEVENS

young widow went to Rome in December 1855. There she studied drawing with one of the best American artists then living abroad, William Page. His wife had just deserted him for an Italian count, and he was in poor health. Sophia took care of him and his three daughters and they fell in love. In October 1857 they were married.

Although he had gained a reputation during the 1850s for striking portraiture, Page soon faded into obscurity because he preferred to create large and unsalable allegorical paintings instead of accepting the lucrative portrait commissions his wife secured for him. After the Pages returned to the United States in 1860, Sophia tried to retrieve their fortunes by writing articles on aesthetic theory that she gleaned from her husband's notes and published under his name. She made little progress in face of Page's deteriorating health and the needs of their four children. Furthermore, most of his paintings turned black within fifty years because of the dark toning he gave them. Fortunately, two of his works survived with their colors intact: one a self-portrait and the other a portrait of Sophia. This last, cleaned and restored in 1936, provides the best surviving image of her. It also brought the recognition of Page's considerable talent that she had struggled so long to secure.

1. FLO to JO, March 12, 1849.
2. FLO to JHO, Feb. 10, 1849.

Additional Sources

DAB, s.v. "Stevens, Benjamin Franklin," and "Stevens, Henry."
Taylor, Joshua C. *William Page, The American Titian*. Chicago, 1957.

THE FORMATIVE YEARS

YEARS

1822 to 1852

CHAPTER I

AUTOBIOGRAPHY

NONE OF THE LETTERS that Olmsted wrote before he was eighteen
has been found, but in later years, while writing on other subjects, he recorded vivid recollections of his childhood which help to fill the gap. The
following chapter presents major passages from these two autobiographical
fragments, while omitting variant drafts and Olmsted's comments on other
matters.

Apparently Olmsted started to write his reminiscences in the middle
1870s: in a prefatory note to the first fragment he referred to his southern
trips of 1852 and 1853 as having taken place twenty years before. According
to Frederick Law Olmsted, Jr., and Theodora Kimball, who printed a version
of some of the fragments in the 1920s, Olmsted began writing "at night when
the strain of his bitter fight for the right development of the Central Park left
him sleepless and he turned with relief to the recollections of a simple harmonious group." To recall pleasure jaunts of his family and New England
village life must have been a solace to Olmsted in the 1870s when he was
landscape architect to the New York Department of Public Parks and so
harassed by Tammany Hall politicians that he came close to a breakdown.

In a prefatory note, Olmsted explained that he intended for the first
fragment to be the start of a book on taste and landscape design in the United
States. He may have intended the second fragment to be part of a similar
book, or it may be simply another version of the same project. The reason he
gave for beginning with a discussion of his childhood was: "This book will
record some general results of observations and reflections from points of
view to which I have been led by causes so far unusual that it will be well
here to give some account of them. I have been influenced even in early
childhood, I believe, to take a little more than common interest in pleasurable
conditions of scenery."[1]

Olmsted realized that he had grown up with a freer and more haphazard education than most of his friends. He wrote these autobiographical fragments to try to explain to himself as well as to others how his background had led him to engage in the new profession of landscape architecture rather than to practice a traditional calling like medicine or the law.

While Olmsted's specific purposes and inevitable memory lapses made him pass over some aspects of his childhood that contemporary letters might have described, his picture of his childhood circumstances is a valuable record of early-nineteenth-century New England life. He brings back a time when the American Revolution and the War of 1812 were still living memories, when the village minister still held some of the authority of his Puritan predecessors, and when romantic taste in scenery and recreational pursuits had begun to appear among the well-to-do like Olmsted's own father.

Olmsted wrote these fragments with many false starts, deletions, and curious addenda that require more flexible treatment than do his letters. The editor has respected the apparent order of the fragments and has presented the narrative in its last stage of evolution. However, when Olmsted deleted a passage adding something fresh to the narrative that he did not later include in a different form, the editor has restored it.

1. *Forty Years*, 1: 44.

AUTOBIOGRAPHICAL FRAGMENT A
PASSAGES IN THE LIFE
OF AN UNPRACTICAL MAN[1]

"The school of the man is the place where he happens to be and his teachers are the people, books, animals, plants, stones and earth around about him."

Philip Gilbert Hamerton[2]

My father was well fitted to live only in a highly organized community in which each man's stint is measured out to him according to his strength. As the world is going he was perhaps as fortunately placed in this respect as he well could be. Yet the world was driving along so fast that a man of any spirit could not but feel himself cruelly prodded up to take more upon himself than he was equal to. My father therefore lived in a state of constant perplexity between his own modesty and self distrust and disposition to acquit himself fully in his proper part, and the confused and conflicting demands which he supposed were made upon him by Mrs. Grundy,[3] made in the name and with the authority of Society, Religion and Commerce.

The affectations by which he aimed to hide his unreadiness to meet these demands were so transparent and his real qualities had so little of brilliancy that he passed with others, even with many of his friends, for a man of much less worth, ability and attainments than he was.

If any one had said to my father that he was highly sensitive to beauty he would have straightened himself, coughed and bridled like a girl, in the desire to accept flattery with becoming deprecation and admission. And he would probably soon after try to justify the compliment by referring admiringly to something which he thought had the world's stamp of beauty upon it, quite possibly something which, but for the stamp, would be odious to him.

He rarely talked even [with] his family on matters at all out of the range of direct and material domestic interests, and in a company where lively conversation was going on would sit silent and even answer questions unfrankly and with evident discomfort.

Yet though his communion with others was never wordy, a decided companionship was always necessary to his comfort, and his silence was never churlish.

His sensitiveness to the beauty of nature was indeed extraordinary, judging from the degree in which his habits were affected by it, for he gave more time and thought to the pursuit of this means of enjoyment than to all other luxuries, and more than any man I have known who could not and would not talk about it or in any way make a market of it.

My mother died while I was so young that I have but a tradition of memory rather than the faintest recollection of her.[4] While I was a small school boy if I was asked if I remembered her I could say "Yes; I remember playing on the grass and looking up at her while she sat sewing under a tree." I now only remember that I did so remember her, but it has always been a delight to see a woman sitting under a tree, sewing and minding a child.

My step mother's[5] character was simpler than my father's but she also had a strong love of nature and her taste was more cultivated and had more of her own respect.

My father when a young man was fond of riding and before I could be trusted alone on a horse was in the habit of taking me sitting on a pillow before him. But while still very young I rode by his side.

The happiest recollections of my early life are the walks and rides I had with my father and the drives with my father and mother in the woods and fields. Sometimes these were quite extended, and really tours in search of the picturesque. Thus before I was 12 years old I had been driven over the most charming roads of the Connecticut valley and its confluents, through the White Hills, and along most of the New England coast from the Kennebec to the Naugatuck.[6]

We were our own servants, my father seldom fully trusting strangers in these journeys with the feeding, cleaning or harnessing of his horses. We rested long in pleasant places; and when at noon we took the nags out and fed them by the road side, my father, brother and I would often wander far looking for a bathing place and for an addition of fresh wild berries for the picnic dinner which my mother would have set out in some well selected shady place.

I had also before I was twelve travelled much with my father and mother by stage coach, canal and steamboat, visiting West Point, Trenton Falls, Niagara, Quebec, and Lake George.[7]

I recollect less of any enjoyment I may then have had than of my impression of the enjoyment my father & mother constantly found in scenery. Yet they could have talked little of it, both being of silent habits; and I am sure that they did not analyze, compare and criticise.

These reflections rise naturally when I review the conditions of my education, for although I was much separated from my father and few men have less aptness, inclination or ability than he had to give oral instruction, I see that the unpremeditated and insensible influence which came to me from him was probably the strongest element in my training. I see also that my father may have unwittingly disclosed to me more of his nature than to any one else. One of two or three incidents that remain in my mind will show what I mean. On a Sunday evening we were crossing the meadows alone. I was tired and he had taken me in his arms. I soon noticed that he was inattentive to my prattle and looking in his face saw in it something unusual. Following the direction of his eyes, I said: "Oh! there's a star." Then he said something of Infinite Love with a tone and manner which really moved me, chick that I was, so much that it has ever since remained in my heart.

Brought up in a superstitious faith in the value of preaching and didactic instruction, and knowing how little he could by deliberate purpose do for me in that way, my father's affection and desire to "do right by the boy" made him always eager to devolve as much as practicable of the responsibility of my education upon ministers.

I was placed successively in charge of six ministers.[8] That this was not a choice of schoolmasters appears from the fact that while living with three of them I was, with my father's knowledge, sent out by them to day schools—twice to the common school[9]—and that only one himself gave me regular personal instruction. In every case too I was for the most part turned over for what is commonly called religious instruction to Sunday school teachers, that is to say vain ignorant, and conceited big boys and girls—parrots or quacks at the business.

The first of these ministers, who became my father by deputy when I was but six years old, was the pastor of a thoroughly rural parish.[10] The surface of the country was rugged, the soil, except in small patches, poor; the farms consequently large and the settlement scattered. The chief dignitary was the justice of the peace, who was a very hard working farmer. There was a little country general store at which the weekly mail was distributed. There was no public house, but near the meeting house there were not only sheds for the horses of worshippers coming from a distance but a range of huts, called "Sunday houses" with fireplaces and in these the people between services during the winter warmed and fed themselves and renewed the hot coals of the foot stoves which they took into their pews. (I think Sunday was then called Sunday and that the fashion of calling it Sabbath came in afterwards or had not yet reached this place.)

The accumulation of results of labor in several generations was chiefly conspicuous in the stone walls which divided the fields. I suppose that the large family in which I lived, enjoyed more luxury than any other but I doubt if, one year with another, four hundred dollars in money passed through its hands. Every household however was self supporting and none so needy that it would not resent an offer of gratuitous assistance unless it were in such neighborly kindness as the poorest might offer the richest. There was a single family of vagabond habits, the father and mother being drunkards, who sometimes came to the store and bartered small peltry chiefly for tobacco and rum, and who once when they had done so betook themselves to a Sunday house and shut themselves up in it for a deliberate drunk. But even this family, which was distinguished and prayed for as "the poor," kept up at least a profession of supporting themselves honestly. They probably owned the cabin they lived in and a small piece of mountain land about it. If not I think they were the only family that did not own some land and till it.

Every one made long days' work; the parson was diligent and travelled far every week on his pastoral duties. He worked with his own hands a little farm from which the family living was helped out. He kept a horse and cow. He entertained a good deal of company—agents of benevolent societies and travelling preachers as well as family friends, parishioners and the families of neighboring ministers—but he had no hired man servant and the only maid was a young girl, probably a relative of his wife's, who often sat at the table with us and before I left was married; perhaps to another minister. There was another young pupil, a big boy who was reading Greek with the parson fitting for college and who paid for his own tutorship by helping in the farm work. On the parson's little farm we had cows and swine and sheep, turkeys, geese, fowls and bees. Besides the commoner farm crops we raised flax and spun it. We had an orchard and sent apples to a neighboring cider mill. I remember seeing the parson grafting scions into the trees. I remember also beating a pan when the bees swarmed, helping to pluck the geese, helping to wash the sheep, setting up the martin box, going with yarn to the weavers, helping to make soap & to dip candles.

It seems to me that while I was here though only six years old I was under no more constraint than a man; that I went where I liked, did what I

101

liked—and especially I had a hand in everything that was going on in the neighborhood. When I saw other boys going barefoot I threw away my shoes and was no more required to wear them except on Sundays. Every house, every room, every barn and stable, every shop, every road and byway, every field, orchard and garden was not only open to me but I was every where welcome. With all their hard working habits no one seemed to begrudge a little time to make life happy to such a bothering little chappie as I must have been. Such a thing as my running into danger even from bad company would seem not to have been thought of.

I remember very distinctly wandering off by myself in the evening to the store and sitting there listening to such talk as happened; going to look in at the window of the Sunday house to see the drunken poor folks; going with the boys to smoke out woodchucks from their burrows, to get rabbits in winter out of stone walls; to trap mink in steel traps and quail in figure four traps. I remember going with rye to the grist mill, riding on the sacks behind some man or bigger boy; going a-fishing on a pond and gathering lillies; going at night to see a charcoal burning and there eating potatoes baked in ashes. I am often reminded of the odor that filled the air—I think it was chiefly burnt turf; spending a day and night at a distant sugar camp and there sleeping in a wigwam of bark; making pastoral visits to sick people with uncle—so I called him though he was no family relation. I seem to remember a bed ridden old woman to whom I timidly handed some flowers which I had been allowed to pick for the purpose in aunty's garden.

I remember when a man came to say that a sick child was dead, and to get the key of the meeting house. I went with him and saw him strike three strokes on the iron triangle which hung suspended by strips of cow hide from the beams of the belfry, by which the tidings were sent to all within hearing, and immediately women began to come from all directions to show their sympathy to the stricken parents. The loss of a single little child stirred every heart in every household.

We were dismissed early from school next day and went to see the coffin made (it was of pine boards). I remember seeing the boards stained with a red wash and varnished—the smell of fresh varnish has often since reminded me of it. We saw the grave dug and helped to take out the bier and dingy pall from the little house in the grave yard where they were kept. All the people for many miles about came to the funeral. Farm work was suspended and the district schools were closed that the children might be present. We walked in the funeral procession.

We had visitors at the parsonage that night and the expressions of grief and sympathy with the parents of the little girl were affecting. Moved by them, after tea I walked to the burying ground and kneeling by the side of the new grave mound prayed God for Christ's sake to raise the girl, intending to lead her over to our house that she might be sent home to her mother. I believe that I did so in good faith and a few years afterwards when I smiled to think of it, I was of the opinion that I had complied with all the necessary formula of effective prayer. I was certain that I had thought so at the time. When, however, my effort proved unavailing, I did not ask myself if I had made any mistake. My attention was probably called off by a whip-poor-will, and by night hawks and fire flies, for these are associated in my mind with the locality. I seldom hear the swoop of a night hawk without thinking of it. I went back to the house and was sent to bed, no one asking where I had been. I never asked the minister for an explanation.

I remember the parson's reading the usual notice in meeting the next Sunday. "It having pleased God to remove by death the infant child of Reuben and Rebecca Wilson, the afflicted parents, with the aged grand-mother, the surviving children and other relatives ask the prayers of the congregation that this bereavement may be blessed to their spiritual and eternal good." As each class of the mourners was designated, they stood up in their pew and many of the women looking on had tears in their eyes.[11]

I remember being taken up by a sleighing party and driven far by moonlight to a large house where I saw flip made by the kitchen fire; saw the "parson's girl" drink it & be merry; saw romping games played around the great chimney, where finally I fell asleep & was put to bed to be taken home in the midst of a furious snowstorm in the bitter morning by one of the boys who treated me to an upset in a snow drift.

I don't quite see how the people old and young—even the drunkard —could be on such good terms with the parson as it seems to me they were. I certainly have seen nothing like it since. I think that the temperance reforma-tion was just beginning and my uncle preached and prayed in the meeting in the school and in the family against intemperance but total abstinence was not yet insisted on. The anti Slavery agitation had not arisen. Divisions on these two questions I understand were afterwards so bitter that half the congregation refused to come to meeting or to contribute to the support of the minister, who finally was obliged to ask for a dismissal on account of the extreme privations to which his family became reduced.

I learned to read in a little brown school house on the bank of a babbling brook in the midst of the woods. I remember chestnut, hemlock, birch and alder trees about it and nearby thickets of mountain laurel. The brook must have been a small one for we made a pool by damming it, into which we put little trout and frogs that we caught with our hands, and from which we filled the drink-water pail of the school. The ground was strewn with rocks and the brook made a crooked way among them with much babbling. I remember beds of fragrant mint along its banks and of pennyroyal on the drier roadside. Here too, by an old stone fence we drew out sassafras roots and in a marshy place at the foot of the hill we pulled the sweetflag root from the black mire.

The narrow road passed on the other side of the school house and sometimes when wheels were heard approaching our mistress would stop short and cry "Your elders are coming; make your manners! make your manners!" and we hastened to stand in line at the road side, the boys to bow, the girls to curtsey. Even when at play and out of sight of the school house the boys would stop and take off their hats if any much older person came near. We were eager to do it, which perhaps is to be accounted for by the fact that we saw so few people and that no man would be in such haste or so absorbed in other duties that he could not acknowledge the courtesy and smile or say a pleasant word to us.

I was a favorite with the mistress; there were not more than a dozen and I loved as a child loves. When she was married and was starting for the Western Reserve in a chaise with a horse hide trunk, studded with brass nails, hung on behind, she stopped at our house to see me. She cried a little when she kissed me. Did I cry also? I think not.

I dimly recall much more that was quaint and that it is harder to believe in (and that would now seem incredible, so rapidly have we shot ahead of that period) of the habits and customs of the parish, but I recall nothing that was not kindly or that I do not thoroughly respect.

One of the most incredible of my recollections is that of the serious and respectful interest taken by all classes of the people in the annual spring parade of the militia, and first that the drummer should have come to the parson for advice as he did weeks before hand in regard to the drum head. Its renewal and the manner of it being determined, I went with a squad to a distant currier's where a sheep skin was selected bargained and paid for in seed potatoes. After it had been prepared & mounted the drummer and fifer practiced at the store every night, Sundays excepted, until the day of the muster.

On the Sunday before, some of the officers appeared at meeting in partial uniform. It was questioned at dinner whether this was a good custom; whether it did not minister more to personal vanity than to any good. The parson, however, regarded it as a suitable mark of respect to the house of God—and remarked that the military arm of the republic had no strength except in its dependence on the Almighty. The approaching occasion was remembered in his prayers.

When the day came and the long roll was beaten in front of the meeting house, about fifty true yeomen fell in and answered to their names. Nearly all wore parts of what had once been uniforms. Very few were without a black and red plume bound in the left side of their hats. The privates all had muskets but I have an impression that the non commissioned officers or some of them carried lances or halberds.[12] The commissioned officers were in full military suits, not that these had been made to fit them for I think that they had been obtained for a consideration from their predecessors and dated back to the last war. They had swords and enormous Chapeaux bras[13] with plumes and also wore leather stocks and silk sashes. The company was drilled, marched and counter-marched, dismissed for dinner, reassembled and, at length, late in the day, a sergeant with a guard of honor was sent to the parsonage and the minister escorted to the ground. On his arrival he was duly saluted by the Company which then formed in hollow square, the minister, commissioned officers, "music" and the Company flag in the centre. The minister delivered a short discourse, made a long prayer and after being thanked by the Captain was reescorted to the parsonage. There were few inhabitants of the parish, old or young, who were not present at this ceremony, as many as possible standing, men and boys with their hats removed, on the long wooden steps of the meeting house, at the foot of which the square had been formed.

The Company being again brought into line the Captain said a few words of compliment closing nearly as follows:

"You are now about to be dismissed for the day and I hope that nothing will occur after the dismissal which will lessen the respect for you as citizen soldiers which your gallant and exemplary conduct while under military discipline has been calculated to inspire in the hearts of the ladies. I will only add that after the dismissal I shall give a little treat at the North Sunday house which you are all heartily invited to partake of." Here a private stepped out and called for three cheers for Captain Fowler, which were given, the drums rolling and the flag waving.

In the Sunday house, pitchers of cider and apple jack, glasses, and plates of crackers, cheese and gingerbread were set out and under their influence the earnestness which had so far characterized the proceedings gave way to a certain temperate degree of hilarity, awkward [and] somewhat forced and creaking. I remember nothing which would indicate that any one imagined there was anything at all funny about it in the whole performance.

After supper a drum and fife concert concluded the solemn patriotic festival, the last piece performed being Old Hundred.

I do not know whether it was before or after this that I spent several months with my uncle at Geneseo,[14] where I remember being taken to see Indians making baskets, to visit at a house in the dooryard of which there was a fawn; and at which a beautiful woman gave me some sweet meats, and that I was sometimes driven rapidly and silently over the turf of the bottom lands among great trees.

I was for months again the smallest boy among sixty at a boarding school,[15] where I was placed under the special care of another clergyman, of whom I remember nothing after my father and mother drove away. Here I suffered in many cruel ways, and I still carry the scars of more than one kind of the wounds I received. I was taken away suddenly when one of the big boys wrote to his father who sent the letter to mine, that a teacher had lifted me up by my ears and had so pinched one of them that it bled. I am glad to remember that when my father questioned at home about it I explained that the teacher had told me that he did not mean to and that I liked pinching better than ferruling. My father had not thought of taking me away when I wrote—I think it must have been in my first letter to him—that there had been a revival in the school; that I had experienced religion, that I had had a prayer party in my bedroom to pray for his conversion and that I wished him to read a certain tract, the title of which I forget.

Then I lived for a few months chiefly with my grandmother,[16] going irregularly to a village school, but being educated more I think through some old novels, plays and books of travels that I found in a sea chest in her garret. I actually read at this time much of Zimmermann on Solitude, Sterne's Sentimental Journey, and the Vicar of Wakefield.[17] I have the same volumes now, and I now have such a puzzling sense of double life as when I see some of Coleman's plays on the stage.[18] I suppose these readings developed the talent which I must have temporarily possessed two or three years later when I could hire other boys to do my chores by telling them stories—no doubt but partially of my own invention.

After this I lived for six months or more at home.[19] But home with me had many branches, for there were no less than ten households of grandparents, granduncles and uncles in which, for all that I recollect, I was as welcome and intimate and as much at home as if I had been born to them. My father's grandfather[20] had five sons, all of whom had I think been sea faring men before the revolution. One had sailed in a letter of marque, was taken prisoner and died in the hulk at the Wallabout.[21] Another who was more successful than the rest in acquiring wealth & honors was carried to a peaceful grave before my day.[22] Another was over ninety years old when I was born;[23] I dimly recollect him, living in a large rambling old farm house, of which he was the only occupant except his housekeeper. The fourth was also over ninety when I rode his knee. He had served the young republic both on sea and land and was the hero of a very daring and shrewd exploit, having with three American seamen and two negroes whom he compelled to assist him, recaptured a valuable prize vessel on the high seas and brought her safely in.[24] They were all infirm from wounds and rheumatism and I remember my grandfather out of his arm chair but once. He then walked a little way with me in a warm spring day, supporting himself with a long Malacca cane, which I now own, held with both hands. Leaning against a fence he pointed out a hang bird's nest in one of a row of elms near us and then told me that he had helped his father to plant the trees, describing how small they were at the time. I wanted my father to let me help him plant trees, and he did, but they were not placed with sufficient forecast and have since all been cut down. But great grandfather's trees stand yet and the hang birds yet have their home in them.

THE JOAB BRACE HOUSE, NEWINGTON, CONNECTICUT

JOAB BRACE

Then I spent nearly five years, vacations excepted, in the home of a minister who undertook with God's help to bring up four select pupils in the fear of the Lord, making no distinction between them and his own children.[25] For their accommodation he had bought and moved a small, old country store along side the parsonage proper, in the cellar of which he stored cabbages and roots, on the ground floor had a workshop and harness room, and in the second story the boys' beds, desks and benches.

The clapboards were warped and shaking and the winter winds swept keenly through them. The heating apparatus was a sheet iron stove, if I am not mistaken made by the Parson himself. The Parson's salary was nominally $500 a year but the people being poor and money scarce he took much of it in "produce:" firewood, for instance, which was invariably delivered when the sledding was good and mostly in logs. As soon as winter came the duty was put on me to keep up the fire one day in four, and to provide wood I had to cut and split these logs; using a beetle & wedges for the larger ones; then carry the wood to the school and up stairs—all in play time—make the fire before day and keep it up till bedtime. I was eight years old and small of my size and had never before been allowed to handle an axe. I do not doubt that I made some progress that winter in acquiring habits of industry.

The parsonage had a small back kitchen in which there was a wooden sink; outside the door stood an open water butt with a spigot at the bottom. After we had dressed by lamp light in the morning and perhaps broken a path through the snow to "the other house," we opened the back kitchen door and in turn drew water in a cast iron skillet about six inches in diameter, out of which with the aid of homemade soft soap, held at a corner of the sink in a gourd, we washed our hands and faces. A roller towel hung upon the wall for the use of all the family. On Saturday night, hot water was furnished us and we were expected to wash our ears, neck and feet. Our meals were eaten in the kitchen & here, on the bare floor, we twice a day kneeled in prayers.

The parson's son, a weakly boy who afterwards died of consumption, lived in the house with the family; the four boarder boys had the "store" all to themselves except in school hours.

They were kept in order in this way: At irregular intervals, when they were expected to be studying their lessons, the parson came to the foot of the stairs, took off his shoes, crept softly up and stood with his ear or eye at the latch. If there were no disorder, he quietly slipped down again and we perhaps knew nothing of his visit. If I were telling a story—my stories were generally of "run aways"—the parson waited until I reached a situation of high interest, where he would break in shouting "Oh! the depravity of human nature!" and seizing a ruler, a stick of fire wood or a broom handle, go at us all pell mell over the head and shoulders. When this first occurred I was stupefied with surprise and terror and was awfully cudgelled. Afterwards I acquired considerable skill in dodging and made a practice of cutting downstairs and off with all my might to the barn where I burrowed deep in the hay. If I came demurely into the house half an hour afterwards, nothing would be said about the matter. It was not often this occurred, partly because we trained ourselves to be quiet and orderly indoors, partly because we cultivated a low tone of conversation and partly because when specially inclined to fun[26]

1. Olmsted's earlier title for this piece was "Passages in the Life of a Wholly Unpracticable Man." He often had to contend with the charge that what he sought to accomplish and the means he wished to use were "unpracticable," and it offended him greatly. The phrase seems to have attached particularly to his career with the New York City Park Department between 1857 and 1878. In 1857 he almost failed in his attempt to become superintendent of Central Park because the park engineer preferred to hire what he called a "practical man" for the position. The story of Olmsted's early encounters with that engineer, Egbert Viele, and his underlings forms the second major segment of the manuscript "Passages in the Life of an Unpracticable Man." Olmsted's sense of the hostility of New York politicians to his "unpractical" nature persisted, and when in 1882 he published a pamphlet attacking the management of Central Park he entitled it "The Spoils of the Park. With a Few Leaves From the Deep-Laden Note-Books of 'A Wholly Unpractical Man.'"

In his manuscript preface to the projected book of autobiographical "Passages," of which this fragment is a part, Olmsted put the whole undertaking in this framework. He was doing it, he wrote, because he recalled "certain passages in my early life in the review of which some light seemed to be cast not only on my own failure in practical ability but in the apparent embarrassment of the public in respect to certain evils of comparatively recent origin which are constantly growing and becoming more and more portentous" (*Forty Years*, 2: 36, 117).

2. Philip Gilbert Hamerton (1834–1894), English artist and essayist, author of a

biography of the English landscape painter J. M. W. Turner and of several books on landscape and art (*DNB, Supplement,* 22).

3. Mrs. Grundy is an imaginary character "who typifies the disciplinary control of the conventional 'proprieties' of society over conduct, the tyrannical pressure of the opinion of neighbors on the acts of others" (*EB*).

4. Olmsted's mother, Charlotte Hull Olmsted (1800–1826), died when he was three years and ten months old (*Olmsted Genealogy,* p. 60).

5. In 1827, a year after the death of Olmsted's mother, his father married her close friend Mary Ann Bull (1801–1894). All of Olmsted's references to his "mother" in the remainder of this autobiographical piece are to his stepmother (ibid.).

6. Most of the traveling outside the state of Connecticut that Olmsted refers to here took place during a single trip when he was sixteen. In August 1838, he went on a trip through the White Mountains in New Hampshire with his father, stepmother, and brother. They went up the Connecticut Valley to Hanover, N.H., toured the White Mountains through Franconia Notch and Crawford Notch, visited Lake Winnepesaukee in central New Hampshire, and ventured as far east as Portsmouth. The mouth of the Kennebec River is some seventy miles east of Portsmouth, and Olmsted did not visit that area until many years later. The Naugatuck River is in west central Connecticut and flows into the Housatonic, which reaches Long Island Sound fifteen miles west of New Haven (JO Journal, Aug. 8–22, 1838).

7. In the spring and summer of 1828, when he was six years old, Olmsted visited his uncle Owen Pitkin Olmsted at Geneseo, N.Y., and at that time saw the Hudson River, West Point, Niagara Falls, and perhaps Lake George. There is no evidence that he visited Quebec before September 1846, when he was twenty-four. That trip, during which he also went to Niagara Falls and Lake George, took place while he was living with George Geddes in Camillus, N.Y. He probably did not visit the cascades of Trenton Falls on the Kanata river near Utica, N.Y. until 1853 (FLO to JO, June 16, 1853; JO Journal, April 20–Aug. 2, 1828, Aug. 27–Sept. 10, 1846, Dec. 9, 24, 1839; Mariana Griswold Van Rensselaer, "Frederick Law Olmsted," *Century Illustrated Monthly Magazine* 46, no. 6 [Oct. 1893]: 861).

8. Olmsted's father first sent him away to live and study with a minister in October 1829, when he was seven years old. The minister was Zolva Whitmore of North Guilford, Conn. Olmsted stayed with him nearly a year, until September 1830 (see note 10, below). Then, from May to September 1831, he was under the special care of a minister while attending Ellington High School in Ellington, Conn. In Oct. 1831 he went to live with the Reverend Joab Brace in Newington, Conn. He remained there, under Brace's casual tutelage, until April 1836 (see note 25, below). At that point he suffered the sumac poisoning that weakened his eyes and interrupted his education. Part of the treatment of his eyes consisted of bathing in salt water, so he spent the summers of 1836 and 1837 in Saybrook, Conn., on Long Island Sound, living with the Episcopal minister George Clinton Van Vechten Eastman (1807–1896). There he received medical treatments and continued his schooling. His last ministerial caretaker was Frederick A. Barton (1809–1881), with whom he lived and studied from November 1837 to May 1840—first in Andover, Mass., and then in Collinsville, Conn.

This means that from the time Olmsted left home in 1829 until he completed his studies with Barton ten and a half years later, there were only two substantial periods when he was living in Hartford and East Hartford and attending schools there. One of these was from September 1830 to May 1831, and the other was from September 1836 to June 1837.

Nothing is known about the sixth minister with whom Olmsted may have lived. He may have been the "Baggs" Olmsted refers to in the following fragment, which he clearly intended to be part of this autobiographical piece:

At Baggs' we were trained to take the best view possible of our superiors, the worst possible of ourselves. Inferiors and subordinates we had none.

I was very active, imaginative, inventive, impulsive, enterprising, trustful and heedless. This made what is generally called a troublesome and mischievous boy. Some thought me a very bad boy, and this was the view which was taken at Baggs's. I had never cared much that I was called so before, but here my exceeding badness (in a world of total badness) was so constantly driven in upon me that it had a strong effect upon a disposition not usually shy. Not that I thought so very badly of myself, but that I got a habit strongly fixed of considering the favorable regard of others as something not to be expected and when obtained as evincing a character to be admired and gratefully looked up to.

(JO Journal, 1829–1840; references for George C. V. Eastman are: Walter E. Howard and Charles E. Prentiss, comps., *Catalogue of the Officers and Students of Middlebury College, 1800–1900* [Middlebury, Vt., 1901], p. 87; Guy S. Rix, comp., *History and Genealogy of the Eastman Family of America* . . . , 2 vols. [Concord, N.H., 1901], 1: 265; *The Churchman's Year Book and American Church Almanac for 1837* [New York, 1837], p. 27. For Zolva Whitmore, see note 10 below).

9. By *day schools* Olmsted means private schools for day students, while by *common schools* he means the local public schools.

10. Reverend Zolva Whitmore (1792–1867), who was pastor of the Congregational church in North Guilford, Conn., from 1821 to 1846. As Olmsted says, he resigned in 1846 because of the controversy caused in his congregation by his antislavery and temperance views.

His obituary notice offers the following description of the man Olmsted remembered most fondly of all his childhood guardians: "A man of very delicate and refined tastes, he especially found delight in contemplating the works of nature. For flowers he had a passionate fondness, and devoted much time to their culture. His garden and dooryard always bore witness to the skill of a connoisseur, and the diligence of an enthusiast" (Jessie Whitmore Patten Purdy, *The Whitmore Genealogy: A Record of the Descendants of Francis Whitmore of Cambridge, Massachusetts, 1625–1685* [Reading, Pa., 1907], p. 78; *Congregational Quarterly* 9, no. 4 [Oct. 1867]: 382–83).

11. In one version of this story, Olmsted makes his attempt to raise the dead girl a response to this Sunday service: "I remembered that I wondered why uncle did not pray that the child should be raised at once and brought back to her parents and tried it myself when I went to bed."

12. A *halberd* is a weapon with a shaft that has on its head an axlike cutting blade, a curved beak, and a spike.

13. A *chapeau-bras* was a three-cornered hat that could be folded and carried under the arm.

14. Owen Pitkin Olmsted (1794–1873), who lived in Geneseo, N.Y. Olmsted left to visit him in April 1828 and returned to Hartford in July (*Olmsted Genealogy*, p. 60; JO Journal, April 20, July 2, 1828).

15. This was probably Ellington High School in Ellington, Conn., which Olmsted attended from May to September 1831. Founded in 1829, the school attracted a number of students from outside the state and during its first ten years was reputed to be one of the best classical schools in the country (Henry R. Stiles, *The History and Genealogies of Ancient Windsor, Connecticut* . . . 2 vols., [Hartford, Conn., 1891], 1: 830–31).

16. Olmsted's grandmother Content Pitkin Olmsted (1752–1839) and grandfather Benjamin (1751–1832) lived in East Hartford. This period, during which Olmsted attended the Hartford Grammar School, was from September 28, 1830, to May 17, 1831. Olmsted was apparently incorrect in remembering it as coming after his time at Ellington High School.

17. The book *Ueber Die Einsamkeit* (1756) by the Swiss physician Johann Georg *ritter* von Zimmermann (1728–1795). At least seven English-language editions of the work were published in the United States between 1796 and 1840, usually titled *Solitude* or *Solitude Considered with Respect to Its Influence on the Mind and Heart*. Olmsted rediscovered the book in 1845, and it was an important influence on his thought thereafter (see FLO to JO, Feb. 2, 1845, note 5 below). The other

books he mentions having read at this time were *A Sentimental Journey Through France and Italy* by Laurence Sterne and *The Vicar of Wakefield* by Oliver Goldsmith.

18. Probably the English dramatist George Colman the elder (1732–1794), whose biographer says of his plays that "the characters are as a rule well drawn, and types of living eccentrically are well hit off" (*DNB*).

19. This paragraph apparently deals with the same period as the preceding paragraph: September 28, 1830, to May 17, 1831.

20. Olmsted's great-grandfather Jonathan Olmsted (1706–1770) of East Hartford was one of the fifth generation of Olmsteds in the Hartford region. His second son, Jonathan (b. 1740), is not mentioned further by Olmsted because he moved to Leyden, Mass., in 1798 and in 1828 began a westward trek that eventually took him to Danville, Ill. (*Olmsted Genealogy*, p. 34).

21. Ezekiel Olmsted (1755–1782) died on one of the British prison ships moored in Wallabout Bay, an inlet on the Brooklyn shore of the East River (ibid., p. 23; James Grant Wilson, *The Memorial History of the City of New York*, 4 vols. [New York, 1892–1893], 4: 8–9).

22. Aaron Olmsted (1753–1806) was a captain in the China trade and a banker (*Olmsted Genealogy*, p. 36).

23. Epaphras Olmsted (1742–1836) of East Hartford, who was eighty years old when Olmsted was born (ibid., p. 23).

24. Gideon Olmsted (1748/9–1845) was no older than seventy-four when Olmsted was born. He marched with six other Olmsteds to the siege of Boston in April 1775. During the Revolutionary War he commanded five privateers, including the sixteen-gun brig *General Green*. He was twice captured by the British while engaged in privateering.

   The exploit to which Olmsted refers occurred in 1779. Gideon had sailed on a trading voyage to Guadeloupe and was captured by a British ship. He was put ashore in Jamaica, signed onto a Jamaican-owned privateer, the *Polly*, and was taken prisoner after a bloody engagement with two ships of the Royal Navy. After a month's imprisonment at Montego Bay in Jamaica he shipped (whether still a prisoner or not is unclear) as second mate of the 130-ton sloop *Active*, carrying provisions to the British in New York. Three of the eleven-man crew were American prisoners released from a prison ship and destined for imprisonment in the prison hulks at New York. On the voyage, in a remarkable show of daring, Gideon Olmsted and the three prisoners seized the sloop and sailed to friendly waters. As they neared the New Jersey capes, however, they met the Pennsylvania cruiser *Convention*, which claimed the *Active* as its prize. Gideon Olmsted bought up the claims for prize money of his three companions and waged a thirty-year court battle for the full amount, some $98,000. The case was one of the most publicized maritime legal controversies in the early years of the Republic, and it brought some sharp clashes between federal authorities and Pennsylvania officials (ibid., pp. 34–35; Gideon Olmsted, "Journal of an Intended Voyage from New London to Gaudalupe in the Sloop *Sea Flower*," original in the Olmsted Papers; *Sundry Documents (Copied from the Original) Relative to the Claim of Gideon Olmsted, Against the Commonwealth of Pennsylvania* . . . [Philadelphia, 1811]; Louis F. Middlebrook, *Captain Gideon Olmsted, Connecticut Privateersman, Revolutionary War* [Salem, Mass., 1933], pp. 19–60, 141; *DAB*).

25. This was Joab Brace (1781–1861), the Congregational minister in Newington, Conn., with whom Olmsted lived from 1831 to 1836. Brace graduated from Yale in 1804 and in 1805 began fifty years of service in Newington. In 1854 he received the degree of D.D. from Williams College. He is described as being "nearly six feet in height, with brilliant black eyes and a commanding presence." He knew Latin, Greek, and Hebrew, and was "a diligent reader of the Hebrew Bible."

   The reason Olmsted was sent to live with Brace was probably the minister's success at fostering revivals, especially among young people. Olmsted's father never had the conversion experience that Connecticut Congregationalism required as a sign of salvation, and he hoped that living in the household of a clergyman would

GIDEON OLMSTED

increase his son's opportunities for such an experience. Brace was a close friend of Asahel Nettleton, who, with Lyman Beecher, promoted revivalism in the Congregational churches of Connecticut as a way of counteracting the effects of the state's disestablishment of that church in 1818. In 1821, at the height of a wave of revivals in Connecticut, Nettleton gave much assistance to Brace's successful efforts in Newington. Then in 1826 and 1829 the children in Brace's school and congregation experienced times of "awakening" and conversion that must have impressed John Olmsted (*Yale Obit. Rec.*, 1st ser., no. 2 [July 1861]: 23; Joab Brace, *Letters of The Rev. Dr. Joab Brace, 1781–1861 to Deacon Jedidiah Deming, 1790–1868 and Milo Doty, 1812–* . . . [Newington, Conn., 1942], p. 3; *DAB*, s.v. "Nettleton, Asahel"; Joab Brace, *Half-Century Discourse. History of the Church in' Newington* . . . [Hartford, 1855], pp. 28–29).
26. The manuscript breaks off at this point.

AUTOBIOGRAPHICAL FRAGMENT B[1]

My father's father and two of my father's great uncles I remember in part by direct memory, for they lived, one at least, till I was nearly ten.[2] But as a baby I was danced on the knee of each of them, and how much of what is in my mind about them I have by memory and how much by personal tradition I cannot be sure.

They had been seafaring men and in the revolutionary war martial

113

men, both ashore and afloat, and their brother captured on a privateer died in the prison ship in the Wallabout.[3] My grandfather himself regarded one of his living brothers as a hero and told me something of an action in which the British sloop of War Ostrich of [16] guns, Captain [Peter Rainier] had been compelled to lower her colors to a French letter of Marque of which my uncle (Captain Gid. he was called) though but a guest on board and serving in the action as a volunteer, was at the moment in command, the French master and every commissioned officer having been killed or sent below disablingly wounded.[4]

Of his own adventures I do not seeem to have ever been able to get any account from my grandfather and the impression he left with me was that though he had been to the most distant parts of the world his life had been quiet and devoid of interest.

Once I had heard an account read from a book of the winter's march through the wilds of Maine of the expedition sent to capture Quebec[5] and I was told that my grandfather had been in it. I wanted to hear more particulars of the matter from him and plied him with questions more than I often dared. I remember only that when I asked if, when they were in a starving condition, he cut the leather off the tops of his boots and fried it, he laughed heartily and called my grandmother to tell her of it.

There was a single exception to his inability, for I do not think it was indisposition, to tell of what he had done and seen. One day I was lying with my head between the roots of a lofty elm, looking up at its swaying boughs and leafage, when he came out of the house and hobbled toward me. It must have been a Sunday or holiday, for he was dressed in his best. His best, although he was in straitened circumstances, was finer than anything we see now. Ruffles on his bosom and wrists; small clothes, stockings and silver buckled shoes; a long silver headed Malacca cane as a walking stick in his hands (I have it now), his gray hair in a queue with a bow of broad black ribband at the end. There was an old cocked hat in the garret with a quadrant, charts, bunting, and small matters of cabin furniture, but I never saw it in his hand. He wore a hat of the then common fashion of real beaver fur.

I rose as he approached and he asked, looking up, did I not think it a fine tree? Then he told me that he himself had planted this tree when a boy. Others near by he had helped to plant, but this one was all his own, and he described to me how he had dug it in the swamp and had brought it on his shoulder and been allowed to plant it all by himself. It came to me after a time as he went on talking about it that there had been nothing in all his long life of which he was so frankly proud and in which he took such complete pleasure as the planting and the beautiful growth of this tree.

Shortly after this I heard a tree spoken of as a Honey-locust, and I got a pod from it and tried to eat the bitter meat I found in it, in order that I might better realize what hard fare that was that poor John the Baptist had to live upon in the wilderness. The seeds, which I could eat no more than the pods, I planted in my garden and a year afterwards I imagined that a sprig of leaves that I found among the weeds then growing had sprung from this seed and I set a stake by it and watched it and it really turned out to be a little honey locust tree and I was proud to show it and call it mine. When I was twelve years old I dug it up and replanted it in another place, a very suitable place in respect of soil and it flourished. Forty years afterwards I went to look at it and thought it the finest honey locust I ever saw. Lately I went again and it had been felled. After a moments thought I was glad of it, for its individual beauty was out of key with the surrounding circumstances and its time had fully come.

I can see that my pleasure began to be affected by conditions of scenery at an early age; long before it could have been suspected by others from any thing that I said and before I began to mentally connect the cause and effect of enjoyment in it. It occurred too, while I was but a half grown lad that my parents thought well to let me wander as few parents are willing their children should.

Within thirty miles of where they lived there were a score of houses of their kindred and friends at which I was always welcome. They were mostly farm houses and had near them interesting rivers, brooks, meadows, rocks, woods or mountains. Those less rural had pleasant old gardens. Of the people, two only shall be referred to particularly. One a poor scholar who, after a deep affliction, lived in seclusion with no occupation but that of reading good old books to which he had formed an attachment in happier days.[6] One of his favorite authors was Virgil, and he took pleasure in reading and translating him to me. He was quaintly mild, courteous, and ceremonious, of musing and contemplative habits, and in this and other respects so different from most men whom I knew that as he commanded my respect and affectionate regard, I recognize him to have had a notable influence in my education.

The other had inherited a moderate competence and been brought up to no regular calling.[7] He lived in an unusually fine old village house with an old garden, was given to natural science, had a cabinet, a few works of art and a notable small library. He was shy and absorbed and I took little from him directly, but he was kind and not so careful of his treasures that I could not cautiously use them as playthings and picture books. He introduced me to Isaac Walton.[8] He had no man servant—indeed no servants, his handmaids being of the order then called help, and he was on precisely the terms with them as it now seems to me that he might have been with helpful sisters, though they did not sit at table with him.

A man came from without the household for the heavier work of

JONATHAN LAW

the place, giving but a small part of his time to it, and there was a boy to do the light chores who received no wages but worked for his board, books and schooling. One of the boys who thus became my play fellow afterwards made his way through college, studied law, and came to be a member of Congress and Governor of a state. For the rest my kinsmen and friends were plain, busy, thrifty people, mostly farmers and good citizens.

If in my rambling habits I did not come home at night it was supposed that I had strayed to some of these other homes where I would be well taken care of, and little concern was felt at my absence; but it several times occurred before I was twelve years old that I had been lost in the woods and finding my way out after sunset had passed the night with strangers and had been encouraged by my father rather than checked in the adventurousness that led me to do so.[9]

It was my fortune also at this period to be taken on numerous journeys in company with people neither literary, scientific nor artistic, but more than ordinarily susceptible to beauty of scenery and who with little talking about it, and none for my instruction, plainly shaped their courses and their customs with reference [to] the enjoyment of it. As a small boy I made four such journeys, each of a thousand miles or more, two behind my father's

STELLA HULL LAW

horses and two mostly by stage coach and canal boat. Besides these, many shorter ones. When fourteen I was laid up by an extremely virulent sumach poisoning, making me for some time partially blind, after which, and possibly as a result, I was troubled for several years with a disorder of the eyes and the oculists advised that I should be kept from study.

It followed that at the time my schoolmates were entering college I was nominally the pupil of a topographical engineer[10] but really for the most part given over to a decently restrained vagabond life, generally pursued under the guise of an angler, a fowler or a dabbler on the shallowest shores of the deep sea of the natural sciences.

A hardly conscious exercise of reason in choosing where I should rest and which way I should be going in these vagrancies, a little musing upon the question what made for or against my pleasure in them, led me along to a point at which when by good chance the books fell in [my] way I was sufficiently interested to get some understanding of what such men as Price, Gilpin, Shenstone and Marshall[11] thought upon the subject.

Rural tastes at length led me to make myself a farmer. I had several years of training on widely separated farms, then bought a small farm for myself which I afterwards sold in order to buy a larger and upon this I lived ten years.[12] I was a good farmer and a good neighbor, served on the school committee, improved the highways, was secretary of a local farmer's club and of the County Agricultural Society, took prizes for the best crops of wheat and turnips and the best assortment of fruits; imported an English machine and in partnership with a friend established the first cylindrical drainage tile works in America.[13]

But during this period also I managed to make several long and numerous short journeys, generally paying my expenses by writing on rural topics for newspapers. As it would have been an extravagance otherwise, however, I first crossed the Atlantic in the steerage of a sailing vessel and nearly always travelled frugally.[14] In all these tours I took more interest than most travellers do in the arrangement and aspects of homesteads and generally in what may be called the sceneric character of what came before me.

The word sceneric flows from my pen unbidden and I venture to let it stand. Some writers of late are using scenic for the purpose it serves, but this is confusing, scenic having been so long used with regard exclusively to affairs of the drama.

All this time interest in certain modest practical applications of what I was learning of the principles of landscape architecture was growing with me. Applications I mean, for example, to the choice of a neighborhood, of the position and aspect of a homestead, the placing, grouping and relationships with the dwelling of barns, stables and minor outbuildings, the planning of a laundry yard and of conveniences for bringing in kitchen supplies and carrying away kitchen wastes, for I had found that even in frontier log cabins a good deal was lost or gained of pleasure according to the ingenuity and judgement used in such matters. Applications also to the seemly position of a kitchen garden, of a working garden, for flowers to be cut for the indoor enjoyment of them, to fixed outer flower and foliage decorations, to the determination of lines of out-look and of in-look and the removal or planting accordingly of trees, screens, bridges, windbreaks and so on, with some consideration for unity of foreground, middle ground and back ground, some consideration for sceneric effect from without as well as from within the field of actual operations. I planted several thousand trees on my own land and thinned out and trimmed with my own hand with reference to future pleasing effects a small body of old woodland and another well-grown copse wood.[15]

Never the slightest thought till I was more than thirty years old had entered my mind of practicing landscape gardening except as any fairly well-to-do, working farmer may, and in flower gardening or of any kind of decorative or simply ornamental gardening—any gardening other than such as I have indicated—I was far from being an adept.

But I gradually came to be known among my neighbors and friends as a man of some special knowledge, inventiveness and judgement in such affairs as I have mentioned and to be called on for advice about them.[16] At

length, growing out of such little repute, I was unexpectedly invited to take a
modest public duty and from this by promotions and successive unpremeditated steps was later led to make Landscape Architecture my calling in life.[17]

1. The material presented in this second fragment discusses more directly the varied experiences of Olmsted's early life that he felt moved him toward a career in landscape design and gave him the ability to deal with practical problems and "practical" men.

   The first section is taken from a larger discussion, never completed, of the relationship of memory to taste and the significance of the idiosyncrasies of childhood memories. The second section is primarily a statement of the unusual elements of Olmsted's upbringing and education that prepared him for his unique career in landscape architecture.
2. Olmsted's grandfather was Benjamin Olmsted, and his two brothers mentioned here—they were Olmsted's great uncles and not those of his father—were Epaphras Olmsted and Gideon Olmsted. Both men marched to Boston to assist the siege there in 1775. Thereafter Epaphras served in the Continental cavalry, while Gideon was master of five privateers and took several prizes (*Olmsted Genealogy*, pp. 23, 34–35; and see Autobiographical Fragment A, note 24, above).
3. Ezekiel Olmsted (see Autobiographical Fragment A, note 21, above).
4. The engagement Olmsted describes took place while Gideon Olmsted was serving on the privateer *Polly*, an American-built brig with a letter of marque and reprisal from the Continental Congress, but with a Jamaican owner and a largely French crew. Gideon and two of his crew from the *Sea Flower* signed on board the *Polly* at Port-au-Prince in early July 1779. They may have intended to serve on the privateer only until she reached American waters, but in any case Gideon was hardly a "guest on board." He states in his diary that he signed on for eight shares. Clearly the French captain of the vessel needed Yankee sailing skill. He signed Gideon's crew member John Buckland for three shares to serve as prize-master, to command any ship the *Polly* might capture.

   Five days out, on July 8, 1779, off the eastern end of Jamaica, the *Polly* encountered the sixteen-gun British sloop-of-war *Ostrich*, commanded by Captain Peter Rainier, and engaged her. After a two-hour battle, some of it hand-to-hand and all carried on with the ships within pistol shot of one another, the *Ostrich* struck her colors. But before the *Polly* could secure her prize, the ten-gun British brig *Lowestoffe's Prize* came up and continued the battle. After two and a half hours the *Polly* surrendered. Gideon Olmsted was at her helm, where three men had been killed before him, during the engagement with the *Lowestoffe's Prize*. The French captain of the *Polly* was killed by a cannonball as he stood by Gideon's side. Half the hundred-man crews of the *Ostrich* and the *Polly* were killed or wounded. The commander of the *Lowestoffe's Prize*, Lieutenant Robert Hibbs, blamed Gideon for the bloodiness of the battle, put him in irons, and threatened repeatedly to kill him (Gideon Olmsted, "Journal of the *Sea Flower*"; L. F. Middlebrook, *Captain Gideon Olmsted*, pp. 30–41).
5. In November 1775 Benedict Arnold led an expedition through the Maine wilderness to attack Quebec City, losing half his men on the march. His attack on the city failed, as did a combined attack he made on December 31 with the Continental forces, under Richard Montgomery, that had taken Montreal. There followed an unsuccessful six-month siege, during which the Continental troops suffered many privations, including an epidemic of smallpox (Curtis P. Nettels, *The Roots of American Civilization: A History of American Colonial Life* [New York, 1938], p. 698).
6. This was Jonathan Law (1784–1859), a lawyer and postmaster of Hartford from 1809 to 1829. He married Stella Hull (1786–1841), an older sister of Olmsted's mother, Charlotte Hull. The Laws took Charlotte to live in their household, and Law is said to have adopted her, although both of her parents outlived her. Olm-

sted's middle name was in his honor. In a letter to Mariana Griswold Van Rensselaer of June 11, 1893, Olmsted gave the following description of him:

Being childless he had been a second father to my own mother. I was much at his house. He was a scholar, often reciting Latin poetry to me, (I had a good drill in Latin as a small boy) often reading the Latin poets for his own edification. He was a personal friend of Whittier and upon occasion wrote verses himself, as upon the death of my mother, of which he gave me copies. He cultivated a garden, and I had beds in it. He loved me and I cared much to have his good opinion.

After his wife died in 1841, Jonathan Law lived alone in Hartford for three years before moving to Cheshire, Conn.

The poet John Greenleaf Whittier boarded at Jonathan Law's house while editing the *New England Weekly Review* in 1830 and 1831 (Franklin Bowditch Dexter, *Biographical Sketches of Graduates of Yale College, V: 1792–1805* [New York, 1911], p. 597–98; *Hartford County*, 1: 614; *Olmsted Genealogy*, p. 60; Headstone Inscriptions, Cheshire, Cemetery 1, Section "B," p. 13; Charles H. Weygant, comp., *The Hull Family in America* [Pittsfield, Mass., 1913], p. 495; Puella Hull Mason, comp., *A Record of the Descendants of Richard Hull, of New Haven, Connecticut* [Milwaukee, Wis., 1894], pp. 34–35).

7. Charles Hyde Olmsted (1798–1878), Olmsted's bachelor first cousin, son of the banker and shipmaster Aaron. Since his inheritance made it unnecessary for him to earn a living, he spent much of his time pursuing literary and scientific interests, especially American history, genealogy, and natural history. He graduated from Yale in 1818 and received an A.M. from Harvard in 1850. He was an active member of the Hartford Natural History Society when Olmsted took part in its activities in the 1840s and served for several years as president of the Connecticut Society of Natural History (*Yale Obit. Rec.* 2d ser., no. 8 [June 1878]: 287; *Olmsted Genealogy*, p. 36; *Eleventh Reunion*, p. 9).

8. Izaak Walton (1593–1683), English writer, author of *The Compleat Angler*.

9. Olmsted gave further evidence of the boldness of his early ramblings, and his pleasant experiences in Cheshire, in a letter to Mariana Griswold Van Rensselaer of June 17, 1893. After saying that his mother came from Cheshire and that he only dimly remembered her farmer father, he continued:

Much more clearly I recall the great fireplace of a house of my aunt Brooks, my mother's sister, in which house and in the brooks flowing by it, I spent many happy months, often walking to it to pass a night as I grew older. I was but nine when I once walked sixteen miles over a strange country with my brother who was but six, to reach it. We were two days on the road, spent the night at a rural inn which I saw still standing a few years ago, and were so tired when we arrived that, after sitting before the great fireplace and being feasted, we found that our legs would not support us and were carried off to bed. It was a beautiful region of rocky glens and trout brooks.

10. Frederick Augustus Barton, a surveyor, civil engineer, and teacher of mathematics at Phillips Academy, Andover, Mass. Olmsted lived and studied with him from November 1837 to November 1838. At that time Barton completed his study for the ministry at Andover Theological Seminary and took a church in Collinsville, Conn. Olmsted followed him there and continued to study with him until May 1840 (Claude M. Fuess, *An Old New England School, A History of Phillips Academy Andover* [Boston, 1917], p. 210; *General Catalogue of the Theological Seminary, Andover, Massachusetts, 1808–1908* [Boston, 1909], pp. 152–53; *Forty Years*, 1: 4).

11. All of these men whose influence Olmsted acknowledges were English writers on landscape and agriculture of the eighteenth and early-nineteenth centuries. Sir Uvedale Price (1747–1829) was a leading proponent of the picturesque style of landscape gardening and the author of *An Essay on the Picturesque*. William Gil-

pin (1724–1804) wrote and illustrated five volumes on the "picturesque beauty" of various parts of England. He also wrote a more general work that strongly influenced Olmsted's ideas on landscape design, *Remarks on Forest Scenery, and Other Woodland Views, (Relative Chiefly to Picturesque Beauty)*. The poet William Shenstone (1714–1763) often wrote on the theme of nature and retired at the age of thirty-one to beautify the landscape and gardens of his estate. William Marshall (1745–1818) was a farmer, writer on agricultural topics, and author of a multi-volume work on the rural economy of England. He also wrote "A Review of the Landscape, A Didactic Poem," and a two-volume work entitled *Planting and Rural Ornament* (DNB).

12. In fact, it was Olmsted's father who bought the farms at Sachem's Head, Guilford, Conn., in 1847 and on Staten Island in 1848, for $4,000 and $12,000, respectively; and he did not sell the former until some time after he bought the latter. Olmsted lived on the Staten Island farm from March 1848 until he moved to New York in April 1855 to begin his editorial work on *Putnam's Monthly Magazine*—a total of seven years (Guilford County Deed Records, 35: 170; JO Journal, Jan. 1, 1848, Aug. 30, 1853; JHO to JO, April 1, 1855).

13. Although the drainage-tile-making machine that Olmsted helped to import for the Richmond County Agricultural Society was one of the earliest imported, perhaps even the second, it was not the first. In 1848, five years after its invention in England, the Seneca County, N.Y., Agricultural Society had acquired such a machine. The *Transactions* of the New York Agricultural Society of 1850 carried the following notice about Richmond County:

> A drain pipe and tile machine has been purchased in England by some officers of this Society, and will be put in operation in this county the ensuing spring. It is of larger capacity than any machine that has been hitherto imported, and of the pattern (Whitehead's patent) that received the highest commendation at the last meeting of the Royal Agricultural Society. It was selected by Mr. Parks, the celebrated draining engineer.

Josiah Parkes (1793–1871), whom Olmsted met while in England in 1850, developed a system of deep drainage of the soil that was an important part of the agricultural reform movement in England (Marion M. Weaver, *History of Tile Drainage (In America Prior to 1900)* [Waterloo, N.Y., 1964], pp. 78–79, 86; DNB; FLO to JO, Aug. 11, 1850, below).

14. While it is true that Olmsted never traveled in extravagant style and did most of his traveling in a way that allowed him to see how the people of the region lived, he exaggerates in this statement the rigors of his European trip in 1850 and the reason for the frugality he practiced during it. He wrote only one letter for a newspaper while on that excursion, and his father paid most of the expense of $300.

Furthermore, Olmsted and his companions—his brother, John, and Charles Loring Brace—did not make the voyage to England in steerage. They engaged a second-class cabin in a sailing packet, the *Henry Clay*. In his book *Walks and Talks of an American Farmer in England*, Olmsted described the cabin as "a 'family room' exclusively for ourselves, in the very large and neatly-fitted cabin of a new, clean first-class packet." This was for dramatic effect, however, and his brother gave a more accurate description to a friend two weeks before they sailed, saying, "The passage is $12-bunks between decks, only separated from the steerage by a bulk head. Jolly."

When Olmsted and his companions went on board they found the steerage area full of freight and the steerage passengers lodged in the second class cabins, and the group barely succeeded in claiming possession of their cabin. This meant that there was little distinction between steerage and second-class passengers, although the captain did agree to provide the Olmsteds and Brace with their meals, permitted them to have a light in their cabin at night, and gave them other special conveniences and privileges.

Much of the frugality of the pedestrian trip through Europe in 1850 was due to Brace's poverty rather than the economic condition of the Olmsted brothers. As John Hull Olmsted noted concerning the voyage to England, "The economy is mostly on Charley's account. I should hardly care to go in the 2nd cabin for my health." When the Olmsted brothers returned from England without Brace in the fall they took passage on a new and luxurious steamship, the Inman Line's *City of Glasgow*. After his return, Olmsted had some second thoughts about their style of travel and advised Charles Loring Brace to spend money with a freer hand during the rest of his trip. "Borrow money," he advised, "and dress well. Travel by railway and pay for the inside of the cathedral and for a *catalogue* to the Picture Gallery" ([Frederick Law Olmsted], *Walks and Talks of an American Farmer in England*, 2 vols. [New York, 1852], 1: 10–11; Arthur George H. Macpherson, *Mail and Passenger Steamships of the Nineteenth Century, The Macpherson Collection, With Iconographical and Historical Notes by Captain H. Parker and Frank C. Bowen* [Philadelphia, 1929?], pp. 61–62; FJK Sketch of FLO, p. 41; *Forty Years*, 1: 5; JHO to FJK, March 16, 1850; FLO to CLB, Nov. 12, 1850, below).

15. Frederick Kingsbury described Olmsted's first major landscaping design, the improvement of his Staten Island farm, in the following way:

> The house was simple yet picturesque. It had been occupied by a tenant. The barns were quite near, and in the rear of the house was a small pond, fifteen or twenty feet in diameter, used for washing waggons, watering stock and as a swimming place for dogs, ducks and geese. There was no turf near it. The whole place was as dirty and disorderly as the most bucolic person could desire. It was on the surroundings of the house that Olmsted first showed his genius in landscape construction.
>
> He moved the barns and all their belongings behind a knoll, he brought the road in so that it approached the house by a graceful curve, he turfed the borders of the pond and planted water plants on its edge and shielded it from all contamination. Thus, with a few strokes and at small expense he transformed the place from a very dirty, disagreeable farmyard to a gentleman's house. This was his first attempt at anything of the sort, and it was as successful as anything he ever did (*Forty Years*, 1: 85–86).

16. Olmsted is said to have designed, or been consulted about the improvement of, the grounds of the following places on Staten Island during the years he lived there: the farm of William Henry Vanderbilt at New Dorp; Colonel William E. Ross's estate, "Ross Castle," in Rossville; and the estate of Theophylact Bache Satterthwaite, on Grymes Hill near Stapleton, with a house designed by James Renwick. Olmsted is also said to have directed construction of a stone wall around the property of Ernest Cazet on Grymes Hill (Margaret Boyle-Cullen, "The Woods of Arden House," Part 3, *Staten Island Historian* 15, no. 2 [April–June 1954]: 14; Charles W. Leng and William T. Davis, *Staten Island and Its People, A History, 1609–1929*, 4 vols. [New York, 1930], 2: 946; Dorothy Valentine Smith, *This Was Staten Island* [Staten Island, N.Y., 1968], pp. 98–99; Charles Gilbert Hine, *History and Legend of Howard Avenue and the Serpentine Road, Grymes Hill, Staten Island, Gathered by Charles Gilbert Hine from Real Estate Records and Long Memories . . .* [New York?, 1914], pp. 42–44, 78; Thomas Edward Satterthwaite, *Biographical and Historical Sketchs of the Sheafe, Wentworth, Fisher, Bache, Satterthwaite and Rutgers Families of America . . .* [n.p., 1923], p. 104).

17. In 1857, Olmsted's friend Charles Wyllys Elliott, a member of the newly formed board of commissioners of Central Park, urged him to apply for the position of superintendent. He was successful in this, and his position on the park made possible a collaboration with Calvert Vaux in creation of the prize-winning design for the park that launched Olmsted on his career of landscape design (FLO autobiographical fragment, quoted in *Forty Years*, 2: 34–35; Frederick Law Olmsted, *A Journey in the Seaboard Slave States in the Years 1853–1854, with Remarks on Their Economy: With a Biographical Sketch by Frederick Law Olmsted, Jr., and With an Introduction by William P. Trent*, 2 vols. [New York, 1904], 1: xv–xvi).

OLMSTED'S CONNECTICUT

CHAPTER II

EARLY LETTERS

1840–1842

OLMSTED'S EARLIEST SURVIVING LETTERS were written in the spring and early summer of 1840 to his brother, John Hull Olmsted, who had gone to Paris for six months to study French and acquire the social graces. The eighteen-year-old Olmsted missed his brother dearly and tried his hand at recording the events and issues of the day for John's entertainment and instruction. One of the most promising topics proved to be the 1840 "Log Cabin and Hard Cider" campaign in which the Whig party's military hero, William Henry Harrison, ran against the Democratic incumbent, Martin Van Buren, and the antislavery Liberty party candidate, James G. Birney. The colorful campaign stimulated Olmsted's awakening political interest, and he wrote several letters about a Whig Fourth of July celebration that included the building of a log cabin, symbolic of Harrison's simple origins.

The best letter, which is included in this chapter, described the cabin and the celebration in the center of Hartford. It is a valuable description of an episode in one of the first presidential campaigns in which slogans, placards, songs, and floats carried more weight than political argument. Olmsted was caught up in the Whig campaign rhetoric, which portrayed Martin Van Buren as a haughty aristocrat reveling in luxury in the White House while Harrison remained a simple frontiersman content with a log cabin and a barrel of hard cider. It apparently did not occur to Olmsted that it might be unfair to the Democrats and Liberty party men in Hartford for the Whigs to dominate the Fourth of July celebration and make it part of their political campaign. The Whig persuasion was the political orthodoxy of his family and native city, as Congregationalism was its denominational allegiance.

Olmsted's pleasant summer in Hartford came to an abrupt end in August, when his father took him to New York to work as a clerk in the dry-goods firm of Benkard and Hutton, importers of silks and other cloth from

France. The work did not appeal to Olmsted and only quickened his interest in other things. He went aboard the ships docked at Manhattan wharves to check consignments and send mail, and felt the lure of the sea. At the same time his residence in the city strengthened his memory of the pleasures of country living. The second letter in this chapter expresses his nostalgia for the joys of rural life and his rebellion against the routinized life of the city. He wishes himself back in the carefree outdoor existence he had previously enjoyed. In his enthusiasm for the country he resorts to a bit of sentimental rhetoric; but he does so only with tongue in cheek and punctures the airy dreams with a bit of humorous realism.

In March 1842 Olmsted left Benkard and Hutton, and spent the following summer happily boating and sailing with his brother. The last letter in the chapter shows him back in Hartford, where he delighted in a carefree life of socializing and travel while his brother was starting college at Yale. Perhaps it was not Olmsted's intention, but he pictures a society with much tolerance for a playful and spirited young man like himself. The letter also shows Olmsted's sense of the great size of his country and the opportunities it offered. His remarks about the "venerable Audubon's" expedition to the Rocky Mountains may have stemmed from his own wish to be there, too.

To John Hull Olmsted

Address: Master John H. Olmsted/C. P. Bordenave/44 Rue de la ferme
      Paris/Per *La Duchesse d'Orleans*[1]
Postmark: Paris/Aout 10

Hartford July 7th 1840

Dear Brother,
      I have some little time left to write you this morn, & although I do not feel very well I must improve it. By great exertions we got all our hay in yesterday. Today I expected to go to East Hartford with Charley[2] & help them there, but it rains. Tomorrow the Boston Light Infantry are expected here on invitation of Light Guards.[3] "The Glorious Fourth" was celebrated here with the *usual* "*eclat*." The *usual* accompaniment of guns, squibs & crackers, kept us awake as *usual* the night before.
      The morning was ushered in by the ringing of bells & the firing a salute of 24 guns. At ten o'clock a procession was formed at the State-house, which proceeded to the Log Cabin corner of Asylum & Trumbull Streets, where an oration was delivered by Matson[4] & the Cabin was dedicated to *Harrison & Reform*. A large procession then formed, attended by the Brass Band, & with numerous appropriate banners, which proceeded through the

125

principal streets & returned about one o'clock to the Cabin, where a collation of crackers, cheese, [. . .] cold meats, &c. with hard cider, iced lemonade, &c, &c, but nothing *ardent*, was attended to.

The Cabin was filled I should think about three times, before all were provided. Addresses were delivered by several celebrated gentlemen, several patriotic toasts were drunk & the meeting adjourned at sundown. The Cabin is 75 by 30 feet & 8 feet high. A Liberty pole over one hundred feet high rises from it. The "fixins" are complete. It is decorated inside with coon, fox, beaver, otter, buffalo & other skins. A live *coon* & hawk have appropriate places. The officer's desk is a hollow tree trunk, 6 feet in diameter & 3 in height, with a door, &c. Stools with natural three legs, a wooden chandelier, being the roots of a tree, &c. were provided by the "Farmington folks." There is also old furniture, some being made in 1620, old basket hilted swords, muskets & rifles, powder horns, canteens of hard cider, decoy ducks, hammocks, banners, "Picturs" with log frames, &c, &c, &c.

In the evening very fine fireworks were thrown up from Bunker Hill on her return from a pleasure excursion in the Sound. Nearly all the Sabbath schools had celebrations: "The Free Church" & "Universalist" schools & Bible classes to the amount of over 600 persons, had an excursion in the cars to Meriden.

Father thinks I can ask you questions & give you hints on what to write about. But I say surely you cannot be in want of material. Don't be afraid. For instance you began your letter about the Western[5] with a very wide margin, &c. but you see you have not room enough for all you want to say. Mr. Norton's letter, published in the Observer,[6] gave us many more particulars. By the [way], he mentions *you*, as the "youth from our city" who was one of the five teetotalers on board. In your letter from Bristol you took a small sheet, but you did not have near room enough. You did not even mention the magnificent bridge you must have crossed (if I understand it) in going to Clifton.[7] Mind & take a big sheet next time.

We are all pretty well. Ada's[8] cough I think is better. We have nearly finished cherries. Raspberries & currants are on hand. Do come home in the Fall. As an *inducement* I mention that it is the intention to pull down the Log Cabin after election & give the logs for fire-wood to the poor. As for improvement I think you must be making all the time, I hope you will attend the "accomplishment" schools this summer & be able to teach me on your return.

Please send us some French Periodicals & remember I am a curiosity hunter.

Yours affectionately,

F. L. Olmsted

If you had my headache you would excuse mistakes.

1. At this time, John Hull Olmsted was beginning a six-month stay abroad. C. P. Bordenave, a Frenchman who taught languages and fencing in Hartford, accompanied him as his tutor. The letter was sent by *La Duchesse d'Orleans*, a packet of the Havre Line (JHO to FLO, June 26, 1840; JO to JHO, May 19, 1840; JO Journal, April 29, July 8, 1840; William A. Fairburn, *Merchant Sail*, 6 vols. [Center Lovell, Maine, 1945–1955], 5: 2784).
2. Probably a reference to Charles Loring Brace.
3. The Hartford Light Guards were an independent infantry company organized in 1835 (*Hartford County*, 1: 186).
4. William N. Matson (1812–1876) was the orator of the day. He was a lawyer in Hartford, a judge of probate, and a reporter of the Supreme Court of Connecticut (*Hartford Daily Courant*, July 5, 1840, p. 1; *Hartford County*, 1: 131; Yale University, Class of 1833, *Fourth Record of the Class of 1833*, George E. Day, comp. [New Haven, 1879], p. 27).
5. The 212-foot steamship *Great Western*, on which John Hull Olmsted made the passage to England. Designed by the great English engineer Isambard Kingdom Brunel (1806–1859) and completed in 1837, the *Great Western* was by far the largest steamship built up to that time and was the first to be designed and built for regular transatlantic voyages. The ship ran between New York and Bristol, which was the terminus of the Great Western railway, of which Brunel was chief designer and engineer (JO Journal, May 9, 1840; *EB*, s.v. "Brunel, Isambard Kingdom"; Celia B. Noble, *The Brunels: Father and Son* [London, 1938], p. 262).
6. A letter by John Treadwell Norton (1795–1869), a gentleman farmer of Farmington, Conn., written during the passage of the *Great Western* to England. It appeared in the *Connecticut Observer*, which was published in Hartford. Norton gave a full description of the ship, its crew, and its passengers, with special attention to the amount of drinking and gambling that went on. "There are but five on board, including a youth from your city," he wrote, "who abstain entirely from all intoxicating drinks" ("Letter from John T. Norton, Esq.," *Connecticut Observer, and New-York Congregationalist* 16, no. 26 [June 27, 1840]: 1; Albert Palmer Pitkin, *Pitkin Family of America. A Genealogy of the Descendants of William Pitkin* . . . [Hartford, 1887], p. 106; *Hartford County*, 1: 213 n).
7. The bridge over the Avon River at Bristol, designed in 1831 by Isambard Kingdom Brunel. It was an iron suspension bridge with a height of 240 feet and a span of 700; the great chains for supporting the span stretched between massive Egyptian-style arches at either end. Construction began in 1836, but the funds were exhausted within thirteen years. The bridge was finally completed in 1864 as a memorial to Brunel (*EB*, s.v. "Brunel, Isambard Kingdom"; C. B. Noble, *The Brunels*, pp. 106–110).
8. Ada Theodosia Olmsted (1839–1846), Olmsted's sickly year-old half-sister, who had caught the whooping cough nearly two months earlier (*Olmsted Genealogy*, p. 60; JO Journal, July 28, 1839, May 14, 1840).

To Mary Bull Olmsted[1]

New York. March 20th 1841.
Dear Mother,

I was very much pleased to receive a letter from you by Father on his recent visit to this city. I received a letter from Father on business, the answer to which I dispatched last night.

Mary's[2] letter pleased me very much. I found it difficult to frame an answer which I thought would please her. I hope I shall see how I succeeded by the next epistle, which I shall expect from her next week. I also wrote a few lines to Bertha[3] to encourage her ambition. I hope to hear from her soon.

I am sorry to hear Ada is suffering so much. Can I send you no rarities for her? If you find it difficult to procure swabs in Hartford I think I could obtain them here. I have succeeded in seducing a pair of doves into a coop in our tower, & they have commenced laying. Could you spare me one of the canaries this summer? I think I could take good care of it. If you have such fine weather as we have had for two days, you must soon find the blue-birds. Indeed, I think that yesterday & today have been two of the finest days I ever knew; though I believe there has not been twenty four hours before, this month, in which there has not been some kind of a storm, generally snow.

Oh, how I long to be where I was a year ago: midst two lofty mountains, pursuing the uneven course of the purling brook, gliding among the fair granite rocks, & lisping over the pebbles; meandering through the lowly valley, under the sweeping willows, & the waving elms, where nought is heard save the indistinct clink of anvils & the distant roaring of water as it passes gracefully over the half natural dam of the beautiful Farmington when the declining Phoebus gilds the snow capt hills & enlightens the venerable tower of Montevideo,[4] then & there to be—"up to knees in mud & sand" chasing mush-squash![5] (Ahem!—I say; I did that, I did. That was I, & nobody else. It's mine "par brevet de invention." Entered according to the act of congress, &c.)

If you had heard all the compliments, thanks, &c, bestowed upon you and yours for those last nut cakes, you would—([I] guess)—"do pretty much as you pleased without any hints perhaps." I believe it in contemplation among those who had the honour of tasting them through my bounty, to present you with a silver turning fork or dipper, skimmer or what you call it, *inscribed* with an appropriate *inscription*. I will endeavour to return the box, if you wish it, soon.

If you have an opportunity please send me a pair of suspenders, ditto gloves. Please send these & sundries as soon as you can make it convenient, for all my old ones are about used up & I am obliged to use "jury's."[6]

I am sorry I could not answer yours before, & that I had forgotten that I was in your debt before. But I find that in that letter (last but one) you say that as "you & Father are one you consider all his letters as yours." "Nuf sed." "You understand."

We are about closing & I must hastily adjourn "sine die."

With love to the children & in hopes of a speedy answer I remain

Your affectionate son

Frederick L. Olmsted

1. Mary Bull Olmsted, Olmsted's stepmother (*Olmsted Genealogy*, p. 60).
2. Mary Olmsted (1832–1875), Olmsted's half-sister (ibid.).
3. Bertha Olmsted (1834–1926), Olmsted's half-sister (ibid., p. 109; *Eleventh Reunion*, p. 9).
4. In this passage, Olmsted is describing scenes near Collinsville, Conn., where he had been living the previous year with Frederick A. Barton. The tower he refers to was on Talcott Mountain, overlooking the Farmington River six miles west of Collinsville (*Hartford County*, 2: 1).
5. A corruption of an American Indian word meaning muskrat (Abram Smythe Palmer, *Folk-Etymology: A Dictionary of Verbal Corruptions* . . . [1890; rpt. ed., New York, 1969], p. 249).
6. Olmsted resorts here to nautical language, saying that his suspenders and gloves are so worn that he is forced to "jury rig" them—that is, keep them functioning with improvised repairs.

To John Hull Olmsted

Hartford 7th December 1842. Wednesday.

Dear Jack,

Nothing but an overwhelming sense of the comparative necessity of writing to you tonight could induce me to keep from bed at eleven o'clock this evening when I am going shooting in the morning & have many preparations to make. I returned from Mr. Ayres[1] at nearly 9 o'clock (I made the morrow's engagement with him), found company here, was up late last night & must be up very early in the morning to clean the gun, &c.

How then can I go into the particulars you wish, & tell you how I made a triumphant incursion to Cheshire—(& carrying their women & children into captivity beyond the grand *canawl*).[2] How the " 'oss run away with me" three times; with what coolness & desperate calmness I guided the rushing *foaming* steed between Scylla & Charybdis. Piloting by Jacobsen in one of the rushes with the skill of a "branch pilot" or old (what's his name—Aeneas' man) himself.[3] How with Jac. I dined, drank & smoked at Farmington. How the court of enquiry (Ego,—judge advocate) decided the hold backs were too long & "no blame was to be imputed to the captain or ossifers." How I got to Brooks' Grove before dark *almost* & attended a "musical sweary" at the residence of our host in my long-togs same evening. How the daughter of our distinguished senator[4] passed the night & was escorted to her residence in his own carriage by a gentleman well known in fashionable circles of west end (of Cheshire) who returned with Lizzy[5] calling on two ladies "by the way." How the same evening I attended a party—should I say a *"route"*[6] at the villa of the honorable statesman whom I have before mentioned. How I did rush it &c. How I kissed (sub rosa!) (whisper it ye ——s) the three pret—no, I can't, I can't!

I have got the old (aunty's[7]) stove up in our room & have been rerigging it, the room, in anticipation partly of the cozy times we & co. will have there one of these (Christmas I was going to say—but two weeks thereafter) days. Not for that have I shifted bedstead & got a truck (not a cart) which takes up about half the room of the old one. Your (that would be) cane or cudgel or spruce shillelagh as Mrs. Kelly[8] calls it awaits your order or somebody's transportation to you, but I *guess* you have best "leave that be," as well as the pictures now, till you are up or I am down.

Mr. Ayres (I took tea, or dinner, or supper with him & or his brother & that pretty sweet little dam'd wife of his,[9] spent P.M. & evening) does very much want a "crane-eye." Do you know any boat man? (Did *that* come off?) Ask him about 'em. The "Governor"[10] said New London harbour was full of 'em. To catch them make a jig ("squid," properly in New York) of a pipe stem on a "pin hook." Troll.

Our boat is gone—gone; & is not in the city waters, I think. I shall try "Ho-can-um"[11] & if not there conclude a sloop has "hauled in the slack" on't.

Mrs. Governor Ellsworth says (did I tell you?) Ol[iver] will go to China *any* how, if he has to go before the mast.[12]

The venerable Audubon dined with Mr. Ayres short time since. Next spring starts for Council Bluff, Yellowstone & Rocky Mountains in search of materials for his new magnificence, "Zoology of America."[13] "Might I be there to see."

Yours,

Fred.

Respects to Peet, Chapin & Co. (Charley in course).[14]

1. William Orville Ayres (1817–1887), a teacher in East Hartford and vice-president and curator of the Natural History Society of Hartford (*Yale Obit. Rec.*, 3d. ser., no. 7 [June 1887]: 370; *Geer's Directory for 1843*, p. 130).
2. The Farmington Canal, connecting New Haven with the Connecticut River in Massachusetts, which ran through Cheshire (Rollin G. Osterweis, *Three Centuries of New Haven, 1638–1938* [New Haven: Yale University Press, 1953], pp. 245–46).
3. Olmsted's socializing in Cheshire was mixed with danger. Because the "hold-backs" on the harness of his horse were too long, he had three runaway experiences. His companion in these adventures was Otto F. Jacobsen, a teacher at the Hartford Grammar School and organist at the South Church in Hartford who tutored Olmsted and his brother in fencing and music (JO Journal, expense account, Oct. and Dec., 1842; *Hartford Daily Courant*, Dec. 7, 1842, p. 1; Isaac N. Bolles, comp., *Directory and Guide Book, for the City of Hartford, for 1842: With a Complete New Map of the City* [Hartford, 1842], p. 40: see Spear 513).
4. Caroline Ives (b. 1821), daughter of Benajah Ives (1798–1868). Benajah was elected to the state senate from Cheshire in 1842 and served his term in 1843 (Arthur Coon Ives, *Genealogy of the Ives Family* . . . [Watertown, N.Y., 1928], p. 61; [Samuel Green], *Green's Connecticut Annual Register and United States Calendar for 1843: To Which Is Prefixed an Almanac* [East Windsor, Conn., 1843], p. 23; *Homes of Cheshire*, pp. 63–64).
5. Probably Elizabeth Ellsworth (1824–1901) who was the daughter of Governor Wil-

liam Wolcott Ellsworth (1791–1868), of Connecticut. She married Waldo Hutchins (1822–1891), a lawyer and politician who was a park commissioner in New York from 1857 to 1869 (Lemuel Abijah Abbott, comp., *Descendants of George Abbott of Rowley, Massachusetts*, 2 vols. [Boston, 1906], 1: 149; death date for Elizabeth Ellsworth Hutchins supplied by Woodlawn Cemetery, New York City; BDAC, s.v. "Hutchins, Waldo"; FLO to John D.˙Crimmins, July 2, 1887).

6. In the letter, Olmsted wrote above the line a partially legible punning phrase on "route":

    (I)   (d some [. . .])
    a "route" at the villa

7. Probably Maria Olmsted (1798–1859), Olmsted's maiden aunt, "a dear kind devoted woman . . . plain as a pikestaff and devoid of vanity" (*Olmsted Genealogy*, p. 36; *Forty Years*, 1: 80).

8. Mrs. Mary A. Kelly (c. 1802–1863) was the Olmsteds' cook from 1840 to 1845 (JO Journal, Feb. 21, 1840; April 9, 1845; Feb. 12, 1863).

9. Jared Augustus Ayres (1813–1886), a teacher at the American Asylum for the Deaf and Dumb in Hartford: his wife, the former Miss S. L. Wilcox (b. 1821): and his brother, William Orville Ayres (*Yale Obit. Rec.*, 3d ser., no. 6 [June 1886]: 298).

10. Perhaps William Wolcott Ellsworth, governor of Connecticut from 1838 to 1842 (see note 5, above; Samuel Hart et al., comps., *Encyclopedia of Connecticut Biography*, 10 vols. [New York, 1917], 1: 40–41).

11. The Hockanum River, which runs through East Hartford.

12. Emily Webster Ellsworth (1790–1861) was the wife of Governor William Wolcott Ellsworth and the daughter of Noah Webster, the famous lexicographer. Her son Oliver Ellsworth (1820–1878) retained the interest in commerce that Olmsted reports here, and spent ten years in commission business in Ecuador and Panama (William H. and Melville R. Webster, *History and Genealogy of the Governor John Webster Family of Connecticut* [Rochester, N.Y., 1915], pp. 780–81; L. A. Abbott, *Descendants of George Abbott*, 1: 149; *Boston Daily Advertiser*, Nov. 12, 1878, p. 11; S. Hart, *Encyclopedia of Connecticut Biography*, 1: 41).

13. John James Audubon (1785–1851), the artist and zoologist, had earlier sought to make use of the resources of the Hartford Natural History Society. In August 1841 he asked William Orville Ayres to procure specimens for him to use in preparing *The Viviparous Quadrupeds of North America*. Audubon left New York for the West on March 11, 1843, to spend two months of the summer at the mouth of the Yellowstone River, gathering specimens (Francis Hobart Herrick, *Audubon the Naturalist: A History of His Life and Time*, 2 vols. [New York, 1917], 2: 229–30, 275).

14. Charles Loring Brace and two of John Hull Olmsted's Yale classmates, William Peet (1822–1895) and Henry Barton Chapin (1827–1914) (*Yale Obit. Rec.*, 4th ser., no. 5 [June 1895]: 301; ibid., 6th ser., no. 5 [July 1915]: 731–32).

CHAPTER III

THE VOYAGE TO CHINA

1843

ON APRIL 23, 1843, Olmsted sailed from New York for China as an apprentice seaman aboard the bark *Ronaldson*. Crammed with a cargo of ginseng and what Olmsted called "Yankee notions," the bark rounded the Cape of Good Hope, crossed the Indian Ocean to Java Head, then sailed north to Hong Kong and Canton. The four-month voyage was a miserable one. The captain, Warren Fox, so kindly and pious on shore, proved a tyrant with little concern for his crew's welfare at sea. Soon after leaving port he made the crew throw overboard many of the barrels of salt beef that the ship was required by law to carry, to make room in the hold for freight he had stored in the cabin. At the same time he put the crew on short rations of water for half of the hundred-day passage to Java. On the *Ronaldson*, Olmsted later judged, he was "worked harder and bedded more gloomily" than a horse in a coal mine.[1]

Although miserably seasick at the beginning of the voyage, Olmsted recovered and took up his duties, including the dangerous work of handling sails aloft. Toward the end of the voyage, however, he was temporarily disabled again with paralysis in one arm.

After the *Ronaldson* arrived at Canton in September 1843, Olmsted's ambitions to see Chinese society were thwarted by a siege of sickness, probably typhoid fever. During the four months that the bark lay at anchor below Canton waiting for its cargo of tea, he made only three brief visits ashore. Despite these meager opportunities for observation, his letters to his family were full of the same vivid description that were to make his literary reputation in his travel books on England and the American slaveholding states. Already he was showing an eye for significant detail and a knack for capturing the flavor of the speech he heard. He learned all he could from the

Chinese who came aboard the ship, and carefully recorded the manners, customs, and dress that he saw when he went ashore.

The politeness and forbearance of the Chinese toward his boisterous shipmates was all the more impressive to Olmsted in face of the sufferings inflicted on them by other foreigners in the Opium War of 1839–1842. During the war the British captured four ports and blockaded Canton, killing thousands of Chinese and committing atrocities against thousands more.

Olmsted saw China at an important time of transition in that country's relationship to the West. Before the Opium War the Chinese had restricted foreign trade to a few merchants in Canton, but the Treaty of Nanking, which ended the war, opened five ports to foreign merchants and ceded Hong Kong to Britain. When the *Ronaldson* sailed up the Pearl River to Canton, British warships were there to enforce the treaty. The Americans at this time were in the process of securing their trading rights in the aftermath of British success, and in February 1844, a month after the *Ronaldson* sailed for New York, the U.S. commissioner to China, Caleb Cushing, arrived in China with a squadron of U.S. Navy ships to negotiate the opening of additional Chinese ports to Americans.

Olmsted did not write letters during his harrowing voyage home from China, but he later recounted some of the incidents in an anonymous article, "A Voice from the Sea," for the *American Whig Review* in 1851 and in a letter of 1891 to the philosopher and psychologist William James.

The *Ronaldson* was short-handed on the return voyage, and there were no passengers aboard to witness Captain Fox working his crew around the clock. The food was so poor that Olmsted and his shipmates suffered from scurvy. Near the end of the voyage the crew almost mutinied because of the brutal flogging of a boy, George Ryckman, mistakenly accused of swearing. As the crew looked on, the first mate whipped the boy while the captain held and kicked him. Olmsted described the response of his shipmates as follows:

"How long are we to let that go on?" asked one, while another counted aloud the lashes—"Twenty-three, twenty-four"—"We are no men if we stand it longer." With this, he sprang forward, and nearly every man snatched a handspike or drew his sheath-knife. I fully expected to see the officers thrown overboard, when in a moment, almost before a step was made, our oldest and best man exclaimed, "Avast! avast! Come back, you fool; put down your knife; what do you want to run your head into a halter for? Can't you wait till we get home and let the law serve them out?" This interruption led to more deliberation, and finally a single man went aft, unarmed, with a remonstrance, which fortunately was heeded.[2]

When the *Ronaldson* arrived in New York, George Ryckman's father charged Captain Fox and first mate Jason Coghlin with assault and battery, and brought them to trial. Olmsted and other members of the crew testified against the captain and mate. Particularly effective was the testimony of the "oldest and best man" of the crew who had stopped the mutiny by urging the men to go to the courts for justice, and who asked to be locked up in the Sailor's Home to keep from getting drunk before the trial. The court ruled against the captain and mate and ordered them to pay damages to the Ryckmans.

The experience of the China voyage had a life-long influence on Olmsted. It gave him a continuing concern for the lot of the merchant seaman and led him to outline a program for proper education and discipline in the merchant marine. Having seen a Yankee sea captain at work, he had an image of physical suffering imposed by arbitrary authority that made the conditions forced on American Negro slaves seem hardly unique, and less brutal than he might otherwise have found them. Captain Fox's actions remained for him a touchstone of harsh assertion of authority. Forty years after his China voyage, he thought the attitude of New England factory owners toward their employees was similar: "They are generally taking the sea captain's view," he said, "and regard every grievance and aspiration of the working man as unreasonable and unnatural."[3]

Despite his hardships aboard the *Ronaldson*, Olmsted retained his love of the sea. He frequently used seafaring terms in his writing and he greatly enjoyed his many later Atlantic crossings. Still, at the very end of his life the nightmarish quality of the China voyage returned to haunt him. In 1899, lost in the half-real world of senility, he dreamed that he was back in his forecastle bunk on the *Ronaldson*, exhausted and sick, with the cold rain and spray dripping down on him.

1. [Frederick Law Olmsted], "A Voice from the Sea," *American Whig Review* 14 (Dec. 1851): 526.
2. Ibid., pp. 528–29.
3. FLO to Charles Eliot Norton, March 16, 1886, Charles Eliot Norton Papers, Houghton Library, Harvard University, Cambridge, Mass.

To JOHN HULL OLMSTED

Address: John Hull Olmsted/Yale College

Hartford, April 8th, 1843. Saturday morning

Dear Jack,

You see I have been obliged to return without again visiting you, very much to my regret. I have shipped or engaged to—any way—& must be in New York on the 18th instant—to sail as soon after as may be—but I'll try if I have time to give you the whole yarn.

Well, let me see. It was last Saturday—no, it was Friday—the "Charleston"[1] arrived from Canton. Goodwin[2] & I went on board when she hauled in to the wharf & were much pleased with the appearance of the ship, & we concluded we would try to ship in her if she went another Canton voyage. Her owners or consignees are Talbot, Olyphant & Co.[3]

Next day, Saturday, George Howard[4] & myself were bound up to look at the "Charleston," & called at Mr. Morton's.[5] He recommended us to go to Gordon & Talbot[6] and enquire & get a letter of introduction to Talbot & Olyphant; Mr. T. of G. & T. being a friend of Mr. Morton's & a member of Dr. Spencer's church.[7] Well, Talbot, said, the Charleston was not going out again. He knew of a vessel that was to sail soon, but he believed all her vacancies were filled now, &c,—good morning. But this kept me over Sunday, as no boat left now 'til Monday morning.

Sunday Mr. Talbot (that is of G. & T.) spoke to Samuel Howard[8] too, saying that if he or his brother would call him Tuesday or Wednesday perhaps he might have some information for this young man. On this (& other) I concluded to hang on over Tuesday, on which afternoon George & I called again on G. & T. Talbot took George aside & said they had a vessel to sail for Canton soon—that he had not been more particular the other day, because he wanted to enquire as to my character, &c. George of course satisfied him immediately & told him if he wanted more information he would refer him to Mr. Morton & others. Very good—he feared they might want to send me to sea because they could not keep me ashore (it might be almost true in one sense) & the lik' o' that. Then he told *us*, that they were about to send the Bark "Ronaldson" (Captain Fox)[9] to Canton. He believed they could take one boy more, was not sure. I could go and see the Captain & ask. "We always dislike," he said, "to take a green hand, but somebody must now & then & we may as well as any else I suppose."

Then we put out for the "Ronaldson" which we found lying at the "Sectional Docks" most up to "Tobacco Inspection" (Great Western's berth).[10] (She is undergoing complete repairs, has just been recoppered, &c.) The Captain was forward to oversee the men working at the new to'gallant for'c'stle. He stepped aft soon after we came aboard. George introduced *ourselves* to him, & our business. He received us & our *business* very kindly. Said he would see Mr. Talbot this evening & if I would call tomorrow morning, etc., &c. So, there's another boat gone.

Well, next morning you may be sure I was there betimes—but no Captain aboard as the repairs were interrupted by the rain. (By the way, I've got the *darndest* sort of a cold.) The mate, Mr. Coghlin,[11] received us (Goodwin was with me this time) & thought the Captain would be on board when he (the mate) went to his dinner—say one o'clock.

Now's the time, as I have a sailor with me, to describe the ship. Bark, I should say.[12] She is of about 330 plus tons, pretty good form, but nothing clipper. Rakish rigging, long black yards (main royal up) (By the way, the only ship I saw out of the Navy Yard with a lightning rod), handsome cabin on deck—high bulwarks, to'gallant fo'c'stle now building; (below before). Has a long boat, quarter boat & whale boat. Carries two bulldogs (6 lb. carronades or so), wheel of the best construction under cover (when wanted) & is about two years old, having been but two voyages to Valparaiso or thereabouts. Mr. Coghlin says she is the best calculated for Canton of any ship he ever saw except the "Morrison."[13]

Well, I went up to the "Home"[14] & amused myself in the reading room & in the Cabinet till noon. When I went aboard again the mate had some friends in the cabin, I believe, & had changed his mind. Now thought the Captain would not come aboard at dinner time—but as he slept aboard if I would come up at six o'clock I might see him. (Of course, I can do nothing after that time, so the next boat's off.) Well, in the evening the Captain told me in a very handsome manner he had concluded to take me. And in the conversation that ensued, he believed he had got three *good* boys & now he hoped he had another. (That was all he could take.) The other boys have all been to sea before & one of them had been a voyage with him & was a very good boy. He was the son of Mr. Braisted of the U.S. Hotel, &c.[15] I asked him about the room (for stowage) I could have. He said he should have us in the steerage going out. In return he should build a house on deck for us as he could not have his boys for'd with the men. (He don't let his boys associate with the old hands.) Well, the end of 'tis, I was much pleased with him, and after making some purchases next day returned to Hartford in the Globe,[16] where we arrived at 5 o'clock yesterday morning. Of the incidents of the passage which are interesting & amusing I must—but the day must close immediately—so—but that need not hinder my hearing from you Monday.

Yours,

Fred

1. The Boston-owned *Charleston* arrived in New York from Canton, China, on March 31, 1843 (Record Group 36, Records of the Bureau of Customs, National Archives, Washington, D.C.).
2. James Seaman Goodwin (b. 1822), the twenty-one-year-old son of Erastus Goodwin, a tailor, who moved from Hartford to New York in 1833. Young Goodwin was in Hartford during March 1843, when Olmsted was looking for a berth, so the two joined forces. Goodwin, who had apparently already been to sea, regaled Olmsted with "good yarns," and the two exchanged books of sea stories and adventures. After several disappointments, they decided in late March to go to the New York waterfront and deal directly with the shipmasters there (Frank Farnsworth Starr, comp., *The Goodwins of Hartford, Connecticut, Descendants of William and Ozias Goodwin* [Hartford, 1891], p. 639; "List of Persons Composing the Crew of the Bark Ronaldson of New York—whereof is Master Warren Fox Bound for East

THE VOYAGE TO CHINA: 1843

Indies," April 22, 1843, Record Group 36, Records of the Bureau of Customs, cited hereafter as "Crew of the Ronaldson"; FLO Pocket Journal, March 1843).
3. Talbot, Olyphant and Company, headed by David Washington Cincinnatus Olyphant (1789–1851) and Charles Nicoll Talbot (1802–1874), one of the most important American firms trading with China (*DAB*, s.v. "Olyphant, David Washington Cincinnatus"; Tyler Dennett, *Americans in Eastern Asia: A Critical Study of the Policy of the United States* . . . [New York, 1922], p. 72; information on Charles N. Talbot supplied by Emily P. H. Talbot).
4. George Howard, clerk, probably the son of Mrs. D. A. Howard. It was at the Howards' house at 120 Henry Street in Brooklyn that Olmsted occupied a room while working in New York from 1840 to 1842 (JO Journal, Aug. 18, 1840; Henry R. and William J. Hearne, comps., *Brooklyn Alphabetical & Street Directory, and Yearly Advertiser, for 1845 & 6* [Brooklyn, N.Y., 1845], p. 108: see Spear 197).
5. Peter Morton (1801–1846), a wealthy businessman, at this time associated with the New England Glass Company, who had an office at 127 and 129 Water Street in New York (William M. MacBean, *Biographical Register of Saint Andrew's Society of the State of New York*, 2 vols. [New York, 1922–25], 2: 146–47; John Lomas and Alfred S. Peace, *The Wealthy Men and Women of Brooklyn and Williamsburgh: Embracing a Complete List of All Whose Estimated Possessions . . . Amount to the Sum of Ten Thousand Dollars and Upwards* . . . [Brooklyn, 1847], p. 31).
6. The New York tea firm of Oliver H. Gordon (b. 1800) and George Augustus Talbot (1808–1885). George was the younger brother of Charles N. Talbot of Talbot, Olyphant and Company. (*Boston Evening Transcript*, June 1, 1885, p. 2; information on George A. Talbot and Charles N. Talbot supplied by Emily P. H. Talbot).
7. Dr. Ichabod Spencer's Second Presbyterian Church in Brooklyn, of which both Peter Morton and George A. Talbot were trustees (James Manning Sherwood, comp., *Sermons of the Reverend Ichabod Spencer, D.D.*, 2 vols. [New York, 1855], 1: 35; Thomas Leslie, Henry R. Hearne, and William J. Hearne, comps., *Brooklyn Alphabetical and Street Directory, and Yearly Advertiser, for 1843 & 4* [Brooklyn, N.Y., 1843], p. 229: see Spear 195).
8. Samuel H. Howard, apparently George Howard's brother (*Longworth's American Almanac, New-York Register, and City Directory* [New York, 1838], p. 34: see Spear 951).
9. Warren Fox (1803–1849) (William Applebie Daniel Eardeley, "Connecticut Cemeteries, 1673–1910," 8 vols. in typescript [Brooklyn, N.Y., 1914–17], 1: 4).
10. The *Ronaldson* must have been refitted at the floating dry dock of the New York Sectional Dock Company, between Rutgers and Pike streets on Manhattan's East River shore. The Tobacco Inspection station and berthing for the Liverpool and Bristol steamships was three blocks farther east at the foot of Clinton Street (John H. Morrison, *History of New York Ship Yards* [New York, 1909], pp. 60–61; *Longworth's American Almanac, New York Register, and City Directory, for the Sixty-Seventh Year* [New York, 1842], second p. 44, at back of directory: see Spear 959; *The New York City Directory, for 1842 and 1843* [New York, 1842–43], p. 377: see Spear 960).
11. Jason Coghlin, the twenty-eight-year-old first mate ("Crew of the Ronaldson").
12. The *Ronaldson* was built in Philadelphia in 1839 for a group of four Philadelphians that included the ship's presumed namesake, James Ronaldson. The ship weighed 320 tons and had an overall length of 102 feet and a beam of 27 feet.

A bark is square-rigged on the mainmast and foremast, with only fore-and-aft sails on the mizzenmast. What Olmsted means in the following description is that the *Ronaldson's* masts were raked, or tilted, toward the stern and that her main royal yard was in place high on the mainmast while she was in port, rather than stored on the deck. The bulwarks, or sides of the ship above the upper deck, were high. Previously the forecastle where the crew had their quarters had been below the deck, but now a free-standing cabin was being built for them above it. The long boat carried sails and was the largest of the ship's boats; the quarter boat was a long, light boat, usually for the captain's use, while the whale boat was strong and buoyant, for use in heavy seas. During the voyage Olmsted learned to call these boats, respectively, the pinnace, gig, and surf boat. Bull dogs are guns on the main deck, and carronades are short, large-caliber ship's guns (Carl C. Cutler card file, Mystic Seaport Library, Mystic, Conn.; see FLO to Parents, Sept. 5, 7, 1843, below).

13. A ship in the China trade, which its owners, Olyphant and Company of Canton, China, named after the British missionary to China, Robert Morrison. The firm Olyphant and Company was organized by David W. C. Olyphant in 1828, after which he returned to New York to found Talbot, Olyphant and Company of that city (T. Dennett, *Americans in Eastern Asia*, pp. 246–48; *DAB*; *DNB*, s.v. "Morrison, Robert [1782–1834]").

14. The Sailor's Home, at 190 Cherry Street in New York, founded in 1841 by the American Seamen's Friends Society. It was a boarding house with accommodations for 500 sailors (John A. Kouwenhoven, *The Columbia Historical Portrait of New York: An Essay in Graphic History* . . . [Garden City, N.Y., 1953], p. 199).

15. Olmsted's shipmate was sixteen-year-old Jacob T. Braisted, who had sailed with Captain Warren Fox on the *America* to China and returned with him on the *Zenobia* in 1841, when the *America* had to be abandoned in Hong Kong because she had been irreparably damaged by a typhoon. His father was probably William Braisted, who with Henry Johnson reopened the United States Hotel in New York in January 1843 ("Crew of the Ronaldson"; FLO to JHO, Sept. 28, 1843, below; *New York Daily Tribune*, Dec. 8, 11, 1841; Isaac Newton Phelps Stokes, *The Iconography of Manhattan Island, 1498–1909. Compiled from Original Sources and Illustrated by Photo-Intaglio. Reproductions of Important Maps, Plans, Views and Documents* . . . 6 vols. [New York, 1915–28], 6: 618).

16. The steamboat *Globe*, which ran between New York and Hartford (*Geer's Directory for 1843*, p. 98).

To John Hull Olmsted   [c. April 10, 1843]

Address: John Hull Olmsted/Yale College

"All in good time"

My dear Jack,

Now then for a splice to the yarn I sent you Saturday. As I was standing by George in the gangway of the "Globe,"[1] a young fellow stepped on board & I said, "There's a midshipman going up with us."

His appearance and manners were so characteristic I could not help noticing him—then, & after the boat had left the wharf; as he stood by the side of the wheel room, in a Spanish cloak & a rakish cap, without lace, & the button half concealed, as if he was pretending "to sink the quality" as those fellows often do. Bye & bye the Captain asked him into the wheel-house & I thought he was "showing off" as he answered that he "liked the wind best." However, I wished the Captain would be as civil to me.

Towards evening after we had passed Hell Gate,[2] as I was pacing the cabin, the quasi middy, coming down the companion[way], run foul of me & immediately apologized as the cabin was dark, &c. I entered into conversation with him & soon learned that he had never been in Hartford, but had once been in Middletown at school. "Since when, I have been at sea."

"In the navy, I presume."

"No, in the merchant service."

"Indeed," I replied, "I expect to go to sea myself in a few weeks."

"You do?" said he, "I have shipped to sail about the middle of the month."

"In the *Ronaldson*?"

"Yes!"

"So have I. I hope we shall make good shipmates."

"Good."

"Come, let's sit down & talk it out."

"Very well."

Now wasn't that a "pretty passage." I saw immediately that he was the "very good boy" Captain Fox had spoken of. You may imagine he "spun right off the reel," & I got just all sorts of information & "most desirable articles for the market."

His father is Braisted of U.S. Hotel, New York, & he knew me from having seen me there. He had been sick & Captain Roath who boards at U.S. Hotel was taking him for "an airing." Of course, we supped & chequered & newspapered & slept & got up to look at the (occasional) ice & "returned in," etc. together. And when the steward woke me up for "Tickets sir, if you please" & I found it was five o'clock & the boat coming 'longside the wharf: didn't *we* go up to the Captain & didn't I tell him we were going to be shipmates, & we might as well be messmates & he must let him go up & take breakfast with me. And didn't we go up to the house before anybody was up & Aunt Maria[3] open the door "en dishabile," and didn't we, & didn't we hang together all the forenoon & get as thick as pickpockets? Didn't we? I recking we did!

Our folks sewed the last stitch of the last thread in the last quilt of the accumulated patchwork of the passing generation, Friday afternoon; & after resting their fingers over Saturday forenoon, began to cut out & contrive the red flannel & check.[4] Oh law.

Aunt Maria has just been telling me that she hoped I would "get a good life preserver & never go way up on to the tip top," without being sure to take it up with me, so when I was blown off I needn't get "drowndered."

Now the "*thing* of 't is": for you to consult & conclude what's best to be done. You see, I must go to New York in the beginning of your Review Week & shall probably sail before the end of it. Now what do you say? Hadn't you better see Thatcher?[5]

Let me hear from you immediately.

And send up the "*Net*" and *Lardner*.[6]

And just recommend any little things which you think I may be likely to forget.

Give my love to Charley[7] & the rest of 'em.

I took a most outrageous cold in New York & am now about (or perhaps a little more than) half sick, nevertheless.

Your affectionate brother,

Frederick Law Olmsted.

All the brood of all the Howards & Joe Black [. . .] love as well as & "Dear Jack—

Don't forget the pigtail!"

1. The first part of this letter describes Olmsted's trip back to Hartford from New York on the steamboat *Globe*. His companion was George Howard (see FLO to JHO, April 8, 1843, note 4; *Geer's Directory for 1843*, p. 98).
2. A narrow, rocky section of the East River with swift, dangerous currents.
3. Maria Olmsted.
4. That is, his family was busy sewing the quilts and clothes that Olmsted would need for his voyage. The merchant sailor of the 1840s wore a loose, checked shirt of flannel, tight trousers with bell-bottoms, a low-crowned, well-varnished black hat with a black ribbon, and a black silk neckerchief (Richard Henry Dana, Jr., *Two Years Before the Mast*, ed. John Haskell Kemble, 2 vols. [Los Angeles, 1964], 1: 4).
5. John Hull Olmsted had to secure special permission in order to leave Yale College while it was in session, as Olmsted said he must do if the brothers were to see each other before he sailed for China. The man whom Olmsted suggested he approach was probably Hartford-born Thomas A. Thatcher (1815–1886), assistant professor of Latin and Greek at Yale (Yale University, *Catalogue of the Officers and Graduates of Yale University, 1842–43* [New Haven, 1842], pp. 4, 30; Increase N. Tarbox, ed., *The Diary of Thomas Robbins, D.D.*, 2 vols. [Boston, 1886], 2: 1014 n).
6. This may be Dionysius Lardner, *Course of Lectures on the Sun, Comets, Fixed Stars, Electricity, Steam Navigation, &c., &c.* (New York, 1842).
7. Charles Loring Brace.

To Parents

Address: John Olmsted, Esq./Hartford, Conn./U.S.

Care of Harden & Co.[1] at
Liverpool, Havre, Amsterdam and New York

Ronaldson, Latitude 11°50′ South,
Longitude 106°10′ East
August 6, 1843

Dear Parents,

Thinking it possible we.may meet some homeward bound English or American Indiaman at Anjer,[2] where we hope to arrive in course of a week, I take occasion to assure [you] of our safety, for which I hope I am truly thankful to God who has preserved us through a long & perilous voyage. (It grieves me very much to tell you it has likewise been in many respects a disagreeable & unpleasant one, for I know [how] much it will pain you.)

We have not seen land since we left New York nor seen a human face out of our "floating (workhouse) castle" [. . .]. Our barque was so loaded & crammed with freight that room for men [and] their effects—necessities of life, food, water, etc.—was scarce to be found. You will recollect remarking how our deck was lumbered up when we left. This has furnished us with a great deal of hard work, & in fact the loading her so deep & heavily has nearly proved our destruction altogether. Again, for want of room she was not certain (say) so well provisioned as she might or I suppose otherwise would be. [For] instance, we were out of potatoes & all fresh fruit & put on an allowance of water the first month.

For nearly a month I suffered exceedingly from sea sickness—during all which time my chest *in which was* [Dr. Taft's[3] remedy]—was stored where it could not be opened. The officers during this time were particularly kind & forbearing to me. In gratitude, I resolved as soon as I did get out, that whatever might after happen I would not growl at them, and I believe I have kept it. I determined to be as contented as possible & although I think I have suffered as much or more than any one, I do think I am as & have generally been happier than any one else of the crew. But a more discontented, grumbling, growling set of mortals than our men are, you can not imagine.

During my sickness I "bunked in" with Jim.[4] What I should have done without him & Dr. Green[5] I don't know. Dr. G. attended me with great care. I shall never forget the kindness I have experienced from him during the whole voyage, & I cannot be too grateful to him for continued favors. Left by seasickness so weak I could hardly stand, I was not able, had they wished, to do active duty aloft for some time. I was set to work filing rust, etc. from tools & such jobs which gave so much satisfaction that I was appointed Armourer & had the muskets, blunderbusses, pistols, cutlasses, etc. which were in horrible condition, to clean & burnish. This employed me a long time. And we were in the latitude of Cape of Good Hope cold weather early in June, but we had thousands of miles of easting yet to make before we could double it, through the most boisterous seas. And now we began to experience the beautiful qualities of our wash tub. She is loaded so deep that most every sea washes over her. From that time to this we have not had a dry deck.

On fourth July we were reefing topsails off "Cape of Good Hope." ("Off" some way to be sure for we were driven to near 40° South.) A few days after, we were shortening sail. I had furled the royal in the A.M. In the P.M. Jacob (Braisted) was slapped off the lee fore-topgallant yard. (I was on lee main-topgallant.) Most providentially he fell between the sail (outside) & the foretack.[6] If he had wetted he would [have] been lost. (No stop). Much to our surprise he has almost entirely recovered. The same night, we had the heaviest squall the captain or mate ever knew. The double reefed main-topsail was split to ribbons before we could close reef it, & the ship so nearly overwhelmed that they (officers) say if it had lasted with the same strength five minutes she would never have come up. We were scudding under bare poles the rest of the gale.

From that time to this we had a succession of gales, being under reefed topsails half the time. Allowance of water was three times shortened: the last off [the] Cape, to three quarts including water for cooking—coffee often each one quart, dinner often another quart, so we have to go without it often.

9th August, "At Anchor off Anjer."

You cannot think how busy we have been since I wrote above. Having [an] unexpected good run, we have not had time to prepare for port. All hands—most of the time getting up anchors &c. guns, gun gear, &c, &c., and continual shifting sails. Oh dear, I shouldn't think it possible to work so as I have.

About a month since, I had a stroke of Paralysis in my right arm, which for a time rendered it useless, but I have now recovered it sufficiently to go on duty again. Still, it [is] extremely weak & if it don't ache now! (dinner time.) The thumb & finger are yet numb, but not so much as they were.

It is so hot here, dead calm & a burning sun.

We have had two or three on the sick list ever since we left.

All old Indiamen on board say this has been the worst voyage (for weather) they ever knew. One of our able seamen proved entirely incompetent & has hardly done any duty since we left. As we had but two others & [are] otherwise half manned, judge you. That man will probably be invalided & sent home. If I [have] another *stroke* I shall expect the same—but don't anticipate it.

(I have told Dr. Green that it would be a great gratification to you to hear from him—& I hope he will add a few lines here.)

At Anchor, Anjer off Java

Dear Sir,

Through the kindness of your son I have the pleasure of addressing a few lines to you. You will please forgive all lack of etiquette in regard to length and writing as we are now in great haste preparatory to going ashore. Presuming that your son has given you particulars of the voyage I will avoid repetition mentioning, however, that we had far from a pleasant one owing to the vessel's having been so heavily freighted. Likewise, we have had much wet weather, and decks wet for some months. Your son is quite altered in appearance and I hope the benefit he will derive from the voyage may be of permanent benefit to his health, and with pleasure having learned that he is not addicted to the vices common among young men of [to]day, have little doubt that such may be the case. I am happy to say that he is convalescent from a slight attack of P. Paralysis.[7] With my kindest regards for yourself and son I remain yours, &c.

J. P. Green

Well now—to the great business of this letter—but I cannot. Words I cannot find to express the love, [. . .] *love*,—what can I say—that accompany this. But I rejoice to think that no one can conceive it, can know it better than all those dearest friends whom if it were possible I should mention. Brothers, sisters, you know what I would say to you. Aunt Maria & Cousin Fanny[8] & you. Don't you, Mary, Bertha, Ada? And if Master Albert[9] don't I hope he will. No! No! None of you can conceive how ties of love are strengthened by distance.

Dear Jack; But brother I can't write to you now. I must. We hope to arrive at Hong Kong in about six weeks or so. Captain appears to think we shall be on the coast (Am.) in winter,[10] but we think he can't do it. You shall hear from [me] again more at length by the first opportunity.

Goodbye & God bless you all,

Your affectionate son,

Frederick Law Olmsted

1. George Harden, importer, was listed in 1842 as having an office at 43 William Street, New York (*Longworth's American Almanac . . . for the Sixty-Seventh Year*, p. 289: see Spear 959).
2. Anjer, or Anger, or Angerlor, a port on the Sunda Strait at the western end of Java, where ships in the China trade often stopped for provisions.
3. Gustavus M. Taft (1820–1847), a homeopathic physician in Hartford who prepared medicine for seasickness for Olmsted (see "The Voyage Out," below, p. 146; *Hartford County*, 1: 149–50).
4. James S. Goodwin.
5. John P. Green of New York, a passenger on the *Ronaldson*. He attended the College of Physicians and Surgeons of Columbia College from 1838 to 1840 but did not graduate (Columbia University, Committee on General Catalogues, *Columbia University Officers and Alumni, 1754–1857*, comp. Milton H. Thomas [New York, 1936], p. 256).
6. The foretack is the line by which the tack, or upper corner, of a foresail is controlled.
7. For partial paralysis, or *paralysis partialis*, the paralysis or palsy of a particular muscle (Robert Hooper, *Lexicon Medicum; or Medical Dictionary . . . by the late Robert Hooper . . . 8th ed., rev., cor., and improved by Klein Grant . . .* [London, 1848], s.v. "paralysis").
8. Maria Olmsted and Frances E. Olmsted (1829–1907), Olmsted's cousin (*Olmsted Genealogy*, pp. 36, 109).
9. Olmsted's three half-sisters and his infant half-brother, Albert Henry Olmsted (1842–1929) (ibid., pp. 60, 109; *Eleventh Reunion*, p. 9; *New York Times*, June 10, 1929, p. 25).
10. That is, Captain Fox thought he could complete his trading in China quickly and return to New York in early 1844. The prospect of returning to such a "cold and stormy winter coast" was not pleasant to his crew (see FLO to JO, Dec. 27, 1843, below).

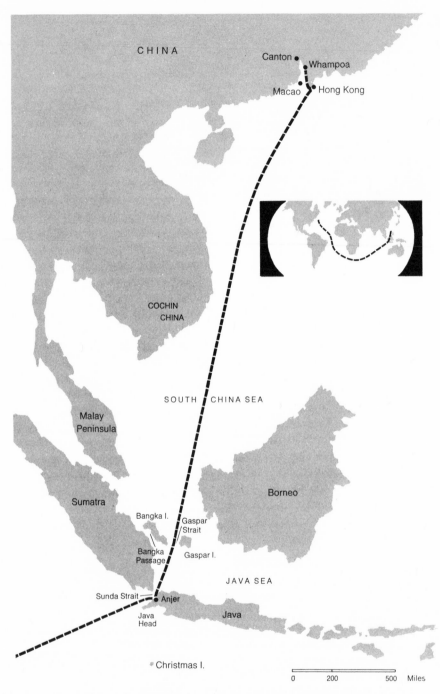

VOYAGE OF THE BARK *Ronaldson* FROM NEW YORK TO CANTON,
APRIL 24 TO SEPTEMBER 8, 1843

THE VOYAGE OUT
[April 24 to August 9, 1843][1]

Monday 24th. Soon after we parted from you, we anchored again, waiting for a change of tide. Soon hove up & stood out with a light breeze in company with quite a fleet, some thirty small craft: Packet "Albany" for Havre,[2] & "Pilot" for Batavia (arrived at Anjer some twenty days before us).

The spout we noticed turned out to be from a *real whale* (a fin-back), not the sea breaking over a rock as you supposed. My chest was now in a room 2½ by 3½ feet wide under two others; two berths in the back. Here were crammed "four boys." (Accommodations for four young gentlemen with sleeping apartments attached.) I was very little sea sick. Chose into the second mate's[3] (Starboard) watch.

Next morning, before daylight, I was set to work at the head pump, which, as I was now quite sea sick I found exceeding hard. Imagine an iron pump handle set close to the floor (much heavier & working much harder than our kitchen pump) so you have to touch it at every stroke; of course, stooping very much. After I had pumped without any interruption about an hour, feeling almost "gone," I ventured to ask the carpenter, who stood to pass the water on of the deck tub at the break of the fo'c'stle, if we were most through (washing decks.)

"Most through!" (Never mind the *exclamations.*) "Well by ———, youngster. You a'n't tired yet, are ye? You may think yourself d——d well off if you get through before 8 o'clock. So look about ye. You bloody young ———."

Acting on his suggestion, I looked about me.
"Sail ho!"
"Where away?"
"Right ahead, sir!" I replied.
She proved to be a brig bound in & ran close under our stern. I was in hopes she would report us. Squally. Reefed topsails, but made sail again towards night.

26th. Clear & pleasant. Spoke a brig from Mobile fifteen days out, bound for Boston.

27th. Breeze freshened. Sail shortened. Sent down royal yard. Towards night a gale: double reefed topsails. Was now quite sick, wet through & could hardly hold myself up. Mate saw my condition & ordered me below. Thought at least I would try to get on some dry clothes, as it was cold. Opened the door of our *room.* That was enough. *Faugh!* Over she goes. Such a sickening stench, you can't imagine it. Crawled to the fo'c'stle which was much better. Turned into Jim's bunk (fortunately very wide one) where I

145

remained nearly two weeks—hardly eating, drinking or thinking. Dr. Taft's remedy would I suppose have relieved, but while the gale continued it was impossible to get it & afterwards only by *great exertions*, as my chest was *all but* inaccessible. Jim did everything he could for me, & Dr. Green attended me daily. After some time he recommended me to eat some gruel & as Jim thought it would do me much good, he got some meal of the steward, & gave it to the cook. *Gruel.* Oh yes. Visions of dear Aunt Maria (how often I thought of her) with the nice thick mess covered with grated nut-meg in a white bowl. Oh yes, it will be very good. My mouth fairly watered for it. Jim brought me at last a mess of stuff in a tin pot, recommending it highly. I put a spoonful in to my mouth.

"Bah! Why Jim—."

"What's the matter?"

"It's sour as. . . ."

"Oh no! That's your mouth. It will taste better in a minute. You must get it down. It will do you a great deal of good."

Well, I try again. "Bah! there's something in it—salts. Why Jim."

"No, nothing of the kind."

"Are you sure? Oh, I know, it's salt water!"

"No, it is not, for I gave the cook[4] the water out of the scuttle-butt."[5]

Well then I concluded, it is my mouth & persevere; swallow, much against my taste, about half a pot full of it.

"Positively, Jim, I have done the best I can."

Jim assures me I never shall get well if I don't keep something on my stomach. But no more can I possibly manage. So Jim means to make a good supper of it himself. He tries a spoonful.

"Why, there is something wrong."

"I knew there was, I knew there was. Try a little more; perhaps it will taste better."

"Bah! Certainly there is something wrong."

It turned out that the steward had given him some sour meal (from the old South American stores) which it was hoped the pigs would take off their hands. (One of the pigs died that night.) The next thing I tried was some beans Jim had saved from the soup & had baked. A few days after codfish scouse[6] (substitute for codfish balls), but it was two weeks before I could eat the ship's allowance.

On the 8th of May, I went regularly on duty—standing watch, working about decks by day & taking my lookout at night.

April 25th.   Blowing fresh—reefed fore topsail.
    26th.   Clear & pleasant.
    27th.   Breeze freshens. Shortened sail, small gale; double-reefed.

28th.	Under double-reefed topsails. In the Gulf Stream.
29th.	Under double-reefed topsails. In the Gulf Stream.
30th.	Sunday. Clear weather. Service in the cabin.
May 1st.	Made sail. Reefs out. Evening: reefed again.
2nd.	Double-reefed topsails. Spoke Brig "Roberts." Heavy sea.
3rd.	Meteor seen in West.
4th.	Flying fish washed aboard. Porpoises seen.
5th.	Shook out reefs. Exchanged signals with British Bark.
7th.	Attended service. Washed & changed clothes.
8th.	On regular duty. Bark to windward, supposed the "Pilot."
9th.	Beating to windward. Evening spoke brig "Pisoria" for Rio de Janeiro. Longitude 41°.
12th.	English brig signaled. (11th signaled ship) Allowance of water. Potatoes stopped.
28th.	Crossed the line.
	Possibly my Anjer letter miscarried. So ———
June 5th.	Met an American brig.
10th.	Heavy squall. Close-reefed. Cooler. Cape Pigeons & Albatross.
	Cape weather commencing. Nearly in its latitude.
23rd.	Passed in the night Tristan da Cunha.[7] Rainy weather.
July 4th.	Procession formed before daybreak. Proceeded to fore topsail yard. Close reefed fore and main topsails. Off cape Agulhas[8] at noon. Longitude 41° South. Very heavy sea. Put on short allowance of water. Killed a pig.
7th.	Jake Braisted fell from fore topgallant yard. The heaviest squall the Captain ever experienced. Main topsail blown away. Furled all sail & scud[ded].
8th.	Still scudding: no sail set. Tremendous sea. Snow storm.
15th.	Woke in the morning with a paralyzed hand. Knocked off.
23rd.	In longitude of St. Paul's & Amsterdam.[9]
August 3rd.	Still reefing every day nearly.
August 4th–6th.	Saw the first tropical bird (a marlinspike). Cape pigeon seldom seen. Latitude 20° South. Morning service in the cabin first time this side the Cape.
7th.	Off Christmas Island. On duty. "Man of War hawks."
8th.	Made Java Head. First land. Saw the first sail.
9th.	Arrived at Anjer.

1. Title supplied by the editor for Olmsted's day-by-day description of his voyage from New York to Anjer on the island of Java.
2. A packet of the Union Line on the New York to Le Havre run from 1831 to 1847

147

(William A. Fairburn, *Merchant Sail*, 6 vols. [Center Lovell, Maine, 1945–1955], 2: 1106; *Doggett's New York Business Directory for 1841 and 1842* [New York, 1841], p. 96).

3. Probably that of twenty-year-old Charles Cotton, Jr., of Newport, R.I., who left the ship in China ("Crew of the Ronaldson").
4. Daniel Staples, twenty-six, of Maine, known as "Mush Dan" by the crew (ibid.; FLO to JHO, Sept. 28, 1843).
5. A cask lashed on deck to hold fresh water for daily use.
6. A sailor's stewed or baked dish; in this case, probably made of codfish and ship's biscuit.
7. An island in the southern Atlantic off the coast of southwest Africa.
8. The southernmost point of Africa.
9. Two islands in the middle of the southern Indian Ocean.

To Parents

Address: 34 Ann Street/Hartford/Connecticut

> At anchor off Hong Kong,
> September 5th, 1843.

Dear Parents,

We arrived at this port day before yesterday, one hundred and thirty-two days from New York.

I wrote you at "Anjer" on the 9th of August, which place we left on the following evening having procured a supply of yams, sweet potatoes, plantains, bananas, cocoa-nuts, tamarinds, fowls, ducks & paddy (rice in the "hull") to feed them on, pumpkins and *fresh water*. Of these, the yams & water alone were intended for the benefit or use of the "people." To be sure, we would occasionally get a plantain or banana smuggled out of the maintop by a boy setting to'gallant studd'n sails in the night, and we were welcome to the cocoa-nuts' shells—rinds, I should say—after the Captain had drunk their contents. East Indians never think of eating them except with a spoon when in a pulpy state, as it were.

We bought "amongst us" two large green turtles—but when the first was killed, the best part of it was taken for the Captain's table & supplied it for some days, while we had but one meal. The other was launched overboard. They called it *sick*, but the way it struck out for Cochin China[1] was a caution to doctors.

We had a most remarkable passage through the "straits."[2] We had anticipated a very hard & dangerous time. There is a beautiful clipper built English vessel now lying by us which was over three weeks getting through; anchoring every night. I think we were but three *days*, and did not anchor once. The second night we were becalmed and all hands kept up some time expecting to anchor. The magazine was opened, guns loaded with grape, &c,

for you know this sea ("Java Sea") is infested with Malay pirates, who *very* often attack vessels. But just as we were about to drop the kedge,[3] a light breeze sprang up. It soon became strong & so favorable that we could lay our course. Sunday (twelfth, I think) P.M. land was made right ahead, and at dark we were almost enclosed by it. Before midnight we passed "Jasper" Island at the head of the ("Jaspar" or "Gaspar") Straits & were in the China Sea.

The next morning I made three sail from the royal masthead. Before night we were near enough to see that they were "Malay Proas."[4] Our course was altered a little & next morning they were out of sight. We were now standing before the regular "monsoons"—which gave us plenty of work. Thus at daylight we are "right before it" carrying lower, topmast, topgallant & *royal* stud'n sails on both sides.[5]

The wind shifts a little over our starboard quarter. "Brace the yards!" "Let go to stab'd." "Man the lee braces." "Fore brace!" "Hold on to starb'd!" "Well!" "Make Fast." "Topsail brace"—"well!"

"To'g'l't brace"—"well!"

"Royal brace a small pull—belay!" "Haul taut to stab'd!" "So!" "All Well."

"Main brace!" And so with all the main braces. (He takes another look.)

"Braces a little more!" "In lower stud'n sail!" (larboard).

It hauls still more. Braces again. We haul the stud'n s'l tacks as taut as possible, but they shake.

"In fore topmast stud'n s'l." "Clap on the downhaul." "Take in to'g'l't stud'n sail, Sir!" "In to'g'l't s'ls." "Up into the top, you boys. Haul in fore & main t'g'l't & royal stud'n sails. Make them up in the top."

By the time all this is done, the wind is coming back again. The first thing is to set the lee foretopmast stud'n sail. (The hardest sail in the ship to set.) Then royal & to'gallant stud'n s'ls or these first, lower stud'n sails. The wind continues hauling and the same operation goes on: bracing to starboard, slacking larboard stud'n sail tacks—tauting the starboard & soon taking them in one after another & perhaps setting spanker, gaff topsail, jib & flying jib. These two operations perhaps occupy us for an hour or two.

A dark cloud is seen rising on our larboard bow. Those that have a chance perhaps put on an oil jacket. The cloud rises small, or rather narrow, but long. Likely, we see a distant water spout (we *did* notice several). The wind is perhaps subsiding. All hands on deck busy washing down, feeding the fowls, &c. & paying no attention to the weather, till: "Stand by fore-royal halyards!" Then we all knock off work & soon one is standing by the main royal & to'gallant & fore royal & to'gallant halyards.

The squall strikes us. Everyone is wet through & those not "standing by" crowd under the lee of the rail. The old man comes on deck having

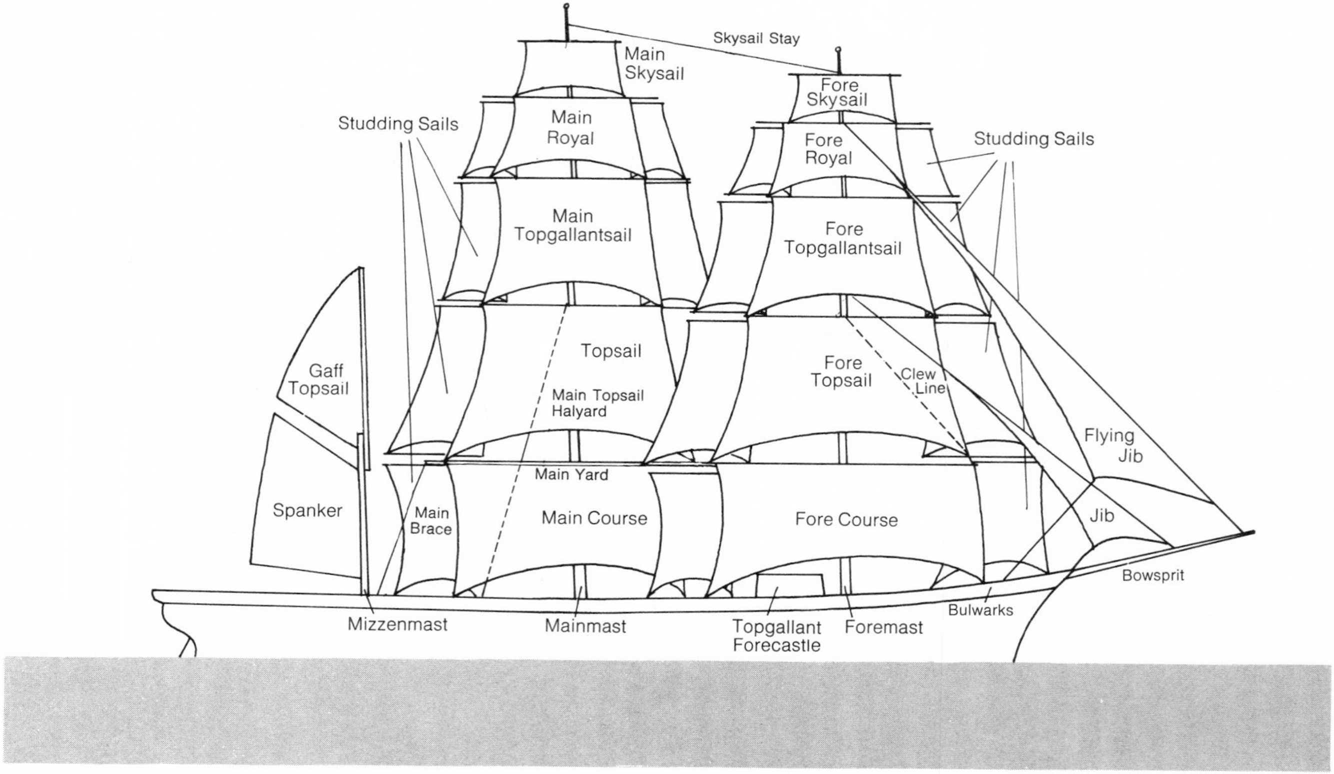

RIGGING PLAN OF A BARK

Skysail Stay

Main Skysail

Studding Sails

Fore Skysail

Fore Royal

Main Royal

Fore Topgallantsail

Main Topgallantsail

Clew Line

Fore Topsail

Topsail

Main Topsail Halyard

Flying Jib

Jib

Bowsprit

Bulwarks

Foremast

Fore Course

Topgallant Forecastle

Main Yard

Main Course

Mainmast

Studding Sails

Main Brace

Mizzenmast

Gaff Topsail

Spanker

noticed the barometer. "Clup fry'l" ("Clew up the fore royal.") "Haul down flying jib." "Clew up main-royal." "Lay aloft you b'ys & furl 'em."

One boy goes to each royal (in the first place, I should have got in all the studding sails & braced her sharp up—for the wind comes out ahead in the squalls & we are not "Full & bye.") By the time the boys are at work aloft: "Look out for yourselves on the to'g'l't yard!" They are hauled from below & the fore & main to'gallant sails are doused, but hardly ever furled.

In ten or fifteen minutes (from commencement) the squall breaks. "Hoist the main-to'g'l't sail!" then the fore. The royals are loosed, sheeted home & hoisted up, flying jib set & gaff topsail. Then we have a bracing spell—or rather a squaring—for as the squall passes, the wind is coming on her quarter again; & one after another, the studdingsails are set.

Oh! This is the weather to kill sailors. Any one of us had rather see a gale & reef topsails, than a light fair wind & the everlasting studding sails. We were often kept at work with scarce a minute's rest the whole night watch. But about two weeks before our arrival to our great astonishment we were becalmed & when we did get a wind it was ahead. And so it continued all day & night. The Captain was expecting it to change every hour, but to our delight we were still braced sharp up. No studding sails for forty-eight hours afforded us great relief. But such a thing in the "regular monsoons" had never been heard of before. It was at least a month too early. What could it mean? Deuce a bit did we care. So it did not mean to come back again.

We now had fine times—working at jobs in the daytime & in the night. "Come on deck to sleep & go below to rest." That is, when it was not squally, as it still often was. But often, if not generally, the watch below slept on deck. At eight bells, perhaps, throwing the blanket off & putting on a pea jacket. Then, if it was not one's lookout or wheel, coiling away on the studd'n sail again.

By day all hands were employed fitting the ship for port & for show. A flying skysail was made & royal stud'n sail soon after we left the straits, & the skin is yet to grow where I barked my shins on the to'gallant & royal shrouds & backstays, becketting & unbecketting that bothering little pocket-handkerchief flying kite.[6] Now three or four hands were sewing on the poop & boat awnings. The guns and gun-carriages were scraped & painted, & much of the iron work was scraped & oiled. The carpenter was employed on the gig which with the surf boat & pinnace were painted in the best manner. The best seamen were pointing & grafting gun gear, making fancy boat gripes &c, &c.[7]

For my part, I had a job which I liked very well: it was making an enlarged (800%) chart of the entrance to Canton River, including Macao & Hong Kong. (By the way, that should be "*Hong* Kong," not "*Hong Kong*.") The Captain was much pleased with it, & I presume on that account, partly, has made me his clerk here.

On the 30th of August we made land (about noon) and next morning were in sight of the island or the islands of which Hong Kong is one. It was not till noon of the 2nd instant that we got up opposite the town—which will show you what kind of winds we have been among lately. (Twenty-seven miles)

Hong Kong, September 7th, 1843

I was three days in the cabin copying invoices, writing (advertising) circulars, &c., during which time I eat at the second table with second mate, carpenter & sailmaker. I wrote the above in knock-off time and such "spells" as I could manage to get while there. I have had no time to go on with it.

Whampoa, Sept. 25th, 1843

P.S. I open to say that it is uncertain how soon the *Talbot*[8] (not the *Panama*[9]) is to sail: but as she has taken on board a chop boatload[10] of sweetmeats, we judge it will be soon.

1. The southern part of present-day South Vietnam; in the 1840s, the Empire of Annam.
2. Sunda Strait and Gaspar Strait between the Indian Ocean and the China Sea.
3. Kedge anchor.
4. A proa is a double-ended outrigger sailing canoe, usually about thirty feet long, used in the Malay Archipelago.
5. The monsoons are seasonal winds: in the region of the China Sea they blow from the southwest from late May to mid-September, and from the northeast from mid-October to mid-December.
   In the passage that follows, Olmsted describes the endless work of handling sails on a square-rigger when sailing before generally light winds that frequently change direction. First, there was the task of setting studding sails outside the usual sails when there was a following wind. When the wind shifted (or "hauled") so that it blew less directly from behind, it was necessary to shift the sails to a more fore-and-aft position by "bracing" the yards. This meant adjusting the braces, which were lines running from the yards to the deck.
   If the wind shifted back astern, the yards were "squared" again. If the wind shifted too far forward, it was no longer possible to carry the studding sails and they had to be taken in. The studding sails and their rigging would then be stored in the "top," a scaffoldlike platform over the head of the lower mast. At this point the square sails would be "braced up" and the fore-and-aft sails, which were more efficient for sailing close-hauled, would be set. These would be the spanker and gaff topsail on the mizzenmast and the jib and flying jib. In the instance that Olmsted describes, the *Ronaldson* sometimes encountered head winds that forced her to sail "full and by"—that is, with the yards braced up sharply but with the sails still full.
   When a squall struck it was necessary to "douse"—or take in—the royals and topgallant sails. This was done by hauling them up to their yards by means of the halyards attached to the lower corners of each sail, and then "clewing up" the flapping middle of the sail to the yardarm by means of "clew lines" attached to the interior bottom edge of the sail. Both halyards and clew lines were handled from the

safety of the deck. If a sail needed to be secured more tightly, the sailors faced the arduous and often dangerous task of going aloft to the yards, where they "furled" the sail by hand. The ship's "boys," of whom Olmsted was one, traditionally had the responsibility of going aloft to handle the royals and skysails.

6. A flying skysail was the highest sail on a ship, set above the royals. It was a temporary sail, easily removable from its yard and attached to it by "becketts," short lines with a small loop or grommet at one end and a knot at the other that slipped through the eye and held. In order to set that "flying kite," as sails carried above the royals were called, Olmsted had to stand where the shrouds and backstays of the upper masts met the mast and so was in constant danger of scraping against them.

7. What Olmsted describes here is the fancywork in cloth and rope with which the sailors adorned the *Ronaldson* as they neared port. *Pointing* involved tapering the end of a rope and weaving some of its yarns around the tapered end. To *graft* was to cover ring-bolts and other objects with a weaving of fine line. *Gripes* were broad bands formed by weaving strands of rope together and were used to secure the ship's boats on deck (William H. Smyth, *The Sailor's Word-Book: An Alphabetical Digest of Nautical Terms* . . . , revised for the Press by Vice-Admiral Sir E. Belcher [London, 1867], s.v. "pointing," "grafting," "gripes").

8. The *Talbot*, a 623-ton ship built by John Currier in 1837 in Newburyport, Mass., arrived in New York on April 7, 1844, after a voyage from New York to Montevideo and Canton that had begun on December 22, 1842 (W. A. Fairburn, *Merchant Sail*, 5: 3041, 3045; Record Group 36, Records of the Bureau of Customs, National Archives).

9. One of a succession of ships owned by the New York tea merchants N. L. and G. Griswold, which made "Panama Teas" a byword among grocers. The *Panama* arrived from China in New York on May 28, 1844 (Robert G. Albion, *The Rise of the New York Port, 1815–1860* [New York: C. Scribner's Sons, 1939], p. 246; W. A. Fairburn, *Merchant Sail*, 6: 3691; Record Group 36, Records of the Bureau of Customs).

10. Chop boats were the licensed lighters used in China for transporting articles of trade.

To John Olmsted

Address: Number Thirty four, Ann St./Hartford, Conn./U.S.A./per *"Mary Chilton."*[1]

> *Ronaldson*, at anchor among the Celestials;
> Whampoa, September 24th, 1843.

Dear Father, and all hands at sweet No. 34: (not forgetting our most worthy Sophomore Yaliensis),

The *Valparaiso*[2] arrived week before last, at Macao; two days after her, the *Ann McKim*,[3] in the remarkably short passage of one hundred and one days from New York. One day passed, and another, and another. No news from home! How disappointed we were. No communication was allowed with her, from commercial considerations, I presume. This gave us a little hope, however, & on the twenty-first, a "sampan" brought some parcels on board. Among them was that dear one from you. How—how rejoiced I was: *All Well, Thank God.*

I wrote you last from Anjer (Island of Java) dated 10th of August. We left there the following evening and arrived at Hong Kong on the 2nd instant. We had a most excellent run through the Straits & Java Sea. There are some ships here which were three weeks or more. (They, however, took the Bangka passage).[4] We passed the island of Gaspar the fourth night from Anjer—at midnight—without having once anchored or seen a pirate, though constantly prepared and expecting both. Coming up the China Sea we had a harder time; shortening or making sail hourly. The last week we were mostly becalmed, with an occasional light breeze or heavy squall. We saw several water-spouts, but happily arrived three days too late for a typhoon, which was experienced at Hong Kong on the twenty-sixth ultimo. We were three days in sight of Hong Kong, or of the islands of which it is one, without wind enough to reach it (27 miles). We found the place very unhealthy—the "red coats" (as a sailor told me) "dying off like rotten sheep, not like men at all." "Young Morrison"[5] had died just before, universally lamented.

There were about forty vessels at anchor in the port: no Americans, four English men-of-war. Finding no market for our "notions," we remained only four days & two days after arrived here. Here there are some sixty sail, mostly English country ships.[6] The Americans are the *Talbot, Panama, Mary Chilton, John G. Coster,* Philadelphia brig, *Wissahicken* (wicked chicken) and now the *Ann McKim* & *Ronaldson.* We have just learned (as a secret) that the "Mary Chilton" has a cargo already to be "shov'd aboard" of her & will go off for New York in a few days. I am just now under the doctor's hands, sick—not seriously—but sufficiently so to make writing a burthen, particularly with the "*ray*ther limited accomodations I ———— *enjoy.*" The *Panama, we are informed*, will take a cargo of old teas, too, & sail in course of two weeks. If so, you may expect to hear from me again by her. We have no news of the East India Squadron.[7]

I have tried with all my heart to think well of the bark in which my lot is cast, to believe that those evils which we have felt—& which have produced so much ill feeling in others, in *all* my shipmates—were the result of accident, negligence & necessity. I have endeavoured to think that it was from the nature and habit of the men & that in other ships I should find as much grumbling—if not from the same, from similar grievances. In this I succeeded pretty well, and as I wrote you from Anjer, there was not so contented a person on board. Since our arrival, however, I am convinced of necessity that our men not only are more discontented, but have much more cause for complaint than the crews of other vessels here, our neighbors. We are worked much longer, if not harder, & have many less privileges than are customarily allowed.

I find, however, all hands expect a much pleasanter time when we are homeward bound (for such reasons as you will find in Dana's *Two Years*),[8] & I hope, if I do not forget past experience of trouble, I shall at

The Whampoa Anchorage

least have written brighter pages to read to you & have pleasanter yarns to spin for the girls to knit by.

I know you expect a more particular account of our voyage than I am now able to give you, & I am much relieved & very glad to find by your letter that you have in some measure anticipated my difficulties & do not expect a regular pen & ink Diary, which if you had once seen my accommodations, quarters & facilities (or difacilities—difficulties (?)) you would immediately perceive the impracticability of attempting. I only wonder the idea I had of writing could have ever entered my head. I did, to be sure, once or twice "take up my pen" after my recovery from seasickness, but after a few accidents (which, if not amusing, were at least so considered by my messmates) I was obliged to give it up. However, I have, as I rejoice to find suggested in your letter, "contrived to use the pencil" quite freely, under [the] circumstances, & have tolerably copious notes of *nearly* the whole voyage—often scratched off in the time devoted by others to rest.

I read your remark recommending me to "take every opportunity of going ashore" & "informing myself, &c." which caused great amusement to my shipmates. My opportunities of observation & investigation are very similar to those enjoyed by Mr. Pickwick while a resident in his Majesty's Fleet Prison. *I have not yet left the ship since we have been here.* I am obtaining a good deal of entertaining information in regard to the customs, laws & habits of this most singular people from our attendant "Eyee" (Sanpan boat man; ship's waiter) an interesting and well-informed young man.[9] Of course, I have had no opportunities of meeting Dr. Parker[10] or of presenting my letters. Remember me with the sincerest assurances of respect to Dr. Hawes[11] & Reverend Mr. Gallaudet,[12] to whom I am under great obligations for the letters with which they honoured me. Also to Cousin Charles, Mr. Ayres, Mr. Monds, Dr. Comstock, Mr. Turner, Mr. Terry & other members of the Society.[13] My great regret at not going ashore is that I can not obtain information & specimens, but I hope yet to do something. The only specimen I now have is of a *White "Bittern"* (as I take it) which, probably driven off by a storm, took refuge in our bowsprit & was captured in the China Sea. The only shells I have seen here, my dear Mr. Monds, are some *"cowries"* we brought from Anjer.

My personal health since we were at Anjer has improved, I think. My arm & hand have entirely recovered. This place is represented as very unhealthy, but we see no reason for it (the representation I mean). We are moored between a graveyard & an extensive paddy field. Eleven of us in the fo'c'stle (we being turned out of our room) nearly devoured by mosquitoes. We have got a great deal of work to do before we leave, which will not be *before*—December! So we come on the coast in summer. No one *knows*, however, when we are to leave.

Our ship is attended by a physician who comes on board every day. There is a hospital ship in the fleet. Several Captains have died, but few men.

I have written off a short sketch of a few days after I left that you may compare. You must have been disappointed very much at not seeing us reported. I have noticed, I believe, all the ships we saw on the other side of Anjer.

If any tolerably decent berth at Canton should offer, I might take it for I am "ship sick," as you may imagine.

Dr. Green has a prospect of associating himself with Dr. Parker at Canton.

Mrs. Gutzlaff[14] has gone to Chusan to find her husband, who I hope will see her better treated than Captain Fox did. She is a very *disagreeable*, notional old granny. I hope I shall get many more such agreeable epistles as that from the dear girls. I shall endeavour to answer it particularly, as well as John's, by the next opportunity.

God bless & protect you all. With an ocean of love,

Frederick

1. A bark engaged in the China trade as early as 1838. She arrived in New York on February 13, 1844 (W. A. Fairburn, *Merchant Sail*, 4: 2582; JO Journal, 1836–1846, end sheets).
2. A bark of 402 tons, owned by Howland and Aspinwall of New York, built in Baltimore in 1836. She sailed for Canton on May 18, 1843, and was back in New York on May 18, 1844 (W. A. Fairburn, *Merchant Sail*, 4: 2174; Record Group 36, Records of the Bureau of Customs).
3. Built in 1832 by Isaac McKim (1775–1838) of Baltimore, the *Ann McKim* was one of the earliest and the most famous of the "Baltimore clippers." She entered the China trade in 1840 and on her third voyage out in 1842 had a record passage of seventy-nine days from New York to Anjer (*DAB*, s.v. "McKim, Isaac"; W. A. Fairburn, *Merchant Sail*, 6: 3905; Carl C. Cutler, *Greyhounds of the Sea: The Story of the American Clipper Ship* [New York, 1930], pp. 89–93).
4. The *Valparaiso* and the *Ann McKim* passed west of the island of Bangka, off Sumatra, whereas the *Ronaldson* passed east of it, through the Gaspar Straits.
5. John Robert Morrison (1814–1843), member of the legislative and executive council and officiating colonial secretary of the Hong Kong government. His father was the prominent British missionary to China, Robert Morrison—hence the sobriquet, "Young" Morrison. His death from malaria in 1843 was regarded by British authorities in China as "a positive national calamity" (*DNB*, s.v. "Morrison, Robert [1782–1834]").
6. "Country ships" were those engaged in the "country trade" between India and China (John King Fairbank, *Trade and Diplomacy on the China Coast: The Opening of the Treaty Ports, 1842–1854* [Cambridge, Mass., 1953], pp. 59–60).
7. The East India Squadron consisted of four U.S. naval vessels, under the command of Commodore Foxhall A. Parker, that were accompanying the U.S. Commissioner to China, Caleb Cushing, to Macao. The squadron did not arrive until February 1844, at which time Cushing negotiated the Treaty of Wang Hiya, opening five Chinese ports to American merchants (*DAB*, s.v. "Cushing, Caleb"; Foster Rhea Dulles, *The Old China Trade* [Boston, 1930], p. 192).

8. The prime reason Dana gave was that on the voyage home, " 'Never mind—we're homeward bound!' was the answer to everything" (R. H. Dana, Jr., *Two Years Before the Mast*, 2: 273).

9. Presumably "Sam," a Chinese man attached to the ship to run errands and act as an interpreter (see "The Real China," below, p. 188).

10. Peter Parker (1804–1888), one of the first Protestant medical missionaries to China from 1835 to 1840 and again from 1842 to 1857. He served as secretary to Caleb Cushing in the Wang Hiya treaty negotiations (*DAB*).

11. Joel Hawes (1789–1867), the Olmsted family's minister, pastor of the First Congregational Church in Hartford (*NCAB*, 11: 186; *Hartford County*, 1: 287).

12. Thomas Hopkins Gallaudet (1787–1851), founder in Hartford in 1816 of the first American free school for the deaf, of which he was the director from 1817 to 1830. In 1843 he was the chaplain of the Hartford Retreat for the Insane. He was a member of Joel Hawes's church (*DAB*; *NCAB*, 9: 138–40).

13. Olmsted is referring to members of the Natural History Society of Hartford:

William Orville Ayres (1817–1887), a vice-president and curator of the society (*Geer's Directory for 1843*, p. 130).

Joseph Monds, a vice-president and treasurer of the society (ibid.).

Charles Hyde Olmsted (1798–1878), Olmsted's cousin and president of the society (ibid.).

John Lee Comstock (1789–1858), a vice-president and curator of the society, surgeon during the War of 1812, popular scientific author, and director of the Hartford Retreat for the Insane (ibid.; *Hartford County*, 1: 142, 172; "Report of the Directors of the Connecticut Retreat for the Insane," 1840, 1842, 1843, 1844 [Hartford, n.d.]).

William Wolcott Turner (1800–1887), corresponding secretary of the society, instructor at the American Asylum for the Deaf and Dumb for thirty-two years, and principal of it for ten years (*Geer's Directory for 1843*, p. 130; *Hartford County*, 1: 428; *Yale Obit. Rec.*, 3d ser., no. 8 [June 1888]: 416).

Henry Wadsworth Terry (1799–1874), a curator of the society and a landscape gardener, later employed in laying out Central Park in New York (*Geer's Directory for 1843*, p. 130; Stephen Terry, Comp., *Notes of the Terry Families, in the United States of America* . . . [Hartford, 1887], p. 73; Headstone Inscriptions, Canton, Cemetery 2, p. 38).

Olmsted spent much time on activities connected with the Natural History Society of Hartford in the period before he sailed for China. He faithfully attended the meetings of the society, acted briefly as corresponding secretary *pro tem*, and visited with one or more of the members almost daily. He frequently joined with them in searching out a comet then visible in the early evening sky. He borrowed books from them on travel and natural history, and made careful note of the unusual flora and fauna encountered by men on long voyages to other continents. William Ayres was presenting a series of papers to the society in ichthyology, which led Olmsted to dissect and stuff some pickerel and perch. Joseph Monds, who gave Olmsted drawing lessons, was an authority on shells and was preparing a series of papers on conchology. He encouraged Olmsted and gave him some snails to keep with a chameleon the society had received as a curiosity and then "referred" to Olmsted. At meetings of the society other members brought reports on their special interests: Henry W. Terry lectured on the propagation of plants and displayed silk strands produced by his own silk worms, and Charles H. Olmsted exhibited the first five plates of Audubon's new work, *The Viviparous Quadrupeds of North America*. These Olmsted thought "Most Perfect." Since he was so caught up in the activities of the society, Olmsted was anxious to bring back specimens that would interest its members (FLO Pocket Journal, March 1843).

14. One of the *Ronaldson's* passengers, Mrs. Karl Friedrich August Gutzlaff (d. 1849), an Englishwoman who conducted a school at Macao. Her husband, Karl Gutzlaff (1803–1851), was one of the Chinese secretaries to the English commission in China in 1835 and was a magistrate at Chusan. At the death of John Robert Morrison he succeeded to the position of Chinese Secretary of the government of Hong Kong

(Kenneth S. Latourette, *A History of Christian Missions in China* [New York, 1929], pp. 221–22; Alexander Wylie, *Memorials of Protestant Missionaries to the Chinese* . . . [Shanghai, 1867], pp. 54–56).

To JOHN HULL OLMSTED

Address: John Hull Olmsted/care of John Olmsted, Esq.
Hartford, Connecticut

Ronaldson, Whampoa Reach,
Sept. 28th 1843

Dear Brother,

Your letter of the 21st May was received per Ann McKim about 3 weeks since. I have written home, twice previously to this date: first from "Angier point," and last, from this anchorage (23rd Ultimo) sent by American barque *Mary Chilton* as perhaps you may know. Private letters by the "overland mail"[1] are seldom taken, and then only as a particular favor, to some established house. We hear nothing yet from your East India Squadron. Jim (alias "Mr. Goodwin") was told the other day that the Brandywine was to leave Mr. Cushing and the prince (our most illustrious emperor's son & heir, as the celestials understand) at the Cape of Good Hope & call for him at Bombay, to which place he was to proceed overland.[2] A very fair specimen of forecastle news, that. I was glad to find by the papers, you were so kind as to send me, that sometime previously all was quiet in China, for we had heard nothing definitely from *there* later than the news by the *Delhi*[3] (arrived just before we left).

I was dreaming the other night, in this wise: Charley Cook, John Buck[4] & you & I were got together & were having a sort of a kind of a oyster supper, you know, at Marmy Dean's. One of those pretty girls was passing me a pot—a cup of coffee, I mean—which I clumsily enough capsized into the oysters. She *gently* placed her taper fingers on my shoulder & growled out, "Fred!"

"What is it?"

"Why, turn out and be hanged to you. It's four bells & your watch. Relieve the deck, will ye!"

It is not necessary to say the fairy form disappeared & in its room appeared that infamous cross grained down east elephant, from "Sackarap," "Mush Dan."[5]

"One hundred days to Cape Town"—rather too much of a good thing. Charley[6] must have thought so, if he found anything good about it indeed. Second time too. We were seventy four days to longitude of the Cape & latitude 41° South or thereabouts. John Buck too must have had a pretty hard time. One good qualification of our vessel—she needed one—was her tightness. In all the bad weather off the Cape, we kept her free enough by half an hour's pumping every other day, & often we would not touch the pump for weeks at a time. Now, here on our quarter is the Ann McKim, the beauty.[7] First thing every morning, *yank*, yank, she has to be pumped out. We have not rigged the pumps since we moored. The *Zenobia*[8] is the ship our skipper returned home in with Jake (Braisted) after losing the old *America*[9] in a typhoon at Hong Kong.

You must have had a glorious vacation: six dozen from [. . .] and pounders at that. Excellent! I feared the freshet would have marred your sport. Horace, Xenophon, Euclid—*ray*ther dry I imagine after that. I think I shall be calculated to appreciate rural comforts, if no other, when I return. With the exception of landing a few moments at the foot of a barren hill at "Contoon" opposite Hong Kong, I have not yet embraced old mother earth since I parted from the rather disguised specimen on the Pike Street wharf.[10] You may imagine, if you can, what a deprivation it is to me. I shall surely do something "disprit" before long—such as paddling ashore in my anchor [watch] some night to *wallow* in the luxuriant paddy swamp along shore—here.

You had just been reading *Wing & Wing*.[11] We had two or three copies on board, but I had no time to read them. This you may think strange, if not preposterous, but the fact is when I had any spare time after writing my notes & paying a little attention to cleanliness, &c, there were my clothes to dry, bedding to air & all sorts of little things, which you would consider necessary. Besides, I have not yet seen the time on board this vessel when I could not turn in—Avast! I think I have seen *that* time—but when having a chance I could not go to the "land of Nod"—the only land I could make anyhow—in about the same time you could go to grass, or I roll overboard. You can hardly have an idea how sleepy I used to be. Why, when first I got started, one morning, the deck tub was in use for some purpose & I was stationed to catch the water as it flowed from the head pump hose in a steady stream. Actually, again & again I got fairly to sleep while the bucket was filling & woke in proper time to pass it & stick under another. What do you think of that for a yarn? The best of it is, it's true. So bothered I was, too, to keep my outlook: it would have amused [you] I believe to see the expedients I resorted to. However, I succeeded pretty well after all—for I have not been rope's ended yet, as two of the boys were for being caught asleep.[12]

I was writing as above, when the mate called me, & after asking if I could swim, told me to get into the pinnace with the other boys. We tried to run up to "Boston Jack's," our "compradore's" at Whampoa,[13] but found the tide had turned & we could not beat up a narrow passage. The shore here was lined on either side with low wooden houses. Some had large porches & verandahs in front and tiled roofs. In one or two barnlike affairs were chop boats, &c, building. Some were shops with gaudy little signs swinging before them. Sanpans, a kind of boats most common here, in which habitate a comparatively small portion of the vast *floating population* of this great empire, with their bamboo gig tops rising one above another, were fastened in great numbers to stakes. The men were generally lying asleep————

"In statu quo," December 10th, 1843

And as for the rest of the above yarn, is it not recorded in the pencil chronicles ("crayon sketches") of Fred. Olmsted? Yea, *"in toto."* I had no business to begin writing so. But at *that* time we were not (speaking as a well man) kept busy *all* the time. And it was the first time I went ashore, and I saw a "Joss house"[14] or two and a mud fort &c., &c., &c., so I felt quite interested and suppose you'd be, as very likely you would. Nevertheless, I can fill up a sheet more profitably and in place of that I'll give you three yarns of going ashore & visiting Canton to boot in a few weeks or months. For the *Stephen Lurman*[15] looks like a clipper & we may not get the new green teas for a month yet, though I hope we shall in a week. In which case we shall be along after this, as quick as the trade winds, & variables, will *drive* us, judging from the new "thundering big" jibs & stud'n sails that "Sails"[16] is stitching at—reefs in 'em & bothering bonnets too; reefed topmast stud'n s'l. Mr. Richard D[ana]!—talk about your *Alert;*[17] why it was every day business with us off the Cape.

Well, how do you like the *sea?* The sea. On the whole, I believe that if I had been in some ships, with some officers, & some crews, & those not *very* uncommon and enjoyed the health I might have expected, I should have been *agreeably* disappointed. *But*—my dear brother, I was not well when I came on board, I suffered most severely from seasickness, in the first place, and since the first of April, say, I don't think I have enjoyed twenty four hours of as good health *and strength* as for years previously. Though I had no regular severe illness, and was not off duty before our arrival, but very little, yet I don't think I ever felt the strength and spirit, that I had a year since. In the severe weather I had a pretty bad fall on the spars, with a heavy coil of manila to settle it & so on to the scuppers—which exposure & wet *rheumatized*—but I never lost a watch by it, though you may be sure that for some days I could not "fly round" aloft so handy as usual. This was a bore, but my general health in the worst weather was better than at any other time. Why so? Well I suppose—I'm pretty sure—it was because we had at that time "watch and watch."[18] If any one you know wishes to try his fortune on the deep, recommend his first enquiry when looking for a ship to be in regard to the time he is likely to have to rest and take care of himself.

I had no idea this was such a sickly place as I find it. For the last month more than half of our crew had been severely sick. And now the

Captain has to live in Canton at the factories,[19] and Mr. King[20] is trying to hurry us off on his account. As for myself—judging from appearances, I must have been pretty sick, for my face is as sharp as a Malay proa (of which I shall yarn) and my arms &c. have a good deal of the living skeleton about them. However, they do say it's nothing to last May when I [was] sea sick. Sails, who is a very intelligent fellow—I tell Jim sometimes when he laughs at my paying so much attention to this, that & t'other, that he (Sails) is the only man (F. L. Olmsted, boy; wages _____, Hartford, Conn.) of observation on board. (How the deuce should I know anything about the cabin!)—Well, said Sail maker (his *Ma* called him John and land sharks, Mr. Chrystal) has often told me since that he never saw me about decks, in those days, but he was reminded of Cruikshank's idea of Smike.[21] And truly, they say my clothes (which in after time required *expansion*) did fit me very much after that remarkable costume of a purser's shirt on a hand spike, which those versed in Nautical literature so often read of.

Well, I was going to tell you that after all, up to the time I lost the use of my arm, *"pro tempore,"* I never desponded of becoming a first rate sailor. I never was really—even when sea sick—homesick, or wished myself clear of the ship. Even in the time of greatest danger, when the Captain expected the barque to go down in five minutes & that old topsail that we'd just got reefed down close, was a crack, cracking away, & I was looking to see the "bloody old sticks" snap out of her, I was laughing to see the old grumblers crowd up to windward, hoping that at last they would allow I'd seen "something like a blow," & thinking what a nice cruise some of their chests, &c. that wan't secured must be enjoying in the fo'c'stle. And when at last we were ordered aloft, I was a better sailor than I ever have been before or since, for I was the first out on the windward yard arm, & the way I hauled in the rags & passed the gasket, made even "old Jess"[22] say that I "had good pluck & did my duty man fashion." But in truth I'd no idea at the time that we were in real danger of going down.

Now I think of it, this letter is just as private as—no place aboard a ship is, particular when you bunk in watch & watch, & have a berth mate with his head full of "Jerusalem crickets" (as I *did* & shall!). You must not even show it to Charley—no objection to your reading passages, if you must—but supposing I put in some that'll stop its going further.

A word (1!) about my ship mates. I'll speak of two of my mess mates to begin with. When at first the Captain (the infernal deceitful old liar—though in spite of everything I won't make up my mind that he is not conscientious—a regular hypocrite, but *what* a conscience!) made such good speeches, such promises & the singing at *service* was such *fun*; the *men* for'd, that the *boys* (he has a son) "must not associate with," at sea (on shore in N.Y.) (though they can be turned in among them & find places to sleep on their chests or on the deck (floor) for three or four months in a foreign sickly port).[23] When the men were concluding to knock off swearing &c & thinking they should come back better men than they left, &c, these boys (moral young men, the Captain called them) were laughing at them, and swore almost as hard as the same men did a month and a half afterwards, when (as it always afterwards was) *all hands* were kept at work Saturday P.M. and they were obliged to wash their clothes, &c in their watch below (in service time) on Sunday. And when they went ashore at "Anjier" (it's spelt every way), they bought a bottle of gin, & the first thing when they get to town— "off to Hog lane to get something to drink after pulling a dozen miles or more." Guess the rest. My watch mate is the most ill natured fellow & when started (easy enough to get steam up too) the most perfect Billingsgate blackguard that ever I heard. But he has some good qualities.

What's our prospect going home? In the first place there is not the restraint of the passengers who outward bound were imminently calculated as such. It is already beginning to show. The mate[24] damns us, up & down, has his brandy on board, &c, blackguards them as sons of (you know) & you can judge. As for the Captain, I don't like to say much, for *"on dit"* he is not only pretty sick at the factories, but he has a very consumptive cough. He is a man of terrible passions, but has a remarkable self command. He used to blast us (the crew) and call us all ugly names you can think of, but hardly ever used profanity, which he *ordered* to be punished in the boys. The other day in administering[25]

John Hull Olmsted S[ophomore]

Postscript to a letter dated at Whampoa, Dec. 10th, 1843

Confound your crossed letters. I have been trying it there with some miserable blue ink, but as it's rather unprofitable business, writing what can't be read. I think I can afford paper (I know Father's wondering I don't use the *packet post* all the time. Fact is, I've got none left fit to write on) sufficient to make myself intelligible.

I have been trying to inform you that partly on account of the absence of the restraint of our late passengers, we are not likely to meet with so much consideration from our officers on the homeward bound passage as formerly, which they are already beginning to show in not being very "mealy mouthed" in their expressions. The mate, for instance, G____d d____n'g a man just recovered from the most severe and dangerous case of fever in the fleet, for weakness, as a "regular soger," "marine," &c.,[26] and applying such complimentary titles as "damn'd son of a _____," "you are a fool & the man that made ye," & the like (*he* swears like a pirate).

Our new second mate,[27] by the way, turns out to be a real horse at work; and a first rate seaman, they think. There'll be no sogering, or slack work in our watch, while he's with us. (He is a Dane I think.) He'd be "right glad he hadn't come aboard," though, he says, as does our new man Nicholas[28]—who comes from a country ship where his time is just out as apprentice. The poor fellow would give all his old shoes, if he had not shipped aboard the "dom'd yonkee work hus." He's "the divil for repale," though, & thinks Dan'l O'[29] the only big man to spake of, in the world.

I scarce ever heard the Captain use a profane expression. (The other day he was about to administer an emetic to a sick boy, who told him Dr. Green disapproved of it, &c., &c. "*Dr. Green may go to hell!* for ought I care—it would make a saint swear.") He has a most remarkable command of temper having evidently most violent passions by nature, which he restrains most admirably sometimes. I've seen him jump half across the poop at the man at the wheel (Oh, She's a wild jade) with, "Blast ye! I'll knock ye over the wheel, ye don't keep the ship steadier, you're the biggest soger," &c. "Blast ye" is common enough. So is "old granny," "old woman," "Want your petticoats," "infernal soger," "Oh, you marine!" &c, "Stupid ass" & the like.

Perhaps I had better not say anything more about Captain—for he is pretty sick, though not confined to his bed. (He never is, over twelve hours.) And "Gallynews" talks of consumption & an awkward cough; & sailors all say that the sea kills or cures that, "*sure.*" Well, he's a most incomprehensible man, truly. He certainly *did* sometimes appear a most devout man, and I have attended the service with great pleasure & I hope some benefit, very regularly. Since we have been in port, the daily service has been given up, as we were worked so late, there was no time for it.

After all, but for one consideration, even supposing I do not recover my health, the voyage will be very profitable to me. I've seen and learned a great deal here considering my comparatively small means of observation. I've heard much more than I've seen, to be sure. And although I've been but once to Canton and was then hurried away almost before I'd time to look about me, I suppose I know *altogether* as much about it as any of 'em.

Besides the different classes of "China men," I've seen plenty of such fry as the John Bulls, Saronies, Paddies, Johnny Crapeaus, Prussians, Dutchmen, Danes, and other Fanquis[30] from that way, and Hindoos, Lascars, Malays, Japanese, Sumatrians, Manilla-men, Kanakas, Seapoys, Sea horses, Sea—

But I must stop there, for I've seen very few of the inhabitants of the sea. We were remarkably unfortunate in that respect. The only thing we took was a porpoise or two coming up the China Sea. I only saw one shark, two or three dolphin— (no mistake in them—by Neptune! They are magnificent), lots of whales though, and of skipjack and albacore, &c, &c, all guesswork. Nothing I've been so disappointed in, as my inability to procure specimens of

Natural History. Off the Cape, acres and acres of various birds, of every variety (some dozen or two) I have slight notes. Plenty of birds alive in town, but is it not strange that amid all their ingenious performances they don't preserve them when dead?

Just now, it's pretty cold & we wear drawers, stockings, &c. (season is backward, too, I believe), but it was terrible hot to be sure when we first got in. At Hong Kong in furling sails, several of us were blistered by touching the naked skin to the yards, and in coming through the Straits, Chips[31] had a tin box entirely unsoldered.

Canton is a queer place, & these Fuckees are a "rum set" anyhow. 'Twould look rather odd down our way, I *guess*, to see Dr. Beresford[32] go to work on an old man in the middle of Main Street—take his eye out, so that it hangs half down his cheek, scrape & clean it with his instruments, swab out the socket & slip it back again as good as new. That's the celestial way of doing business. And by the way the old cove he's operating on takes it very coolly; without a cringe or sigh as if 'twas an every day performance to him as well as the leech.[33] But the prettiest sight (say in front of the Phoenix Bank)[34] is a couple of incendiaries sitting in stocks with their tongues cut out undergoing the pleasant operation of starving to death. Rich, that, decidedly _____!

2nd P.S. to a letter dated "Whampoa reach Dec. 10th, 1843" to John Hull Olmsted

And then my dear Soph. as to what I've learned, seen, &c, let me see. Oh, I've seen lots of human nature to be sure. It's perfectly *ridiculous* how mistaken I was in my estimation of the character of my shipmates. Not one but what I've changed my opinion of, except Sails. I got him down about right on first acquaintance.

There's "old Davis."[35] How or when he came on board I don't know. He certainly lay in his bunk all the first afternoon. The first I saw of him was during my first anchor watch. James was gone I think to strike the bell, & hearing a noise forward, I met a man as I went to see the cause. The only answer to everything I said was "Where's the scuttlebutt?" or to that effect. I did not know, more than you do, now. And as the poor drunkard was in danger of breaking his neck, constantly tumbling among the lumber as he was, I called Jim who got him to his bunk after finding the water he so much wanted. He was not there long, though, but continued all night reeling among the casks, hen coops, hawsers, stores, &c. in search of the "scuttlebutt."

Next day, he was well enough, for he had got his brandy from his chest. He was the only one that did not attend service that night, and he never has, since. He was constantly "growling," from his first return to sanity. He had been shipped while on a spree, didn't know where he was bound, and wouldn't go a long voyage, particularly to Canton, for fifty dollars a month, in the best craft that ever sailed out of heaven.

While I was seasick I was disgusted with him in every way. He never stopped growling & prophesying how all this stuff would turn out. No one could be calculated to make us all miserable better than "Old Davis," I would often think. Then he looked like "Old Davy:" with half his nose "knocked to buggery's island" against some curb stone, pale, dirty, a nasty outré, nondescript dress; regular banged up, round top, old "rum heaver." The mate came to the forecastle door third morning aboard—fourth day I mean. "Well! how long do you intend to soger here?" &c "_____I believe you are_____drunken soger." (There's been some pen trying on this side.)

A month out or so, I saw my detestation, Sunday morning. He was sitting in the shade of the foresail attentively reading a very old, worn-out Bible, smoking from a new clean pipe. The dress he always wears is entirely of stout canvas. He cuts and sews them himself. A white jumper of peculiar cut & sew, & trousers ditto; straw hat in warm, white wool in cold, and a stiff painted ditto in rainy weather.

To make the matter short, he turns out one of the best of seamen. All his predictions are verified. After the second mate left, the mate gave him entire charge of the rigging. I once heard the captain & mate speaking of him & it seemed as if they were vying with each other to find sufficient terms of praise for him: "the best seaman I ever knew," "first-rate sailor," "worth all the rest of the able seamen we've got," &c, &c. A day or two after, he dropped the hatch on deck—then 'twas— "dom yer sule! [If] I ever see the lik of thot agin, gov ye a kack in the ayes," "I'll knock ye threw the side!" "D'ye think the deck's made of airon & be dom't till ye!"

Give my heartiest expression of friendship to "Charley," Mr. Peet, Harding[36] and the rest of 'em; "all enquiring friends." Also to the Washingtons, Frank, Dud & Bill.[37] I am sorry I can't write to them.

I must stop now at any rate, though I had some more to say. I hope that in—the course of time, say—you'll "come down to York" & find me, Sailor's Home, U.S. Hotel, Howard's, Mr. Morton's,[38] any rate.

I shall give more time to seamanship (knots, &c) & navigation if possible going home. I'll keep a sort of a mere log like & occasionally write out a scene, or description at length rather than journal. Oh Jack, if you & I were *passengers*, eh! The old sea is glorious (sublime) after all, but the fo'c'stle is—No—it's too grave to be ridiculous. Dear brother Jack. God bless you. I'm crying like a baby.

Your loving brother Fred all the world over.

1. The overland mail was the service by the British Post Office that ran to India and China by way of the Mediterranean and the Isthmus of Suez (*First Report of the Postmaster General on the Post Office* [London, 1855], p. 18).

2. John Olmsted sent his second letter to his son in China by the frigate *Brandywine*, one of four U.S. Navy ships that set out in May 1843 to escort Caleb Cushing to China for treaty negotiations. The flagship of the squadron, the new steam frigate *Missouri*, burned and sank at Gibraltar on August 25, whereupon Cushing proceeded to India by way of Malta and Egypt while the three remaining ships sailed around Africa. Cushing rejoined the squadron at Bombay in November 1843 and arrived at Macao on the Bay of Canton on February 24, 1844. The son of the "Emperor of the United States" was not a member of the diplomatic mission, but its secretary was Daniel Fletcher Webster (1813–1862), eldest son of Daniel Webster, who was secretary of state when the mission was being organized. (Claude Moore Fuess, *The Life of Caleb Cushing*, 2 vols. [New York, 1923], 1: 416, 422–25; JO to FLO, July 17, 1843).

3. The *Delhi* arrived in Boston from Canton on April 12, 1843, just eleven days before the *Ronaldson* sailed from New York for China (Record Group 36, Records of the Bureau of Customs).

4. John Buck (c. 1822–1847), apparently of Hartford, sailed to England before the mast some time after Olmsted went to China. Charley Cook was apparently another Hartford boy (JO to FLO, July 17, 1843; JO Journal, March 21, 1847).

5. Olmsted was not complimenting the cook, Daniel Staples of Maine, by saying he was from Sackarap. Either from reading Dana's *Two Years Before the Mast* or from listening to his shipmates, he knew the incantation pronounced by sailors over the salt beef left to them after the captain had his pick:

> "Old horse! Old horse! What brought you here?"
> " 'From Sacarap' to Portland pier
> I've carted stone this many a year;
> Till, killed by blows and sore abuse,
> They salted me down for sailors' use.
> The sailors they do me despise:
> They turn me over and damn my eyes,
> Cut off my meat, and pick my bones
> And pitch the rest to Davy Jones." (2: 278 n)

6. Olmsted seems to be including Charley Cook and John Buck on his voyage because he brought them along in his dream.

7. Isaac McKim spared no pains or expense in making the *Ann McKim* the handsomest merchant ship of her day. Her total cost was nearly $50,000. One historian describes her as follows: "Her frame was of live-oak, and the carving of her figurehead and stern was carried out with grace and beauty. On deck the gleaming brasswork of her bells and trimming was reflected in the polished Spanish mahogany of her rails, hatch coamings, and skylights. She mounted twelve brass guns . . ." (Helen La Grange, *Clipper Ships of America and Great Britain, 1833–1869* . . . [New York, 1936], p. 41).

8. The *Zenobia* was owned by Talbot, Olyphant and Company of New York. She sailed from New York before the middle of June, carrying John Olmsted's third letter to his son (JO to FLO, July 17, 1843).

9. The *America* was a 346-ton vessel built in Portsmouth, N.H., and owned by George A. Talbot and Associates of New York. Captain Fox was her master in 1841, when she was damaged in a typhoon and condemned at Hong Kong (C. C. Cutler, *Greyhounds of the Sea*, p. 390; *New York Daily Tribune*, Dec. 8, 11, 1841).

10. The pier on the East River where the *Ronaldson* was moored before she sailed for China (see FLO to JHO, April 8, 1843, above).

11. *Wing and Wing* was a tale of adventure about a French privateer by James Fenimore Cooper, published in 1842.

12. This problem persisted, in a form at least as severe, on the return voyage. Although Olmsted wrote nothing about it at the time that has survived, he recounted some of his difficulties and expedients in a letter to the philosopher and psychologist William James (1842–1910) on July 8, 1891. The relevant portion of the letter, taken from a signed duplicate typescript in the Olmsted Papers, is as follows:

Dear Professor James:—

I have received your note in which you say that you would be glad to have a fuller narrative of my experiences in what I believe to have been a condition of sleeping with open eyes.

The first was when I was twenty years old, one of the crew of an American ship, in the South Atlantic, homeward bound from China. I was at the time but imperfectly recovering from typhoid fever, on such unsuitable diet that it resulted in scurvy before we reached home. The ship was short-handed and the time usually allowed for sleep had been curtailed, "all hands" being kept on deck during the morning and the afternoon watches.

At two o'clock in the morning, it was my turn to keep the lookout on the forecastle. I realized that I was in a state of cruel drowsiness and struggled resolutely to get the better of it. Soon, while still standing erect and looking vigilantly ahead, I fell sound asleep and was awakened by falling upon the deck. I then determined not to allow myself to stand still for a moment. The ship was being painted and some spars had been temporarily lashed upon the forecastle so that I could find no place for walking which would allow me to move more than five steps each way, back and forth. In walking this distance, if I staggered sidewise towards the stern, I should fall over the break of the forecastle down upon the main deck, and if I moved more than five steps, there was nothing at one end of my beat but a small life-line at the height of my knee, to prevent me from stepping overboard. Walking to and fro in this situation, I repeatedly struck my forehead and temples with my fists, trying to overcome the inclination to sleep. Nevertheless, I three times went sound asleep between one end of my beat and the other and the third time was saved from being pitched into the sea only by catching the life-line with my hand. I reflected that to continue this walk would be suicide and looked about for some more effective means of keeping myself awake. The expedient I adopted was to sit on a spar at a point where the heavy bolt-rope forming the bottom of the foresail would, as the ship rolled, first strike me from behind; then rake my head, compelling me to bend downward and let it pass, and then strike me in front and force me again to move as it swung backward. Thus I should be sharply struck and compelled to crouch uncomfortably two or three times a minute. So situated, I looked forward upon the sea; imagined that for an instant I had caught sight of a dipping light on the horizon; roused myself to the utmost vigilance in searching for its reappearance, and, while so vigilantly searching, lost consciousness, as I have no doubt, with my eyes wide open. How long I remained in this condition I do not know, but it must have been a number of minutes; possibly half an hour. When consciousness began to return to me, I felt the stroke of the sail upon my head as it swung forward, and, at the same time, knew that I had been seeing, before my mind took hold of the fact, a pair of eyes looking into mine. Then I heard a voice, asking: "What is the matter with you?" It came to me as if part of a dream, but waked me completely and on the instant I knew that the Captain was standing on the windlass and so bending over and turning his body as to look me in the face. I was able to answer promptly and in a quick, natural, decisive way: "There is nothing the matter with me, sir." "Why don't you answer when you are hailed?" "I have heard no hail, sir." "What do you mean? I hailed you from the quarter deck; I hailed you from the waist, and when you did not answer I came to the windlass and hailed you within three feet of your ear. I thought you must be asleep until I saw that your eyes were open." "I don't understand it, sir; I certainly did not hear you." The Captain believed me and turned away, saying: "Keep a sharp lookout," and I did not fall asleep again until after I had been regularly relieved.

In a manuscript fragment describing this experience Olmsted wrote, "I was asleep to sound and touch—even to pain, for my head had been pounded painfully, but awake to vision."

Olmsted gave another description of the situation on the *Ronaldson* at this time: "For two weeks, in mid-ocean, in the finest weather, our crew had less than seven hours on an average in the twenty-four allowed them for sleep, washing, dressing, eating their meals, cleaning their dishes and their abode, mending and taking care of their clothes, &c" ([Frederick Law Olmsted], "A Voice from the Sea," *American Whig Review* 14 [Dec. 1851]: 529).

13. "Boston Jack" was so named because he had been to Boston, Mass., in his youth. Olmsted discusses him at length in his letter of Nov. 30, 1843, to Aunt Maria (below). Like other compradores, he supplied merchant ships with food and naval stores.

14. A Chinese temple. A joss was a Chinese household divinity and idol before which worshippers burned "joss sticks," or incense.

15. The *Stephen Lurman* left New York for Canton on June 15, 1843, and was home again A,ril 1, 1844 (C. C. Cutler, *Greyhounds of the Sea*, p. 115; Record Group 36, Records of the Bureau of Customs).

16. John Christal, twenty-six-year-old crew member and sailmaker on the *Ronaldson* ("Crew of the Ronaldson").

17. The *Alert* was the ship on which Richard Henry Dana, Jr., returned to Boston from California in 1836. Dana wrote: "We had a new topmast studding-sail made with a reef in it,—a thing hardly ever heard of, and which the sailors had ridiculed a good deal, saying that when it was time to reef a studding-sail, it was time to take it in" (*Two Years Before the Mast*, 2: 316).

18. That is, keeping the usual system of watches that entailed four hours on duty followed by four hours off duty, or "below," varied only by two two-hour "dog watches," usually between 4:00 and 8:00 P.M. (R. H. Dana, Jr., *The Seaman's Friend* [Boston, 1851], pp. 167–68).

19. The factories were the places in a riverfront section of Canton outside the city walls where foreign traders—that is, "factors"—resided and carried on their business (James C. Thomson, Jr., "A Cycle of Cathay," *American Heritage* 23 (Aug. 1972): 7).

20. Charles William King (c. 1809–1845), merchant, who was a partner in the firm of Olyphant and Company of Canton, where he spent most of his active life after 1826 (*DAB*).

21. The emaciated Smike was a character in Charles Dickens's *The Life and Adventures of Nicholas Nickleby*, which appeared in 1839 with illustrations by "Phiz." Olmsted assumed that "Phiz" was the English caricaturist and illustrator George Cruikshank (1792–1878), but the work was actually that of Hablot Knight Browne (1815–1882) (*DNB*, s.v. "Browne, Hablot Knight").

22. William Jessup of New York was forty years old when he joined the crew of the *Ronaldson* and must have been a veteran seaman. The oldest crew member on this voyage was forty-nine ("Crew of the Ronaldson").

23. In his autobiography, Olmsted's friend Frederick Kingsbury recounted an apocryphal story of Olmsted's concerning Captain Fox's treatment of himself and the other boys: "Capt. Fox promised to look after him as he did after his own son, who was going in the same position. Fred said he thought Captain Fox redeemed his promise, for on the voyage out young Fox jumped overboard to escape his father who was chasing him with a marlin-spike" (*Kingsbury Autobiography*, Part 3).

24. Jason Coghlin.

25. The letter ends abruptly at this point; the postscript that follows is on a separate sheet of paper and was written at a later time.

26. In *Two Years Before the Mast*, Dana explained these terms as follows: "*Soger* (soldier) is the worst term of reproach that can be applied to a sailor. It signifies a *skulk*, a shirk—one who is always trying to get clear of work, and is out of the way, or hanging back, when duty is to be done. 'Marine' is the term applied more particularly to a man who is ignorant and clumsy about seamen's work,—a greenhorn, a land-lubber" (1: 128 n.).

27. Martin Lewis, discharged from the *Ianthe*, replaced Charles Cotton, Jr., as second

mate of the *Ronaldson* while the ship was at Whampoa ("Crew of the Ronaldson"; FLO to Parents, Nov. 20, 1843).

28. Nicholas Donnally, from Belfast, Ireland, who was about twenty years old ("Crew of the Ronaldson"; [F. L. Olmsted], "A Voice from the Sea," pp. 531–32).

29. Daniel O'Connell (1775–1847), Irish political leader devoted to the repeal of the union of Great Britain and Ireland and to the reform of the Irish government (*DNB*).

30. The term *fanqui* or *fan-kwai*, meaning foreign devils," was applied by the Chinese to foreigners (Samuel W. Williams, *The Middle Kingdom: A Survey of the Geography, Government, Literature, Social Life, Arts and History of the Chinese Empire and Its Inhabitants*, 2 vols. [New York, 1833], 1: xiv; C. Toogood Downing, *The Fan-Qui in China in 1836–7* [London, 1838], p. v).

31. The ship's carpenter.

32. Samuel B. Beresford (1806–1873), Hartford physician, born in Dutch Guiana, who had studied at the University of Edinburgh and was a member of the Royal College of Surgeons, London (*Hartford County*, 1: 144).

33. What Olmsted in fact must have seen was a common practice of Chinese barbers: turning over a customer's eyelids and clearing them of any mucus lodged on the inner surface (S. W. Williams, *The Middle Kingdom*, 2: 129).

34. Located on Main Street, Hartford (*Hartford County*, 1: 336).

35. "Old Davis" was probably the "oldest and best man" of the crew, who, according to Olmsted, stopped the near-mutiny on the *Ronaldson*'s return voyage. No man named Davis appears in the official list of the crew. Perhaps the man known as "Old Davis" was Edward Omer of Pennsylvania, age forty-nine, the oldest member of the crew by nine years ([F. L. Olmsted], "A Voice from the Sea," pp. 528–29; "Crew of the Ronaldson").

36. Charles Loring Brace, William Peet (1822–1895), and John Wheeler Harding (1821–1896), all students at Yale College at this time (*Yale Obit. Rec.*, 4th ser., no. 6 [June 1896]: 380).

37. Students at Washington College, Hartford: Francis Joseph Clerc (c. 1817–1907), class of 1843; Oliver Dudley Cooke (c. 1822–1895), class of 1844; and William Upson Colt (c. 1824–1848), also of the class of 1844 (*Hartford County*, 1: 440; Trinity College, *Catalogues Senatus Academici Collegii Sanctissimae Trinitatis Harfordiae . . .* , 6 vols. [Hartford, 1872–1900], vol. 1890: 37–38).

38. Mrs. D. A. Howard and Peter Morton (see FLO to JHO, April 8, 1843, notes 4 and 5, above).

To Parents

Address: Per Ship Lucas[1]/John Olmsted Esq./Hartford/Conn/U.S.
Postmark: New York/Ship/Mar./19

Whampoa Nov. 20th. [1843]

Dear Parents,

You must have been much disappointed at not hearing from us by the Ann McKim (In fact, all my letters have been such mere apologies that I have been ashamed to send them), but I have a very good reason for it, as for the last three weeks I have been confined to my bunk with Typhus Fever, which has had a most debilitating effect on me. For two weeks I eat nothing, but now I have appetite enough to eat a bowl of weak soup. I am getting better, having little or no fever.

The last time I had the pleasure of hearing from you was I think October 20th when I received a most welcome parcel of letters and papers, dated June 1st, which probably came by the Zenobia, owned by Gordon & Talbot. I wrote last by the Mary Chilton.[2] Oh! Aunt Maria, Oh! Johnny, Fanny, Mary & Bertha,[3] how I grieve that I cannot answer your invaluable letters. I feel guilty, but if you could have seen me in this Work House you would pardon me. However, in a few weeks after you have read this I hope you will need no letters from me. Oh! Aunt Maria, to be sick in a ship's forecastle is the extent of human misery.

Our Second Mate left us more than a month since, and this week a deaf Dutchman, for four years a mate, and now discharged from the Ianthe[4] because he had no command over the men, has taken his place.

James[5] was, unfortunately, severely ill at the same time with me, which made it much worse for both of us, particularly for me. He has however recovered, and will be able to resume his work tomorrow. At the time, our three best men were sick, and one of them nearly died, so that at one time, his pulse could not be felt. Besides, the steward is sick and pretends to be crazy. The Captain of course sent him to the forecastle (where he has no more right to be than the livestock) where he keeps all hands awake all night.[6]

And the boys have been turned out of a house, which we were miserable in, the passage out, and crammed in the Forecastle, where there was hardly room for the men. And I am indebted for a place to lay in, and he has to sleep on deck. The fact is we are moored in the most unhealthy place in the river and the Captain says he would not come up here again, if he should come to Canton forty times. We've had a dozen American ships close around us. Two or three have dropped down, and we probably would do the same, if we were not going away so soon.

The Captain accidentally discovered I could pull an oar, so I made one short visit to Canton. But I had little more time than sufficed to make a most agreeable call on Dr. Parker, where I had the pleasure also of meeting his young and beautiful wife (late Miss Webster of Washington).[7] I made no purchases at all. In fact, it is considered that most all their knick-knacks can be obtained as cheap or cheaper in New York, especially since the fire, as most of the business part of the city is destroyed, which has advanced the price of everything. But some kind of thin clothes are much cheaper. I have got nothing of the kind but a pair of bright brown grass cloth pants, which I purchased to call on Dr. Parker.

This you will probably get by the Lucas which has been here but about a week. However she is chartered by our owners, Gordon & Talbot, and we can get no cargo until she is full. If she had not come we should probably have been off. She sails next Tuesday the 22nd[8] and then we can complete our cargo in a few days. And as we are all tarred and painted we will be after her in a week. We give her (our barque) four months home. I don't think we will be longer than that unless we lose some of our spars or meet with some accident. And we *ought* to have a shorter passage.

Will you be kind enough to send down my coat and "Old Grey" immediately on receipt of this to Mr. Morton, requesting him to keep them at his store. I can expect no more letters from you, for if a ship arrives we do not get them under a week. After all, we may not sail as soon, but that is the probability. The *Talbot* and *Splendid*[9] will sail, and likely other ships in two weeks, so it will be carry on, to get home first. I hope you have saved the paper containing the account of the fire in Canton, as I should like to see the account of it.[10] Ours and the Ann McKim boat were the first that arrived (about 1 o'clock A.M.).

I wish to finish myself, James having been kind enough to write the above after me.

My dearest love to you all. I am sorry I could obtain no presents at all, but I have had no opportunity.

Homeward bound! The prospects are favorable—except that some of the stores are in a *rather* poor condition & the water will not be as good as coming out. Otherwise, I think we shall have a pleasanter time than coming out.

Don't think because of my writing that I am very sick. It's only weakness & a trembling hand.

God grant that we have a good passage & that I find you all well. Poor Ada,[11] I shall bring her some candy, if she has not passed from this world of pain. But I hope I shall find her recovered and able to enjoy the pleasures of the world. Good-bye!

Your affectionate son F. L. Olmsted.

1. Perhaps the 280-ton *Lucas*, built in 1828 at Castine, Maine. She left Canton on November 25, 1843, and arrived in New York on March 18, 1844 (W. A. Fairburn, *Merchant Sail*, 5: 3459; JO Journal, 1836–1846, end papers).
2. The *Mary Chilton* left Canton on October 1 carrying Olmsted's letter of September 24 and arrived in New York on February 13, 1844 (JO Journal, 1836–1846, end papers).
3. Olmsted's aunt Maria Olmsted, his brother, John, his cousin Frances, and his half-sisters Mary and Bertha.
4. Martin Lewis had replaced Charles Cotton, Jr., as second mate ("Crew of the Ronaldson"; see FLO to JHO, Sept. 28, 1843, note 27).
5. James S. Goodwin.
6. During this time of sickness on board, Olmsted witnessed some striking examples of what he later called the *Ronaldson*'s officers' "contemptuous disregard of the common needs of mankind . . . the mockery of a man's most sacred feelings; aggravations of the horrors of death; total neglect and repudiation of all fellow-feeling." In "A Voice from the Sea," he described one of these instances: "One of us, when nearly the whole crew were sick below with the jungle fever, was shrieking so heart-rendingly that I held my ears. An officer called loudly through the scuttle, 'Will you stop that infernal noise?' 'O God! O God!' exclaimed the sufferer. 'God! God!

What good is there in yelling to God? Do you think He'll help you?' 'Oh, let me die, sir; let me die!' 'Well, if it will stop your jaw, die, and be damned!' " (p. 527).
7. Harriet Colby Webster Parker (1818–1896), wife of the medical missionary, Peter Parker, and the first foreign woman permitted to live in Canton (Oak Hill Cemetery Records, Washington, D.C.; George Barker Stevens, *The Life, Letters, and Journals of the Reverend and Honorable Peter Parker* [Boston, 1896], p. 229).
8. The *Lucas* left on Saturday, November 25 (JO Journal, 1836–1846, end papers).
9. The *Talbot* arrived in New York on April 7, 1844. The 473-ton *Splendid*, a Baltimore clipper built in 1832, owned by N. L. and G. Griswold of New York, had left New York on May 26, 1843, after a record run from Canton of 102 days (Record Group 36, Records of the Bureau of Customs; W. A. Fairburn, *Merchant Sail*, 4: 2173; 5: 2746–47; 6: 3690).
10. On the night of October 24, 1843, a great fire swept through Canton, consuming over one thousand houses, the Danish and Spanish hongs, and the British Consulate. At three in the morning American merchant ship crews arrived from Whampoa to help. The fire consumed nearly a square mile of the city before it burned out at the river's edge on the following morning (*New York Daily Tribune*, Feb. 23, 1844, p. 3).
11. Ada Theodosia Olmsted.

To Maria Olmsted   [November 30, 1843]

Address: Miss Maria Olmsted/and/The Misses F, A, B, O & Co.[1]
Care of/John Olmsted Esq./Hartford/Conn./U.S.
by Mary Ellen[2]/Per package, Harden & Co.

Bark *Ronaldson* at anchor, Whampoa,
Thanksgiving day, 1843

Dear Aunt Maria, dear coz. & my dearest sisters,

It's just about the right time of day, & I am imagining you just about well to work on the turkeys & cranberry. Though, in matter [of] fact, you are more likely preparing for Dr. Hawes'[3] *great* yearly discourse. Miss Fan, the *Dido*, British man of war, has just struck four bells—afternoon watch. Can you calculate what time it is where you are?[4] I wonder if you girls are at a side table this year. I suppose Mother has the "boiled & oyster," as usual, while Father performs on the roast & criticizes the dressing. So? as the Frenchman says.

As for me, being yet on the sick list, I luxuriate on broth; while the few well men yet on deck have an hour or two ago helped themselves out of two iron bound wooden tubs to rather dry, tough, but fresh buffalo and *"taro"* (which is a kind of yam—which is a tropical substitute for our excellent potato) eating it without salt, from their tin pans, cutting it with their sheath knives or jack knives (which they are now using with the tar bucket or slush pot in the rigging) & using the forks that nature provided—hardly as white (clean!) as your silver ones. Take care, Bertha. That's a big drum stick, but I guess you'll manage it with one hand.

I hope you *won't* think I've neglected answering your letters—the pleasure of receiving which, you can scarcely imagine—any longer than I could help.

I was obliged to give up my attempt to write you, as above, as I found I was not well enough. It is now about a week later and I am considerably better, but I have to write with caution. For if the mate should see me, he would be very likely to say I was well enough to "turn up," when in fact I am so debilitated that Dr. Green[5] assures me I should be very likely to be laid up with a relapse, which would prove very dangerous. But the mate tells the men they must not mind what the Doctor says, but get to work as soon as they are able. This morning he has hustled a poor fellow out, to work at sennit,[6] (under a bamboo shed, as it rains) who will most certainly have the *"shakes"* this afternoon, as usual. But the old hazer says—"work while you are able."

By the way, it is the same man, that a few weeks ago, was not expected to live fifteen minutes, who made his will (sailor), gave his *real* name, which no body in the ship knew before, his father's direction, &c., &c.—who turned to long before he was able, and in consequence has been laid up again on the sick list, with the fever & ague & other complaints.

A most agreeable circumstance occurred to me last evening. The mate was gone to Canton with a boat's crew, when Dr. Green came on board and invited me to take a sail with him in his sanpan—equivalent to "taking a ride or airing in his sulky." Nothing could give me more pleasure as I had not left the ship for more than a month. But I must not be particular. I'll spin the whole yarn to you one of these days, I hope. I laid down on a mat with a bamboo pillow, & we proceeded to Boston Jack's[7] at Whampoa—this a noted Chinaman who visited Boston in his youth, & has since amassed a fortune as "Compradore" or "provider" of naval stores (to American ships mostly) from a mast, anchor or long boat, to a half dozen of eggs (duck's) or a roll of soft tuck[8] (which I get of one of his clerks or assistants every other morning). On Dr. Green's expressing a wish to see him, he came out from his residence in the rear, into his office. Doctor told I had been sick, &c., &c. & he told me to come in. So I entered & rested myself on a cushioned chair. You must recollect I'm a sailor, swinging in tarry trousers, check shirt, with the lanyard of a jackknife in place of a cravat, monkey jacket, &c.

After resting myself some time I took a short walk with the Doctor & Chinese attendants, in the streets of Whampoa, occasionally entering the shops & stores, & seeing the Chinese in their every day life. Old *gentlemen* of fortune with rich dresses & robes reaching to their feet, their long tails richly interwove with silk cord, little black satin skull caps with bright turk's heads[9] or topknots on the *unshaved* part of their crowns. These "old knobs" we often saluted, which they gravely returned, each repeating *"chin chin,"* which like a great many of their phrases means many things of a similar character—

as "Good evening," as in the present instance, "Good bye," "Thank you," &c. Their sons of every age,—little covies, not much bigger than Mister Albert[10]—strutting about in precisely similar dresses, as gravely as Dr. Cox, or Parson Brace[11] in the "marriage ceremony." However, speak to any [of] 'em big or little, & you find [them] full of fun enough, & they'll joke and laugh from Dan to Beersheba.[12] Ay, & talk all the time as much nonsense as the main to'gallant studding-sail topping lift blocks, that we had stuck aloft without any thing rove through 'em all the way from New York here.

And you "women kind" will be glad to know I had an opportunity of seeing the fashions, for I met three *ladies*. That is as much of ladies I suppose as Whampoa can boast, for the *rale ginuine ladies*—of Hong merchants families, for instance—are never seen in public. But I was glad enough to have an opportunity of seeing 'em hobbling (exactly as if with wooden legs) on their tiny peg tops—what would you call 'em—not feet certainly— about three inches long. The shoes they wear are shaped something like that. If I get well enough to go to Canton, I may possibly get a pair—but I very much fear I shall not be allowed to go up. And if so, I shall come home, with my chest as empty of anything Chinese, as when I left.

If I could afford it I'd get a tail; for they *can* be procured. Some of the crew of the *Congress*[13] had two or three, which they whipped off the thieves they took, with their cutlasses. A sufficient punishment I hope the Mandarins thought it. For our sanpan boy, Jo, says, "Suppose you gi' me vive undret dollar no cut him off, suppose gi' me dis sip—suppose de whole fleet—not cutty him," &c.[14]

But the ladies' head dresses, they would be as great curiosities to you I presume as the men's. They were all bare headed except I suppose a large quantity of what you call "false hair." Why, I saw a wash woman dressing her hair in a sanpan fastened to our quarter, & she had three or four *hanks* yet to be put *on*, & the Lord knows how many she had built on before. But these, had—mercy! as much again as I had ever seen before—say as much as Mr. Stearnes would care about lifting on the big pitch fork. Each of them had a parasol or umbrella—bamboo, I think they are. I mean to get one of them, too, if I can, and a Chinese gentleman's straw hat. The rest of their dress was plain enough: Nankeen I think—loose gown kind of jacket, *long*, & trousers—blue. But law! if I ran after the women in this style I shall get in a scrape & no mistake. Never get where I started for, at any rate.

But I must mention one thing more before I go back to Boston's. Now *gals*—I was looking into the doors to see a good interesting place to sit down at, for I wanted to rest every half minute. Passing a half open door, I thought the noise inside, which was low, sounded sort o' kind o' natural, as if it was familiar to me at sometime. A moment's thought & I had it. I feared to intrude (I fear a *native* would not believe *it*).

"Sam," to the attending Fuckee. "This China (*chiny*) school—make learn, Eh? Catchy read?" (That's the way Fanquis talk to the common people or generally to all.)

"Ya (yes). Suppose & want ya—can go." (If you wish you can enter.)

So opening the door, we entered. It was a long room, not very light. The pupils generally were standing up, though there were a few desks, with books on them. I suspect they study at home mostly, as I met some boys afterwards in different places with books, who I think were going to recite. The boys all stared & generally laughed as I came in, and some young rascals [said] in a low tone "Fanqui!" I suppose the master half rose & bowed to me, but coming in from the open street, I did not perceive him at first.

At any rate, the little fellow before him never once looked up or altered his tone as he followed the letters on his book (with his young nails some half inch long). He read with a kind of singsong—first high & then low—about two pages; closed his hornbook; about face, & was trotting off without taking the least notice of me, when I took the liberty of stopping him by catching hold of his tail (about eighteen inches long). He whipped round and laughed in my face! However, I gave him a bit of Mandarin cake (which I had bought for Jack[15] on board) (composed, they say, of rice flour, sugar & dry lard—very delicate & nice they are, too) for saying his lesson so perfectly. He chin chin'd me & went about his business.

I looked at the "boss," who bowed & smiled. He was about forty years old, I think, & looked very sedate. Before I turned, though, there was another young Celestial singing away as before. On the desk, there was a earthen vase, with brushes (pens), &c. and a *large rattan* split a dozen times half down. I took it out. All the boys laughed and the old man, too, for that matter. He took & laid it over one of them—two or three coming up for him to show us what it was for—not hard, of course.

But enough of the school. Returning with the Doctor, I looked at some pickles in what appeared a mere huckster's shop, but which proved to be a very extensive preserve factory & storehouse, having a salesroom in Canton. I passed through half a dozen rooms, in which men were at work chopping all sorts of vegetables, &c, or which were filled with chests, cases and jars of sweetmeats, &c. & a yard as large as the "orchard" full of jars, the size of a half barrel, containing "soy," a fish & soup sauce; I presume, as the jars were uncovered, not yet completed. I tasted his ginger, (the doctor would not allow me to eat a plateful that was handed me,) as sample. It was far superior to anything of the kind I ever saw before: extremely delicate & rich, and a beautiful color. I should have taken a small 50 cent jar then, but he refused to take (copper) mace,—cash—which was all I could offer, wanting silver. A case of four jars, he asked three dollars for.

But at this rate I shall never get you back to "Misser Boston's" which the Doctor & I did about sunset. Outside were three young buffaloes, the number he has killed every night, to supply the ships next day. We found Jack at tea with his partners—two—on the platform by the waterside, in front of the store. On the table were various dishes of vegetables, or rather of "greens," two of lobsters, and crabs, shrimp, and the invariable large dish of rice, probably curried, stood near at hand. There was *soy*, too, which Boston said they had eaten with their soup.

Apparently they had been engaged some time, and were now enjoying their tea, wines, and liqueurs, of which there were several choice kinds on the board, such as sherry in a beautiful cut glass, short octagonal perfume bottle, Cherry brandy in a queer old fashioned Dutch concern, with a copper plate and a jaw-breaking name of the maker on one of the sides, three or four wines and French liqueurs—London porter, &c. while the old boy smuggled "Samshew" (a wretched fiery Chinese spirit, which has killed more English soldiers than any of their weapons) out of a tea pot, drinking from a cup the size of a large thimble.

Some of these, however, were unnecessarily brought on for our special benefit—I mean the Doctor's—though I was soon invited to a seat at the "board" where I had an opportunity of enjoying the best supper of cold ham, excellent eggs, bread, &c. and such capital tea, with loaf sugar, (such a contrast to our shushong with molasses).[16] I was soon on intimate terms with our polite entertainers, and was induced by their gentlemanly and complaisant manner, imperceptibly to drop the fo'c'stle. All that I've been writing, dear Aunty, will have been but the shell to you. Now "stand by" for the "meat."

"Mr. Boston," says I, "do you happen to remember many years since, an American Captain by the name of 'Olmsted?' "[17]

"Humstet?—no—I no. . . ."

"Ha!" interrupted one of his partners, an old man sitting next to me; "*Me sabé* (know—Portuguese) him. No come here, long time—twenty year, more. S'ip 'untress[18]—I think—he come."

"Yes sir! Yes sir. That's him. I am very glad you recollect him."

" 'hem! You *sabe* him?"

"I have the honour of being his nephew."

"Eh?"

"He my uncle—you sabe? My father's uncle."

"Me sabe! Me sabe!"

"I sabe him children[19] you know."

"Ah! he no come long time. Suppose him catchee die."

"Yes—long time since—before I was born." And quite a conversation, very much as above, ensued. (I have endeavoured to follow as much as possible the words we used, to show you a specimen of the Anglo, Macao (Portuguese) Chinese always used here.)

I suppose, I rose very much in their opinion, when they found I was

AARON OLMSTED

"connected," (as Boston expressed it) with a rich and honourable *captain*.
The old man enquired about his family, &c., with apparently much interest, &
you may be sure I was not backward in satisfying him. I told him they would
be glad to hear from their father's old acquaintance, which appeared to please
him very much. If I am not mistaken, he was his boat attendant or "sanpan."
And it is customary if a captain once has a man, he is pleased with, for him
to obtain his services for successive years, if he is not engaged.

About this time it threatened to rain. A large close awning was
spread and lights brought on—Chinese candles about the size of your little
finger of wax with stems, so they stood three or four inches above the candle-
sticks (after the Fanqui fashions). Before we left, the doctor called for a
glass of water. An attendant, of which perhaps twenty stood near us, brought
two. But our hosts would by no means allow me to drink it, as it would not
do for my stomach, recommending me to drink cherry brandy or tea instead.

178

They were undoubtedly right as this river water, unless it has been a long time "settling," produces violent dysentery &c.

I don't suppose I have drunk a half a pint for a month past. But *tea*, Lord bless you! morning & night. It's a caution to Dr. Alcott to say nothing of Dr. Taft[20] (to whom my best respects). Gracious! but you ought to see these "China-men." When the ginseng[21] merchants were aboard of us, they had some thirty or forty coolies employed along our decks, sifting it, sorting it, &c. Then there were two hands who did nothing else but bring up large waiters of tea from their boats & pass it around to them. I don't recollect whether it was another one or not that kept them supplied with little paper cheroots. But their masters on the poop had I think each one a pipe bearer, who also managed the tea cup performance. The gang of stevedores, too, in heaving out our bale goods, had a tub of tea standing at hand, and every few minutes would file off and bale it out, having one man whose business it was to keep it ready for them! There's one ship near us, that I am told allows the men to drink no water, but furnishes her men with tea—hot from the coppers —four or five times a day.

So the youngster eats more than John and I both, eh? Aunty— perhaps you'd think Fred would do better than all three, if you could have seen him sometimes last July putting down the salt—Oh! I have it—"*junk*" and hard tack.[22] How many slices of *bread* (how my mouth waters, when I think of Mrs. Kelley's *soft* bread)[23] would you think he'd be likely to eat in a bowl of milk, if you could see him devouring a couple of (mouldy) "iron-bound sea cakes" soaked in a quart of tea dashed with 'lasses? And then "retiring" on the (so-called) "*beef*" kid,[24] to get well ballasted, for a four hour's—I don't know what to call it;—sleep won't do—for "lubbers, along shore," pretend to sleep—say, four hour's—"below"—"bunked in"—that "overhauls fair"—or a two hour's "bright lookout there for'a'd!" ("bright lookout it is, sir!") and a caulk under the lee of the long boat;[25] unless interrupted by "Clew up fore & main r'yal!—lay aloft you b'ys & furl 'em"— or, "You, Frederick! Up there and unbecket the main skysail"—or—"Haul down that starb'd main-to'gallant stud'n sail.—Into the top & roll it up one of you boys. Send the gear down on deck, & rig in the boom!" or some such agreeable intelligence from the Mr. "Cock of the walk" on the weather side of the poop.

And you've nobody to "*taze* ye, have ye." Faith! Wait a day (or a month or two for that matter perhaps) and if that's what bothers ye (as appears by your letter), nevar belave me, if I don't aze yer mind of it.

(Postscript)-No. 3. To Miss Maria Olmsted & Co. 34 Ann St.

Remember me with respects to Coz Charles and Mr. Ayres.[26] I regret he does not succeed better with his school. I am sure he must deserve to.

We have had some five or six days of severe storm. As our "Re-pealer"[27] says, "Och! It don't rain then? Faith! It's for want of time to pour." The to'gallant forecastle deck not having the usual "wetting down" has leaked a good deal. In truth, the cook and one man have been *flooded* out of the berths. Fortunately, Chips[28] had just the new "boys' house" finished, and two of them "moved in" that night. Next morning, Jake,[29] one of them, was found sick; the house leaking considerably. I have since been much troubled by sundry aches and pains in head, back, ears, neck, chest, stomach, thighs, groin, legs, knees, ankles, arms, &c., resulting probably from two *trickles* of water, which would have been much more acceptable when we were at sea.

However, we were all enlivened yesterday (Sunday) the 17th by the arrival of a "chop" with some cassia which the Stephen Lurman could not take, and a letter informing the mate that the teas would be coming down immediately. And, as the Doctor says, we may sail, the latter part of the week. The Lurman hove up to drop below to the 2nd bar this morning—but a remarkably fair wind having since arisen, it is not improbable she may have sailed immediately to get down the river. In which case I shall send by the *Mary Ellen* bound for New York, to sail tomorrow. Other ships will probably be leaving all the week, by one of which John & perhaps Father may expect to hear from me. If we get away before New Year's day, you may expect to hear considerable louder from me, perhaps by May Day. That, after all, I may put off to first of June as you did last year.

It was pretty cold, certainly, for a week after we left, but I did not suffer much, having a powerful Homeopathic remedy. Except the first day, be-fore I could get out thick clothes from the "Combin," which as happens Chips was employed all Sunday razeeing.[30] He swears that the maker was either out of work or was in debt to "y'r old man," and wanted to make a "high" job of it; that he owned a share in a nail factory & was creditor to a hardware dealer. He has already recovered eighty screws, & expects some days more work on it: cutting it down one half—as the Captain advised him to "throw the lumber overboard."

My kind friend, Jim, became pretty well acquainted with you while I was seasick. He begs to be mentioned with his compliments to you—whose name, by the way, he says he always associates with ginger nuts. You'll hardly believe that I eat many of them 4th July—and a few left nearly a month after—though partly injured by salt water, which penetrated my chest at last, with some damage to sundry articles.

I don't think, girls, you could write with much pains, or be as successful as you [were] in what you wrote me, if your light came from a window 6 inches long and another the space of an auger hole; three men shaking their sides with laughter at a good yarn or joke. This with brandy [. . .], "to be well-shaken," being their only remedy for the shakes, with which

180

each expects to be attacked during next 24 hours; as their shipmate in the lower bunk there is fairly making the bowsprit appear a divining rod. Then your ink must have the interesting property of coming out of the pen a beautiful white—& not tarnishing for some time. I meant to have said more & talked about the fruit, my "[. . .] little cabin," the new horse—but apologizing for shortness of letter & sending, instead, therefore, *love*, I remain "Freddy."

1. Olmsted's aunt Maria Olmsted, his fourteen-year-old cousin Frances, and his half-sisters: four-year-old Ada and eight-year-old Bertha.
2. The *Mary Ellen* had left New York on May 31, 1843; she arrived back in New York on April 8, 1844 (Record Group 36, Records of the Bureau of Customs).
3. Joel Hawes.
4. At four bells, or 2:00 P.M., in Whampoa on Thanksgiving Day, November 30, 1843, it was 1:00 A.M. on the previous day in Hartford. On Thanksgiving Day in Hartford, the day after Olmsted wrote this letter, his father noted in his journal, "Fred's company much wanted"—one of his few expressions of personal feeling in thirty-seven years of journal-keeping (*New York Daily Tribune*, Feb. 23, 1844, p. 3; JO Journal, Nov. 30, 1843).
5. John P. Green of New York (see FLO to Parents, Aug. 6, 1843, note 5).
6. Sennit is "flat cordage, formed by plaiting rope-yarns or thread together." When there was no other work to do, sailors were put to work weaving hats from sennit of grass (*A Naval Encyclopedia*, [Philadelphia, 1881]).
7. "Boston Jack" was the favorite Whampoa compradore of American sea captains. He was one of the few Chinese who had visited the United States, having once made a passage to Boston as a ship's steward. He returned to Whampoa on the 200-ton schooner *Cossack*, whose supercargo was Oliver H. Gordon, later a partner in the firm of Gordon and Talbot, which owned the *Ronaldson* (William C. Hunter, *The 'Fan-Kwae' at Canton Before Treaty Days, 1825–1844* [London, 1882], p. 63; information on Gordon and Talbot supplied by Emily P. H. Talbot).
8. A term for sweet foods, especially pastry, jam, or candy.
9. An ornamental knot, resembling a turban in appearance.
10. Olmsted's one-year-old half-brother.
11. Arthur C. Coxe (1818–1896), at this time rector of St. John's Church (Episcopal) in Hartford; and Joab Brace, whose school in Newington, Conn., Olmsted attended from 1831 to 1836 (*DAB*, s.v. "Coxe, Arthur Cleveland").
12. An expression taken from Judges 20:1, meaning from one extreme to the other; as Dan was the northernmost city in ancient Israel, and Beersheba the southernmost.
13. The *Congress* was a 376-ton ship built in 1831 for E. K. Collins of New York (W. A. Fairburn, *Merchant Sail*, 5: 2790).
14. In the early seventeenth century the Manchus imposed their own hair style, the queue, on Chinese men in regions under their control as a sign of allegiance. By the nineteenth century what had first been compulsory had become traditional. An American resident in China during the 1840s testified that "The people are vain of a long thick queue . . . nothing irritates them more than to cut it off" (S. W. Williams, *The Middle Kingdom*, 1: 761–62).
15. Jacob T. Braisted.
16. The concoction of tea and molasses that the crew of the *Ronaldson* drank was probably similar to that described by Dana in *Two Years Before the Mast*: "The proportions of ingredients of the tea that was made for us, (and ours, as I have before stated, was a favorable specimen of American merchantmen) were, a pint of tea, and a pint and a half of molasses, to about three gallons of water. These are all boiled down together in the "coppers," and before serving it out, the mess is stirred

up with a stick, so as to give each man his fair share of sweetening and tea-leaves."
(2: 296 n)
17. Aaron Olmsted, Olmsted's great-uncle, who was one of the first Americans to go
    into the China trade as captain of his own ship (*Olmsted Genealogy*, pp. 36, 442).
18. Perhaps the 270-ton full-rigged ship *Huntress*, built between 1800 and 1804 in
    Newcastle, Maine (W. A. Fairburn, *Merchant Sail*, 5: 3357).
19. Of Aaron Olmsted's children, Olmsted knew best Charles Hyde Olmsted, who had
    encouraged him in his scientific interests (see Autobiographical Fragment B, note
    7, below).
20. William A. Alcott (1798–1859) educational and dietary reformer, and Gustavus
    M. Taft (1820–1847), the Olmsted family's homeopathic doctor. In his book *Tea
    and Coffee*, Alcott argued that tea is a narcotic and poison, and supported his views
    with numerous instances of its debilitating effect on the human system and its
    deadly effect, in concentrated doses, on birds and animals (*DAB*, s.v. "Alcott, Wil-
    liam Andrus"; *Tea and Coffee* . . . [Boston, 1839]).
21. An aromatic root found in North America as well as in China. Because it was
    prized by the Chinese as a medicine it was imported to China by American ships
    and sold for return cargoes of tea and Chinese goods (Kenneth Scott Latourette,
    *The History of Early Relations between the United States and China, 1784–
    1844* [New Haven, 1917], pp. 10, 14, 27, 29, 73).
22. Junk is salt beef; hardtack is bread or biscuit made of flour and baked without salt.
23. Mary A. Kelly, the Olmsteds' cook.
24. A wooden tub holding salt beef from which the sailors served themselves (*Naval
    Encyclopedia*).
25. That is, Olmsted suppered on hard, stale sea-biscuit and salt beef in order to get
    sustenance for one of two things, depending on the timing of his watch: either four
    hours of inadequate rest in a bunk below, or four hours of watch divided into two
    hours of keeping "bright lookout" and two hours of uncomfortable rest on deck. A
    "caulk under the lee of the longboat" meant catching a bit of rest while on watch,
    usually without the approval of the officers. Under the longboat, for instance, was
    the spot that Richard Henry Dana's watchmate chose to spend the first watch he
    stood on the *Pilgrim* while still at anchor in Boston harbor (*Two Years Before the
    Mast*, 1: 6).
26. Charles Hyde Olmsted and William Orville Ayres, both members of the Natural
    History Society of Hartford.
27. Nicholas Donnally.
28. The ship's carpenter.
29. Jacob T. Braisted.
30. Perhaps a storage locker that the ship's carpenter was cutting down.

To John Olmsted

Address: John Olmsted Esq./Hartford/Conn./U.S.
         Per Ship Talbot[1]
Postmark: New York/Ship/Apr. 7

Ronaldson Whampoa December 5th 1843
Dear Father,
        I wrote you by the *Lucas*[2] which sailed some ten days since. We
were then expecting to sail last week: but orders having been received for us
to take Green teas, we are detained. How long?

"Perhaps a week—perhaps a month," *Captain Fox.*

"Say two or three weeks," (*F.L.O.*)

"Sooner the better," (*all hands.*)

The internal navigation is interrupted to a great degree by drought, low water, so the teas don't come down. Meantime the old Hong merchants hold up for enormous prices. So there you have it.

I have had a bad time the last week, hardly able to hold up my head—owing to constipation (same illness you understand). As Dr. Green dislikes unnecessary purgatives as much as I do, tried to get along without them using syringe, &c., but yesterday obliged to resort to medicine, & this P.M. much relieved by it. But hardly able to sit up long enough to scrawl off as quick as possible, as I get sick, if long out of a lying posture. I now anticipate a speedy recovery.

All the boys are now down, & two men, but none seriously ill: (that is very.)

Steward of English ship arrived yesterday says they have eleven hands on sick list.

Probably several ships sail now before us. [I will] write more at length, & I hope to Aunt Maria, John, Fanny, & the children, or some at least.

I am getting the nausea & must turn in. I know sickness will excuse everything & the ship sails to-morrow morning. With all love,

Your affectionate son,

F. L. Olmsted

1. The *Talbot* sailed with this letter sometime after September 25, 1843, and arrived in New York on April 7, 1844 (see postscript to FLO to Parents, Sept. 5, 1843, above).
2. See FLO to JO, Nov. 20, 1843, note 1, above.

To John Olmsted

Address: Mr. John Olmsted/Hartford/Conn.
Postmark: Ship/New-York/Apr 20.
    Per *Natchez*[1]

Ronaldson, Whampoa Reach,
December 27th 1843

Dear Father,

I had given up my intention as expressed in my letter to Aunt Maria & the girls, of writing you, as it appeared there was nothing to sail before us. But yesterday, very unexpectedly, I went to Canton, passenger in the boat as "liberty man," & most rejoiced I was to hear from [you] again before we left, in a letter I obtained there (date June 11th—18th), & this morning the Doctor informs me the *Helena*[2] will get under weigh tonight. How long she may stay at Macao I can't say. But even if we get to sea before her, which is not likely at all, I doubt not you may receive this some weeks before we arrive as she is one of the crack ones, & made a most remarkable passage out, 'round the "Horn."

Your last previously by *Zenobia* received October 21st. We expect our last chop of tea tomorrow & shall probably sail Saturday, to anchor some four miles off Macao for a day or two. And then Hurrah for blue water, & if ever a poor beshaken & befevered set of fellows could send home their topsails nimbly, we shall, for everyone thinks that he shall recover his strength & spirits & be somewhat less certain of being on the sick list in course of a week.

I enclose the "finale" of John's letter.[3] I meant to have written you a caution to read what you pleased loud to the family, &c., as I presume you did. I wanted to give you an idea of the altered manners of our mate. By the way, I have to complain of no personal ill treatment. The only punishment—besides "working up"[4] which is going on with some body all the time—I have had, has been being kept up part of my watch, or at work during part of dinner hour, or something of that kind. The other boys have been each ropes' ended; one "at the wheel" (particularly forbidden by law) pretty severely. I have no fear of its happening, that's more. But I get my full share of *abuse*, which is unavoidable by any course of conduct. Our stores are not in the best condition: sour flour, sour meal (sour "mush,") the beans have a confounded queer taste, not the most desirable—which is *too* bad—for a pan of baked beans by favor of the cook—saved from the "sodiment" as our mate would say of the soup—used to be the best thing I could get in the ship. Nobody complains of the beef, salt, but when it was taken from the coppers it would almost bring tears to my eyes at twelve feet distance. Yet all hands are growling because the Captain has stopped it entirely—because we [have] but just enough to last home—& "will be glad when we get to sea & rid of this _____ fresh buffalo beef." After all, don't think we are going to suffer. I anticipate a pretty comfortable & pleasant passage. Coming out when not sick I was happy enough, half the time enjoyed myself, I presume, better than anybody aboard.

We had a fine warm day yesterday, though I had hardly more time than before, as in going up we had such a strong tide against us that we did not get there till afternoon. After we had got dinner, some went one way & some another. Some soon found the second mate after them, who told them to look for the others & send them down to the boat; others soon got the same message. I for one took care to look for myself & made some purchases. We managed to humbug about "looking for" each other for some hours & did

[not] get away much before night—having the tide against us again. I enjoyed it very much, & got besides a Mandarin (everything is Mandarin that's peculiar to China & want[ed] to be sold I suppose) cap, sword (1st chop), knife, chop-sticks, [. . .] a few etceteras.

Confoundedly tired, a headache & the slightest degree sick—which will account for the excessive dullness of this letter, the whole of which I believe only informs you of my returning health & strength & the prospect of our soon being on our way home. Home! home!! The thought of seeing you once more—Oh my, I can't sit still, to think of it.

Poor Jim, he turned to[5] again yesterday morning, & when I returned from town, I found him back with a fever. Today he feels pretty well again, but has a slight dysentery. Since his first severe illness in which for a short time he was very low, he, like every one else, has had a constant succession of attacks, only his have come oftener & lasted longer. One week at sea and we shall all be as well as ever—so he says—& I think he's right.

We have now but five sick; one turned to this morning & probably one or two will to-morrow.

Well—there will be one advantage in our having remained so late— we avoid a winter coast, a sailor's dread when coming from warm climates.

Give her four months, and begin first January.

The overland arrived yesterday I hear & news, the mate said, was unfavorable—but to what I don't know.

Here it is again, "Knock-off!" I do hate the finishing of a letter. You all know there, how I love you, well then have a kissing match all round & tell each other Fred sent it.

1. The 523-ton *Natchez* was built in 1831 as a New Orleans sailing packet and was owned at this time by Howland and Aspinwall of New York. Robert H. Waterman was her master. The postmark on this letter indicates that Olmsted got back to New York from China five days ahead of the *Natchez* and the letter (W. A. Fairburn, *Merchant Sail*, 6: 3603, 3659; JO Journal, April 15, 1844).
2. The *Helena* was a ship of 598 tons built in 1841 for N. L. and G. Griswold of New York. She was one of the first really fast clipper ships. She left Canton on December 31, 1843, and arrived in New York on April 5, 1844 (W. A. Fairburn, *Merchant Sail*, 2: 1503; 6: 3691; JO Journal, 1836–1846, end papers).
3. Presumably the "2nd P.S. to a letter dated Whampoa Reach, Dec. 10th, 1843, to John Hull Olmsted" included here at the end of FLO to JHO, Sept. 28, 1843, above.
4. *Working up* was "keeping men at work on needless matters, beyond the usual hours, for punishment" (W. H. Smyth, *Sailor's Word-Book*).
5. To *turn to* is to return to work.

AMERICAN BARK OFF THE CHINA COAST

THE REAL CHINA[1]

In early life I once lived for four months on a vessel lying at anchor near the mouth of the Great South river of China. The Opium War had just ended and British frigates which had brought desolation and more bitter poverty to many a poor household on its banks were moored near us. It was naturally to be supposed that the traditional antipathy of the people to foreigners had been greatly exasperated, and when we first began to go on shore we were cautioned that we could not be too careful to avoid offending the prejudices of those we might meet, not to go far from our boats and to keep together for common defence in case of necessity. It was said that some English merchant seamen had been roughly handled and that one who had strayed away and not reappeared was supposed to have been murdered.

From the first, however, such warnings were little regarded by most of my shipmates, some of whom were rough and reckless men such as sober quiet people anywhere in the world are shy of. Some too would at times be a little the worse for liquor, heedless, boisterous and quarrelsome.

Once a man in this condition lurched against a woman who was carrying a child in one arm and an earthen jar in the other, striking her with his elbow in that to save herself from falling she had to drop the jar. As I saw the jar fall I thought that he had knocked it out of her hand and it looked as if he might have struck her. There was a little outcry and something like a mob at once gathered about us, looking at us menacingly, but the woman apparently explained that she thought there had been no wrong intention, the rest of us expressed our regret, and in a few moments there was a general bowing and smiling and a way was opened for us to go on.

As a rule at all the villages and even at lone farm houses where the people had been accustomed to see foreigners we were allowed to wander freely and were treated with a degree of civility that in view of all the circumstances seems to me now quite wonderful.

If I had been a full blown admiral in a "brass coat" greater respect could hardly have been paid to me. I was in fact a very insignificant working man in my shirt sleeves. I am not sure that I was not barefooted and I much doubt if my hands were free from the slush and tar of the rigging in the repair of which I had just before been engaged.

On another occasion I boarded an armed Chinese vessel, said to be the floating quarters of a Mandarin or high officer, and met with even warmer hospitality, dishes of stewed meat, rice, fruit and a little cup of spirits being set before me as well as tea and tobacco.

Once, when on shore, hearing a hum like that of an infant school, I looked in at the window of the house from which it came and saw an elderly man with great spectacles teaching about twenty little boys. As soon as he observed me, he laid down his book, came forward and throwing open a door invited me to enter and then proceeded with great cleverness by gesture and example to show me how he taught the boys to read.[2]

Once when we were fatigued and dry while one of these little mobs was hanging upon and jeering us we saw a boy who was carrying a pot of water. By motions we made him understand that we would pay for a drink from it. After a little while a bolder boy took the pot and bringing it near to us, set it upon the ground and with a laugh ran away. After we had satisfied ourselves we laid some "cash" by the side of it and drew back, whereupon the same boy, a ragged, half starved Chinese hoodlum, took the jar and kicked the money toward us, laughing again and shaking his head.

We had a man known as Sam attached to our ship while she lay in the river who ran errands with a small shore boat for the Captain, acted as an interpreter, and made himself useful in any way he could either in the cabin or on deck. He was a willing and skilful servant and the Captain tried to engage him to go to America with us. At last our steward falling ill, the Captain offered him very high wages, double as much as he had proposed to pay at first. Sam persistently declined and told me if the Captain doubled his offer again he would not go. I remonstrated with him for we would all have liked him as a shipmate, when he explained that he was the only son of an aged man and that it would therefore be infamous for him to go away from home. If his father did not need his care he would have jumped at the Captain's offer.

I had made a friendly acquaintance with a merchant's clerk by giving him some lessons in the English alphabet. Shortly before we went to sea he came on board and remarked to me that when Chinamen ventured upon the ocean they set up Joss in their cabin before which from time to time they set cups of tea and burned joss sticks and paper prayers.[3] He did not see any Joss in our cabin and he asked me if I would not be more comfortable when a great storm arose if such a recognition of our dependence upon the good will of a Superior Being has been observed? It was a simple friendly inquiry made in a perfectly well-bred way.

Following some other sailors at a little distance I once entered a building which, though no idols were to be seen, I took to be a place of worship of some sort. It was dark and overhead and in recesses on the right and left rafters, wainscot and tile were to be dimly made out through a thin veil of smoke. A table or altar stood opposite the door upon which joss sticks were burning. There were numerous inscriptions on the walls and on paper and silk lanthorns, banners and tags hung from them and from the ceiling. There were also several quaint bells and gongs. The sailors had made their way through a little crowd of Chinese who stood before the altar and some of them had gone behind it and were lifting the banners and shaking the lanthorns. Others were striking the bells and gongs with their fists and knives. As I stood peering in at the door and gradually making out what I have described, a sailor called out to me with an oath: "What are you keeping your hat off for in a heathen temple?"

Presently, as my eyes became accustomed to the gloom, I saw an old gentleman observing me from a side door. As our eyes met he bowed and directly came forward and beckoning me to follow him, led the way into a little room where there were piles of books and manuscripts. He laid open one of them which appeared very ancient, and showed me that it contained plans of the building and tried in a gentle, patient way to make me understand something of its origin and purposes. He could use a very few words of Pigion English, and, rightly or wrongly, I made out that the object of the structure was to keep the memory green & preserve the sayings of some good men who lived many generations ago. Afterwards the old gentleman took me through the main room calling my attention to the decorations of the bells and other things which he thought admirable and when I left he gave me several printed papers which I presumed to be religious tracts.

It was only when we pulled up some of the creeks or bayous to a distance from the fleet, where the people had had no direct dealing with foreigners and knew them only as rapacious enemies, that we met with anything but kindness and hospitality. These were holiday excursions. Leaving our boat in charge of a hand or two, we would be making our way along the dykes of the rice fields toward a pagoda, burial ground or village when we would hear a shrill cry, soon repeated by other voices, and presently see boys running together and shouting in concert a phrase which it was understood among us was equivalent to "Here come the heathen!" It seemed to be a make-believe rather than a real alarm. People nearby would look up as they heard the cry and regard us curiously. Idlers perhaps would smile, women would pick up their children and draw back out of our way, but nobody stopped work or looked at all threateningly except the vagabondish boys and they seemed more disposed to make fun of us than to injure or repel us. Sometimes as these gained boldness with numbers they would get behind us and menace us with brick-bats and pelt us a little with balls of mud. But though we heard that some other sailors had been driven into a miry place out of which they escaped with difficulty, I doubt if it had not been after some aggravated provocation.

We roved wherever inclination led us, hardly ever saying by your leave but taking that for granted, much as I have since seen a band of saucy Comanches do in a Mexican border village. Thus we made our way, often interrupting men and women at their work, into shops and factories, boat builders' yards and potteries, gardens, cemeteries and houses of worship; even into private houses; seldom receiving the rebuffs or rebukes which I am sure that we deserved, often invited and assisted to gratify our curiosity.

This good natured disposition was, as far as I can remember, univer-

189

sal. We met, to be sure, few but the poor and lowly. Yet we occasionally encountered some of the more fortunate classes. Once, for example, we had alongside of our ship an elegant yacht in which a wealthy merchant had come to deal for some part of our cargo. After quitting work in the afternoon I went to the gangway of this singular craft (which was very like those described by Marco Polo in the [Thirteenth] Century) and, by lifting my eyebrows to one of the crew, asked if I could come on board. The man stepped into the cabin and returned with a well dressed young fellow— perhaps the owner's son—who at once offered his hand to assist me in coming on board and then extended it as an invitation toward the cabin into which he followed me. The cabin was rich with carvings and contained some pretty furniture of black work inlaid with ivory and mother of pearl, and a number of musical instruments. All these were shown to me in a pleasant way. In a corner there were two gentlemen over a table, playing chess I think. When we came near them they bowed and smiled and, the servant at this moment bringing in the tea things which were placed upon another table, they rose and one of them handed me a cup of tea. Delicious tea it was. They each took a cup of it with me, then offered me cigarettes and finally waited upon me to the gangway and bowed me over the side with perfectly grave suavity.

I suppose that civilization is to be tested as much by civility as anything else. And I have recalled these incidents as illustrations of a personal experience which made a strong impression upon me, tending to a higher estimate of the social condition of the masses of the Chinese people than I think generally prevails.

1. Olmsted apparently wrote this essay early in 1856; he finished it at 3:00 A.M. on the day he left New York for Boston on his way to Europe in February 1856. His ship sailed on February 13. He expected *Putnam's Monthly Magazine* to publish it, but his friend and partner Joshua A. Dix could find only part of the text after his departure, and it remained unpublished (FLO to Joshua A. Dix, Aug. 3, 1856, Dix, Edwards & Co. Collection, Houghton Library, Harvard University, Cambridge, Mass.; *Forty Years*, 1: 6).
2. This episode is mentioned in FLO to Aunt Maria, Nov. 30, 1843, above.
3. See FLO to JHO, Sept. 28, 1843, note 14.

CHAPTER IV

CONNECTICUT
INTERLUDE

1844–1845

WHEN THE *Ronaldson* docked in New York in April 1844, Olm-sted was thin and worn. His first task was to restore his health, and the remedy was near at hand. As he had written his brother from China, "I think I shall be calculated to appreciate rural comforts, if no other, when I return."[1] He was soon out in the countryside collecting specimens and reporting back to his friends at the Hartford Natural History Society. By summer he was taking camping trips and enjoying picnics with his friends and Hart-ford girls.

The fall of 1844 found him casting about for something more sub-stantial to do. Farming, the occupation of many of his Connecticut forebears for two hundred years, attracted him, and he decided to live for a few months with his uncle David Brooks in Cheshire, near Hartford. During the winter of 1844–1845, Olmsted found time to re-read Johann Zimmermann's book *Solitude Considered with Respect to Its Influence on the Mind and the Heart*, and was pleased with its reaffirmation of his conviction that the rural pursuits he enjoyed were healthier for the body and the mind than any occupation he could pursue in the city.

Olmsted was ready to put Zimmermann's views into practice, and in the spring of 1845 he went to live on Joseph Welton's farm near Waterbury, Connecticut. He enjoyed his stay there and felt in retrospect that Welton was the most conscientious, healthy, and moral of all his teachers. To a reader of Zimmermann, Welton's virtues would have been no surprise.

Olmsted settled into his new life in May 1845, well pleased with his choice. To be sure, the darker side of rural life intruded in such forms as the ignorance of farm hands, the sterility of the Connecticut soil, and the macabre life at the town's poor house; but Olmsted referred to these in his letters as if they were but comic relief or picturesque interludes in an otherwise benign rural world. The satisfaction he felt was due in part to his freedom to come and go at the Weltons' almost without restraint—a welcome change from the iron discipline of the *Ronaldson*. He worked intermittently at the farm until the end of the haying season in August, and then, well before harvest time, returned to Hartford. There he spent much of his time boating and picnicking with his family and friends.

As a result of his stay at Welton's, Olmsted became increasingly convinced of the value of country life. The traditional "professions" were not the only honorable pursuits, he declared: farming combined the proudest aims of science and fostered the development of man's aesthetic sensibilities. No other way of life, he was sure, was so beneficial.

In the fall of 1845 Olmsted further sought to legitimize his chosen profession by studying subjects related to scientific agriculture at Yale. He attended the lectures of Benjamin Silliman and participated in laboratory experiments with his brother and friends. His friends at Yale traveled in the highest circles of New Haven society, and Olmsted felt shy and ill at ease because of his own haphazard education. He was deeply flattered, therefore, when the bright and pretty young Elizabeth Baldwin took him seriously and encouraged his intellectual interests. This New Haven interlude, during which he cemented his lifelong friendship with Charles Loring Brace and Frederick Kingsbury, and tasted the rarefied atmosphere of the Baldwin family's intellectual soirées, lasted only three months. Late in the fall he had a series of fainting spells, resembling apoplexy, which moved his father to bring him home to Hartford to recover. Brief though it was, his time at Yale broadened his horizons and strengthened his self-confidence while he pursued his dream of becoming a gentleman farmer during the next half-dozen years.

1. FLO to JHO, Sept. 28, 1843.

To JOHN HULL OLMSTED

[May 31, 1844][1]

Address: John Hull Olmsted/Quasi Soph—/Yal. Coll./New Haven

Vale! Soph. quasi![2]

The staff arrived last evening (Thursday), having received a salute of rain during the hour or two previous, "Choctaw & Kate" making some sixty miles over bad roads in the day. Father insists that the savages in some of those Loco-Foco regions cut out the miles a deal longer than among us. Reasoning from their known meanness, however, I think it quite as likely that our "'pikers" habitually give short measure.[3] During their absence (K. & C.'s), I have put up a new back to their stable, whitewashed it & made some other improvements. Being Major Domo (acting), I marketed, & the first day we rushed on eels, clams, custard & chocolate.

In the evening the Natural History Society were to meet at Smith's rooms, but there was not a quorum present owing to some misunderstanding as to the place. Mr. Monds, Prof. Jackson, E. Smith & myself were there only.[4] Smith had some fine fossils. M. don't like the Atheneum building, particularly as connected or associated with the name. He thinks it should have been à la Grec. S. highly approves of the name, thinks that the inscription in front ("Wadsworth") added $500.00 to the subscription list. Wishes there was a similar one on the rear, for that matter (_____sabi?) We are expecting to have our rooms towards the close of July.[5] Mind ye, there'll be bad blood yet about the distribution of these same rooms.

Professor Jackson very rightly argues that a single noble piece of art (in sculpture) would be better worth having than fifty ordinarily fine paintings. He also advocates procuring casts from the most celebrated works of antiquity—(these from Florence.) Speaking of Powers' "Eve,"[6] he says it is conceived in the idea that she was before her fall: a perfectly pure, sinless being *without shame.* She is represented *per*fectly nude, not even a leaf of cover, & the spectator is to observe her with the same conception of perfect purity.[7]

He is curious to see how it will be received here. Monds says she'll have to put petticoats on in New England. Then I said I had seen a statue in New Haven where the privates were hid by a blue handkerchief drawn over one thigh. (Did you ever hear old Major Terry's[8] orders? *"Foot Guards!* You'll appear on parade, Monday, twenty-first May next, eight o'clock, forenoon, front of the State House! Full uniform, white gloves, ruffled shirt, powdered hair, and *tally wags*[9] *dressed on the left side!* Carry arms! Eyes right! You are dismissed!")

Then, M. says, you may see this day in Salem the "Laocoon" & "The Boy & Thorn in His Foot,"[10] all the _____ well clothed in cambric, an old maid having been engaged in fitting them—probably because she was at home in the business—as Yorick's merchande des gants with the gants d'Amour![11] In a similar case here, Miss Smith[12] would be deputized by the Moral Reform Society. The Professor relates how Powers' servant girl in blundering through the studio by night knocked the _____ off a model of a boy. She knew enough to stick it on again, unfortunately wrong out. On being told of it, she answered that she "never saw but one & that *pointed so.*" Nasty fellows! How they do talk!

Stopping at Monds' coming home, we three, Miss Monds[13] & I had each a few yarns to spin of our individual experience of the sea. Mr. Monds' had a gloomy strand twisted in: his beautiful protégé returning to her friends

—dying of Consumption—on the third week out, during a most awful gale, at midnight, the water in the cabin washing her mattress, tremendous sea on, & everything about her in dreadful confusion, but within, calm as a setting star.

Friday

Hartford (as I did not hear service read yesterday, don't know the date.)
Dear Brother,
This is to inform you that I remain, as usual, yours up to fashion.
Frederick Law Olmsted

N.B. P.S. *Forgot* to tell you that your letter with the kind information in regard to their "honors" came to hand a day or *two* after the fact. In regard to the small matters I think you mentioned wanting in the P.S., I suppose you did not care much for them. So being very busy building a hen coop (going to start an egg factory—think we may charter mathematical music mill—"Euclidodeon" or what ever you call it; if the market chokes) didn't attend to "monopo*lize* the hookfrocking and lacestaying" affair. (Hope 'twill benefit your eyes.) However, the letter is knocking round below stairs and I should not wonder if you did secure it after all.

By—(golly) if you didn't allow yourself more recruiting when in college—it's no wonder you got the Consumption. Lord bless—'twould give a *cat "fits"* to be mewed up in the style you propose. Better it?—hang me if I could not, I'd go mummify myself in a Book case. Yes—here—now—5 to—15 wash—20 dress—35 to Mrs. _____ in the Avenue to enquire if Miss _____ is suffering at all from fatigue in walking from the theat—church (I mean) last night. Till breakfast—down to the bay—swim some-times—or look to the boat. See that your oars dont split (oil 'em (paint oil) *thoroughoughly*). Go look at the schooner on the stocks (rather slippery modeled ain't she?)

After breakfast study & read (your selection'l do) ten or fifteen minutes, or from that to a couple of hours. Then make your calls—till twelve. Take an observation, square the yards, & write up your log. Bear a hand with it, so as to have time to write a few pages (of postscript) to Fred. Then go to soup—("Soup's ready sir!" Steward) with a clear conscience. Tuck your napkin—take your fork in your right hand. "Eat slow, & masticate your food well." "Sit up straight in your chair." "Don't *toss*." Be very polite, particularly to John Olmsted the Hull. Decline segars, drink your wine slowly & grace-fully, & when you're offered hot punch don't drink it ("damn'd weak") but dip your fingers in the glass—& hang up in front of your nose to dry. If you give the "all shaking" touch it will be emphatically appropriate.

Then P.M. half, at least half, to exercise & recreation. You'll have a capital chance to make a collection of native shells. Ayres[14] got a specimen of every species known in the Sound while in college. But at all events whatever rules you make stick to 'em in spite of temporary inclination.

1. Although the date "June? 1844" is penciled on this letter, Olmsted probably wrote it on Friday, May 31, 1844, just after his father returned to Hartford from taking John Hull Olmsted and his baggage back to college in New Haven. John Olmsted's journal entry for May 30, 1844, fits Olmsted's description of the trip in his letter: "returned via Savin Rock, Derby, Naugatuck, Waterbury, & Southington. 58 miles on the 30th. Rain came @ 8 A.M." (JO Journal, May 28, 29, 30, 1844).

2. Olmsted hails his brother as a quasi-sophomore because of the anomalous situation to which he was returning at Yale. John Hull Olmsted had made little progress in his studies during his sophomore year because of illness. What must have been the beginnings of tuberculosis forced him home to Hartford for short periods during November and December 1843, and in late January 1844 he left for a three-month trip to the West Indies to recoup his health. When he returned to Yale at the end of May he became a member of the class below his original one. He graduated in 1847, a year after his closest friends and former classmates (JO Journal, Nov. 1, 7, 29, and Dec. 4, 9, 1843; Jan. 27 and April 30, 1844; Yale University, *Biographical Notices of Graduates of Yale College, 1816–1909* . . . [New Haven, 1913], p. 373).

3. Both Olmsted and his father supported the Whig party with its program of internal improvements, while the inhabitants of the region through which John Olmsted passed were "Loco Foco" Democrats unwilling to tax themselves for good roads. Olmsted's humorous alternative explanation for the seeming length of a mile when traveling on their bad roads was that the turnpike builders in such improvement-minded parts of Connecticut as Hartford gave "short measure" in calculating the length of their turnpikes, in order to increase the tolls they collected.

4. Joseph P. Monds, a friend of Olmsted's who taught him drawing and encouraged his interest in natural history; Abner Jackson (1811–1874), clergyman and professor of intellectual and moral philosophy at Washington College (renamed Trinity in May 1845) in Hartford; Erastus Smith (1803–1878), recording secretary and librarian of the Natural History Society of Hartford (FLO Pocket Journal, 1843–1844; *Appleton's Cyc. Am. Biog.*, s.v. "Jackson, Abner"; *The Connecticut Annual Register for 1843* [Hartford, 1843], p. 119; Connecticut Historical Society, *Hartford Historical Documents and Notes: Genesis and Development of the Connecticut Historical Society* . . . [Hartford, 1889], p. 89; Headstone Inscriptions, Hartford, Cemetery 13, p. 57).

5. The Wadsworth Atheneum in Hartford bore the name of the man who was the moving force in its creation, the banker and insurance executive Daniel Wadsworth (1771–1848). In 1841 he began to promote the founding of a gallery of the fine arts in Hartford by donating a valuable site for it. He was also the first and largest contributor to the subscription used to raise the necessary funds. He offered the land on the condition that the building erected there should house an art gallery and provide rooms for use by the Connecticut Historical Society and the Hartford Young Men's Institute. The Historical Society was also to make rooms available for the Natural History Society of Hartford, "so that under the same roof art, literature and science should be cultivated." The architects chosen to design the Atheneum were the popular and influential partners Ithiel Town and Alexander Jackson Davis. Their Gothic Revival structure was completed on July 31, 1844 (*Who Was Who in America, 1607–1896* [Chicago, 1942], s.v. "Wadsworth, Daniel"; *Hartford County*, 1: 541; Roger H. Newton, *Town & Davis, Architects: Pioneers in American Revivalist Architecture 1812–1870* . . . [New York, 1942], pp. 238–40; *Wadsworth Atheneum Handbook* [Hartford, 1958], p. 5).

6. Hiram Powers (1805–1873), American sculptor, began work on *Eve Tempted* in

1839 at his studio in Florence, Italy. The first version, in clay, was nearly complete by 1841, and a plaster cast was made sometime thereafter. The plaster statue was greatly admired by many, including Bertel Thorwaldson, the Danish sculptor and critic who, when Powers remarked to him that *Eve Tempted* was his first statue, replied, "Any sculptor might be pleased to call it his last" (Clara Louise Dentler, "White Marble: The Life and Letters of Hiram Powers, Sculptor," typescript, National Collection of Fine Arts, Smithsonian Institution, Washington, D.C., pp. 105, 109, 138).

7. Hiram Powers once wrote to a friend: "I claim that in all my works there is no impure thing or sentiment. I have always aimed at the pure image of God and they who shrink from beholding it and fear contamination should try to purify their own minds, for it is out of the minds of men that evil cometh" (ibid., p. 138).
8. Nathaniel Terry (1768–1844), Hartford banker and insurance executive, who had been a member of Congress from 1817 to 1819 and mayor of Hartford from 1824 to 1831. He commanded the Governor's Foot Guard from 1802 to 1813 (*BDAC*).
9. Male genitalia (Harold Wentworth, *American Dialect Dictionary* [New York, 1944], s.v. "tallywags, tarriwags").
10. Copies of two famous Hellenistic statues of naked male figures: one the Laocoon group from Rhodes, and the other the "Boy Pulling a Thorn from His Foot" in the Palazzo dei Conservatori in Rome, or a similar statue in the British Museum in London (Margarete Bieber, *The Sculpture of the Hellenistic Age* [New York, 1955], pp. 104, 134–35, 138).
11. Olmsted is referring to the beautiful Parisian shopgirl in Laurence Sterne's *A Sentimental Journey*, who combined flirtation with her attempts to sell gloves. Olmsted read the book at the age of nine, when he discovered it in a trunk that his grandmother Content Pitkin Olmsted kept in her attic in East Hartford (*A Sentimental Journey through France and Italy by Mr. Yorick; To Which Are Added The Journal to Eliza and A Political Romance*, ed. Ian Jack [London, 1968], pp. 51–56; *Forty Years*, 1: 56).
12. Presumably Catherine Smith, the Olmsteds' chambermaid (JO Journal, expense account, Dec. 1844).
13. Maria Monds (c. 1819–1845), daughter of Joseph P. Monds (JO Journal, Oct. 22, 1845; *Hartford Daily Courant*, Oct. 25, 1845, p. 3).
14. Jared A. Ayres (1813–1886), teacher at the American Asylum for the Deaf and Dumb at Hartford, who in 1843 was secretary of the Natural History Society (FLO Pocket Journal, March 1, 7, 11, 22, 24, 1843).

To CHARLES LORING BRACE   [August 4, 1844]¹

Address: Charles L. Brace/Yale College

Hartford. "I keep no note of time."
My dear friend,
It occurs to me that if you and I correspond much this term, according to agreement, it will be requisite to begin pretty *soon*. I only fear it is already so near Commencement, with you—that I shan't get an answer. I had an idea that you'd start the wagon; but as you don't, I think I'll give you a push.
Our Commencement came off last week with great eclat, so far as I

VIEW OF HARTFORD, CONNECTICUT

can judge. I went into the church Thursday to hear our friends, & was very much gratified. Bill (late—now brevet Reverend William Upson Colt, A.M. (or B.A.?))[2] succeeded excellently well—both in composition and delivery. I think with others whose opinions I have heard, it was the best performance. And then when I was congratulating him & trying to compliment him, he must not understand, but twist it all off onto his class, like a gentleman as he is every inch of him, & there's a good many. Then the Poem & Sterling & Kelly,[3] all very good—so also the music, which I take it is nothing rare from that choir.

I was disappointed in not hearing Dud.[4] I suppose he'd never worry himself for an appointment.

Like a fool—as if I had not enough experience already of perils by land and sea—I must allow myself to be prevailed upon to attend a small circle of particular, *I* mean a large soc[iable] party, the other night. And if ever again I am caught in such a scrape, may I be jam'd, bang'd, cram'd, slam'd, and ram'd into something small enough and shot out of't.

You see, they wanted me to *dreadfully*. Mother must go & somebody must go with her. Father could not. Nobody else but Fred. Fred's somebody —ergo—Fred must go—quod erat ridiculous. With a great, heavy, hot, uncomfortable, fashionable, big, black, coat, in addition to feeling remarkably small, as a matter o'course,[5] I was likely to evaporate to nobody,—a coat; = a coat, minus somebody. To avoid which, I wing'd a couple of old maids & stood for the balcony where I backed & fill'd 'em among the sensible folks that had already got out of the ovens—till they were tired. Then moored in the first vacant berths on a sofa, where I cooled off with a caution. As in a few minutes my back was so lame I could just get to the dressing room containing a big bed &c, a bureau glass and comb, very useful, very to me (no brush) a washstand establishment, two clean towels and a dirty one, a thing-amaree and half dozen peacocks' feathers. Then I managed to get home in a very pleasant humour and have been laid up ever since, which was just what I deserved & be hang'd to't.

I've been trying to discover any mortal pleasure in this business. I examined the women folk very particularly. As far as I could reach, the motive for sacrificing one's comfort so—with perhaps some desire to oblige others—is to see and show fine dresses; (I can't imagine it at all as a market where every one appears under such very disadvantageous circumstances personally) & to taste sweetmeats & flippery. Some pretend they go to enjoy social intercourse. As if rational conversation was allowed in good society, so-called. Oh pshaw! Now do you, or any body but old maids, and scandal mongers, really like these hot beds? I don't.

Now I'll tell you the truth, as to how I allowed myself to be sucked in to this scrape. I thought these Condits would be there. They've just come —to Commencement. I did want to see them, particularly the youngest.[6]

She's an angel, so to speak, and I'll tell you why pretty soon. She used to look one in every expression. That is, three years ago. I haven't seen her since, in the body. And I never conversed with her. I doubt if I could. I don't speak the language. But—now please don't laugh & keep your lip down. When I was sick—I was delirious in the Indian Ocean—she used to come. Particularly one night she came and took me ashore on Christmas Island and brought Father and Mother & _____. Well, it's a fact the next morning I was a great deal better.

And now, when I've been sick enough to be down, I've been on the qui vive to see her and can not. Once they were going out—and Sarah[7] turn'd and looked right in my face—Lord! What eyes she's got! Heh? *But* Frances kept poking her head round the other way, as I verily believe on purpose to avoid me.

I wonder if I really shall be an old bach. What a shivering idea—oh my! I tell you it's haunted me like a nightmare since this last scrape. No! No! Sooner would I take up with one of those country girls—six of whom kissed me—oh—before I went to sea. My dear fellow, what shall I do?

I know your first enquiry if you should see me would be in regard to "the girls." Why man, there an't but four in the city I know. The rest I look at sometimes, when I can do it safely. But my tongue's tied.

When's *my cousin*[8] going to be married?

Father wants me to go to New London & Newport tomorrow—but I shan't leave *now*.

Yours with high regard,

Fredk. Law Olmsted.

1. Commencement at Washington College in Hartford was on August 1, and Olmsted's father went to New London on August 5, which makes August 4 the probable date of this letter (*Hartford Daily Courant*, Aug. 1, 1844, p. 2; JO Journal, Aug. 5, 1844).
2. William Upson Colt (1824–1848) of Hartford, a half-brother of the inventor and arms manufacturer Samuel Colt. Originally a friend of Brace's, he became a warm friend of the Olmsteds and their Yale student friends during their college years. After graduating from Washington College in 1844 he spent the academic year 1844–45 studying at Yale Divinity School and teaching at the Episcopal Academy in Cheshire. During much of this year, Olmsted was also in Cheshire, living with his uncle David Brooks. In 1848 Colt graduated from Andover Theological Seminary. He died on September 28, 1848, soon after becoming principal of Ellington Seminary in Ellington, Conn. (Martin Rywell, *Samuel Colt, A Man and An Epoch* [Harriman, Tenn., 1952], p. 83; FJK *Sketch of CLB*, p. 71; Washington College, *Catalogue of the Officers and Students of Washington College, Hartford, for the Academic Year 1843–44* [Hartford, 1843], p. 6; Yale University, *Eighth General Catalogue of the Yale Divinity School, Centennial Issue, 1822–1922*, 19th ser., no. 2 [New Haven, 1922], p. 95; Cheshire School, *Catalogue of the Officers, Teachers, and Alumni of the Episcopal Academy of Cheshire* [New Haven, 1916], p. 20; *Life of Brace*, pp. 59–60).
3. John Canfield Sterling (1822–1874) of Sharon, Conn., and John Howard Kelly (c. 1821–1864) of Stockport, N.Y. (Albert Mack Sterling, *Sterling Genealogy*, 2 vols. [New York, 1909], 1: 514; Washington College, *Catalogue of Washington College, Hartford, for 1843*, p. 5).

4. Oliver Dudley Cooke (1822–1895), son of a Hartford publisher and bookseller of the same name. He spent his childhood in New York, where his father had moved before he was born. He attended Washington College, where he was a roommate of William Upson Colt, and was graduated in 1844. He then taught for a time at the American Asylum for the Deaf and Dumb in Hartford. In 1851 he received a Master's Degree from Trinity College there (*Hartford Daily Courant*, March 27, 1895, p. 6; *Wheeling* [W. Va.] *Sunday Register*, March 24, 1895, p. 1; *Hartford County*, 1: 624).

5. The "Crew of the Ronaldson" of April 1843 listed Olmsted as five feet, six inches tall; this is corroborated by a notation on the inner cover of "The Kingsbury Family Record for All Matters of General or Particular Interest," a manuscript in possession of Mrs. Ludlow Bull, Litchfield, Conn., which states that Olmsted's height in December 1860 was five feet, five and three-quarter inches.

6. Frances P. Condit (1826–1889), the youngest daughter of Stephen and Phebe Condit of Hartford. She married William B. Babbitt on August 12, 1846 (Jotham H. and Eben Condit, *Genealogical Record of the Condit Family, Descendants of John Cunditt . . .* , rev. ed. [Newark, 1916], p. 45).

7. Sarah M. Condit (1824–1894) was the Condits' eldest daughter (ibid., p. 102).

8. Perhaps Cornelia Olmsted (1821–1869), the daughter of Olmsted's distant cousin Danison Olmsted (1791–1859), a professor of mathematics and natural philosophy at Yale. She was married on August 29, 1844. The nearest common ancestor that Olmsted shared with Denison Olmsted was Joseph Olmsted (1654–1726) (*Olmsted Genealogy*, pp. 16, 19, 25, 26, 44, 72, 73, 122; *DAB*).

To Abby Clark[1]

South-end [Cheshire][2]

Saturday evening
Jan. 18th, 1845

Our reverend friend at the "nursery"[3] was going to have a letter written to you today, Miss Abby. And I agreed to come up and add an answer to the postscript with which you honored me, as I promised you. But circumstances have hindered my leaving home, and I must beg the liberty of using a separate paper. I feel as if I had returned to common air, after breathing in an atmosphere of exhilarating gas for a couple of weeks. Pray Miss Abby, do they breathe anything else at your house? However, I like Cheshire pretty well and I would rather be here just now, than anywhere else (saving your presence).

Recollect that this was the "icy Saturday" (any bones broke your way?) And I tell you, it pays for a good deal of previous self denial to enjoy its splendour as we do here. Look in what direction you will, the prospect is equally striking. For every blade of grass or sprig or ragged fern or old tangled briar bush—even the old stone wall and Virginny fence—as well as the stately trees or rugged mountain are equally encased with clear, silvery ice. I wish you could have seen the woods when the sun's rays were slanting across and through them. Such enchantment was never conceived in Arabian Nights. The scene this evening is so brilliant and I am admiring so much, that I am tempted to describe it to you. If I could impart to you but a slight share of the pleasure I receive from it, I should be delighted.

The effect of the ice on the evergreens is peculiarly rich. There are half a dozen young hemlocks, which I set out by the window here in the fall, and they do appear magnificent. Two of them (as I address you) have bowed their beautiful heads crown'd with fleecy light to the very ground. But where they stretch up out of the shade of the house, how splendidly their dark green feathery spray, waving and trembling with its load of twinkling brilliants, shivers and glistens in the clear bright moonlight—like the green tresses of a mermaid toss'd in the foam of a breaking wave.

And there's another most exquisite tinge of green—the like of which you'll only find in Fairy Land—in those sprouts and weeds struggling through the snow crust and ice which forms a dazzling mosaic pavement over the garden. How the sparkles from the drooping boughs of the willow where it sweeps the brook kindle up and reflect the dancing eyes of the ripples! And oh! Miss Abby, if you could but look up here at the moon through the thick little sprigs of the old maples, it is beyond description.

Well, I'll stop. Who! (ough?) Pegasus! And *apropos* of coming down—*that shoe*—I had it in my pocket Monday morning when I called for Bill's[4] letter. But not seeing you, it escaped my mind and I have it here. I will send it up to you by the first opportunity, and if you will direct the other to me in "care of Mr. Charles Brace" and send it through Miss Mary,[5] I shall be extremely obliged to you.

Did you "keep shady" with Mr. Harding?[6] I am interested in the result of that affair. Remember that I am "the Knight of the shorn (*scissored*, alas!) lock."

There's hardly anything talked of here now but the great "tea-party" for the "benefit of the first Presbyterian meeting house in Cheshire," which is to come off Valentine's evening. As for the rest, you know they do talk in the country. They say that Miss Bradlee has jilted young Hitchcock, poor fellow. The new Academy teacher has been twice to the Presbyterian church and in the evening went home with—but that's scandal. As also, if you care to know it, is the ridiculous yarn, which *is* going the rounds, that I am going to be married. I've no thoughts of it. Miss _____[7] but never mind what am I doing.

I set down to write an apology for not writing a postscript and to tell you how I "like Cheshire," and I have been making a newspaper—for which I offer a thousand apologies. Will you do me the favour to sit down & write me a scolding—I forgot you said you never scold. Well, hardly anything would give me more pleasure than to receive under your hand and seal a pardon for all the errors I have been guilty of this evening. But did you ever try to write a letter in a kitchen full of women and children "getting ready for Sunday?" You see what queer work it makes. But at all events you won't have the *same* complaint to make of my letter that I did of your postscript.

> With compliments to your sisters[8] and with great respect, I remain
> Your obedient servant,
>
> Frederick Law Olmsted

1. Abby Morton Clark (c. 1820–1871) of Hartford, the daughter of Ezra Clark (c. 1790–1870) and Laura Hunt Clark (c. 1788–1862) (*Hartford Daily Courant*, May 5, 1862, p. 2, and Jan. 12, 1870, p. 2; Connecticut State Department of Health, Bureau of Vital Statistics, Hartford, death record of Abby M. Clark).
2. On January 13, 1845, Olmsted had left Hartford for Cheshire to visit the family of his mother's sister, Linda Hull Brooks (1796–1865), and her husband David Brooks (1791–1873). He often visited them during his childhood and had spent part of the fall of 1844 on their farm learning about farming from his uncle (JO Journal, Oct. 30, Dec. 25, 1844; Jan. 13, Feb. 26, 1845; Florence McCutcheon McKee, comp., *McCutcheon Family Records* [Grand Rapids, Mich., 1931], pp. 287–88).
3. Probably William Upson Colt, who at this time was teaching at the Episcopal Academy in Cheshire and studying at Yale Divinity School (see FLO to CLB, Aug. 4, 1844, note 2, above).
4. William Upson Colt.
5. Mary Brace (1820–1903), sister of Charles Loring Brace (John Sherman Brace, *The Brace Lineage*, 2d. ed. [Bloomsburg, Pa., 1927], p. 104; FJK Journal, Nov. 11, 1903).
6. John Wheeler Harding of East Medway, Mass., graduated from Yale in 1845 and from the Andover Theological Seminary in 1849. He then became the pastor of the Congregational Church in Longmeadow, Mass. (*Yale Obit. Rec.*, 4th ser., no. 6 [June 1896]: 380).
7. Miss Basset (see FLO to JO, Feb. 2, 1845, note 16, below).
8. Laura, Harriet, Martha, Mary, and Ellen Clark were the sisters Olmsted might have known ("Last Will of Ezra Clark, late of Hartford, Deceased," Feb. 7, 1870, Connecticut State Library, Hartford, Conn.).

To John Olmsted

Address: Mr. John Olmsted/Hartford
Postmark: Cheshire C-/3 February

Cheshire, February 2nd, 1845

Dear Father,

I did not want to write to you until I could say something definite in regard to Bear Mountain.[1] When I got here I found Mr. B.[2] had not begun to go to Wolcott, & he assigned as a reason the sickness and death of Uncle

Andrew.[3] Various occurrences delayed us till last week when by great exertion I managed to get off with 'Lonzo[4]—cart, baggage & provisions for a week's use. Got to the shantee about 8 o'clock at night without accident, except that while I was gone ahead to hunt up the shantee, the bedclothes got off & 'lonzo found them half a mile back, wet & muddy. We made a fire, cooked our supper & turned in.

The next day we went to cutting, & the two succeeding days to dragging off the wood, that was scattered about the land, getting it in piles, that it might not be covered up by snow falling, and be more accessible when we shall have sledding. I cooked—we had a leg of beef, ham, potatoes, bread, etc., gridiron, spider, kettle, etc. There was a big spring—dug out for cattle close by the shantee—in which, or out of which, I had a bath every night & then turned in—after the first night being all alone a mile from anybody (Alonzo being sick of the shantee). I liked it very much.

Sat up with a hot fire reading Zimmermann on Solitude[5] (which will rank next to the Bible & Prayer book in my Library. I think it is one of the best books ever written. I wish everybody would read it) till 10 o'clock or so. Turned in & rolled up in a buffalo [robe] till 'lonzo woke me the next morning. Had breakfast about sunrise. Then A. would go off carting, & I'd stay to wash the dishes etc., after which I'd take my gun & dog, & go exploring, and I found some of the most picturesque & sublime scenes I ever saw—within a mile or two. The mountains are remarkably grand, and every few rods almost is a brook which winds about in the gorges till it finds the most effective spot for a display—when [it] jumps off & comes tumbling & smashing through the rocks, over the side of the mountain in the most astonishing manner. From the highest summit—which is entirely bare of any vegetation higher than *tear trousers*[6] and is, I believe, on our land—I saw at the same time all the country between here & [Mount] Tom & Holyoke with the Tower—away off east, the mountains over the river—& south to Long Island etc.,[7] I don't know where you'd find a more extensive or beautiful prospect.

Shot one partridge. Tore my clothes—old pantaloons & jacket—all to rags. Kept my feet wet & everything else, but couldn't catch cold. On the contrary, cured my old one.[8]

Well, Friday morning, "Alonzo had one o' his turns." You know he's been crazy once, & they can't or won't do anything with him. Botheration. I tried to reason with him. Might as well talk to the cattle. Then I pretended wrathy: "What do you mean, Sir!" & all that. No go. All I could get out of him was: "I know what I'm about. Ain't a-goin' to have our things in this damned old smoke house any longer."

I knew there was nothing to be done with him. He wanted to go board at Frost's,[9] & thought I should go too, I s'pose, when he'd taken off the things from the shantee. So without saying a word to me he goes about it. We had been as good-natured, & chatty, & confidential as could be, half an hour before at breakfast. Of course, I told him I did not want anything more of him, & he "might go home." Then good-humoredly I lent him a hand till I saw him on the road home, when I took my gun—& making a circuit of ten miles over the mountains West—I got home about 8 o'clock P.M. somewhat hungry (Friday night.)

He told the folks, "we were a'most out of provision, & the cattle out o' fodder, & *we* thought we'd come home day afore Saturday." I told his father[10] how 'twas. He laughed and said something about "one of his turns —since he was sick that time—'fraid he'd be crazy," & so & so—hem. I s'pose he expects to go up again this next week. Don't know whether he will or not, but I think I shall go & live alone in the shantee & let him & his father stay at Frost's—if they choose.

I think we had better turn most of the wood into coal which is worth $18 a ton. Very high now. Wood very low. If you wish, send down your Irishman,[11] to stay with me in the shantee. Wages are $12 or $13 per month. Alonzo expects $13, but that will depend. He is a first rate with the axe. A man offered to chop for me at 25 cents a cord. He said wages were from 12 to *16* dollars & he'd had $*18*—liar.

Andrew died of western fever & doctors—was cheated out of what he was worth by one of those rascally Toledo sharpers—blades—swindlers— merchants or speculators—last summer. Has left a wife sick, with one child & another born since he died.[12] Her father & uncle both died in the same house within three weeks before Andrew—nine heirs, estate not able to pay its debts.[13] I've seen, loved & pitied his little daughter "Meribah," aged seven or so, boarding at her aunt's in town—that she may attend school—first time this winter—very interesting—confiding & pretty.[14]

There's to be a festival or tea party or fair or humbugging auction [. . .] of some sort to come off here on Valentine's evening: for the benefit of the Presbyterian church & all that. They seem to expect great things of me. I don't know what reason they have to, I'm sure.

Gov. Foote's darter,[15] a young old maid in specs, wanted to know how many valentines I'd engage to prepare! Thunder! Then they came to our house with a sleighing party. Invited to go with 'em—went—kept up till morning, eating raw meat of some sort & drinking hot coffee water—for which, I suppose, they left a dollar unpaid for me to *settle*—after I'd made a speech thanking 'em & all that bosh!

One of the girls—Judge Basset (a loco-foco)'s daughter from some- where near New Haven—got sick.[16] As there was nobody else seemed to care a cuss for her, & she was decidedly the best lady of the whole of 'em, I devoted myself to her—the whole night. And she appeared very grateful & all that. Of course we are engaged after that, & I shan't be surprised at all to hear our *publishment* one of these Sundays. And now they talk as if it was a matter of course that I should hire a horse & sleigh her up to it, etc.

I wish you'd order me home or else send me some money & a ream of light blue note paper.

Y.w.y.r.

F.L.O.

[P.S.][17]

If you send the Irishman, let him bring blankets enough.

I can buy you the handsomest 'coon skin (New York make, tails & all) sleigh robe you ever saw for $20—which I believe would be cheap for it, the materials being worth nearly that—*new, neatly* trimmed lion's head, &c.

Tell Dr. Taft[18] his sulphur (2 drops every other night) only made the eruption worse—a great deal. Stopped taking it & was cured—pretty much.

1. Most of this letter describes a trip Olmsted took in January 1845 to cut wood on a ten-acre lot on Bear Mountain in the town of Wolcott, Connecticut, which he owned jointly with his brother. The land was probably part of Southington Mountain, whose eastern side descends steeply to the Quinnipiac River valley and whose highest points provide the distant views that Olmsted describes (Connecticut Land Records: *Town of Wolcott, Connecticut, Register of Deeds*, 9 [1845–1860]: 212, on microfilm in the Connecticut State Library, Hartford).
2. Olmsted's uncle David Brooks.
3. Andrew Hull (c. 1811–1845) died on January 1, 1845 (*Connecticut Courant*, Jan. 11, 1845, p. 3; Myron A. Munson, comp., *1637–1887. The Munson Record: A Genealogical and Biographical Account of Captain Thomas Munson . . .* , 2 vols. [New Haven, 1895], 1: 286).
4. Olmsted's cousin Alonzo Brooks (d. 1887), one of nine children of David and Linda Hull Brooks (*Homes of Cheshire*, p. 81).
5. The book *Ueber Die Einsamkeit*, or *Solitude Considered with Respect to Its Influence on the Mind and the Heart*, by the Swiss physician Johann Georg *ritter* von Zimmermann (1728–1795) had a lasting influence on Olmsted's thought. Zimmermann taught the superiority of rural over urban life. He summed up the purpose of his book in a passage whose spirit runs through many of Olmsted's statements during his years as a farmer:

   . . . if I shall be able to convince the innocent votaries of rural retirement, that the springs of pleasure soon dry up in the heat of the metropolis, that the heart remains cold and senseless in the midst of all its noisy and factitious joys; if they shall learn to feel the superior pleasures of a country life, become sensible of the variety of resources which they afford against idleness and vexation; what purity of sentiment, what peaceful thoughts, what unfading happiness, the view of verdant meads, the sight of numerous flocks and herds quitting the fertile meadows on the close of day, instil into the mind; with what ineffable delight the sublime beauty of a wild romantic country, interspersed with distant cottages, and occupied by freedom and content, ravishes the soul; how much more readily, in short, we forget all the pains and troubles of a wounded heart, on the borders of a gentle stream, than amidst the concourse of deceitful joys, so fatally followed in the courts of princes, my task will be accomplished, and all my wishes amply gratified! (*Solitude Considered, with Respect to Its Influence Upon the Mind and the Heart . . .* , J. B. Mercier, trans. [New London, Conn., 1807], p. 13.)

6. A colloquial term for low, prickly bushes: in this case, probably scrub oak (Mitford

M. Matthews, ed., *Dictionary of Americanisms on Historic Principles* [Chicago, 1951], s.v. "tear coat, tear blanket").

7. From the height of Bear Mountain, Olmsted could see up the Farmington River valley to Mount Tom and Mount Holyoke fifty miles to the north and across the Connecticut River to the line of high hills some fifteen miles east of it. He could also see Long Island Sound and perhaps the low shoreline of Long Island, to the south.

8. This paragraph is written around the margin of page two of the letter.

9. Perhaps the house of David Frost (1767–1850) on Southington Mountain (Samuel Orcutt, *History of the Town of Wolcott from 1731 to 1874* [Waterbury, Conn., 1874], p. 480).

10. David Brooks.

11. Possibly John Stannis, whom John Olmsted employed as a gardener (JO Journal, expense account, Dec. 1844).

12. Catherine Munson Hull (1813–1894) survived with her daughters Meribah and Garafelia (M. A. Munson, *Munson Record*, 1: 286).

13. Levi Munson (1783–1844), Catherine Munson Hull's father, died at his house in Cheshire on Christmas Day 1844. An inventory of his estate on January 3, 1845, set its value at $5,713 (ibid., pp. 260–62).

14. Meribah Hull probably was living with her mother's older sister Abigail Munson Bristol (1810–1889), wife of Ryer Bristol (1811–1871) of Cheshire (ibid., pp. 285–86).

15. Samuel Augustus Foote (1780–1846), congressman, senator, and governor of Connecticut, had six sons but no daughters. Perhaps Olmsted thought Eliza S. Foote (b. 1812) was Samuel's daughter. Her father was William Lambert Foote (b. 1778), resident of Cheshire, who had been at different times town clerk and probate judge (Abram W. Foote, *Foote Family, Comprising the Genealogy and History of Nathaniel Foote, of Wethersfield, Connecticut, and his Descendants . . .* , 2 vols. [Rutland, Vt., 1907–32], 1: 187–88; *DAB*, s.v. "Foote, Samuel Augustus").

16. Sheldon Basset (d. 1865), town clerk, justice of the peace in Derby, Conn. who had several daughters (Samuel Orcutt, *The History of the Old Town of Derby, Connecticut, 1642–1880* [Springfield, Mass., 1880], pp. 365, 698).

17. These sentences are written around the margin of page three of the letter.

18. Gustavus M. Taft, who introduced the practice of homeopathic medicine in Hartford in 1842. Homeopathic methods differed sharply from the "heroic measures," bleeding and purgatives, of orthodox medical practice. Homeopathy, which gained a wide following in the United States during the 1840s and 1850s, was founded by the German physician Samuel F. C. Hahnemann (1755–1843). He taught that "similars should be treated by similars," and used drugs that could produce symptoms like those of the disease being treated. He prescribed drugs in very small doses, believing that they were most effective when highly diluted.. He taught that drugs effected their cures by stimulating the spiritual action of the body's vital force. Because of this emphasis on the interrelation of physical and spiritual elements in man, homeopaths were often at least partial adherents of the doctrines of Swedenborg and the spiritualists. Social reformers Hugh Doherty and James John Garth Wilkinson, whom Olmsted met in England in 1850, were both Swedenborgians and homeopathic physicians (see FLO to JO, Aug. 11, 1850, below; *Hartford County*, 1: 150; Martin Kaufman, *Homeopathy in America: The Rise and Fall of a Medical Heresy* [Baltimore, 1971], pp. 1–47; *EB*, s.v. "Homeopathy"; Richard H. Shryock, *Medicine and Society in America, 1660–1860* [New York, 1960], pp. 123–26, 144–45; Henry B. Shafer, *The American Medical Profession, 1783–1850* [New York, 1936], pp. 96–115).

To Charles Loring Brace   [May 16, 1845][1]

Address: Mr. Charles L. Brace/Care J. P. Brace Esq.[2]/Hartford

Dear Charley,

It's a great bore to have to write with poor ink like this, a'n't it? But that's not what I was going to say. I'll tell you what I've been about and leave the little miseries for the last page, if there's room.

After *that*, that morning, *Kingsbury*[3] could not get to the cars without calling on Miss Abby,[4] and I was glad of another opportunity to dun her (hoping to save my attorney the trouble of collection). I've got her blessing, but not *the* shoe, and parted from those regions & went & came unto the coasts which lie around about the Caravanserai at Meriden,[5] where we had to wait an hour or two, waiting the moving of the mail coach. K. found an honorable shad eater[6] with whom he discussed the Railroad Question,[7] and I employed myself with the newspaper till I had used up all my lead. Then we drank a bottle of ginger pop. After this, instead of smoking to pass away the time, I studied nature—a much more stupid and sensible "aid to digestion." The richest subjects as usual were exposed right before us.

I was considerably interested in a couple, male and female species, genus *Homo*. They were in full feather and deep colored and though young, appeared to be in "mating season." The male had his feet confined in such small toed, tight little fire buckets, & his nether plumage so cruelly strapped over them, that he found it difficult to walk, and at first I thought him a cripple, from the odd style in which he planted his *motives*. Poll—*spinate*; hair, *soapy*: covered with a cloth cap, with a long tassel & square visor, cocked with a rake to his *weak* side & worn continually in the ladies' parlour. He handed the she one a pamphlet from the table, & she looked at it a moment & said, "It's a novel!"

"Yes, I guess 'tis."

"Why! You don't real novels?"

"O, yes, I've read more'n one, I tell you. I *admire* to read 'em."

"How can you! I never read a novel in all my born day."

"You never? Well, I have. I tell you if I ha'n't!"

When the agent opened the office, he flung himself onto his extremes, & after gaining his balance progressed to the pigeon hole and sung out "Tickets for two!" And I took the opportunity to get an envelope for the *news*paper which we sent by Jackson[8] who was in the cars—& I suppose she got it, didn't she!

The driver over was a pretty good sample, too. He was good natured as a blind cow. Only as he had driven over early that morning & was out late the night before—sparkin'—(wonder if he is better off than I) he was somewhat *sleepy*. He remembered me (as Collins)[9] and asked kindly after the "Harford gals." Then he had a "great team." Only one of 'em lame, and so far from vicious that he had the utmost confidence in them & let them do just as they pleased, except—sometimes when he was catching a nap, when as the wheelers were trying to get out of the way of the old coach as it was rattlin' down the hill into 'em, then, as we pitched over a *riser*, & he was all but tossed over their heads, he would fetch up on the footboard, & waking suddenly, recover the reins & sing out "Hey! old brown!"

As we got into Cheshire he was kind enough to describe the country to me, pointing out the various objects of interest to an enlightened traveller: the roads, the "center," the *ragin' canawl*, &c., till, as we were getting towards (*my*) Bear Mountain,[10] K., in calling my attention to the prospect (which *is* rich), hap'd to tell me we were crossing the road to Cheshire. I corrected him & told him that was the "Morse's Farm's road"[11] and went down under the Mountain, where the Barnes girls live.[12] The driver looked at *me some*, but did not offer any more information about the roads for some time.

Among the passengers was a young old maid of less than forty who *boasted* that she had got a new set of teeth that would not wear out quite *so quick* as those she'd *shed*. At last K. says "we've arrived," and you know what kind of a place we were at. I *like* it. What a good natured, smooth pated, contented old gentleman his pater is?[13] I like him all the better, I suppose, for telling me that a young man couldn't have a more rational view of happiness than I did—which most folks would think queer. But he's right, for he has just such himself & he's happy withal. He says he don't want anything except about $5,000, well invested. And I don't know anybody [who does not] feel a good deal so,[14] and there are a few that *need* it less.

The next morning I went with K. up the river, a mile or two, to Mr. Joseph Welton's,[15] the farmer with whom I am now living. The next morning we went surveying some cord wood on wild lands of Mr. K's on Drum Hill[16] & came home after noon tired & hungry. Eat *some* dinner & went to sleep soon after. I recollect K.'s finished a letter to you and it seems to me I tried to write a postscript,[17] but I have not a very distinct idea whether I succeeded or not. Anyhow, we both slept till near supper time, when it was raining, and it has been keeping a doing so almost ever since, except sometimes when we dared it by going out without an umber*ill*.

Did you "go into *s'ciety*" any here? I have visited the Kendricks[18] *which* is the aristocracy & Martha which plays something Grand March on the piano—who are most beautifully turned out—and Miss Johnson[19] that they pester Fred about, & Fred's Gran'ma & 'lisha[20]—and they are all good clever folks, besides several more.

Yesterday I came up here. I found *boss* had gone over the hill to help the men what keeps the "town poor." (I am now next door to the workhouse.)[21] So I got a *hoe* & went and helped plant corn all the P.M. Don't you think I shall do? We had two or three of the paupers with us, and I was exceedingly edified by their conversation. One chap—built like a table fork—only he had a horrible fever sore—informed me that he did not associate himself with every old tramper that came along and I felt highly flattered, you may be sure, that I was allowed to have the next row to him. There was another one with an outlandish name, something like "Ham," who hail'd from "Guntown,"[22] and said he had been a soldier & could tell of moving accidents—&c., &c. Very entertaining, but I was more interested in the view of "work hus" economy that he uncurtained for me.

As he had been used to night watching they made him *nurse*, & he opened rich with an account of sitting up with an old woman who finally got so "she couldn't scold no longer." "And then," says he, "I was in hopes she was goin', but she held on, & when I woke up again she had [her] old mouth wide open, a breathin' like all possessed. I was a good mind to cram down a big junk of *opium*, but remembered the doctor said 'twouldn't have no effect on her, she'd drank so much gin. And so I put it in my pocket, & I got a piece on't now. And the darn'd old thing han't cum out the winder yet & she can scold now like the devil. She mends stockins & has to get old blind Eunice to thread her needle for her." I found the stairs were so arranged that they could not move a coffin through them, but had to go out the window, till it has got to be a common phrase. Says he, "I likes to have 'em die—coz they never gives me no rum only to pay for digging a grave."

When I came *home* here I found the school-marm, who is "boarding 'round" the district, and I suppose will stay here a week or so. As she is young, pretty, and rather intelligent, I "didn't mind" till bed time, when Mrs. W.[23] asked me if I should prefer to "sleep with a companion!" I told her I would rather be by myself. "Then we'll put you here till the schoolmarm's gone. Then you go into her *chamber*." And she showed me into a little box, pretty nearly filled with a feather bed.

It is a pleasant place, and I think I shall like it pretty well as a school, but it will be *awful* dull if I don't hear from you and the rest now & then. Welton is an old schoolmate of F.K.'s and has taught school some himself. By the way, he is a *churchman*, and when he reads prayers you would think he was trying to read so as to show the Examining Committee that he did not have to *spell* the *hard words*. He is tolerably well-informed and has been very successful as a farmer. He's got a good farm and he's proud of it, and he's a good & rather pretty wife with a kind expression, and he loves her like—as I mean to mine.

On the whole I think I am tolerably well off and I feel very much obliged to Kingsbury for finding the place for me. I am to work or play, come or go just as I please, but I mean to stay and work, till after haying anyway.

I am writing in the next room to *the* bedroom, and if you will put me in mind of it when I see you, I will tell you a good female Yankee trick I was just witness to. (Is *hearing*, witnessing?)

I cannot close without telling you how happy I am as a Christian. I trust I am not over-confident, but I do think a man ought to be able to be better satisfied with himself, by the grace of God, in the country rather than in the city. One has so much more opportunity and inclination for reflection and prayer that he must be better improving his time.

I don't know when I shall mail this letter, so I can't say whether it is to find you in Hartford or Yale; but you will write me before long—do. Not the first few days of the term though, if you love me, not till you are over the first attack of the blues. Love to Clint.[24] Hope he found the prison Democratic enough. 'Twould just suit him if we could all live so lovely; baiting the keepers who are the convict's aristocracy. It's queer that such a sensible fellow as he shouldn't see that what he calls the aristocracy is the more Democratic portion of the people (in feeling), and what he calls the Democratic are just the ones that *wish* to be Aristocratic (really.)

Yours affectionately,

F. L. Olmsted

P.S. I've been writing to Emma,[25] and I've a mind to appoint you censor to "suppress publication" if you see fit. For indeed, I don't think I've much sense of propriety. My ideas are so different in matters of etiquette from most folks, &c., that I know I must be liable to be making blunders; however, I don't think there's any danger with E. who generally gets one's *meaning* before he's fairly got it himself.

P.S. Saturday P.M.

I find a letter here at the office that looks as if it was from you, but it's altogether illegible, so try again. Mr. W. has a very good glass, & with that assistance I may be able to study it out, this evening. I hope it's not very important, but I wish you would use common paper, at least till July.

Yours,

F.L.O.

1. Olmsted and his friend Frederick Kingsbury left Hartford on May 12, 1845, for a trip to Meriden by train, and from there by coach through Cheshire to Kingsbury's home in Waterbury. On May 15, Olmsted moved to the home of the Kingsburys' neighbor, Joseph Welton. He wrote this letter the next day, and it can therefore be dated May 16, 1845 (FJK Journal, May 12, 15, and 16, 1845).
2. John Pierce Brace (1793–1872), father of Charles Loring Brace.
3. Frederick Kingsbury.
4. Abby Morton Clark, mentioned frequently in Frederick Kingsbury's journal, was a student at the Hartford Female Seminary (FJK Journal, Nov. 27, 28, 1844; July 16, 1846; Jan. 12, 1847; see FLO to Abby Clark, Jan. 18, 1845, note 1, above).
5. The Meriden Hotel, which opened in 1842 (Charles Bancroft Gillespie, comp., *An Historic Record and Early Pictorial Description of the Town of Meriden, Connecticut* . . . [Meriden, Conn., 1906], p. 364).
6. A slang term for members of the Connecticut state legislature, who were reputed to be exceedingly fond of Connecticut shad (M. M. Matthews, *Dictionary of Americanisms*, s.v. "shad eater").

7. This was a period of active railroad promotion in Connecticut. In 1844 New Haven interests had secured a charter from the legislature for a railroad to New York, and were, at the time this letter was written, negotiating for use of a track into New York City from the Connecticut border. In 1845 pressure was mounting among stockholders of the Farmington Canal, which ran from New Haven north to the Massachusetts border, to gain permission from the legislature to replace the canal with a railroad. This occurred the following year. Before that time Hartford-based interests had prevented the legislature from giving aid to the financially troubled canal company (Rollin G. Osterweis, *Three Centuries of New Haven, 1638–1938* [New Haven, 1953], pp. 247–49; Julius Gay, *Farmington Local History—The Canal* . . . [Hartford, Conn., 1899], pp. 13–16).

8. Jefferson Franklin Jackson (1821–1862), a member of the Yale class of 1846 from Alabama (*Yale Obit. Rec.*, 1st ser., no. 3 [July 1862]: 73; Thomas M. Owen, *History of Alabama and Dictionary of Alabama Biography*, 4 vols. [Chicago, 1921], 3: 893).

9. Isaac Clinton Collins (1824–1879), member of the Yale class of 1846 from Lowville, N.Y. (*Yale Obit. Rec.*, 2d ser., no. 10 [June 1880]: 403).

10. See FLO to JO, Feb. 2, 1845, note 1, above.

11. Moss Farms Road runs along the base of Peck Mountain, west of Cheshire.

12. The four daughters of Ambrose R. Barnes, member of the Connecticut state legislature in 1846 (Joseph Perkins Beach, *History of Cheshire, Connecticut, from 1694–1840* [Cheshire, Conn., 1912], p. 448; Connecticut General Assembly, *Roll of State Officers and Members of the General Assembly of Connecticut from 1776 to 1881* [Hartford, Conn., 1881], p. 315).

13. Charles Denison Kingsbury (1795–1890), landowner and merchant in Waterbury, Conn. (Frederick J. Kingsbury and Mary K. Talcott, eds., *The Genealogy of the Descendants of Henry Kingsbury, of Ipswich and Haverhill, Massachusetts* [Hartford, Conn., 1905], pp. 255, 318).

14. The material in brackets has been added by the editor to clarify the apparent meaning of the passage.

15. Joseph Welton (1814–1894), Waterbury farmer and nurseryman whose farm on the Naugatuck River Olmsted and Frederick Kingsbury visited on May 13, 1845 (FJK Journal, May 13, 1845; Joseph Anderson, ed., *The Town and City of Waterbury, Connecticut, from the Aboriginal Period to the Year Eighteen Hundred and Ninety-Five*, 3 vols. [New Haven, 1896], 2: 31–32; William J. Pape, ed., *History of Waterbury and the Naugatuck Valley, Connecticut*, 3 vols. [Chicago, 1918], 3: 252–55).

16. On May 15 Frederick Kingsbury and Olmsted surveyed Drum Hill in Waterbury (FJK Journal, May 15, 1845).

17. Frederick Kingsbury wrote Charles Loring Brace on May 15 (ibid.).

18. Green Kendrick (1798–1873), originally from North Carolina, married Anna Maria Leavenworth, the daughter of the Waterbury manufacturer Mark Leavenworth. He had a distinguished career in Connecticut politics and in 1851 was elected lieutenant governor. Martha Kendrick (b. 1829) was their daughter. Olmsted and Frederick Kingsbury called on them on the evening of May 13, 1845 (J. Anderson, *The Town and City of Waterbury*, 2: 266–70; Elias W. Leavenworth, comp., *A Genealogy of the Leavenworth Family in the United States* . . . [Syracuse, N.Y., 1873], p. 230; FJK Journal, May 13, 1845).

19. On May 14, Olmsted and Frederick Kingsbury called at the home of John Davis Johnson (1793–1887), a Waterbury manufacturer. His daughter was Cornelia Maria Johnson (b. 1823) (FJK Journal, May 14, 1845; J. Anderson, *The Town and City of Waterbury*, 2: 307).

20. Fanny Johnson Leavenworth (1796–1852), Frederick Kingsbury's maternal grandmother, was the widow of Frederick Leavenworth (1766–1840). Elisha Leavenworth was her son. (E. W. Leavenworth, *Genealogy of the Leavenworth Family*, p. 144).

21. Waterbury built a combination almshouse, house of correction, and town farm in 1839 (J. Anderson, *The Town and City of Waterbury*, 3: 882–83).

22. Gunntown was a settlement in the western part of the township of Naugatuck, Conn., where the Gunn family had acquired large landholdings in the eighteenth century (ibid., 1: 697).
23. Mary Salina Pierpont Welton (b. 1817), wife of Joseph Welton (ibid., 1: Appendix, pp. 103, 151).
24. Isaac Clinton Collins had egalitarian beliefs that conflicted with Olmsted's view that men like himself cared more for the common good than did many of "the people." Collins combined his democratic beliefs with allegiance to the Democratic party, a strong family tradition. His father, Ela Collins (1786–1848), was a New York State assemblyman, delegate to the Constitutional Convention of 1821 and Democratic congressman in the 18th Congress (1823–1825). Collins's brother, William Collins (1818–1878), was a Democratic congressman from New York in the 30th Congress (1847–1849). Collins kept up this tradition in his own career. He became a lawyer in Cincinnati and was active in the Democratic party. He served in the Ohio legislature (1857–1858) and was the unsuccessful Democratic gubernatorial candidate in 1873. (BDAC, s.v. "Collins, Ela" and "Collins, William"; J. Fletcher Brennan, ed., Biographical Cyclopaedia and Portrait Gallery of Distinguished Men . . . [Cincinnati, 1879], p. 158).
25. Emma Brace.

To JOHN HULL OLMSTED

Address: Mr. John H. Olmsted/Hartford Ct—
Postmark: New Haven/Jun/24/Ct.

Chateau L'eau roche[1] Jeune 18th, 1845

Mon Cher Jean,

But—I think I'll write in English this time.

Your package of Tribunes by mail thankfully acknowledged.

Pleasant ride, very, I had, up, that day—but I survived with the assistance of an occasional pull at the pocket flask, its effects as usually known illustrated or held up in a Temperance lecture by the driver—who appears, by the way, a pretty clever honest fellow, fully competent to take charge of a small sack of oranges, cocoa nuts, &c., just received and landing from Brig So & So from St. Kitts, Barcelona, Barbados, I mean, or any such sort of thing.

I have been ploughing, since, breaking up old—old enough—old as the hills I'm sure, though they say it was ploughed thirty years ago—fallow—without no rocks nor roots nor nothin'. All as smooth as the lee side of the sand spit in a north*weas*ter or that favor'd bit of Connecticut, that the sailors told about, where they have to grind the sheeps' noses to a point 'fore they send 'em to pasture, so they can get 'em down between the stones. I haven't dislocated my hips nor my right wrist nor my neck yet—have, all the rest.

Received also last night a grand bundle of newspapers &c. from home—a summer jacket, for which I am obliged to you—a frock of same stuff as your plaid. I mean to send your jacket down but shall not have it wash'd here.

I sent a letter to Father yesterday in answer to one I received from him last week in which he gave me a lecture on Rash marriages, &c., saying that matrimony was a subject for me not to think of for years. I've no intention of marrying for three or four years. But I'd just as lief as not be engaged, if I came across a suitable person, before I took a farm on my own account, fearing that after that I should have no good opportunity of selection. I think I should like to cruise for about a year, then fall desperately in love & lay off and on till I could bring about an engagement. At any rate I should hope to be married before I am twenty eight. Don't you think I am reasonable? Well, under favorable circumstances I should do better than that, but I've "got a pretty large *caution*," Gibson[2] says.

This fellow makes fun for me with his Phreno-lingo. "That 'ar' man," says he, speaking of an overgrown chap that drawls out his talk like a psalm tune in slow time on a hand organ, "That 'ar' man's got a pretty considerable development of the lympfatic narve." "He wouldn't be afraid o' nothin'. D'ye 'spose he would? D'ye obsarve his head? He 'ant got no caution. Not none 'tall." He gives me a pretty good character: large caution, large firmness, small destructiveness, large veneration, large philoprogenitiveness, small hands, large eyes, small mouth, large belly. What do you think of it?

Let me hear from you and the boat as often as possible.

I write this to have ready when opportunity occurs.

I have some great "settoos" with Gibson. How do you spell that? "Set-to?" I s'pose so. He's strong & has the advantage of me by long odds, but he does not. He isn't quite sure of it yet. He guards altogether too well & hits—very palpably.

18th. I've been all day hoeing potatoes & am gratified to find that I can keep up with Mr. Welton very well without much fatigue. I find by breakfasting on bread & milk I can do without drink between meals. I think I shall live on it, pretty much. They don't have anything else—proper good—but butter & cheese, which is very superior. They have a miserable mess of soured switchel which they think is "beer," and they pay dear for their infatuation. I'm too temperate for it—by a pailful.

We've had a horse—mare, filly. No! She wasn't a *dumb* baste at all, but a Yankee hoosier gal "to tea"—a character, rich! Regular Miss *Higgins* —Miss Squeesh. I've a good joke to tell you—fat! Awful! Enclosed for home, etc. as you'll see.

    Your'n

                agr—ic' (ula)
                A Greek

---

1. For "Waterbury."
2. One of Joseph Welton's hired men. Gibson was caught up in the current fad, phrenology, which provided an analysis of character and mental ability through examina-

tion of the contours of the skull. Different parts of the head were held to be the seat of different characteristics. Gibson's examination of Olmsted revealed the presence of the following traits in large amounts: Cautiousness, which was "Solicitude about consequences—apprehension of danger—instinct of fear—care—anxiety"; Firmness, which was "Stability—decision of character—fixedness of purpose—desire to continue—aversion to change"; Veneration, which was the "Sentiment of adoration and worship for the Supreme Being—reverence for what is considered above us—respect for superiority, &c."; and Philoprogenitiveness, which was "Parental affection and tenderness—love of offspring, and of children generally—fondness for pets, especially young animals, and for the infirm and helpless." Gibson found that Olmsted had little of the trait of Destructiveness, which was the "Propensity to destroy, exterminate, and inflict pain." (Orson Squire Fowler and Lorenzo Niles Fowler, *Phrenology Proved, Illustrated, and Applied, Accompanied by a Chart . . . Together With a View of the Moral and Theological Bearing of the Science . . .* , 2d ed. [New York, 1837], pp. 61, 82, 103, 119, 147.)

Gibson also got involved in the fad of mesmerism and attempted to hypnotize Joseph Welton's hired boy. Olmsted described his efforts in a letter that Frederick Kingsbury quoted in part in his biographical sketch of Olmsted:

You recollect my telling what sort of a chap this Gibson is—of Washington—Joe's man—with his phrenology and all that. He was taken all of a sudden with a fit of Animal Magnetism, and one day he told me that when he was hoeing corn with Henry—Henry Pratt, you know, the boy—he thought he would try him. So he seated him opposite to him on a 'tater hill' and commenced the willing and passes. He succeeded remarkably well for the first time—so that before he was interrupted, the boy could not open his eyes, though he was conscious, and able to speak, &c. I agreed that Henry must be a good "subject" and advised him to persevere. He made other attempts—but short and unsuccessful—during the week after. One night as soon as we had finished supper he and Henry went off to bed. I went at nine, and after sitting up reading half an hour turned in, and had got to sleep when I was woke by Gibson, dressed at my door.

"Mr. Olmsted, Sir, will you please come up stairs?"
"Come up stairs? What for, Gibson?"
"Oh, nothing sir—only I wish you would, sir, I want to show you something—something I wish you would look at sir."
"What is it? I dont want to turn out for nothing. Is there a ghost there, man?" (He appeared very much excited.)
"No, sir, I'm sorry to disturb you, sir, but I've mesmerized Henry, sir—complete; and I just wish you'd step up, so you can tell the folks—'fraid they won't believe me."

So I went off with him conjecturing it was a natural sleep—for I thought it was time the boy should be sleepy. But he assured me there was no mistake—he had tried several experiments and he could paralyze his limbs, etc.

As we entered the room, the boy was in two chairs leaning on the bed and bolstered up with four pillows. "See," says he, "just as I left him exactly; ha'n't moved a jot. Now look here"—and he began to draw his paws down Henry's arm in a knowing manner, till the arm was elevated horizontally. "See, paralyzed—stiff as a stake—can't be moved"—striking it to show me. Then the other arm the same way. "There—now don't you believe he's mesmerized?" "Well, no, I replied. Then tapping the boy under the chin, "Henry." "Sir," says he, opening his eyes and mouth, dropping his hands and grinning like a Cheshire cat. Oh, poor Gibson's face changed more than Henry's. How chap-fallen he did look. I told of it—as that was what he wanted me for—and how the school mistress does run him. Henry's a smart child for his age.

To CHARLES LORING BRACE

Address: Mr. Charles Loring Brace/Yale College/New Haven

Waterbury, June 22nd, 1845

Dear friend,

I have this evening received a letter from John, dated Thursday, in which he informs me that he has had another bilious attack and was about returning home.[1] I am very sorry to hear this. I did not approve of his re-entering this term at all, and I am glad he has left—and hope he will keep out for the present—this summer at least. Don't you?

Would you advise him to give up college altogether? I doubt if he will ever have permanent good health, while he continues a student. He writes I presume in a more cheerful manner than he feels, that he need not pain me, but I can see that he begins to despair studying a profession. He says to me, "To think of quitting college altogether is bad enough. Do you suppose I *could* ever be contented as a farmer?—or businessman?" "I'd rather be a healthy *Irishman* than a sickly professor," &c. Why; if he saw the necessity of giving up a profession or rather of giving up *study*, I'm not afraid but what he'd be contented enough as a farmer. The man that could not must have a very vitiated taste, or bad mind, but then—he never could work any. In the first place, he's no inclination to, and next, no ability.

As to the "business"—which I suppose amounts to writing at a desk all day & half the night, or practising assumed politeness or eulogizing a piece of silk or barrel of lamp oil—I would sooner recommend to study the profession of butcher and learn to stick a hog with accuracy and dispatch, or something as manly and refined.

For myself, I have every reason to be satisfied with my prospects. I grow more contented—or more fond of my business every day. Really, for a man that has any inclination for Agriculture the occupation is very interesting. And if you look closely, you will be surprised to see how much honorable attention and investigation is being connected with it. The "Cultivator" has now *five regular* monthly European correspondents. Scientific men of the highest distinction are there devoting their undivided attention to its advance.[2] And I think here the coming year will show a remarkable progress.

For the matter of happiness, there is no body of men that are half as well satisfied with their business as our farmers. At least I never have met with them. And as for profit—it is sufficient to know that our farmers as they now are, with their miserable plan, can *live*. Amos Kendall (the father of celebrated Amos' children) has said a good thing for Agriculture—I came across in a paper & cut it out.[3] I've a mind to copy it for you.

Though, while I have *room* I'll state the object of this letter, which was to say to you that Friday morning I sent *John* a bundle with an enclosure for you containing a letter for Emma[4] from me, which if worth your while you can probably obtain by calling for at the Professor's.[5] Now to return to our sheep (wolf)—black (but about the best Loco-foco, I reckon outside of 82 if that's your number and Albany).[6]

Alluding to his new occupation, after stating that he will devote a portion of his time to writing & the rest to manual labor, he says; "It is the occupation in which we spent the earlier part of our life; and in the midst of party strife, oppress'd with the labors of public station, we have never ceased to look back with regret to this honorable and peaceful employment. There is no malignity in the earth we till; there is no ingratitude in the plant—flower, or tree we nurse. . . ." By the way, is not he the very man that was so shamefully ungrateful to the noble Henry?[7] Bah! I'll copy no more.

The Cultivator for this month notices John Harding's article and Yale Lit.[8]

The birthday of Freedom—what's [to be][9] did?

I expect after I've got this letter [in the m]ail shall get one from you.

The omnibus for Miss Abby[10]—[. . .] drove up, or broke down, or "got sot." "Stuck," I presume.

I am lighted by a miserable "dip," which don't give light enough to kill a mosquito by. Fortunately, there are not *many* here. (Slap!) (Retiring music—)

Yours affecti—(whack!—got enough now I reckon.)

F.L.O.

1. John Hull Olmsted had been forced by illness to go home from college on May 28. He returned June 10 and went home again on June 20 (JO Journal, May 28, June 10, 20, 1845).
2. The *Cultivator*, founded in 1834 at Albany by the agricultural reformer Jesse Buel and edited in 1845 by Luther Tucker, was the best agricultural journal published in the East, if not the country, before the Civil War. Among its contributors were many of the best American authorities on agricultural science and horticulture. In June 1845 the *Cultivator* had three American correspondents writing regular letters from Great Britain and Europe. John Pitkin Norton (1822–1852) was studying chemistry at Edinburgh; he returned in 1846 to help in preparations for the founding of the Sheffield Scientific School at Yale. Eben Horsford (1818–1893) was studying chemistry with the German chemist Justus von Liebig at Biessen; he became professor at Harvard when he returned in 1847 and was one of the major figures in the early development of the Lawrence Scientific School there. The third contributor was the agriculturalist, landscape gardener, and author Donald Grant Mitchell (1822–1908), who was touring the British Isles and the Continent (Albert L. Demaree, *The American Agricultural Press 1819–1860* [New York, 1941], pp. 340–44; *DAB*).
3. Amos Kendall (1789–1869), Massachusetts-born journalist, leading adviser of Andrew Jackson, and postmaster-general from 1835 to 1840. From 1840 to 1845 he remained in Washington, D.C., engaged in journalism and farming (*DAB*).
4. Emma Brace.
5. Denison Olmsted.
6. During his freshman year at Yale, Charles Loring Brace had lived with John Hull

Olmsted at No. 83 North Middle College (Yale College, *Catalogue of the Officers and Students in Yale College 1842–43* [New Haven, 1842], pp. 21–22).

7. Amos Kendall became an associate of Henry Clay's when he moved to Kentucky in 1814, and gave Clay strong support after 1816 as editor of the *Argus of Western America*. In 1826 he broke with Clay and became a partisan of Andrew Jackson. For this he was accused of being ungrateful and self-seeking (*DAB*, s.v. "Kendall, Amos").

8. John Wheeler Harding, an editor of the *Yale Literary Magazine*. The *Cultivator* judged the magazine to be well managed, interesting, and useful, and made special note of an article (perhaps by Harding) on agriculture in the January 1845 issue (*Yale Obit. Rec.*, 4th ser., no. 6 [June 1896]: 380; *Cultivator*, n.s. 2, no. 6 [June 1845]: 185).

9. The words in brackets in this section of the letter are the editor's reading of words partially obliterated by the cutting out of the stamp.

10. Abby Morton Clark (see FLO to Abby Clark, Jan. 18, 1845, note 1, above).

To JOHN HULL OLMSTED

Address: Mr. John Hull Olmsted/John Olmsted Esq./Hartford/Conn.
Postmark: Waterbury/Jun

Waterbury, June 23rd, 1845

Dear John,

Your letter of Thursday, informing me of your illness, I received last evening. I was very sorry to hear of it, but I must confess I never hardly thought you'd get comfortably through this term. I do think these colleges are a most grievous nuisance, and I'd almost make one of a mob to raze 'em all down about the besotted faculty's ears, if I could not make reason reach 'em any other way.

I don't think we were placed in *this* world to ruin the body in an attempt at perfection of the soul, which we can only look for in another, and not there, if we live as murderers or suicides here. Moreover, it can't be. For on a healthy state of one depends the proper action of the other—while here. And if it didn't, is there no credit to be given to physical excellence? If not, why is it placed in our power, by proper cultivation & study, to excel? The German universities—the best in the world in other respects, too—are right in having their Gymnastic Department with its professors and other machinery rank with the Classical and Mathematical.

I suppose you will have left now for the summer, and I shouldn't be careless in advising you to keep away—if it were not in deference to Father's wishes and if you had a reasonable taste or inclination for anything else of your own. At all events, I hope you won't again subject yourself to the routine with all its absurd requirements, merely for a bit of sheep's skin, the acquirement of which would never be of value except to disguise a jackass. That is, I should hope you wouldn't re-enter at all, unless you are convinced

Yale College

—as I presume you may be—that you can safely do so, and that it will be the readiest manner of obtaining all the *useful* knowledge which you would get by being tackled to your, or a, class.

I hope that anyway, you will let your views and wishes be known without reserve. You are old enough to judge yourself, and as father's observation has not trended much near this line, he will be willing to give yours some credit. I think, like most persons who did not when young enjoy those privileges which he has so liberally afforded us, he considers as too important the advantages of a superior education.

I see from some of your reflections—as your "rather" choosing to "be a healthy" laborer, "than a sickly professor"—you're in a measure prepared to give up your favorite pursuits, if it should prove advisable. You ask if I think you could ever be contented as a farmer or merchant. As the latter, I'm sure you ought not to be, nor any other man. No man of respectable mind is altogether, I believe. The best of them are either half engaged with other things, or are looking forward with impatience to the time when they shall be.

I believe that was a true remark; that the passengers by the Drydock omnibuses[1] were of a better & bolder physiognomy than most of the omnibus freights taken elsewhere. And accounted for by the effect of their different habits in business—they being mostly mechanicks & men whose labor always *commands* their support—their *smiles* & *manners* not being business capital, like one whose suavity furnishes him with his salary or income, and who must appear pleas'd, anxious, indifferent, or sad according to his customer's humor and not his own. And I think you'd be no better off, for the matter of health, either at the desk or counter.

Rural pursuits, on the other hand, tend to elevate and enlarge the ideas, for all the proudest aims of Science are involved in them. They require a constant application of the principles and objects of the Chemist, Naturalist, Geologist, Mechanic, &c. More than all of *them*, it cultivates, or should, the taste & sentiment. And there is no more occasion for anything vulgar or offensive in its operations, than in theirs.

The objects of a farmer, too, are such as to relieve him from the annoyances which the envy and opposition of rivals constantly inflict on most other active occupations. And the higher you rise in distinction, the more are you marked with the shafts of malice. Even lawyers and politicians, too, have proverbially a crafty look. And did you never notice what a mysterious, self satisfied air all young ministerial railroad passengers and [. . .] have? Meaning "I'm driving the right team, I don't care what you say, and I'll bring arguments & curses till I've hollered my lungs out of me, if you won't take my ticket."

But the objects of a farmer are such as benefit others, and will not subject his motives to harsh investigation. For my part, I believe that our farmers are, and have cause to be, the most contented men in the world. And for the matter of profit, it is sufficient to know that they live & bring up their families in what they consider comfortable circumstances, with their usual system & management. I should think by the use of the proper tools and machinery which a man of intelligence and information would procure and invent, at least half of the most disagreeable and hard labor of our old-fashion'd farmers might be dispensed with to advantage.

But I doubt whether taste for its peculiar pleasures, or inclination or ability for its manual exertions, will make you a farmer. If you could, however—and of this you are the best judge—become interested in its operations for a year or two & connect yourself with its present rapid advance as an honorable & learned profession, you would not only find it a sufficient means of support, but an agreeable and healthful pursuit.

I sent your jacket with a letter—by Express—last Friday to be left at the Professor's.[2]

Very affectionately, yours with what I have to look at—only, unfortunately I've forgot to put in the sashes, if I have not the curtain.

Fred

Send me a crow quill and I'll do better.

P.S. I wish to make a chemical analysis of soil. I believe I have all the materials that will be necessary for my purpose or can procure them here, except a small pair of exact balances and a little "prussiate of potash."

P.S. Express Office Monday night. Have this moment received Father's of Friday. Nothing to add. Hope to see you soon.

Affectionately,

F.L.O.

---

1. The Dry Dock omnibuses, among the first in New York, ran from City Hall Park and must have carried shipwrights and mechanics to the dry docks on the East River ([Asa Greene], *A Glance at New York* . . . [New York, 1837], p. 260).
2. Denison Olmsted.

To CHARLES LORING BRACE

Address: Mr. Chas. Lor. Brace./Yale College/New Haven

Waterbury, July 9th, 1845
July 10th

My dear Charly,

I received a letter from you some time last week. What a complete blunderer you are anyhow. But I had entirely forgotten that there were letters in that bundle except for Emma and you and John.[1] I'd no intention of troubling you with them. They were of no consequence, but I'm obliged to you, all the same.

I have been in Hartford luxuriating on green peas and ripe cherries for some days, and now returned half sick to bread (half-baked rye dough by accident this week) and milk. By the way, I had the gratification of eating some of Emma's own bread at your house, and it was as good as could be, I assure you. I was at your house twice. Nobody there but your father[2] and Emma, but I could not have had a much more agreeable time than I did.

I went up on the Fourth, and was fortunate enough to hear Mr. Case's[3] performance, of which you have seen some notice. Oh! It was *rich*, though, I tell you. Decidedly a stupendous splurge. In the first place, I believe Mr. Case inquired of some friend if he knew any town that was desirous of obtaining the services of an orator for the Fourth. Certain public spirited individuals having learnt this, and it having come to their knowledge also that he had been engaged in the composition of an Independence address two years before, it was resolved that the result of so much distinguished labor should not be lost, but if possible secured for the edification of their own fellow citizens. Accordingly, a *self-constituted* Committee waited on the notable author and very readily obtained his acceptance of the appointment of "orator of the day."

So, on the morning, appeared on every lamppost and nuisance wall a handbill headed with a spread eagle with the flying motto of "Keep up the Spirit of '76" informing the public that *the* oration would be delivered at the foot of the State House yard by Seymour N. Case, Esq., after the reading of the Declaration of Independence, &c, "per order *Com. of Arrangements.*" Agreeably to this call at four o'clock I found perhaps a thousand persons, or half of it, waiting there in lively anticipation.

Considerable apprehension of disappointment (is that a bull?) was evident, but it was said Mr. Case had been called on early in the afternoon and found rehearsing before a glass. However as he did not appear a committee went to look him up. He had locked himself into his room, and refused them admittance, telling them indignantly that he was not to be imposed upon. (Some friends had advised him that he was *sold*. It is supposed to have been Mr. Toucey.[4]) Admission having been obtained however by a match key, his various personal acquaintance (who are they not?) severally assured him that there was no hoax, at least as far as they were aware. And each as friends privately advised him that if such had been the case, it would be much to his credit & renown to get the better of them, by carrying it through in a masterly manner, at the same time offering their countenance and protection.

Colonel Waterman (the Sheriff)[5] came in hoping anxiously that he would delay no longer, as the people were getting excited and he feared it would be impossible to restrain them much longer. There were ten thousand men waiting impatiently and he did not know where it might end, &c. This evidently affected him and he inquired who was to be the *reader. Chas. T. Bull*[6] was mentioned and several others, to each of which he objected (as guises I suppose). Mr. *Skinner*[7] he thought would be just the man (quite complimentary to John wasn't it!) Mr. S. accepted and was agreed upon.

A procession was started immediately—thus: Marshall of the day (Colonel Waterman), Orator of the day carrying his roll, Reader of the Declaration of Independence with a big sheep covered book (arm in arm), Erastus Goodwin, Esq.[8] (solus), assistant grand marshall, Committee of Arrangements, and the escorting committee with faculty and students of Trinity College, as an escort armed with canes; citizens (two deep) and strangers, three young ladies from the country in white dresses (accidentally), young gentlemen of the public schools, &c.

The crowd parted respectfully and permitted the "set" to enter the American Hotel,[9] on the lower balcony of which they presently appeared. The adjoining windows and other balconies were crowded with beauty and white dresses. A table with chairs and a small awning were provided. And the meeting having been called to order by the Marshall, Mr. Skinner read the Declaration, after which the Orator was presented and received with every demonstration of delight. The cheers subsiding, Mr. Case unrolled a scroll of close written foolscap, which frightened some of the country folk who wanted to go home that night.

He commenced reading very loud and continued amidst general cries of "louder!" When it was evident he had reached the highest capacity of his voice, the Marshall requested the audience to keep order and silence was partially restored. The most rapturous applause, however, hailed every sentiment—generally in the middle of its delivery—and a running accompaniment of laughter, "good!" "louder!" "great!" "That's fine!" "Splendid!" "My!" &c., &c. was kept up.

Bouquets were thrown from the windows behind him, which he acknowledged with peculiar grace & benignancy. His modesty however would not allow him to wear a wreath, with which a young gentleman with the best intentions, acting as the representative of the ladies, endeavoured to adorn his brows.

When he had finished, Mr. Chapman, Major Ely, Lawyer Goodman, the Comptroller (Tyler),[10] and others of our first public men were called upon, but severally excused themselves mostly on the plea that they dare not risk their reputation in extemporaneous speaking after such a well prepared and brilliant production as they had listened to. No lawyer could better the *case*, &c.

But the best of [it] was to see him try to look calm and composed sitting in the sunshine burning with blushes, his hair *wilted*, chin & nose dripping with sweat, & holding a bouquet as big as your hat, tied to a broom handle. He was escorted by the enthusiastic crowd to the City Hotel, where he held a levee where many distinguished strangers were presented to him, each retiring with a deep impression of his *peculiar* affability, &c.

It struck me as a peculiar feature of the affair that the whole crowd in which there must have been many strangers, appeared to understand the thing perfectly. Do you suppose that *he* did? Not a bit of it. John Skinner said he made a congratulatory call on him the next morning and he remarked "Ah! Mr. Skinner, yesterday was the happiest day of my life! The proudest moment of my existence!" &c. "Ah Sir! There is nothing—there is nothing, Sir, so cheering to the soul, as the murmurs of popular applause!" I hope the address will be published for your benefit.

I will try to recall one sentence: "The proud bird of liberty *clap'd* his wings, and scouring through the etherial element perched upon the topmost cloud of heaven's array, proclaimed to the sordid scions of royalty, *America is free!*"

John started with "liph,"[11] on Monday for New Hampshire, and perhaps Montreal. I rode up with them as far as "Alford's"[12] where I left them in good spirits. Frank and his step brother[13] were in company in a buggy. I do hope this journey will set John up again.

I should like to know when you expect to be in Litchfield. Our folks are to visit that way sometime in August, and I think *I* shall, if *you* do at that time.

Yours,

Fred

1. Emma Brace and John Hull Olmsted.
2. John Pierce Brace, at this time principal of the Hartford Female Seminary.
3. Seymour N. Case (1817–1872), an eccentric lawyer, who practiced law in Hartford for thirty years (*Hartford County*, 1: 132; *Hartford Daily Courant*, Nov. 27, 1872, p. 2).
4. Isaac Toucey (1792–1869), a prominent Hartford lawyer in whose office Seymour Case worked during his early years of law practice in the city. Toucey became governor of Connecticut in 1846, attorney general of the United States in 1848, U.S. senator from Connecticut from 1852 to 1857, and secretary of the Navy under James Buchanan (*DAB*; *Hartford Daily Courant*, Nov. 27, 1872, p. 2).

5. Nathan Morgan Waterman (1815–1871) of Hartford was deputy sheriff of Hartford in 1845 and commanding officer of the Connecticut First Regiment, Hartford County (Donald L. Jacobus, comp., *The Waterman Family, Descendants of Robert Waterman of Marshfield, Massachusetts* . . . , 3 vols. [New Haven, 1939], 2: 653; *Geer's Directory for 1844*, s.v. "Waterman, Nathan Morgan"; *Hartford County*, 1: 180).
6. Charles Tyron Bull (1816–c. 1853) of Hartford (Gurdon W. Russell, *Contributions to the History of Christ Church, Hartford, Conn* . . . , vol. 2, *Additional Contributions to the History of Christ Church* [Hartford, Conn., 1895–1908], p. 49).
7. John Warburton Skinner (1818–1889), journalist and lawyer. After graduating from Yale College in 1843 he studied law in Hartford and was part-time editor of the *Hartford Daily Courant*. When he completed his legal training he practiced law in St. Louis. He married Charles Loring Brace's sister Mary in 1852 (Yale University, Class of 1843, *A Record of the Class of 1843, Yale College. Prepared by Request of the Class.* [New York, 1859], pp. 101–2; Yale University, *Catalogue of Officers and Graduates, 1701–1915* [New Haven, 1916], p. 127).
8. Erastus Goodwin (1795–1882), cloth merchant and tailor of Hartford (Frank Farnsworth Starr, comp., *The Goodwins of Hartford, Connecticut, Descendants of William and Ozias Goodwin* [Hartford, 1891], p. 639).
9. The American Hotel was on State Street in Hartford (*Geer's Directory for 1845*, p. 12).
10. Charles R. Chapman (1799–1869), Connecticut lawyer and politician; possibly William B. Ely, who was the commanding officer of the Governor's Foot Guard in 1840–41 and a grocer in Hartford; Edward Goodman (1805–1882), lawyer and city politician, long active in the state militia; and Daniel Putnam Tyler (1798–1875), lawyer, politician, and proprietor of the Brooklyn (Conn.) Academy (*BDAC*, s.v. "Chapman, Charles R."; *Hartford County*, 1: 191; I. N. Bolles, *Directory and Guide Book for* . . . *Hartford, 1842*, p. 128; *Hartford Daily Courant*, July 29, 1882, p. 2; Willard I. Tyler Brigham, 2 vols., *The Tyler Genealogy* [Tylerville, Conn., 1912] 1: 170, 336–37).
11. Eliphalet Terry (1826–1896) of Hartford, son of the prominent Hartford businessman Eliphalet Terry (1776–1849) and a schoolmate of Brace. He became a landscape and animal painter. In 1846–47 he studied in Rome with his cousin, the portrait painter Luther Terry, then maintained a studio in Hartford for a few years and moved to New York c. 1851 (FJK Sketch of CLB, p. 7; *Hartford Daily Courant*, Nov. 5, 1896, p. 4; George C. Croce and David H. Wallace, *The New-York Historical Society's Dictionary of Artists in America* [New Haven, 1957], p. 622).
12. Perhaps a tavern owned by E. J. Alford in Windsor, Conn. north of Hartford on the Connecticut River. Alford took over the management of the United States Hotel in Hartford in 1842 (*Connecticut Courant*, Jan. 15, 1842, p. 3).
13. Frank Terry (1827–1874) and Henry Warner Birge (1825–1888). Birge's mother, Lucy Ripley Birge, married Terry's father, Roderick Terry, after the death of her husband, Backus W. Birge (Stephen Terry, comp., *Notes of the Terry Families, In the United States of America* . . . [Hartford, 1887], pp. 81, 317).

CHAPTER V

THE SEARCH FOR
LOVE AND CERTITUDE

1846

In Many Ways, 1846 was a decisive year for Olmsted. He suffered a rebuff from the girl he most admired, received his best training in agriculture from a gentleman farmer he would later emulate, reached important conclusions about his religious faith, and expanded his political concerns amid questions raised by the Mexican War.

Olmsted began the year in Hartford recuperating from the series of fainting spells he had suffered while at Yale in the fall of 1845. When Elizabeth Baldwin came from New Haven on a visit, he was delighted at the attention she paid to him and the serious talks they had. It hurt him deeply, therefore, when she refused to correspond with him after she returned to New Haven.

That spring she played an important part in a religious revival among Olmsted's friends in New Haven that led many of them to feel they had attained salvation. Olmsted's parents urged him to join his friends so that he, too, might benefit from the revival. He went to New Haven and reveled in the atmosphere, holding long talks with Miss Baldwin and others. As a result, he had a conversion experience, but he was not sure whether the change of heart he felt came from the direct action of God's grace or was simply a response to the "Human Sympathy" that his friends held out to him. This question of the reality of religious experiences that took place during revivals was an old one, and in debating it he was trying to find a reasonable answer to one of the many religious questions then troubling his contemporaries.

Throughout Olmsted's youth, the traditionally stable religious condition of Connecticut was unsettled. In 1818 dissenting groups forced the legislature to abolish the position of the Congregational church as the official state church. Fearful of what the effects of disestablishment would be, Congregational ministers launched a series of revivals that brought many converts and halted the spread of Unitarianism in the state.

At the same time there were doctrinal quarrels within the Congregational church itself. Nathaniel Taylor of the Yale Divinity School evolved a "New Haven Theology" that expanded the area of free will and limited the concept of natural depravity. To combat Taylor's doctrine, the strict Calvinists, centered in the Hartford region, founded the Hartford Theological Seminary. The seminary's president, Bennet Tyler, carried on a long rear-guard action against the rising liberal theology in what was known as the "Taylor-Tyler" controversy. Further divisions within the Congregational church arose in the 1840s over the teachings of Horace Bushnell on Christian nurture and the nature of Christ.

Olmsted was aware of these religious issues as he grew up, since Hartford's leading Congregational ministers, Joel Hawes and Horace Bushnell, often clashed on doctrinal questions. The aversion to controversy over points of doctrine that Olmsted expresses in his letters was probably due in part to this continuing rancor in Hartford. His father apparently found this controversy distasteful, too, because when Joel Hawes and other orthodox Congregational ministers in the Hartford region tried to convict Bushnell of heresy for his book *God in Christ* (1848), John Olmsted left Hawes's church and joined Bushnell's.

Although influenced by both Hawes and Bushnell, Olmsted did not restrict himself to the teachings of Congregationalists. He read Unitarian doctrine, examined the beliefs of Catholics, Episcopalians, and Quakers, and almost joined a Presbyterian church.

Before the New Haven revival had run its course, Olmsted left his friends and traveled to Camillus, New York, where he continued his agricultural education with George Geddes. His letters describe his experiences as a farmer's apprentice and show that while he was learning the techniques of prize-winning farming he still had time to pursue the religious questions that had occupied him in the spring.

His religious experience in New Haven in March 1846 made him anxious to take the next step that was expected of him: make a profession of faith and join a church. But most churches required members to follow religious practices and profess beliefs that Olmsted considered narrow and sectarian. He tried to resolve his religious difficulties through wide and thoughtful reading of theological works and the Bible, but could not reconcile his views with the admission requirements of the churches. He joined no church while at the Geddes farm and disappointed his family by not becoming a church member when he returned to Hartford in the fall.

During the summer of 1846, his reading of Thomas Carlyle's spiritual autobiography, *Sartor Resartus*, strengthened his resistance to joining a doctrinally narrow church. The book made a strong impression on Olmsted and defined for him what the fruits of conversion should be. He sympathized with the hero, Teufelsdröckh, who, like himself, had suffered uncertainty about his role in life, had loved and lost a lady of high station, and felt himself a talented but poorly educated lover of nature. In Carlyle's affirmation of life and his assertion that salvation lay in doing the duty that lay nearest, Olmsted found a message that met his needs. Therefore he turned from questions of doctrine and concerned himself with what he considered to be his duties toward others.

His immediate role in life was to take up the profession of scientific farming. He had learned much from George Geddes, and by the end of the summer he was ready to start farming on his own. In November 1846 his father bought him a farm on Sachem's Head in Guilford, Connecticut, to which he moved the following spring and began to work the land.

To CHARLES LORING BRACE

Address: Mr. Charles L. Brace/from Fred Olmsted/per valisse

Hartford, February 5th, 1846

My dear friend,

I seat myself to acknowledge the receipt of your very acceptable letter, which came to hand yesterday P.M. with an enclosure for Emma[1] (which met with an accident before it got to her, but I presume remained legible) and one from John.[2] I don't intend to answer you at all now, having a cold which has only become decisively a *bad* one this afternoon and not feeling at all in the humor. (Here he blows his nose.)

As to what I've been doing? I'll do the best you can expect under the circumstances.

I've rode horseback some. The day (Saturday) after you left I recollect I rode out on the Albany turnpike to a road going over Prospect Hill. You've been that road *perhaps?* Well, after you get over the hill a spell, there's a road that brings you into town by the Asylum,[3] you know. So I came in that way—I did—stopping some. Oh yes! Thomas C. Perkins'. I did call there and saw his wife, a very intelligent woman with whom I conversed some about various matters & things.[4]

She's been to the West and told me something about the country and people—not forgetting, of course, the Cincinnati porkascope.[5] Then we talked some about people & society. Miss Baldwin[6] of New Haven—perhaps you may know her, some of the students do, I believe—has been visiting her and she spoke in very good terms of her. Then I rode into town.

While fastening my horse at the store I noticed a lady with her face turned round, down street (as if waiting for somebody), whose gay long-shawl, and *couleur de rose* ashes (ashes of roses-colored) pelisse coatcloak, seemed not altogether new to my eyes. When I had *hitched*, she turned round and presented the smiling face of Lizzy Baldwin. Bless her good little soul. Wasn't she clever to stop and talk there on the *trottoir* with me for five minutes. Then, when I read the paper & had just got suited to a pair of gloves (standing by the counter near the door), *she*, in passing down, looks in & turns to me again. I go out & find her waiting with her face round a few steps below. How many girls would not care more for *appearances?*

With a face and eyes like a look-out's in a gale—with riding in the wind—and with boots & spurs and ragged gloves & mud & horse hair, I walked down in earnest & close conversation with her, westside Broadway time, twelve meridian, all white kid-dom creaking in their new boots. Governor's daughter. Excellent princess. She's a dove. Whew! I shall fill up my letter with her. Didn't call Monday. Oh, yes! Monday morning rode out with your folks' invitation [in] about ten minutes—doing well! Knitting (knit or not) that splendid scarlet purse.

A real jolly time on the hill that night. I acted like a sheep, as I knew I should—in the tableaux more particularly I mean—she as an Irish girl as if she was born in Tipperary and was *raised* on taters and kellen.

Wednesday didn't go out till late in P.M. Called at Day's. When I was going, Mary said she was going to have me stay to hear. So I did, and in the evening Livia did sing.[7] Oh! Most gloriously! As if she was singing herself and not her music master. Between Miss Mary and some old singing books, I found lots of things she knew once and hadn't forgotten. She goes into it so good and sings so naturally, and as if she loved to. I don't know anybody I'd rather hear. She's a regular brung up good girl anyhow, or I don't know everything. When you are seeing her give my heartiest regards and all such sort of things.

Didn't see any of them Wednesday. Miss Baldwin called (What! Fourth page!) that evening. Reading Society at Mr. Terry's.[8] Very pleasant. Tried to be entertained by Sarah Cook and succeeded very well. Nice girl, half love her. Good time dancing. Went into it like a bear, but with Mary's kind instruction succeeded better than I had anticipated.

Miss Baldwin called at the store[9] that day to send word to me that she was going out of town soon and hoped to see me before she went & she would be at Mrs. Perk's[10] next morning, etc. Of course, I went out. Had a pleasant call: subject of conversation "marriage," etc., (not the "wedding"). Liked her views of the subject very well. Mrs. Hooker[11] of Farmington there.

Asked Miss B. to ride—be driven. Took her out to West Hartford. Had a good time, but no sentiment or confidential stuff at least—but a few sentences. Concert that night, fine. Emma'll tell about it. I wish there were five pages in a letter sheet. But to conclude, *they* went the next morning in those cruel cars that have carried off so many good people[12] and so endeth this chapter.

I meant to have continued on another sheet, but you must wait (for chapter second) a day or two.

Tell Collins & Hill to write to me as well as Charley Trask.[13] Compliments to [. . .] & Inf. Chem. A.[14] in general, & the *fellows* in particular. Read this if you can. Written in *your* library.

A bundle from Miss Mary Day for Miss Olivia. My regards to her & to Miss Baldwin—[. . .]

1. Emma Brace.
2. John Hull Olmsted.
3. The American Asylum for the Deaf and Dumb in Hartford.
4. Thomas Clap Perkins (1798–1870) was a Hartford lawyer and sometime member of the state legislature. He married Mary Foote Beecher (1805–1900), the daughter of Lyman Beecher and sister of Henry Ward Beecher and Harriet Beecher Stowe. They were the parents of Emily Perkins. Mrs. Perkins was the "only purely private Beecher." Her cousin-in-law Mary Hallock Foote said, "It was the general opinion that for an all-around endowment, including common sense, she was blessed beyond any of the geniuses of the family" (Lyman Beecher Stowe, *Saints, Sinners, and Beechers* [New York, 1934], p. 152–53; Mary Hallock Foote, *A Victorian Gentlewoman in the Far West: The Reminiscences of Mary Hallock Foote*, ed. Rodman W. Paul [San Marino, Calif., 1972], p. 81; *Perkins Genealogy*, Part 3, pp. 80–81).
5. Mrs. Perkins had probably been to visit her parents in Cincinnati, where they had been living since 1832 when Lyman Beecher became the first president of Lane Theological Seminary. By 1840, the number of meat packing plants there and the volume of their business had earned Cincinnati the name "Porkopolis of the West" (*DAB*, s.v. "Beecher, Lyman"; Ray A. Billington, *Westward Expansion: A History of the American Frontier*, 2d ed. [New York, 1960], p. 330).
6. Elizabeth Baldwin.
7. The activities Olmsted describes took place at the Hartford home of the Hon. Thomas Day (1777–1855), judge of the county court of Hartford, reporter of the Connecticut Supreme Court of Errors, editor of many volumes of court reports and sometime secretary of state of Connecticut. He was one of the most active promoters of benevolent and scientific enterprises in the Connecticut of his time. His daughter, Mary Frances Day (1826–1895) was one of the girls Olmsted and his friends most admired. Olivia Day (1826–1853), whose singing Olmsted praises, was the daughter of Thomas's brother, Jeremiah Day, president of Yale College (Thomas Day Seymour, *The Family of the Rev. Jeremiah Day of New Preston* . . . [New Haven, 1900], pp. 15, 17, 23; FLO to FJK, June 12, 1846, below).
8. Probably the home of Henry Wadsworth Terry, recording secretary of the Natural History Society of Hartford and landscape gardener.
9. The dry-goods store of Olmsted's father at 158 Main Street, which became "Olmsted, Thacher & Goodrich, Dry Goods," in March 1845 (*Geer's Directory for 1847*, p. 88; FLO to JHO, March 13, 1846; JO to FLO and JHO, Oct. 6, 1845).
10. Mary Beecher Perkins (see note 4 above).
11. Probably Mary Beecher Perkins's sister, Isabella Beecher Hooker, who lived in nearby Farmington, Conn. and whose husband, John Hooker, had a law partnership in Hartford (*Notable American Women*, 2: 212).
12. A reference to the Hartford and New Haven Railroad Company, which began service between the two cities in 1839 (Forrest Morgan, ed., *Connecticut as a Colony and*

as a State; Or, One of the Original Thirteen, 4 vols. [Hartford, Conn., 1904], 3: 292).

13. Three members of the Yale class of 1846 who became Olmsted's friends. For Isaac Clinton Collins, see FLO to CLB, May 16, 1845, above, notes 9 and 24. George Edwards Hill (1824–1915) of Boston, Mass., was the son of Henry Hill, the treasurer of the American Board of Commissioners for Foreign Missions. After graduating from Yale he became a Congregational minister. Charles Hooper Trask (1824–1905) of Manchester, Mass., was the son of a sea captain. After graduating from Yale he studied to be a minister, but recurring throat trouble led him to abandon his plans and become a merchant instead (*Yale Obit. Rec.,* 6th ser., no. 5 [July 1915]: 729; ibid., 5th ser., no. 6 [June 1906]: 541).

14. For "Infantile Chemistry Association" (see FLO to CLB, July 30, 1846, note 8, below).

To CHARLES LORING BRACE

Hartford, Sunday Evening, Febr. 22nd, 1846

Dear Charley,

I ought now to answer yours of some three weeks—Sunday night—since, but I shan't find it easy to say much worth troubling you with on the subject. The first thing that occurs to me about it is that I don't father "the fear of death is a hangman's whip,"[1] but Burns or Hogg[2] or Scott or Shakespeare. Secondly, I don't believe I applied it as you seem to think.

The fact is I don't believe the fear of death does speak much or very effectually as a *driver.* What's the reason? For if we sit down and talk it over in your style, it certainly cuts us up terribly. I rather believe we must all—even among the best of Christians—have more or less sceptism (spell it right, I can't.) We are religious too much from the thought: "It can't do any *harm* at all events," and have not a good substantial foundation for our belief (not faith). Were you not startled to see how little we all knew about the evidence those Sunday evenings and how much doubt we all had? I do not think Collins[3] was right about examining the whole thing thoroughly and making up one's mind without prejudice from the *evidence,* disregarding what other men think.

If we do so, I can not see how we can be wrong. And if that French infidel gave a true and candid account, I don't see—I wish I could—how he, with all his endeavours after the truth, can suffer the pangs of remorse to all eternity in a deeper hell than you and I who merely rely upon a *blind* faith in a *mystery.* That poor fellow is a heart-sore to me. I wish I could think there was a purgatory and I could *spend myself* to get his truth-loving soul out of it.

I abhor infidelity and I think have convinced myself sufficiently of its absurdity. But it is seldom the needle stands firm and direct to what in my soul I believe is the true faith. At present, it is dipping at (or against) Unitarianism.

I think Charley Lamb in a letter to Coleridge (they both appear to have been Unitarians) uses language something like this: "What is this," (He is reprimanding him for some liberty of speech with sacred things) "What is this better than what they would say who make believe the" (or, a) "man, (Christ Jesus) equal to God" or "who think God a man," or something of that sort.[4] It is a long time since I saw it, and I can't give it to you now, so it will [not] strike you as it did me. But my idea is if *these folks* are right and if hearts that prompt to goodness and acts of kindness, and searching heads, were to find what was right, we should be as likely to find it with them as with us perhaps. But I say if they should be right, should not we be guilty—no, not guilty—but are we not in the habit of a constant blasphemy and a dreadful one, too?

Now, here are some of our greatest men and best scholars & philanthropists—letting alone the Foreigners, German Philosophers and their co-workers in England (Carlyle &c)—Franklin and Jefferson (and I have a much better opinion of Jefferson every way, lately) and Adams (Franklin & Jefferson are more Unitarians at least than anything else I think) [and] our first Theologian (so considered in the Edinburgh [Review]) Channing[5] —all these men, and plenty of others will occur to you, that on other subjects we consider almost as authorities, the results of whose investigations and reasoning we pay the greatest respect to.

Is it not at least our duty to try to be *sure*—to know that we have a reason, a right to be satisfied—that what we look upon and act upon as truth and duty is not as they think (and are equally confident with us) as rank and horrible blasphemy?!

I've somewhere got Jefferson's ideas on this and I'd like to give them to you if I find them.

My sheet anchor (in reasoning about this) is the truth of the Bible, new and old. If 'tis true—and I can't see how it could be otherwise—Unitarianism can't bear up against it. I've given you about all my Unitarianism in the above reflections. I am not much afraid of it, but I shouldn't like to study their books and reasoning without preparation.

I've rambled so far (and since I began I have been to hear Mr. Hasting's[6] lecture on Moses' psalmody, etc.), I've really forgot 'twas I had to say on "the subject before the meeting," i.e., fear of death. But thus much: I feel just so as you do. Only I have cause to feel ten times *"more so."* Our consolation must be that we in preparation and in the hope of *yet* doing something for the good and help and salvation of our fellow sinners and the honor & glory of Christ through whose *all-powerful atonement* and *mediation* —*as we believe*— we can hope to be saved from *Justice*.

1. This letter clearly illustrates Olmsted's reluctance to accept any religious faith for which he did not have a well-reasoned foundation. The question under discussion here—whether the fear of death drives one into faith—must have been a poignant one for him: his half-sister Ada had died at the age of seven only a week before. The actual quotation is from Robert Burns, "Epistle to a Young Friend":

> The fear o'hell's a hangman's whip
> To haud the wretch in order;
> But where ye feel your honour grip
> Let that aye be your border;
> Its slightest touches, instant pause—
> Debar a' side pretences;
> And resolutely keep its laws
> Uncaring consequences.

(James Currie, comp., *The Complete Works of Robert Burns* [Halifax, 1845], p. 128).
2. James Hogg (1770–1835), Scottish poet and friend of Sir Walter Scott (*DNB*).
3. Isaac Clinton Collins.
4. Lamb believed that it was blasphemous to consider man in any way equal to God, because of the unbridgeable distance between the Divine Mind and the human intellect. "The New Testament," he wrote, "instructs us that the proper relation between man and God is that of a humble, dependent child to a kind parent, our heavenly father." Coleridge tried to console Lamb after his deranged sister Mary murdered his mother, writing, "You are a temporary sharer in human misery, that you may be an eternal partaker of the Divine Nature." Lamb replied, "What more than this do those men say who are for exalting the man Christ Jesus into the second person of an unknown Trinity?—men whom you or I scruple not to call idolators. Man, full of imperfections at best . . . in the pride of speculation, forgetting his nature, and hailing in himself the future God, must make angels laugh" (Charles Lamb to Samuel Taylor Coleridge, Oct. 24, 1796, in *The Works of Charles Lamb*, ed. Thomas N. Talfourd, 4 vols. [Boston, 1860], 1: 31–32).
5. William Ellery Channing (1780–1842), leading figure in the founding of American Unitarianism. From his reading of the Scriptures he drew a system of belief that differed radically from the doctrines of New England Calvinism and asserted "the goodness of God, the essential virtue and perfectibility of man, and the freedom of the will with its consequent responsibility for action" (*DAB*).
6. Thomas Hastings (1784–1872), Connecticut-born composer, who wrote some one thousand hymn tunes and compiled numerous editions of psalms and hymns. He was one of the most influential men of his generation working to improve American church music (*DAB*).

To CHARLES LORING BRACE   [March 27, 1846][1]

Address: Mr. Chas. L. Brace/Yale College/New Haven

Old Hartford, Friday night
Dear Charley,
I have but a short time to spare just now to answer your good favor of Wednesday, now on hand. But as I have not written you for some time and am going out of town tomorrow,[2] I'll try, for somewhat.
Thank God for Miss Baldwin and all the rest.[3] What an angel she

232

will make! How glad I am! Do you recollect our wondering how such a sensible girl could live without religion. I knew she must think about it a great deal, and I thought sh'd be coming out. But I did not think—I don't know but I did too—that 'twould be so soon. But I did not think it would be so sudden. I should have *picked her out* for a *gradual*, I think. I can't understand it.

We used to talk about answering prayer. I think, and always have, Revivals and Conversions, etc., etc. were more connected with prayer than anything else and seemed more directly the result of prayer. I'd like to know how many folks have remembered her (and them) in their devotions the last three months. If you and I have, how much more a *good* many others! I believe those girls Hetty Blake & Miss Bacon⁴ & _____ have saved many souls this spring.

I wish you'd tell me more about her and the operation—the process. Ask her—pray—does she really think 'twas a miracle, or the like of one? I wish you would. A case of "special interpose" etc. or anything like it? If she thinks so and you do, I'm *swamped* on that tack. You say "would be more gradual with such fellows as," etc. Now I should say *she was just one of those fellows.* I wish you'd tell her so, and see if *she would not have* thought so. You say you are in a mist of doubts. Why, bless you, I'm in a real old bank fog and becalmed without steering way, at that, almost. But the sun does shine through occasionally.

Spirit of God or Human Sympathy? I expect to see people as excited tonight at the Whig Caucus as I ever saw them in a Methodist camp meeting. If 'twas a Loco Foco meeting you might say Spirit of _____ —something else. But it is not. And if 'twas a church meeting to elect a deacon, it might be all the same.

My character might be changed as much by an intimate acquaintance with Miss Baldwin or anybody else I admired and respected so much. As much as some people I know have been changed by an acquaintance with Christ—to my poor judgment—and good Christians, too, I suppose. Now I'll bet Miss Baldwin wouldn't believe that possible. Perhaps she'll be more likely to next year. The fact is I don't quite believe it myself. But change of heart, etc. does puzzle me. I don't believe mine has been *orthodoxically* anyhow. I've got a confoundly filthy one now, and I believe it's been growing cleaner and softer—a *considerable spell* at least—ten years I should think.

I wrote John hoping to draw his attention to religion. His answer don't show much feeling, but perhaps that is my fault. Among other things, I urged him to read the Bible daily, etc. He replies that he has been in the habit of reading the *Bible, some.* "Never could perceive any good effects or great advantage from it"(!) How much is some? Why, I did not see him read it but once, and then in French, all last term.

He says he means to "do as near right as the imperfections of human nature will allow and, repenting of the rest, put his trust in Christ," and "It don't seem to me I should be much changed—except in my motives. They might be less selfish, & look more to God's glory. *Cant,* I abhor."

I don't know but I ought to make a public profession, but I can not tell you all the reasons why I do not.

I have been out to your folks'. All well and send love. Mary[5] declares she don't go to New Milford (Blast it, as much as you are a mind to. 'Twill ease you) until she knows who is going to have *them peaches.*

It's too bad, but so we go. "Where" I go I don't know—New York —Albany—West to Syracuse down to Owego. Expect to find a place somewhere.[6]

I meant to have told you about my jolly ride up that time: Getting *spilt* with all the *things* & the *luncheon* into *soft* snowdrifts, carrying a *lady* (of 150 pounds) and baby (of course) several miles over bare ground, getting out & pushing up hill & being offered six and a quarter cents, & no thanks for it. Meeting and bowing to young ladies while Jerry, all jaded out, was dragging (on a slow walk), me in a dashing cutter & furs *down through* Asylum Hill. Some clay there, but not a speck of snow. God bless you, Charley. Write again after you have seen her immediately. A little more time to spare; I'll go on.

While I think of it, where is the fourth of Sterne—Sterne's Letters?[7]

I begin to think I *do* love Miss B. Really. The fact is—never mind. If I never did before I do now. What a blessed thing she must be.

Pshaw! I am going to be Clodpole. I should be a scamp to think of making her Mrs. Clodpole. She ought to be a queen—or a martyr—or a missionaryess or a schoolmistress—or an angel. She's too good for any course vulgar *man* merely, is not she? I don't see how you can stay in College while she is in the same town. Don't she run away with you altogether? Oh, I'd give considerable if not more to go *there* with you tomorrow night. Well, Well. There's plenty more good fish in the sea. But shall we ever look upon her like again. No Sir! I don't believe it. I vow I wish I'd never seen her. Farewell, Miss B!

I go to Collinsville tomorrow. Tell Fred I mean to try to write him before I go if I can, but if I don't he must not wait. I hope to find letters from both of you by Wednesday when I return—by Lucius[8]—your valisse anyway.

Stick to Old Hartford, Charley. We all love you here. Au revoir.

1. This letter was probably written on Friday night, March 27, 1846, the night of the Whig rally Olmsted mentions (*Hartford Daily Courant,* March 27, 1846, p. 2).
2. Olmsted left for Collinsville, Conn., on March 28 (JO Journal, March 28, 1846).
3. Elizabeth Baldwin and the others converted during the New Haven revival in the spring of 1846.

4. Henrietta Blake (1825–1901), daughter of Eli Whitney Blake, a New Haven manufacturer and inventor. She attended Delia Bacon's classes in New Haven for a time and was reputed to be an excellent Greek scholar and adept at Hebrew. Later in 1846 she was the ringleader in the publication of a newspaper, "The Gallinipper," which satirized Yale faculty members and students, and which the college quickly suppressed by threatening to expel the Yale students involved. Rebecca T. Bacon (1826–1878), was the daughter of Leonard Bacon, minister of the First Church (Congregational) of New Haven from 1825 to 1866. She and Henrietta Blake experienced conversion and joined Leonard Bacon's church in New Haven in December 1845. Their conversion began the period of religious seriousness among Olmsted's friends in New Haven during the early months of 1846 (Franklin Bowditch Dexter, comp., *Historical Catalogue of the Members of the First Church of Christ in New Haven, Connecticut, A.D. 1639–1914* [New Haven, 1914], p. 238; *New Haven Daily Morning Journal and Courier*, June 30, 1880, p. 2; Thomas W. Baldwin, *Bacon Genealogy: Michael Bacon of Dedham, 1640, and His Descendants* [Cambridge, Mass., 1915], p. 279; *Yale Obit. Rec.*, 3d ser., no. 7 [June 1887]: 351; Vivian C. Hopkins, *Prodigal Puritan: A Life of Delia Bacon* [Cambridge, Mass., 1959], pp. 102–3, 226; Alida (Blake) Hazard, *The Blakes of 77 Elm Street; A Family Sketch* . . . [New Haven, Conn., 1924], pp. 38–42; *DAB*, s.v. "Bacon, Leonard").
5. Mary Brace, sister of Charles Loring Brace. The Brace family lived in New Milford.
6. Although Olmsted had already corresponded with George Geddes about the possibility of staying with him at his farm in Camillus, N.Y., he did not finally decide to do so until he had spent a few days there (FJK Sketch of FLO).
7. The fourth volume of Laurence Sterne's works published in England contains the letters. This is not true of other editions (Laurence Sterne, *The Works of Laurence Sterne*, 4 vols. [London, 1819]).
8. Lucius Olmsted (1827–1862), son of Denison Olmsted (*Olmsted Genealogy*, pp. 73, 122).

To FREDERICK KINGSBURY   [April 1, 1846][1]

Hartford, *Wednesday* P.M.

Dear Fred,

I wish I could feel properly grateful to God, for the glad news in your letter of last Monday, which I have only just now read on my return from Collinsville.[2] I am very much obliged to you for writing again so soon, though it would be strange if you should refrain when you had so much to tell me. How thankful we should be for these crowning mercies.

Oh! I do hope he will prepare us for a state in which [we] can render him more worthy praise. I do feel, Fred, that I am a most ungrateful man. I so much want God's help to make [me] more thankful for all these mercies and blessings which he is heaping on our heads. I am so much & so continually glad, and so little thankful. I try to thank and bless him and rise from my knees, unsatisfied and perplexed, for I have not begun to thank him with all my heart. Yet I can not command any more of it. I feel that I have tried to do my duty and wonder that I can not do it better. I pray for his assistance and ask forgiveness for my great deficiencies. Yet I have no great *longing*, though I try to hope for heaven, where I shall have no more such troubles.

Do you have such sort of feelings? I have had daily for a great while. I recollect your feeling about—(can't think of the word)—death of the soul. I used to feel just so and sympathize with you. I don't quite so much now. I believe it shows a great want of *faith*. Discussing it with George Hill[3] once, something he said set me a-thinking. And it seems as if 'twas one's own fault, and—in short wicked.

I might say, Fred, I am "full of doubts," but that don't express it—by a long shot. I believe it's perfectly impossible for me to express myself with any sort of clearness and with truth on Religious subjects, though I feel a great desire to. I know I cannot. My ideas are so *indefinite*. I do not know *what* I think. I can't begin to satisfy myself. I hardly have an opinion. How can I tell others what I don't know myself?

But I do know I am glad, very glad, to hear that such good news of my friends. It seems as if I was more glad to hear that Charley[4] is saved, than I was for all the rest. I don't know why, I'm sure—perhaps because I thought he was in more danger. I do trust I am even more than them, grateful and thankful. And I hope it is because I am better prepared to be. I had thought of Charley a great deal. What a great thing it is! How much happier, how much more useful he will be! Fred, I do most *heartily* sympathize with you. I regularly love you this afternoon and feel as if I could kiss you.

I've been *thinking* like a—human-being here for an hour or two. I want to tell you what I'm thinking & how, but I can't. I wish I could express my thoughts—like, as you do—but subjects that I like to *hear* and *read* & *think* about I can't talk [about]—I can't even ask questions. And that's the reason I like such folks—Miss Baldwin—and you, so much—who can & will guess and know what a fellow thinks & feels & *wants*, and sympathize with him so easily.

Speaking of Miss B.—seems to me—she must be now one of the happiest persons in existence. I think she will do immense good there. Her influence will be so great and so beautifully exerted.[5]

Father (to avoid Jury duty I presume) has unexpectedly found business called him to New York while I was absent. I hope he did not take John off.

John[6] is a singular fellow. I feel as if I knew less of him, of the constitution, and *method*, the *way* of his mind than any body else's. He must be approached very delicately and influenced—I think. Danger I fear of *avoiding* rather than *following* a *direction* he is *not* inclined to receive. I wish I could come down. (By the way, I suppose you know I sent you a letter Saturday.) I shall start for Albany with letters and introductions—in course of a fortnight, at most, after *election*. (I fear Toucey[7] will be elected.) Norton of Farmington, where I was last night, is very kind to me in advice and recommendations, etc.[8] John P. Norton expected now daily. D'ye know he was appointed Professor in Union? Has not accepted. Do write again Fred & believe me warmly your friend.

1. This date is based on the fact that the Connecticut state elections were held the following Monday, April 6, and Olmsted left for New York on April 4, 1846 (*Hartford Daily Courant*, April 6, 1846, p. 2; JO Journal, April 4, 1846).
2. Kingsbury's good news evidently concerned the religious conversions that Olmsted's friends in New Haven were experiencing as a result of the revival there. Kingsbury, Charles Loring Brace, and John Hull Olmsted, as well as several others, were converted at about this time (Mary Bull Olmsted to JHO, April 2, 1846; Mary Bull Olmsted to JHO, April 3, 1846; FLO to JHO, April 3, 1846; Owen Pitkin Olmsted to JHO, April 5, 1846).
3. George Edwards Hill, a Yale classmate of Kingsbury's.
4. Charles Loring Brace.
5. Olmsted means that Elizabeth Baldwin would be using her new-found faith to bring about the conversion of others as the revival in New Haven progressed.
6. John Hull Olmsted.
7. Isaac Toucey, lawyer and Democratic politician, was elected governor of Connecticut in 1846 (*DAB*).
8. John Treadwell Norton, a gentleman farmer in Farmington, Connecticut, had just given Olmsted a letter of introduction to use in his search for a farm at which to study. His son John Pitkin Norton (1822–1852), an agricultural chemist, was returning from three years of scientific study at Edinburgh and Utrecht. He refused a position at Union College in Schenectady, N.Y., to become professor of agricultural chemistry at Yale (*DAB*, s.v. "Norton, John Pitkin").

To JOHN HULL OLMSTED

New York, April 16th, 1846.[1]

Dear John,

I wrote you very hastily yesterday from a most uncomfortable situation at Lovejoy's.[2] I will now tell you what I have been about since then, as much as I can before dinner. As I don't have time to write for myself I wish you'd send both these letters to me when you can that I may keep them for a Log.

When I had closed the letter of yesterday, I gave the clerk another blow up, about the room, and then went over to Park Place, where a Regiment of the "Jefferson" somethings were on parade.[3] One company—of rifles, in frocks, dark green and black, looked effective—and one of heavy infantry, grenadiers, looked ridiculous. The whole poorly drilled and awkwardly marching to poor music. The staff officers shabbily mounted. In the P.M. I saw a fine company of "Fusileers" with an excellent band. 'Till two o'clock I spent my time among the book stores &c. Then went and had another jaw about room. (Lovejoy and all his folks are remarkably civil or I should have packed off long ago.)

Then down to Bunels—or Bonnards'[4] rather—Restaurateur Francais —and here as was to be supposed the tide turned. I came away contented, quietly digesting a nice little dinner. Called at Richard's place again and made the girl show me up to his room. His comfortable sofa with a luxurious heap of cushions and pillows was too much for me, and when he came in he caught me asleep. I was in a situation to make "Mark" perfectly miserable. I got a good nap while he dined, and afterwards we had a jolly chat over his— fire. For it has been, whew! chilly.

He took me into Trinity[5] and left me there, delighted. You have seen it or will. At B & H's[6] everybody welcomed me and—so forth. Jo brought me a piece of board which he had saved from the bottom of my old drawer, when the alterations were made. It had on it a list of all hands connected with the establishment at the time it was written upon from Mr. Benkard down to the carman's *mare*, with some remarks of title attached to each. Then some observations about myself: a record of my taking the responsibility of Petit Cashier and in virtue of my office the command and keys of that desk. (In the margin was a note that B & H suffered to the amount of the worth of a steel pen which I had spoiled in the above "humbugging.") There was a closing inscription made at the time I left resigning the office to H. W. Priest[7] &c, &c, concluding "Sic transit" &c.

Mr. Benkard was very civil which was more than I had expected. In truth he was very kind, for him. He gave me a (sealed) note to Captain Robinson,[8] his father-in-law, a fancy farmer at Newburgh. Went to the Sailor's Home[9] and heard a little about several of our hands—nothing very gratifying or interesting at all to you.

Finally at eight o'clock, having strengthened myself by a little supper at Florence's,[10] I got a porter, and squeezing through the mob in Lovejoy's bar room and office, we attacked the pile of baggage, of which there was a stack big enough for a freight train. 'Twould have puzzled half a dozen locomotives to start it all at once, the whole belonging to folks that had arrived, all but five, since I did—and were fools enough to wait there expecting the house would be vacated. Half an hour after, I was in a big comfortable easy chair, in a good big comfortable room, with a good big comfortable fire—and everything else just so. The clean white sheets, mellow pillows, and rosy blankets were so inviting I could not help—just seeing how 'twould feel—and the next thing I knew 'twas nine o'clock to-morrow morning, the fire out, and the stand with the books and the chocolate and the *unwritten* letters to Emma and Poole[11] by the window, and out the window the great cross of St. Peter's[12] gilded by the sun, the North River all alive with the morning boats that I was going to Albany in. There goes the gong and after dinner here goes to Newburgh in the "Santa Claus,"[13] to Albany to-morrow night.

I send the Bible. I can't find anywhere in New York Thomas Barne's Manual of Prayer. Ask *Henry* or Jim to procure me one.[14]

My cold's better. I've had a glorious Astor House[15] breakfast, my hair cut just as I remember *Stella's*[16] telling father was the new fashion twelve years ago, parted down the middle behind and brushed forward &c and swelled. And I've been shampooed, and my head's as light as a bird, and I've flirted with a pretty girl that grew in New Haven or Hartford, I could swear, all down Broadway Omnibus. And I've got a summer heavy plaid cap &c &c.

1. Olmsted wrote this letter just before taking a steamboat up the Hudson on his way to George Geddes's farm at Camillus, N.Y. A note at the end of the letter added by John Hull Olmsted in New Haven before sending it on to his father in Hartford has been omitted.

2. A hotel located at 34 Park Row and Beekman Street in New York (*Doggett's New York Business Directory for 1846 & 1847: With a Map*, 4th publ. [New York, 1846–47], p. 126: see Spear 971; John Kouwenhoven, *The Columbia Historical Portrait of New York, An Essay in Graphic History* [New York, 1953], p. 191).

3. The Jefferson Guards were the Fifth Regiment of Infantry of the New York State Militia (Frederick Phisterer, Comp., *New York in the War of the Rebellion, 1861–1865*, 6 vols. [Albany, N.Y., 1912], 1: 531).

4. A refectory owned by John Bonnard at 5 Nassau Street (*Doggett's Business Directory for 1846 & 1847*, p. 203).

5. Trinity Church, designed in the Gothic Revival style by Richard Upjohn, was just reaching completion at the time Olmsted visited New York and was dedicated a month later (Everard M. Upjohn, *Richard Upjohn, Architect and Churchman* [New York, 1939], p. 64).

6. The Beaver Street store of James A. Benkard and Benjamin H. Hutton, New York importers of French silks, where Olmsted worked as a clerk from 1840 to 1842 (JO Journal, Aug. 18, 1840, March 11, 1842; *Rode's New York City Directory for 1850–51* [New York, 1850], s.v. "Benkard, James A.," "Hutton, Benjamin H.": see Spear 990).

7. Henry D. Priest, associated with Benkard and Hutton, who lived at 6 Carlisle Street (*Doggett's Business Directory for 1846 & 1847*, p. 318).

8. Henry Robinson (d. 1866), a retired sea captain, lived in the Washington Heights section of Newburgh, N.Y., on a 267-acre farm that was "a beautiful landscape, wonderfully adorned by Nature" (John J. Nutt, comp., *Newburgh, Her Institutions, Industries, and Leading Citizens* [Newburgh, N.Y., 1891], pp. 65, 121).

9. The Sailor's Home in New York, a boarding house run by the American Seamen's Friends Society.

10. An oyster saloon owned by William H. Florence at 413 Broadway (*Doggett's Business Directory for 1846 & 1847*, p. 174).

11. Emma Brace and William Frederick Poole (1821–1894); the latter was from Salem, Mass. He entered Yale College in 1842 with John Hull Olmsted and Charles Loring Brace, and had the room next to theirs in North Middle College. At the end of his freshman year Poole left college to earn money by teaching and did not return to Yale until the fall of 1846. At that point he began the creation of an index to periodicals that became the standard reference work in the field: *Poole's Index to Periodical Literature, 1802–1881* (*Yale Obit. Rec.*, 4th ser., no. 4 [June 1894]: 225–26; Yale College, *Catalogue of the Officers and Students in Yale College, 1842–43* [New Haven, 1842], p. 22).

12. The first Roman Catholic church in New York. It was built in 1785–1786 and re-

THE PAPERS OF FREDERICK LAW OLMSTED

built in 1835–1836 (William Thompson Bonner, *New York, the World's Metropolis, 1623-24—1923-24* [New York, 1924], p. xi).

13. The *Santa Claus*, a steamer commanded by Captain B. Overbagh (*New York Daily Tribune*, April 16, 1846, p. 4).

14. Albert Henry Barnes (1826–1878) and James Nathan Barnes (1827–1892) were sons of Albert Barnes (1798–1870), a Presbyterian clergyman who played a prominent role in the contest between the Old and New schools of American Presbyterianism. The book Olmsted wanted seems to have been written by the elder Barnes and was probably his *Prayers for the Use of Families*, published in Philadelphia in 1833 (*DAB*, s.v. "Barnes, Albert"; *Yale Obit. Rec.*, 2d ser., no. 8 [June 1878]: 302; 4th ser., no. 1 [June 1901]: 109).

15. The Astor House was built in 1830. With three hundred rooms furnished in heavy black walnut, it was one of the wonders of its day (W. T. Bonner, *New York*, p. 151).

16. Stella Hull Law, Olmsted's aunt.

To CHARLES LORING BRACE

Fairmount, May 27th, 1846

Dear Charley

I was very glad to get your letter, very glad indeed. I have not answered it before because—it is not very easy to *tell*—probably pretty much the same reasons that you did not write it before. I am kept pretty busy—and can't set down to write calmly & deliberately as I want to—never. I am going to try now to get this done if I can before the mail closes.

I have not yet written Emma,[1] though I have been "agoing" to—every day—and thinking I would before I went to bed again. But I don't like to scribble off a letter without thinking what I am going to say or how I am going to say it, or whether it is likely to bore her or please her—to a lady, even though so good and charitable a friend as Emma. Besides, after working perhaps in the dust—coming in tired and *sweaty*, and with one's head full of mould board and furrow slice—it is a great deal easier to *read* than to write. If you doubt, just try the experiment some night after a hard trouting where you have toiled all day & *caught nothing*. Do you remember—of course you do—*our trying* to write to Miss Abby that night at Can*aa*n Falls?[2]

I need not assure you of my sympathy—on the death of your uncle. Your Aunt Mary must feel it sadly;[3] but how much less so than she would if he had departed without the happy change in his character you speak of. Doubtless his conversion was in answer to much prayer. What an encouraging thought it is, too, Charley. "The effectual fervent prayer of the Righteous availeth much."[4] How much—more we realize than we used to.

How did you like Dr. Bushnell's letter to the Pope?[5] I suppose folks laugh at him a good deal. It does seem a little self conceited—(*pardon!*) but that's the way to do the business—if you could only get the old fellow to read the letter. I believe we can do a great deal more for deluded men—Catholics

—or Unitarians, drunkards, & Slaveholders—by praying *for* them than by *spotting* them, blackguarding them through the newspapers, and exasperating them. Acting as if we hated them as much as we did their doctrines. Let us agree to pray for the Pope. And treat them kindly. Reason with them as though *we might* be the mistaken ones—for truly I think in my heart we *may* be. Be more anxious to show them the lovely features of our own faith than the absurd and shameful ones of their own. Men are oftener drawn to Truth and the Christ, I believe, than driven.

I think myself the Pope and his adherents have got to "come out of that," pretty soon. It will attend the next great stirabout of this big kettle of ours. Perhaps this little war with Mexico will be the pudding stick. Speaking of guns do *you parade* from eleven till one daily, Sundays excepted? I *calculate* you Seniors feel altogether too large to play soger. *"Martial Exercises"* I presume don't accord with your dignity.

They are having an interesting time there though, are they not? Will you vote for Taylor—the hero of Chaparral?[6]

This is an interesting country. John will have read you all I have written about it. The brooks so full of Carbonate Lime, tufa[7] is deposited over anything dropped in them for a year or two. The soil is much of it Gypseous—Gypseous shale—tufa & limestone the common rocks.

There are a good many Indians about here. I see them occasionally. The women almost always with a white blanket over their heads—blue dress—pantletts—or pantaloons. I saw one here with a pair of genteel *half gaiter* black pants—buttoned over her moccasin. They generally have bangles of white metal—beads. Huge silver rings, &c., too.

I am pleasantly situated enough—and I think advantageously—as regards farming—pretty much as I wished to be. A pleasant and well informed family.

I am glad to hear your family are well. Give my love to Mary[8] when you write. How does your father like to teach boys?[9]

There are *not* "any girls here" to console me. Nor any where—else. So—you know. Write as often as you can conveniently—& tell me *all about* the girls—and the college & the fellows. Sorry to hear the P.C. is broken up. Where are you now—and all of "ours?"

Your exiled friend

Fred.

---

1. Emma Brace.
2. Abby Morton Clark. Canaan Falls is a town in northwestern Connecticut.
3. James Pierce (1779–1846), Brace's great-uncle, brother of his great-aunt Mary Pierce of Litchfield, Conn., died on May 10, 1846 (Charles Thomas Payne, *Litchfield and Morris Inscriptions* [Litchfield, Conn., 1905], p. 40).

4. The quotation is from the General Epistle of James, 5:16, which reads, "Confess *your* faults one to another, and pray for another, that ye may be healed. The effectual fervent prayer of a righteous man availeth much." Olmsted felt the truth of this statement strongly at this time because of his experience in New Haven during the previous month. He came away feeling that he had been saved and that his salvation was due primarily to the prayers and "Human Sympathy" of his friends (FLO to JHO, April 7, 1846).

5. Horace Bushnell joined with other Connecticut ministers in 1843 in forming the Protestant League—later the Christian Alliance—for the purpose of opposing the Catholic church. In 1846, after traveling in Italy, he published "A Letter to His Holiness, Pope Gregory xvi," in which he called on the pope to permit groups like the Christian Alliance to carry on their evangelical work in Catholic countries, and to submit the Catholic church to "the open trial of truth in the field of religious liberty. . . ." He referred to the eighty-one-year-old pontiff as an old man "at his grave's edge" and, ironically, dated his letter the day after Gregory's death.

    In the letter Bushnell made a scathing attack on the secular power of the papacy, saying the papal states had the "worst government in Christendom," priest-ridden and poverty-stricken. He also criticized the superstitious use of holy relics, papal claims of infallibility, the pageantry of the papal mass, and the show of luxury in the Vatican (Barbara M. Cross, *Horace Bushnell: Minister to a Changing America* [Chicago, 1958], p. 81; Horace Bushnell, "A Letter to His Holiness, Pope Gregory xvi" [London, 1846], reprinted in Horace Bushnell, *Building Eras in Religion* [New York, 1881], pp. 356–85).

6. Olmsted had just learned of General Zachary Taylor's victories over the Mexican army in his first encounters with it at the battles of Palo Alto and Resaca de la Palma on May 8 and 9, 1846. The early newspaper reports did not give names for the battles, simply stating that they took place near the wide strip of thick chaparral growth that ran parallel to the Rio Grande a few miles east of the river (*New York Daily Tribune*, May 25, 1846, p. 2).

7. Tufa is a porous limestone deposit.

8. Brace's sister Mary.

9. After a long career of teaching girls, first at his aunt Sarah Pierce's school in Litchfield, Conn. and then for fifteen years as principal of the Hartford Female Seminary, John Pierce Brace was teaching boys at an academy in the small village of New Milford, Conn. He left that position within three years and never taught school again (*DAB*).

To Frederick Kingsbury[1]

Fairmount, June 12th, 1846

Dear Fred:

I don't know what I have got to write about except your letter. I might string out considerable I suppose in answer to that—but there's no particular occasion to.

I am very sorry and anxious for Miss Bacon[2] and you may tell her so if you please—and for the rest of them. I can only congratulate you—I hope you will get well acquainted with Miss Mary Day.[3] She's another of them and well—but I told you all I could about her that night in the Avenue before the bell began not to stop. Thank you for what you say about _____. I'd just that sort of idea of her. I fell in love with her after my fashion last winter. She's got a regular angel face that would do first rate to stick into a Prayer Book, as well as answer more practical purposes. Did you see Mary Warburton[4] in Hartford?

I think you are right about being sad. I do not think I am apt at all to be sorry or sad, without occasion, but I do very often have a day or two of gloom arising from a consciousness of neglect of duty of some sort, and in this way I am oftener miserable than you'd think perhaps. But I do think it is a man's duty to be happy, at all events to appear happy. It's one's secret faults and not, rather than, those which are noticed by the world that make him displeased with himself. We ought to appear cheerful and contented (resigned) as well as kind and charitable. I don't know but fretfulness and the blues bear the same relation to suicide that unkindness, uncharitableness, hard dealing and oppression do to murder.

I want to make myself useful in the world—to make happy—to help to advance the condition of Society and hasten the preparation for the Millennium—as well as other things too numerous to mention.

Now, how shall I prepare myself to exercise the greatest and best influence in the situation of life I am likely to be placed in? You know perhaps as well as I what that is. I suppose it's no very great stretch of ambition to anticipate my being a Country Squire in Old Connecticut in the course of fifteen years. I should like to help then as far as I could—in the popular mind—generosity, charity, taste &c.—independence of thought, of voting and of acting. The education of the ignobile vulgus ought to be much improved and extended.

The Agricultural Interest greatly preponderates in number and wealth in the state—but perhaps has the least influence in Legislation. Lawyers—whose sense of right and truth is blunted by profession—the sense of law—and traffickers who value themselves as they can make their own interest appear—whether truly or not—the interest of another, make our laws, make public opinion, because they have had their intellectual faculties sharpened by practice—and education. Now the people—farmers and mechanics—the producing classes that the rest live on—want to think and judge for themselves, to cultivate the intellectual.

But my intellect wants a good deal of cultivation before I write an Essay on Political Economy; and you may—now—give me such advice as you please as to how to cultivate it. And my intellect wants a good deal more of it, I presume, than you are aware of. Few children that would have to strain harder than I to get their head outside a problem of E,—and since that fit last winter,[5] I have been afraid to strain much for fear I should break something.

In study I am wonderfully lazy or weak and very soon get tired out. I am romantic—fanciful—jump at conclusions and yet always find headaches or convenient excuses when I want them. I have a smattering education—a little sum, from most everything useful to such a man as I—learned as I took a fancy to it. Of Arithmetic, I cypher slow and without accuracy. Grammar I know nothing of—nor the rules of Rhetoric or writing. Geography, I know where I have been. History, nothing but of my own country—except what I have got incidently. I can't even spell such a word as that right. But W. Trumbull can't either—I believe they say so.

Fire away! It's rather difficult to know where to begin or how, isn't it? But withal I ought to be studying my *profession* all the time (instead of writing to you). And a bit of that difficulty just checks my symptoms here. Recollect brother, I don't have but just time every day to say prayers and brush my teeth. You may as well tell me, too, how I am going to learn to write and speak to a whole school room full, &c.

I've told John[6] and I suppose he will tell you how I have got my hands full of Sunday School. I have got to go down to Syracuse to purchase a Library.[7] I think some of being sent to London as delegate to World's Convention.[8] If I go I shall get them to pass a Resolution that the Pope be informed that he is barking up the wrong tree and not hold any longer that he is a d____d rascal and the son of the host of sin.[9] About war I have concluded that if I am drafted I shall go and kill all the Mexicans I am told to—learn to eat frijoles, see a live Cathedral, and learn what they measure the floating gardens with.[10] If there's war with England[11] I am not sure but I shall volunteer (so you needn't worry). Get taken prisoner and see the world at their expense.

What's become of Danbury R. R.? What do you think about the bridge? Are they laying up the tow-path—and what else is going on?[12] How are all the fellows? Does Miss (you know)[13] feel any way delicate about me? When is she coming this way? When do you hear from Emma?[14]

  Truly, yours,

       Fred.

1. The text of this letter is taken from a typescript version in FJK Sketch of FLO. The original has not been found.
2. Rebecca T. Bacon.
3. Mary Frances Day of Hartford.
4. Mary Warburton (1827–1906) (Headstone Inscriptions, Norwich, Cemetery 4, p. 378).
5. Olmsted is referring to the fainting spells he suffered in late 1845, which forced him to leave Yale and return to Hartford to recuperate.
6. John Hull Olmsted.
7. At this time Olmsted was teaching Sunday school at a church in the Fairmount neighborhood, where he was a teacher, the librarian, and member of a committee to select and purchase books (FLO to JHO, June 11, 1846).
8. The World Convention of Christian Protestant Ministers, to which the nearby Methodist conferences wished to send George Geddes as a lay delegate (see FLO to JHO, June 19, 1846, note 15, below).
9. This is one of many expressions by Olmsted at this time of his dislike of the narrow

outlook he found in the Protestant churches. He is referring especially to one of the sections of the Westminster Confession of the Presbyterian church. It stated: "There is no other Head of the Church, but the Lord Jesus Christ; Nor can the Pope of Rome, in any sense be head thereof: but is, that Antichrist, that Man of sin and Son of Perdition, that exalteth himself, in the Church, against Christ, and all that is called God" (Presbyterian Church in the United States of America, *The Constitution of the Presbyterian Church in the United States of America: Containing The Confession of Faith, The Catechims* [sic] *and The Directory for The Worship of God* . . . [Philadelphia, 1850], p. 114).

10. The floating gardens were on shallow Lake Xochimilco near Mexico City. They were created by laying soil on top of floating masses of water plants and then securing them by poplar stakes that took root in the lake bottom. The last phrase in the sentence may have been wrongly transcribed by the person who made the typescript copy of this letter: it should perhaps read "and learn what they manure the floating gardens with."

11. The prospect of war with England over the Oregon boundary question had existed for some time. The Democrats made the cry "Fifty-four Forty or Fight!" part of their successful campaign of 1844, and during 1845 all attempts at compromise failed. In his message to Congress in December 1845, President James K. Polk revived the demand for all of Oregon and set off belligerent responses in England. On April 27, 1846, he approved and signed a joint resolution of Congress empowering him to terminate the joint occupation with England of the Oregon country. This proved the prelude to peace rather than war, however. On June 6 the British minister Packenham proposed the adoption of the compromise line of 49° and on June 15, 1846, such a treaty was signed (Thomas A. Bailey, *A Diplomatic History of the American People*, 8th ed. [New York, 1969], pp. 225–35).

12. Olmsted is referring here to three of the many railroad promotion projects underway in Connecticut at the time. The interior city of Danbury was seeking to find a railroad link to Long Island Sound, having been bypassed a few years before by a railroad running inland from Bridgeport. At the same time there was great concern in Hartford about a bill before the state legislature authorizing construction of a railroad bridge across the Connecticut River at Middletown that would block navigation above it to Hartford; and the trustees of the Farmington Canal, which ran north from New Haven to the Massachusetts border, were in the process of building a railroad along the course of the canal (Susan B. Hill, comp., *History of Danbury, Conn. 1684– 1896, From Notes and Manuscript Left by James Montgomery Bailey* [New York, 1896], p. 272; FLO to CLB, May 16, 1845, note 7, above; FLO to JO, July 1, 1846, note 13, below).

13. Elizabeth Baldwin.

14. Emma Brace.

To John Hull Olmsted

Address: Mr. John H. Olmsted/Yale College/New Haven/Conn
Postmark: Syracuse/N.Y./Jun 20

Fairmount,[1] June 19th, 1846

Dear John,

I don't know but I am working too much now. For somehow when I *come in*, I don't feel like anything but singing or hearing Mary[2] play, or lying down on the floor & kicking the carpet and thinking about the girls or some nonsense. I can't read, write, or study, without getting to sleep.

We got our Sunday School underweigh last Sabbath—in great style —fifty scholars. I had the biggest class—overgrown boys.

We purchased about 83 (increased to 97 when I close) books for Library. I added three of mine that I had finished and shall have contributed and expended about a dollar more. I still have my class at Amboy. The school there is not large or well conducted as ours at Fairmount.[3]

I think I shall join the Church at Amboy in July. I have talked about it with the pastor, a very good youngish man—his wife from Meriden. His name Lathrop, brother of some missionary's wife that died in Smyrna.[4] I wish they hadn't Articles of Faith &c. I don't see the need of them. A man ought to be able to receive the Communion when *he* considers it desirable, without professing any particular religious views—and when perhaps he has none except Christ & him crucified.

The truth is, I do believe the Episcopal Church is the only true *Catholic* (I mean not *exclusive*, not *sec*tarian. The *Creed* is all that a man is obliged to own.) Church amongst all of them. Though I should hate to identify myself with such a bigoted set as most of them (churchmen) are, I must honestly confess that as far as creeds go I am much better satisfied with theirs than any other.

I am not sure now if I was to cut loose from prejudices of education, &c., conquer all family and personal and sectional and hereditary and national *pride*, as I know I ought to—and all regard for wounding the pride— feelings—of my friends, &c., I would be a member of the old true church of our ancestors—what the Episcopal Church *was* and yet intends to be. And then again perhaps I would *not*. At any rate, I don't think it of sufficient importance to worry myself about a great deal. There's nothing in the Prayer Book (or the Bible) to prevent my receiving all the sacraments tomorrow, if I choose. And if they were offered to me I am not sure I should decline.[5]

I'd like to know what you think of Baptism. What's the use of it to babies. Is it not a "means of grace?" And if it is, what is that but the beginning of the "work of Sanctification." I believe my heart began to change at Baptism and has been changing ever since. And I hope it will continue to be in a renewing state.

I believe that I was brought up to regard it in a very different light. And if I had seen it as I now do I should have been a better man or should have begun to try to be a better man much sooner than I did begin to try to be. I believe that in partaking (as to partaking unworthily, *who can* judge?) of the body & blood of my Redeemer, my supplies of grace—of light from on high, of assistance and comfort—will be increased. And I believe that I ought to have begun to partake of them years ago. Penitence is a work of grace. If I was not then sufficiently penitent—and was aware of it, if I was not then convicted of sin (but I was), if I did not then see the way of salvation clearly, if I was not then devoted to God, and if this (sufficient or abundant—or whatever may express the quantity or strength of the necessary) conviction, conversion, & devotion is the result of Divine Grace, why should I be refused —or be instructed to wait until I had received it before I accepted and partook of these appointed means for receiving enlarged supplies?

Considering it in this way, am I *now* a member of the church of Christ? This, I suppose, is the Episcopal doctrine. If I did not disagree with the common views held upon this subject by most of our folks—and such as you entertained when you shrunk from thinking (from "conviction") of the subject, falsely supposing that your *duties* or your great *duty* and responsibility would be dreadfully increased (or commence?) by *beginning* to do your duty, I would not I think join any church without being *re*baptised. The *sacraments* must be more than symbols. Well, I'll drop the subject for the present—perhaps to take it up in connection with something else before this goes.

As to farming I am doing well, and now have a good deal of faith in myself as a farmer. I wrote to father a day or two ago very hastily and concluded very abruptly, being interrupted by tea bell and the mail cart. And at this moment it is ding dinging again. Mr. Geddes gone and I have to head the table.

Post Tea. We had the greatest rain storm this morning you ever saw. I had just got the garden in fine order, and it is half washed downhill. The gate to our irrigating canal was carried away, and the pen a-bursting out gullied up the ground the worst kind before I could get a wheel barrow load of stuff into the gap. Fence blew down and horses into the meadow—so I learned how to build bear-a-hand fence.[6] Our garden is placed thus:

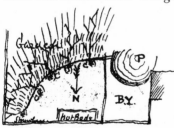

B.Y. Barn Yard, P. Pool, C. Canal. Side hill S.E. exposure. You see how nicely we can tap our canal or main drain and irrigate all below. (As at "T" "T".)

I wish I knew your plan for vacation and father's with dates. And I wish I could calculate how long I am to stay here &c. I wish to get my time between this and then staked out. I have promised to go to Skaneateles and to the Indian Onondaga Castle.[7] I have some thoughts of going to Auburn to see Mr. Skinner[8] "and things" 4th July.

In writing to father I mentioned the visit of Mrs. Geddes' brothers and niece.[9] They came while we were shearing. And the first they saw of me, I was "all in a sweat" and smock frock—pretty considerably dirty and *rum* looking anyway—on the barn floor laying across a sheep's belly. By and by

Geddes[10] said "Come Mr. Olmsted—supposing you knock off. Come in and cool off and see what's in the papers."

So after I had washed & "slicked up" a little, I walked into the parlour and rather *astonished* the young gentlemen by my transmogrification. The young Medic was a fine clever fellow—and the girl—faith! I believe I more than half got in love with her. I'll tell you how that was, bye and bye. She is tall and handsomely proportioned. And the first interview, I got the impression that she was a goodish gay jolly sort of thing—somewhere between 16 and 21—pleasing healthy face—More like *unto* Frank Condit's[11] than somebody else's. And you know how ridiculously resemblances strike some eyes. They say—when I came here—folks talked of my reminding them of her—and I liked to be taken for her brother.

After tea, we went down to her cousins—the Jerome girls.[12] And I found she had no city airs or starch—or anything of that. You'll believe it, I suppose, when I tell you three of *us* swung together. (Finally swing broke, nobody hurt, and I shinnied up the *standing part* to repair it and displayed sailorship.)

From what I have told you of Geddes you will have judged that I feared his Religious views were very—unsound—too Rational and self glorifying. And I had hoped for an opportunity to provoke him to an avowal and discussion of them. That evening it was providentially afforded. He thinks the Apostles preached faith, and not works so strongly, because at that time it was entirely new and strange—difficult to be understood &c., &c. Our divines or fathers, in protesting against and opposing the penance doctrines &c. of the Roman church, carried their views altogether too far—and works are sacrificed &c., &c.

We were in a dark(ish) room—he on the sofa, she and I in front. As I said, I took her for a gay girl, and I thought that I was rather impolite to occupy the conversation entirely on such matters as I supposed were entirely uninteresting to her, or worse than that, but I did not like to lose the opportunity. Well, I had forgotten her entirely and got quite warm. Finally having got him fairly open, I told him I did not believe most people even among the most constant church goers and priest and sermon ridden communities really understood the mediation of Christ, &c., *now*. I then described (what I feared was his own mistake—as) the common feeling of the world. And then with all the warmth and eloquence I could, I gave my views, concluding I believe with some strong expressions—and "that is *my* opinion!"

Miss Sarah, who had been entirely silent hitherto, immediately said, "and I uphold you in that opinion, Sir!" After that I gave it up pretty much to her—finding she was both able and anxious. And her views and assistance, and her earnest and sweet manner of expressing herself encouraged and delighted me.

She only stayed over night. [. . .][13] Heighho! Speaking of guns—

MARIA PORTER GEDDES

when she left in the morning after she gave me a real Baldwin[14] squeeze or shake. And somehow these hearty open souled girls that are not afraid folks'll think something always do melt me right down—and all others too, I suppose you'll say,—no! because I keep clear of them!

Now for Geddes' view of Baptism—which I meant to speak of when I dropped the subject. I got them that same night. He thinks Baptism was never intended for anything but proselytes. We are brought up—not Heathen, not Jews—nothing but Christians. And (except for converts from Paganism, Ismailism, &c.) it is entirely useless and never intended.

Mr. Geddes was asked by an agent for the three adjoining Conferences to allow them to appoint him their lay delegate to the World's Convention.[15] His business interfered. They offered to pay expenses. He corresponds with and often entertains Bishop Hedding.[16] He has *not* had children baptised.

I wish you'd tell me all the news from Emma and New Milford as well as *up street*.[17] And by the way, I should most decidely like to know why Charley[18] don't write me. You may read this letter to him and to Fred,[19] for I don't expect to write another this summer. And tell Fred I wrote him last week. I mention it because I think it possible the letter miscarried, but he may *answer this one*—whether or no!

Mr. Geddes is gone to Plank Road[20] a good deal of the time. Mrs. G. is a good sort of woman, but says but little for herself. However she took a private opportunity to express her agreement and sympathy with the views I had advocated in regard to Baptism, the Influence of the Spirit, &c. She and her husband are Methodists—the old lady,[21] a Presbyterian. By the way, the old lady claims to be a cousin (she was a Jerome from Berkshire County) of Miss Dwight of New Haven.[22] And some of her relations out here married a Colonel Olmsted of Connecticut. I had looked for a letter from you this morning. You ought to write more—hadn't you?

June 20th

Your affectionate brother

Give my love to Charley Trask.[23] Let me hear how all the fellows get on. Do you speak in Society yet? I suppose a sense of duty will make you now.[24] It is a long time since I've heard from you. When does Miss Baldwin come this way?[25]

---

1. The Geddes farm, "Fairmount," which gave its name to the nearby area and post office in the town of Camillus, was located on the south side of the north branch of the Seneca Turnpike at the corner of the old military road that ran from Onondaga Hill to Oswego, later New York State routes 5 and 173 (information supplied by Richard N. Wright).
2. Mary Geddes (1834–1891), George Geddes's daughter (Pearl S. Cossitt, *The Cossitt Family: A Genealogical History of Rene Cossitt, A Frenchman Who Settled in Granby, Conn. A.D. 1717 and of His Descendants* [Pasadena, Ca., 1925], p. 66).
3. In addition to teaching Sunday school and serving as librarian for a church in the Fairmount neighborhood, Olmsted was teaching a Sunday school class at the Presbyterian church in the village of Amboy, two and a half miles away. He described his Amboy class of the previous week as "seven little shavers that pretend to learn seven verses—every week—and when each has made believe repeat some of them, he thinks he has nothing else to do—but play—or quarrel—until the books are given out, and then to snatch his hat & *cut*" (FLO to JHO, June 11, 1846).
4. Alfred Crafts Lathrop (1811–1888), first pastor of the Presbyterian Society of Amboy in Camillus, N.Y. His wife was Stella Desire Hough (1813–1873) of Meriden, Conn. His sister Judith Sabrina Lathrop (1813–1844) was early "consecrated to the missionary work" and married Ashael Grant (1807–1844), a missionary at the Nestorian Mission in Persia. She died at Oroomiah, Persia, not Symrna (*General Biographical Catalogue of Auburn Theological Seminary, 1818–1918* [Auburn, N.Y.: 1918], p. 69; James M. Crafts and William F. Crafts, *The Crafts Family: A*

Genealogical and Biographical History . . . [Northampton, Mass., 1893], pp. 346–47; W. Woodward Clayton, *History of Onondaga County, New York* [Syracuse, N.Y., 1878], p. 309; Thomas Laurie, *Dr. Grant and the Mountain Nestorians* [Boston, 1853], pp. 13, 31–32).

5. This passage and those that follow in this letter show some of Olmsted's most immediate concerns as he searched to reconcile his beliefs with the creeds and practices of particular churches. He was drawn toward the Episcopalians because they required only affirmation of the Apostles' Creed, not acceptance of a whole series of points of doctrine. Since he felt that the sacraments served as a means of grace (that is, helped to make the participant a recipient of God's grace), he wished to avail himself of them as freely as possible. His desire for the sacraments to be more than symbols led him to the unorthodox position, held by the Anabaptists of the early Reformation, that the sacrament of baptism, in order to reflect the reality of becoming a Christian, should take place after one's conversion rather than in childhood. At the same time, Olmsted's belief in sacraments as a means of grace led him to believe that his own baptism—which had occurred in 1827, when he was only five—had nonetheless marked an important stage in the process of his becoming a Christian (JO Journal, June 3, 1827).

6. "Bear a hand" is a nautical phrase meaning "hasten" or "hurry up."

7. The "Castle," or Indian village, on the Onondaga Reservation eight miles from Fairmount was the site of Indian burial grounds and the central longhouse of the Iroquois confederacy (information supplied by Richard N. Wright).

8. Thomas Manwaring Skinner (1791–1880), publisher and bookseller of Auburn, N.Y., founder of the *Auburn Gazette*, and publisher of the *Farmer's Almanac* (information supplied by Richard N. Wright).

9. George Geddes's wife, Maria Porter Geddes (1810–1870), was the daughter of Samuel Porter (1778–1843), a physician who moved from Williamstown, Mass., to Skaneateles, N.Y., in 1799. Two brothers who may have visited her at this time were Evelyn Hart Porter (1801–1875), a physician, and James Gurdon Porter, a carriage maker, both of Skaneateles. The niece mentioned was eighteen-year-old Sarah Maria Porter, Evelyn's daughter (William M. Beauchamp, *Past and Present of Syracuse and Onondaga County, New York, from Pre-Historic Times to the Beginning of 1908*, 2 vols. [New York, 1908], 2: 25–26; Edmund N. Leslie, *Skaneateles: History of Its Earliest Settlement and Reminiscences of Later Times* [New York, 1902], pp. 326, 332, 405; Dwight H. Bruce, ed., *Onondaga's Centennial*, 2 vols. [Boston, 1896], 1: 367; birth and death dates of the above have been verified from the records of the Oakwood Cemetery, Syracuse, N.Y., by Richard N. Wright).

10. George Geddes.

11. Frances P. Condit of Hartford, to whom Olmsted had been strongly attracted a few years before and about whom he dreamed while sick and delirious on his China voyage (see FLO to CLB, Aug. 4, 1844, above).

12. Probably Laura, Anna, and Francis Jerome, daughters of Isaac Jerome (1793–1829) and Clarinda Patchem Jerome (1794–1876), who lived on a farm one mile east of the Geddes farm. George Geddes was their first cousin (Oakwood Cemetery Records, Syracuse; Franklin H. Chase, *Syracuse and Its Environs: A History*, 3 vols. [New York, 1924], 2: 122).

13. Three lines crossed out and made indecipherable.

14. Referring to Elizabeth Baldwin.

15. The World Convention of Christian Protestant Ministers, which met in London in 1846 (Emory Steven Bucke, ed., *History of American Methodism*, 3 vols. [New York, 1964], 1: 674).

16. Elijah Hedding (1780–1852), Methodist bishop from 1824 to 1852. He was one of the founders in Boston in 1823 of *Zion's Herald*, the earliest exclusively Methodist journal (*DAB*).

17. Emma Brace. The Braces lived in New Milford, Conn. "Up street" is a version of the expression "down town," and by it Olmsted apparently means that he wants to hear the news from Hartford as well as that from New Milford.

18. Charles Loring Brace.
19. Frederick Kingsbury.
20. At this time George Geddes was the engineer in charge of construction of what is claimed to have been the first plank road built in the United States. It ran fifteen miles from Syracuse, N.Y., to the foot of Oneida Lake. It was completed in July 1846. A post office with the name of Plank Road was established in Centreville, on the plank road, in March 1846 (Joseph Austin Durrenberger, *Turnpikes; A Study of the Toll Road Movement in the Middle Atlantic States and Maryland* [Valdosta, Ga., 1931], pp. 144–45; George Geddes, *Observations Upon Plank Roads, Together with the General Plank Road Law of the State of New York* . . . [Syracuse and New York, 1850], p. 3; information on Plank Road post office supplied by Richard N. Wright).
21. Lucy Isaacs Jerome Geddes (1779–1857), mother of George Geddes (Donald L. Jacobus, "Families of Ancient New Haven," *New Haven Genealogical Magazine* 4 [1927]: 942).
22. Lucy Isaacs Jerome Geddes had moved with her parents and family from Stockbridge, Mass., to Fabius in Onondaga County, N.Y., in 1794. The Miss Dwight of New Haven referred to was probably Julia Strong Dwight (1824–1853), granddaughter of Yale president Timothy Dwight, whose wife's mother was an Isaacs from Connecticut (F. H. Chase, *Syracuse*, p. 122; D. L. Jacobus, "Families of Ancient New Haven," p. 942; Joshua V. H. Clark, *Onondaga, or Reminiscences of Earlier and Later Times* . . . , 2 vols. [Syracuse, N.Y., 1849], 2: 331; Benjamin W. Dwight, *The History of the Descendants of John Dwight of Dedham, Massachusetts,* 2 vols. [New York, 1847], 1: 140, 144, 171–73).
23. Charles Hooper Trask.
24. John Hull Olmsted had recently joined one of the junior class's secret societies at Yale, the Alpha Delta Phi (FLO to JHO, April 26, 1846; Lyman H. Bagg, *Four Years at Yale by a Graduate of '69* [New Haven, Conn., 1871], pp. 106–7).
25. Elizabeth Baldwin made a visit to the Charles P. Kirklands in Utica, N.Y., in September 1846 (FJK Journal, Sept. 18, Oct. 23, 1846).

To John Hull Olmsted

Address: Mr. John H. Olmsted/Yale College/New Haven/Connt.
Postmark: Syracuse/N.Y./Jun 26

Fairmount, June 26th, 1846

Dear John,

Your very acceptable letters of the six o'clock—day—came this morning. I have not been hurried at all for a week back and have written— once to you & twice to Father, besides to George Bissell.[1] We are just getting in a great hurry again. So if I write—it must be without delay. So I'll take up your letter regularly to answer.

Sorry to hear you were not well.[2] I am glad you put your turns to such good account. About staying home from church—I always think so. It does me more good to read a sermon, and meditate and carry out such ideas from it as I choose—digest—some—such as I want—at leisure, than to hear three. By the way, I do most fervently wish—on all accounts—this custom of two regular sermons per diem were abolished and a single sermon of half the usual length—and four times usual strength—substituted.

I never can sit down when I want to and make a business of meditation—successfully. About *Reading*, it *is* just so exactly with me and *I* too *am* trying to overcome it. I now generally run over after my usual fashion a chapter of *Upham*,[3] anytime in the day, when I can snatch it up. And when I am ready to retire I read it over again, dwelling upon the most important ideas & taking a short note or memorandum of them.

I am trying to read a little of something else—to cultivate mental powers to make me think, too, every day. I have been reading Randall on Mental & Moral Culture.[4] *The Psalms* I read about half in course, but gave them up and am now in Hebrews, reviewing & studying the last half dozen chapters. Besides I have two Sunday School lessons to study by Comments, &c, per week. A few Sabbaths since, one morning before church, finding there was some choice of expressions, between the prayer book version and the modern Revised Standard editions, I wrote off to suit my own taste and learned by heart that beautiful Psalm, the XXIII ("The Lord is my Shepherd," &c.)

I generally get a half hour for retirement in course of the day and always write my Journal & read a little at bedtime.

I have been in the corn field two or three hours since I began the letter. I am still thinking a good deal on the subjects I wrote you last week. I have been almost determined not to join a church which required anything more than Christ and the Apostles did. As if a man could not be a Christian without being a Presbyterian! If I were to follow my own judgment, now, I doubt very much if I should not at once partake of the communion—without troubling any so-called church to qualify or elect or permit me. It seems very absurd to me.

Now here, this minister[5] knows—at least I told him, I knew nothing of his Articles of Faith or the particular tenets of the Presbyterian Church. He does not ask me to examine them, and I shall not, I presume. But he thinks it right and proper that I should join his church, that I shall not do right if I do not. So would think a Baptist or something else.

Now I could go to a *"Catholic"* Church and be qualified in their opinion—(so I think, though the *Prayer Book* says nothing of it) to drink of that cup and eat of the bread when and wherever it is offered me, without professing any particular tenets, but such as are held in common by all professing to be Christians. Do you know, that in the Episcopal Church it is not even required to be confirmed to partake. Dr. Arnold[6] says, "Nay, I would even say what the Church fully authorizes me in saying, let not your not having been confirmed restrain you;" from "getting for your souls the help they need." I shall be "propounded"[7] I presume next Sunday, and I shall try to have a talk with Mr. Lathrop before the day.

Speaking of *guns*, I was told by two of the committee of arrangements that either I or Cooper[8] would be called upon to deliver the oration at the Fairmount celebration of this 4th. I told them about Mr. *Case*.[9]

Yes. I got the papers and send you one.

I have written Emma.[10]

Capron[11] is *good* for Grammar School.

Who is Hetty B.[12] going to take those lessons of?

Great time you had on the mountain.

What does "A & C" mean and how do you like it.

Tell me more particularly about your coming out here. We can not keep more than two of you very well—for a day or two. I don't know about being on hand in August, but I guess I can after sowing wheat. Must be back before 16th.

P.S. Jim's teacher,[13] being engaged preparing for the 4th this P.M., he had half holiday and caught us a fine trout supper.

Tell Charley Brace to mind his business. I *should* like to know why he don't write. It's six weeks since I wrote him.

I send on a scrap that has been lying on my desk till it is pretty much filled, the plan(s) you ask for. A little study will explain them. The one of half or quarter mile each way from us. The other of the homestead. Geddes is Gedes: "ge-d-ez."

We might knock the boat to pieces and be worth $5.00. I suppose I would let Savage have it for that if he would take [it] out of the yard. It's worth that if not more, honestly.

1. George P. Bissell (1827–1891), of Hartford. In 1854 he started a mercantile firm that Olmsted's half-brother Albert joined in 1865. In 1876 the firm became "G. P. Bissell and A. H. Olmsted" (obituary notice in the Scrapbook Collection, Connecticut State Historical Society, Hartford, Conn., 16: 42).

2. John Hull Olmsted became sick on June 23, 1846, and went home from college. He returned on June 30 (FJK Journal, June 23, 1846; JO Journal, June 30, 1846).

3. Thomas Cogswell Upham (1799–1872), professor of mental and moral philosophy at Bowdoin College from 1824 to 1867. He set out to refute Kant's philosophy in his *Philosophical and Practical Treatise on the Will*, published in 1834. Olmsted might have been reading this or one of his many other books, such as *Principle of the Interior or Hidden Life* (1843), which was considered to be a religious classic (*DAB*).

4. Samuel S. Randall (1809–1881), author and educator; his *Mental and Moral Culture, and Popular Education* was published in Boston and New York in 1844 (*Appleton's Cyc. Am. Biog.*).

5. Alfred Crafts Lathrop.

6. Olmsted was quoting Thomas Arnold (1795–1842), headmaster of Rugby School and Anglican clergyman, later Regius Professor of History at Oxford. His actual words were:

> Entirely separate as the communion here is from all school regulations, and earnestly as we endeavour to abstain from any mere human and personal influence to persuade you to come, I have the more right to entreat you in your turn not to let such an idle reason as that of being in a lower part of the school

prevent you from getting for your souls the help which they need. Nay, I would even say, that the church fully authorizes me in saying, let not your not having been confirmed restrain you; above all, take care that you do not make it an hypocritical excuse for putting off a little longer the duty of serious thought and self-examination. And now in these days, when the opportunities of confirmation occur so seldom . . . we cannot be justified in willingly depriving ourselves of a great means of grace, on such a reason as this. (*Sermons Preached in the Chapel of Rugby School with an Address Before Confirmation* [New York, 1846], p. 40; *DNB*).

7. Proposed as a candidate for membership in the Presbyterian Society of Amboy.
8. Probably Edward Cooper, editor of the *Teacher's Advocate* in Syracuse, who had recently published an address by George Geddes to the local teachers' association. Olmsted must have thought, however, that the Cooper the people in Fairmount were talking about was the novelist James Fenimore Cooper. He lived ninety miles away in Cooperstown and was probably the only Cooper in the region that Olmsted, in writing to his brother, would refer to simply by his last name (W. W. Clayton, *History of Onondaga County*, p. 196; information on Edward Cooper supplied by Richard N. Wright).
9. Seymour N. Case an eccentric lawyer whom several leading citizens of Hartford prevailed upon to deliver a flowery Fourth of July oration in 1845, as a joke (see FLO to CLB, July 9–10, 1845, above).
10. Emma Brace.
11. William B. Capron (1824–1876) of the class of 1846 at Yale became the principal of the Hopkins Grammar School in Hartford, which was incorporated into the Hartford High School as its classics department in 1847 (*Yale Obit. Rec.*, 2d ser., no. 7 [June 1877]: 264; *Hartford County*, 1: 640, 644).
12. Henrietta Blake.
13. The teacher of James Geddes (1831–1887), George Geddes's son (D. H. Bruce, *Onondaga's Centennial*, 2: 1039).

To John Olmsted

Fairmount, July 1st, 1846

Dear Father,

Yours and John's of 26th reached me only this morning. (Why so long?)

Our folks are expecting a visit from Mr. Randall and family of Cortland.[1] The rain may prevent their coming today. Mr. Geddes seems to think Randall a very great man.

We have some cherries, and within a mile is a cherry orchard which sends some bushels to market daily. We are eating pies from *them*. We live well. Mr. Geddes is very abstemious himself, not eating much besides potato, bread, coffee, tea, and gravy—the latter more particularly. But we have fresh meat well cooked and served, half the time at least—and *silver forks every day*.

We are unfortunately late with our garden. Lettuce we have had all the time. I never eat it. (beet tops, ditto). We shall have new potatoes and some green peas for Randall. Also (for him) pines[2] and melons—(cost 4¢) cucumbers, &c purchased in Syracuse. Tomatoes blossomed. Sweet corn backward. Currant pies, lamb, and veal—and good beef, mashed potatoes (always for dinner), &c, &c., old stories. Very Yankee Indian pudding. Very light & white bread and milk always. Chickens as often as Jim[3] gets a chance to shoot them for trespassing in the new sowed fields, &c. A make shift dinner now and then. Not of boiled pork &c. but pork disguised as a pancake—fried in butter.

We have excellent water and an ice house so handy that they never think it is not worth the trouble to use it. Mr. Geddes drinks Congress Water and a little brandy for the stomach's sake. And we have tea three times a day and very good coffee for breakfast.

I think now you and John will be satisfied.

Skaneateles is at the head of Skaneateles Lake, not Seneca. The member of Congress you *did* probably call on there was, I believe Mrs. Geddes's father.[4] The Shotwell farm[5] is in Seneca, is it not? The woman that entertained you, I suppose, was here last week. She is in a premature dotage from an affection of the brain. She lives, they say in the finest place on the lake.

You ask who Sara Porter is. She's a plaguy fine girl I calculate. And my business over there is probably to fall in love with her. She is Dr. Porter's daughter. Your old member of Congress's (who was also M.D.)'s granddaughter. Lives *somewhere* in Skaneateles and don't play very well (or very much) on a vile piano—*they say.*

I think *Greeley* "is indefensible" and Polk pretty "near right."[6] Tell me, John, where you think Polk so far out of the way (in regard to Mexico). I like Cassius M. Clay[7] and would vote to make him Vice President at least. For President my choice first would be to nominate old Harry, next Judge McLean, Crittenden, Clayton, and I would vote for Taylor or Soup before I would for Calhoun or Wright.[8] Perhaps Taylor would make an excellent President. The skilful disposition, management, and partisan diplomacy of a frontier army is prima facie evidence of a talent for government—governing. It was in Old Jackson. He showed it. To be sure, he did show also (but equally after and before his nomination) strong passions and a hasty temper. But Taylor has no Ambrister and Arbuthnot[9]—what's their names—on his hands. I suspect Scott is a vain, ambitious, though talented man. His defence of himself[10] (which Major Kirby[11] says he *knows* he wrote himself, though it is commonly denied) is thought to be a very able, talented production.

There is a good and I think very correct article on Greeley in the last *True American.*[12] I will try to send it to you. The T. Am. is a real *good* paper.

I am pretty confident the Supreme Court will nullify the Bridge. It would be a very dangerous precedent.[13]

I have acknowledged Mr. Dixon's kindness and express my "high respect."

"Boggy Stow"—quaint name. I don't know what "Stow" means—but I hope it is more promising than the rest.

I have learned to file the knives and all about our mill.[14] It grinds more cob-corn than Fitzgerald's promises, too—but does not grind flour.

The postmaster promised to mark that letter single, or I should not have sent it. My postage account for this quarter (ending yesterday) was just $1.00.

That reminds me of what I am sorry to say. I am afraid I shall get out of money before you come. You will wonder how. I have been more liberal than I should have been if Mr. Geddes had not, entirely out of kindness and to save me the payment of forty to fifty dollars board, taken me in and entertained every way so handsomely. But I have not been at all extravagant. My Expense Book accounts for nearly $10.00 and I have nearly that amount left. But I was thinking, between postage, puppy, ($2.00), picnic, & Porter, it would some of it be gone pretty soon.

1. Henry Stephens Randall (1811–1876), agricultural expert of Cortland, N.Y., biographer of Thomas Jefferson, and author of many books and articles on farming (*DAB*).
2. Pineapples, which were cultivated in hothouses called "pineries" (Bernard M'Mahon, *The American Gardener's Calendar: Adapted to the Climate and Seasons of the United States* . . . [Philadelphia, 1857], p. 110).
3. James Geddes.
4. From this statement and the one in the next paragraph about Sarah Maria Porter's parentage, it appears that Olmsted thought Mrs. Geddes's father, Samuel Porter, had been a congressman as well as a physician. In fact, it was Samuel's brother James Porter (1787–1839) of Skaneateles who served in the Fifteenth Congress, from 1817 to 1819 (see FLO to JHO, June 19, 1846, note 9, above; *BDAC*, s.v. "Porter, James").
5. Perhaps the farm of Benjamin Shotwell (1759–1848) in Wayne (formerly Seneca) County, N.Y. His wife was Bathsheba Pound Shotwell (1763–1848) (Ambrose M. Shotwell, comp., *Annals of Our Colonial Ancestors and Their Descendants* [Lansing, Mich., 1897], Part 2, p. 95; FLO to JO and JHO, May 4, 1846).
6. Horace Greeley (1811–1872), Whig editor of the *New York Daily Tribune*, accused President James Polk of fomenting the Mexican war. "No honest man," he wrote, "ever doubted that the President deserved impeachment" (*New York Daily Tribune*, June 8, 1846, p. 2; *DAB*).
7. Cassius M. Clay (1810–1903), a distant cousin and supporter of Henry Clay. Although a native Kentuckian of the planter class, he was an outspoken critic of slavery and its effect on the society of the South. In 1845 he founded the weekly antislavery newspaper, *True American*, in Lexington, Ky., which Olmsted was reading during his stay at Geddes's farm (David L. Smiley, *Lion of White Hall: The Life of Cassius Clay* [Madison, Wis., 1962], pp. 71–86).
8. This list of Olmsted's choices for president gives some indication of the strength of his loyalty to the Whig party and its aging leader, Henry Clay (1777–1852). In 1846 it was doubtful that Clay would again seek the Whig presidential nomination, and many Whigs were turning their attention to younger men. John J. Crittenden, senator from Kentucky, and John Clayton, senator from Delaware, were close friends and political lieutenants of Clay's. Crittenden, who had succeeded to Clay's senatorial seat in 1842, was viewed by many as his logical successor as standard-bearer of the Whig party. Apparently, Olmsted preferred Supreme Court Justice

John McLean of Ohio to either of these men. As postmaster general under James Monroe and John Quincy Adams, McLean had gained a national reputation for his efficient and nonpartisan administration of that department. He moved to the Supreme Court after Andrew Jackson's election in 1828, in part because he refused to make the wholesale removals and appointments for political reasons that Jackson's advisers demanded.

In the summer of 1846 the move to attract General Zachary Taylor to the Whig party as its candidate for 1848 was already under way, given impetus by his defeat of the Mexican army at the battle of Palo Alto in early May. The Mexican War also strengthened the presidential hopes of General Winfield Scott, whom Whig leaders had considered nominating in 1840 and 1844. Scott earned the nickname "Soup," or "Hasty Plate of Soup," because of his letter of May 25, 1846, to Secretary of War William L. Marcy upon being informed that President Polk was removing him as general-in-chief of the U.S. Army. He wrote, "Your letter of this date, received about 6 p.m., as I sat down to take a hasty plate of soup, demands a prompt reply."

Olmsted preferred these men, Whigs and nationalists that they were, to the more sectionally oriented leaders of the Democrats. The two examples he chooses here are John C. Calhoun, the leader of the Southern Rights faction of the Democratic party, and Silas Wright, governor of New York, ex-senator, and one of the leaders of the antislavery "Barnburner" faction of the party (*DAB*, s.v. "Calhoun, John Caldwell," "Clay, Henry," "Clayton, John Middleton," "Crittenden, John Jordan," "Taylor, Zachary," "Wright, Silas"; Albert D. Kirwan, *John J. Crittenden: The Struggle for the Union* [Lexington, Ky., 1962], pp. 201, 203–4, 207; Charles W. Elliott, *Winfield Scott: The Soldier and the Man* [New York, 1937], p. 439; Allan Nevins, *Ordeal of the Union*, 2 vols. [New York, 1947], 1: 189; Francis P. Weisenburger, *The Life of John McLean; A Politician on the United States Supreme Court* [Columbus, Ohio, 1937], pp. 31–47, 67).

9. Robert Ambrister and Alexander Arbuthnot, British subjects, were condemned to death by Andrew Jackson during his invasion of Spanish Florida in 1818 for inciting Indian hostility on the border. This act, along with his aggression against Spanish Florida, spoiled Jackson's early chance at the presidency created by his defeat of the British at New Orleans in 1815 (Andrew Jackson, *The Correspondence of Andrew Jackson*, ed. John S. Bassett, 7 vols. [Washington, D.C., 1927], 2: 367; *DAB*, s.v. "Jackson, Andrew").

10. In May 1846, General Winfield Scott wrote a letter to the secretary of war that was interpreted as an attack on President Polk, who thereafter relieved him of his command. Scott's "hasty plate of soup" letter of May 25 was his attempt to defend himself. He went on to command a victorious campaign against Mexico, but Polk tried to undercut him again by holding a court of inquiry to investigate his actions as commander. The defense Olmsted mentions might have been a pamphlet. Scott was finally vindicated (*DAB*).

11. Presumably Captain Ephraim Kirby Smith (1807–1847), whose wife was living with her parents, Geddes's neighbors, while Smith was fighting with Scott in Mexico (see FLO to JO, July 23, 1846, note 21, below).

12. The article on Greeley praised him as "one of the noblest instructors of our country." The same issue of the *True American* ran a prospectus of Greeley's *New York Daily Tribune*, affirming its advocacy of reform ("Horace Greeley," *True American*, June 24, 1846, pp. 2–3).

13. The Connecticut legislature passed a bill, over the governor's veto, authorizing a railroad company with routes between Boston and New York to build a bridge over the Connecticut River at Middletown, blocking navigation above it to Hartford. The citizens of Hartford hoped that the Connecticut Supreme Court would declare the bill unconstitutional (*Hartford Daily Courant*, June 15, 18, 19, 1846, p. 2).

14. The Geddes farm had a portable Pitt's Corn and Cob-Cutter for grinding corn. Fitzgerald's mill was a portable grist mill (FLO to JO, July 23, 1846; *Cultivator*, n.s. 2, no. 10 [Oct. 1845]: 324; n.s. 3, no. 11 [Nov. 1846]: 351).

To John Olmsted

Fairmount, July 23rd, 1846. Thursday evening

Dear Father,

Letters from you and from mother (& papers) received this morning. Paper (Mr. Brooks'[1] death) from John, and his Valedictory Oration from Kingsbury,[2] yesterday.

I am obliged to write in considerable haste.

The proposed arrangement for vacation is satisfactory to me. I shall expect you then, if nothing interferes, the 29th of August. You would like to visit Plank Road[3] and Oneida Lake, perhaps. And John would want to spend one day mineralizing hereabouts. I don't suppose you would enjoy yourself here much—at home.

I will suggest nothing more in regard to the *Fall* at present.

Mr. Randall's[4] invitation is not of the greatest consequence. I should (if I did) visit him rather as an act of friendship than for other advantage or pleasure.

In regard to the winter—if you should find a seashore farm, *that* would make some difference. Otherwise, I don't know but Mr. Norton's[5] would be the best place. Wherever I am I shall study more than I work a good deal. If it was not for trespassing altogether too strong on Mr. Geddes' hospitality and kindness, I should not probably desire a better place than this, because I could study and cultivate mental powers to such advantage here. You forgot, perhaps, that I *have* had *some* experience of winter Farming—at Cheshire.[6]

The death of Old 'Miah will throw a beautiful farm into market I suppose—in Cheshire.[7] For inland farming I should not want a prettier place but for its proximity to Sleepy David and the rest of the kit of *borrowing* and pettifying neighbors. It would require a considerable capital to get it underweigh perhaps.

The greatest objection to the Sachem's Head Farm[8] is its smallness and perhaps its bleakness. Probably not over 40 acres would be in tillage at a time—hardly enough. If there were 70 acres of wood and pasture to the back of it, there would be a good deal such a farm as I want. I should think it was priced too high. If there is a good deal of land—pasture, as I understand you—a good deal of it certainly is rock, and some sterile—stunted wood I think growing on it. Altogether—nearly as high—considering position, as Morris's.[9]

Considering Morris's is just the place you want, seems to me it is queer you don't take the trouble in course of a year and a half to see, examine, and value it. Perhaps the old fellow would sell it cheap, if he had a chance. Townsend[10] says he thinks he would. I have thought a good deal about that Sachem's Head place without knowing it was for sale. (So I have of 'Miah's.) There is no fruit there I suppose & perhaps no soil for it. I should like to hear more about it.

There is the prettiest ground for a *ferme ornée*[11] in that place of 'Miah's I ever saw almost—a beautiful nook under the mountain—or dell— with a fine large trout brook running through it. A quarter of a mile from David's, half a mile from the railroad canal. The farm has been miserably cultivated by the old miserly tyrant that has gone to his account, but there is by nature excellent land and every convenience and beauty desirable.

Of course Uncle Owen won't go by here without calling. If he and Fanny[12] will be kind enough to stop here overnight, which will be convenient, I shall be glad to see them and Geddes won't be sorry, to say the least. Let me know, if possible, when to expect them—whether they will want their "baggage carried up," &c. The cars stop for supper at Syracuse and will (if requested) land here one quarter hour after. Our house is on the hill Southwest opposite the 5 mile post. Must be seen a little before that though.

Mr. Geddes has been quite unwell: dyspepsia, &c, cross as a sawhorse. Tuesday I went with him and James[13] over the Plank Road to Brewerton at the outlet of Oneida Lake. There is a good house there and it is used as a watering place. There is very fine sport fishing. I caught some fine Oswego bass, chub, and perch and saw my first cat-fish.

Do you recollect the little pleasure steamboat, perhaps 30 feet long, that came into Sachem's Head in her first trial trip from Bridgeport—one day about eight or ten years ago? The *"Dream"* she was then. She came into Fort Brewerton while I was there. Her principal business is towing. The lake is the largest sheet of fresh water I was ever on. Larger than I had supposed. Can't see across it—some thirty miles—length.

The agent for Fitzgerald's Mills has been putting up one here yesterday & today. It seems to do very well, except the bolting is not perfect. Cost 75 dollars. Will probably grind 4 bushels wheat in an hour. Does not compare for *cob* grinding with Pitt's—the one we have.[14] That will grind a bushel of long clean ears in four minutes! Our man ground 20 bushels, as they came, last Friday *forenoon* after 8 o'clock.

I meant before to have suggested to you to plough & fence off a piece of ground at the lot and plant with [. . .] &c. (If there is any good any where near Hartford). It could save much *time* **or** *expense* on a farm for me.

My corn is dreadful. I think of having a surgical operation performed on it, cutting out all [. . .] and taking off the skin opposite, binding the toes together, so they will grow—one.

I have got my terrier. The finest pup you ever saw. I call him "Pepper" (5 weeks old).

We have the best physician in the country living with us (as much as anywhere) now. His name is Healy[15]—an eccentric, kind-hearted, deaf, cigar-smoking old cock—that goes about doing good without asking for a fee. He never eats meat, has an independent fortune, is always where you don't expect to find him, and never where you do. He nurses more than he prescribes and his patients have the greatest faith in him.

I don't get the *Monthly Journal of Agriculture*.[16]

Do you take the *Horticulturist*?[17]

I am about writing Uncle Law[18]—and shall write mother, John, George Bissell,[19] & Charley Brace as soon as I get time. I have about a week of my Journal to write up now. Captain *Smith*[20] from *Texas* will probably be here in course of a week for a day or two.

A gentleman from Mississippi dined with us today.

1. Jeremiah Brooks (c. 1792–1846), Cheshire farmer, who died suddenly "while at work in his hay field, July 7, 1846, at 54 years of age" (*Homes of Cheshire*, p. 83).
2. Frederick Kingsbury was elected senior class orator by the members of his class, and he delivered the valedictory oration at Presentation Day, July 1, 1846. The class orator for the graduation ceremonies that took place six weeks later was chosen by the faculty. The position of orator was the highest office a class could confer on one of its members, and the orator was supposed to be the best representative "of the general talent of the class, as distinguished from scholarship . . ." ("A Poem by Edwin Johnson and the Valedictory Oration by Frederick John Kingsbury Pronounced before the Senior Class in Yale College, July 1, 1846," in Sterling Memorial Library, Yale University; L. H. Bagg, *Four Years at Yale*, p. 484).
3. The new plank road between Syracuse and Oneida Lake (see FLO to JHO, June 19, 1846, note 20, above).
4. Henry Stephens Randall.
5. John Treadwell Norton, from whom Olmsted received advice and letters of introduction before leaving for Fairmount in March 1846. The house on his farm had thirty-four rooms, and he surrounded it with ten acres of flower gardens and trees. Olmsted understandably thought that it would be a pleasant place to spend the winter learning about farming (FLO to JHO, March 18, 1846; *Hartford County*, 1: 213 n, and 2: 200; Albert Palmer Pitkin, *The Pitkin Family of America: A Genealogy of the Descendants of William Pitkin* . . . (Hartford, Conn., 1887), p. 106; Mabel S. Hurlburt, *Farmington Town Clerks and Their Times, 1645–1940* [Hartford, 1943], pp. 210, 249–50, 312–13).
6. In late 1844 and early 1845, Olmsted had spent some time living at the farm of his uncle David Brooks in Cheshire (JO Journal, Oct. 30, Dec. 25, 1844; Jan. 13, Feb. 26, 1845).
7. The farm of Jeremiah Brooks, a cousin of Olmsted's uncle David Brooks, in Cheshire (*Homes of Cheshire*, pp. 81–83).
8. This is probably the seventy-acre farm on Sachem's Head, near Guilford, Conn. that Olmsted's father bought him in December 1846. See his description of the farm in FLO to JHO, Feb. 16, 1847, below.
9. Perhaps Amos Morris (b. 1750), who owned a farm on the coast near New Haven that had been in the family since 1671 (*Commemorative Biographical Record of New Haven County, Connecticut* . . . , 2 vols. [Chicago, 1902], 1: 94).
10. William Kneeland Townsend (1796–1849) of East Haven, Conn., whose farm and livestock won many prizes from the New Haven County Agricultural Society. Olmsted considered staying at his farm, "Prospect Hill," after he left Geddes's farm in the fall of 1846 (Doris B. Townshend, *Townshend Heritage: A Genealogical, Biographical History of the Townshend Family* . . . [New Haven, 1971], pp. 122–3, 143–50; FLO to FJK, Aug. 22, 1846; FJK Journal, Nov. 22, 1845).

11. The term *ferme ornée* originated with the English poet William Shenstone, who could find no English word to describe the elaborate landscaping he carried out on his estate after 1745. The English landscape gardener Humphry Repton (1752–1818) referred to the term in *The Art of Landscape Gardening*, which Olmsted read as a youth, but criticized Shenstone's overly ambitious and incongruous attempts to extend park scenery throughout all parts of his farm. The American landscape gardener and horticulturist Andrew Jackson Downing defined the term in his *Cottage Residences*, with which Olmsted was probably familiar. "The *ferme ornée*," he wrote, "is a term generally applied to a farm, the whole or the greater part of which is rendered in some degree ornamental by intersecting it with drives, and private lanes and walks, bordered by trees and shrubs, and by the neater arrangement and culture of the fields. But it may also be applied to a farm with a tasteful farmhouse, and so much of the ground about it rendered ornamental, as would naturally meet the eye of the stranger, in approaching it the first time" (*EB*, s.v. "Shenstone, William"; Humphry Repton, *The Art of Landscape Gardening*, ed. John Nolen [Boston, 1907], pp. 136–41; Andrew Jackson Downing, *Cottage Residences; Or, A Series of Designs for Rural Cottages and Cottage-Villas, and Their Gardens and Grounds. Adapted to North America* [New York, 1842], pp. 93–94).

12. Olmsted's uncle Owen Pitkin Olmsted of Geneseo, N.Y., and his daughter Frances made a trip to Niagara Falls during the next month (Frances E. Olmsted to JHO, Aug. 11, 1846).

13. James Geddes, son of George Geddes.

14. Fitzgerald's and Pitt's were portable grinding mills (see FLO to JO, July 1, 1846, note 14, above).

15. Dr. Samuel Healy (1788–1854), graduate of the College of Physicians and Surgeons in New York City, who began practicing medicine in Onondaga County in 1816. The "nursing" of his patients that Olmsted refers to frequently involved venesection, or bleeding. George Geddes's father James (1763–1838) had a long illness under his care and became, judging by Healy's day book, "probably the most venesected man of the doctor's large number of patients" (information on Samuel Healy supplied by Richard N. Wright; "Relic of Bygone Days," Syracuse *Journal*[?], May 16, 1896, at Onondaga Historical Association, Syracuse, N.Y.).

16. The *Journal of Agriculture*, edited from 1845 to 1848 by the agricultural writer and reformer John Stuart Skinner (1788–1851). Through June 1846, its title was the *Monthly Journal of Agriculture* (*DAB*; Frank L. Mott, *A History of American Magazines*, vol. 1, *1741–1850* [Cambridge, Mass., 1938]: 442).

17. In July 1846, Andrew Jackson Downing published the first issue of his periodical, the *Horticulturist and Journal of Rural Art and Rural Taste* (*DAB*).

18. Olmsted's scholarly uncle, Jonathan Law, who took in and perhaps adopted Olmsted's mother when she was a young girl. He shared his interest in literature and gardening with Olmsted, who often visited him as a boy (see Autobiographical Fragment B, note 6, above).

19. Probably George Bissell, who was later a Hartford merchant and a partner of Olmsted's half-brother, Albert.

20. Ephraim Kirby Smith, Connecticut-born soldier and graduate of West Point. He married Mary Jerome (b. 1814), the eldest daughter of George Geddes's relatives and neighbors, Isaac and Clarinda Jerome. At this time Smith was on leave to visit his family following the death of his father. He returned to his command in Mexico in late August 1846, and died on September 11, 1847, from wounds suffered in the battle of Molino del Rey (Emma Jerome Blackwood, ed., *To Mexico with Scott: Letters of Captain E. Kirby Smith to His Wife, Prepared for the Press by His Daughter* [Cambridge, Mass., 1917], pp. 3, 8, 9, 55; FLO to CLB, July 30, 1846, below; information on Mary Jerome supplied by Richard N. Wright and from records of the Oakwood Cemetery, Syracuse, N. Y.; George Washington Cullum, *Biographical Register of the Officers and Graduates of the U.S. Military Academy, from 1802 to 1867*, rev. ed., with supplement continuing the register of graduates to Jan. 1, 1879, 3 vols. [New York, 1879], 1: 307).

To CHARLES LORING BRACE

Address: Mr. Chas. L. Brace/Yale College/New Haven/Conn.
Postmark: ·Syracuse/Aug 4

Fairmount, July 30th, 1846

Dear Charley,

Your Letter of the 20th inst. reached me this morning. There's a letter to you partly written in my portfolio dated July 9th. I was interrupted in writing it and have not had the time convenient to finish it since. I intend to, however, whenever I happen to feel in a Metaphysico Theologo humour. I mention it that you may consider that I have not formed any of the strange conclusions that you deprecate.

I was highly pleased and interested with your account of "the *folks*" and description of your uncle's house and grounds and the surrounding scenery. There was no occasion for you to tell me where Beverly was and *all that!*[1] "Aunt Mary's"[2] vivid descriptions are not so easily erased.

I'll tell you how you'll oblige me now—and you can do it well *enough* if you'll try—I'll answer. Give me a rough plan of the place—showing the grounds, relative situation of the house, garden, fields, *sea*, &c.—with a sketch of the mansion and as much more—barns—ground plan, etc. as you've a mind for.

Your uncle's Book farming—so much as you detail—don't *astonish me.* You forget I am on the *"Premium Farm* of the Empire State." (You'll find Geddes' Report in the last Albany Cultivator and in the Quarterly Journal. By the way, Dr. Emmons, in introducing it, pays Geddes a handsome compliment.)[3]

Father thinks—or is looking at the farm west & north sides of Sachem's Head Harbour. I should think it might be situated a little like your Uncle's, and if I should take it, I should want to visit your uncle's.

It seems like an age since I saw you or have heard from you before. And I want to know how you have changed, what kind of a man you have got to be, &c. How you've grown, &c. I'd like to compare you with what you was when we had that daguerreotype taken. You recollect it, don't you? There in New Haven, the last term of Senior year. You don't forget those old-fashioned daguerreotypes. It took us a whole forenoon, if not a whole day, to get five faint smoky stiff-grouped impressions—which we called daguerreotypes.[4]

There was not a single line of telegraph in the city then.[5] Ah, there have been great changes in our day, old fellow. I hope some of them are for the better, and that we have not ourselves had the influence of clogs upon the advance of society, happiness to man, & Glory to God.

That good old Saint, Jeremiah Day,[6] was "Prex" then. "Little Miss

263

OLMSTED AND FRIENDS IN NEW HAVEN, 1846
Back row, left to right: CHARLES LORING BRACE,
JOHN HULL OLMSTED; *front row,* FREDERICK KINGSBURY,
FREDERICK LAW OLMSTED, CHARLES TRASK

OLMSTED AND FRIENDS IN NEW HAVEN, 1846
Back row, left to right: CHARLES TRASK, FREDERICK KINGSBURY,
JOHN HULL OLMSTED; *front row*, CHARLES LORING BRACE,
FREDERICK LAW OLMSTED

Prex!"[7] don't you recollect, we used to call one of his daughters so—a queer, bright eyed, big nosed girl—full of life and striking expression. Did you ever hear what became of her. They used to say Fred Kingsbury (That Valedictory of his was a sensible thing was not it?—he was one of our Infantile Chemistry Association you know.[8])—they used to say Fred (so we called him then) was in love—with her—Miss Day. What was her first name? Something like *"ice?"* Somehow, that's associated with her—to me. I never believed it though, did you—except as we all loved one another. How odd it sounds now.

There was old governor Baldwin, one of the old school Whig Connecticut governors. His daughter, pretty girl—sensible too.[9] Recollect how she *sung?* Her favorite, something about a little Indian boy that was lost & found again or something. Didn't she make poetry & such things. I believe I was more than half in love with her myself one spell—wasn't you? But she "hated cats"—and I couldn't go that.

Bishop Bacon's daughter[10]—and—But I expect you remember all those dear *young* saints as well as I. It's pleasant to think of 'em a little now & then, isn't [it] though? I hope we shall all meet again.

Talking of daguerreotypes—that you may prepare yourself and look destiny in the face—I give you a prophecy and a compliment from a very discerning and *clever* man to whom I showed that *plate.* He put his finger on your head after studying it a minute and said, "That's the greatest man in the crowd." "Now mind what I say, that man will make a great noise in the world!" So you may as well be loading up to your calibre.

As for me, I am "the same old two and six." Not quite so soft perhaps as I used to be—for at these presents, I do not know that I am violently in love anywhere. I think my taste for study and reading has rather increased. I am afraid it will interfere some with my character for business and I find it harder to write & take pains than ever.

This has been a good place for me. I have looked on and talked more than I've worked; but I've considerable faith that I shall make a good farmer. In fact, I don't doubt it at all, if I can only get (a good wife and) a place to suit me and am not badly shaved in purchasing it. I'll write you another letter—one of these days. You were so confounded impudent—a spell ago writing to me—I did not mean to write about anything else (but "war") this time.

Captain (Kirby) Smith[11] is here on a short furlough. Now Captain Smith is a tall, straight, well-made man, with an honest, frank, sun-burnt face, short curly hair and handsome whiskers. A fine looking fellow is not he in a neat undress uniform. But then, too, he is sociable, courteous, well-bred, unassuming, modest, gallant, well informed and all that—no extravagance. Splendid fellow isn't he? You have only to ask him questions, and he'll answer just as you want to have him, not as if you did not know anything, and yet not above particularizing. It's real *fun* to tap him and draw off the stirring incidents of the battles, the mess table jokes, and campaigning anecdotes.

In the first place it did not take long to discover the news-papers lied tremendously. That whole affair of Captain Martin Scott & the Texan rangers —sixty killed—was so nearly without foundation, that even now, he knows nothing of it.[12] And Captain S. is a particular and confidential friend of his. He makes him out to be a great fellow. That keeping communication between the forts was desperate business. He admires General Taylor but General T. is not a classical scholar. He told May to take it *"nolus volus."*[13] They make a great deal of fun about it. There was a report in camp that "the Penn. University had conferred the degree of LL.D. on General T. on account of the classical erudition he displayed in the action of the 9th May." Gen'l Taylor heard of it and enjoyed the joke.

Smith breakfasted with Major Ringgold[14] on the morning of the 8th.

"What did you have for breakfast?"

"Cold ham"—(do *you like* it?) "hard bread and a bottle of claret."

The first shot that hit his company knocked a man down at his feet. He looked up at him.

"I am killed, Captain!"

"Oh no, you are not. A dead man can't speak."

"But look here, Captain."

The ball had struck him in the temple. Captain T. put his finger on the wound and told him the ball had not gone through his skull.

"Well then, by George, Sir, I am good for another."

And he picked up his musket and marched on. The next man that was shot, the ball passed between the Captain's legs.

The first day they had little to do but to stand fire and repulse the Mexican Cavalry in hollow square (Fifth Infantry). At the Resaca de la Palma[15] his company were among the first and longest engaged. The whole country is full of chapper*el* (so accented) and underbrush with little openings and cowpaths amongst it. They scouted up through the bushes on the left side of the road till they reached a low bank (near A. "A") under cover of which they lay a few minutes protected from the fire of the Mexican Entrenchment (at E) while Smith & the officers reconnoitered. The main body with General Taylor were on the road (T) which was commanded by the battery (B).

They saw the immediate necessity of taking this and when they had drawn all the men they could collect into a body on the edge of the brush, gave the word to charge it (the battery). His company had been stationed at Fort Winnebago,[16] and as they went down into the ravine on a full run they raised the *Winnebago yell*. Before they reached the battery they heard the cavalry coming down behind them and opened to the right and left for them to pass through. The cavalry were all yelling too—and came like a thunderbolt.

After they had taken the battery, they pushed on to the left where posted irregularly among the bushes were the "Tampico Guardo Costa," who fought desperately hand-to-hand.[17]

"Take care, Captain," said a man by his side, "That fellow's aiming at your head."

He looked, and saw an *esquibo* (?) (large bored, heavy fire arm) ranging right at his head. He *ducked* as the man's arm moved in pulling the trigger and the ball went over his head. Then he chased him (the Mex)—firing his pistols at him and hit him in the shoulder—and was just grabbing him when he found himself right in a squad of about twenty of the enemy. He defended himself with his sword till his men rushed in and succored him.

"Captain," said another man, "that rascal yonder just shot at you—see his hat there through the mesquite bush. He's loading again. If you'll let me rest across your shoulder, I think I can fetch him—sure." So he did. The puff of smoke blew off.

"Did you hit him?"

"*He ain't **there**—Sir!*"

We have his blood-stained sword and two or three of the copper balls.

There's a good story about the "Great Western"[18]—that six foot and over Amazon, the heroine of Fort Brown, but it's too long to write now. The story of the Mexican supper all ready and the grand feast on after the action is a yarn. But after it was all over, they brought the train up and got the mess chest and had a capital supper with some glorious hot coffee of their own. Smith was "officer of the day." Had all the *camp* duty to attend to that night.

In strolling about looking up the bodies of his men, &c, he stumbled into a beautiful—kind of an arbour—very neatly made of bushes. It turned out to be General Vega's bivouac—and in it he found a bundle of correspondence with Paredes, Arista, & government and other matters.[19]

You'll be glad to learn (at least I was) the truth about that young officer that Leander like swam the Rio Grande in his uniform, *being captivated by a Mexican damsel*. He was a friend of Colonel Cross—who you recollect disappeared (cut off by rancheros) and his object is supposed to be to discover what had become of him. If this had been known by the enemy, you see, he would have been hung as a spy. The general opinion among the officers was that he was acting with the approbation of General Taylor though he said nothing about it:[20]

Cry "enough!" now & I'll stop.

I don't know just where to direct this letter, but I suppose you will be in New Haven at Commencement at any rate.

And if you are you will have to sketch those plans from memory. I should really be much obliged to you for them.

Truly your friend,

Fred

P.S. I've just received a letter (at last) from Em. She appears to be very pleasantly situated.[21]

She tries to stuff me with a yarn which I *may* tell you and Fred K.—but I *shall* not.

1. Brace's uncle Charles Greely Loring (1794–1867) had a farm in Beverly, Mass. Brace visited him there in the summer of 1846 and thought Beverly his "very ideal for a summer residence" (*DAB*; Charles Henry Pope and Katherine Peabody Loring, *Loring Genealogy* [Cambridge, Mass., 1917], pp. 166–68; CLB to JHO, Aug. 6, 1846).

2. Brace's great-aunt Mary Pierce (1781–1863) of Litchfield, Conn. who was the aunt of Charles Greely Loring's first wife, Anna Pierce Brace (C. T. Payne, *Litchfield and Morris Inscriptions*, p. 40).

3. Ebenezer Emmons (1799–1863), geologist, physician, and teacher, co-edited the *Quarterly Journal*, so Olmsted assumed he had written the unsigned introduction to the article praising the detailed description of the Geddes farm that followed ("Prize Farm Report," *American Quarterly Journal of Agriculture and Science* 4, no. 1 [July 1846], frontispiece; *DAB*).

4. The five friends were Charles Loring Brace, Charles Trask, Frederick Kingsbury, John Hull Olmsted, and Frederick Law Olmsted. Two of the daguerreotypes are reproduced on pages 264 and 265.

5. The telegraph line through New Haven from New York to Boston had been put into operation on June 27, 1846, only a month before this letter was written (Robert L. Thompson, *Wiring a Continent: The History of the Telegraph Industry in the United States, 1832–1866* [Princeton, N.J., 1947], pp. 59–61).

6. Jeremiah Day (1773–1867) was president of Yale from July 23, 1817 to October 21, 1846 (Yale University, *Historical Register of Yale University 1701–1937* [New Haven, Conn., 1939], p. 33).

7. Olivia Day. In December 1849, she became engaged to Thomas K. Beecher. The engagement dismayed John Hull Olmsted, who had "hoped for a union" of Kingsbury and Olivia. She and Beecher were married in September 1851 (T. D. Seymour, *Family of Jeremiah Day*, p. 15; *DAB*, s.v. "Beecher, Thomas Kinnicut"; JHO to FJK, Jan. 9, 1850).

8. A small group of students including Charles Loring Brace, Frederick Kingsbury, and Charles Trask began attending Benjamin Silliman's lectures to the upper classmen on chemistry, mineralogy, and geology. In their senior year Olmsted joined them in studying chemistry with Silliman's assistant, Thomas Terry Hunt (1826–1892). They went well beyond the regular course in experimentation and studied "to the profit of some and to the solid satisfaction of all" (FJK Sketch of CLB, pp. 2–8).

9. Elizabeth Baldwin.

10. Rebecca T. Bacon.

11. Ephraim Kirby Smith (see FLO to JO, July 23, 1846, note 21, above).

12. Martin Scott (1788–1847) was not involved in the incident. On April 28, 1846, Captain Samuel H. Walker of the Texas Rangers set out from Fort Texas to take

important news about Mexican troop movements to General Zachary Taylor at Point Isabell. On the way Mexican cavalrymen attacked and dispersed his force. Walker reached Point Isabell with six of his men and returned safely to Fort Texas, which was then under shell fire, with the news that Taylor would soon come to its aid (*New York Weekly Herald*, May 23, 1846, p. 1; Walter Prescott Webb, *The Texas Rangers* [Austin, Tex., 1965], pp. 80, 93–94).

13. Contemporary newspapers reported that when Taylor reached Fort Texas to relieve it, he said to Captain Charles A. May, "Your time has come. Here are the enemy's batteries, Sir. Take them *nolens, volens*"—that is, no matter what the cost. Taylor's Latin was not equal to the occasion, and he actually used the meaningless phrase "*nolus, volus*." May understood the command, nonetheless, and led a successful charge in which he lost a third of his men (*New York Weekly Tribune*, May 30, 1846, p. 2; *DAB*, s.v. "Taylor, Zachary").

14. Samuel Ringgold (c. 1800–1846), soldier, native of Washington, D.C., graduated from West Point in 1818 and died of a wound received in the battle of Palo Alto (G. W. Cullum, *Biographical Register of the Officers and Graduates of the U.S. Military Academy*, 1: 174).

15. The battle of Resaca de la Palma on May 9, 1846, was the first major engagement of the Mexican War.

16. Fort Winnebago was in Wisconsin on the Fox River opposite the portage to the Wisconsin River.

17. The Tampico Guarda Costa's flag was the last to disappear from the field in the battle of Resaca de la Palma. The Mexican color sergeant bore the standard until his regiment was totally destroyed by American gunfire (Horatio Ladd, *History of the War with Mexico* [New York, 1883], p. 64).

18. "Great Western" was Lieutenant Braxton Bragg's laundress. She won the right to march with Bragg's company because of her excellent care of the wounded during the bombardment of Fort Texas (Edward J. Nicholas, *Zach Taylor's Little Army* [New York, 1963], pp. 90–91; Robert Selph Henry, *The Mexican War* [New York, 1961], p. 54).

19. Romulo de la Vega (1811–1896), a brevet brigadier general, was commander of the Mexican troops before Fort Texas. Paredes y Arrillaga (1797–1849) was then a general and president of Mexico, and Mariano Arista (1802–1855) was commander of the Mexican army (Fayette Robinson, *Mexico and Her Military Chieftains, from the Revolution of Hidalgo to the Present Time* . . . (Hartford, Conn., 1851), pp. 263–65; *Webster's Biographical Dictionary*, s.v. "Arista, Mariano"; *Diccionario Porrua de Historia, Biografía de Mexico* [Mexico City, 1964], s.v. "Arrillaga, Paredes y").

20. On April 12, 1846, Colonel Trueman Cross (d. 1846), quartermaster of the U.S. forces, strayed from the army encampment by the Rio Grande. His close friend Lieutenant Edward Deas (c. 1812–1846) swam across the Rio Grande in an attempt to find him and was captured by the Mexicans (G. W. Cullum, *Biographical Register of the Officers and Graduates of the U.S. Military Academy*, 1: 404; E. Nichols, *Zach Taylor's Little Army*, pp. 50, 57–58; E. J. Blackwood, *To Mexico with Scott: Letters of Captain E. Kirby Smith to His Wife*, p. 38).

21. Emma Brace, having graduated from the Hartford Female Seminary with the intention of being a teacher, had left home to start a school in Garrettsburg, Kentucky, in the summer of 1846 (*Life of Brace*, p. 14).

TO JOHN OLMSTED

Fairmount, August 12th, 1846

Dear Father,

I wrote mother last week mentioning incidents in my visit to Skaneateles. There is a lady there who says she knew you—in the way of shop-
ping I suppose, twenty years ago—Mrs. Clark.[1] I don't remember her
maiden name—something not common in Connecticut. The scenery about S.
is perfectly beautiful, nothing else. The long sweeping roll and easy slope of
the hills is charming. They run off into the Lake. There is no flat land or
marshes about it. Farther up, the hills grow bolder and descend with more
abruptness into the water, till at the head of the lake, sixteen miles south of
Skaneateles, they are mountains a thousand feet in height and the lake is
probably of equal depth—the features changing to grandeur. It is a pleasant
day's excursion there, either by boat or carriage. A ride around the lake—
about forty miles—with a dinner at the cascades is the common *pleasuring*
there.

I have been looking for a letter from you and the Monthly Journal
for two or three days. I am anxious to hear about the Head farm.[2] If the
Farmer's Library can be had separately at half subscription price, I would
drop the Monthly Journal—though it is very good—in favor of Drs. Emmons
& Prime's Quarterly Journal of Agriculture and Science, a very able, practical
scientific periodical—$1.50.[3]

I have thought of writing an article about Fuller's farming,[4] &c for
the Cultivator but have given it up because I have not myself sufficient
reliance on the correctness of the statements.

All our grain has been a good deal lodged, most of it mowed and
much made and stored in bulk—like hay. It does not make much difference,
when it is to be machine thrashed. I have not worked much during harvest—
cradled till my hand was horribly blistered. The fact is I have not had but
very few hard days work this summer. But I think my time has been as
profitably spent as it would have been any where else. You will have noticed
the article on Judge Van Bergen's farm in last Cultivator.[5]

I have trimmed all our grape vines.

Mr. Geddes leaves Saturday. Leaves his mother[6] to visit friends in
Rochester, goes on to Lockport—mineralizing—and Niagara. Has given up
going to Detroit. Returns in about a week—say 10th prox. After the October
fairs (say the 10th), he goes with Mrs. Geddes[7] to New York and Boston.

I was disappointed in not seeing or hearing anything of Uncle Owen
& Co.[8]

Captain Smith's[9] furlough has been extended 30 days.

I have two copies of Elihu Burritt's "Christian Citizen" sent me
from the publishers. Though like every newspaper of pluck it will look at

ABIGAIL ANNA HULL BROOKS

things with rather coloured glasses and take contemptible advantages, playing with words in a way that a plain honest man would call lying, it is on the whole a capital good paper—and less faulty than most to say the least. Burritt is in England now, himself, and all he writes is striking and original, worth a whole mail car of common namby pamby editorials.[10] I would advise you to take it instead of the Herald,[11] if you do take that. And for my part, though I do like the Observer,[12] I'd rather have [it]—and I'd take it sooner than any or all the sectarian publications in the country.

I am at war with all sectarianism and party trammels. The tyranny of priests and churches is as great a curse to the country and the world as Negro Slavery. I very much doubt if I shall join or array myself under any communion that is not open to any "follower of Jesus Christ."

I have been reading Sartor Resartus. It took me about three weeks, but I was intensely interested before I finished. And now if anybody wants to set me down for an insane cloud dwelling Transcendentalist, because I like Carlyle, I hope they'll gratify themselves. I do think Carlyle is the greatest genius in the world, with a greater intellect than Scott, Bulwer, Dickens, Hemans[13] and all the lady writers of the age together. I perfectly wonder and stand awe-struck as I would at a Hurricane. Have you read his Cromwell?[14]

A letter was advertised for me in the Syracuse P.O. Of course it was from Cheshire—and has been there—let's see—dated June 10th but post-

272

marked July 18th—from 'Lib.[15] It seems then A. Anna Abigail A. Anna A. Abagail—came home to—get married. I congratulate her heartily and still more—the Rev. Mr. Le Conte.[16] He'll have an excellent wife or a kitten won't make a cat. I suppose they've been engaged some years. She's a sensible girl.

What have you done, or what's proposed about the Seminary? Give it up—I, say—to Miss Thatcher.[17] Private enterprise, better than trustees. You can't make a college of it. Send the girls to Abbott's or the Rutger's[18]— somewhere where all the energies and skill is not to be bent and devoted to getting up a new or *reviving* an old reputation. The science of education has made great advances in ten years and Connecticut is behind the world.

The new tariff,[19] I hope, will give us a Northern President at least. War with Mexico has saved us from war with England.[20]

Texas with slavery, will I hope give us California as well as Oregon *without*. If we can but secure that before the lines are irretrievably drawn, then at least I hope it will be North & freedom vs. South and slavery. And then Hurrah for gradual Emancipation and a brisk trade with Africa.[21] Senator Niles ought to have a coal medal with a steam-boat just cast off and a man jumping overboard *at* the wharf, in *bold* relief—motto, "Better late than never."[22]

I hope you will come on as early as you can, and go by way of Oswego. The *sooner* the better.

Your affectionate son,

Fredk L.O.

John run over and see Captain Kimberley.[23] The old woman's dead you know.

1. Probably Sarah Morison Clarke, widow of Joseph T. Clarke (c. 1798–1845), minister of Saint James Episcopal Church in Skaneateles where the family of Mrs. George Geddes worshiped. John Olmsted had probably known the Clarkes when they lived in Bethany, Conn. near Hartford, where one son was born in 1827. She was the daughter of a Scottish coffee planter in Jamaica (information supplied by Richard N. Wright).
2. The farm on Sachem's Head in Guilford that Olmsted's father was thinking of buying for him.
3. Olmsted proposed to drop the *Farmer's Library and Monthly Journal of Agriculture*, established by John Stuart Skinner, in favor of the *American Quarterly Journal of Agriculture and Science*, started in 1845 in Albany, New York by Ebenezer Emmons and A. J. Prime (Albert L. Demaree, *The American Agricultural Press, 1819–1860* [New York, 1941], p. 25 n; *Union List of Serials*, s.v. "American Journal of Agriculture and Science").
4. William Fuller (1799–1867), owner of "Sherwood Farm" near Skaneateles, was one of the leading farmers of the area. He introduced fine breeds of cattle, was on the Committee of Arrangements for the New York State Agricultural Fair held in Auburn on September 15, 1846, and in 1849 became president of the New York State Agricultural Society (E. N. Leslie, *Skaneateles*, pp. 143; *Cultivator*, n.s. 3, no. 8 [Aug. 1846]: 243).

THE PAPERS OF FREDERICK LAW OLMSTED

5. Anthony A. Van Bergen (1786–1859) had a farm at Coxsackie, N.Y., where he tried out many innovations in farming ([Frederick Law Olmsted], *Walks and Talks of an American Farmer in England*, 2 vols. [New York, 1852], 1: 181–82; Sebastian Visscher Talcott, comp., *Genealogical Notes of New York and New England Families* [Albany, N.Y., 1883], p. 301; "Successful Farming," *Cultivator*, n.s. 3, no. 8 [Aug. 1846]: 250–51).
6. Lucy Isaacs Jerome Geddes.
7. Maria Porter Geddes.
8. Owen Pitkin Olmsted and his daughter Frances (see FLO to JO, July 23, 1846, note 12, above).
9. Ephraim Kirby Smith.
10. Elihu Burritt (1810–1879), "The Learned Blacksmith," was the leading American figure in the international peace movement at this time. In 1844 he founded the *Christian Citizen*, in which he advocated pacifism and international brotherhood. In the summer of 1846, when he and his followers failed to convince the American Peace Society to take a firmer stand against all war, he left that organization and spent most of the next decade in England. There he organized the League of Universal Brotherhood and promoted a series of international peace conferences (*DAB*; Alice Felt Tyler, *Freedom's Ferment: Phases of American Social History from the Colonial Period to the Outbreak of the Civil War* [1944; rpt. ed., New York, 1962], pp. 419–22).
11. Olmsted is probably referring to the *Missionary Herald*, the organ of the American Board of Foreign Missions, to which John Olmsted had subscribed in previous years (F. L. Mott, *A History of American Magazines*, 1: 133–34).
12. Probably the *Congregational Observer*, published in New Haven. It was formed in 1840 as a result of the merger of the *New Haven Record* with the *Connecticut Observer*; Olmsted refers to an article in the latter in FLO to JHO, July 7, 1840, above (*Union List of Serials*, s.v. "New Haven Record").
13. Sir Walter Scott, Charles Dickens, the English novelist Edward George Earle Lytton Bulwer-Lytton, and the English poet Felicia Dorothea Hemans.
14. The first American edition of *Sartor Resartus; The Life and Opinions of Herr Teufelsdröckh* by Thomas Carlyle (1795–1881) was published in 1846. His *Life and Letters of Oliver Cromwell* was published in England in 1845 (*DNB*).
15. Elizabeth Laura Brooks (1829–1899), Olmsted's cousin, daughter of David and Linda Hull Brooks of Cheshire (Puella Follet H. Mason, comp., *A Record of the Descendants of Richard Hull, of New Haven, Connecticut . . .* [Milwaukee, Wis., 1894], p. 61; Headstone Inscriptions, Bridgeport, Cemetery 4, p. 311).
16. Porter Le Conte (1817–1847), a Congregational minister, married Olmsted's cousin Abigail Anna Brooks (c. 1818–1879) of Cheshire, on September 27, 1846 (P. F. H. Mason, *A Record of the Descendants of Richard Hull*, p. 34; Cheshire Vital Records, 1780–1840, p. 430; Franklin Bowditch Dexter, *Biographical Notices of Graduates of Yale College: Including Those Not in the Annual Obituary Records* [New Haven, 1913], p. 329–30; *Homes of Cheshire*, p. 81; Headstone Inscriptions, Cheshire, Cemetery 1, p. 12).
17. The Hartford Female Seminary, of which John Olmsted was a trustee and of which John Pierce Brace had been head, continued under Helen A. Swift in 1846 and Mary M. Parker in 1847. A Miss Thacher ran a private school for girls in Hartford (*Hartford County*, 1: 649; *Geer's Directory for 1847*, p. 162).
18. Abbott Academy at Andover, Mass. founded in 1838, and Rutger's Female Institute in New York, incorporated in 1837 (A. F. Tyler's *Freedom's Ferment*, p. 245; *Rutger's Female College Catalogue, 1867–1868* [New York, 1867], p. 25).
19. The Walker Tariff, passed by Congress on July 30, 1846, was a Democratic measure that considerably reduced the protection afforded a number of important industries by the previous Tariff of 1842. At the time the Walker Tariff was enacted there were dire predictions that it would have a disastrous effect on American industry, which was located primarily in the North (Frank William Taussig, *The Tariff History of the United States . . . Including a Consideration of the Tariff of 1930*, 8th. ed. [New York, 1931], p. 114).

THE SEARCH FOR LOVE AND CERTITUDE: 1846

20. During the first half of 1846 the possibility of war between the United States and Britain arose over the Oregon boundary question. The issue was resolved in June 1846 by a treaty adopting the compromise line of the forty-ninth parallel (see FLO to FJK, June 12, 1846, note 11, above).

21. This is the only time in his extant letters or published writings that Olmsted expressed the view that emancipation should be followed by colonization of the freed slaves in Africa. Many opponents of slavery at the time, however, viewed colonization as a natural and desirable corollary of emancipation. The late 1840s, which saw the growth of the political antislavery movement in the North and the rise of the Free Soil Party, also saw increased support for the American Colonization Society. This trend was much more marked during the early 1850s, however. Olmsted's father had contributed money to the American Colonization Society four times in the previous five years, and Olmsted may have made this statement on his account (Philip Staudenraus, *The African Colonization Movement, 1816–1865* [New York, 1961], pp. 240–44, 251; JO Journal, Sept. 5, 1841, Jan. 1843, Dec. 1843, Dec. 24, 1844).

22. On July 28, 1846, John Milton Niles (1787–1856), Democratic senator from Connecticut, deserted his party to vote with Daniel Webster and the northern Whigs against the Walker Tariff (*DAB*; U.S., Congress, Senate, *Congressional Globe*, 29th Cong., 1st sess., 1846, 15, pt. 1: 1158).

23. Possibly Dennis Kimberly (1790–1862), a New Haven lawyer with a decided taste for the military, one of the first captains of the New Haven Grays (Edward E. Atwater, *History of the City of New Haven to the Present Time* [New York, 1887], pp. 245–46).

To Frederick Kingsbury[1]

Fairmount, August 22, 1846.

I have not been very well for a few days—ate too many apples &c. and then took brandy to counteract them—and then not being better off, took apples to counteract the brandy. And so I have been going on, but it's confounded hard to make the proper average. This morning I felt stupid as an owl at noon day—and tried to balance accounts by eating half a dozen green pears and drinking a stiff dose of brandy, and going to bed. Now I have got up—but don't feel any better. Under such circumstances I should never think of answering a letter that came from anybody but you, unless a mere business inquiry as to how I'd have the money sent, or the like. I suppose that sounds like anything but a compliment, but 'tis one.

I am very sorry you cannot come; that's all I've got to say about it. I guess I shall be here in September, and I shall hope to see you then. I don't know where I shall be this coming winter. Perhaps I shall try to get onto Norton's farm in Farmington—perhaps with Townsend in East Haven[2]— perhaps on *my own*. I shall try to be situated so as to be likely to study more than to work. Do you think I shall be contented on a farm—15 miles from New Haven, and three miles from neighbors? I mean civilized ones, gentlemen, doctors, lawyers and ministers.

By the way, I am beginning to have a horror of ministers. They are such a set of conceited, dogmatical, narrow minded, misanthropic, petty mind tyrants. I am most afraid to have such opinions but the fact is, I have acquired for good or evil a great many independent and agrarian and revolutionary ideas and ways of thinking which would frighten such kind folks as my good mother, or Mrs. Baldwin,[3] not a little.

And now I am about it, it was just on this account that I wanted to see you. I don't know what to think about many things—and I wanted you to help me. Nobody can understand what I mean but you. I am full of speculation; and I respect one set of men so little above another, that now I have no very decided opinion on any subject that I have not examined for myself. I mean that I am not to be led by the nose any longer by any man or men—by any teacher, priest, party or church. I give no man leave to call me Whig or Presbyterian, and no man has the right to say I am not a Patriot and a Christian. I have not joined any church—I cannot believe it is best I should —nor am I likely to at present.

As for identifying myself with that set of men, the most bigoted, self complaisant, pharisaical, anti-advancing, anti-reforming, stiff necked old Jew Christians, agreeing on one thing, and that without a true meaning—to call themselves Presbyterians—if I am to have my feelings, dispositions, and opinions, I might almost say, known by my name I would prefer to be called Unitarian or Universalist. I suppose you would be very sorry to hear that I was one—so I tell you I am not by any means—but I should be neither frightened or horror struck to hear that you or John was. I suppose every reasoning creature must be full of "doubts" and in my opinion the more a man doubts, the more of a thinking animal he is. How intellectual I must be! I doubt everything pretty near—but understand such doubting does not affect (at least for worse) my happiness.

In fact my doubts are built on this—I will think and act right, I will find Truth and be governed by it, so far as I can, with the light God is pleased to give me. I will be accountable to no one but God for my opinions and actions. Trusting in Him for light I will not fear for nor care for what man thinks of, or does towards me. I am liable to mistake myself—but so far as I *do* judge myself, this is my paramount governing principle. I hope so anyway, and except from the consciousness of yielding to temptation, and thinking and acting contrary to my own more solemn, more rational and better intentions—as I often do most wickedly—what can I be sorry for? Whether it is because I am endowed with a sluggish, unfeeling heart, or I am a Philosopher or a Christian I do not know, but I certainly do not feel disappointments much or have gloomy anticipations.

I certainly have been declaring Independence this summer, and cutting myself loose from the common rafts of men. I shall hitch on again I suppose when I think there's occasion—but I shall attach myself not by proxy. I don't give my helm to Father, Mother, Schoolmaster, editor or minister, again.

I suppose it was because perhaps a little, I had this vagabond feeling that I fancied Sartor Resartus. Why, it took me three weeks to read through the first book, but when I got along about the "Everlasting No!" I was enchanted with it and some parts I have laid on my bed and read and thought over by hours—again and again.[4] One of my temptations in the wilderness is coming off now, and the very consciousness of fighting the devil with a posse of Presbyterian priests and Methodist elders, and infidels and so forth at his back and fighting for Truth and God's glory is better than 'tis to be following your file leader like a machine.

But the mail won't stop for me to write nonsense. I am very glad Charley is not more broken down by the loss of his father.[5] I had written a letter of sympathy and condolence to him but so unsatisfactorily expressed, and looking so much like a ceremony I would not send it.

We are all cursedly selfish—guess you are not worse than the rest except when you have got the dyspepsia blues. You are not romantic—imaginative enough to be in love. Otherwise you are reasonably in love as much as I am.

Ask John how to direct—or direct here so 'twill be forwarded. Love to the "46."[6]

Yours truly,

Fred.

1. The text of this letter is taken from a typescript version in FJK Sketch of FLO. The original has not been found.
2. John Treadwell Norton, and William Kneeland Townsend of East Haven, Conn. (see FLO to JO, July 23, 1846, notes 5 and 10, above).
3. Mary Bull Olmsted, and Emily Perkins Baldwin (1796–1874), wife of Roger Sherman Baldwin and mother of Elizabeth Baldwin (DAB, s.v. "Baldwin, Roger Sherman; Perkins Genealogy, pt. 3, p. 79; Thomas Townsend Sherman, Sherman Genealogy Including Families of Essex, Suffolk, and Norfolk, England . . . [New York, 1920], p. 293).
4. The chapter entitled "The Everlasting No" comes in the middle of Sartor Resartus, in book II, which recounts the life of its protagonist, Teufelsdröckh. It tells of his sufferings after being rejected by his beloved, Blumine, and describes his loss of religious belief and his despair. By the end of the chapter he casts off this rejection of life and begins the progression that leads to his affirmation of "The Everlasting Yea." The chapter concludes, "It is from this hour that I incline to date my Spiritual New-birth, or Baphometic Fire-baptism, perhaps I directly thereupon began to be a man."
   The tone of this letter, with its brave assertion of independence, shows how thoroughly Olmsted had absorbed the spirit and message of Sartor Resartus (Thomas Carlyle, Sartor Resartus; The Life and Opinions of Herr Teufelsdröckh [Boston, 1846]).
5. Charles Hooper Trask, whose father, Captain Richard Trask (1787–1846), died of cholera on August 6 and was buried before his son learned of his death (FJK Journal, Aug. 6, 13, 1846; Darius Francis Lamson, History of the Town of Manchester, Essex County, Massachusetts, 1645–1895 [Manchester, 1895], pp. 32–33).
6. The Yale class of 1846.

To JOHN HULL OLMSTED

Hartford, Dec. 13th, 1846

Dear John,

Your letter with Disputation and oranges was received in due time per extra valisse. I have lost your letter (just now) but can probably answer it about as well. The dispute is not by me either, but I interlined a little commentary or criticism in it and will return by valisse.

We read it—I did—to all hands, in parlour assembled, as I afterwards did the President's message.[1] They were all much gratified with it, except perhaps father, who thought you ought to have written more carefully as you had time enough (and if you had not you ought to have made time) and claimed the credit himself of all the original ideas—what he called the "best things." You having got them from him when you was here.

I was myself much pleased with your views, which I generally coincide in. You have got my opinions. Only I doubt I should have known them if you had not shown them up for me. But there are some sentences with or without meaning, that I'm sure you wrote without much *consideration*, that will do well enough to be heard (read rapidly) in a dispute, but would not be the thing to be read carefully and reflected about even perhaps "after dinner."

I am much pleased with the view you take of the *tendencies* of Carlyle's writings—with his object—and the distinction in that respect between him and Macaulay.[2] I must go further than you, however. You say (or quote) in your letter, "C. is not a believer." I must wish to believe that he is. And can you give a reason why I should not? At least, tell me why you will not consider Carlyle a *converted* man.

Can we not follow him by his own account through his *"experimental" knowledge* of the "successive states and stages of growth, entanglement, unbelief, and almost reprobation into a certain clearer state of what he himself seems to consider as *conversion* whereby the Highest came home to the bosoms of the most limited"? What was that, in common with "the poorest Pietists and Methodists," from when he dates his Spiritual Majority—whence forth (from which) *"we are to see him* work in well-doing with the spirit and clear aims of a" (true) "man?"[3]

For what does he "thank the Heavens that he has found his Calling; wherein, with or without perceptible result, he is minded diligently to persevere"? Considering himself a priest—and if but the meanest of that sacred hierarchy, it is honor enough to spend & to be spent, speaking boldly forth what is *in* him: "what God has given; what the Devil shall not take away."[4]

Are not these sentences (below) which I copied—while reading

Sartor Resartus—the very reflections or mottoes of a sanctified or super-worldly heart?

"Make thy claim of wages, a zero, then; thou hast the world under thy feet." (Let (new) Life begin with *Renunciation* (of self). What *right* hast thou to happiness? Thou canst love the earth while it injures thee, and *because* it injures thee (through much tribulation we enter a better world.)) "Love *not pleasure*, love God." (Man) can do without Happiness and instead thereof find Blessedness."[5]

You admit his writings show that he endeavours to do good. He himself says again, "conviction is nothing till it has converted itself into conduct." So he says to himself in continuation, "Whatsoever thy hand findeth to do"—&c. and—"Work while it is called today," &c.[6]

I do hope and believe, though I would do it with the most profound humility, that I shall see among the jewels of our infinitely merciful Father and Saviour, Thomas Carlyle, and Milton, who never "joined a church," and Sanctus Socrates, and Ann Boyd[7] whom God saw fit to make the instrument of the conversion (at least of removal) of one soul to the hopes and intentions at least, of Christianity—from the gaping jaws of a sleeping church (so-called) together with the Sages and Martyrs and Poets and Priests who have in all times spoken and suffered, bearing testimony of the God-like which is in man —which by the way wouldn't be there if He had not put there, man being totally depraved by nature.

What is this we call Conversion? Some change from the natural character of man by the action of the Spirit, and manifesting itself by the *fruits* of the Spirit. But how much action? How much change? How much fruit shows the point is past? Which fruit is the cultivated and which the wild? Which the wheat—which the chaff—until at the harvest they shall be separated?

Dr. Hawes[8] says there is a definite moment when a real *change* takes place—though we may not be able to distinguish the minute in which it occurs, or the hour, or day or week or month or year or years. He says, too, that a child is converted so young that its earliest memories will be devoted to God. Paul says, the children of a single believing parent are holy.[9] Schleusner's comment is "Now are they counted members of the Christian Church."[10] And this I find quoted approvingly by a Presbyterian commentator.

The Reverend E. Chapman[11] says they are holy enough for *religious ordinances*, at any rate. Is that holy enough for conversion? Is conversion holy enough for that? Mrs. Harriet Beecher Stowe says that an individual passing from what is *at present expected* or attempted or asked ("If you have got *so far*, you may have the privileges which we hold the keys of from the apostles. If you have not, you must wait till you get up to, and profess, *our* standard.") to the Christian experience of the Apostolic age, would feel as if delivered from the bondage of corruption into the liberty of the children of God. Were they converted when in that bondage?

The Reverend Mr. Snyder thinks no man is a Christian who does not denounce the abolition of Capital Punishment. The reverend father Harvey[12] thought no converted man ("follower of Christ") would hesitate to go as far as the most enthusiastic apostle of—Temperance. The reverend Mr. —— of Cincinnati assures his flock that they must be drunk to receive the grace of God. The right reverend and sainted father Cotton Mather thought any one who defended the witches or refused his assistance in drowning them was an alien from Christ's kingdom.[13]

Who shall separate the tares from the wheat? Who shall attempt to decide where D.D.'s disagree? Verily, the "church committee!" They shall make a standard to *suit themselves*—and if you don't come up to it you can not come in. And if you do not stay up to it, or down to it, you shall be warned publicly, or finally kicked out in disgrace. "You can't come in now. Go next door. We consider it a gate of Hell, but you can get in there. They say whosoever will, let him come and drink *freely*. Get out—we are too good for you! Your example would be bad. What would folks—we mean sinners —say?"

Fred,[14] please hand this to John—but read it, beginning over the page and tell me what you think of Carlyle?

Lib[15] wishes me to tell you the Campbells are coming—and sends her love.

1. President James Polk's message to Congress on December 7, 1846, was a review of the injuries the Mexican government had inflicted upon the United States, the causes of the war with Mexico, and its progress since its inception (*New York Daily Tribune*, Dec. 9, 1846, p. 2).
2. Thomas Carlyle and Thomas Babington Macaulay.
3. Thomas Carlyle reflected his own "spiritual new birth" of June 1821 in *Sartor Resartus* in the episode in which Professor Teufelsdröckh decides to defy death and the devil and assert his own freedom. The actual words in *Sartor Resartus* are: "Thus have we . . . followed Teufelsdröckh through the various successive states and stages of Growth, Entanglement, Unbelief, and almost Reprobation, into a certain clearer state of what he himself seems to consider as Conversion. . . . The old world knew nothing of Conversion: instead of an *Ecce Homo*, they had only some *Choice of Hercules*. It was a new-attained progress in the Moral Development of man; hereby has the Highest come home to the bosoms of the most Limited; what to Plato was but a hallucination, and to Socrates a chimera, is now clear and certain to your Zinzendorfs, your Wesleys, and the poorest of their Pietists and Methodists. . . . It is here then that the spiritual majority of Teufelsdröckh commences: we are henceforth to see him 'Work in Well-Doing,' with the spirit and clear aims of a Man" (*DNB*; *Sartor Resartus*, p. 87).
4. Carlyle's words are: "I thank the Heavens that I have now found my Calling; wherein, with or without perceptible result, I am minded diligently to persevere." And, "Higher task than that of Priesthood was allotted to no man: wert thou but the meanest in that sacred Hierarchy, is it not honor enough therein to spend and

be spent?" And, before that, "Awake, arise! Speak forth what is in thee; what God has given thee; what the Devil shall not take away" (*Sartor Resartus*, p. 88).

5. Carlyle's words are "So true is it, what I then said, that *the Fraction of Life can be increased in value not so much by increasing your Numerator as by lessening your Denominator*. Nay, unless my Algebra deceive me, *Unity* itself divided by *Zero* will give *Infinity*. Make thy claim of wages a zero, then; thou hast the world under thy feet. Well did the Wisest of our time write: 'It is only with Renunciation (*Entsagen*) that Life, properly speaking, can be said to begin.' . . . What Act of Legislature was there that *thou* should be Happy? . . . Small is it that thou canst trample the Earth with its injuries under thy feet, as old Greek Zeno trained thee; thou canst love the Earth while it injures thee, and even because it injures thee; for this a Greater than Zeno was needed, and he too was sent." Also, "Love not Pleasure; love God. This is the EVERLASTING YEA, wherein all contradiction is solved; wherein whoso walks and works, it is well with him," and "there is in man a HIGHER than Love of Happiness: he can do without Happiness and instead thereof find Blessedness" (ibid., p. 85).

6. Carlyle's words are: "But indeed Conviction, were it never so excellent, is worthless till it convert itself into Conduct," and "Up, up! Whatsoever thy hand findeth to do, do it with thy whole might. Work while it is called To-day, for the Night cometh wherein no man can work" (ibid., pp. 86–87).

7. Ann Boyd, a children's nurse employed by the Olmsted family (JO Journal, Jan. 1, 1845; Mary Bull Olmsted to JHO, Dec. 31, 1846).

8. Joel Hawes.

9. Olmsted may be referring to the passage in Saint Paul's First Epistle to the Corinthians, in which he says, "For the unbelieving husband is sanctified by the wife, and the unbelieving wife is sanctified by the husband: else were your children unclean; but now are they holy" (1 Cor. 7:14).

10. Perhaps a comment by Johann Friedrich Schleusner (1759–1831), Lutheran theologian who specialized in New Testament exegesis (*Schaff-Herzog Encyc.*, 10: 247).

11. Perhaps the Presbyterian commentator was Ezekiel Jones Chapman (1781–1866), who graduated from Yale in 1799. Olmsted might have looked for quotations in his *Critical and Explanatory Notes on Many Passages of Scripture* ([Utica, N.Y., 1831]; Franklin Bowditch Dexter, *Biographical Sketches of Yale College with Annals of the College History*, 6 vols. [New York, 1911], 5: 345–46).

12. Joseph Harvey (1787–1873), clergyman and graduate of Yale College in 1808. From 1835 to 1838 he edited a religious weekly, the *Watchman*, published in Hartford. One of the numerous religious pamphlets he wrote was "An Appeal to Christians on the Immorality of Using or Vending Distilled Liquors as an Article of Luxury or Diet" (ibid., 6: 197–200).

13. Cotton Mather, clergyman, scholar and author, who played an important role in the furor over witchcraft in Massachusetts in the early 1690s (*DAB*).

14. Frederick Kingsbury.

15. Olmsted's cousin Elizabeth Laura Brooks of Cheshire. She was staying with the Olmsteds in Hartford while attending the Hartford Female Seminary (JO Journal, Jan. 1, 1847).

CHAPTER VI

THE GENTLEMAN
FARMER

1847–1849

Bᴏʟsᴛᴇʀᴇᴅ ʙʏ Cᴀʀʟʏʟᴇ's Mᴇssᴀɢᴇ that work and sacrifice would lead to salvation, Olmsted flung all his energy into his farming at Sachem's Head in 1847. His brother, skeptical from past experience, hoped this new love would prove less ephemeral than some that had preceded it.

Olmsted quickly found the farm a formidable challenge: the soil was rocky and worn out, and most of the land had been left as unplowed pasture or hay field for at least ten years. The "central feature" was a swamp, and the house was set in the middle of it. To transform the place into a model farm, Olmsted plowed up the fields and fertilized them, consulted with the famous New York architect Alexander Jackson Davis about a design for a new farmhouse, and planned improvements with an eye to their landscape effect.

Sadly enough, the nearby community of Guilford also needed improving. The contentious local churches showed little Christian charity toward one another: instead they reflected divisions in the town that were political (and medical) as well as religious.

The spectacle of faction-ridden Guilford sharpened Olmsted's growing distaste for intolerant sectarianism and party spirit. In his letters he upbraided Charles Loring Brace for wanting to be settled and firm in his religious beliefs. Once he became so, Olmsted warned, he would no longer be able to appreciate the merits of reasonable beliefs that differed from his own. He also warned Brace not to be so sure of the rightness of his abolitionist views that he condemned proslavery advocates as un-Christian. Olmsted's sense of the limits of reason strengthened his plea for charity and forbearance between the adherents of rival doctrines. At the same time, he greeted some of the reforms of the day with enthusiasm, welcoming a free public high school in Hartford and the prospect of universal manhood suffrage in Connecticut.

As the year progressed, Olmsted tired of Sachem's Head and prevailed on his father to buy him a more promising farm, with better access to market, on Staten Island. He moved there in early March 1848, and the letter he wrote describing the voyage brought out the best of his nautical prose.

On Staten Island, Olmsted had a better farm and less cantankerous neighbors. Besides being skilled farmers, they carried on a much more genteel social life than had his neighbors at Sachem's Head. Some of them were distinguished men, like publisher George Palmer Putnam and newspaper editor and poet William Cullen Bryant. In the fall of 1848, Olmsted was further cheered by the arrival in New York of his brother, John, who had come to study medicine, and Charles Loring Brace, who planned to teach school and study for the ministry. They often came out to Olmsted's farm for weekends and continued the wide-ranging discussions of religion and politics they had begun at Yale.

The farm needed a great deal of work, and in the process of making improvements, Olmsted showed increasing talents for administration and landscape design. In the midst of farming, he kept attuned to the progress of civilization. He greeted the republican revolutions of 1848 in Europe with enthusiasm and eagerly read John Ruskin's newly published *Modern Painters*. In all of this he was preparing himself for a larger career than that of a gentleman farmer.

To CHARLES LORING BRACE

Hartford, Jan. 27th [1847][1]

Dear Charley,

I am really sorry and mad with myself, that I should have let so long a time elapse without writing to you. I have put it off from time to time—and now that I should be really excusable, because I have got so much that I must do this week before I leave home (*forever*), I can't help purchasing a letter from you to cheer me in my voluntary exile to the rock bound head of Sachem. For though you never will take any direct notice of a fellow's letters to you, the coincidence of mail following (those from you) and never coming at any other time is so invariable that it may almost be relied upon as a rule—whether it may be cause and effect or not. It won't to be sure seem like an exchange of equivalents, unless you value commodities not by their intrinsic worth but by their rarity or the pains taken to make them.

The fact is, it is confounded [difficult] for me to write decently—to write a letter. Just think, since I came from school it has been growing harder. With you on the contrary, it is more & more an everyday business. It's your trade to think and write—and every day adds facility to your handiwork.

Your mind, cutting book leaves daily, is a self-sharpening tool. Mine rooting dirt and floating downstream grows dull, waterlogged and rusty.

Now mine friend, [. . .] every time you run your pen against me, you scrape me a little brighter.

I believe I know what your idea of Mary Day[2] is. I do so because I had ideas. Only I didn't feel so certain of them or so definite as you of the same kind. But now I have had some good opportunities and I have not misimproved them. But I have studied her (and this is a science not learned in books). And now you may rely upon it, Sir—she's all that I pretended to believe she was (and didn't, only wanted to). She's all—and more also. I don't believe there's a piece of clay nearer Perfection since the day Eve cottoned to the old snake. Unless 'tis her sister.[3] But she's all my fancy painted her & considerable more. Hurrah! (N.B. I have not *now* the least mite of doubt about it.) But then a man couldn't love an angel, I believe. (Not till he was translated.) Could an angel love a man? Real soft love? No! I reckon 'twould only be a sort of patronage. But Charly, Mary Day is not conscious of this *patronage*. She *means* to *love* and to *like* and to make folks easy and happy and good.

Well, and I guess she does too. At any rate, she thinks to be right as far as she can. And she has got a good long rope, and it's stretched tight.

I believe she's a first-rate specimen of the Christian of the 19th century and a beau ideal of a *she-gentleman*.

I have enjoyed myself a great deal at the little dancing parties this winter. Did anybody tell you about our sleigh ride to Alvord's? The greatest piece of real right now good time I ever saw connected with what they call *gay*—blast the word. It has melancholy association. "*Gay*"—used to be "Watkinson sociable"[4] but I have got over that or the Watkinsons have. For I really enjoyed an evening there not long since and a real change seems to ha' come over the spirit of my dreams. For I am actually pretending to stay another day in town for the purpose of attending Mrs. Trumbull's[5] rout—which a year [ago] I would not have touched the invitation to with a ten foot pole.

Mary Warburton's[6] all right. Emily Perkins is acquiring a confirmed habit of being pretty and entertaining—which, owing to her peculiar locality, is cruelty to animals.

Charly Trask[7] was here this morning. Gone to Andover (from New Haven—a day or two).

John says he has written you nine pages, so you won't stand in need of any of my cooking after such a meal on your stomach. By the way, isn't it queer they find *raw* raw oysters digest (I think it's) an hour sooner than stewed. The same with eggs. You are wrong about trout. There's nothing goes through the mill so soon as that, (you said) particularly when *it's* fried.[8]

May I write a letter to your uncle to enquire about *Lucerne*?[9] From my reading I should not suppose it at all likely to succeed in this cold climate. Nor should I suppose it could be afforded to be cultivated in the English manner.

I have read the Tales of the Devils[10] with much interest and pleasure. The Book your father published last spring—(on conversion &c.) I have enquired for in vain at Andrus's and all the book shops—.[11]

I sent you Bushnell's Sermon as you wished. Fault is in the P.O., not me, if you don't get it.

Yours affectionately,

Fred Olmsted

1. This letter is misdated 1846. Olmsted moved to Sachem's Head the first week in February, 1847.
2. Mary Frances Day (1826–1895) of Hartford, with whom Olmsted had fallen in love during the winter of 1845–46. In December 1847 he told Frederick Kingsbury that he still loved her "and wish some of my friends would marry her one of these days, because she is my perfect beau ideal of one sort of woman—and could not be beat for an educated gentleman" (FLO to FJK, June 12, 1846, above; Dec. 5, 1847, in FJK Sketch of FLO; Thomas Day Seymour, *The Family of the Rev. Jeremiah Day of New Preston* . . . [New Haven, 1900], pp. 17, 23).
3. Ellen Day (1829–1850), whom Olmsted saw frequently during the summer of 1847, while she was at the Sachem's Head House (a summer hotel). Her family had heard rumors that she had been "very intimate" with Olmsted during the summer and looked him over carefully when he appeared at a family party at her parents' house in Hartford on Thanksgiving evening in 1847 (FLO to FJK, Dec. 5, 1847, in FJK Sketch of FLO; T. D. Seymour, *Family of Jeremiah Day*, p. 17).
4. Edward Blair Watkinson (1813–1884) was a prominent Hartford businessman and financier (*Commemorative Biographical Record of Hartford County* . . . [Chicago, 1901], p. 238).
5. Eliza Storrs Trumbull (1784–1861), the second wife of Joseph Trumbull (1782–1861), banker, congressman, and governor of Connecticut from 1849 to 1850 (*Appleton's Cyc. Am. Biog.*, s.v. "Trumbull, Joseph"; *A Genealogical Chart of Some of the Descendants of John Trumbull, of Newcastle-on-Tyne, Northumberland, England, and Rowley, in the Colony of Massachusetts Bay* [n.p., n.d.]).
6. Mary Warburton of Hartford (FLO to JHO, March 13, 1846).
7. Charles Hooper Trask.
8. Olmsted may be referring to the investigations of the process of digestion carried out between 1825 and 1833 by Dr. William Beaumont, a surgeon in the U.S. Army. While Beaumont was stationed at Fort Mackinac in Michigan, a French Canadian named Alexis St. Martin had much of his side blown off by a shotgun. The hole made by the charge exposed the man's stomach to view and gave the astute doctor a unique opportunity to discover the digestion time of various foods. As Olmsted indicates, he found that raw oysters took less time to digest than stewed, and hard-boiled eggs less time than soft-boiled—a difference of half an hour in each case. Broiled bass—the food most like trout Beaumont fed his subject—took much longer to digest than oysters or eggs in any state (*DAB*; William Beaumont, M.D., *Experiments and Observations on the Gastric Juice and the Physiology of Digestion: Facsimile of the Original Edition of 1833 Together with a Biographical Essay, "A Pioneer American Physiologist," by Sir William Osler* [1833; rpt. ed., New York, 1959], pp. vii–xii, 41–44, 180).
9. The legume alfalfa.
10. A book published in 1847 by John Pierce Brace, Charles Loring Brace's father, por-

traying the condition of the wicked between death and resurrection. It describes in particular the fate of the soul of Ernest Maltravers, part of whose torment after a prosperous but dissipated life on earth is to see his illegitimate son become a successful congressman and lead the virtuous and happily married life he himself might have had (*Tales of the Devils, By J. P. Brace* . . . [Hartford, Conn., 1847]).

11. Olmsted is probably referring to John Pierce Brace's *Lectures to Young Converts, Delivered to the Pupils of the Hartford Female Seminary, During the Revival of the Winter Term of 1841* (Hartford, 1846).

To JOHN HULL OLMSTED

Guilford, Feb. 16th, 1847

Dear John,

I really am not at all in the way of writing letters to you. I have written home five times, mere business letters about tools, stock, etc. Your letter or excuse for one last Wednesday, with Father's enclosed, reached me. I am very sorry to hear your eyes fail. Your papers—*Tribunes* Sunday, and *Yankee*[1] yesterday—are received. Shall send latter to CLB.

Whatever you may think, I *am* very busy. Looking up tools, advice, and hired man and his wife and my wife—and cattle and so forth. You recollect our friend Jonathan Leete that went with his boat blackberrying with us to the Thimbles.[2] He drives the Sloop *Branford* now, and I have sent by him for some tools. I have bought an ox-cart for $25.00. I have a scow-boat of the burthen of a cartload and a half—building—for rock-weeding etc., to cost $20.00. I have a good man with his wife in view that I can probably get for pretty high wages.[3]

I have been to Sachem's Head[4] but once, and then did not go into the house. I am going there again this P.M. It does look real nasty and forlorn about the house. And I do hope visitors will keep away from me next summer. The farm generally pleases me well. There is a good deal more beautiful and valuable wood on it than I had supposed. But then—again— there's more rocks, and there are not so many apple-trees, and the barn and house are in worse condition than I had thought them to be.

Father writes that he shall send my things tomorrow, Wednesday. If your eyes will excuse you, won't you bring them over—and so look at the farm with me? I would like to have you look at it in winter because it will do away with that bugbear, "*bleakness*," I think. There's nothing bleak at Sachem's Head. That is, on my point.

At this season, it is all a swamp for several acres about the house: real juicy. And a stream from the barn yard empties itself near the front door—into the sea. The whole farm is very moist, which makes it backward in the spring. I shall try draining.

There are several educated men in the village. I have not seen any

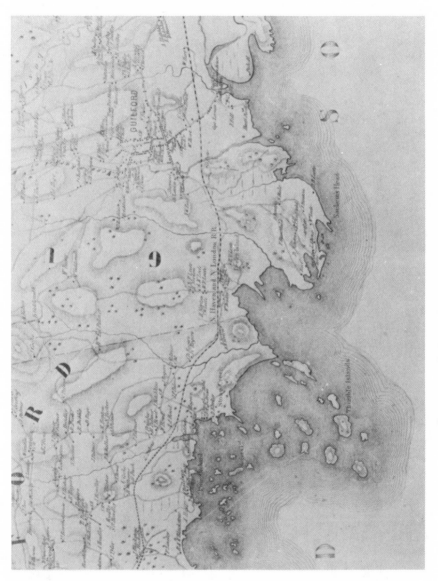

GUILFORD, CONNECTICUT AND SACHEM'S HEAD

society yet. Called on Mr. Hall[5] yesterday. Tolerably pleased with him, but I am afraid he's not the sort of man to be my friend. I shall try it, however. Somehow theology seems apt to have a cursed be-littling, hardening effect on a man's heart. It seems as if a minister almost always "spoke for effect," like a politician. I *scarce* know a clergyman that I think an honest man. There's just the *damnedest* kind of Christianity here raging that ever I saw.

May God forgive me if I judge them and remember not their sins to visit them against their children. Mr. Hall himself told me with a smile of good pluck that the churches hated each other with all their might. Having a strong Whig church, of course, Mr. H. is a violent Whig. And he boasts that there is not but one member of his church that is a Loco Foco.[6] It will be hard if they can't excommunicate him before long. More than that, there are only two Locos that dare to enter the meeting house.

There's a true Whig physician, of course. He gets no employment out of their church, and I suppose any of them would die and be _____ before they'd call in a heretic Loco. This fortunate doctor[7] was a partner of Chittenden's in Hartford, but heard of this rare chance for a monopoly of killing and jumped the counter. The Abolition church is just the same— doctor and all. They've all got sore eyes trying to go past the Whig church, Sundays, without winking.[8] The Methodist church they call the Tory church. They are all steamed to death—go the whole hog for Polk, Texas, and slavery—for Thomson. Hot drops and steam to Heaven.[9] Glory! Amen! "The Episcopal is a Tory church," says Mr. Hall, "but there are some very respectable wealthy men in it and they are Whigs."

The Old Man always confounds "Tory," "Democrat," and "Loco" and "Federalist" and "Whig," much to my horror.

Oh! I would already, it seems to me, give my life to induce in this people a spirit of charity and brotherly love. May God, for Christ's sake, help me to be the means of encouraging it. They are naturally remarkably intelligent and large minded and kind hearted, I believe. Did that sheep with a wolf's stomach, the Reverend Mr. Dutton,[10] bring this pestilence among the flocks? God send medicine. The soul of improvement is the improvement of the Soul.

If the gun &c. comes, call at the Stage Office and ask Phelps[11] to call for them, if you please. You must *know* Phelps. Send them Thursday. Call at Trowbridge's,[12] if perfectly convenient, and ask if he has a Geddes' Harrow.[13]

I did think of coming to New Haven but give it up for the present. My love to Fred.[14]

I have written to Geddes, Joe (Welton), & old man David.[15]

Tell father I want the *Horticulturist*. Nothing of the kind here but the *Boston Cultivator*.[16]

Dear John, P.S. I enclose a letter; I do not wish to be post-marked here. Please send immediately to the *"Boston Cultivator."*[17] I wish you'd send a better copy or something like it if you have time. I have not now.

P.P.S. Of course, mind, *pay* the postage on that.

1. Olmsted is perhaps referring to the *Yankee Farmer and New England Cultivator,* published in Boston.
2. Jonathan Fowler Leete (1823–1860) engaged in the coasting trade between Guilford, Conn., and New York. The Thimbles are a group of islands two miles west of Sachem's Head (Edward L. Leete, comp., *The Family of William Leete, One of the First Settlers of Guilford, Connecticut* [New Haven, 1884], pp. 65–66).
3. Olmsted hired Henry Davis and his wife for $365 a year, plus room and board and such privileges as cow pasturage and chicken feed. Davis worked on the farm and his wife cooked and kept house. All of them—Olmsted, Davis, and his "clever quiet wife and converse baby," as John Hull Olmsted described them—shared the single farm house on the property (JHO to FJK, June 18, 1847; FLO to JHO, Feb. 26, 1847; FLO to JHO, May 11, 1847; JHO to FLO, Jan. 19–20, 1848).
4. The location of the seventy-five-acre farm in Guilford that Olmsted's father had purchased for him (JO to JHO, July 26, 1846; JO Journal, Jan. 1, 1847; FLO to FJK, Feb. 19, 1847; *Guilford County Deed Records,* 35: 170, microfilm, Connecticut State Library, Hartford).
5. Eli Edwin Hall (1814–1896), pastor of the First Congregational Church in Guilford from 1843 to 1855 (*Yale Obit. Rec.,* 4th ser., no. 6 [June 1896]: 415).
6. That is, a Democrat. Although the "Loco-Focos" were only a faction of the Democratic party, opponents of that party tended to call all its supporters by that name.
7. Probably Alvan Talcott (1804–1891), who graduated from Yale in 1824, obtained a medical degree in 1831, and settled in Guilford in 1841. Talcott married Olive N. Chittenden, sister of Henry Abel Chittenden (1816–1895), a Hartford dry-goods merchant (Alvan Talcott, comp., *Chittenden Family: William Chittenden of Guilford, Connecticut, and His Descendants* [New Haven, Conn., 1882], pp. 72, 125, 127; Bernard Christian Steiner, *A History of the Plantation of Menunkatuck, . . . and Guilford, Connecticut, . . .* [Baltimore, 1897], pp. 413, 502; *Yale Obit. Rec.,* 4th ser., no. 1 [June 1891]: 6–7).
8. The "Abolition Church" was the Third Church of Guilford, Congregational, formed in 1843 as a result of a schism in the First Church. In 1842 the members of the First Church refused to permit the local antislavery society to use the church building for its meetings. Because of this their minister, Aaron Dutton (1780–1849), left the church and went to Iowa for the American Home Missionary Society. The next year the abolitionist faction of the First Church separated from it and formed the Third Church. Dutton returned to Guilford in order to make preparations for moving to Iowa permanently, but was never healthy enough to do so. He was living in Guilford at the time Olmsted was at Sachem's Head.

   During this period the slavery controversy also spread to the Second Church, in North Guilford. The minister there was Zolva Whitmore, whom Olmsted remembered so fondly in his "Passages in the Life of an Unpractical Man." Whitmore was a strong antislavery man and an ardent revivalist, and both issues caused deep division in his church in the early 1840s. Only his "uncommon degree of prudence" permitted him to keep his position during the crisis that split the First Church in Guilford in 1842–43. But his congregation remained so divided that he resigned in 1846, a few months before Olmsted moved to Sachem's Head (B. C. Steiner, *History of Guilford,* pp. 285–87; *Congregational Quarterly* 9, no. 4 [Oct. 1867]: 382–83).
9. The Methodist Church of Guilford had been formed in 1837–38 by Charles Chittenden, an impressive revivalist preacher. The pastor of the church in 1847 was the Reverend Charles R. Adams (1816–1865), who left the next year.

   According to Olmsted, the members of the Methodist or "Tory" church were not only ardent proslavery and expansionist Democrats but also enthusiastic followers of Samuel Thomson (1769–1843) a New Hampshire herbalist who founded a system of medicine that gained a considerable popular following. He believed that disease resulted from a reduction of body heat and supplemented his herbal preparations with hot steam baths. These were so universally used by Thomsonian practitioners that the latter were known as "steam doctors," or "steamers." To increase body heat Thomson also prescribed "hot drops," which were a mixture of cayenne pepper, whiskey, and gum of myrrh (B. C. Steiner, *History of Guilford*, p. 388; Martin Kaufman, *Homeopathy in America: The Rise and Fall of a Medical Heresy* [Baltimore: 1971], pp. 17–22; Reuben Chambers, *The Thomsonian Practice of Medicine* . . . [Bethania, Pa., 1843], pp. 57–58; Gurney S. Strong, *Early Landmarks of Syracuse* [Syracuse, N.Y., 1894], pp. 262–63).

10. Aaron Dutton (1780–1849), a clergyman, graduated from Yale in 1803, then studied with Timothy Dwight and was ordained in Guilford in 1806 (see note 8 above).

11. Elihu Phelps, livery stable agent of Hartford (*Geer's Directory for 1845*, p. 78).

12. Henry Trowbridge and Sons, shipping merchants at U Wharf in New Haven (*Benham's City Directory for 1846–7*, comp. J. Madison Patten [New Haven, 1846], p. 21: see Spear 823).

13. The Geddes harrow had the form of two V-shaped sets of beams attached to a central beam. Its narrow leading point permitted it to bypass large rocks and stumps more easily than could the wide, rectangular conventional harrow (John J. Thomas, *Farm Implements and the Principles of Their Construction and Use* . . . [New York, 1854], pp. 141–43).

14. Frederick Kingsbury.

15. These were the three men under whom Olmsted had studied farming between 1844 and 1846: George Geddes, Joseph Welton, and Olmsted's uncle, David Brooks.

16. The journal that Olmsted wanted was the *Horticulturist and Journal of Rural Art and Rural Taste*, founded in 1846 and edited by Andrew Jackson Downing. The weekly *Boston Cultivator*, established in 1839, attempted to serve as a family newspaper as well as an agricultural journal. It had a separate column devoted to "Moral and Religious" topics and was "cluttered with 'sob' verse" (Albert L. Demaree, *The American Agricultural Press, 1819–1860* [New York, 1941], pp. 78 n, 181).

17. Olmsted preserved his anonymity; what must have been his letter appeared in the *Boston Cultivator* of March 13, 1847, with no address and signed "Munhaden." It was a request from "A Young Farmer" for advice on the best way to use seaweed and fish for manure.

To Charles Loring Brace

Guilford, March 22nd, 1847

Dear Charley,

Your letter of 3rd &+ instant has reached me. I am extremely obliged to you for the very lucid, satisfactory & business-like instructions in regard to Lucerne, &c.[1] I shall lay them up and probably use them one of these years.

I have been to Hartford & bought my tools, oxen, dog (a noble Newfoundland), and engaged a nice young wife (with her husband) to keep house for me.[2] I have already begun carting manure (and it's quite a luxury of manure, this clean green rock-weed.) I have got a lighter building, and am going to New York to buy a life-boat.

John, poor fellow, is in Hartford on account of his eyes again. He has probably written you before this. He is under Dr. Beresford's[3] care and takes blisters & stingers & counter-irritants & calomel.

They have had the jolliest, funniest, time in Hartford discussing the "High School Question," in great crowded meetings at the City-Hall.[4] The Governor & the Terrys—Taintor, Allyn & some scurvy fellows—opposed to it,[5] and Bushnell, Burgess, Clark, Baptist, Unitarian, Robinson, James Bunce, Chapman, & almost every body else in its favor.[6] There was the most exciting debates, personal attacks, sharp cross firing, &c. for two or three nights I ever heard. Bushnell vs. the Governor, as to who was the most Democratic, &c. You would have enjoyed it. 'Twas finally carried by a tremendous triumph of the clergy and sans-culottes.[7] A most glorious and happy union. I was with them heart & soul. Down with the Aristocrats! Up with the rags and hearts!

I can only *deny* that I ever did call—or think—you "sanctified"—or any of those things (except as a manifest joke.) Nor did I ever apply the term Pharisaical (or such) to you directly or impliedly. My letters must get infernally shook up to have the words come together as you read them now-a-days.

I am glad to hear you had such a grand time in Boston. It must have been a great pleasure and benefit to you. I tell you what, Charley, I believe would do you more good than—something else—a vast deal—to spend a year or a season in some well conducted though rough business or mercantile establishment. The fact that it would be so repugnant to your tastes is evidence of the benefit it would be—the discipline would be to you. Think of it, Charley. How ridiculous? Well, sir, every time you laugh 'tis at the expense of some most respectable and tasteful men. Isn't it? Pshaw!

I must make a short letter of this, for I have but little time left.

"We are certain of some things—let us act on them," you say. Very good, so I do & will. At least I intend to. "The various opinions great minds have held ought not to deter us, &c." Well I think they had. Now, the very fact that J. C. Calhoun[8] thinks *so* of *Slavery* is evidence to me that Slavery is not the greatest sin in the world—that a Slaveholder may be a conscientious Christian. And it is just exactly such reasoning as this would prevent my joining a church that forced me to profess to believe Slaveholding to be *either* a unforgiveable sin or a "beneficial Institution sanctioned by God"—a church that refused either Slaveholders or Abolitionists its communion.

I doubt if God has left us with so little light on whatever it is you call "Important Points" that men equally good, equally discriminating, equally judicious, equally unprejudiced, &c. (both of them too far superior to us in those qualitites) must be at sword's points, ever fighting—fighting—anathematizing & excommunicating each other, yet pity full & charitable, and equally anxious for the Glory of their professed Head, equally good, kind, benevolent, Christian, in their relations to their neighbor.

I can't believe the whole duty of man is on either side *alone*. Now, I believe J. C. Calhoun is wrong. And I would (if I thought 'twould do otherwise than make him stronger in his prejudices) tell him so & my reasons. But he *may* be right. God knows—I honestly believe he *may* be right. My belief is only strong enough to make me act to a certain extent.

Now I say the *Omniscient Judge may* pronounce him a Christian or Heretic. *I* have no *right*—it is not my business to unchristianize him—to decide at all. I am not called upon to act. I won't act upon it, nor will I make it my business at the option of ever so many small minds to ever act upon it. Nor any more than I can help will I make it their business to act upon me.

The Congregationalists insist to take it upon them to decide whether or no I am a Christian (*small* minds, too). The Episcopalians do not. Therefore, though I am a *Congregationalist*, I have and shall communicate with the Church Catholic under Episcopal government.

Yours affectionately,

Fred Olmsted

1. In his letter of January 27, 1847 (see above) Olmsted expressed his desire to get information from Brace's uncle, Charles Greely Loring, about lucerne, or alfalfa.
2. Henry Davis and his wife (see FLO to JHO, Feb. 16, 1847, note 3, above).
3. Samuel B. Beresford, Hartford physician.
4. This series of public meetings in 1847 was the culmination of nearly a decade of agitation in Hartford for a tax-supported high school available free of charge to all qualified students in the town, girls as well as boys. On March 8, 1847, the high school was approved by an overwhelming vote at what was described in 1886 as "the largest town meeting ever held in Hartford." The exclusive Grammar School with its classical curriculum was merged with the new Hartford English and Classical High School, which opened in 1847 (*Hartford County*, 1: 641–44; *Hartford Daily Courant*, March 9, 1847, p. 2).
5. Isaac Toucey, Hartford lawyer and governor of Connecticut, 1846–47. The Terrys were probably Eliphalet Terry (1776–1849) and Roderick Terry (1788–1849), sons of Judge Eliphalet Terry (1742–1812) of Enfield, Conn. They owned the largest of the Hartford mercantile houses engaged in the West Indies trade. They may have been joined by another brother, Seth Terry (1781–1865), a Hartford lawyer. Other opponents were John A. Taintor (1800–1864), a prominent Hartford wool merchant and livestock importer, and Timothy M. Allyn (1800–1882), a merchant and one of the wealthiest men in Hartford (*DAB*, s.v. "Toucey, Isaac"; *Hartford County*, 1: 127, 213, 385, 500–502, 546, 662; 2: 157; Stephen Terry, comp., *Notes of Terry Families* [Hartford: 1887], pp. 17, 38; *Boston Daily Advertiser*, Aug. 29, 1882, p. 8; *Yale Obit. Rec.*, 4th ser., no. 22 [July 1863]: 93; *Hartford Daily Courant*, March 9, 1847, p. 2).
6. The leading clerical supporters of the free high school were Horace Bushnell, who had written a powerful report on the subject in 1841 that was widely circulated, and George Burgess (1809–1866), Episcopal clergyman, rector of Christ Church in Hartford, and soon to become bishop of Maine. Other leaders in the movement were David F. Robinson (1801–1862), Hartford book publisher, and probably Charles Chapman, lawyer and editor of the *New England Review*. The most active promotor of the high school during the final stages of the agitation was James M. Bunce (1806–1859), a Hartford merchant (*DAB*, s.v., "Burgess, George"; *Hartford County*, 1: 115, 406,

623, 644; Donald L. Jacobus, *A History of the Seymour Family: Descendants of Richard Seymour of Hartford, Conn.* [New Haven, Conn., 1939], p. 230; *BDAC*, s.v. "Chapman, Charles"; William R. Cutter, ed., *Genealogical and Family History of the State of Connecticut* . . . , 4 vols. [New York, 1911], 1: 535–36).

7. The *sans-culottes* of the French Revolution, the ultra-democratic and egalitarian faction. Olmsted uses the term to mean "the people," those without wealth or privilege.

8. Olmsted seems here to be referring to John C. Calhoun's general stance as a defender of the institution of slavery. Calhoun's usual defense was a constitutional and political one, but a month before this letter was written he made one of his infrequent personal statements concerning the "peculiar institution." He did this while presenting his resolutions on the slave question to the Senate on February 19, 1847. The *Hartford Daily Courant* reprinted his speech on March 10, 1848, and quoted him as saying: "I am speaking as an individual member of the South—one who drew his first breath there—and whose hopes and feelings are centered there. A planter, a slaveholder—and none the worse, I believe, for being a slaveholder . . ." (for another version of the statement, see John C. Calhoun, *The Works of John C. Calhoun* . . . , ed. Richard K. Crallé, 6 vols. [New York, 1851–56; rpt. ed., 1968], 4: 347–48).

To John Hull Olmsted

Guilford, March 23rd, 1847

Dear John,

I wrote shortly to Father, yesterday, and now reply to yours of 18th instant.

I note what you say about Alsop's[1] and trees. I intend to plant (trans-) but few ornamental trees and with them to take great pains. Until I know where to put my house exactly, I can not arrange the lawn very well. The *Lawn* is to be the grand feature of my gardening. The ground is naturally graded and finely adapted for a broad smooth green plat (X) broken only by a few trees or clumps. Along on the rear edge of it and so circling towards the shore, some low thick shrubbery (a) is wanted. Back (cornering on b.) I suppose will be a good place for an orchard (beyond the proposed barn). 'Tis there we are carting our manure now and mean to plant corn & potatoes this year.

I expect Davis[2] will move in next week. We are going over to trim apple-trees, &c. this week, and to cart rock weed as fast as Roberts[3] brings it in any quantity. It's very unfortunate that I must pay for all my manure so. About four loads of seaweed, though, I got from the Rossiter-lot-beach for the trouble of carting. Potatoes are selling here now at 95 cents a bushel. At this rate, seed is going to cost something.

Tom[4] never would answer my purpose, I am confident. That is, I should kill him or he will kill me. Still, perhaps I ought to take him as discipline to my impatience. If Father thinks so I'm content; (but I actually would for the sake of comfort rather have no horse at all.) Charles (Leete)[5] has a very pretty mare; the neatest beast under a saddle I most ever rode— i.e., she rides easy, trots free, & capers or (now having not been out of her stable in a month) is playful. She is nine years old, and I suppose he would sell her cheap as he has no use for her.

The cow ("Tilly") I have bought is nothing remarkable. Mr. Griffing[6] got her for me. I buy her of Hubbard[7] (a cattle jockey) for $30.00 to be kept till 1st of April. Had not she better rather be named "Mother Hubbard"? She has a very handsome dark red bull calf by her side. Give him a name. Bartlett[8] seemed inclined to back out from selling me his best cow for $30.00. I don't want her or any of his, because any of them would teach my whole stock to cross the flats and be off by the bathing house road.

I don't hear from Mr. Ayres[9] yet, nor from Geddes or Van Bergen.[10] I don't get papers now. What a shameful, rascally, inconvenient, & tyrannical law this new Newspaper postage is. It has gone into operation now, too, the postmaster tells me, not waiting till July as the papers say. Papers coming from New York being paid 3 cents. My postage on the Tribune from New Haven would be $9.00 a year. Repeal! Repeal![11]

Try Nimrod again.

If you return this way to New Haven, let me know, if possible, a day or two before-hand that I may not be gone to New Haven myself. The copper-boats *are* life-boats.[12] How long the (two) chambers would remain tight in ordinary usage I can not tell. But if they should happen both to get stove or cracked a *little*, it would take a good while to exhaust the air from them. Mr. Norton's boat—only 12 feet long—will carry 10 persons easily inside and dry. Water logged, they would not sink with most anything. No ordinary ballast begin to take them down, and one will float as many men as can get hold of her. I think it is quite a consideration.

There were eleven sail put into the Head, one night, last week. While we were at work there there were forty sail in sight at once.

You have wonderfully improved your writing hand. I'd no idea it was yours until I had read some ways. This secret of it is—*large letters.*

I can't get anybody to make my lighter's sail. I propose to have it a lug as I shall seldom want to beat her and it will have a *look.* She is to be twenty feet long. What sized sail would you give her? This sail is easiest to hand & reef—least in the way. The mast holes to the surf boats I suppose are placed forward— or perhaps I would rig thus:

"Nep."[13] flourisheth.

He does not mind very quick, but improves. Griffing says these dogs never do mind very well. That Rossiter beach is complete for bathing, at any time of tide. *Long* clams are real good, well cooked. Round don't compare with them.

1. Olmsted is probably referring to one of two Alsop mansions in Middletown, Conn., both of which had extensive grounds planted with unusual and ornamental trees. One was built c. 1810 by Joseph Wright Alsop (1772–1844); the other was begun by Richard Alsop IV (1789–1842) in 1838, but not completed until after his death (Mary Alsop Cryder, "Alsop Genealogy, Being a Brief Account of the Descendants of Richard Alsop Who First Appeared in Middletown, Connecticut, in 1750 . . ." [typescript in the Genealogical Section, Library of Congress], pp. 13, 16, 17, 22; The Architects' Emergency Committee, *Great Georgian Houses of America*, 2 vols. [1933–1937; rpt. ed., New York, 1970], 2:195–97; information on the Alsop family supplied by Joseph Alsop).
2. Henry Davis, Olmsted's hired man.
3. Luke G. Roberts owned land to the north of Olmsted's farm. Roberts and his three sons helped Olmsted prepare the ground for the trees he bought in New York (*Town of Guilford, Connecticut, Register of Deeds*, 35 [1846–1850]: 170; FLO to JO, Nov. 4, 1847).
4. Tom, a spiritless horse owned by Olmsted's father (JO Journal, April 8, 1847, Feb. 28, 1848; JO to FLO, Feb. 10, 1847).
5. Charles Frederick Leete (1820–1907), a Leete's Island farmer at whose house Olmsted stayed before moving into the Sachem's Head farm (E. L. Leete, *Family of William Leete*, p. 43; Headstone Inscriptions, Guilford, Cemetery 1, p. 58).
6. Frederick Redfield Griffing (1798–1852), a Guilford businessman who owned land adjacent to Olmsted's farm (Clara J. Stone, comp., *Genealogy of the Descendants of Jasper Griffing* [New York, 1881], p. 81; FLO to JHO, Feb. 26, 1847).
7. John Hubbard (1804–1891) of Guilford, who was "an enterprising farmer and high authority on cattle" (Edward Warren Day, comp., *One Thousand Years of Hubbard History, 866 to 1895. From Hubba, the Norse Sea King, to the Enlightened Present* [New York, 1895], p. 257).
8. Probably Ebenezer Bartlett, previous owner of the farm at Sachem's Head, who, in Olmsted's judgment, had badly mismanaged the place during his nine years of ownership (FLO to FJK, Feb. 19, 1847; Guilford County Deed Records, 35: 170).
9. Either Jared A. Ayres or his brother William Orville Ayres, both of Hartford.
10. George Geddes and Anthony A. Van Bergen. The latter tried out many innovations on his farm at Coxsackie, N.Y. ([Frederick Law Olmsted], *Walks and Talks of an American Farmer in England*, 2 vols. [London, 1852], 1: 181–82; Sebastian Visscher Talcott, comp., *Genealogical Notes of New York and New England Families* [Albany, N.Y., 1883], p. 301).
11. The new postal law established a charge of three cents for newspapers mailed from places other than the place of publication (*Hartford Daily Courant*, March 10, 1847, p. 2).
12. Olmsted is probably referring to Francis' Metallic Life-Boat, which was already being used by some ships of the U.S. Navy, or a lifeboat of similar design. The Francis boat had a hull made of sheets of corrugated copper and had watertight copper compartments for buoyancy (*Francis' Metallic Life-Boat Company* . . . [New York, 1852], pp. 14–15).
13. Olmsted's Newfoundland puppy, "Neptune," often referred to as "Nep" (FLO to CLB, March 22, 1846).

To Charles Loring Brace[1]

Address: Mr. Chas. L. Brace/Catskill/N.Y./care of Dr. Brace[2]
Postmark: New Milford/Se 11/Ct

Sachem's Head, Sept. 9th, 1847

Dear John,

The Doctor[3] and I had a *jolly time* in the "Susan Nippers." She brought us before a famous breeze to the Sachem's wharf in two hours from the Light House.[4] The Doctor said he never enjoyed a sail so much and such sort of things. But in fact he did seem to be delighted with it and you would have imagined he was born for a sailor.

By the way, speaking of jolly time with "the Doctor" reminds [me] that Geddes[5] was hugely pleased when he came to hear that the Doctor had been playing ninepins. There was here then—you remember that clever old fellow—the famous Judge Bronson.[6] He is Chief Justice of New York and the beau ideal of that character—very highly honored at home. Geddes says, "In our parts they would kill a Doctor of Divinity for playing ninepins. Last year they tried to excommunicate or unlicense one for boarding at a house where some of the boarders were permitted to dance," and so on. He would like amazingly to tell at home that he had play'd ninepins with a Yankee Doctor of Divinity and the Chief Justice of the State of New York.

So he set me to plotting it and without any difficulty I got the Doctor to join sides with me against the Judge & Geddes—Connecticut against New York. They thought they could beat us easy, but the Doctor and I took off our coats. The Doctor got the highest string, I the next, and Geddes least of all. It tickled Bushnell very much. He crowed about it a great deal, till Geddes vowed he'd never roll with a D.D. again. "He has mistaken his profession," says he, "he was cut out for a gambler."

Au revoir. We did not talk much about Christian Nurture[7]—and what he said I was not particularly pleased with. There seemed to me to be too much want of respect to his opponents. The matter of the Church—I enlarged upon and gave my opinions somewhat freely. We did not discuss it, properly—for it is a matter I will not argue upon—if I can help it. I do not feel able to—but the fact is there was nothing to argue.

I was not surprised to find the Doctor considered the matter a good deal as I did—to a certain extent at least. That is, he agreed that the present *orthodox view* or plan of the local churches was very objectionable—not warranted by scripture, and that a reform or change was very desirable. He was not prepared to say that the local churches should be abandoned, but he had made up his mind that a member of the *church* at large (i.e. anyone who *himself* called himself a follower of Christ) should not be excluded from the sacraments because he was not a member of a particular association of

296

believers—(local church.) And he wished that his church could be organised on some plan whereby anyone could partake with them in the communion (of the church of Christ) and any parents themselves not members of the church could have their children baptized, &c.

He was very glad indeed that I had joined his church in communion, although I had not professed to join it in faith. He did not at all disapprove (I mean he did not say that he did) of the course I have been led to pursue. And though he did not intimate what he should have done if he were in my place, he said that his own views had changed very much since he joined the church by profession of Faith, and he thought it was an open question and one of great difficulty. It was troubling him more than any other similar question. If the local church organization was necessary—and he was afraid of the consequences of abandoning it—and if the Profession of Faith was necessary to such an institution, then it should [be] in the simplest form.

I have but little idea when you will be in New Milford—but I believe I shall direct there as the quickest way to get this to you.

We have an Easterly storm here now—which if it reaches you will be likely to cool your pedestrian ardor. It is very cold and disagreeable. I suspect if I had time I should feel lonely and all that, but we have a great deal to do. I believe I shall have to go to New Haven to get another hand, next week. The Hotel[8] has closed.

I hope that you are going to be in New Haven. I suppose indeed that you are, as I hear nothing to the contrary. I have given my advice in favor of John's[9] anchoring there another year.

I took a big sheet. I hope it will not cost you double postage. There! I've lost my pen in the inkstand. It's not double postage, I know—don't tell me it is. I've taken a big sheet—and—after all I shall not fill it. I wish I'd lost my pen two lines sooner. 'Twould ha' been a good reason for not droning on.

Yours affectionately,

F.L.O.

1. Although the letter is addressed to Charles Loring Brace, the salutation is to John (John Hull Olmsted). The contents of the letter, and the reference in it to John in the third person, make it clear the letter is intended for Brace.
2. Brace's uncle, Dr. Abel Brace, who lived in Catskill, N.Y. (John Sherman Brace, *Brace Lineage* . . . , 2d ed. [Bloomsburg, Pa., 1927], p. 104; *Yale Obit. Rec.*, 5th ser., no. 2 [June 1902]: 133).
3. Horace Bushnell, who had received an honorary doctorate of divinity from Wesleyan University in Middletown in 1842 (Wesleyan University, *A Catalogue of The Officers and Students of the Wesleyan University, 1845–46* [Middletown, Conn., 1845], p. 15).
4. That is, from Lighthouse Point at the mouth of New Haven harbor to Sachem's Head, a distance of ten nautical miles.
5. George Geddes.

6. Greene Carrier Bronson (1789–1863) was at this time chief justice of the Supreme Court of the state of New York. He had practiced law in Utica, been attorney general, and was candidate for governor in 1855 (*NCAB*, 3: 387).
7. In 1847 Horace Bushnell published two sermons on Christian nurture, his first publication on a concept that he later treated more fully in a longer book (Horace Bushnell, *Views of Christian Nurture, and of Subjects Adjacent Thereto* [Hartford, Conn., 1847]).
8. The Sachem's Head House, built in 1832. It was the largest summer hotel between New York and Newport (B. C. Steiner, *History of Guilford*, p. 209).
9. John Hull Olmsted.

To CHARLES LORING BRACE

Address: Mr. Chas. L. Brace,/Care of John P. Brace Esqr./New Milford/Ct. Postmark: Guilford/Sep 23/Ct.

S.H., Sept. 20th, 1847

Dear Charley,
     Did you ever examine the "creed" of the "Society of Friends?" I *should* have said, I suppose, the "Profession of Faith." If you have not, very likely your first thought is *not* one of surprise or regret at your ignorance or neglect. You have no particular reverence for a shad-bellied coat,[1] nor do you think much of the reasoning faculties of the man who is convinced by the arguments of the wearer of one for not conforming his garments to those of his "fellow creatures." Yet you must respect that body of men, whatever their garb or language, that have so perseveringly upheld what they were convinced was right—suffered shame, persecution, and contempt, principally for practices based entirely on doctrines which we are ready to acknowledge *abstractly*, and are getting ready to acknowledge practically perhaps. We must respect while we smile at these ridiculous martyrs. Think of William Penn. Think of him even in connection with our own boasted Puritan fathers. Think of the Quakers of Ireland in the Rebellion,[2] the Quakers of Ireland, I might add, at this day—the Quakers of England, who to this day never bend the knee to Mammon by paying *tithes*, and from them they have never been taken except by forcible seizure.
     Do you recollect the origin of these "Articles of Faith"? You can not easily forget Carlyle's apostrophe to the "Cordwainer of Leeds."[3] Throwing aside the broad principles which they have so earnestly, so meekly, so painfully, so boldly *professed* by the actions which associate with them immediately in our minds—did it ever occur to you that these people, that George Fox & Co. had distinctive opinions on other matters as well as on Conformity to the world and Pride and War—and the ministry and the sacraments? Do you know what these—Feeders of the hungry and clothers of the naked—

prison visitors—Slave-freers—what Gurney and Mrs. Fry[4]—*think* on the subjects that Theologians and Princes of the church *fight* about?

Well, it's a queer-mess. They differ a little in nearly every ingredient from the churches "of the World" in their hodge-podge. Things were likely to taste a little different to a frugal cobbler than to a university-indoctrinated cook. The grand feature perhaps is the manner in which or extent to which they recognize the Influence of the Spirit—together with their contempt for *forms* and certain sorts of *means*. About Natural Depravity, original sin, or "Christian Nurture," I forget, because I never paid any attention to anybody's views upon them except the latter, I suppose.

I was thinking to-day of the Inspiration of the Scriptures, and an idea of the Quakers bearing upon this subject led me to bring them before you. They refuse to speak of the Scriptures as the *"Word of God."* Any natural inference as to a doctrine you would draw from this fact they object to, in some way or other explaining it away. (They think the term irreverent to Divinity I believe.) But it has often occurred to me in my heretical and unshackled moments of dissipated wandering on the borders of what the Pharisees of the present day term infidelity, whether we had sufficient authority to call all parts of the "Book" the "Word of God."

I should like to know all the meanings that a Professor of Greek, if he had occasion for them to sustain an argument, would find for the words "Inspiration of God." (Not that this authorizes the use of the term.) And then I would be glad if he could convince me perfectly that the word *"all"* in the text alluded to did *not* refer to a—well, no matter how much of the Old Testament.

I should like to read a real Unitarian argument on this subject. Then a Review of that argument by Dr. Tyler,[5] and *then* a letter of Dr. Bushnell[6] upon the subject—without any *particular* reference to the last, but full of Love and charity to the first. I think it would settle my very *riley* views of the subject as a piece of cod-fish does a pot of coffee. I should find bottom for the *grounds* of my belief or unbelief. There is, however, a great deal which I can hardly hesitate to receive as (what we understand by) Inspired.

Several volumes[7] Our Saviour alludes to in such a way as we can hardly imagine he would, if he had but now appeared, to the words of —Ireneus,[8] or—Luther, or—Shakespeare, or—many whose words *are* quoted now, often with as much respect, *as if they had* been inspired—the "immortal Milton" (never *"joined the church"*) or the Father of "Orthodoxy," Jonathan Edwards. I once heard a "New England Divine" express some doubt as to Isaac Watts[9] *not* being *inspired*. Whereto a "True-Church" man enquired if he thought all his poetry was inspired? Certainly he did not. Does anybody suppose the poetry of the Hebrew minstrel was inspired? I believe some do.

Do you suppose that Paul was divinely led to say one word of his own and to stipulate that that should be excepted in order that it might be known that all (the rest) was unexceptionable? The Apostles certainly were *not* Divinely inspired in *all* their ways—in all their *counsels*—even after the Day of Pentecost. Is it not possible that they sometimes put their counsel—such for instance as Peter might have given at Antioch, and for which Paul "withstood him because it (he) was to be blamed"—on paper?[10]

Solomon certainly was not always Divinely Inspired, any more than Byron was. I must confess, I think there's room for doubt whether he was when he wrote the Canticles any more than Byron when he wrote his "Devotional Poetry." I think so because I have heard or read of some dignitary-of-the-church's saying he considered it a "vile bawdy song," &c. I never read it myself since I used to "read the *Bible* through"—a good while ago. I did read Scott's[11] Introduction to it, however—but stopped there because he frightened me out of it.

The principal argument, I believe, (for I never felt sufficiently doubtful to spend a great many years studying the Rabbis) is that (of the Old Testament) they were received and held sacred by the Jews. You know I suppose (but do you think a man might be damned for doubting?) whether the Priests had made a mistake about it. The Jews—were they inspired to know which was sacred? Some of the Psalms are. *Is it* possible some are not? May there be interlopers? Is it certain that Christ should have mentioned it, if there were?

This reminds me of what strikes me as a failure in Scott's argument in regard to Diabolical possession, &c. He says (in effect) that Christ always reproved the errors and superstitions of the Jews. Now did he, unless they were dangerous errors? He did not tell them, that we know of, that the earth was round, that you could not see from the top of a mountain ever so high—all over it—except by miracle. We do not know that he even instructed his disciples in Geology, or the length of Moses' day. I should not be surprised if even Peter thought the world made in 6 × 24 hours, each measured by the swing of a pendulum × 60, 'til he met Moses himself in heaven.

By the way, what do you suppose Moses thought about it? I sometimes have been appalled with an idea that Moses did not know any thing more about it than Dr. Robbins[12] does of the establishment of the First Church in Conn., but inspired by the spirit (as we or Dr. Robbins might be, *now*) he wrote what *he* thought from tradition, etc., to be true, &c. as Delavigne[13] does now, of Luther's day.

But as to the "Word of God," and this application of [the] term: I do not know as it is of any consequence. Though I was going to [say] if Christ had himself written—*that* we might call the Word of God in distinction from the rest of the *Bible, written* by men. I don't know as the difference is worth noticing. Now don't suppose at all that I *do not believe* in the Inspiration of Scripture. I simply give you an idea of an unsatisfactoriness that occasionally crosses my mind, and to start you upon the subject a little, if you think best.

I should like to hear you, too, on the subject of Politics and the principles to govern the bestowment of your vote or influence, or for *not using your* influence or vote? I have read the address of the Liberty Party National Convention.[14] It is very long, but far from convincing to my mind. The main object is "Religious men should support candidates who go for religious measures." But Religious men even do not agree on every measure. And the whole argument is based on opposition to one-idea-ism—which is Garrisonism[15] I suppose.

1. A kind of coat worn by Quakers; it is cut so that it slopes gradually away from the front to the tails (*OED*).
2. Olmsted may be referring to the persecution of the Quakers in Ireland by Puritan authorities during the Irish Rebellion of 1641 (Great Britain Public Record Office, *Calendar of the State Papers Relating to Ireland. September 1669–December 1670, With Addenda, 1625–70*, ed. Robert Pentland Mahaffy [London, 1911], pp. 373–77).
3. The "Cordwainer of Leeds" was George Fox (1624–1691), founder of the Society of Friends, or Quakers. In *Sartor Resartus* Carlyle gave a glowing account of young Fox's religious quest. For Teufelsdröckh, Carlyle's clothes-philosopher hero, the "most remarkable incident in Modern History" was Fox's creation of a suit of leather with which to clothe himself while he retreated to the wilderness in search of spiritual truth (Thomas Carlyle, *Sartor Resartus; The Life and Opinions of Herr Teufelsdröckh* [Boston, 1846], pp. 92–94).
4. The English Quakers Joseph John Gurney (1788–1847) and Elizabeth Fry (1780–1845) were brother and sister. Her career, especially, fits Olmsted's description. She early visited the poor and sick, sought to educate their children, and promoted the formation of societies for the purpose. Her chief concern was prison reform: she cared for and taught the women in Newgate Prison, and in 1817 founded a society to carry out such a program. Thereafter she traveled through England seeking to improve conditions at other prisons, and urged more humane provisions for prisoners transported to New South Wales. Her brother shared her desire for prison reform, and worked closely with the leaders of the English antislavery movement (*DNB*).
5. Bennet Tyler, Congregational clergyman, an ardent defender of Calvinism as interpreted by Jonathan Edwards and Timothy Dwight, and an opponent of the innovations of Nathaniel Taylor of Yale. He was president of the Hartford Theological Seminary until 1857 (*DAB*).
6. Horace Bushnell.
7. That is, several books of the Old Testament.
8. Saint Irenaeus (c. 130–200), early church father and bishop of Lyons. The first great Catholic theologian, he was the earliest church father to systematize Christian doctrine and is often called the father of Christian orthodoxy (F. L. Cross, ed., *The Oxford Dictionary of the Christian Church* [London, 1958]; Richard A. Norris, Jr., *God and World in Early Christian Theology* [New York, 1965], p. 72).
9. Isaac Watts (1674–1748), the greatest hymnist in the English church. His *Catechisms* (1730) and *Scripture History* (1732) were still standard works in the middle of the nineteenth century. His *Psalms and Hymns* became the religious textbook of the dissenting churches in England (*DNB*; Harry Escott, *Isaac Watts, Hymnographer: A Study of the Beginnings, Development and Philosophy of the English Hymn* [London, 1962], pp. 256–67).
10. The passage Olmsted had in mind is Galatians 2:11, which reads: "But when Peter

was come to Antioch, I withstood him to the face, because he was to be blamed." This is part of Paul's account of the argument he had with Peter over the question of the demands of Jewish law on Christians.

11. Thomas Scott (1747–1821), Anglican clergyman. His religious beliefs changed from Unitarianism to traditional Calvinism. His *Collected Writings* totaled ten volumes, of which four were the Biblical exegesis *The Holy Bible, with Notes* (*DNB*).

12. Thomas Robbins (1777–1856), Congregational clergyman and antiquarian. In 1815 he published a series of biographical sketches entitled *An Historic View of the First Planters of New England*. At the time this letter was written he was librarian of the Connecticut Historical Society (*DAB*).

13. Jean François Casimir Delavigne (1793–1843), poet and playwright, published *Une Famille au temps de Luther* in 1836 (Paul Harvey and Janet E. Heseltine, comps. and eds., *The Oxford Companion to French Literature* [Oxford, 1959], p. 192; *EB*).

14. The Liberty Party was formed in 1839–40 with the sole purpose of opposing the expansion of slavery. It polled 7,000 votes in the presidential campaign of 1840 and 62,000 in 1844. In 1847 some of its members undertook to expand both its program and its appeal. They gathered in upstate New York in June, nominated the philanthropist and abolitionist Gerrit Smith for president, and formally abandoned the Liberty Party. They took the name Liberty League and issued an *Address of the National Nominating Convention* that was widely circulated. It is to this address that Olmsted refers. It called for antislavery voters to abandon the narrow position of the Liberty Party and to create an organization that would take a consistent stand on other political issues of the day. This gave impetus to the formation of the Free Soil Party, which occurred the following year (William Goodell, *Slavery and Anti-Slavery, A History of the Great Struggle in Both Hemispheres with a View to the Slavery Question in the United States* [New York: William Goodell, 1853], pp. 468–77; Ralph V. Harlow, *Gerrit Smith, Philanthropist and Reformer* [New York, 1939], pp. 178–79).

15. William Lloyd Garrison (1805–1879), editor of the abolitionist newspaper, the *Liberator*. Despite the wide range of his reform interests, Garrison was for many people the symbol of "one-idea" reform that concentrated all its attention on a single issue—in his case that of slavery—in the belief that the solution of that problem would lead to the righting of many other wrongs of society (Russel Blaine Nye, *William Lloyd Garrison and the Humanitarian Reformers* [Boston, 1955], pp. 113–15, 201–2).

To FREDERICK KINGSBURY

Sachem's Head September 23d, 1847

My dear Fred,

Your favor of the 20th inst. reached me last night. I shall try if it is possible for me to leave home just at that time to be in Waterbury at the Fair,[1] and the proposal you are kind enough to make, will be a very great additional inducement. Please offer my compliments to your father and mother, and I think you may add that I accept their obliging invitation with great pleasure. I really hope you will not be gone, but I do not know that I can say anything to keep you. I did not tell you of the talk I had with Bushnell[2] in the boat—I'll keep it till I see you.

How oddly we met Jackson[3] at Meriden—and what the deuce had become of you, that *we* could not find you sooner? When shall we three come so near meeting again? Next Sunday perhaps.

Mary Buel[4] I never saw except in the street and at *meeting*. I did not see anything to the contrary then. It's a long ways to Litchfield though—and I don't know how I could court her: particularly as I am busy in the trouting season. I don't know but I might go up to look at the Winchester man's[5] cattle—and run away my horse in L. and so break my leg—and court on convalescence. It would not take long if the roads were open to find if she ate clams.

I have not heard nor heard of Bill Colt.[6]

Can not you look me up a mason—that can lay stone? I saw one in Collinsville.[7] He wouldn't undertake my job for less than $2.00 a perch. Geddes said he could get it done at Syracuse for 50 cents. I believe I shall send out there. There is no one here that knows anything about it.

Your uncle[8] must have been in the very hottest of it in that battle—that last—battle (God grant it may be). I am happy to hear of his promotion. That was not *my* Captain Smith. His name is something Kirby, or Kirby something Smith[9]—he is thar' though.

The Hotel[10] has been closed these three weeks—and I do keep on thinking—and don't do anything else—I might almost say—though I am tolerably busy—one of [my] men having gone and potatoes digging. I am getting along very well. Shall have a better crop than my neighbors—though some rot. I shall send a parcel of them to New York next Monday at 37½ cents.

What do you think of Free Suffrage?[11] You are the greatest Southerner for a sensible Northern man I ever saw. I most want to have a talk with you about Abolition &c. Come now for once just give me a letter on the Wilmot Proviso &c.[12] And the abolition principle in politicks. I never have discussed or spoken upon the subject with a single man—but I keep thinking occasionally and I don't know but I am growing into an Abolitionist. It seems to me reason has mighty little to do with politics. To all practical purposes I am a vigilant neck or nothing *foxy* Whig—never hardly losing an opportunity even if it is an equivocal one of helping my party. And yet on my conscience I am a very lukewarm half blooded coon only. The *rationale* of it is I suppose I am tremendously patriotic (I am, if you'll believe me, it's the strongest principle in my nature, if it is a natural instinct. It's stronger than love, hatred, selfishness, or even I do confess Religion or the love of life itself—now laugh). And wanting to do something for my country I fall hold of the Whig rope because I can clutch that easier than any other. I am going to be a Peace man, too—I am afraid: afraid I say, because it will not be pleasant for me—as I have naturally a wonderful taste for the pomp & circumstance of glorious war. If I could only be persuaded that it was right, there's really nothing I should like so well as to lead the *forlorn hope*.[13] How different I am from you in all this—and yet we are a good deal alike, some. You've no sort of sectional feeling—I have the strongest in the world.

I do wish I had not a vote to give for several years to come. And I wish I could keep clear of politics all together till I had a little more judgment, than I have now. I wish you'll think or talk more on Politics and such subjects of general interest a little more. You are just the right sort of man to arrive at correct conclusiòns and you ought it seems to me to be using a little more influence among the populus. At any rate with me. You could do more good in one day writing newspaper articles on Political and Moral subjects than you can in writing for the Yale Lit., or for that matter the $5.00 Quarterlies—or a year in a course of law. Don't you think so? I have often most devoutly wished you would. Pray do write to me now & then.

> Yours affectionately
>
> F L Olmsted

1. The New Haven County Agricultural Fair, held in Waterbury on October 6, 1847 (*Cultivator*, n.s. 4, no. 11 [Nov. 1847]: 350).
2. Horace Bushnell.
3. Jefferson Franklin Jackson, a classmate of Kingsbury's at Yale.
4. Mary Buel of Litchfield, whom John Hull Olmsted had apparently recently met and thought a likely prospect for his brother.
5. Probably Lemuel Hurlbut (1785–1856) of Winchester, Conn., the first breeder of Devon cattle in the state, whose herd received special praise at the Litchfield County Agricultural Fair in 1847 (John Boyd, *Annals and Family Records of Winchester, Conn., with Exercises of the Centennial Celebration, on the 16th and 17th Days of August, 1871* [Hartford, Conn., 1873], pp. 98, 99; *Cultivator*, n.s. 4, no. 11 [Nov. 1847]: 350).
6. William Upson Colt.
7. Collinsville, Conn. where Olmsted had gone with George Geddes earlier in the month (FLO to JHO, Sept. 5, 1847).
8. Julius J. B. Kingsbury (c. 1801–1856), a West Point graduate, who was promoted to bvt. major on August 20, 1847 for his "gallant and meritorious conduct" in the battles of Contreras and Churubusco. He was in the battle of Molino del Rey, Sept. 8, and the assault and capture of Mexico City, Sept. 13–14 (George W. Cullum, *Biographical Register of the Officers and Graduates of the United States Military Academy, at West Point . . .* , 2 vols. [New York, 1868], 1: 248).
9. Ephraim Kirby Smith (see FLO to CLB, July 30, 1846, above).
10. The Sachem's Head House, near Olmsted's farm.
11. The question of universal manhood suffrage was before the voters of Connecticut at this time. In May 1847 the General Assembly had approved an amendment to the state constitution passed by the previous legislature giving the vote to all male citizens of the United States who had resided for a year in the state and for six months in the town where they voted and who sustained "a good moral character." The question then went to the towns, who voted on it on October 1, 1847. The proposal was defeated, 19,148 to 5,353.

    Olmsted and his friends reached different conclusions on the question. Kingsbury opposed the amendment, while Olmsted apparently argued for it, "as a Whig and a democrat." Charles Brace "was growling away in his old Federal fashion about the ignorance, meanness and prejudice of the lower classes that would decide the question as he supposed in accordance with their degradation," but never-

THE GENTLEMAN FARMER: 1847–1849

theless wanted an even greater expansion of the suffrage (*Hartford Daily Courant*, Nov. 9, 1847, p. 2; FLO to FJK, Dec. 5, 1847, in FJK Sketch of FLO).

12. The proposal offered in the summer of 1846 by the Democratic representative from Pennsylvania, David Wilmot, calling for the exclusion of slavery from all territory acquired by the United States as a result of the war with Mexico.

13. Olmsted apparently uses "forlorn hope" in its military sense: a picked body of men who lead an attack with little hope of surviving it (*OED*).

To Charles Loring Brace [October 12, 1847]

Address: Mr. Chas. L. Brace/New Haven/Ct.

I wish you were here to-night Charley. (Sachem's Head, Guilford, Oct. 12th, 1847) It is what the ballad writers call a wild night, sailors would call it very dirty, though if one can judge sitting on the weather side of the house it will sweep some decks clean. Common folks (on the lee side) would simply say perhaps it was very windy. And if a deputy sawbones was of the party he would observe "*flatulent*," though the penny a liner would say the wind is *high*. We farmers might reply—our *corn* will be *flat*.

The house shakes—it's fairly awful! Even Nep looks at the window as if he meant it shouldn't *come in*. Due *South*—the only point from which

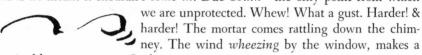

we are unprotected. Whew! What a gust. Harder! & harder! The mortar comes rattling down the chimney. The wind *wheezing* by the window, makes a noise like a snow storm. Such a *roar*.

Charley, I do wish you were here on my own account. It is really getting awful! Here comes hail! Prit! Prit! What a noise! Everything trembles! My God! How could I trifle about it? But really, Charley, I have written just as fast as you please to imagine, hardly stopping to think a second—so fast did the storm increase and so fast did my feelings change with it. As I write this sentence there is, thank God, a lull.

I had just stepped out to *enjoy* it. Dark as pitch. But you could hear and feel—and you *could* see the breakers. It occurred to me to walk down towards the point—where it must be most grand—but I gave it up saying to myself, If Charley Brace was here we would go down to-gether, but I do not want to go alone. Then I came in and thought I ought to write to you (for why, anon) and as I took my pen there came a harder puff, and I wrote my thoughts—"I wish you were here," and it *grew* and *grew*, harder—till the lull. And now again the house begins to tremble.

What an awful time to make Fire Island Light.[1] Certain death! God have mercy on them!

That is not hail—only drops of rain. With what force they must be driven!

305

I don't hardly think *I* am frightened at all. I can not believe there really is any danger of the house's blowing over. Yet, I know I shall not take my clothes off to go to bed while it blows like this. *Why*, I can not tell you, but I suppose it is a relic of sea feeling and habit. And I have once or twice half turned my head towards the door with a sort of half idea that a woman, pale, and with a shawl over her night clothes was coming in. And I am all ready to tell her, "There's no danger. It's impossible for the house to blow away. I have seen harder blows than this." (I know if I have, I was in something that knelt before it—and got away and ran as fast as she could. Didn't stand and resist without so much as stooping or bowing to it like this slab sided affair.) If I have got to live in a house at Sachem's Head it shall be something stronger than this—if I can get it.

I have been out to see if the barn stood it. I can not see that it is gone. It stands against a great rock and I suppose that held it. Positively, I heard something like a shriek! I do hope it was a loon.

There is a very singular *boom*ing roar, which you hear through all. I suppose it is what the folks here often talk about and call the surf breaking on the south side of Long Island. I never heard it before.

Here is another terrible puff. I involuntarily lift myself in my chair with the surge of the gale. Nep has got used to it and gone to sleep. And even I begin to [*take hold*][2] again. I believe I should be more com[*fortable if*] I was asleep. So, good night, Charley. [*I wish*] there was a light house here. Just think of spending the night on Falkner's Island,[3] and then of going up, up, to trim the lamps. But have not I been up (& down, too) to furl the close reefed main topsail in such a time? I think there must have been some comfort in feeling the ship cotton to it if I have. I don't know. It don't seem now as if any canvas could stand to it to this time.

I send you this letter (nearly forgot to mention it) that you needn't come here while I am gone. There are not any ducks feeding in shore yet, either. Guess if any of them are about tonight, they'll be going ashore. I am intending to go to Hartford tomorrow—at any rate, God willing, next day—and think of going to New York before I return. Two Sachem's Head boys were to leave New York in a small sloop to come home today. They have *most likely* got in to harbor—but how anxious their parents must be! And two Falkner's Island boys sailed in a 30 ton smack to the eastward today.

Yours affectionately,

Fred.

1. A lighthouse on Fire Island near the entrance of New York harbor, on a dangerous lee shore in a southerly gale.
2. The three sets of brackets in this part of the letter result from the cutting out of the stamp. The editor has restored the probable words used, some of which were only partially obliterated.

3. Falkner's Island in Long Island Sound, about three miles off Sachem's Head and the site of a lighthouse.

To John Hull Olmsted

Southfield,[1] March 6, 1848
Monday
10 A.M.

Dear John,

We worked till after dark that night and got all the potatoes that were fit for the market on board, and nearly all the furniture. Then it blew very hard, and we gave up going that night. *Next* morning, Wednesday, I got *everything* on board before nine o'clock, but it kept on blowing. And we waited & waited—all the time looking for a lull—for the Captain was in a great hurry on account of the market. We did not finally get off till noon of the *next* day, Thursday.

The *Julliet* was a fine craft, built in New London for a *packet* 22 years ago. Since rebuilt once or twice, but the same cabin, large & comfortable with two spacious state-rooms. My sofa went lengthways in her. The chests, chairs, &c., were in the state-rooms. I propose to give you a particular account of our trip because there was some seamanship—or boatmanship—which you will like to examine—and appreciate—& perhaps it will be of use to you. I hope not.

The "Old Jule" is very deep, drawing more water than the largest river steamboats (i.e., 7 feet) with good beam, sharp, staunch, & weatherly. Will carry sail equal to a smack,[2] almost. Of course, she is very *wet*. The Captain, (Clancy[3]) a fine man of great experience and skill, accommodating, polite, and *jolly*, though suffering terribly with *tic-douloureux*[4] all the time. He was not fit to be out at all and would not have been, but for the prospect of relief and chloroform in New York. The hand, old Dr. Sweet's son,[5] a very queer fellow—at sea almost from a baby and as competent a boatman as the Captain, Benoni—*Nony*, for short—his name. George Roberts[6] shipped because the captain was sick—after we left the wharf *of course*. Jim, a boy, for cook. A good for nothing booby. Been a canal driver and cook on the lakes.

We were becalmed off New Haven—weather looked bad—put her head in. A sloop to westward put about, too. Calm continuing at sunset, began to row. At dark, a breeze from S.E.; stood up the harbor. I went below—and to sleep. Was woke up by a strange—very strange—noise. Jumped on deck and found we were trying to drive through the ice—fetched up by it—all hands trying to break a passage through with handspikes and crowding sail on her. Snow storm commenced.

307

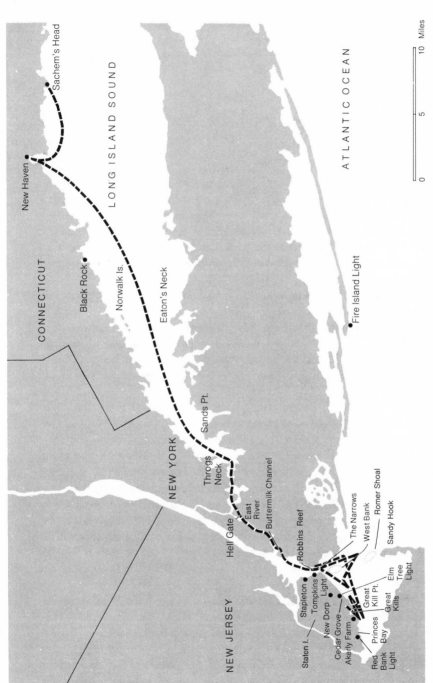

CRUISE OF THE SLOOP *Julliet* FROM SACHEM'S HEAD
TO STATEN ISLAND, MARCH 1848

"Sloop ahoy! What sloop's that?"

"*Alert!*"

"Hallo Sol!"

"Hallo! What sloop's that?"

"*Julliet.*"

"Hallo Bill. What's the matter? You fast?"

"Yes—fast enough—in *the ice.*"

"The Devil!"

So the Alert puts her helm down, tacks, and tries to pass someways to windward to us. Pretty soon she fetches up in the same way. Now, I never saw anything so dismal: snow storm, very thick, cold and ice. White with snow all about.

At length, I saw the light—over her stern bearing S.S.E. I sung out to the Captain that the ice was drifting (and carrying us) on to the west flats. He sounded and found it was so and let go anchor. She soon fetched 'round and held. The ice below pushed by us, and we were soon clear. Hailed the Alert, and she did the same. Hove up and beat up for the cove. Alert followed. Anchored when we sounded two fathoms muddy bottom. Alert ditto. Went below, got supper & turned in.

Next morning (Friday), put out under jib and afterwards got reefed mainsail on her. Afternoon cleared, off Norfolk islands. Took breeze from S.W. dead ahead. Set topsail and *put her into it.* Alert hull down, probably put in to Black Rock. Very heavy sea. Off Eaton's Neck at sunset, wind increasing. I never saw a sloop *go* as we did from Sands Point to Throg's Point! We carried whole mainsail–nothing else out. We came to anchor in a harbour a few miles east of Hell Gate at 11:30, and it was blowing a regular gale then.

Next day, Saturday, wind the same. Beat down through the Gate on so on. In going through Buttermilk Channel, just as we were tacking below the *cut* of the Atlantic Dock, she *grounded.* 15 feet of water, according to chart, close along side of us. Tide running ebb like a mill tail.[7] Took in all sail and waited—very low neap tide[8]—till half past three o'clock P.M. Got off then, and beat down. A'hazing breeze. Lots of vessels coming in. Beat everything going out.

I undertook to pilot her round from Fort Tompkins. Wind—a snorter—West, dead ahead as it could be. I kept Tompkin's Light open by Robyn's reef light, and stood out towards Sandy Hook. About halfway there, tacked and went to the Southward of white buoy on end of West Bank. Laid up towards the Elm Tree. Tacked and stood off shore—intending to lay up nearly to Red Bank light in Prince's Bay. Sun set, wind increasing. Captain afraid to be out. Smacks putting back, so we followed them and stood back very much disappointed. Went inside of West Bank. Dark and threatening. Worked up under lee of Staten Island, anchored off Stapleton.

Got supper. After supper George & I took the boat and boarded smacks till we found Mart' Kimberly in his new smack, the "Robert Bruce." He was very glad to see us. Spent the evening with him.

Sunday morning, Captain went on deck and immediately ordered the bonnet[9] to be unlaced from the jib. It looked very nasty in the North West. We had breakfast. The wind same as last night yet. I advised the Captain to remain where he was (I wanted to go ashore). No, he said. It was going to blow from N.W. and he had rather be South side of the island.

After breakfast found all the smacks (half a dozen) getting under weigh and mostly going up to the city. We weighed, and stood out under jib. Mart' run across our bows and told the Captain it was going to blow so he would not be able to land my stuff if he got 'round. But the Captain thought he would run into the Kills[10] and lay there till tomorrow. It was blowing a good reefing breeze then. We reefed the mainsail, but before we set it the wind increased and we put two reefs—close reefed it. "We'll get under snug sail and then take it leisurely along down," said the Skipper.

We got below the Narrows and began to haul up on the wind—S.W. I went to help the men hoist the close reefed mainsail and stood to leeward with the throat halyards.[11] We had got it about up when the Captain yelled out "Lower the mainsail. Let it go by the run."

Only it would not run. We pulled away at the down haul, but as Nony said, all the men in New Jerusalem could not get it down soon enough. Before I knew what was to pay, the sloop jumped all under almost. I ran aft and stood by the helm.

The northwester had come butt-end foremost—a regular gale. Now you may suppose with jib and helm to contend against it we were going to leeward about as much as any way. And the first thing that way was the West Bank—with one foot sounding at low water—beyond that the Romer shoal, beyond that the coast of Africa. It was absolutely necessary to have some *aft* sail on her, so we passed a lashing 'round the leach[12] and set the head of the mainsail—a sort of lazy reef or bob-mainsail.

Now she went along a good deal easier, and made better weather of it. But I can tell you, when the puffs came, if she did not shake herself, my imagination is pretty strong. The Captain, his face all quivering, had the helm. I stood alongside of him, and wished I was ashore and had gone to meeting like a good boy. I had my life-preserver on, by the way, and blew it up. (As to what I thought of it: At one time I really thought we should have put off to sea, and I reckoned how long our water would last. Of course, with all my trumpery we had *wood* enough without calculating on the carlines[13] of the "Old Jule," and potatoes, turnips, & fowls enough to go to China with. I actually went and studied the chart that I might pilot her out without hitting.

George stood by the break of the quarter-deck, catching things that were going overboard, lashing our deck load, and slapping his hands & kicking his feet. For you must understand, *ice was making* all the morning. Nony stood by the halyards—and stand there he would, the water breaking over him all the time, though the Captain ordered him half a dozen times to come aft. *Jim* was shut in the cabin with Nep' and Minny.[14] At length, Nony came aft. "It's worse than a voyage to West Indies," says he. George and he then went below.

"What are you going to do," said I to the Captain. "Nothing to do but to anchor her," he replied. And I went below—to see if I could find any shoal mud anywhere about[15] (on the chart.)

"He's going to anchor, Nony."

"She won't hold a minute."

I went on deck again and asked the Captain if he could not get her about.

"I don't know," says he, "Her mainsail is all forward. I don't think she can be brought up. I'll try it bye & bye when we get a lull."

"Nony, do you think we can get her about?"

"We can try."

And we did and succeeded. You know how it's done in such a case. Nony tended the jib, of course, and of course got well washed.

We now headed up N.E., perhaps, or better, towards Staten Island. The sail set a great deal better on this tack and we worked to windward some. We had a very large anchor and chain.

"Nony," says the Captain, "don't you think *big Jonathan* would hold her if we dropped him close in shore here?"

"The Devil! No! Nothing but hard sand there."

"Well, I shall try him anyway," says the Captain.

Forward goes Nony, and overhauls chain, &c.

We were nearly off *the cedars*—the elm tree if you remember in New Dorp plain—a quarter of a mile from shore when we came to anchor in this wise.

"Haul down the jib!" You know how confoundedly hard a jib always does come down when you need it in a hurry. That is, when it is blowing. (I sprang forward and caught hold the down haul. I was wet to the skin in an instant, and in another, all iced over.) "Haul down the mainsail. Let go the anchor (as soon as she begins to gather stern way. Not before or the chain may get foul the stock)."

Furled the jib. (Think of it.) And I tried to help the Captain smother the mainsail, but my fingers were so stiff with the icy water.

"Now you go below, Mr. Olmsted," says the Captain, "and dry yourself; we can take care of the deck."

I can tell you I was glad to go. Jim was there before me. And Nep, how glad he was to see me. Oh! how my fingers did ache, directly. The Captain came down.

"Your fingers ache? Run them through your hair," says he.

I did and found it relieved them.

We had nearly forty fathom of chain in two fathoms water. Nony stood in the bow with the lead line to feel her drag for some time. We then took ranges and concluded she held. As Nony opened the door to come down, the spray from over the *bow* reached my bookcase in the *back* of *the cabin*.

All the ships going to sea were close-reefed. A brig under close reefed fore topsail and reefed foresail. Imagine what it was in the Ben' Swan under that sail—*going free*, recollect. And think what a time for a sloop to *work to windward*. Never mind how we spent the day, only Nony got us a first rate dinner. Frigsoup, he called it—a cross between a fricassee and a chowder.

P.M. Nony was mending our sails, for they were torn some in the morning. Towards evening it lulled a good deal. Got the anchor up, close reefed mainsail & jib (bonnet off), beat down opposite Ackerly.[16] Standing in easy. Run aground. Down anchor. She swung to it. Down sail; Captain came ashore & took tea with me. 8 o'clock wind light. Arranged to boat ashore at high water in the morning.

In the night, I heard the wind up again—a regular howler. Early in the morning I went to the beach. 'Twas blowing like fury. Saw they were heaving up[17] (high water). She paid off and run under head of the jib 20 rods and grounded again. Down jib. Up again after a while, and there she lay when I commenced this letter, bumping and thumping—stern to windward and sea making a breach over it.

She finally got off and ran on under bare poles till inside the *Kill point* where she came to anchor. This P.M. it lulled again, and we got all my things ashore and most of them carted home—all of consequence, (boating them in the Kills). At 12:00 last night the Captain found the wind was up again (hauled down West) but he was aground and nothing could be done till high water. So he turned in. At *one* he was woke by being shot out across the cabin floor, the sloop having heeled down[18] of a sudden.

---

1. Olmsted is writing from his new farm in the Southfield section of Staten Island. In this letter he describes the arduous sailing trip he had when he moved from Sachem's Head to Staten Island. Apparently his brother, John, had been at Sachem's Head on Tuesday, February 29, the day on which most preparations for the trip were completed, but had left before night.
2. Fore-and-aft rigged fishing boats, often with a well for keeping fish alive.
3. Perhaps William L. Clancey (b. 1820), a mariner residing in Guilford (*Guilford Vital Records*, 3: 3).
4. Severe facial neuralgia.

5. Benoni Sweet (c. 1822–1894), son of Benoni Sweet (c. 1760–1840) of Guilford, who was a skillful bone-setter (*Commemorative Biographical Record of New Haven County, Connecticut* . . . , 2 vols. [Chicago, 1902], 2: 1066; Thomas R. Hazard, *Recollections of Olden Times: Rowland Robinson of Narragansett and His Unfortunate Daughter* [Newport, R.I.: 1879], pp. 274, 287; Guilford Vital Records, 2: 375; Connecticut Church Records, Guilford, Christ Episcopal, 1744–1909, 3: 459, in Connecticut State Library, Hartford; *Hartford Times*, Sept. 4, 1840, p. 3).
6. Very likely one of the sons of Olmsted's next-door neighbor, Luke G. Roberts.
7. The water flowing rapidly through a mill race or sluiceway.
8. A tide that occurs after the first and third quarters of the moon when the sun and the moon do not exert gravitational force in the same line; it is the smallest of tides.
9. A piece of canvas laced to the foot of a jib in moderate weather to increase sail area.
10. All references to Kills in this letter are to the Great Kills, a well-protected cove on the southeast coast of Staten Island near Olmsted's farm (William T. Davis, "Staten Island Names, Ye Olde Names and Nicknames," *Proceedings of the Natural Science Association of Staten Island* 5, no. 5 [March 14, 1896]: 30).
11. The throat halyard is the line used to raise the forward edge of a gaff-rigged sail.
12. The leach is the back edge of a fore-and-aft sail.
13. A carline is the short timber ranging fore-and-aft in a ship from one deck beam to another.
14. Olmsted's cat Minny (JO to Dear Boys, June 5, 1847).
15. That is, any nearby shallow spot with good holding ground for an anchor.
16. Samuel Akerly (1786–1845) was the previous owner of Olmsted's Staten Island farm (Margaret Boyle-Cullen, "The Woods of Arden House," *Staten Island Historian* 15, no. 1 [Jan.–March 1954]: 7–8; idem, "Arden House," ibid., no. 2 [April–June 1954]: 13).
17. That is, the men on the *Julliet* were raising the anchor.
18. The sloop had tipped far over while aground.

To CHARLES LORING BRACE

South side March 25th 1848[1]

Dear Charley,

I received a letter from you coming by way of "Guilford Sachem's Head" and Hartford, last week, in which like a good humored savage you raked me and particularly my amiable but unfortunate brother for transgressing your right angled laws of friendship. Well, as long as there are circumstances in the events of the world, or digestion in my body, or variations in the humours of my mind, I shall hold out an outlaw. So don't be *inclement.*

There is not much room for argument in regard to the *metaphysics* of your letter, as your positions are matters of opinion which reasoning has little to do with. Still the drift of some of it I must protest against. I think, Charley, I never knew the man that had graduated at a Theological Seminary that showed ordinary *charity* in his heart. I do believe it is harder for an editor and a clergyman to enter the kingdom than for a rich man. This was an observation independent and had no connection with your letter. So don't feel bad.

I believe it was suggested, however, or followed the groan I gave on noticing how much importance you do in your heart attach to matters of belief—questionable matters which can not be decided in this world and which I think it is right down wicked—absurd—filthy to look upon and act upon as absolutely decided. "Doing," and "settling" on questions of *"Belief"* —you write on the same line—as of equal importance—and the amount accomplished of each (acts and opinions) (doing good and *thinking* not good, but some way, decidedly, not *acting* decidedly) you speak of as companion labors in the work you have to do—as equally progressing you towards the object of your existence.

Now I thank God, Charley, you are not *settled* yet, not absolutely pinned down to any or but comparatively few Theological dogmas—(I hope *political* too.) May this unsatisfactory state that you weep and mourn about so much—in God's name—bother, fret, and spur you till you are perfected in the fullness of light. For just as soon as you reach the state I must infer from your letter you pray for, it will be perfectly impossible for you practically to have charity for those that differ from you. And I believe that one spark of charity is of more value than all the *results settlings*, of all the study, the light (or Grace of Belief), the candid beginning of Investigation (for candor can not progress with growing opinion) of Drs. Taylor, Edwards,[2] Luther, Calvin (whose opinions have been a terrible curse), the Holy Fathers, or the Apostles to the Hebrews & Gentiles. Without the Charity and Love they preached and which made them preach, they would stand a poor chance to be saved. Without half their opinions, in my opinion, they would have borne more sweet fruit and less bitter, sickening, cursed high taxes on Goodness.

(Except the absurdities I have written—one or two back there.) Why the devils themselves (if there are any) believe and tremble, but what good does it do 'em? Why don't they accomplish more good? How much satisfaction it must be to Beelzebub to reflect "how much he has settled upon in belief." "Life is hurrying away and how much have I *done* or *settled upon* in Belief?" That's what you say.

Take all the Commandments God has given through the Scripture and through the natural impulses of your heart, as far as they agree with conscience or reason. Can not you perform them without being firmly settled on the damnation of infants—or the salvation of infants, if you believe God's mercy is consistent with both? And if you don't, is not the belief in God's mercy a vast deal the most important of the two—more important than settling on authenticity of the passages from which you might draw the arguments against it?

What in the world do you want? *Pure Religion*, don't you—to save you—and that is "to visit & relieve the widows and fatherless."[3] It *"is before God."* Now can you not do that without believing in—"what you do not understand," as your ridiculous conscience tells you you ought to, and makes you half miserable for not doing.

You ask—and I think it is the very damndest piece of unbelief even you ever started—whether, if you are "investigating *honestly*," [the] Just and Merciful Father "will forgive" your "*mistakes?*" Why, what blasphemy! What would your earthly father do? And who was it said "Forgive them, for they know not what they do?" Is it not a good reason? And we believe that He shall come to be our Judge.

Now is your belief more culpable than that which led those men to the acts which seemed to need forgiveness? How any man can believe that Jesus Christ is one with the Father and yet be *settled* in his belief of eternal punishment to those who do—they know not what—does puzzle me as much as the Trinity itself. God has given me the Bible but I should never know it to be His word if he had not given me Reason to judge it by. And my Reason—it condemns a good deal of it. The Bible is not consistent with itself. Well, I *do not* believe the Bible to be the Word of God.

I have tried hard to believe the Bible, but I'll be hanged if I can. That is, I am not settled on it, and I never expect to be in this world. What earthly (or other) motive you can imagine yourself to have for being dishonest I can not imagine. Really, are you not splitting hairs?

You say you don't know as I can help not settling on points of belief. I can (practically) but not without, Pharoah-like, hardening my heart. You must conclude when you are settled, that every one who differs is wrong; and in consequence that their salvation is doubtful. Now, what rule have we to judge men by, but their fruits?

A Bishop of the Church of England lately preached a sermon on the death of a man that had never been baptized, never communed, and that differed in creed most essentially from the xxxix Articles.[4] (What a fence about truth xxxix makes.) "Can we doubt" (said he) "that he was in danger whose whole life was an unwearied comment on evangelical Christianity? To give a moment's heed would be a libel on Christianity itself." His life was his preparation. In death he gave no sign. His life was the sign & seal. And can you not find scores of *Christians*—as Orthodox in belief as the Devil himself, for all you know—whose life is anything but a sign of their Heavenlymindedness? And can you find the man whose actions tell, speak, a heart of Love—who imitates Christ in mercy, who is eloquent against tyranny & vice, yet charitable to the vicious even, whom you can feel God will not be merciful to? I had for my part rather be in Horace Greeley's shoes, an Infidel as your schoolmen call him, than in Dr. Bacon's or Dr. Taylor's.[5]

You ask if it is possible for a man to have true Repentance, without that knowledge of his sin which can only be obtained by a knowledge of the Infinite Sacrifice which was necessary to *wash his guilt* away. I do not believe that I ever had that knowledge (in your sense) and I do believe that I am a Christian. This can not be argued upon (this necessity). I believe that God did appear in the world as Christ: that as God, with His power and goodness, and as man with his weakness—his temptation to use the Power to punish those who injured him (or sinned) and man's capability of suffering, he came for the salvation (from temporal, perhaps eternal misery) of His children. Here He displayed His Infinite Goodness, which the natural man was incapable of trusting without, whilst He showed us the Height of excellence and triumph over Human failings we might strive to attain, in the forgiveness of His enemies. He led us to worship such goodness (and thus presented us with a true God to worship). To Love such Goodness and to Love Him—consequently to hate sin—to hate ourselves. Not to worship Happiness. To worship Goodness. Not to love our depraved selves. To love God and the God-like in ourselves.

So as a lamb that suffered for the sins of men, He poured out his blood freely and gladly that we might see and believe that no atonement was necessary to reach His Mercy: that we might have Faith in His Infinite Goodness, Mercy, and through this Faith we might be led to Love Him. Worship Him. Strive to be like Him. Strive for a new life. More! Knowing the frailty of our fallen nature and the temptations that beset us; pitying us as a Father pitieth His children and as a Father ready to give good gifts to them that ask him, He has promised that to them that have this Faith—if they heartily believe (for if so they will heartily desire it) that He is so good and so ready to help them—He will quicken and renew in their hearts His holy spirit, that as new creatures in Christ they may hereafter live to Him & Goodness, not to Sin and themselves.

"God judgeth the heart." It is not the past sin, but the present purpose which *is* a man's heart.

I skipped this page accidentally. It comes after the next leaf.

When I say I don't believe the Bible, of course I mean that I do not firmly, fixedly, *settled*-ly believe it: and I really rather think we can not depend on it, as a settling thing for all doctrine, for it does seem there is a good deal of man's handiwork in it.

I ought to fill this page out with the *French Revolution*. But—as everybody else says, wait till the next steamer arrives.[6] I think that scene in the Deputies, with those bold presaging words—the voice of Divine decree as it were—that low, calm voice, to be for the next twelve-months the nightmare of all tyrants—*It is too late*. I think it will stand as about the most impressive scene in History.[7]

I wish I were that man. Jeremiah will stand no higher. It is too late. Hear it, fools. Hear it, slaves, and have Faith. Hear it, Nicholas![8] Hear it, Metternich! Hear it Irish landlords! Hear it Scotch lairds and English hunters. Hear it Slaveholding sons of America and prepare to meet—or avert—your fate. (Whoop!)

I wish I was a German now. I wouldn't stay here long. I am going to join the European Revolutionary Vigilance Committee. Hurrah for a General

War—only a short one. I only wish now Henry Clay was President or Daniel Webster or any statesman. Only there is not any other. Oh, if I was a Pole now wouldn't I! I'd open a recruiting office in five minutes. Give you the chaplaincy—Blackcoat.

I really revel in a *Righteous* War. As it is, I don't see as you and I can do much but pray & praise—and burn tar barrels and hurrah. I mean to do that thing next week. I keep a bright look to Sandy Hook for the "*Caledonia.*" Horrid ship wreck wasn't it?[9] See you perhaps next week.

P.S. Just in time it comes! I congratulate you on the *Republic!* God bless Lamartine![10]

Stoned from under, House of Lords!

1. "South side" was the local name for the section of Staten Island where Olmsted's farm was located (W. T. Davis, "Staten Island Names," p. 64).
2. American theologians Nathaniel W. Taylor and Jonathan Edwards.
3. This statement, with its emphasis on good works and lack of concern for doctrinal questions, indicates the direction Olmsted's religious convictions were to take. It anticipates his last formal statement on the subject, which he included in his *Walks and Talks of an American Farmer in England:* " 'True religion is this: to visit the widows and fatherless in their affliction, and to keep oneself unspotted in the world' " (1: 245). Both statements are close paraphrases of the Epistle of James 1:27: "Pure religion and undefiled before God and the Father is this, To visit the fatherless and widows in their affliction, *and* to keep himself unspotted from the world."
4. The Thirty-nine Articles were formulated by the Church of England during the sixteenth century as the statement of its doctrinal position. The clergy, but not the laity, were required to subscribe to them. In 1801 the Protestant Episcopal church in the United States adopted them, with some modifications (William Stevens Perry, ed., *Journals of the General Conventions of the Protestant Episcopal Church in the United States, 1785–1835* [Claremont, N.H., 1874], 1 [1785–1821]: 279–80).
5. Horace Greeley, editor of the *New York Daily Tribune,* was an enthusiastic supporter of many innovations of the day, including spiritualism. Leonard Bacon, minister of the First Church of New Haven, was "regarded as the most formidable polemical writer and speaker in the American Congregationalism of his day."

    Nathaniel W. Taylor was a Congregational theologian, a student and intimate of Timothy Dwight (1752–1817). He became Dwight Professor of Didactic Theology at Yale Divinity School in 1822 and was still preaching when Olmsted and his friends attended the college. His name was apparently a byword among the students for brilliance and skillful argument. In the same year this letter was written, Charles Loring Brace wrote of Olmsted: "I must say Fred is getting to argue with the utmost keenness,—a regular Dr. Taylor mind in its analytic power!" As a theologian, Taylor challenged the Congregational doctrine concerning freedom of the will as formulated by Jonathan Edwards, and his teaching split New England Congregationalism into two camps. On one side were his supporters, the "Taylorites," while on the other were the "Tylerites," adherents of the Calvinist president of the Hartford Theological Seminary, Bennet Tyler. The controversy carried into the Presbyterian church and was the main theological reason for its disruption in 1838 (William H. Hale, *Horace Greeley, Voice of the People* [New York, 1950], pp. 91–107; *DAB,* s.v. "Bacon, Leonard," "Taylor, Nathaniel William"; CLB to FJK, Oct. 1848, quoted in *Life of Brace,* p. 61) .
6. The *New York Daily Tribune* of March 20, 1848, had brought the news of the abdication of King Louis Philippe of France and the formation of a provisional government with the poet and politician Alphonse de Lamartine (1790–1869) as its

most important member. The fate of the regime—and whether it would retain some form of monarchy or declare a republic—was unknown.

7. Olmsted is referring to a scene at the Chamber of Deputies on the day after Louis Philippe's abdication in favor of the young son of his dead son, the duc d'Orleans. When the Deputies met on that day, the duchesse d'Orleans appeared with her son, the heir-designate, in hopes of gaining approval for his succession and her regency. As the *Tribune* described it:

> She makes her way with difficulty through the crowd, and reaches a seat. The presence of the child impresses the assembly, but does not put an end to the uproar.
> At last silence is obtained, and then a member rises and says that the King has abdicated and conferred the Regency on the Duchess. That is a critical moment. Shall the act be confirmed? Will the Chamber and the people accept the new King and Regent? No! a voice from the gallery cries, "It is too late!" So it is all over with the House of Orleans. The shrewd statesman, the great manager, LOUIS PHILIPPE, has waited till it was too late.

(*New York Daily Tribune*, March 20, 1848, pp. 2–3).

8. Nicholas I (1796–1855), czar of Russia, who worked from the time of Napoleon I to forge an alliance among the monarchies of Europe to withstand and suppress revolutionary movements. He had wished to use armed force to put down the revolutions of France and Belgium in 1830, and used Russian troops to crush the Polish insurrection of that year. Prince Clemens Lothar von Metternich (1773–1859), the chancellor of Austria, was the leading diplomat in this attempt to protect the European *status quo*, and during the previous decade he had become "a hated symbol of repression and reaction" (*EB*).

9. The *Caledonia* was a steamship of the Cunard Line, which began fortnightly mail service to New York from Liverpool on January 1, 1848. The shipwreck to which Olmsted refers was that of the *Omega*, which sailed from Liverpool for New York with 315 passengers on January 16, 1848. She was disabled in a storm and drifted on the Grand Banks for a week. Then the bark *Aurora* sighted her and took off 166 passengers, of whom 60 died of cold and hunger before reaching Nova Scotia. On February 11 the *Omega* met the brig *Barbara*. All but 30 of her remaining passengers and crew had been transferred to the *Barbara* when the ships were separated by a gale in which the *Omega* foundered. The *Barbara* attempted to reach St. John's, Newfoundland, but was wrecked on that coast in a blizzard and left fewer than 40 survivors (David B. Tyler, *Steam Conquers the Atlantic* [New York, 1939], p. 91; Robert G. Albion, *The Rise of New York Port, 1815–1860* [New York, 1939], p. 325; *New York Daily Tribune*, March 24, 1848, p. 1, March 27, 1848, p. 2.)

10. The *New York Daily Tribune* of March 28, 1848, brought news of the flight of Louis Philippe and his family to England and the declaration of a republic by the French provisional government. It also told of the provisional government's abolition of the Chamber of Peers, created with the Restoration of the Bourbons in 1814, and the abolition of titles of nobility.

To CHARLES LORING BRACE [July 4, 1848]

South side, 1st, 73 I., U.S.[1]

Fellow Citizen,

Hurrah for the Republic! I always get up early on the glorious anniversary. This morning I found it was half past three (a few minutes after I went to bed). Turned out with alacrity, rushed to the window and according

OLMSTED'S STATEN ISLAND FARMHOUSE

to my old custom—that is, the costume of a night gown and hair *au naturel*—I welcomed the blush in the east (becoming a *modest* sky as she is reminded of the birth of liberty), which announced the approach of the glorious (no other word) day (*Day* reminds of Horace of that ilk.[2] If you see John[3] ask him to tell you something about him. If not, remind me of it) and waked up the drowsy household & disturbed the fowls with the discharge of both barrels and the pistol, concluding with a feu de joie of crackers. (Aunty[4] thought I had just discovered that Nep had gone mad and was putting an end to his misery.) I have sent all the men and women[5] off to the city—and stay at home myself to see the hay spoil—and write to you.

I have given up writing all those letters of my Fancy, the hope for the leisure for which has delayed me so long. I have a great deal to talk to you—but can write but little. Sacred be this day to Patriotism and Politics. I was much pleased, Charley, with the political part of your last letter. I think I sympathize very closely with your feelings. And so far as you expressed *opinions*, I even agree with you more than usual. I am willing to admit that I exalted Clay too highly. His northern tour[6] did seem to me to show a little of the imbecility of age. Before the Convention[7] met, my zeal for him had cooled, but in favor of a northern man—no 10th-rate availability man—no fierce sectional—but for Daniel Webster.[8] *Not all I could ask*, but on the whole far the best man for President now living I think. But if I did exalt Clay I do not think it began to be as much as you depreciated him.

I confess, I do think you took a more bigoted, mean, partisan view of him than I know you to of anything else. It makes me afraid of you as a partisan. Loving your friends or favorites superabundantly is a very different thing from despising and refusing to consider favorably an enemy. I think that there was something entirely wrong at the bottom of your view of Clay—or rather your distortions of him, for you refused to view him.

319

THE PAPERS OF FREDERICK LAW OLMSTED

I am not sorry to see the prospect of General Taylor's election. I think much good will be done by that, besides the somewhat dubious good you think so much of. It will break old parties. And the fact that the respectable old, Federal, moral, orthodox Dr. Hawes Whigs of little Connecticut stand almost to a man to their guns, "without a why or wherefore," after such a flag has been run up over them, shows how much any influence against party trammels is to be desired.[9]

Mind you, I am not despising them for thinking General Taylor *is* good enough Whig for them, but because they evidently in Connecticut—the main body of them—have not thought at all. They either consider their delegates supreme judges, against whose decision their reason cannot appeal, or they think how a turncoat would be despised—not a turncoat from principles, but from men, with whom he has acted, i.e., from party.

This I think is plainly indicated by the fact that so few of those who speak have disagreed from the main body—or the Convention. I do not doubt they will be surprised to find (at the election) how many have thought for themselves and come to a different opinion from the delegates.

You understand that I do not consider it a matter of course, nor do I mean you shall imply that I think it equally probable that honest men should come to a different decision from the delegates that nominated Taylor. I do think they had a very hard question indeed to decide. I do not believe a body of clergymen—under similar circumstances—would have conducted themselves as reasonably and gentlemanly to a decision.

If they had simply declared themselves unable to agree as "*Whigs*" and then, as many as pleased, organized a new party, made a declaration of objects and principles on which they or a certain respectable number of them could agree—such as (objects) union (opposition to sectional action), opposition to War Policy—the reduction of the Army and Navy without prejudice to the *old* officers[10]—a moderate increase of Protection to certain manufactures—Internal Improvement, and in general opposition to the besotted *laisser aller* (faire) principle (pretended) of Loco Focoism,[11] and nominated Taylor as the leader of these or such measures—I should have honored them—and been quite as likely to vote with them—as now.

After all, I am not at all sure but they were right as they were. If they had nominated anybody but Taylor (just then), they could not calculate on the Barnburners[12] as allies. Cass would very probably have cursed and disgraced the country as its President. I think it is right of two evils to choose the least. If you thought your vote would elect Taylor over *Cass*, should he not have it, even though by permitting Cass' election you gave expression to your dislike to *both* of them? I think the Philadelphia Convention was in such a predicament. Fortunately you and I are not, I think.

1. The date of the letter is the first day of the 73d year of the Independence of the United States, or July 4, 1848.
2. Horace Day (1816–1892), a New Haven bookseller and, later, superintendent of the New Haven schools (Yale University, Class of 1836, *Historical and Biographical Record of the Class of 1836, in Yale College for Fifty Years from the Admission of the Class to College* [New Haven, 1882], p. 39).
3. John Hull Olmsted.
4. Maria Olmsted, who had come to the Staten Island farm to act as housekeeper (*Forty Years*, 1: 79).
5. Olmsted's hired help: two Irish girls and a boy, six regular Irish field hands, and two harvest hands whom he boarded (FLO to FJK, May 10, and July 16, 1848, in FJK Sketch of FLO).
6. In late February and early March 1848, Henry Clay made a trip from Washington to Philadelphia and New York in an attempt to strengthen his bid for the Whig presidential nomination.
7. The Whig National Convention met in Philadelphia on June 7, 1848.
8. When the Whig convention opened, most of the New England delegates favored the candidacy of Daniel Webster. They quickly threw their support to Gen. Zachary Taylor, however, justifying their action with the claim that he was the only Whig capable of winning the election (Allan Nevins, *Ordeal of the Union*, 1: 198–201).
9. The Dr. Hawes to whom Olmsted refers was Joel Hawes, for many years the Olmsted family's minister and pastor of the First Congregational Church in Hartford. Part of what chagrined Olmsted about the work of the Whig National Convention was that after choosing its candidates it quickly adjourned without drawing up a platform (ibid., 1: 202).
10. This policy of reducing the army and navy was not part of the Whig party program of the time, and Olmsted's espousal of it was probably due to the influence of George Geddes. While at Fairmount he wrote Frederick Kingsbury that Geddes "goes for disbanding all armies and navies. Let the frontier take care of itself and commerce take care of itself. Insurance Companies build men of war, etc." (FLO to FJK, May 15, 1846; see also FLO to JO, Aug. 12, 1846, above).
11. In this phrase Olmsted expresses his belief that the principles of the Democratic party, especially its Loco-Foco wing, left too many activities in the hands of private citizens who pursued their own profit rather than the public good. He wanted an active government that met the needs of the community and promoted the well-being of those without wealth and power (FLO to CLB, Dec. 1, 1853).
12. The Barnburners were the radical antislavery faction of the Democratic party.

To FREDERICK KINGSBURY
Entepfuhl[1]

Nov. 17th, 1848
Wednesday

My dear Fred,

I received your kind letter last night—by the post mark it was a week and a half old.

I do not feel like answering much to your remarks on the condition of my heart and mind. The fact *that* I do not, is perhaps indicative of an improvement since I wrote you last—and I thank God heartily that I believe there has been some. Although the same mental difficulty would arise—or is yet obvious—I do not feel inclined so much to look at—and be querulous. Perhaps in short, it is nothing more in Bible language than a brighter Faith.

Though I should like to have your view a little more distinctly expressed (Is it not rather indistinct to yourself?), I believe I understand it pretty well. I think if I had been in your place I should have tried to say about the same thing. But I wonder if you would not hesitate to follow it out, and use it as a foundation of further opinions. I would not, I think. It is a very important point—to all Christians, to all just men. I should think it might be particularly interesting to [those] interested in Criminal Law. I never saw a cool opinion about Moral Insanity. Most men think it necessary to be violently enraged when it is mentioned to show that they are safe. I always proclaim myself a "dangerous man." I know that I am. I know that there is danger in my opinions—danger to the "basis of society" and all that. But sweeping fires—whirlwinds &c sometimes make way for good. I am not afraid of Revolutions though I may dread them. (This flight is not based you understand simply on "Moral Insanity" but on the general tendency of my opinions—or my Faith.)

Of Moral Insanity (you will see what I call so) I can have no doubt. Set up a Moral point—an ultimate, on which Morality shall be to a certain extent founded. To the mind's eye of Charley Brace it is—White. To Henry Brace[2] it is Red, to me they are both absurd, and I know—and see as plain as I see this ink—and it is Black—stark, staring Black—and the man must be mad who can doubt it. Charley says sometimes I seem to see or think I see something the rest do not, & hang me if I don't—not what they do not—nor what they can not—but as it seems to me, what they *will* not. They refuse to, or else they lie, or are crazy.

I know how apt a man is to deceive himself, and to hug his opinions that he has taken up almost accidentally. But about these things I feel very sure that I am honest. They are not matters of Conscience, but of Reason—and sink or swim I hold them, and if they burn, I must burn with them. I know this much, that in prospect of death I can not throw them overboard. My own Reason must pilot, and if she runs down the Bible, my own heart & my own friends, I can not take the helm from her.

As to "Theories & Creeds," there I should like to fight you. I know that if I could get at half the ammunition I have stowed away somewhere, and aim it with any sort of distinctness I could stand you a pretty good game. But I am all fogged up with a horrid cold in the head this P.M., and if I think any more I shall be having a fit.

I will write you again in a few days perhaps. Meantime I wish you would think a little about this "morbid action of the mind," &c. & write me.

That is as long a sentence as I can write without my head's throbbing.

It is a good subject for a Christian to think about too. Do what you will with the facts the consideration must provoke charity.

Your view of Farming and Pears was very commonsensible, but I could tell you some circumstances that you did not consider—that are necessary to a correct idea of my position.

We did have a pleasant time with Emma Brace. She had the worst of the worst gale of this year, but got safe through it; that's all we know.[3] I think you said something about her that was not *precisely* honest. I'll see when I come up.

My regards to Dudley[4]—and with congratulations to Mrs. Russ and—no the baby is too green yet. I'll spare you.

I called on Ellen Day,[5] thank you.

I'll say only just enough more to fill out the page.

Yrs

F. L. Olmsted

1. In relation to this heading, Kingsbury noted in the margin, "A name which he proposed for his place, taken I think from Sartor Resartus." Entepfuhl was the village where the hero of Thomas Carlyle's *Sartor Resartus* spent his idyllic childhood.
2. Henry Martin Brace (1828–1901), a cousin of Charles Loring Brace and Yale classmate of John Hull Olmsted (J. S. Brace, *Brace Lineage*, p. 104; *Yale Obit. Rec.*, 5th ser., no. 2 [June 1902]: 133).
3. Emma Brace had sailed for Charleston, S.C., on her way to Georgia, on November 4, 1848 (JO Journal, Nov. 4, 1848; JO to FJK, Oct. 30, 1848; JHO to FJK, Feb. 10, 1849).
4. Oliver Dudley Cooke, who was teaching at the American Asylum for the Deaf and Dumb in Hartford. At this time Kingsbury was in Hartford studying law with Thomas C. Perkins (*Kingsbury Autobiography*, pt. 3).
5. Ellen Day of New Haven (see FLO to CLB, Jan. 27, 1847, note 3).

To John Hull Olmsted

Hartford, Friday, February 10th, 1849

Dear John,

I worried up to 32nd St. and found I had to wait an hour and a half for the Express train. So when the accommodation came along I took that.[1] Waited over half an hour in New Haven for the boat; which not arriving, we were sent on by an accommodation train.

The time keeps being cut up by short snow squalls here, and every day seems to be the last of the sleighing, and then the bare spots are covered again. I have taken Fanny, Mary, Bertha[2] in the cutter and had a short ride with Mrs. Robinson, Sarah, and Emily in the big sleigh yesterday, landing them at Mrs. Perkins',[3] where I spent the P.M. reading Macaulay[4] to them, and am asked to do the same at Mrs. Robinson's this P.M.

I spent the evening reading and discussing *Modern Painters*[5] with

Miss Stevens[6] who is much interested in it—alternating it with Noctes Ambrosianae.[7] Fred K.[8] left the morning I reached here. Jim Beecher is here and I see him. He goes to New York next Monday to sail in the (that same) "Samuel H. Russell."[9]

Mother is in Northampton and is trying to draw all the world after her. Father received yesterday from her a letter urging and begging him to go about preaching water cure[10] to Mrs. Robinson, Pomeroy, Tainter, Gill,[11] and I don't know how many more—whom she is convinced stand greatly in need of the cure. Also a lot more who have female children between 14 & 15 years of age are urged by every consideration of duty to posterity to bundle and walk—to the *Hall* of Vigor and Regularity. Bertha & Mary Robinson[12] it is thought *will* be *baptized adults*. Father is converted, I think, and will have a serious talk with Mr. Robinson. Mrs. Robinson is anxious—and will let her husband decide. Mrs. Perkins[13] is also getting the Missionary Spirit.

To fill out the page: George Olmsted has failed;[14] the Irishman that whipped his children is dead and denied a Christian burial. Miss Imlay[15] is dead. Mother has taken a decent little girl to bring up.[16]

Monday morning. The "American Hall" was burnt Sunday morning (4 o'clock). The lower story was not injured much, but pretty much all above was consumed. Walls standing. Cardelli the artist suffered most. His paintings and his grand piano were burnt.[17]

Jim Beecher goes this evening. That is, if his friends do not persuade him not to. I was just now at Mrs. Perkins' where there were three of them at him—hard. I could not get any last weekly papers to send by him. They are all sold out or burnt up at the news offices. If you *can*, give him one before he goes and a paper with the last steamer's news.

I read Macaulay every P.M. with or to the Robinsons and Perkins', and call every morning to see *whether I shall*. The conclusion is that Emily is the most lovely and loveable girl. Oh, she is. Well, I really think she has the most incomparably fine face I ever saw. And she is a real tender sensible downright good woman.

The Modern Painters improves on acquaintance and Miss Stevens forms an amalgam with it in my heart. She is just the thing to read it or have it read to one by. She is very sensitive to beauty—thoughtful, penetrating, enthusiastic. There is a capital review (very flattering) of it in *North British Review* (Feb.) 1847[18] which is worth your reading—as it gives the cream of the book. I am very anxious to get the second volume.

Roderick Terry, senior,[19] is dead.

There is a great snowstorm coming now—just in time again—for the sleighing stopped yesterday.

Mother is writing communications for the Courant on Hydropathy.

Aunty & I send love to Julia[20] & you, and suppose she knows "Julia Lafaette" is about to be married to a southron—lawyer.

324

Bertha has stopped going to school.

If you have an opportunity, borrow the 2nd vol. Modern Painters of Mr. Hoppin and send us.

Miss Stevens had been admiring the clouds with 'Livy Day[21] the other morning. She (Miss S.) said, "I have been reading the—."

(Livy,) "*Modern Painters*. I thought so. So have I."

1. Olmsted went from Staten Island to Hartford via New York on February 6. An accommodation train was one that made all local stops needed by its passengers (JHO to FJK, Feb. 10, 1849; *OED*).
2. Olmsted's cousin Frances Olmsted and his half-sisters Mary and Bertha.
3. Olmsted's sleighing companions were Anne Seymour Robinson (1801–1892), wife of David Franklin Robinson of Hartford, her daughter Sarah Amelia Robinson (1829–1909), and Emily Perkins. He drove them to Emily's home on Asylum Street in Hartford (D. L. Jacobus, *History of the Seymour Family*, p. 230).
4. The first two volumes of Thomas Babington Macaulay's history of England, which Olmsted was reading with his friends, had been published only three months before. It met with immediate success in England and had a reception comparable only to that given the novels of Sir Walter Scott and Charles Dickens (*DNB*).
5. John Ruskin's great work, which had a strong influence on Olmsted's aesthetic views. In 1847–1848 Willey and Putnam of New York published the first two volumes, which Ruskin had published in England in 1843 and 1846.
6. Sophia Stevens.
7. The series entitled "Noctes Ambrosianae" began in *Blackwood's Magazine* in 1822. It contained "discussions in the form of convivial table-talk, giving occasion to wonderfully various digressions of criticism, description and miscellaneous writing." After 1825 it was mostly the work of the Scottish writer John Wilson (1785–1854), who wrote for *Blackwood's* under the pseudonym of "Christopher North." The American edition of these pieces, published by Carey and Hart of Philadelphia in 1843, contained those that had appeared in *Blackwood's* between 1825 and 1835 (*EB*, s.v. "Wilson, John").
8. Frederick Kingsbury.
9. James Beecher (1828–1886), youngest son of Lyman Beecher. After graduating from Dartmouth in 1848 he spent five years on vessels in the East India trade, first as a seaman and then as an officer. In 1853 he returned to study for the ministry at Andover Theological Seminary, but he could not leave the sea behind completely. After his ordination he took charge of the Seamen's Bethel in Hong Kong, where he remained until the outbreak of the Civil War. The first ship on which he sailed was the fast *Samuel H. Russell*, built in New York in 1847 and owned by Abiel Abbot Low of Brooklyn, partner of one of the largest firms in the China trade. Before Beecher left on his first voyage, Olmsted gave him extensive advice about what gear to take with him (Lyman Beecher Stowe, *Saints, Sinners, and Beechers* [New York, 1934], pp. 384–85; [*The Original American Lloyd's Register*], *New York Marine Register: A Standard of Classification of American Vessels* [New York, 1857], p. 59; *DAB*, s.v. "Low, Abiel Abbot"; FLO to JHO, Feb. 13, 1849).
10. Mary Bull Olmsted made several trips to the water-cure establishments at Northampton, Mass., in early 1849. She often took along friends and relations, and generally approached the subject in evangelical fashion. She went to the Round Hill Water Cure, started by Samuel Whitmarsh in 1847, and occasionally visited the older Ruggles' Water Cure Establishment, run by David Ruggles, a Connecticut-born Negro, and the newer Springdale Water Cure, started in 1848 by Dr. E. E. Denniston. All these water-cure centers followed the methods devised by the German hydropathist Vincent Priessnitz (c. 1829). They involved hot and cold baths, compresses and poultices, and the drinking of water (JO Journal, Jan. 18 to April

19, 1849; Dorothy B. Porter and Edwin C. Rozwenc, "The Water Cures," in *The Northampton Book: Chapters from 300 Years in the Life of a New England Town* [Northampton, Mass., 1954], pp. 121–26; *EB*, s.v. "Hydropathy").

11. Anne Seymour Robinson; Elizabeth Russell Collins Pomeroy (d. 1881) wife of Alexander Hamilton Pomeroy of Hartford, who lived on the same street as the Olmsteds; Mrs. Adelia Croade Taintor (1804–1881), wife of John Taintor, wool dealer; Mary Elizabeth Southmayd Gill (1814–1880), wife of Alfred Gill, lumber dealer (Albert H. Pomeroy, *History and Genealogy of the Pomeroy Family* [Toledo, Ohio, 1912–22], p. 613; *Geer's Directory for 1847–1848*, pp. 56, 92; Headstone Inscriptions, Hartford, Cemetery 4, p. 67; *Yale Obit. Rec.*, 1st ser., no. 4 [July 1863]: 93; Headstone Inscriptions, Middletown, Cemetery 1, p. 121).

12. Bertha Olmsted and Mary Caroline Robinson (1834–1903), daughter of Anne and David Robinson (D. L. Jacobus, *Seymour Family*, p. 230).

13. Mary Beecher Perkins, mother of Emily Perkins.

14. George Olmsted (1793–1849), a relative who died March 7, 1849 (*Olmsted Genealogy*, p. 63).

15. Henrietta Imlay (1823–1849), daughter of William and Phoebe Imlay (Hugh and Nella Imlay, *The Imlay Family* [Zanesville, Ohio, 1958], pp. 49, 51; JO Journal, Feb. 7, 1849).

16. JO Journal, Oct. 3, 1849: "Rec'd from Brooklyn Orphan Asylum, Sarah Jane Muir, born May 8, 1841."

17. The American Hall, a public building in Hartford, burned on February 11, 1849. Liberto Cardella, an Italian painter living in Hartford, lost many paintings in the fire (JO Journal, Feb. 11, 1849; *Geer's Directory for 1849*, p. 31; *Hartford Daily Courant*, Feb. 12, 1849, p. 2; George C. Groce and David H. Wallace, *Dictionary of Artists in America, 1564–1860* [New Haven, Conn., 1957], p. 108).

18. The laudatory review of the first volume of John Ruskin's *Modern Painters* was an anonymous article in the *North British Review* 6 (Feb. 1847): 401–30.

19. Roderick Terry, grocer, whose store was in Hartford. He died on February 9 (S. Terry, *Terry Families*, p. 38; *Geer's Directory for 1847–1848*, p. 113).

20. Probably Olmsted's cousin Julia Mason Olmsted (1832–1880), daughter of Yale professor Denison Olmsted (*Olmsted Genealogy*, p. 73).

21. Olivia Day, daughter of Jeremiah Day, president of Yale.

To John Hull Olmsted

Address: Mr. John H. Olmsted/Care of Mrs. Lewis[1]
36 Fourth St./New York
Postmark: Hartford Ct./26 Feb. 5

Hartford, Feby 24th, 1849. Saturday

Dear John,

It is very hard to get in a mood of writing. One does not feel like repeating in a letter what he has been saying. And I don't think about anything now that I care about, or that could be written about, that I don't immediately blab it to Miss Stevens or Miss Emily.[2]

The principal subjects upon which I am *exercised* now are (in the neighborhood of Sundays): Dr. Bushnell's Theory of Language—Instinctive (apparently) perception of Truth and subjects adjacent thereto—Landscape

Beauty and the Beauty of all nature, and of faces which beat all nature;[3] the Theory, Economy, and Moral Philosophy of Love and Courtship or Courtship and Love; Past Depravity of Human Nature as shown by Macaulay in Lord Jeffries and James 2nd and his devilish queen[4] (one of Mrs. Strickland's angels[5]), and present perfection as evident in Emily.

All these I enjoy in company with Miss Stevens and Emily—and sometimes with Mrs. Perkins & Mrs. Robinson & Sarah, Livy Day[6] and Tom Beecher. With the latter I have got on very thick and careless terms. Have stayed late with him two evenings and he has opened his private box a good deal to me. I think he is a great man (with some weak links) and I shall not be at all surprised if he turns society completely over here in a few years. He'll do something great among ideas here if he stays long.[7]

I continue to meet the Macaulay Club every day at Mrs. Robinson's and enjoy it very much. Walking home with Emily often and going in sometimes (when her mother stops on the way) to finish the conversation, I have got very intimate with her and gallantry and joking aside, really think her a very fine girl. Really one of us, "one of ours," and enjoying our things more than any of us except perhaps Charley.

I had the most delicious sleigh ride with her yesterday—on the ice, double team in the cutter. We went to Farmington River and back; *weather mild* and sleighing of course capital—though the streets are wholly bare in the city. I have never enjoyed anything of the sort nearly as much and she said the same.

In the evening after school I had another delightful one with Miss Stevens and Miss 'Livy—who sang richly.

Later in the evening, I went to the *Sociable* at Mrs. Bunce's.[8] I confined my attention to Miss Brognard and Fanny[9] *and* the refreshments, and enjoyed myself from sympathy with the rest of the company, which was quite large. Strange enough, I was able not to speak to either Emily or Sarah. I went home with Tom Beecher and stayed late with him.

Dud and 'Liph[10] I have met once or twice.

I have read Dr. B's first discourse—and want to read it again. Miss Stevens has read the second.[11] She says it is just what I want.

Spring weather. Nothing new from Northampton.[12]

That letter was from Mrs. LeConte, not Elizabeth. The main object of it was to learn whether I would be willing to take Edwin this summer.[13] She and all the girls are very anxious I should—for his improvement—and I am not surprised. I replied that I would and tried to have them understand that it would not be convenient for me to take anyone else.

I have been reading (part of) Dr. Bushnell on *atonement* and do like it very much. The sermon on the Trinity,[14] I was not much interested in—that is, not nearly as much, because personally it is not important. I have had all sorts of belief in regard to the Trinity and all shades, my impression never very strong. Sometimes I have acknowledged myself a Unitarian—as much as any thing. Never have been at all satisfied, and never very much worried about any of them. Lately I have thought it of very little practical consequence and could hardly have expressed any opinion as to the Trinity and Unity.

But in regard to the atonement, so-called, that is the subject of Dr. B's second Discourse. I have found the "doctrine" he advocates very important to me.[15] It has influenced me to good. I have grown better for believing it. I have never assented with understanding or cordiality to any other. Yet, I have not held it clearly and distinctly enough, and I have seen a good many difficulties in regard to it. I could not reconcile certain passages of the Scripture with it and perhaps false views falsely based on those passages.

But I think Dr. B has set it all right. It's a glorious, reasonable view; I believe it will be generally received. And when our ministers will not feel it their duty to preach Christ solely to the understanding, but let Christ come as Love and not as Logic, the world will grow better faster than it ever has done before. The Devil will draw up Logic against Logic wherever he thinks it will pay to all eternity, but he can't do much against the sword of the Spirit when it's pointed against Spirit. Heart answereth to Heart and not to Head.

We expect to hear from you this evening. If so, you may expect to hear again from me soon.

I hope to hear in regard to H. William Blaken,[16] as I want if I can be sure of getting rid of him, to take Terry the Orphan.[17]

Monday noon. Charley Trask[18] and George Hill[19] have been both in town since Saturday night. They called on me this morning, and Charley remained with me till they left this noon. They are both looking very well indeed, better than ever before. Charley you will probably see tomorrow *en route* to St. Petersburg. He will tell you all about himself. If he don't I will when I come down. I enjoyed his visit *entirely.*

Last evening owing to a storm I was permitted to enter the "Sunday Sociable" (*private* club) with Miss Stevens. There were only Sarah Day, Emily, Sarah, Eliz. Hammersley, 'Livy, Miss S., the Day's boarder, Tom,[20] & myself. The subject of conversation and Bible study was something like "The Apostolic Expression of Christian Character." What was it? Shown in their writings and actions. Of course, it was very pleasant, though Tom was rather frightfully earnest.

After conversation we had some singing. Is it not a most useful and agreeable way of spending an evening, particularly Sunday evening? Next Saturday night they meet again at Mrs. Hammersley's.[21] Sarah Day told me to come under her protection, and I shall be very glad. The subject—The "Magnanimity of Christ" as displayed anywhere and everywhere—&c., &c. I proposed it. Sarah Day showed a quick perception of me in immediately remarking that I thought that *smallness* was commonly thought a necessary part of Christian Character rather than greatness. "So do I," she added.

Why have I not heard from J. Van Peet[22] about the turnips that were in the schooner? Do you know anything about them? The hay also.

I shall remain till after next Sunday on account of Communion. May probably leave immediately after with Aunty,[23] who would like to [*visit Cheshire on the way*],[24] and may remain a few days next week on Aunty's account.

I gave Charley a scrawl to introduce him to Buck Bull.[25] I wish you could give him another instead of it.

1. John Hull Olmsted boarded with an Abby Lewis at 362 Fourth Street while a student at the New York College of Physicians and Surgeons (JHO to FJK, Oct. 30, 1848; FLO to JHO, Jan. 6, 1849; *Doggett's New York City Directory, 1847–48* [New York, 1848], p. 247).
2. Sophia Stevens and Emily Perkins.
3. Olmsted is speaking here of the various elements of his intellectual fare during his stay in Hartford in early 1849. He was attending Horace Bushnell's church and perhaps reading his new book, *God in Christ: Three Discourses . . . with a Preliminary Dissertation on Language* [Hartford, 1849]. In the first section of the book, "Preliminary Dissertation on the Nature of Language, as Related to Thought and Spirit," Bushnell asserted the symbolic nature of language and the impossibility of reducing Christian truth to statements of dogma. The mixture of other subjects is explained by John Hull Olmsted's report to Frederick Kingsbury that "Fred is reading Macaulay loud to Emily Perkins & 'Modern Painters' to Miss Stevens—and is somewhat intoxicated between the two" (JHO to FJK, Feb. 10, 1849).
4. George Jeffreys (1648–1689), First Baron of Wem and Lord Chancellor of James II. As Macaulay noted, "the depravity of this man has passed into a proverb." He is remembered as the "hanging judge" of the so-called Bloody Assizes held in 1685 for the trial of participants in the Duke of Monmouth's Insurrection. As a result of the assizes over three hundred persons were executed and hundreds more sold into slavery in the West Indies. Macaulay also judged James II harshly, observing that his administration of Scotland "was marked by odious laws, by barbarous punishments, and by judgments to the iniquity of which even that age furnished no parallel. . . ." Macaulay characterized James's queen, the Catholic Mary Beatrice of Modena (1658–1718), as possessed of "princely greediness and unwomanly cruelty" (*EB*, s.v. "Jeffreys, George"; Thomas Babington Macaulay, *The History of England from the Accession of James II*, 5 vols. [New York, 1849–1861], 1: 253, 417, 606).
5. Agnes Strickland (1796–1874), English historian, thought that Mary Beatrice of Modena had "conjugal tenderness and passionate maternity, like one of the distressed queens of tragedy" (Agnes Strickland, *Lives of the Queens of England, From the Norman Conquest . . . , Private as Well as Public*, 12 vols. [London, 1840–1848], 9: x).
6. Mary Beecher Perkins, Anne Seymour Robinson, Sarah Amelia Robinson, and Olivia Day.
7. Olmsted's estimation of Thomas K. Beecher (1824–1900) was perceptive. His father, Lyman Beecher, felt that Thomas had as good a mind as any of his children, including the much more famous Henry Ward and Harriet. He was so impressed by young Thomas's scientific studies that he almost relinquished his determination for all his sons to be ministers.

    At the time of this letter, Thomas was going through a period of questioning of the current religious orthodoxy that coincided with Olmsted's own. He was a strong admirer of Horace Bushnell, and when he finally presented himself for examination prior to becoming a Congregational minister he patterned his statement of doctrine closely on that of the Hartford theologian. Even at this age, Beecher was a man of strong and often unorthodox beliefs. As principal of the Hartford High School from 1848 to 1850 he gained the admiration of many people and (apparently) the antagonism of the school board. These traits persisted and helped keep him in obscurity. In 1851 he lost the opportunity for a church post in Baltimore because of his insistence that he be free to preach against slavery, and he was dismissed from a church that he formed in Williamsburgh, N.Y., because he chastized leading members of the church for dishonesty. In 1854 he accepted the call of a small church in Elmira, N.Y., and in that city fulfilled the predictions that Olmsted made for him.

He showed his independence by refusing to be "settled" in his church and served from month to month for forty years. He flouted contemporary standards for ministerial conduct by drinking beer, dancing, and playing billiards. He cared little for preaching and refused to make pastoral calls. Instead, he sought to teach his parishioners the ways of Christ by his own example. Although opposed at first by the other ministers in town, he gained great influence and became Elmira's leading citizen. At the same time he kept up a flow of pronouncements on current issues that led to the remark that he was "everything and its opposite." In time, his influence extended beyond Elmira. This was due especially to the fame of the new church he had built in 1875 embodying his concept of the "Church Home." It contained facilities for a variety of social and cultural activities including dancing, theater, gymnastics, and billiards, and was one of the first examples of what came to be known as the "Institutional Church" (*DAB*; L. B. Stowe, *Saints, Sinners, and Beechers*, pp. 354–83; W. S. B. Mathews, "A Remarkable Personality: Thomas K. Beecher," *Outlook* 82, no. 9 [March 3, 1906]: 555–61; Congregational Churches in Connecticut, General Association, *Contributions to the Ecclesiastical History of Connecticut* [New Haven, Conn., 1861], p. 330; FLO to CLB, May 27, 1951).

8. Elizabeth Chester Bunce (1807–1861), second wife of James M. Bunce. They lived at 32 Ann Street, near the Olmsteds' home in Hartford (Headstone Inscriptions, Hartford, Cemetery 13, p. 33; *Geer's Directory for 1849*, p. 28).

9. Mary B. Brognard, an assistant teacher at the Hartford Public High School, who boarded with the Olmsted family. Fanny was probably the daughter of James M. Bunce and his first wife Frances Ann (Brace) Bunce (1808–1838) (*Geer's Directory for 1849*, p. 189; JO Journal, Feb. 28, 1849; Headstone Inscriptions, Hartford, Cemetery 13, p. 33).

10. Oliver Dudley Cooke and Eliphalet Terry.

11. The first discourse in Horace Bushnell's *God in Christ* is "Concio Ad Clerum: A Discourse on the Divinity of Christ," and the second is "A Discourse on the Atonement" (for elaboration, see note 15, below).

12. Olmsted's stepmother made several visits to water-cure establishments in Northampton in early 1849 (see FLO to JHO, Feb. 10, 1849, above).

13. Olmsted's cousins Abigail Brooks Le Conte (c. 1818–1879), Elizabeth Brooks, and Edwin M. Brooks (1831–1860), children of David and Linda Brooks of Cheshire (*Homes of Cheshire*, pp. 81–82).

14. "Concio Ad Clerum: A Discourse on the Divinity of Christ" (Horace Bushnell, *God in Christ*, p. 121).

15. In "A Discourse on the Atonement," Bushnell rejected the Unitarian doctrine that Christ was "a man, a human teacher, who is sent to reform us by his words and his beautiful human example," and the concept of Him, held by traditional New England Congregationalism, as "a *sacrifice*, an *expiation for sin*, a *vicarious offering*. . . ." Instead, drawing from the text of 1 John 1:2, he asserted that "the Life of God was manifested in Jesus Christ, to quicken the world in love and truth, and reunite it to Himself." By manifesting the "common vivifying life of God" in which alone "all souls have their proper life," Christ reunited the world to the "Eternal Life" from which it had been separated by the "withdrawal into self and self-hood" of sin (ibid., pp. 187–89).

16. Henry William Blaken, a farm laborer (FLO to JO, March 14, 1849).
17. Terry Callaghan, an orphan in the care of Father John Brady (c. 1798–1854), pastor of the Church of the Most Holy Trinity, Hartford (ibid.; JO Journal, Nov. 18, 1854; *Geer's Directory for 1849*, p. 24).
18. Charles Hooper Trask, classmate of John Hull Olmsted at Yale, who traveled in Russia during the summer of 1849 (JHO to FJK, Oct. 6, 1849).
19. George Edwards Hill, a friend of John Hull Olmsted's at Yale.
20. Sarah Coit Day (1814–1899), Emily Perkins, Sarah Amelia Robinson, Elizabeth Hammersley (1830–1898), Olivia Day, Sophia Stevens (T. D. Seymour, *Family of Jeremiah Day*, p. 17; Headstone Inscriptions, Hartford, Cemetery 3, p. 93; *Hartford Female Seminary Reunion of 1892* [Hartford, 1892], pp. 85, 88).
21. Sophia Cooke Hammersley (1805–1869).
22. John Van Peet, one of Olmsted's hired men (FLO to JHO, March 14, 1849).
23. Maria Olmsted.
24. The words in the brackets have been supplied by the editor, the words in the letter being nearly obliterated by a crease in the page.
25. Buckland Bull (1824–1885), son of Mary Bull Olmsted's brother, Ebenezer Watson Bull (Edmund F. Peters and Eleanor Bradley Peters, comps., *Peters of New England, A Genealogy, and Family History* [New York, 1903], pp. 137–38).

APPEAL

TO THE

CITIZENS OF STATEN ISLAND,

BY THE BOARD OF MANAGERS OF THE
RICHMOND COUNTY AGRICULTURAL SOCIETY.

[December 1849][1]

"AGRICULTURE—*The most useful, the most healthful, the most noble employment of man.*" "*I know of no pursuit in which more important service can be rendered to any country, than by improving its Agriculture.*"— WASHINGTON.[2]

In requesting the attention of the citizens of Richmond County to the constitution of their Agricultural Society, we desire them to consider whether it should not obtain their cordial support.

Associations for the encouragement of Agriculture and Horticulture, and for mutual assistance in Rural Improvement, have for years existed in forty-three of our sister counties. The advantages that have accrued to their respective localities from their institution are most gratifying and undoubted. We have hitherto disregarded their example and their success, and neglected the encouragement offered to these enterprises by the enlightened policy of our State. Has it been a reasonable pride that has permitted us to remain thus distinguished?

How is this, Fellow Citizens? Is the very best method of Farming which can be adopted universally practised among us? Is it by any one of us? Is Agriculture, as a science, sufficiently understood in our community? Can no luxuries be added to our orchards—no new beauty bloom in our gardens? Are there no incongruities or inconveniences in our Domestic Architecture? Is the want of refined Rural Taste nowhere observable on our island? Are we quite satisfied with our *Roads*—confident that our breeds of cattle are unsurpassed, and that no improvements can be added to the implements of our Husbandry, that we should neglect or refuse to combine our knowledge and influence in these matters? May we not want a little of the patriotic sentiment, the neighborly feeling, the cordial good understanding among ourselves, that would be promoted by a free interchange of our thoughts, opinions and observations, and by manifesting a unity of purpose with regard to these subjects of common interest?

The average yield of wheat on Staten Island is less than twenty bushels from an acre. Some farmers in the county have obtained at the rate of forty and even fifty bushels. The average crop of Indian corn has been estimated as not far from thirty bushels. We know that one farmer has obtained for the last five years an average in each year of over sixty bushels, and in one of over ninety; and this, he assures us, at no greater cost than is often expended to obtain the ordinary crop. Another, we are informed, has this year, without extravagant expenditure, taken from an acre one hundred and seven bushels, as the reward of his intelligently directed labor. One hundred bushels, it is supposed, will cover the yield from an acre of the land devoted to potatoes. Three hundred bushels from an acre have been raised here.

What occasions these differences? It may be asserted that owing to long culture, some of our lands are impoverished and rendered incapable any longer of producing large crops. "Old Richmond is getting worn out. Our toil is wasted upon her." We have no doubt of it; so is the whip wasted on a starved horse. But we know that there are lands that have been driven longer than ours, that yet show wind and bottom, and seem far from being run out. We find in the Agricultural Report of the "Old Colony" of Plymouth, on the rock-bound shore where the famished Puritans first gathered their scanty supplies of corn: seven crops in one year, of this grain reported of over one hundred bushels, the premium crop being one hundred and forty. The fields of England were tilled ages before the first furrow was turned on Staten Island, yet they are made to produce larger crops than the largest we have mentioned. Instead of *running out* they actually grow more productive. From official returns it appears that within the last few years the average crop of all England has increased eight bushels per acre. Mr. Colman[3] tells us of some of those old farms being made to produce year after year, an average crop of fifty bushels of wheat, and one of them of fifty-six, from the acre. Of potatoes, a yield per acre of six hundred and sixty bushels, is reported.

Farmers of Staten Island! it is the application of Science, of

THOUGHT TO AGRICULTURE, that does this! What results might we anticipate if the Thought, the Skill, the Enterprise, the Energy, should be brought to bear upon our noble employment, which have given to the world the Steam Engine, the Cotton Gin, the Steamboat, the Railroad, the Electric Telegraph! And why shall we not ask it? No man expects the Merchant, the Mechanic, the Manufacturer of the present day to succeed in his calling while stupidly shutting his eyes to the light of Science, or scornfully pushing aside the proffered aid of the student. They readily avail themselves of aid from all sources. It is time the Farmer did so too. They have no patent right to improvement. Progress is no *half-hardy* plant that must be trained to the walls of cities. Why is it, then, that in all the pursuits of Human Industry we see such rapid advancement, while in our Art, the art on which all other arts depend, the wheels of progress move so strangely slow?

The simplest explanation, as we conceive, is forcibly presented in a speech lately delivered before the Norfolk County Agricultural Society, by the Hon. Daniel Webster.

"In all other professions," he says, "men have had opportunities of comparing ideas and assisting one another. What one knows, all know. What is the experience of one, all soon become acquainted with. It is conversation; it is the meeting of men face to face, and talking over what they have common in interest; it is this intercourse that makes men sharp, intelligent, ready to communicate information to others, and ready to receive instructions from others, and ready to act on those which they receive only by this communication. The great practical truth of the present generation is, that public improvement is brought about by voluntary combination."

It is in this point of view, Fellow Citizens, "in this great practical point of view," that we urge upon you the importance of your hearty aid to Agricultural Association. Its great power for good depends at last on individual cooperation. Shall it fail for the want of the influence of your names, of your knowledge, of your experience, of your experiments, of your assistance in its investigations, of your attendance at its meetings, and of your use of the benefits it may offer?

It is not in its effects on mere physical comforts that this subject rests its claims upon your serious consideration. The benefits of our support to this society, we warmly trust, will not end here. With the Farmer must rise the Man. The mysteries of God are ever opening to his observation. Give us to read aright their unwritten word, and our hearts shall hear His voice. With increased knowledge of the operations of nature, with our eyes opened to a thousand wonders hitherto unseen, our sensibility to the Beautiful will be awakened. We shall mutually cultivate true taste, and its fruits will ripen not only to gladden our eyes by the adornment of our Island, but to nourish in our hearts all that is true and good.

We ask you, then, Fellow Citizens, one and all, to associate in this Society. We entreat you to support it. We believe it will increase the profit of our labor—enhance the value of our lands—throw a garment of beauty around our homes, and above all, and before all, materially promote Moral and Intellectual Improvement—instructing us in the language of Nature, from whose preaching, while we pursue our grateful labors, we shall learn to receive her Fruits as the bounty, and her Beauty as the manifestation of her Creator.

1. Olmsted wrote this document as corresponding secretary of the newly formed Richmond County Agricultural Society. It was issued in early December 1849 (FLO to JO, Dec. 12).
2. The first of these quotations is apparently a toast and does not appear in George Washington's published writings. The second comes from a letter of July 20, 1794, to Sir John Sinclair of Caithness, Scotland, president of the British Board of Agriculture, established in 1793. Washington writes: "I know of no pursuit in which more real and important service can be rendered to any Country, than by improving its agriculture, its breed of useful animals, and other branches of a husbandman's cares. . . ." (George Washington, *The Writings of George Washington from the Original Manuscript Sources, 1745–1799,* ed. John C. Fitzpatrick [Washington, D.C., 1940], 33: 437; *DNB,* s.v. "Sinclair, Sir John").
3. Henry Colman (1785–1849), Massachusetts clergyman and agricultural writer. He traveled in Europe from 1842 to 1848 and at the end of his tour published two books on European agricultural and rural economy (*Appleton's Cyc. Am. Biog.*).

Cortelyou Farm, Greenridge, Staten Island

CHAPTER VII

ENGLAND
AND AFTER

1850–1852

AFTER TWO YEARS of farming on Staten Island, Olmsted began to move toward the career of traveling and writing that would absorb much of his energy in the next ten years. His first opportunity came in the spring of 1850, when John Hull Olmsted and Charles Loring Brace were planning a walking tour of England and the Continent. Olmsted pleaded with his father for permission to leave the farm for most of the growing season and join his friends in their travels. His father agreed, but even his brother thought his decision to leave the farm for so long would confirm the widely held view that he was changeable and lacked fixed purpose. "Won't it add to the preconceived notions people have of his stability," John wrote Frederick Kingsbury, "—the stability of change!"[1]

The two surviving letters that Olmsted wrote during the trip are included in this chapter. One is an account he wrote for the *Hartford Daily Courant* of a long debate in the House of Commons that was Sir Robert Peel's last appearance there. The other tells of his visit to Olmsted Hall, the ancestral dwelling of the family in Cambridgeshire. It also recounts some of the activities of Olmsted and his friends in London, where, as John said, they saw "the best pictures, best buildings, even the best gardens and parks, and not only these things but the best men."[2]

When Olmsted returned to America in October 1850 after an absence of six months, he was depressed by what he found. In place of the exciting procession of earnest thinkers and reformers he had encountered on his trip, there were his frivolous and materialistic countrymen. He decided that some good should come of what he had learned on his trip and began to seek a way to exert "increased influence . . . over others."[3] He urged Charles Loring Brace, who was still in Europe, to prepare to join in this effort, and his brother John echoed his thoughts. "We want ten thousand such apostles of ideas as you to come and work, and work against the material tendency that is swamping us," John wrote his friend. "That will be your exact post when you return. . . ."[4]

Olmsted chose to influence his countrymen by writing on important social issues. During the voyage back from England, he wrote an article about the life of merchant seamen in which he proposed new educational and recreational facilities to improve their lot. He published it anonymously the following year in the *American Whig Review* as "A Voice from the Sea." Meanwhile he wrote a glowing description of "The People's Park at Birkenhead, Near Liverpool," which appeared in the May 1851 *Horticulturist*. He then went on to write a two-volume account of his English walking tour entitled *Walks and Talks of an American Farmer in England*. The first volume was published in February of 1852 and the second in October. At the same time he began to search out American subjects to investigate and describe.

In the summer of 1852 he visited the North American Phalanx, a Fourierist community at Red Bank, New Jersey. He described it in the letter to Charles Loring Brace included in this chapter, and in an article published in the *New York Daily Tribune* on July 29, 1852. His concern, as in his book on England, was to find social practices and innovations that might improve American society. These writings of 1852 were the prelude to Olmsted's major literary enterprise, his travels in the South from 1852 to 1854 and the three major books of description and analysis of the region that he wrote during the following five years.

1. JHO to FJK, March 16, 1850.
2. JHO to Mary Olmsted, July 4-5, 1850.
3. FLO to CLB, January 11, 1851.
4. *Life of Brace*, p. 109.

To John Olmsted   [March 1, 1850][1]

Southside, Feb. 29th, 1850

Dear Father,

I wrote you hastily from New York yesterday. Returning from there in company with Judge Emerson,[2] I accepted an invitation to dine with him, and then, on account of the storm to spend the night. An exceedingly agreeable visit. Excellent family: Mrs. Emerson,[3] lovely character. He wishes to borrow the ("Man's Power") book,[4] and I shall take the liberty of keeping it for him. He said he would show it to Putnam,[5] & ask him to republish it. (I did not have the book with me.)

He had The Knickerbocker with Charley's critique on Emerson[6] with which he was much pleased, and is anxious to know the author. You had better read it.

We had a thunder storm—breaking up the S.E. storm—towards morning. Blustering wind today, water spouts on the bay. I came home by the new road on the ridge from the "Academy of Sacred Music" to the Moravian Church.[7] Delightful prospect: fine woods through which the road passes. Mr. & Mrs. E. had heard of John's engagement and warmly congratulated me.[8] Mr. Emerson is not on friendly terms with Frank.[9]

E. knew Captain Fox. Had had him as a witness and had formed a correct opinion of his character. Captain Fox died lately at Stamford, leaving a handsome amount of life insurance to his family.[10]

Mr. Field[11] yesterday gave me some useful information for John in regard to travelling in England, and invited me to bring John & Charley to his house—as also did Mr. Emerson—that he might help them. He says the pedestrianic dress does not debar him from any objects of interest or the attention of gentlemen, because it [is] very common now for men of the higher class to travel in that way. His brother, a large Birmingham manufacturer, would be [of] use and he would be glad in any way to assist him.

John thought I did wrong not to let you know how it tries my whole *manliness* to have such a trip as this brought so close to me. If I had thought I could do it with sufficient control of myself not to have excited your contempt for anything reasonable I might wish to say, I would have done so. But I confess the idea, if I give it the rein of contemplation at all, is so exciting that I can not control it with impartial reason, and so, for the present I try to forget it. For I exceedingly fear my dangerous liability to enthusiasm, and mean to guard against it with all my mind in future. If I did not suppose that you would look upon it with violence of prejudice against my unreasonably strong feeling, I should think you a great deal better able to judge about it than I. I should be content not to allow my mind any labor with it.

I have had a just barely controllable passion for just what John is thinking to undertake, beginning certainly as long ago as when I read Silliman's Tour[12]—17 years ago, and year after year—& never so hardly as this last winter, restrained only by filial gratitude from being accomplished by any desperate means.

This winter I made up my mind that I would make no engagements, but on the contrary arrange every thing that there might be as little in my business as possible to interfere with the plan to go to England in a year from next November—when I calculated that John would be in Europe, and either the farm would be sold, or the question of its ability to support me at least as a bachelor favorably settled.

The little sum that would be absolutely necessary to accomplish all I could hope for, Charley & I concluded we could manage to obtain on the way. Charley, after maturely considering its practicality, made a compact with me: if nothing extraordinary—which he could not anticipate—occurred, to join me, though he did not like the idea of winter, while I dared not calculate on my ability to be gone in summer.

The idea of settling down for life without having seen England seemed to me cowardly and unreasonable—and I determined, God prospering me, not to do it, if I had to sell the farm and spend half my fortune. For I considered that with my whole fortune, *and* a family if I was ever blessed with it, I should have to do it at greater extravagance than by a very large pecuniary sacrifice I could before I married.

Talking over particulars put into our heads the idea of John's going there instead of to the Prairies which he has been talking of all winter, and which was very distressing to me—for the reasons I gave you in Hartford. Then, Charley to go, too—and I saw at once he & they ought to—certainly the very best thing for both of them—and I gave my consent at once. But it does make me miserably lonely: and certainly, if it would not be very unpleasant to you, I would make any other necessary sacrifice.

My ambition to make this farm *profitable*—to carry out my ideas of husbandry and humanity successfully—is very great, and if I thought I must surrender it, it would be very hard for me. But considering the knowledge I should obtain which would particularly be available to my situation, more perhaps than to any man in America with the facilities for obtaining just what I want which some recent events have offered me—considering also certain arrangements I believe it is practicable for me to make, the necessary loss of time would not I conclude, with perhaps too strong a bias from my hope, materially affect the question of my success as a farmer. You can not say that is entirely preposterous I am sure, and I only desire you to consider it as candidly as I try to myself. Do not then estimate without a little calculation of money value, the loss to the farm by my absence from after the planting season, which by reason of having all my land plowed and manure carted on already, will be earlier than usual this year, until the time John wishes to return—before the fall of the leaf—corn cutting, tree planting, fall plowing and draining. The study of the English practice of draining done by the present system reduced ½ in expense, and greatly more valuable according to the Quarterly Review—(January, please read it)[13] would pay any land owner, for what it would cost me.

Robert Cronin—or Mr. Field or Judge Emerson's gardener, or any professional man of the sort, could be obtained easily enough on the island for at the most $10, who would be better able than I, a great deal, to do what after the 1st June might be desirable for my trees.

Harvest is the only important time at which I should be needed. You would expect to be here then, and you know how hard it would be to get along safely without me. I have found that my men are all ambitious to do their best when I am absent. There are 24 acres in three fields, adjoining the barns, of hay—very much less than usual—but of wheat there is more than last year.

Please reckon up the *money* loss by absence, and compare it with the money value of my experience among English & Scotch farmers. The manner in which I have so far managed this farm certainly shows that I should not make a careless application of it.

The use I should be to John is worth some dollars. My experience and aptitude to *roughing it,* his diffidence and Charley's awkwardness in obtaining information and services of men, would make my confidence and sympathy and experience with common and rough men of great assistance— to his comfort, his health, & his purse.

The possible vigor of constitution I should gain is worth some bushels of wheat. I had to take medicine every week or two this winter to check the bowel complaint I contracted last summer, and during the last three weeks it has reduced me a good deal. If we have such another season here as from the complaint now at Quarantine[14] seems not unlikely, I think it will go hard with me. The sea voyage would probably set me up and the walk establish me. I only say it's worth something.

I am ten times as able (by disposition) as John to rough it cheaply —more so than Charley. I believe that my *necessary* expense for the trip would not be over $140 to $160. I enjoy and use the advantages of travelling vastly more than John—always did. I remember what I see and hear when travelling very much better than he. I can manage better than he, and in money matters can manage better for him—better than he can for himself.

In case of his sickness, I have experience among hardships, and boldness and confidence that he has not to obtain assistance and comfort. I have tact and caution in nursing and understand his powers of endurance better than Charley or he himself. All might be, I say, worth a great deal to him.

The very strongest reason that urges me I can not urge at all. And another which cruelly strengthens my desire there's no use in pressing upon you, because you have not made up your mind as I have that I must at any time go to England. It is that it will be *so much* more practicable for me to go now, cheaply, in the best company, with the best preparation to obtain *useful, profitable* information; with the vigor of youth and enthusiasm which would accomplish so much more than the comfortable caution of a little maturer age—so much more practicable for me to go this summer than any *summer* for any period that I can look forward to.

Next summer my trees may come in bearing, and after that I shall have to take the winter passage and see the farms froze up, the trees leafless, roads muddy, and the country gone to *"town."* But even this I shall very gladly encounter the first October I find myself the owner of one hundred dollars.

I can have now the advantage of letters from Norton[15] to the Scotch farmers, from Field[16] to the English, from Antisell[17] to the Irish. They all have warm friends there, yet, among just the men I want to learn from. Parsons[18] will introduce me to the gardens and nurseries. Prof. Johnston[19] returns to Edinburgh. Judge Emerson and Stevens[20] direct me to the lions of London, and Field opens the manufacturies.

I did not mean to argue the matter much, but I hope you won't consider my opinions as if they were those of a mere child, nor my desires as senseless romantic impulses *only*. I acknowledge so *much*, that if you can give my position candid and earnest consideration, you are in a position to judge more correctly than I, and I will make myself contented.

I will put the moral and intellectual advantage which I should expect to receive from such a journey at such a time which such men (and between you and I, I look upon John & Charley as two of the very greatest and best men in the world—certainly the two very best travelling compagnons, and which I should otherwise consider to be obtained cheaply at any cost which left friends and health) as to be compensated to me in the everlasting justice of Providence by the discipline and strength which I acquire by a reasonable conformity to your judgement.

There now! Bang away!

We finished corn planting last year, middle of May—and this year have but half as much to plant.

I am sorry to have troubled you with so long a letter. You will be interested in that article in The Quarterly (Jan. 1850).[21] The first part is historical. The modern practice commences on the 55th or 56th page. The Josiah Parkes[22] is an old neighbor and school-mate of Mr. Field's. 26 inches of rain falls in England per year, 30 inches in New York.

The use of drains in drought are not treated of in this article as they ought to have been. Norton shows their advantage—from Science and practice—very conclusively. They say our clay soils on the island suffer much more in time of drought than even the dry lands at the west end. The rental of farms is improved by draining immediately from 2£6 to 4.6.

Yours affectionately,

Frederick

---

1. Since 1850 was not a leap year, the date of this letter is actually March 1, 1850.
2. William Emerson (1801–1868), lawyer and, for a time, judge of the Court of Common Pleas for Richmond County (Staten Island). He was Ralph Waldo Emerson's brother and lived on Richmond Road in Concord, approximately four miles north of Olmsted's farm (Benjamin Kandall Emerson, *The Ipswich Emersons, A.D. 1636–1900* [Boston, 1900], pp. 176, 264–65; Dorothy V. Smith, *Staten Island: Gateway to New York* [Philadelphia, 1970], p. 220).

3. Susan Woodward Haven Emerson (1807–1868) (B. K. Emerson, *The Ipswich Emersons*, p. 176).
4. Olmsted refers to the book elsewhere as "Man's power over himself" (FLO to JO, fragment, c. Feb. 22, 1850).
5. George Palmer Putnam (1814–1872), New York book publisher and friend of Judge Emerson (*DAB*).
6. This was apparently an enthusiastic unsigned review of Ralph Waldo Emerson's published essays, addresses, and lectures that appeared under "Literary Notices" in the *Knickerbocker* 35, no. 3 [March 1850]: 254–63.
7. The Moravian Church with its cemetery in New Dorp, Staten Island, was at the foot of Todt Hill Road.
8. John Hull Olmsted became engaged to Mary Cleveland Perkins (1830–1921) of Staten Island sometime before February 15, 1850. He met her in the spring of 1848 while visiting his brother, who was her neighbor. They were married October 15, 1851 (Frances E. Olmsted to JHO, Sept. 8, 1848; JO Journal, Nov. 7 and 8, Dec. 21, 1848; Jan. 1 and 2, 1849; JHO to FJK, Feb. 10, 1849; *Olmsted Genealogy*, p. 109).
9. Francis Perkins (1808–1889), an uncle of Mary Perkins, who had been Collector of the Port of New York and lived in South Brooklyn (Edmund J. Cleveland and Horace G. Cleveland, comps., *The Genealogy of the Cleveland and Cleaveland Families . . .* , 3 vols. [Hartford, Conn., 1899], 1: 876, 2: 1612; *Forty Years*, 1: 79).
10. Warren Fox died at Stamford, Conn., around November 3, 1849.
11. Alfred T. Field (1814–1884), English hardware manufacturer and merchant, son of the Unitarian clergyman William Field (1768–1851) of Leam, near Warwick, and brother of the law reformer Edwin Wilkins Field (1804–1871). In 1850 Field was acting in New York as commission merchant for the hardware firm he and his brother Ferdinand had established in Birmingham, England, in 1836. He was a neighbor of Olmsted's on Staten Island and worked with him to build up the Richmond County Agricultural Society. When Olmsted was planning his trip to England, Field gave him much advice and drew up a comprehensive itinerary. In 1854 his brother left the hardware business and Field returned to England to take charge of it. Olmsted kept up his friendship with Field and his wife and exchanged visits and letters with them through the next thirty years. In 1864 Field's sister-in-law Harriet Errington went with Olmsted's family to California, where she served for two years as governess and tutor (*New York Times*, May 28, 1884, p. 4; "Edgbastonians Past and Present: Mr. Henry Cromwell Field, J.P.," *Edgbastonia; a Monthly Illustrated Magazine*, 27, no. 325 [June 1908], pp. 119–22; FLO to JO, March 14, 1850; Georgiana Errington Wheeler to Stella D. Obst, Oct. 18, 1851; *DNB*, s.v. "Field, William," and "Field, Edwin Wilkins").
12. Benjamin Silliman (1779–1864) published his three-volume work, *A Journal of Travel in England, Holland, and Scotland*, in New Haven in 1820.
13. This was an article on the history and theory of land drainage in the *Quarterly Review* 86, no. 171 (Dec. 1849): 79–126.
14. The quarantine station for the Port of New York was located at Tompkinsville on Staten Island, and infectious diseases often spread from there to the surrounding population. Olmsted was sick with dyspepsia and other complaints for most of the summer of 1849, but was afraid to take the usual medicine for fear of lowering his resistance to cholera, of which there was then an epidemic (FLO to FJK, July 21, 1849; Charles W. Leng and William Davis, *Staten Island and Its People: A History, 1609–1929*, 4 vols. [New York, 1930], 4: 263–65).
15. John Pitkin Norton, professor of agricultural chemistry at Yale, who had spent two years studying in Scotland.
16. Alfred T. Field.
17. Thomas Antisell (1817–1893), Irish chemist and physician. He was exiled in 1848 for participation in the "Young Ireland" movement and at this time was practicing medicine in New York. Before leaving Ireland he had written books on the soils of Ireland and the sanitary improvement of Dublin, and manuals of agricultural chemistry and elementary geology (*NCAB*, 29: 448–49).

18. Samuel B. Parsons (1819–1906), horticulturist, nurseryman, and landscape gardener of Flushing, N.Y. (*DAB*).
19. James Finley Weir Johnston (1796–1855), an agricultural chemist and professor at the University of Durham. He was returning after a tour of North America (*DNB*).
20. Henry Stevens (1819–1886), American bookman and bibliographer, brother of Sophia Stevens. After 1846 he lived in London, where he collected Americana for the British Museum and supplied such major collectors in the United States as James Lenox, John Carter Brown, the Smithsonian Institution, and the Library of Congress (*DAB*; Wyman W. Parker, *Henry Stevens of Vermont, American Rare Book Dealer in London, 1845–1886* [Amsterdam, 1963], pp. 163, 220).
21. See note 14, above.
22. Josiah Parkes, whose *Essays on the Philosophy and Art of Land Drainage* [London, 1848] was one of the works reviewed in the December 1849 article in the *Quarterly Review*. Parkes was an Engineer of the Royal Agricultural Society and the inventor of a system of deep drainage of soil through the use of tile. His system became an important part of the agricultural reform movement in England, and Olmsted sought to promote it on Staten Island. Such deep or "thorough" drainage was an important element in many of Olmsted's later landscape works (*DNB*; and see Autobiographical Fragment B, note 13, above).

To THE *Hartford Daily Courant*

The House of Commons—A Ministerial Crisis Night—British Republicanism—Cobden—Sir Robert Peel's last speech.

London, June 29th, 1850.

We were so fortunate as to obtain through Mr. Lawrence's[1] attention, cards of admission to the Speaker's gallery of the House of Commons, on the night of the debate of the proposed vote of approval of the foreign policy of the Government.[2]

The hall used is intended to be occupied only temporarily; it has the appearance of a large, oblong school-room, and is very inadequate to the accommodation of the members. It is, however, most admirably lighted and ventilated. The Speaker has an easy seat at one end; before him is a table, at which three clerks sit. They are all in black gowns and long white horse hair wigs, which latter in my opinion rather detract from than add dignity to their appearance. There are galleries running all around the hall, those on the sides being occupied by the members. The seats are plain oak benches, with rails behind to rest the back upon. There are no desks. The benches on the Speaker's right are occupied by the Ministers, and their supporters, the Whigs; the more advanced Liberals, with Cobden and Bright[3] at their head, are nearer the door on the same side; opposite to them, on the other side of the Speaker, is Disraeli[4] and the Tories; Sir Robert Peel[5] and the Free Trade wing of the Conservatives being on the same side, nearest the Speaker. The gallery behind him is used by the Reporters.

The Speaker's gallery is in front of him at the opposite end of the

343

hall and will seat about thirty persons; behind it is the Strangers' gallery, which accommodates eighty. Behind this there is said to be a kind of closet, from which the debate may be heard through an aperture in the wall. Six persons can get into it, and on this night Lady Peel and Lady Russell are said to have been in it among others.

The privilege of a seat this evening was a most valuable one, the debate being considered the most important and interesting that has occurred for four years, or during the present Parliament. It was understood that if the Foreign policy which, as to Greece in particular, had been reproved in the Lords, should not be sustained, there would be a dissolution, and if a small majority only was obtained in their favor, the Ministry would resign.[6] On the previous night it had been found, to the consternation of the Whigs, that a large party of their allies on the Free Trade field were preparing to desert them on this ground. The Hall was densely filled during much of the night, particularly during Sir Robert Peel's speech—it is said there has rarely been so full an attendance. I liked the looks of the members of the House very well. There was no more aristocratic *air* about them than in our own Representatives. It seemed to me that those qualities which make a man most valued among his equals, such as generosity, frankness, tact, and good-fellowship, had been found of more importance at the hustings than all the influences of wealth and family importance.

I will not attempt to give you a sketch of the speeches; you will probably have their substance sent you from another source. They were all it seemed to me *perfectly* reported in the Times a few hours after, and we read them over at breakfast. There was in them all, four members of every party, a recognition of the most liberal ideas and principles of Government:—quite as liberal in their spirit though not as distinctly and loudly proclaimed as any thing that is usually heard in our assemblies. In proposing the Resolution (which was adopted) Mr. Roebuck[7] said that by it the House of Commons declared that

> "We are favorable to those efforts of man by which he endeavors to raise himself in the scale of nations, and by his own enlightenment and a confidence in his own power to govern himself and resist *that tyranny which under the name of legitimacy*, has ever sought to crush him in all those powers which we as Englishmen consider to be *the very birth right which nature has given us*."

Nor did Sir Robert Peel, in opposing this, object at all to the liberal sentiment, but only to the implication that England was prepared to assist the people of any other nation that chose to adopt it and act upon it.

It was gratifying to see how the whole tendency of the debate and of events connected with it was to encourage the adoption and profession of ideas of national duties which even with us might be considered ultra and

344

premature. Though not distinctly admitted, it seemed to me it was left as generally understood that the views of Cobden with regard to the disposition of questions of international dispute, were destined inevitably to be eventually adopted by the Government—a happy day that will be for England and the world. The desire expressed and practicability asserted by Cobden in his speech that the attitude of nations with regard to each other, should be changed, as that of individuals has been in the discontinuance of the practice of always being ready for violent quarrels, with arms worn on the person, was very loudly applauded by both sides of the House, and was received by the handful of *"people"* in the galleries with still more enthusiastic, though silent expressions of pleasure.

From the conversation I have had with people of all classes here, I have been generally gratified in a similar manner. From the sentiments expressed among the people indiscriminately, you would suppose they were as much imbued with free and democratic ideas, as New Englanders. Indeed I do think that the relationship between us is more truly obvious in this respect than any other. We may differ greatly in forms, quarrel like brothers or theologians about details and words; we are both sadly recreant to our principles sometimes in practice, but in nothing, and nowhere else, can an American find greater sympathy if he is willing to meet it, than in his National and Patriotic sentiments here, among his Father's sons.

Their loyal love to the queen, which is often manifested with absurd extravagance, is not servile respect to her person, or vulgar homage to a throne. The very fulsomeness of ceremony shows that a very different thing is meant from what is expressed, as one is often most *polite* to those he wishes to have least to do with. The true motive of their loyal demonstrations, is, rather the same zealous and proud patriotism that sometimes makes people a little ridiculous on our side the water; the queen being considered the impersonation of the spirit of their country, (as Henry Clay has been said to be "of Whig principles"). Added to this is the impulse of gallantry, or romantic respect to a very good lady who has been placed by circumstances in a position of trial and danger, which she may be supposed to endure, not only for the sake of gratifying ambition and avarice, but also from regard to the true honor of such responsibility and duty.[8] It is some cause for gratitude too, that her Majesty has been "graciously pleased" not to abuse the right which law they are sworn to sustain gives her, to *govern* them. It seems to me, too, that the ideas of physical weakness and dependence, connected with the throne when occupied by a woman have not been without their value in soothing jealousy and rebellion towards the government in those, whom the love of freedom and of exercising the right of self-government might otherwise have excited into revolution during the republican *stampede* which lately untethered all Europe.[9]

The whole aristocratic establishment of England, the estates, the privileges, the decorations of the nobility are secured to their possessors by the same principles of law, and, as is yet understood, of justice, by which all other property is conveyed from man to man—from father to son. And all the cumbrous machinery of royalty and nobility is borne with, because it seems necessary to stability,—stability, not of ideas, not oppressions, not power; but of property. The Conservatism of England, (that is of England as a thinking people—not of a party, for the party to which the name is applied seems rather the exception to this,) may be then time-serving, cowardly, and selfish, and compared with the reckless spirit of the Socialist Republicans, I believe it is; but is in no other sense slavish or despotic.

The throne is the central tower of the old feudal castle they have had the misfortune to inherit from our ancestors. The less imposing and ostensible outworks in which its real strength consists, must be quietly and conservatively removed, and used for the foundations of a new edifice, better adapted to cope with the moral and intellectual engines of modern warfare, more appropriate and more convenient to modern and more enlightened life. When the new structure now rising incongruously among and out of the tottering bastions and crumbling buttresses, and which even now betrays its simple Republican style over the old battlements, shall be sufficiently complete and tried to sustain the shock, the old Royal stronghold may be expected to fall. Possibly when the present notable house-wife[10] leaves it, its empty honors may be resigned peaceably and happily to inevitable fate.

The first speaker we heard was Mr. Cockburn[11] (pronounced Coburn.) His speech and his manner was characterized by great life, humour, and personality. It was quite like much of the better kind of speaking in our own House of Representatives. He is a rather small, *thick-set* man, has spoken noticeably but once before in Parliament, but has considerable reputation as a legal orator. (The sessions of the Courts and of Parliament are so arranged that they do not interfere with each other; though there is not the same proportion of lawyers in the political arena as there is with us.) While he was speaking the house was full. He was much applauded and sometimes groaned, and at his conclusion three-fourths of those present left the hall, a great many of the Whigs crowding around to thank and congratulate him.

The two following speakers—Mr. Walpole, and Mr. Moncton Milnes[12] (pronounced Miles)—spoke to almost empty benches, the members—it being near seven o'clock—having gone I suppose to dinner. On this account, perhaps, they were not very animated or interesting.

Then followed Cobden, and though he was not loudly welcomed, it was immediately evident that he was listened to with the greatest interest. He seemed yet a young man, and his sentiments and delivery were full of energy and generous, fearless, independent progression. In leaving his friends (and for this occasion standing—and yet not sympathizing—with those who owed defeat of their favorite policy and their own everlasting position of political decrepitude, mostly to his talent and activity) to refuse his approval to what he had always contended to be the unwise policy of interfering in the domestic concerns of other governments, he was pursuing a most unpopular course. At his conclusion, nevertheless, he received most hearty cheering from both sides of the House; an honorable testimony to the confidence he had obtained in his sincerity.

"Sir Robert!" exclaimed several voices around me, as a fine, tall and venerable man rose and bowed with grace and dignity to the Speaker. After a burst of cheering, the still, fixed attention of all the House showed how much was expected from him. His speech was feeling, eloquent and impressive; his tone and manner, courtly, refined, and grave often almost to sadness, and though his popular reputation with all parties here seems to be for shrewdness, policy, and diplomatic talent, rather than for noble, far-reaching statesmanship, I received the impression of a sincere, earnest, truthful man, which I shall have the pleasure of retaining and associating with the part he plays in history.

[It was the last scene in which Sir Robert Peel was to appear before the public in the Act of this world.—While every cabinet and crowned head in Europe was listening to him, he was called from the stage of history to appear before the "King of Kings." It is remarkable that the very hour in which I was writing these words the great statesman to whom they referred was thrown to the ground in helpless prostration and that noble body, was soon all that was left of him *here*.][13]

There was one passage occurring at the very commencement of his speech which produced so great an effect on the house, and impressed me with such glowing admiration of the man at the time, and is now so honorable to his memory, that I must try to give you an idea of it.

Mr. Cockburn had been sneering at the policy which could have induced Sir Robert and his party to become the friends of the Protectionists in this debate. He could imagine but *three courses* they could have in view; two of these he showed to be impracticable or impolitic. The third was to obtain power by sacrifice of their old principles, by what he termed an unholy alliance with their common enemy. "I tell you," said he, "that I believe that the compromise will involve a deviation from principle on your part." There was *no other course*, he said, and he called upon "the right Honorable Baronet" with impertinent personality to "speak out."—"Be for once frank and fair with us, give us an answer." He demanded with reiterated sarcasm that they should know the conditions of what he "could not help calling a very pitiful and mean combination."

I wish I could convey to you a conception of the almost sublime attitude, feeling, and spontaneous eloquence with which Sir Robert, looking down sternly upon him replied. Speaking very slowly and distinctly, he said—

"There has been no such compromise. He (Mr. Cockburn) demands which of the three courses, which of the three combinations by which office may be obtained, we intend to pursue. Now is it not possible for the honorable gentleman to suppose there may be a fourth course? Is it not possible for him to speculate upon the possibility that men in this House may intend to give their votes without reference to political combinations? Does he exclude the possibility of that fourth course of action which arises from a conscientious conviction as to the truth? Is that excluded from his contemplation? Is it not possible that without reference to party or personal interests men may decline to affirm a resolution which deals with principles of greater importance to the welfare of this country than have ever been under consideration of this House?"

This was but the introduction to a logical defence of his position which, with an air of magnanimous superiority to such unworthy admissions as had been presumed upon, was well calculated to carry convictions of his sincerity and honest, catholic patriotism.

Lord John Russell[14] followed, defending his Ministerial policy in a speech that commanded respectful and studious attention. He appeared a fine polished man, and spoke in a low and rather persuasive tone, and with a calm, deliberate, energetic, but self confident manner. I heard him somewhat indistinctly, and it was partly owing to this perhaps, and in part to fatigue, for we had not left our seats or had any refreshment for more than eight hours, that I was less interested by him, and he seemed to me much less of an orator than either of the great men that had preceded him. The moment he took his seat, Disraeli was on his feet and begged the generosity of the house to give him attention. He seemed to me a greater man than he is usually represented to be. He spoke with fluency and with almost impatient eagerness to carry his convictions to his audience, but without very vigorous or effective arguments.

When he had concluded, at 3 o'clock in the morning, after a few explanatory remarks from Mr. Roebuck, the House divided, (when the spectators are turned out from the galleries) and greatly to the relief and joy of the liberals, both within and without, a majority of forty-six was found to sustain the ministry. F.

1. Abbott Lawrence (1792–1855), Massachusetts merchant and manufacturer who served as U.S. minister to Great Britain from 1849 to 1852. Olmsted and his companions had a letter of introduction to him from Charles Loring Brace's uncle, the eminent Boston lawyer Charles Greely Loring (DAB; John Pierce Brace to CLB, March 22, [1850], John Pierce Brace Correspondence, Connecticut Historical Society, Hartford, Conn.).
2. During the revolutionary era that began in Europe in 1848, the British government, led by the prime minister, Sir John Russell (1792–1878), occasionally tried to strengthen liberal regimes in Europe by granting them loans and other forms of aid. This foreign policy was contested by the Conservatives in Parliament, particularly by Sir Robert Peel, who, though he was allied to Russell in favoring free trade, did not approve of Russell's intervention in the affairs of Europe. Olmsted was witnessing

the debates that led to a vote of confidence sustaining the Russell government on the night of June 28 (Sigfrid H. Steinberg, ed., *The New Dictionary of British History* [New York, 1963], p. 110; *Hansard Parliamentary Debates*, 3d ser., 112 [June 18–July 18, 1850]: 721, 739; John Morley, *The Life of Richard Cobden* [Boston, 1881], pp. 352–82).

3. Richard Cobden (1804–1865), British statesman, a leading advocate of free trade and consistent opponent of British military intervention on the Continent, and his close friend and political ally John Bright (1811–1899). As Olmsted notes, Cobden sided in this instance with the Tory opponents of the foreign policy of his own party, although the repudiation of the Tory policy of protective tariffs that occurred with the repeal of the Corn Laws in 1846 was due in large part to the agitation of the Anti-Corn Law League, of which he was "the presiding genius and the animating soul" (*EB*, s.v. "Cobden, Richard"; *DNB* and *DNB Supplement*).

4. Benjamin Disraeli (1804–1881), first Earl of Beaconsfield, British statesman and man of letters (*DNB*).

5. Sir Robert Peel (1788–1850), English statesman. As prime minister from 1841 to 1846 he abandoned the traditional Tory policy of protective duties on imports, and supported free trade measures. His most important accomplishment in this regard was the repeal of the Corn Laws in 1846, which, however, brought about the downfall of his ministry. He gave important support to the Whig government that then came to power until foreign policy questions brought him into opposition (*DNB*).

6. The immediate cause of the debate on the foreign policy of Russell's government was the British intervention in support of claims against the Greek government by a British citizen, Don David Pacifico (1784–1854). He was a Gibraltar-born Jew whose house in Athens was damaged by an anti-Semitic mob while he was serving as Portuguese consul there. A show of force by the British navy enabled Pacifico to collect his large claim for damages (S. H. Steinberg, *New Dictionary of British History*, p. 110; *Hansard Parliamentary Debates*, 112: 478–596, 609–743).

7. John Arthur Roebuck (1801–1879), British Liberal politician and supporter of Richard Cobden (*DNB*).

8. In speaking of the trial and danger of the position of Queen Victoria, Olmsted is referring to the fact that in the previous month she had suffered two violent attacks upon her person. One occurred when an Irishman in a crowd fired at her carriage; and, on the day that Olmsted arrived in England, a deranged man attacked her with a cane and severely bruised her forehead (Cecil Blanche [Fitzgerald] Woodham-Smith, *Queen Victoria: Her Life and Times*, vol. 1, *1819–1861* [London, 1972], p. 310).

9. Olmsted is referring to the European revolutions of 1848.

10. Queen Victoria had been the devoted wife of Prince Albert for a decade and was the mother of seven children.

11. Alexander J. E. Cockburn (1802–1880) served as a barrister and a member of Parliament, and in 1859 became Lord Chief Justice of England (*DNB*).

12. Spencer Horatio Walpole (1806–1891), a Conservative member of Parliament, and Richard Moncton Milnes (1809–1885), author and Conservative member of Parliament (*DNB*).

13. The brackets around this paragraph appear in the *Hartford Daily Courant* article: Olmsted evidently wrote the paragraph as an addendum to his article when he learned of the death of Sir Robert Peel, who was thrown from his horse in London on June 29, 1850, and died from the resulting injuries on July 2 (*DNB*).

14. John Russell (1792–1878) had a long career in Parliament, beginning in 1813. He led the Whig opposition during the period of Robert Peel's second ministry, from 1841 to 1846, and formed the ministry that succeeded it, which lasted until 1852 (*DNB*).

THE PAPERS OF FREDERICK LAW OLMSTED

To John Olmsted

Address: Mr. John Olmsted/Richmond/Staten Island
    New York/United States of America[1]
Postmarks: Oxford/Au 16/1850/B
    [. . .]/Aug 30/24/

Saffron Walden,[2] Aug. 11th, 1850

Dear Father,

    I came here by rail this morning. Finding the roads were very intricate and the weather threatening, I took a pony chaise with a boy as a guide and drove over a pleasant country abundant in picturesque old houses to Castle Champs—or Camps—near which are ruins of Camp Castle, and traces of field works.[3] The guide posts here directed us to "the Bumpsteds": Bumpsted Helions and Bumpsted Steeple.[4] The first is called by the people generally "Helens." Having reached it we were directed by the sign post again to Homsted Green.[5]

    This turned us down a narrow, ill kept lane, which after following a crooked mile became a narrow irregular common or green. I stopped at a farm house here and asked for Olmsted Hall. It was the next farm. Turning into another and meaner lane, we came to a collection of Barns and farm buildings. I asked a boy in one of them if it was Olmsted Hall. He said it was.

    I desired to see the gentleman who resided in it. He called another boy who was driving the horses of a threshing mill. He was a mere clown and not of age I should think. He said he was Mr. Ambrose—and what did I wish? I gave him my name and country and said I desired to see the Hall—giving him reasons for my interest in it.

    He conducted me to the house.[6] It was a mere cottage of one story with a steep slated roof, two long low windows, walls of stone, white-washed. I went in through a narrow entry, to the kitchen. It was a room perhaps 15 ft. by 20 in size—with a brick floor—had one of the long windows and really was remarkable for an immensely wide fire place (eleven feet). This had been bricked up and furnished with a grate on each side of which were boxes, or closets, which formed seats when they were closed. I introduced myself to the boy's Aunt here, who had lived in the house nearly 50 years, and who was pleased to see me and talk about it.

    She could tell me nothing though of interest and never thought of it in any other way than as a farm house. It still belongs to the Queen's College, Cambridge, and had been tenanted by this family for the last half century.

    Passing through a short entry, out of which a narrow staircase ascended to some *attic* rooms (all very plain and common place), we entered another room of the same size as the kitchen, rather better furnished, the

350

OLMSTED HALL, COUNTY ESSEX, ENGLAND

walls plastered and whitewashed in the same way, and having the other large, long, low window—the only one in the room.

The woman said that this had once been a fine large room, with oak wainscot. "And they used to call it *the Hall*." But Mr. Ambrose had divided it, making another little room by a partition and had lathed & plastered it. The old fire place had been all bricked up (if there was one) and a large coal grate let in to the wall in its place. There was nothing whatever of the old room left unless it might be the window, which was seven sashes wide of small square panes of glass set in lead. But it had been a real *"hall,"* that's certain.

Back of the house, hall or cottage was a little garden, well kept and well filled with sundry fruit trees, gooseberries, &c. It was well sheltered and fenced by a thick high hedge of hazel and hawthorn. Peeping through this I saw the water in the old *Moat*.

I went through the house again and passing out another door crossed the moat by a rude foot bridge. It was about ten feet wide, and not more than three to four deep. The whole inner bank was grown over by the hedge to within 1 foot of the water. There was just about *enough* in it for the ducks to swim in.

I followed it round the garden on three sides of the house, and for a considerable distance in front. A few rods had been filled up by Mr. Ambrose within fifty years. From the direction in which the ends pointed where they were stopped by the filling up, I should judge it had enclosed at least half an acre about the house, perhaps including the stables, &c.

I thought at first the original house might have extended in that direction, but I could find no evidence of it. There was a building which might have been once connected with the Hall, now used as a dairy and Brew house, formerly probably servants apartments and offices. The barns, &c. are modern, large, and numerous.

There are three hundred acres in the farm, some portion being grazing land. Ten laborers are employed upon it. The surface is low and undulating slightly. Near the house is the end of an extensive wood belonging to a nobleman. It may have been formerly a park.

I stayed an hour and a half around the house, and from two positions took a hasty outline of the premises, with minute notes from which an artist could paint you very correct and picturesque views. I don't know as this rather diminutive *Hall* will much gratify your family pride. I rather think it does mine—quite as much as to have found the arms of some big murdering Baron over a dungeon door.

At all events, as I imagined the simple country life that had probably been enjoyed there, the narrow moat that sufficed to defend the home of the peaceful family and the kind lord of the secluded manor, the little hall and great hospitable fire place, I enjoyed in a considerable degree the pleasure of

OLMSTED HALL AND ENVIRONS

a sympathizing relationship, and the good influence of a worthy ancestry.

I picked a few leaves &c. as relics—among the rest, a branch of *yew*, the roots of which may have been planted by an Olmsted.

I then drove to Bumpsted Helions, and found the Parish Clerk. He had no old records, but said there was a chest of them at the Vicarage. He did not know how old. The Vicar was lately dead, and I could not see them.[7] He expected a new vicar soon.

He promised that when he could he would examine them, and if he found the name of Olmsted, would inform me. I told him he should be paid for any trouble he took if he wrote me. He went with me to the Parish Church, a rather interesting little plain old edifice. There were no very old tombstones with legible inscriptions.

We then returned to Saffron Walden (generally called *Walden*). (It is about ten miles from Olmsted Hall.) There I visited the Parish Church. It is considered a very fine specimen of the Pointed Gothic,[8] but after getting familiar with the Norman and Romanesque Gothic on the Continent, I am out of patience with the taste which prefers this flimsy frippery style, and can hardly enjoy it as I used to. I could not find the name of Olmsted among the tombstones. (There were several Catlens.)[9]

I asked two persons who told me they were conversant with a great part of Essex if they had known any families of our name. They had not, nor had ever heard it except as applied to "the *Hall*."

I finished this in Oxford. I wished to have written a letter to Cousin Charles about Olmsted Hall, but I can not possibly get time, and you must send him this with my love.

It would be easy to have the parish records of any town in Essex searched, by directing to the Parish Clerk. And I presume the Heralds[10] in London would rake up the *arms*, &c., for a consideration. Stevens[11] would make enquiries if you care to know more about it. I congratulate myself that if I have not learned that we are from Olmsted Hall, I have not discovered the contrary.

We remained in London a day or two longer than we wished to. I wanted to see Mr. Parkes,[12] the great draining engineer, which I could not do till Tuesday. And John's bowels not recovering a healthy state, he thought it prudent to keep quiet.

Yesterday we left—travelling by rail to Windsor. We saw little at Windsor—some fine trees, and a great overgrown castle-palace, which looked anything but comfortable and *homely*. We walked six miles and dined under a hay stack at noon. Our afternoon's walk from Great Marlow to Henley[13] was about the most charming we have had. I believe as far as such scenery goes I enjoy it as much as the Rhine.[14]

This morning we walked to Reading and then here by Rail, where we overtook Charles.[15] It's midst of long vacation. The town streets dusty in repairs and disappointing. We shall spend Sunday at Stratford on Avon.

John stood the walk better than he had expected to—indeed is quite well and reinvigorated. Only he got so foot sore yesterday, we could not well have walked much further than we did (eight miles) this morning.

Sunday last, we were at Reverend Mr. Morell's, the author of Philosophy of Religion—reviewed in three or four numbers of the North British [Review] last year. A friend of Dr. Bushnell's. He is young, clever and very kind to us.[16] He took us to Wilkinson, the English translator of the voluminous works of Swedenborg.[17] He showed us manuscripts of S's. He is a noble-man—was very genial and good with us. I have not [seen] men that impressed more as a character mingling the good with the great. We also saw here Hugh Doherty the French Socialist—a leader—and correspondent of Greeley's.[18] We had some conversation with him which improved our opinion of him.

We have engaged our passage (Paid it, J. & I) in the City of Glasgow,[19] 4th October.

Our expenses from Liverpool to London for board & lodging were 71 cents a day! Tell it to the unbelieving Jews! (Our other expenses add about equal sum for rail, guides, &c.)

We received a short letter from you day before yesterday. Some letters (about Sir. R. Peel's death, &c.) you seem not to have received. I wrote a long letter last week. I have several business letters to write by this steamer and at this time for England—which must excuse my shortness now.

John is quite well and in good spirits.[20]

Dear Father, Fred has told you that I have got quite well again & that we are on our way towards home. We had a very pleasant walk here. That is, we walked 25 miles & rode 40—rather hurrying on, in consequence of our detention at London.

Next week we shall be occupied with Warwickshire & after that shall hurry on to Ireland & Scotland—where everyone says Fred will find his great objects in far greater perfection than in England. I can hardly imagine finer farming than we see here.

The thing most noticeable in it is the immense prodigality of labor—nothing shirked, or slurred over for want of time. We pass immense fields of turnips of 30 acres often. One we saw must have been 60—all broad cast. You can imagine the labor required to thin them out & keep clean. The tops of some the earliest planted cover the ground. Others later are scarcely making their appearance.

The harvest is going on—the wheat harvest nearly over. A great many occupied in making stacks—of great size & beautifully covered & finished. So far as we can judge, the corn harvest is very fine.

The stubble fields take from the lively aspect the scenery had in spring, but most of them are immediately turned under, harrowed & rolled, so that the brown earth contrasts very prettily with the green of the rowen grass & the turnips.

Fred is very sorry that things should have got behind hand for want of labor, at the farm; he was so particular in cautioning John about it. However, now it can't be helped. Tell us please whether there were any *pears* on the young orchard in front of the house—and whether the grafts on the big, unfortunate pear tree succeeded in living?

I must try & write some of you at home next week. At present, good-bye.

J.H.O.

1. This address was later crossed out and the letter was addressed to Mr. Chas. H. Olmsted, Hartford, Conn., and received the additional postmark of Richmond, N.Y., Sept. 6. This indicates that John Olmsted complied with Olmsted's request in the letter that he send it on to his cousin Charles Hyde Olmsted, who was interested in genealogy and history.
2. Saffron Walden was a municipal borough and a "handsome market town" forty-two miles north of London (William White, *History, Gazeteer & Directory of the County of Essex* [Sheffield, 1848], pp. 654–55).
3. Castle Camps, or Camps Castle, had been a seat of the de Vere family. They received the estate on which it stood from William i, who constructed most of the earthworks that Olmsted notes in the letter. The castle was built by Aubrey de Vere, earl of Oxford, c. 1068 (William Page and J. Horace Round, eds., *The Victoria History of the County of Essex* [London, 1907], 2: 21; Daniel Lysons and Samuel Lysons, *Magna Britannia: Being a Concise Topographical Account of the Several Counties of Great Britain* [London, 1808], 2, part 1, pp. 156–57; Nikolaus Pevsner, *Cambridgeshire*, 2d ed. [Harmondsworth, 1970], p. 314).
4. Helion Bumpstead was a "pleasant village" of some 900 inhabitants, eight miles northeast of Saffron Walden. Steeple Bumpstead was a village and parish two miles farther east (W. White, *County of Essex*, p. 654; John G. Bartholomew, *Bartholomew's Survey Gazeteer of the British Isles*, 7th ed. [Edinburgh, 1927], p. 523).
5. Olmsted Green was a hamlet of five hundred acres in Cambridgeshire, about one mile west of Helion Bumpstead. At one time it belonged to the Olmsted family (W. White, *County of Essex*, pp. 654–55; J. G. Bartholomew, *British Isles*, p. 523).
6. Olmsted Hall was part of the de Vere family's Lordship of Bumpsted Hall, and the Olmsteds held it from them. The earliest recorded date of Olmsted possession of the hall was by Maurice de Olmstede in 1242, although a Martin de Olmstede held it sometime earlier. The Hall remained in the family until the late-fourteenth or early-fifteenth century. It later became the property of Queen's College, Cambridge, and when Olmsted's brother-in-law William Niles visited the bursar there he was told that the vegetables for his supper came from Olmsted Hall (Philip Morant, *The History and Antiquities of the County of Essex, Compiled From the Best and Most Ancient Historians . . .* , 2 vols. [London, 1768], 2: 532; *Olmsted Genealogy*, ix; D. and S. Lysons, *Magna Britannia*, 2, part 1, 157–58).
7. John Hodgson (1802–1850), vicar of Helion Bumpstead since 1833, had died on June 16, 1850 (University of Cambridge, *Alumni Cantabrigienses: A Biographical List of All Known Students, Graduates and Holders of Office at the University of Cambridge, From the Earliest Times to 1900*, John Venn and J. A. Venn, comps. [Cambridge, 1947], pt. 2, vol. *Gabb to Justamond*, p. 400).

8. St. Mary's Church in Saffron Walden was built between 1470 and 1540 (C. Bright-wen Towntree, *Saffron Walden Then and Now* [Chelmsford, 1952], p. 30).
9. Members of the Catlin family were among the early settlers of Hartford. At the time this letter was written, Julius Catlin ([1798]–1888) ran a dry-goods store on Main Street not far from John Olmsted's firm (*Geer's Directory for 1847–1848*, pp. 34, 88; *Boston Evening Transcript*, April 24, 1888, p. 1).
10. The Herald's College, a royal corporation founded in 1483 to exercise jurisdiction over the use of coats of arms.
11. Henry Stevens.
12. Josiah Parkes (see FLO to JO, March 1, 1850, note 23, above).
13. Great Marlow is a town on the north bank of the Thames thirty-one miles northwest of London. The walk from there to Henley-upon-Thames would have taken Olmsted and his friends some seven miles farther up the river.
14. Olmsted and his companions had traveled in Germany earlier in the summer (FLO to Maria Olmsted, July 4 and 5, 1850).
15. Charles Loring Brace.
16. John Daniel Morell (1816–1891), English philosopher and educator. He took a B.A. and an M.A. at the University of Glasgow in 1840 and 1841, and was ordained in 1842. He then studied with the German philosopher Johann Fichte, whose think-ing influenced him strongly. His first book, *Historical and Critical View of the Speculative Philosophy of Europe in the Nineteenth Century*, published in 1846, so impressed Lord Landsdowne, president of the Privy Council, that he appointed Morell inspector of the schools, a position he held until 1876. He published several books dealing with elementary education as well as numerous philosophical works. Olmsted read his *Philosophy of Religion* in 1849, the year it was published, and judged it "very fine." One aspect of Morell's thought that must have appealed to both Olmsted and Bushnell was a "broad religious faith" that permitted him to wor-ship at one time with Protestant nonconformists, later with the Anglican church, and finally with Unitarians (*DNB*; FLO to JO, June 25, 1849; *North British Review* 11, no. 22 [Aug. 1849]: 293–336).
17. James J. G. Wilkinson (1812–1899), translator, biographer, and foremost English proponent of the Swedish philosopher, scientist, and mystic, Emanuel Swedenborg. Wilkinson's commentaries on Swedenborg earned him praise in America as well as in England. Both the elder Henry James and Ralph Waldo Emerson extended him their admiration and friendship because of that work (*DNB*, s.v. "Wilkinson, James John Garth").
18. Hugh Doherty (d. 1891), philosopher and disciple of François Marie Charles Fourier. Doherty met Fourier in Paris in 1836 and devoted considerable time to spreading his doctrines in the following years. He was a contributor to the American Fourierist journal, the *Phalanx*, which Horace Greeley helped establish, during its short exis-tence (1843 to 1845). At the time Olmsted met Doherty in London, Doherty was preparing an English edition of Fourier's *The Passions of the Human Soul, and Their Influence on Society and Civilization*. He wrote critical annotations, a general introduction and a biography of Fourier for this edition, for which the translator was John Reynell Morell, a cousin of John Daniel Morell. After the publication of this work in 1851, Doherty embarked on his great undertaking, a five-volume opus entitled *Organic Philosophy; or, Man's True Place in Nature*, which he published between 1864 and 1878. Believing that "harmonic numbers and definite proportions are the true basis of positive science," he extended into other areas the method that Fourier had applied to his studies of human psychology and social organization (François Marie Charles Fourier, *The Passions of the Human Soul . . .* , 2 vols. [London, 1851], 1: v; Hugh Doherty, *Organic Philosophy; or, Man's True Place in Nature* [London, 1864], 1: v; *The Phalanx: Organ of the Doctrine of Association* [New York, 1843–45], 1: 356; *DNB*, s.v. "Morell, John Daniel").
19. The Inman Line's *City of Glasgow* was a three-masted, single-screw steamship built in 1850 and noted for its provision for the comfort of passengers. In 1854 it was

lost at sea without a trace (Arthur George H. Macpherson, *Mail and Passenger Steamships of the Nineteenth Century* . . . [Philadelphia, 1929?], pp. 61–62).
20. This is the end of Olmsted's part of the letter. The rest of the text given here was written by John Hull Olmsted on a separate sheet of paper.

To Charles Loring Brace

Southside, Nov. 12th, 1850

Dear Charley,

I am very glad to hear you are so well off in Hamburg.[1] I should like to be with you. I advise you to stay as long as you can afford to. The fact is evident now that when we were travelling we were living a great deal more, getting a great deal more out of the world, loving oftener, hating oftener, reaching a great many more mile stones. Everybody at home seems to be superficial, frivolous, absorbed in a tide of foam, gas and bubbles.

Dear me, I am very old. I have not, nor am I ever now expecting to have, trying to have, any earnest sympathies with the fellows. And as for women in distinction from men, money would almost buy the use of my right and expectation of ever really conversing with one again. I am a thoroughly used up young man. If all the rest of the world should die it would not disappoint me much. It's just Fate—and there's no use crying, and that's the only reason I have not and do not continually die of a broken heart. My balloon is smashed. Daylight has walked into my theatre. A half crazy Philosopher, I am woke up, my feet shackled and my hands tied, a mask on my face, carried downstairs with the rest of the crowd. The sun shines, ice is cold, fire is hot, punch is both sweet and sour, Fred Olmsted is alone, is stupid, is crazy and is unalterably a weak sinner and unhappy and happy. This is my truest and most solid and sustainable standpoint.

I am quite as much what everybody, even you and I, calls an infidel as I am a Christian in belief and perhaps in practice; but not I hope in Faith. I never expect to be a real good man and I always expect to be in this world a downright sinner. I believe circumstances make it morally impossible for me to come up to even the ordinary standard of Christian life. I expect it less than ever. If there's a Hell, besides, I'm bound to suffer it. There's no use whining about it now—very much the contrary. The fear of it will do me no good. I have to take my chance of it, but meantime I'll enjoy the pleasure of doing all the good my chains will let me reach to.

The love of money is the root of considerable evil. How it does narrow and degrade and blind most everybody here. They actually let nothing come in competition with *business*. They will not pay their respect to God until they have free leave from Mammon. The common people are ill natured, desperately selfish and incapable of friendship of more than words. Not

358

so beastly and stupid as the English but more crafty and hypocritical—yet better according to their light than the rich.

Stay where you are as long as you can. Get the good and happy characteristics of other nations. Shake off and resist their badness and unhappiness and come and preach with Faith, if you can, when you cannot stay away any longer. For my part, I am not the least bit glad to get back. (I won't say home for home is poetry.) Stay away. See good people, happy people, or people who are not unhappy only because they can not get more money, or money's worth.

I wish that I had seen more of the better, more polished classes. I wish that I had spent more money. I wish that I had borrowed money if necessary. I advise you to. Borrow money and dress well. Travel by railway and pay for the inside of the cathedral and for a *catalogue* to the Picture Gallery. Conform now, when you come to America *fight*. Most of all do I wish I had seen more of the Saints, the earnest men. Their memory is my bottle of water keeping my Faith alive in this desert. See all you can of them, going to London or Bingen[2] or Paris on purpose for this. Even Neill and the ladies I love.[3] I believe I would half marry one of them if she were here. Indeed I do.

Give my love to them if you see them. Don't tell them how mad I am that I did not swim ashore that time I was last in Belfast Loch[4] to see them. I'd rather be there than here a big dam sight. Luxury is killing everybody I know.

We had Fred Kingsbury here last Sunday. We did not [have] a very good time, but rather better than I expected. I knew long ago I'd lost him along with the rest. On the whole Fred seemed better off than you'd suppose. He must be doing others and the world a great deal of good. I doubt if he is himself much. Still he is moving yet and, if slowly, perhaps with more weight and certainty.

I saw his wife[5] under unfavorable circumstances. I closed right in as if she had been a part of old Fred and I had a right to be careless and sociable or silent. She took it well. At first she seemed very unpromising, but fetching another stand point, I understood her differently and have faith enough in Fred at least to say I liked her after half an hour very—well,— much. Better than *most* anybody else I have seen since I came back.

She is nothing but an old fashioned sub[terranean][6] half man though. Good enough for a wife or a servant—no equal friend. Is it impossible, must equality make misery, must unity depend on submission? Thank god—if it must be so yet, there is a better time coming. But we must live while we do live. It is home though wherever we take Christ's Spirit. Don't come this side of the water for it. Find it where you are, and ev[*en among stra*]ngers.[7]

The Fugitive Slave Act[8] is raising a great dust. You will see from

Greeley[9] there is a fearful reaction. The free principles of the North can not stand against the danger of losing Southern trade. The virtue spouted last year was but gas and sentimentality. I think both sides now very wrong. Fred Kingsbury does not read Beecher's articles in *The Independent*.[10] Meantime from the South the mutter of discontent is growing into a roar for disunion. A majority for resistance to—I don't know what the devil the oppression is—is claimed in some states—resistance and nullification.[11] Money is at the bottom of the sin on both sides.

Our 1st County Agricultural Fair went off unexpectedly well. I expect to have towards $20 worth of premiums, notwithstanding my absence.[12] But the farm does look shockingly shabby after Scotland. See a German farm if you can. I mean as much a German farmer. The character and condition of the better farmers as well as the mere laborers I know very little of—in Germany.

I want you to get or order in London in addition to what I asked previously; *Morton on Soils* (up to $2); *Hutchinson on Spring Draining* (Not over $2); Hewitt Davis on Thin Sowing, (a pamphlet); Prof. Johnstone's *Tables of Experiments in Agriculture* (A pamphlet, very important).[13]

You had better write to Stevens[14] and ask him to hand a list of books you and I want to the American book agents, or *his* agents in London, if you are not going to be there any time. Have them sent to you at Liverpool if you like. I'll pay freight and all charges willingly.

I went out yesterday to see Mrs. West[15] &c., but John wanted to come down and so I returned without. Mrs. Dr. Parker has had a baby.[16] There is no news amongst us. The fact is nobody now, we either when we are with them, knows we have been away, or that you are away. It's just the same old story. Bertha[17] has begun to wear long dresses. The last frost finished the leaves. Ice every night now. John has engaged a small room back, with a bed and fire in Wooster St.—224, opposite Bond.[18] Nearly 3½ without board. John Neill[19] has been very sick, gone south. Do not know when he will go home. They are going to build a Dutch uninformed church house here at Bloomingview on Faith & Credit. A Catholic church trying to raise the wind at Rossville.[20]

You have only been gone 8 months, which [. . .] here is no time. Stay long enough to make it a real *life*. Adieu.

1. After the Olmsted brothers returned to the United States in early October 1850, Brace spent six months in Germany. For the first two months he lived in Hamburg, learning the German language and investigating German family life (*Life of Brace*, pp. 96–98, 124; Charles Loring Brace, *Home Life in Germany* [New York, 1853], pp. 1–19).
2. A German city on the Rhine near Mainz. Neither Olmsted nor Brace mentions the city in his writings and it is not clear if they met a circle of reformers and philanthropists there. It may be that they simply had a chance encounter with humble men

who had democratic beliefs and the courage of their convictions. Olmsted's only reference to this came in a letter he wrote Brace in 1853 in which he declared, "I am a Democrat of the European School—of the school of my brave porter of Bingen, and these so called Democrats [Southern slaveholders] are not. They are of another sort, material, temporary, temporizing, conservative" (FLO to CLB, Dec. 1, 1853).

3. Robert Neill. Charles Loring Brace married one of his daughters, Letitia Neill (1822–1916) in 1854. Neill's other daughters were Dora (d. 1921) and Eliza (d. 1912?) (Life of Brace, pp. 90, 197–98).

4. The day after the Olmsteds' steamer sailed from Glasgow it encountered a fierce gale. The captain put about and ran for the shelter of Belfast Lough. The ship spent twenty-four hours there waiting for the storm to abate, and during that time Olmsted wished he could go ashore to see the Neills (New York Daily Tribune, Oct. 24, 1850, p. 3).

5. At this time Kingsbury was engaged to Alathea Ruth Scovill (1828–1899). They were married on April 29, 1851. He had known her as a child, renewed their acquaintance after meeting her at West Point in 1844, and came to know her well when he returned to live in Waterbury in 1849. At this time he was impressed by her "profound refinement of character," which led him "to think and feel that she was a person with whom I could take the joys and trials of life, year in and year out, under all circumstances with the hope of a reasonable degree of happiness." She had an intelligence and capacity for sympathy that caused many people to seek her company and counsel. She also had a basic simplicity that may have made her seem unimpressive to Olmsted (FJK Autobiography, part 3; Homer W. Brainard, A Survey of the Scovills [Hartford, Conn., 1915], pp. 300, 377–81).

6. The material in brackets was crossed out by Olmsted.

7. The material in brackets is supplied by the editor to replace words lost by a tear in the paper.

8. The Fugitive Slave Act, part of the Compromise of 1850, was signed into law by President Millard Fillmore on September 18, 1850. The law authorized the use of federal marshals for capturing fugitive slaves and levied heavy fines against officials who refused full cooperation and citizens who sought to interfere with the return of a slave. Northerners particularly objected to the law's denial of trial before a judge or jury. Instead, cases went directly to federal commissioners who received a fee of ten dollars for a ruling against a fugitive and only five dollars if they ordered him released.

9. Horace Greeley, editor of the New York Daily Tribune.

10. In his articles in the Independent at this time Henry Ward Beecher (1813–1887) counseled disobedience to the fugitive slave law (DAB).

11. When southern extremists failed to get the Nashville Convention of July 1850 to issue the "ultimatum" to the North they had hoped for, they embarked on a campaign to secure secession by individual states. South Carolina, led by Robert Barnwell Rhett, was in the vanguard. When the Nashville Convention reconvened in November it called for a southern convention that would either move to restore the rights of slaveholders threatened by the Compromise of 1850 or provide for the "safety and independence" of the South. At this time there was agitation on the question in Georgia, where elections were held on November 3, 1850, for a convention to express the views of the state on the issues raised by the compromise. During October the secessionists carried on a furious campaign. The unionists overwhelmed them at the polls, but the "Georgia Platform" that the convention adopted when it met in December nevertheless asserted that Georgia should resist, to the point of secession, any abolition of slavery in the District of Columbia without the consent and petition of slaveholders there, or any refusal by Congress to admit a territory as a state because it permitted slavery. It also warned that the preservation of the Union depended on the "faithful execution of the Fugitive Slave Act by the proper authorities" (Allan Nevins, Ordeal of the Union, 2 vols., [New York, 1947], 1: 315–18, 354–57; Henry Steele Commager, ed., Documents of American History, 9th ed. [New York, 1973], p. 323).

12. Apparently Olmsted did as well at the county fair as he anticipated. On December

21, 1850, he wrote Fred Kingsbury, "Our society does well. I have near $20 worth of premiums" (FLO to FJK, Dec. 21, 1850).

13. Olmsted probably was referring to John Morton's *On the Nature and Property of Soils to Which is Added an Account of the Proceedings at Whitefield Example-Farm* (London, 1842); Henry Hutchinson's *A Treatise on the Practical Drainage of Land* (London, 1844), or Simon Hutchinson, *Practical Instructions on the Drainage of Land* (Grantham, 1847); and Hewitt Davis's *The Injury and Waste of Corn from the Present Practice of Too Thickly Sowing* (London, 1843).

14. Henry Stevens.

15. Elizabeth Green Giles West, wife of Charles Edwin West (1809–1900), the principal of the Rutger's Female Institute in Brooklyn, N.Y., from 1839 to 1851. Charles Loring Brace taught Latin there while studying for the ministry in 1848–49 and won West's approbation (*NCAB*, 8: 235; *Pittsfield* [Massachusetts] *Sun*, March 15, 1900, p. 4; *Life of Brace*, p. 61; John Pierce Brace to CLB, Sept. 3, 1849, John Pierce Brace Correspondence, Connecticut Historical Society, Hartford, Conn.).

16. Mary Ann Bissell Parker (1815–1896), wife of Willard Parker (1800–1884), professor of surgery at the College of Physicians and Surgeons in New York. She was a first cousin of both Elizabeth Baldwin and Emily Perkins. The baby was Willard Parker, Jr. (1850–1907) (*Perkins Genealogy*, part 3, pp. 39–41; *DAB*, s.v. "Parker, Willard"; *New York Times*, June 21, 1896, p. 5; June 26, 1907, p. 7).

17. Bertha Olmsted, Olmsted's fifteen-year-old half-sister.

18. John Hull Olmsted had returned to his studies at the College of Physicians and Surgeons in New York City.

19. John Neill of Belfast, Ireland, son of Robert Neill and brother of Brace's future wife Letitia, who spent some time in New York (information supplied by Gerald Warner Brace).

20. Bloomingview (later Huguenot) and West Rossville were both villages in the southern part of Staten Island (William T. Davis, *Staten Island Names, Ye Olde Names and Nicknames* [New Brighton, N.Y., 1896], p. 74).

To Andrew Jackson Downing

Southside, Staten Island

Nov. 23, [?] 1850[1]

Dear Sir,

I wish to thank you for your kindness in sending me, through Mr. Field[2] last spring, a letter of introduction to Mr. Thompson of London.[3] I did not arrive in London in season to attend the exhibition you wished me to:[4] but I twice visited the gardens and enjoyed valuable conversations with Mr. Thompson, who was very obliging and communicative. I took his advice as to what I should see in Paris, and I had thought to offer you some account of what most interested me there. But nearly all that was new and valuable of my observations there has already now appeared in the *Horticulturist* in the article by Mr. T. from the Journal of the London Society.[5]

I spent only about one month on the Continent, mostly Germany, where I much enjoyed the social out door life, and the frequent approaches to realizations of your *ideal village*.[6] The custom of taking meals in the gardens or summer houses is very common; and it seemed to me the middle classes at least *lived* in the open air more than even the English. Nor did it seem to me, as is frequently asserted, that their habits in these respects injured the *family* influence, or made Home any less home*like* and lovable, but the contrary.

I saw the best parts of England, spending two months travelling through it on foot, seeing the country of course to great advantage, so that I feel as if I had not merely seen the rural character, but lived in it, and made it a *part* of me. I was then two months in Ireland and Scotland.

I wish you would, when convenient, do us (your disciples in Horticulture) the favor to explain distinctly the terms used to describe the different ways of growing pears, &c.[7] I think your correspondents of the *Horticulturist* have generally used the term *Standard* to designate pears grown on pear stock only, and *dwarf* for those on Quince or Thorn. But in Europe does not dwarf mean a low ill shapen tree, or a maiden tree that has lost its leader, and is only suitable for walls? And *standard* is used only, is it not, as you use it when speaking of Mr. Rivers' garden:[8] you say he has 2300 standard trees of Louise Bonne of Jersey, etc.[9] (That name will never do to take to *market*, by the way. I wish you would practicalize it.) I apprehended that some of your readers here would misunderstand you then, and I find they did.

Rivers I believe does not grow the L.B.J. on Pear stock at all, but condemns it. Nor does he grow the Copiaument or Bartlett[10] on quince. I was disappointed at not finding the pear grown on quince more abroad. Even at Paris I saw but few in open culture. Those at the *Jardin des Plantes* and at the Luxembourg are splendid full grown trees, and even this bad season were as full as could be desired of fruit.[11] At Versailles they were mostly on trellis or walls. Those *en quenouille*[12] invariably looked unhealthy.

I saw your Fruits of America[13] in France and England and Scotland; always shown as something for me to be proud of as your countryman.

Yours Respectfully,

Fred. Law Olmsted

Mr. A. J. Downing

1. The following text is from a typescript in the Olmsted Papers, Library of Congress, dated November 33 [sic], 1850. On it is the statement, "Copy from Bowyer Vaux who has the original among other Downing papers." Bowyer Vaux was the son of Calvert Vaux, who was Andrew Jackson Downing's assistant and partner from 1850 to 1852, codesigner of Central Park with Olmsted and his partner from 1865 to 1872. The original of this letter has not been located. A nearly complete version of the same text, dated November 23, 1850, appears in *Forty Years*, 1: 89–90 (*DAB*, s.v. "Vaux, Calvert").
2. Alfred Field. Field may have known Downing through his and Olmsted's mutual friend, the poet and newspaper editor William Cullen Bryant ("Edgbastonians, Past and Present," p. 122; FLO to JO, March 14, 1850).
3. Robert Thompson (1798–1869), superintendent of the fruit and vegetables department of the Royal Horticultural Society's Chiswick Gardens, near London (James Britten and George S. Boulger, comps., *A Biographical Index of Deceased British*

and Irish Botanists, 2d ed., rev. and completed by A. B. Rendle [London: Taylor and Francis, 1931], p. 299; *Proceedings of the Royal Horticultural Society,* n.s. 1, no. 7 [Feb.–Mar. 1867]: c, clxix–x).

4. The Royal Horticultural Society held an exhibition of plants in July 1850 at Chiswick Gardens that attracted nearly eight thousand visitors (John Lindley, "The London Horticultural Society's Exhibition," *Horticulturist* 5, no. 3 [Sept. 1850]: 142–43).

5. Robert Thompson, "Report on the Fruit Gardens Near Paris," ibid., 4, no. 12 [June 1850]: 549–55.

6. Downing called for a village with a park of twenty to fifty acres at the center that would be "the nucleus or *heart of the village,* and . . . give it an essentially rural character." Lots fronting on the park should be at least a quarter-acre in size, while the lots on wide streets running out from the park on each side would have frontage of at least one hundred feet. This would ensure the rural character of the town, "first, by the possession of a large central space, always devoted to park or pleasure-ground, and always held as joint property, and for the common use of the whole village; second, by the imperative arrangement of cottages or dwellings around it, in such a way as to secure in all parts of the village sufficient space, view, circulation of air, and broad, well-planted avenues of shade-trees." In time, he hoped, the residents would make the park of grass and trees into a pleasure-ground with flowers and shrubs, and rustic seats and arbors ("Our Country Villages," ibid., 4, no. 12 [June 1850]: 537–41).

7. As this letter indicates, Olmsted became something of an authority on fruits as a result of his own orchard planting and the observations he made on his European tour. As he pursued this interest, Olmsted directed a number of inquiries to the *Horticulturist,* including: "Queries on Sea-Coast Culture," signed "F. L. Olmsted, Sachem's Head, Guilford, Ct.," 2, no. 2 (Aug. 1847): 100; and "Pears—FLO (Staten Island)," 4, no. 9 (March 1850): 439–40. Other inquiries that Olmsted probably wrote were: "Pear Orchards—Southside," 3, no. 5 (Nov. 1848): 254; "Peach Orchards.—A Young Planter, (Southside, Staten Island)," 4, no. 4 (Oct. 1849): 198; and "Importation and Exportation of Fruit," signed "Yours, O. Southside, Staten-Island, Jan. 1851," 6, no. 2 (Feb. 1851): 90–91. Olmsted also contributed two longer essays to the *Horticulturist,* "A Note on the True Soldat Laboureur Pear," 7, no. 1 (Jan. 1852); 14–15, and "Apple Orchards in England," 7, no. 12 (Dec. 1852): 549–52, a passage excerpted from the second volume of *Walks and Talks of an American Farmer in England.* As a result of his pomological efforts, Olmsted received a silver spoon for his pears from the Staten Island Horticultural Society in 1852. The spoon is now in the possession of Charles C. McLaughlin.

8. Thomas Rivers (1798–1877), English nurseryman. Beginning with roses, he went on to improve native fruit trees so that British fruit growers could compete with their rivals on the Continent (*DNB*; [Andrew Jackson Downing], "Visit to Mr. Rivers' Nurseries, Sawbridgeworth, Herts," *Horticulturist* 5, no. 4 [Oct. 1850]: 181–87).

9. Louise Bohne de Jersey is a kind of pear (*Horticulturist* 5, no. 4 [Oct. 1850]: 182).

10. Capiaumont and Bartlett pears (ibid.).

11. The Jardin des Plantes in Paris was a botanical garden, with conservatories and palm house, comparable to Kew Gardens in England. The Luxembourg Gardens in Paris was more parklike and was noted for its trees (Robert Thompson, "Report on the Fruit Gardens Near Paris," ibid., 4, no. 12 [June 1850]: 549–55).

12. Pear trees artificially shaped by careful pruning to assume a regular, narrow, conical shape (Thomas W. Field, *Pear Culture* [New York, 1858], pp. 164–66).

13. Downing's *The Fruits and Fruit Trees of America,* first published in 1845, established him as the leading American authority on the subject (*DAB*).

TO CHARLES LORING BRACE

South Side, Jan. 11th, 1851

Dear Charley,

It was a great selfish disappointment that you did not come, but I am glad and thankful that you concluded to remain.[1] I fear John will not succeed in getting more correspondences for you, but I should be very glad to hear that you felt able to go on next summer as you propose. Even if you give up Hungary, I would stay late enough in the Spring to see the World's Fair.[2] I wish you could get up to Sweden and see something of domestic life there, and the same for Italy—and for a similar reason.

Do you recollect my old Theory of Compensations in National Character?[3] The good side of Swedish character (by character I mean development) we know from Miss Bremer[4] and others. Go you and see, not its faults, but the dangers [that] belong to these good customs and impulses. Of the misery and sin of Italy we have heard enough. I want you to go and appreciate the happiness and nobleness that produce or belong to those particular sins & miseries. I am sure they are there, as I am that I am high because I am low, weak because I am strong.

If you could get to Hungary and really know the people, take an unprejudiced view of their condition & character, learn what really is their Revolutionary impulse, it would be most rare, interesting and valuable. For my part I really am anxious to get some advice about that people from a man that really knows something about them; and I think others must be.

Your letter about yourself and the good you thought you were getting was delightful. I do think so, too. I am more and more constantly aware of the good I received—direct effect on my—*spirit*. I should say that I had more independence, freedom of thought—was less influenced by the mere fact of others' opinions—cared less for their opinions—or at least was influenced less by them than before. At the same time I may, and hope I have (or shall have) more personal regard and respect for them—certainly more charity and brotherhood with those who differ totally with me. I *am* less dependent decidedly on the approval of others and have more faith in myself and *dignity* of *mind* (even less of *exterior*, perhaps).[5]

I have no doubt that you will have grown greatly. But I meant to speak of another effect. I am disappointed in the increased power I have over others, as yet. The mere fact of having been to Europe is worth nothing. To me, in looking at another, it always was an expectation of an increased value to the man—rightly so. But I have now this impression that here people do not *respect* anyone sincerely. Representatives only it seems to me they bow to—as clergymen of religion, &c.

Everybody does seem horridly selfish and wrapped up in personal concerns, as you described the Manchester editor to us. The show of interest they make seems to be merely formal. They, in the closet, think nothing of you except as you have something to buy or sell. Surely I, who am going cross and reserved, do really love and pray for them, though they go to California or I to Europe.

You have very greatly improved in your style of writing, it seems to us, since you have been in Germany. Do you not take more pains to finish and unite your letters than you did?

I was alone when I opened The Horticulturist this month. And when I turned to the article, "Domestic Life in Germany" and saw it was yours, I threw the book down on the floor and laughed, I was so glad. It was about economy, stoves, and my friend's house in Hamburgh—and credited "C.L. in the Independent."[6] I have written to Downing[7] to tell him who you are.

He wants me to write him in familiar letters Rural Impressions of Germany, &c. I find I can not do it. I saw and know too little of Germany to write distinctly upon it. But I agree with him that whoever could do it would be in the way of doing a good deal of small good. Our rural character is *in transitu* and wants help from Germany. What I do wish very earnestly, Charley (and if I could, would urge most seriously) is that Mrs. Gray[8] [do it]—every way fitted, just the person of all others. It is our women that are at fault in this Rural taste, or rather in their entire want of Rural taste. And what a woman like Mrs. G. would see, would *tell*, would, even [if] it seemed trite and common place coming from a woman of her taste and information, would influence them. I wish you would persuade her to write a letter or two for *The Horticulturist*. There is this month the most sensible ideas on the architectural character of churches that has appeared in this country.[9] Do make a serious *appeal* to Mrs. Gray. I am much in earnest.

In The Courant this week (recollect weekly and daily, great circulation) is an abstract with extracts of your Holstein—farm house letter.[10] Very good. You did the farming very well. Don't be afraid to go into particulars. You know a good deal of agriculture. The remark on draining will really be worth something in Connecticut. This from *The Bulletin*.[11] *The Saturday Evening Gazette*[12] in which your letters are also published used to have a considerable number of subscribers at Collinsville, I remember, and I presume has an extensive circulation in such places.

Your remarks on colleges read very good[13]—reasonable & convincing. Your German letters, particularly the Hamburg & *country* letters, have been the most *popular* you have written, I guess.[14]

If you go to Swiss land I can get you a letter to Hall's father in law there, an ultra evangelical, rear guard professor at Geneva.[15]

I had a very pleasant visit from Hen Barnes.[16] Did I tell you? He intended to be here again when you came. He is terribly in love, as usual, with the sex in general—or ideal. But there is nobody here to suit such men as he and I. I honestly advise you to look out [for] a wife in Europe. I don't believe there are any left here to suit us.

Princeton works admirably as an Emetic with Henry. That is, you understand, they give him such a stiff dose of poisoned doctrine that instead of being injured by it he throws up something else with it. He says right out they are perfect jackasses the whole concern of them.

"What do you understand [by] that Mr. Barnes?"

"Why, I understand just what it says, and I think *St. Paul was mistaken about it.* That's the way I explain it."

"But I don't understand you Brother Barnes. Do you not think St. Paul was inspired?"

"Inspired?—yes, inspired—but, that's no reason he should never make a mistake."

He has preached some sermons in Philadelphia that the ministers have blowed him for. He says he wishes he could get once permanently settled, a wife and a salary, and he'd tell 'em something. Dam the whole trade I say. If you are determined to get into the shoes of the devil to do good, when there are so many other honest and honorable ways, I shall think myself a fool.

I don't know but two priests in the country that have not gone with the majority (of church paying citizens) in this damnable Fugitive Slave Law reaction—Beecher and Storrs.[17] God give them better company.

You know, perhaps, Dr. Taylor has addressed a "Union Meeting," and his lickspittle has been published in the Journal of Cotton with half a column of leaded type of flattering introduction. Ditto Dr. Cox—*ditto* two other Doctors whose very names it is not becoming a free man to write.[18] Can't you touch upon this matter in your letters? What do sincere Christian Democrats say about it in Germany?

They have a new Principal at the High School—Hartford—a regular mean lying Compromiser I should think.[19] John probably tells you about him. Their great hope would be that you would come back and take the place when they kick him out—but I have a greater hope.

Congress and the New York legislature have only talked on unimportant subjects yet. There is fun in Massachusetts. The Free Soilers bargained to get a U.S. Senator for 6 years—if they gave the Governor to Locos. The Locos hardly dare to do it.[20] Oh, if the Whigs & F.S. would put in Horace Mann, would it not be capital! Or if they could make a Union Whig Governor & Phillips, Senator. But there's no promise of any such thing.[21]

Mr. Atwood—I beg pardon, (of course, such a man is the) *Reverend* Mister Atwood, Locofoco candidate for Governor in New Hampshire turned three somersets in a week writing as many letters, each condemning the sentiments of the other in regard to Fugitives. He is likely to be promoted to the excellency.[22] Don't despair of the country, Charly. Recollect ten years ago and the Gag—law.[23]

I have begun writing a book. But if I go on *far*, I cannot finish it this winter. I have not landed at Liverpool yet, but have faith that I shall get there pretty strong.[24] I have been invited to take the Whig nomination for Town Clerk, and Justice of Peace, and to deliver an agricultural address at East Windsor (Wouldn't I give their Orthodox fits?)[25] but have declined principally on account of wanting the time if I write.

I have a great lot of trees coming. 5,000 shipped 29th November and not here yet. Some of the packets are making seventy days passage. Think of it! More than *two* months of the Henry Clay![26]

That remark of yours about tenacity of attachment is worth more than a paragraph if it is worthwhile to write upon it [at] all. I won't go into it, but merely say that I think you are quite wrong about me. That in *character* I am much more so than you and John. It is simply previous caution and a subjection to duty which would make me appear otherwise. Else do you not think I should marry?

As it is, I am likely to be all along a bachelor or to marry believing that the "highest element of love" is not of earth, and so secure from disappointment if I shall not find it. Anyway, I am convinced that in this I am less likely to lose my own love—to change my love, as you say, than you are or John.[27] But not for the reason that you suppose. Improbable as it may sound to you, I do not love rashly—foolishly. I do not *Love easily*. My attachments are always worth more than I reckon them. I always find it so. I see but one exception to the rule that I always underestimate rather than otherwise the character and talents of those I am most a friend to. In that exception my attachment increases. While yours and John's decrease. I say my attachment increases, but it is a *grievous* sad attachment, and constantly moved to active, improving kindness. Your attachment is weakened and you are moved to despise and neglect. Of course, I speak in extremes. It's a painful subject anyway.

I doubt if I shall ever "love" till I marry (or am engaged) but I shall not marry a woman that I shall not be very likely to love very dearly when I safely can. I do not know such a one. I am not sure but Miss Neill comes as near it as any, as John thinks.[28] I wish you would ask her what she thinks of it.[29]

I want Murray's *Rhine*[30] to put in my book, if you can send it by anyone. I want those books much. If there is no quicker way, without a great deal of trouble, send me back the list & I will order by a New York house— or send it to Stevens[31] and ask him to hand to a New York house in London and pay or become responsible for it, & I will remit. Or send them & I will pay the house in New York. I am in a hurry.

1. Charles Loring Brace was spending the winter in Berlin, studying politics and theology (*Life of Brace*, p. 102).
2. The International Exhibition that opened in London on May 1, 1851. Sir Joseph Paxton, the designer of the park at Birkenhead that so impressed Olmsted, designed the great Crystal Palace that housed the exhibition (George F. Chadwick, *The Park and the Town: Public Landscape in the 19th and 20th Centuries* [New York, 1966], pp. 68–72, 91–94).
3. Olmsted modeled his theory of compensation on that of Ralph Waldo Emerson, who posited a dualism in nature by which every force or trait was balanced by an antithetical one. "Every excess causes a defect; every defect an excess," he wrote. "Every sweet hath its sour; every evil its good. Every faculty which is a receiver of pleasure has an equal penalty put on its abuse. . . . For every grain of wit there is a grain of folly" (Ralph Waldo Emerson, "Compensation," in *Essays*, first series [Boston, 1841]).
4. Fredrika Bremer (1801–1865), the Swedish writer, who portrayed everyday life in Sweden in her novels of the 1830s (*EB*).
5. One instance of Olmsted's earlier concern for preserving a dignified appearance was the time in 1847 that he drove his oxen and other possessions from Hartford to the farm at Sachem's Head. He chose to wear "a nice cap & dress-coat" on the trip, which his brother said "made it all the more ludicrous, tho perhaps not less 'dignified' " (JHO to FJK, March 29, 1847).
6. Charles Brace's letter, "Domestic Life in Germany," first published in the *Independent*, was republished in the *Horticulturist* ("C. S.," "Domestic Life in Germany," *Independent*, no. 105 [Dec. 5, 1850], p. 1; "Domestic Life in Germany," *Horticulturist* 6, no. 1 [Jan. 1851], p. 43–44).
7. Andrew Jackson Downing.
8. Jane Lathrop Loring Gray (1821–1909), cousin of Charles Loring Brace and daughter of Charles Greely Loring. She married the botanist Asa Gray in 1848 (Charles H. Pope and Katherine P. Loring, eds., *Loring Genealogy* [Cambridge, Mass., 1917], pp. 166–68).
9. In "A Short Chapter on Country Churches," Andrew Jackson Downing set forth several themes that would recur in Olmsted's own writings on landscape and architecture. Repeating one of the basic lessons of the theorists of the Gothic Revival, he declared that a building in its "form and feature" should express its use. ". . . Right expression in a building for religious purposes," he wrote, "has as much to do with awakening devotional feelings, and begetting an attachment in the heart, as the unmistakable signs of virtue and benevolence in our fellow-creatures have in awakening kindred feeling in our own breasts." He assailed the current Greek Revival style of church-building as improper, since the leading idea of Greek architecture was the horizontal line, the *"level line of rationality."* Such a style was fitting for "all civil purposes where the reason of man is supreme," whereas the Gothic style, with "its upward lines—its aspiring tendencies," was far more fitting for churches. Downing was also concerned that country churches should have a proper setting in a spot of green lawn, surrounded by shade trees and covered by ivy or Virginia Creeper. This would help to make the country church more "rural and expressive" and would make the church structure, as well as the sermons delivered within it, "something to become a part of the affections, and touch and better the hearts of the whole country about it" (*Horticulturist*, 6, no. 1 [Jan. 1851]: 9–12, rpt. in Andrew J. Downing, *Rural Essays* [New York, 1853], pp. 260–64).
10. *The Hartford Daily Courant*, Jan. 6, 1851, p. 2, contained an abstract of Brace's article in the *Independent*, no. 106 [Dec. 12, 1850], p. 1.
11. The *Philadelphia Bulletin*, for which Brace wrote letters while in Europe.
12. The *Saturday Evening Gazette* was published in Boston from 1814 to 1906 (Frank L. Mott, *A History of American Magazines*, vol. 4, *1885–1905* [Cambridge, Mass., 1957], p. 69 n).
13. In his letter on German colleges, Brace compared German and American students, deploring the lack of intellectual enthusiasm in the United States and praising Ger-

man students as dedicated, serious, and mature (*Independent*, no. 108 [Dec. 26, 1850], p. 2).

14. These letters appeared in the *Independent*, no. 105 [Dec. 5, 1850], p. 1, and no. 106 [Dec. 12, 1850], p. 1.

15. Eli Edwin Hall (1814–1896), minister of the First Congregational Church at Guilford, Conn., while Olmsted lived at Sachem's Head, married Cecile Malan, the daughter of César Malan (1787–1864), a minister in the Swiss Reformed Church who was expelled from the ministry for his evangelical preaching. Malan continued to preach, however, and made many effective tours of European countries from his base in Geneva (*Schaff-Herzog Encyc.*, s.v. "Malan, César Henri Abraham"; *Yale Obit. Rec.*, 4th ser., no. 6 [June 1896]: 415).

16. At this time Albert Henry Barnes was studying at the Princeton Theological Seminary, a bastion of Old School Presbyterianism. He was married in 1854, the same year he was ordained a minister by the Presbytery of Pennsylvania (Princeton Theological Seminary, *Necrological Report*, 5, *1875–1889*, April 29, 1879 [Philadelphia, 1879], p. 53; *Yale Obit. Rec.*, 2d ser., no. 8 [June 1878]: 302; Winthrop S. Hudson, *American Protestantism* [Chicago, 1961], pp. 103–9).

17. Henry Ward Beecher argued from his pulpit and in the pages of the *Independent* that the Fugitive Slave Law went directly against the fundamental principles upon which the country was founded. Richard Salter Storrs (1821–1900), minister of the Church of the Pilgrims, rivaled Beecher in importance in Brooklyn and edited the *Independent* from 1848 to 1861. Like Beecher, he spoke out strongly against the Fugitive Slave Law, saying that it was against the higher law of God and that one should not violate God's law even to preserve the Union (*DAB*, s.v. "Storrs, Richard Salter"; Theodore Davenport Bacon, *Leonard Bacon, A Statesman in the Church*, ed. Benjamin W. Bacon [New Haven, Conn., 1931], pp. 311, 341; Richard S. Storrs, Jr., *The Obligation of Man to Obey the Civil Law: Its Ground, and Its Extent* [New York, 1850], pp. 32–40; Lyman Beecher Stowe, *Saints, Sinners, and Beechers* [New York, 1934], pp. 236, 280–81).

18. During the fall of 1850 the merchants of New York, who traded extensively with the South, became concerned about the growing support in the North for disobedience to the Fugitive Slave Law, and warnings from the South that such action could lead to disruption of the Union. On October 27, 1850, a great "Union Meeting" of Whigs and Democrats in support of the Union and the Constitution was held at Castle Garden in New York. The meeting declared its support of the compromise measures passed by Congress in 1850 and sought to find ways to quiet the controversy over the Fugitive Slave Law. Soon other cities followed suit, and at a Union meeting in New Haven on Christmas Eve, 1850, the Yale theologian Nathaniel W. Taylor delivered "a most stirring and effective appeal in behalf of the Constitution and the Laws."

The paper in which Olmsted read the speech was, presumably, the New York *Journal of Commerce*—which he calls the "Journal of Cotton" because of its close identification with the New York mercantile community and its active support of the Union meeting movement. In fact, the *Journal of Commerce* sometimes replied to those who criticized the movement as the work of the cotton interests by praising the ability of cotton to unite the nation. On December 20, 1850, it declared in an editorial entitled "Cotton": ". . . Behold how it quickens the sympathies of the North towards the South, and of the South towards the North. Blessed be cotton! It defeats the schemes of agitators, nullifiers, and disorganizers. It strengthens the arms of Union men, in every part of the land."

On December 28, 1850, the *Journal of Commerce* published Taylor's speech at the New Haven Union meeting and introduced it by saying, "There is hardly a name in all New England which will carry with it greater moral effects than that of *Nathaniel W. Taylor*. Wherever in our broad land Christianity is known, the words of this eminent theologian and exemplary man will be heeded." In his speech, Taylor attacked the "higher law" assertion that both the Fugitive Slave Law and Article 4, Section 2 of the Constitution, which provided for the return of slaves who escaped across state lines, were contrary to the law of God and should not be obeyed. He warned that such agitation could plunge the country into civil war and ended his speech with an impassioned plea for the defense of the Constitution.

Samuel Hanson Cox (1793–1880) was pastor of the First Presbyterian Church in Brooklyn, N.Y., and one of the leading clergymen of the city. In a Thanksgiving sermon reported in the *Journal of Commerce* on December 18, 1850, he argued that the Constitution forbade interference by any state or the federal government in the internal affairs of a state. He also criticized members of Congress who expressed "higher law" views about sections of the Constitution. Members of Congress, Cox declared, should either keep their oath to uphold the Constitution or else refuse to take it (Philip S. Foner, *Business & Slavery: The New York Merchants & the Irrepressible Conflict* [Chapel Hill, 1941], pp. 34–45, 55–60; New York *Journal of Commerce*, Dec. 27 and 28, 1850; *NCAB* VII: 557).

19. The new principal of the Hartford High School was Cephas A. Leach (d. 1887), who lasted in the post only until May 1851 (*Quindecennial Catalogue of the Hartford Public High School* [Hartford, Conn., 1910], p. 63).

20. Daniel Webster's speech of March 7, 1850, in which he gave his support to the Compromise of 1850, broke some of the ties between the Whig and Free Soil parties in Massachusetts and made possible a coalition between the Whig and Free Soil politicians and antislavery Democrats in that state. This coalition easily carried the state legislature in the fall elections of 1850. When the legislature met in January 1851, the Free Soilers fulfilled their part of the plan to share state offices, including the election of the Democrat George S. Boutwell as governor. But the Democrats balked at their earlier promise to elect Charles Sumner as U.S. senator and held out for more than three months before doing so (Richard H. Abbott, *Cobbler in Congress, The Life of Henry Wilson, 1812–1875* [Lexington, Ky., 1972], pp. 35–36; David Donald, *Charles Sumner and the Coming of the Civil War* [New York, 1960], pp. 190, 199, 202, 224).

21. Horace Mann (1796–1859), the educational reformer, had been elected to Congress in 1848 as a Whig, but his antislavery stand and his opposition to the leading Massachusetts Whig, Daniel Webster, offended that party. In 1850 he returned to Congress as a Free Soiler, and in 1852 he was the unsuccessful Free Soil candidate for governor. Stephen C. Phillips (1801–1857) had three times been the Free Soil party's gubernatorial candidate and was angered at being bypassed in favor of Sumner for the Senate seat in 1851 (ibid., pp. 185, 225; R. H. Abbott, *Cobbler in Congress*, pp. 31, 34, 42, 48–49; *NCAB*, 11: 489).

22. John Atwood (1795–1873), a Baptist minister, received the Democratic nomination for governor in traditionally Democratic New Hampshire in 1850. When a Free Soil Party committee demanded to know his views on slavery and the Fugitive Slave Law, Atwood at first said that he opposed the law because of its harsh provisions, especially the denial of jury trial to accused fugitives. He soon repudiated this stand, then re-adopted it. This so embarrassed his party that when it met in 1851 it chose another candidate for governor (Ezra Stearnes, *Genealogical and Family History of the State of New Hampshire: A Record of the Achievement of Her People*, 4 vols. [New York, 1908], 3: 1431; John McClintock, *Colony, Province, State, 1623–1888: History of New Hampshire* [Boston, 1889], p. 601; *Hartford Daily Courant*, Dec. 24, 1850, p. 2).

23. In 1840 the House of Representatives ended nearly a decade of debate over the handling of abolitionist petitions by adopting a standing rule that forbade the House to receive them. As a result of the furor that followed, abolitionists in the North gained much wider acceptance for their activities; the greater part of the newspaper-reading public soon "honored the abolitionists while they opposed them, as champions of the rights of the free as well as of the slaves." This new climate of public opinion in the North helped to foster the growth of the antislavery movement. Olmsted apparently means to suggest by this reference that the unjust Fugitive Slave Law could have a similar beneficial result for the antislavery cause (Gilbert Barnes, *The Anti-Slavery Impulse, 1830–1844* [New York, 1933; rpt. ed., 1964], pp. 118–20).

24. Olmsted devoted the first four chapters of his *Walks and Talks of An American*

371

Farmer in England to a description of the ocean passage from New York to Liverpool.

25. East Windsor, Conn., was the home of the doctrinally conservative Hartford Theological Seminary (see FLO to CLB, Sept. 20, 1847, above).

26. The ship on which Olmsted, John, and Charles Loring Brace had sailed to England in 1850.

27. In the accompanying letter that he completed on the address panel of this letter, John Hull Olmsted wrote, apparently in reference to this question, "I thought you wrong about Fred there, too, Charley—that he would not revolt as soon as we at insufficiency of 'character.' "

28. Olmsted is referring to one of the daughters of Robert Neill, whom he and his companions met during their tour of Ireland in 1850. Brace married one of them, Letitia Neill, in 1854 (see FLO to CLB, Nov. 12, 1850, above, notes 3 and 4).

29. At this point the extant part of this letter by Olmsted ends. The paragraph below is one he added in the margin of an interior page.

30. A book entitled *The Rhine*, part of a series called *Murray's Handbooks for Travellers*, projected by the London publisher John Murray (*Webster's Biographical Dictionary*, s.v. "Murray, John"; *The London Catalogue of Books Published in Great Britain with the Sizes, Prices, and Publishers' Names, 1816–1851* [London, 1851], p. 395).

31. Henry Stevens.

To John Olmsted   [December 5, 1851][1]

Address: John Olmsted Esqr/Hartford/Conn.
Postmark: New York/Dec 6

New York, Nov. 4th, 1851
Thursday night

Dear Father,

The things came safely, Monday.

Charley has not yet arrived.[2]

Weather holds cold, hardly any thaw during the week. Can not pull cabbages. You were right about the cabbages—as you understood me, 20–25,000 gone to market and that number still left which with favorable weather would have marketed profitably. Wheat still looking up in town. No movement on the island. I am thrashing and shall sell as soon as I can get a dollar. Hay also improves—quoted at 56. Probably sells better.

I begin after the fashion of the Newspaper: Cotton and Corn, then Kossuth, etc.

The illustrious[3] arrived last night. I had been appointed on Committee of Reception and heard his first speech this morning from Doane's balcony.[4] Afterwards in the procession I carried the large Hungarian Color, immediately behind the carriage in which he rode. While there, he turned and took my hand and I had some conversation with him about the harbor & fortifications. Mentioned Charley, he didn't seem to know anything about it.[5] Afterwards, I had the honor of kissing Madame Kossuth's hand.[6] Stood by and presented ladies, etc.

372

He does not look like his portraits. Younger and less *distingué*. He has a wide and peculiar forehead, somewhat bald with long thin hair a little lighter than mine falling over it, moustache and thick curling beard. His eye is very fine. And when speaking he has a peculiarly animated, cheerful, face, highly expressive and interesting. His eye and the upper part of his face, particularly when speaking, reminds one of Webster.[7] His manner too is like his.

He was dressed in a graceful Hungarian costume; black coat, with small close jet buttons—to the collars; a cloak coat (pelisse) of black velvet with braiding, [. . .] with black lamb's wool, wide, collar. Hungarian hat (which has got to be common since arrival of Mississippi in New York).[8] A handsome felt, low steeple crowned hat with broad band & buckle and small black plume.

He began to speak very hesitatingly and slow and with long pauses in the midst of sentences, as if troubled to recollect words. Afterwards faster, and towards the close freely and rapidly. But then with frequent small errors in his English, as *what* for *that*.

I was very sorry they troubled him on the island, but he took it very easy and I think was not much fatigued. The arrangements were absurd and with no order or precision, everybody ordering & not the slightest attention to order. Nevertheless, it went off well. The unterrified crowded in and kept him shaking hands, which he didn't pretend to much like, a long time. Major Hagadorn[9] couldn't do anything with his soldiers. They charged bayonets & the crowd charged back and upset them and broke their ranks just as they pleased.

You will see the speeches. Our orator[10] was not drunk, nor stupid for want of drink as he was at the Agricultural Society Address and the address was very tolerable—not extra gazy.

I shall stay here tonight—go down in the morning and probably accompany the City Corporation, etc. on the Oregon. There's no sign of preparation tonight that I can see, but doubtless it will be a great affair.[11]

I have read a large part of my book to Field,[12] who likes it much—and arranged with Putnam[13] who has read all I have written (which tells pretty well) to pay me 10 per cent on retail sales after expenses are all paid. The retail sale price to be 25 cents. The cheapest original book ever published in the country. Will require a sale of 3 to 5000 to pay cost. Ten per cent is the highest usual payment to authors. The Harpers pay Barnes for his Notes, one of the most profitable books in the country, 16 per cent. Barnes Jr. thought 5 per cent was the usual payment.[14]

Yours, &c.,

FLO

1. Olmsted must have written this letter on the night of Friday, December 5, 1851, since Kossuth's steamship arrived at the Staten Island quarantine station at 1:00 A.M. of that day (*New York Daily Tribune*, Dec. 5, 1851, p. 4).

2. Charles Loring Brace returned to New York from Europe on December 13, 1851 (ibid., Dec. 15, 1851, p. 7).

3. Lajos Kossuth (1802–1894), Hungarian nationalist and revolutionary, the head of the provisional government established during the short-lived Hungarian insurrection against Austrian rule in 1848. Kossuth escaped from Hungary when the movement for independence was put down, and found asylum in Turkey. In 1851 President Millard Fillmore sent the American steam-frigate *Mississippi* to transport him to the United States as an official guest, and the country received him enthusiastically. Each city on his triumphal tour sought to outdo the others in the warmth of its welcome. Kossuth was a guest of the president while in Washington and addressed a joint session of Congress. Americans hailed him as a great fighter for human liberty, but he found their overwhelming welcome was no true gauge of their willingness to aid the Hungarian struggle for freedom. After seven months he returned to Europe disillusioned, without the diplomatic and financial aid he had sought (Otto Zarek, *Kossuth* [London, 1937], pp. 260–68).

4. Dr. Augustus S. Doane (1808–1852), health officer at the Staten Island quarantine station, was Kossuth's host while he was at Staten Island (*Appleton's Cyc. Am. Biog.*; *New York Daily Tribune*, Dec. 5, 1851, p. 4).

5. Charles Loring Brace's imprisonment by Austrian authorities may have escaped Kossuth's notice, but by July 1852 he had read Brace's book, *Hungary in 1851*, and told him in "a long confidential interview" that it had "done more for him than any other thing . . ." (*Life of Brace*, p. 148).

6. Zsuzsanna Kossuth (1820–1854).

7. Daniel Webster.

8. Kossuth had left the American warship *Mississippi* at Gibraltar in mid-October in order to visit England. The *Mississippi* proceeded to New York with a group of his Hungarian friends and supporters, arriving on November 11 (*New York Daily Tribune*, Nov. 11, 1851).

9. Francis L. Hagadorn (b. 1819), publisher and sometime editor of the local newspaper, the *Staten Islander*, and a major in the New York State Militia. He was the commander of the militia troops that served as guard of honor during the reception of Kossuth at Staten Island (*Annual Report of the Adjutant General of the State of New York, Jan. 17, 1854* [Albany, 1854], p. 23; C. Leng and W. Davis, *Staten Island and Its People*, 2: 758–59).

10. The orator at Kossuth's reception at Staten Island on December 5 was Richard Adams Locke (1800–1871), an English-born journalist who lived on the island. His best-known work was the "Moon Hoax," which he wrote for the fledgling New York *Sun* in 1835, reporting the discovery of animals, winged men, and strange sea creatures on the moon (*New York Daily Tribune*, Dec. 6, 1851, p. 4; *DAB*).

11. Olmsted described the next day's activities in a later letter to his father: "I went down Saturday morning, was admitted to Dr. D[*oane's par*]lor—where I saw Kossuth come down about 10 o'clock (ha[*d been*] writing till then in his room) & go to breakfast. He [. . .] talked with the children—moved about very rapidly and when he sat down appeared to enjoy it—lounging right down as if rest felt good. It was a shameful performance getting him on board the Vanderbilt—and all the arrangements were bad. Stupid asses all around. I kept out of the scuffle and was left & went up with Judge Clawson and others in the 11 o'clock ferry" (FLO to JO, Dec. 8, 1851).

    Kossuth had reason to be tired. The Atlantic passage had been very rough and fatiguing, and he hardly got to bed at Dr. Doane's on the morning of December 5th before he and his party were roused by a welcoming cannonade at 6:30 A..M. That day, after the formal speech-making in the morning, the Staten Islanders insisted that he make a long tour of the island, to see it and be seen. As Olmsted notes, his departure from Staten Island on Saturday, December 6, was pandemonium. When the steamer *Vanderbilt* (which came in place of the *Oregon*) docked at the wharf at Staten Island Quarantine to take on Kossuth and his party, the crowd rushed aboard, heedless of the bayonets of the honor guard, pushing Hungarians and local dignitaries aside (Ferencz and Theresa Pulsky, *White, Red, Black. Sketches of Society in the United States During the Visit of Their Guest*, 3 vols. [1853; rpt. ed., New York: 1968], 1: 51–65; *New York Daily Tribune*, Dec. 6, 1951, p. 4; Dec. 8, 1851, p. 4).

12. Olmsted was apparently reading parts of his book *Walks and Talks of an American Farmer in England* to his English friend Alfred T. Field (see FLO to JO, March 1, 1850, note 11, above).

13. George Palmer Putnam, New York publisher, who published Olmsted's *Walks and Talks*.

14. Albert Barnes, father of Olmsted's and Brace's friend Albert Henry Barnes, was the author of a multi-volume series of commentaries on the New Testament, Isaiah, and the Psalms published under the title of *Notes: Explanatory and Practical* (*DAB*).

To CHARLES LORING BRACE   [c. July 26, 1852][1]

Address: C.L. Brace./Care of Chas. W. Elliott.[2]/New Haven./Conn.
Postmark: South Side N.Y./July 26/Paid 9

Dear Charley,

Mr. & Mrs. Field, Rosa, Dr. Neidhard & myself were the party.[3] Dr. Neidhard is an unusually sensible, reliable, good-hearted, stout, heavy, common-looking, democratic, socialistic, Christianic, German Homeopathic physician, standing high in this profession & having a profitable practice in Philadelphia. Had seen your letters in Bulletin—not your book. Was sorry not to see you & would be glad to do so when convenient to you.[4]

The Navesink Highlands[5] are a narrow range of hills extending down the shore but little further than we went with Benny.[6] Then along their southern base comes the Shrewsbury or Neversink River, embouching into the *inlet* opposite the ocean house a few miles below our *peach-harbor.* Going up this 7 miles or so to Redbank—a very beautiful country. The south shore flattish & rather marshy. North, hilly with beautiful slopes to the shore —on which are woods, orchards & cultivated fields—very charmingly mingled. Finer than Staten Island.

From Redbank we start for the Phalanx by a *diligence.*[7] Country very pretty—sandy & sterile but by marl & capital culture bearing fine crops.[8] Hilly, well wooded & watered. Further you go less pretty—more half cleared land, less diversity of surface &c.

About ten miles—you come to the domain—no indication of approach—woody country—large old brown mill—water & steam power, saw & grist &c.[9] Enter a farm gate & by a good road through pretty wild wood 50 to 100 rods to the phalanstery. No grounds[10]—an old barrack attached to a little old Dutch cottage, & back of this a few rods, a rather fine neat large, brown colored, wood, hotel looking building.

We land on the piazza of it & enter a cold reception room. Plain, matted floor—engraving, head of Fourier & Swedenborg[11] & plaster angel & a vase or two. Visitors' register on table. Nobody in sight for some time & we *waiting.*

I am looking out of window & see from the aforesaid barrack a human being approaching. It is Horace Greeley in a Bloomer. The same high expansive noble benevolent forehead & eye—rather withered in the sensual. The same floxy hair—& a devil may care air about looks & a take it easy carriage & expression. She is between 30 & 50 & looks healthy & good spite of the outrageous oddity.

She comes & salutes us mildly. Tells us most of Field's acquaintances are not here. (Spring[12] for one, for your luck.) But others are brought, dinner ordered, & Mrs. Arnold,[13] as good a specimen of the best sort of New England little oldish woman as I ever saw. Mild, loving, earnest, simple, thin, and monstrously over-worked. She is our hostess & we are made guests—dine, and Field & I, with a young pair of Arnolds, look over the crops, the marl pit &c.

There are about 100 members & 50 visitors, children, & probationers. No one can join until after a year's probation he or she is accepted by a majority vote. Visitors pay cost (same as members for dishes at table & $2 a week for profit & 37¢ for rent. So it costs as a mere boarding-house $3 to 5 a week.)

The attention of the community has thus far been evidently given to merely financial success. They have evidently worked hard & constantly. And though from inexperience they made a good many errors at first and have had a great many peculiar difficulties, they have succeeded in *making it pay.* A great success. They have done little but in agriculture to make money by. And when you consider how hard it is to live by agriculture in general, you will acknowledge they have shown a great advantage in the co-operative principle as applied to it.

They have, as I intimated, neglected anything else almost in the endeavor to make money. There has been little thought of beauty or moral or mental advancement. Education of the young has been forgotten in a great measure. There is surprisingly little [concern] for appearances. They all talk and act *naturally,* simply and unaffectedly. Evidently care little, too little, about the *world* outside. Pay but little attention to visitors and greatly love one-another.

They generally are very strongly attached to the Phalanx, feel confident that it is the right way to live. Have enjoyed it & succeeded in their purposes in it much better than they had expected to. "I *wouldn't* leave for worlds." "Couldn't live any other way." "It is heaven compared with the life I had before," &c., we heard from different individuals.

It is considered a great privilege to be permitted to join them and they reject a great many. I can not tell what sort of people they were. Mostly New Englanders I should think—of various classes—the majority working people. Few or none independently wealthy. Whether any considerable number were actually mere laborers living from hand to mouth, uneducated and uncouth, I could not be satisfied. Some of the later ones were. Many of the old ones might have been and if so have been a good deal refined and civilized by the associative life.

If we compare their situation with that of an average of the agricultural class—laborers & all—even in the best of New England, it is a most *blessed* advance. They are better in nearly all respects. And I don't see why, if such associations were common, and our "lowest class" (I mean poorest & least comfortable and least in the way of improvement moral & mental) of laborers could be drawn of their own will into it, they should not be in the same way advanced in every way. Put a *common-place* man (if a common-place man would choose to be so put) of our poorest Agricultural or Manufacturing laboring class into *such circumstances*, and it looks to me every way probable that he would be greatly elevated—be made a new man in a few years.

On the other hand, take the average of our people of all classes, including the wealthy and gay fashionable—including our merchants & shop-keepers & lawyers & ministers—and I think on the whole the influence of the system, if they would keep to it, would be favorable. They would live more sensibly, be happier & better.

If you take our most intelligent religious & cultivated sensible people, I think it would depend on individual character, on individual tastes. I half think (though my taste would say otherwise) it would be better for me. For you & J.H.O. & Field it would require a change, a good deal of a struggle, to come handsomely and profitably into it.

The long & short of it is I am *more of a Fourierist* than before I visited the Experiment. The conglomeration of families even works better than I was willing to believe. Nevertheless I am not a Fourierist for myself: but for many, a large part of even an American community (people) I am. It wouldn't suit me—certainly not Field or J.H.O. But I think it would the majority. An Associationist—a Socialist—I very decidedly more am than I was before I went to the Phalanx. The advantages of cooperation of labor are manifestly great. The saving of labor immense.[14] The cheapening of food, rent, &c., very great. It would make starvation, abundance. The advantages by making knowledge, intellectual & moral culture, and esthetic culture more easy—popular—that is, the advantages by *democratizing* religion, refinement & information, I am inclined to think might be equally great among the *associated*. They are not at the N.A. Phalanx & yet are manifest among some.

Those who came there refined, religious, (moral at least) & highly intelligent may have suffered. I saw no evidence that I know that they had, but I should have thought they would. Because they have given themselves up to too narrow ranges of thought—have worked too hard to make the association succeed—or, if you please, too hard for the benefit of others.

It is not, by any means, yet a well-organized & arranged establishment. They are constantly improving—seeing errors and returning to do up matters which in the haste of a struggle to get started were overlooked. Yet they see an immense deal to be attended and better arranged when they get time. Nor are they *very* intelligent people or very refined and genteel and of high ideals—*any of them*. There are lots of conveniences they might have— that would be necessary to the comfort of some wealthy people, even for you & I prospectively; that they know nothing about &, of course, care nothing about. They are not any of them *first class* people, or if so they have forgotten some of their 5th Avenue notions. I mean *silver-forks* & such like—(napkins.)

One great thing they have succeeded in perfectly. In making *labor*, honorable. Mere *physical* labor they too much elevated, I think, but at any rate the "lowest" & most menial & disagreeable duties of civilized community are made really reputable & honorable. A man who spent a large part of his time in smoking & reading newspapers & talking and recreative employments only would feel ashamed of himself, would feel small & consider it a privilege to be allowed to black boots & sweep and milk for a part of the time.

It is in this way it would do me good to go there. No, not in making labor honorable, but in making idleness disagreeable & labor of all sorts (moderately) agreeable—in removing much that is disagreeable. Thus I should hoe corn very comfortably, if I had you in the next row to talk to about the Shuss cogsslocken del Espelntatzellin,[15] and should black my own shoes & yours too if you paid me for it, if all that I needed to do was to toss them into a hopper and turn the stop-cock and let on the steam.

The whole of work of the community is apportioned to different *groups*. Rather, first to series; as the "Agricultural Series," the "Domestic Series," "Live Stock Series," &c, & the series into groups. Thus, the Agricultural into the market garden, orchard, experimental, marling, &c., groups. The Domestic Series into—Cooking, Washing, Ironing, Baking, Dairy, &c.

On joining the community I enter my name on the list of whatever group I please—thus on the dairy, the orchard and the market-garden. I work an hour, say, at the churn, six hours at picking apples for market, and three at sorting potatoes. I am credited by so much on each of the groups' books. Each group votes on what the time of each member is worth. The ordinary "day's work" is from 90 cents to a dollar.

The *chiefs* of all the groups of a Series hold conclaves with the "chief of a series" & arrange matters for the series. The series chiefs also meet under a head chief or *chief of the phalanx* & legislate on matters of more general character.

THE NORTH AMERICAN PHALANX, c. 1850

A man works at anything that he finds himself suitable for. Many are members of a good many groups. If a man does not work with any group with which he has registered his name during two months, he is considered to have left it, &c. If a man works only occasionally, irregularly, his time is valued at a lower figure.

The dining room is much like that of a first class hotel—spacious & neat & comfortable. Tables arranged as in an eating-house, but large enough for perhaps a dozen to each. The *carte* of each meal lies on the table (*carte du jour*) with the prices (cost) of the dishes, which as you know are very low. But every little item counts. Bread 1 cent, butter ½ cent or 1 cent, plate of ros' beef, 3 cents, &c. Ice cream *"a la français"*—a big saucer full, 2 cents. The cost varies with the season. During drought & short pasture, buttercakes are graduated in stamping a little smaller, &c.[16]

The waiters are the prettiest & most refined and graceful young ladies of the community mainly—some of the "most respectable" young fellows, too. You are introduced to the waitress of your table.

Miss Mundy[17] mine was, a very good-looking, lady-like young woman, intelligent accomplished & well informed—dressed with great taste. It was odd enough & not altogether agreeable to hold a conversation with her upon *social* topics in which she showed a philosophical mind and a cultivated and refined judgement, she bending over my shoulder. She takes part in the general conversation of the table, but comes & goes as there is occasion. Is a very good waiter indeed—clean, sweet, and good-natured.

Why do all the best of the young people choose to be waiters & so be deprived of the social enjoyment of the meals with their friends in a great measure? They all dine to-gether afterwards, and as they *are* the *best*, it is a privilege to dine with them—of course to wait with them. If it was not, they would be paid the best—(or should be.) So the most cultivated of the men are *attached* to the domestic groups (more or less—they generally also attach themselves to some of the out-door-exercising groups as well.) The chief of the series is a French physician.[18] There are other foreigners, fine-looking gentlemen, also in it and among the waiters, head waiters, carvers, &c.

There is one I must speak of particularly. He was son of a wealthy, aristocratic family. Brought up in style; "got religion," became an Episcopal clergyman, was eloquent & much beloved & esteemed. Had a country church with a salary of $1,000. Didn't see that he was doing good. Worried & fretted & studied & prayed & fasted. Concluded the system was wrong & he was not sincere. Gave it up sick of life. Wandered & wasted. Accidentaly came hither. Stayed a week. And one night ran out & threw up his hat & declared the problem was solved. Here was a Christianity as was a Christianity & a church as was a church. Threw off his black coat & asked leave to work. Got tremendously tired, feverish &c. Found it wouldn't [do]. But was determined to work with his hands—"in labor is prayer."—& went into domestic series. And we were introduced to him, a fine, sad, quiet gentlemanly fellow— *peeling potatoes.*

N.B. Nobody blushes or boasts or seems to consider such employ- ments at all to be kept in the dark or anything less of a regular thing than taking off their clothes for themselves when they go to bed. The fact is they have reconstructed a world for themselves & have forgotten the ways of the world *outside.*

I must tell you something of Mr. Arnold's history.[19] He was a merchant in N.Y. greatly interested in Five Point philanthropies.[20] Gave himself much up to them—so too his wife. Both Massachusetts saints. He was finally so much interested in his reforming labors that he gave his whole time to them & the Unitarians made him *minister at large* with a roving commission much such as you would like.

He then threw himself into it. Gave himself to the work—until he got perfectly sickened, disgusted, and overwhelmed. With large means & doing nothing else, he found it was stopping leaks in a rotten ship. The more you stopped the breech up the more it was *widened.* Had a conviction much like that of the Episcopal clergyman that the system was wrong, that the so- called Church of Christ was wrong. That it was not Christianity he was preaching—that Christians did not love-one-another, &c., &c., &c.

Went to the West and found the most solitary place he could & there lived hermit-like with his family for several years. His wife says, it was the greatest relief & happiness to her to feel that there they could do others but *little* harm & others could do them but *little.*

While so situated, Mr. Spring (his wife's brother) went to Europe with * Fuller[21]—& while gone certain Fourierite periodicals that he had taken were sent to him (Arnold). He did not like them, but read them. So did his wife, until after a year both suddenly found each-other converted. They came to the Phalanx & are fully convinced that it must be by this way only that the kingdom shall come.

The arrangement of the dormitories is much like that of a hotel; a large number of small bed-rooms for single parties and suites of rooms for families. There are three or four tenements adjoining the main-house, built into it like a *block* with no communication with it or with each other except by a gallery in the rear to enable the inmates to go to the dining-hall or the work rooms (kitchen &c.) dry shod. There is also one entirely detached cottage.

These families could have their meals sent to them (by some addi- tional payment) but in fact none do—all preferring the common refectory. Here families have their usual tables separate from others if they choose. Families separate, though, a good deal. Husband & wife & the younger children generally together, but the older children "follow their attractions." That is, being generally *engaged* as soon as they are big enough, they sit with their espoused.

In the evening from supper till 10 o'clock or later there was a good deal of recreation, walking parties, rowing parties, dancing & music. There are 6 pianos in the establishment & several guitars, &c. There was a music teacher & a French teacher. Also one of the French refugees[22] teaches fencing & dancing, &c. But recreation of this sort was not *general*. The less cultivated however spent the evening much more elevatingly than most country people do—in conversation & discussions. There is very little reading done.

Most of the young ladies & some of the older men dressed *à la Bloomer*, generally not very tastefully. Some appeared to much greater advantage when so than in long skirts. A graceful *action* was much more graceful and gratifying where the movement of the leg could be seen. Some were very short skirted. Usually the kilt reached an inch or two below the knee, or enough to reach over it in sitting. Not always though. There was the most perfect natural propriety & good sense among them all. The Bloomer has been naturalized, and in an hour you are as accustomed to it as you would be in China. It is "all right." Many who wore Bloomer in A.M. were in "evening dresses" later. Some appeared better & some worse for the change.

As to creeds, the majority are Swedenborgians, but there is nothing peculiar to the community. I should think persons of all the great nominally Christian churches from Catholics to Unitarians, or rationalists.

The very shortest Bloomer had me by the button sitting under the trees for half the evening telling me of her Spiritual Supping experience. She had had, during two months, frequent intercourse with her father who died eight years ago while she was a child, & received most delightful words from, and practical advice and assistance. She believed it all as fully as she did or could anything not absolutely tangible. She recognized the influence of spirits constantly upon her as she did heat & light. It was a regular thing. Thought there was much humbug. Foxes & Fishes were imposters.[23] Others fools—self deceived. Her yarn didn't amount to much. She was a person that would be easily imposed upon.

I have been, since last sheet, reading Tribune of Saturday (23rd.) If you haven't it's worth it—on Spiritual Manifestations & the *Shekinah* article on Judge Edmonds.[24] And I add a little more.

She was convinced or held her faith entirely from the *moral* evidence —the general character of the communications she had received. First, though, she was startled by receiving answers to questions and suggestions in her own mind which she had not uttered or expressed in any way. As for material manifestations, she had certainly seen tables lifted and taken across a room. She had stood on a table and been moved gently and steadily across the room & back to the exact spots on the carpet that the legs occupied before—no person being near the table, at 4 o'clock P.M., open daylight. It was in Massachusetts last spring or winter. The table was moved at her request to give evidence of the ability of the spirits to exercise material agency. Was guided as she directed, &c. As I said, she was the sort of person that would be easily imposed on and be run away with by her own imagination. Nevertheless, her facts & her faith impressed me with a little more respect for the matter.

As to the people of the community in general, I have a strong respect for them as hard-working, earnest, unselfish livers in the faith of a higher life for man on earth as well as "above." There were fewer odd characters than I should have expected to find. Generally, there was much simplicity and self-containedness among them. I think they are living devoutly & more in accordance with the principles of Christ—*among themselves*—than any equal number of persons I ever saw living in the usual neighborhood intercourse together.

There is a certain class that they very much need to have associated with them. I could not help wishing Charles Elliott had joined them. Believing a good deal in their principles as I believe he does, he would have been exceedingly useful to them. They much need mechanics, but I think it is the fault of their theory that they do not have them. Their success without them is the more wonderful. I believe they have only one carpenter & a watch maker, or some such nearly useless thing to them. Having to pay high, of course, for all mechanics brought to do work for them from a distance.

What they need for improvement as a community of moral creatures is more attention to the intellectual. They want an *Educational Series* very much. They have no fit teacher—a Frenchman for want of a better acts as schoolmaster to the fry. But there is no proper nursery department & the children, & not the children alone, are growing without any proper discipline of mind.[25] A rum set one would think they would make. But I must confess those who are breaking into manhood & especially into womanhood tell well for the system. They are young *ladies* & young *gentlemen*. Naturally and without effort or consciousness, so.[26]

You had better go there next fall. I'll go with you. Mr. Arnold was sorry you didn't come with us. And others would be glad to see you. If you could give them a lecture on Hungary they would be gratified. Hadn't you better get one up—with some reference to present position of things? Remodel your old one a little. I told them you would come bye & bye.[27]

If we can make a boating-party for several days it will be pleasant in peach season—*October* rather too late. Charles Elliott ought to go with us. Be valuable to him as a market gardener.

All the folks here. Nothing of importance. Beckwith not yet bought. In a fortnight I may leave home for a little while.

Yours Affectionately,

Fred.

P.S. I have condensed this for the Tribune. Told them if they didn't want to print it to direct to you & you would get it at the office.

1. This letter describes a visit Olmsted made to the North American Phalanx, a Fourierist community at Red Bank, N.J., fifteen miles south of his Staten Island farm. At its creation in 1843 it was intended to be the prime demonstration in the United States of the validity of the theories of social organization of the French psychologist, philosopher, and social reformer, François Marie Charles Fourier. Albert Brisbane, a student of Fourier's and his leading American disciple, helped to organize the venture, and Horace Greeley provided some of his own funds and the publicity of his *New York Daily Tribune*.

By the time Olmsted made his visit to the North American Phalanx, the Fourierist phase of American social reform had almost run its course. Of the many phalanxes founded in the mid-1840s, the North American alone remained, and Olmsted saw it in the last year of its success. In 1853, a decade after its founding, a large group seceded and formed the Raritan Bay Union nearby. The North American struggled on, but the destruction of its mills by fire in September 1854 dealt it a deathblow, and by early 1856 it had broken up.

At the same time that he wrote Brace about his visit, Olmsted sent a similar letter to the *New York Daily Tribune* that appeared on July 29, 1852 under the heading "Association," with the title "The Phalanstery and the Phalansterians. By An Outsider." Olmsted signed the letter "An American Farmer" (John Humphrey Noyes, *History of American Socialisms* [1870; rpt. ed., New York, 1961], pp. 449, 487–99).

2. Charles Wyllys Elliott (1817–1883), author, landscape gardener, and interior decorator, born at Guilford. In 1838–39 he studied landscape gardening and horticulture with Andrew Jackson Downing and followed those pursuits for the next eight years in Cincinnati, Ohio. He then spent a decade in the iron business in New York with his brother Henry. During that time he became one of the founders of the Children's Aid Society, of which Charles Loring Brace was director, and was a commissioner of Central Park from 1857 to 1860. In 1857 he told Olmsted of an opportunity to become superintendent of the park and helped bring about his appointment to that post, which soon led to his collaboration with Calvert Vaux in creating the prize-winning "Greensward" design for the park. After the Civil War, Elliott was manager of the Household Art Company of Boston. He wrote books on a variety of subjects. Two of them, *Cottages and Cottage Life* and *The Book of American Interiors* show that he shared Olmsted's concern for fostering taste and domesticity in American society (*NCAB*, 13: 465; Wilimena H. Emerson, Ellsworth Eliot, and George E. Eliot, comps., *Genealogy of the Descendants of John Eliot, "Apostle to the Indians," 1598–1905* [New Haven, 1905], pp. 124, 159–61; Charles W. Elliott listed as a park commissioner in the first, second, and third annual reports of the Board of Commissioners of Central Park [1858–60]).

3. Alfred T. Field, his wife, Charlotte Errington Field (c. 1817–1880), and their daughter Rosa (d. 1931).

Dr. Charles Neidhard (1809–1895) of Philadelphia was one of the founders of homeopathic medicine in the United States. Born in Bremen, Germany, he migrated to the United States c. 1825 when his stepfather, the political economist Georg Friedrich List, was banished from Germany. After receiving medical training in Philadelphia, Neidhard was converted to homeopathy. He practiced it continuously after 1836 and built up a large practice in Philadelphia. He had visited the

North American Phalanx at least once before, in 1847 (London *Times*, March 3, 1931, p. 19; *DAB*, s.v. "Neidhard, Charles"; J. H. Noyes, *American Socialisms*, pp. 471–73).

4. That is, Brace's letters on Hungary in the *Philadelphia Bulletin* and his book *Hungary in 1851*, published in April 1852 (*Life of Brace*, pp. 122, 149).
5. The Navesink Highlands are in northeastern New Jersey, south of Sandy Hook between Sandy Hook Bay and the Navesink River.
6. Benjamin Pierce, a Staten Island neighbor, who sailed a sloop for John Hull Olmsted on a September excursion (JHO to Mary Olmsted, Sept. 20, 1948).
7. A public stage coach.
8. In his letter in the *New York Daily Tribune* of July 29, 1852, Olmsted wrote, "There are six hundred acres of land in the domain of the Association, most of it of the ordinary quality of 'Jersey land.' About two hundred acres are under cultivation, much improved within a few years by dressing with marl, two beds of which, of superior quality, are on the property." Marl is a deposit of clay mixed with calcium carbonate and was used to fertilize soils deficient in lime. In the region of Red Bank there are many outcroppings of sedimentary Hornestone marl, a mixture of greensand marl or glauconite, clay, sand, and marine fossils. It was used extensively in the area after 1820 for restoring the fertility of worn-out soil (Hubert G. Schmidt, *Agriculture in New Jersey; A Three-Hundred-Year History* [New Brunswick, N.J., 1973], pp. 129–31).
9. In his *Tribune* letter Olmsted wrote, "A stream of water running through it, gives a small milling-power. . . . The Association have a grist and saw-mill driven with the aid of a steam engine that they have added to the small water-power" (*New York Daily Tribune*, July 29, 1852, p. 6).
10. In his *Tribune* letter Olmsted expanded this description: "There is some pretty natural wood and a picturesque ravine near the house, but no garden or pleasure ground; indeed the *grounds* about the house are wholly neglected, and have a shabby and uninviting appearance. It is evident that the Association have neglected everything else in their endeavor to make the experiment successful, financially" (ibid.).
11. Emanuel Swedenborg (1688–1772), the Swedish philosopher and mystic whose doctrines had considerable appeal for a generation of reformers fascinated by spiritualism and convinced of the perfectibility of man and society. Olmsted asserts that a majority of the members of the North American Phalanx were Swedenborgians. He seems to be alone in this: at least, none of the accounts compiled by John Humphrey Noyes in his *History of American Socialisms* make that claim. The Fourierists did, however, attempt to attract members of the Swedenborgian Church of the New Jerusalem by asserting the basic unity of the teachings of Fourier and Swedenborg. As one propagandist said, "The doctrines of the two men cannot remain separate. Their union constitutes the union of Science and Religion" (see Marguerite Block, *The New Church in the New World: A Study of Swedenborgianism in America* [New York, 1932], pp. 150–60).
12. Marcus Spring (1810–1874), a New York commission merchant and promoter of associational experiments. He was a director of the North American Phalanx, in which he invested $5,000. In 1853 he was one of the group that seceded from the North American and formed the Raritan Bay Union at Eagleswood, N.J., outside Perth Amboy. His wife, Rebecca Buffum Spring, was the daughter of Arnold Buffum, a Rhode Island Quaker and first president of the New England Anti-Slavery Society (Records of the Phalanx Realization Fund Society in North American Phalanx Papers, Houghton Library, Harvard University, Cambridge, Mass.; Maude Honeyman Green, "Raritan Bay Union, Eagleswood, New Jersey," *Proceedings of the New Jersey Historical Society* 68, no. 1 [Jan. 1950]: 4–8, 19).
13. Lydia Spring Arnold (1801–1854), sister of Marcus Spring, born in Northbridge, Mass. She was the wife of George B. Arnold, president of the North American Phalanx (*Vital Records of Northbridge, Mass., to the Year 1850*, comp. Thomas W. Baldwin [Boston, 1916], p. 78; Greenwood Cemetery Records, Greenwood Cemetery, Brooklyn, New York; M. H. Greene, "Raritan Bay Union," p. 7).

14. In his *Tribune* letter Olmsted took special note of the way communal sharing of domestic tasks and the application of mechanical power to them lessened the burden on women: "A small steam-engine is employed for washing, mangling, churning, &c., and the arrangements of the domestic department are all admirably contrived for saving labor. I should guess roughly that one woman could do the work of ten, with the ordinary farm-house kitchen conveniences—in other words, as far [as] this goes, farmers would save their wives and *women folk* all but one-tenth of their now necessary drudgery by living on the associated plan" (*New York Daily Tribune*, July 29, 1852, p. 6).
15. Olmsted apparently intended this as a ponderous German nonsense-phrase.
16. This painstaking system for distributing the cost of food fairly was devised only after the failure of a system of common sharing of food and expenses. Apparently some slackers or "birds of prey" hovered near the refectory as meal-time approached and grabbed the choice morsels for themselves, causing the adoption of the procedure Olmsted describes (J. H. Noyes, *American Socialisms*, pp. 503–5).
17. Either Lucy Munday or Hannah Bell Munday, both of whom were at the Phalanx in December 1852 ("Records for the Council of the Chiefs of the Phalanx" for March 5, 1854, MS at Monmouth County Historical Society, Freehold, N.J.; J. H. Noyes, *American Socialisms*, p. 467).
18. Emile Guillaudeu, Jr. (b. 1812), was listed as chief of the Domestic Series in 1849 and 1854, and probably held that position in 1852 ("Records for the Council" for Dec. 12, 1849 and Jan. 6, 1854; U.S. Census Records for 1850: Red Bank).
19. George B. Arnold (1803–1889), president of the Phalanx, served as minister to the poor for the Unitarian societies of New York City from 1834 to at least 1837. From 1837 to 1849 he lived in Alton, Ill., where he established a nursery.

He returned to the East for the sake of his children and joined the North American Phalanx. In 1853 he took part in the secession from the North American that led to the formation of the Raritan Bay Union, and became president of that society. After the failure of this experiment he turned his attention to mechanical invention, which he had already practiced at Raritan Bay and the North American. He devoted his later life to scientific pursuits and the practice and investigation of spiritualism (*DAB; New York Times*, Feb. 3, 1889, p. 3; Fredrika Bremer, *Homes in the New World*, pp. 76–77, 84; M. H. Greene, "Raritan Bay Union," pp. 4–8; J. H. Noyes, *American Socialisms*, pp. 488, 508–11).
20. The Five Points section of Manhattan was notorious for its squalor and traffic in vice, and was the focus of concern for several religious and humanitarian groups. At this time Brace was working at the Five Points House of Industry, run by the Reverend Lewis Morris Pease (*Life of Brace*, p. 153; *Monthly Record of the Five Points House of Industry* 41, no. 3 [July 1897], pp. 33–34; Robert H. Bremner, *From the Depths: The Discovery of Poverty in the United States* [New York, 1956], p. 5).
21. Sarah Margaret Fuller (1810–1850), American journalist, critic, and social reformer. When she served as literary editor of Horace Greeley's *New York Daily Tribune* in the mid-1840s she signed many of her articles with a large asterisk. She accompanied the Marcus Springs to Europe in August 1846 and they returned without her in 1847 (Thomas Wentworth Higginson, *Margaret Fuller Ossoli* [Boston, 1884], p. 216; Margaret Bell, *Margaret Fuller, A Biography* . . . [New York, 1930], pp. 191, 195, 246).
22. A number of refugees from the French Revolution of 1848 and its aftermath became members of the North American Phalanx (Norma Lippincott Swan, "The North American Phalanx," *Monmouth County Historical Association Bulletin* 1, no. 1 [May 1935]: 62; Julia Bucklin Giles, "Address of Julia Bucklin Giles before the Monmouth County Historical Association," November 18, 1922, typescript in Monmouth County Historical Association, Freehold, New Jersey, p. 16).
23. The spiritualist mediums Margaret Fox (c. 1833–1893), Catherine Fox (c. 1839–1892), and Ann Leah Fox Fish (c. 1818–1890). In 1848 Margaret and "Katie" began to hear spirit rappings, and within two years, under the management of Leah,

they embarked on public demonstrations of their ability to contact the spirit world. These served as a powerful impetus to the spread of belief in spiritualism in the United States and in England and Europe as well (*Notable American Women*, s.v. "Fox, Ann, Leah, Margaret, and Catherine").

24. John Worth Edmonds (1799–1874), New York Supreme Court justice, prison reformer, and spiritualist. On July 24, 1852, the *New York Daily Tribune* reviewed the first volume of the *Shekinah*, a spiritualist journal, and reprinted from it an account of Edmonds's reception of spiritual messages from his wife (*DAB*; Alice Felt Tyler, *Freedom's Ferment: Phases of American Social History from the Colonial Period to the Civil War* [1944; rpt. ed., New York, 1962], pp. 419–22).

25. An educational series was not set up until November 30, 1853. By that time the seceders who founded the Raritan Bay Union had improved greatly upon the situation at the North American. They brought in the famous abolitionist preacher Theodore Dwight Weld, his wife Angelina Grimké Weld, and her sister Sarah Grimké to run a school there. It was a great success and attracted students from afar (M. H. Greene, "Raritan Bay Union," pp. 10–12; "Records for the Council" for January 3, 1854).

26. In his *Tribune* letter Olmsted added, "If I had a boy to educate, who at sixteen had acquired home habits of continued persevering application of mind in study, and who was tolerably stocked with facts and formulas, I would a good deal prefer that he should spend the next few years of his life as a working member of the North American Phalanx than at Yale or Harvard" (*New York Daily Tribune*, July 29, 1852, p. 6).

27. Brace delivered a number of lectures on Hungary after his return from there in December 1851 (*Life of Brace*, p. 148; FLO to JO, Feb. 24, 1852).

APPENDIXES

1

CHRONOLOGY
OF FREDERICK LAW OLMSTED

1822–1852

1822

April 26   Born in Hartford, Connecticut.

1825

September 2   His brother, John Hull Olmsted, born.

1826

Febuary 28   His mother, Charlotte Law Hull Olmsted, dies.

April   Begins schooling at the first of three "dame's schools" he will attend in Hartford.

1827

April 25   His father, John Olmsted, and Mary Ann Bull marry.

June 3   He and his brother are baptized.

1828

April 20 to
August 2   Visits his uncle Owen Pitkin Olmsted in Geneseo, New York; goes to Niagara Falls.

1829

November 9 to
September 27,
1830   Boards and studies with Zolva Whitmore in North Guilford, Connecticut.

1830

September 28 to

May 1831   Attends Hartford Grammar School.

1831

May 18 to

September   Attends Ellington High School in Ellington, Connecticut.

October 8 to

April 30,

1836   Boards and studies with Joab Brace in Newington, Connecticut.

1836

Spring   Suffers severe sumach poisoning, causing temporary partial blindness.

July 1 to

August 16   Boards and studies with George Van Vechten Eastman in Saybrook, Connecticut.

September 5   He and his brother, John, attend Hartford Grammar School.

December 1 to

June 1837   Attends academy (Edgar Perkins, principal) in East Hartford.

1837

November 19 to

November 9,

1838   Boards and studies with Frederick A. Barton at Andover, Massachusetts.

1838

August 8 to 22   Travels to the White Mountains and New Hampshire coast with his father, stepmother, and brother, John.

December 19 to

April 6,

1840   Boards and studies with Frederick A. Barton in Collinsville, Connecticut.

1839

December 9

to 24   Travels with his father to Washington, D.C.

1840

May 9 to
November 3   His brother, John, travels to Europe and studies in Paris.

August 18 to
March 1842   Works in New York for dry-goods importing firm of
Benkard and Hutton.

1842

September 28   His brother, John, enters Yale College.

Fall   Visits John at Yale.

1843

March 27 to
April 7   Goes to New York, ships on bark *Ronaldson*, bound for
Canton.

April 23   *Ronaldson* sails for Canton.

September 8   *Ronaldson* anchors in Whampoa Reach, near Canton.

December 30   *Ronaldson* sails for New York from Whampoa.

1844

January 27 to
April   His brother, John, goes to West Indies for his health.

April 15   *Ronaldson* arrives in New York.

October 30 to
March 21,
1845   Visits and studies at the farm of his uncle David Brooks
in Cheshire, Connecticut.

1845

May 12 to
August 13   Lives and studies farming with Joseph Welton in
Waterbury, Connecticut.

October 1 to
January 7,
1846   Attends lectures of Professor Benjamin Silliman at Yale
College.

1846

February 16   His half-sister Ada Theodosia dies, age six.

April 10   Leaves Hartford and goes to George Geddes's farm in
Camillus, New York.

August 27 to
September 10   Travels with his father and brother to Niagara Falls, Montreal, Quebec, Lake Champlain, and Lake George. Returns to Geddes farm.

October 4   Returns to Hartford.

November 10   His father buys him a farm at Sachem's Head, Guilford, Connecticut.

1847

February   Moves to Sachem's Head.

August   His brother, John, graduates from Yale.

1848

January 1   His father buys him a farm on Staten Island.

March 5   Moves to Staten Island.

October   His brother, John, arrives in New York to study medicine.

1849

February 6 to
March 8   In Hartford: reads Macaulay's *History of England* with Emily Perkins, and Ruskin's *Modern Painters* with Sophie Stevens.

Fall   Is elected corresponding secretary of the newly formed Richmond County Agricultural Society on Staten Island.

1850

February   His brother, John, and Mary Perkins announce their engagement.

April 30   Sails for England with his brother, John, and Charles Loring Brace.

May 27 to
c. June 21   Travels from Liverpool to London, much of the way on foot.

July 9 to
August 10   Travels in France, Belgium, and Germany.

August 10 to
October 4   Travels in England, Ireland, and Scotland.

October 4   Sails from Glasgow.

October 24   Arrives in New York.

1851

April 29	Frederick Kingsbury and Alathea Scovill marry.
May	"The People's Park at Birkenhead, Near Liverpool" published in the *Horticulturist*.
August	Briefly engaged to Emily Perkins.
August 5	His brother, John, suffers severe lung hemorrhage, confirming that he has tuberculosis.
October 16	His brother, John, and Mary Perkins marry.
December	"A Voice From the Sea" published in the *American Whig Review*.

1852

January	"A Note on the True Soldat Labourer Pear" published in the *Horticulturist*.
February 18	*Walks and Talks of an American Farmer in England*, volume 1, published by George Palmer Putnam.
July 29	"The Phalanstery and Phalansterians" published in the *New-York Daily Tribune*.

II

GENEALOGICAL CHARTS

HULL FAMILY

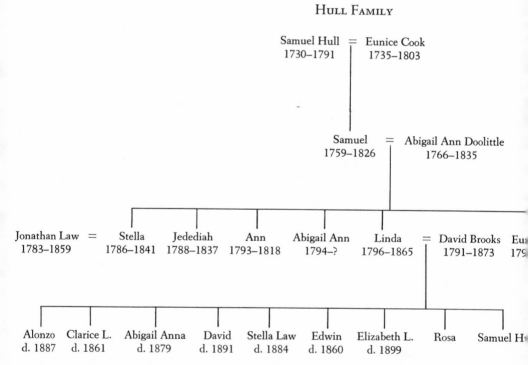

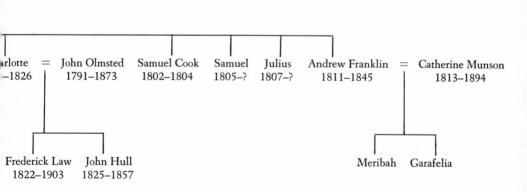

rlotte = John Olmsted   Samuel Cook   Samuel   Julius   Andrew Franklin = Catherine Munson
–1826   1791–1873   1802–1804   1805–?   1807–?   1811–1845   1813–1894

Frederick Law   John Hull   Meribah   Garafelia
1822–1903   1825–1857

OLMSTED FAMILY I

Jonathan Olmsted = Hannah Meakins
1706–1770   1717–1806

Joseph   Jonathan   Epaphras   Mary   Hannah   Gideon   Benjamin   = Content Pitkin   Aaron   Ezekiel   John
1739–?   1740–?   1742–1836   1744–1825   1746/7–1814 1748/9–1845 1751–1832   1752–1839   1753–1806   1755–1782   1761–?

Elizabeth   Frederick   Theodosia   Ezekiel   John   Owen Pitkin   Maria
1776–1825   1779–1818   1782–1822   1785–1829   1791–1873   1794–1873   1798–1859

Olmsted Family II

Samuel Hull = Abigail Ann Doolittle
1759–1828   1766–1835

Benjamin Olmsted = Content Pitkin
1751–1832   1752–1859

Isaac D. Bull = Mary Watson
1774–1849   1773–1859

Charlotte Hull
1800–1826

John Olmsted
1791–1873

Mary Ann Bull
1801–1894

= (John Olmsted = Charlotte Hull)

= (John Olmsted = Mary Ann Bull)

Children of John Olmsted and Charlotte Hull:

Frederick Law   John Hull
1822–1903   1825–1857

Children of John Olmsted and Mary Ann Bull:

Charlotte   Mary   Bertha   Owen   Ada Theodosia   Albert Henry
1828–1832   1832–1875   1834–1926   1836–1838   1839–1846   1842–1929

Frederick Law = Mary Cleveland Bryant Perkins
1822–1903   1830–1921

John Hull children:
John Charles   Charlotte   Owen Frederick
1852–1920   1855–1908   1857–1881

Frederick Law children:
John Theodore   Marion   Son   Frederick Law
1860   1861–1948   1866   1870–1957

NAME INDEX

Italic numbers indicate illustrations.

Basset, Sheldon (d. 1865), 204, 206
Baumann, Eugene A., 33
Beaumont, Dr. William, 285
Beecher, Henry Ward (1813–1887), 89, 229, 360, 361, 367, 370
Beecher, James (1828–1886), 324, 325
Beecher, Lyman (1775–1863), 68, 89, 113, 229, 329
Beecher, Mary Foote. *See* Perkins, Mary Beecher
Beecher, Thomas Kinnicut (1824–1900), 89, 269, 327, 329, 330
Beelzebub, 314
Bellows, Henry Whitney (1814–1882), 24, 25
Belmont, August, 19
Benkard, James A., 5, 238, 239
Beresford, Samuel B. (1806–1873), 165, 170, 291, 292
Billings, Frederick (1823–1890), 30
Birge, Backus W., 224
Birge, Henry Warner (1825–1888), 223, 224
Birge, Lucy Ripley (Mrs. Backus W. Birge; Mrs. Roderick Terry), 224
Birney, James G., 124
Bissell, George P. (1827–1891), 252, 254, 261, 262
Blake, Eli Whitney, 235
Blake, Henrietta (1825–1901), 233, 235, 254, 255
Blaken, Henry William, 328, 331
Bonaparte, Napoleon, 318
Bonnard, John, 239
Bordenave, C. P., 125, 127
"Boston Jack," 160, 169, 174, 176, 177, 178, 181
Boutwell, George S., 371
Bowles, Samuel (1826–1878), 31, 32
Boyd, Ann, 279, 281
Brace, Abel, 296, 297
Brace, Anna Pierce (Mrs. Charles G. Loring), 269
Brace, Charles Loring (1826–1890), 7, 8, 9, 10, 12, 16, 19, 40, 72, 80, 81, 82, 86, 89, 121, 122, 125, 130, 139, 140, 162, 166, 170, 192, 196, 201, 202, 207, 216, 224, 234, 235, 236, 237, 239, 240, 250, 252, 254, 261, 264, 265, 269, 282, 283, 286, 291, 292, 304, 317, 322, 327, 329, 336, 337, 338, 339, 340, 341, 354, 360, 361, 362, 368, 369, 372, 374, 384, 386, 387, 394; biography of, 67–71
Brace, Emma (1828–1850), 8, 210, 216, 221, 227, 228, 229, 238, 239, 240, 241, 244, 245, 250, 251, 254, 255, 269, 270, 323; biography of, 71
Brace, Henry Martin (1828–1901), 322, 323
Brace, James, 67
Brace, Joab (1781–1861), 4, 108, 108, 109, 110, 112, 175, 181, 392; house of, 107
Brace, John Pierce (1793–1872), 67, 68, 71, 207, 210, 221, 223, 241, 242, 274, 285
Brace, Letitia Neill (Mrs. Charles Loring Brace). *See* Neill, Letitia
Brace, Lucy Porter, 68
Brace, Mary (Mrs. John Warburton Skinner) (1820–1903), 201, 202, 224, 234, 235, 241, 242
Brace family, 234, 235, 241
Brady, John (c. 1798–1854), 331
Bragg, Braxton (1817–1876), 270
Braisted, Jacob T., 136, 138, 139, 141, 147, 160, 176, 177, 180
Braisted, William (father of Jacob T.), 138, 139
Bremer, Fredrika, 365, 369
Brewer, William (1828–1910), 31
Bright, John, 343, 349
Brisbane, Albert, 384
Bristol, Abigail Munson (Mrs. Ryer Bristol) (1810–1889), 206
Bristol, Ryer (1811–1871), 206
Brognard, Mary B., 327, 330
Bronson, Greene Carrier (1789–1863), 296, 298
Brooks, Abigail Anna Hull (Mrs. Porter LeConte) (c. 1818–1879), 272, 273, 274, 327, 330
Brooks, Alonzo (d. 1887), 203, 205
Brooks, David (1791–1873), 6, 191, 199, 202, 204, 260, 261, 274, 288, 393
Brooks, Edwin M. (1831–1860), 327, 330
Brooks, Elizabeth Laura (1829–1899), 273, 274, 280, 281, 327, 330
Brooks, Jeremiah (c. 1792–1846), 259, 260, 261
Brooks, Linda Hull (1796–1865), 120, 202, 274
Brooks family, 396, 397
Brown, John Carter (1797–1874), 343
Brown, Lancelot "Capability," 10
Browne, Hablot Knight, 169
Brunel, Isambard Kingdom, 127
Bryant, William Cullen (1794–1878), 18, 19, 283, 363
Buchanan, James, 223

Mary Beatrice of Modena (1658–1718), 329

Mather, Cotton (1662/63–1727/28), 280, 281

Matson, William N. (1812–1876), 125, 127

May, Charles A., 267, 270

Mayne, Sir Richard (1796–1868), 22

Mead, William R. (1846–1928), 44

Melville, Herman (1819–1891), 17

Metternich, Clemens Lothar von, 316, 318

Mill, James, 7

Milnes, Richard Moncton (1809–1885), 346, 349

Milton, John, 279, 299

Mitchell, Donald Grant (1822–1908), 216

Monds, Joseph P., 156, 158, 193, 195, 196

Monds, Maria (c. 1819–1845), 193, 196

Monroe, James, 258

Morell, John Daniel (1816–1891), 355, 357

Morell, John Reynell, 357

Morris, Amos (b. 1750), 259, 261

Morrison, John Robert (1814–1843), 154, 157, 158

Morrison, Robert, 138

Morton, John, 362

Morton, Peter (1801–1846), 135, 137, 166, 170, 172

Moses, 231, 300

Muir, Sarah Jane (b. 1841), 326

Munday, Hannah Bell, 386

Munday, Lucy, 386

Munson, Levi (1783–1844), 204, 206

Murray, John (1808–1892), 368, 372

Neidhard, Charles (1809–1895), 375, 384

Neill, Dora, 361

Neill, Eliza, 361

Neill, John, 360, 362

Neill, Letitia (Mrs. Charles Loring Brace) (1822?–1916), 69, 361, 362, 368, 372

Neill, Robert, 69, 359, 361, 362, 372

Nesfield, W. E., 10

Nettleton, Asahel (1783–1844), 113

Nicholas I (czar of Russia), 316, 318

Niles, John Milton (1787–1856), 273, 275

Niles, William, 356

North, Christopher. See Wilson, John

Norton, Charles Eliot (1827–1908), 29, 40

Norton, John Pitkin (1822–1852), 216, 237, 341, 342

Norton, John Treadwell (1795–1869), 126, 127, 236, 237, 259, 261, 275, 277

Nott, Eliphalet (1773–1866), 19

Nott, Joel B. (1797–1878), 19

Noyes, John Humphrey (1811–1886), 385

O'Connell, Daniel (1775–1847), 164, 170

Olmsted, Aaron (1753–1806) (great-uncle), 112, 178, 182

Olmsted, Ada Theodosia (1839–1846) (half-sister), 126, 127, 128, 172, 181, 232, 393

Olmsted, Albert H. (1842–1929) (half-brother), 143, 175, 254, 262

Olmsted, Benjamin (1751–1832) (grandfather), 106, 111, 114, 119

Olmsted, Mrs. Benjamin. See Olmsted, Content Pitkin

Olmsted, Bertha (1834–1926) (half-sister), 91, 128, 129, 171, 172, 173, 181, 323, 324, 325, 326, 360, 362

Olmsted, Charles Hyde (1798–1878) (cousin), 115, 120, 156, 158, 179, 182, 354, 356

Olmsted, Charlotte (1855–1908) (step-daughter), 88

Olmsted, Charlotte Hull (Law) (Mrs. John Olmsted) (1800–1826) (mother), 4, 84, 86, 99, 110, 119, 262, 391

Olmsted, Content Pitkin (Mrs. Benjamin Olmsted) (1752–1839) (grandmother), 106, 111, 114, 196

Olmsted, Cornelia (1821–1869), 200

Olmsted, Denison (1791–1859), 200, 216, 220, 235, 326

Olmsted, Epaphras (1742–1836) (great-uncle), 112, 119

Olmsted, Ezekiel (1755–1782) (great-uncle), 112, 119

Olmsted, Frances E. (Fanny) (1829–1907) (cousin), 143, 171, 172, 181, 183, 260, 262, 274, 323, 325

Olmsted, Frederick Law (1822–1903), frontispiece, 264, 265

Education and formative experiences:
——agricultural training, 6, 7, 191–92, 212, 235, 339
——formal schooling, 4, 6, 100, 103–4, 105–6, 108–13, 120, 192, 269
——informal learning, 100–105, 117, 119–20, 158, 165, 226

Olmsted, John Charles (1852–1920) (step-son), 22, 31, 39, 41, 45, 87
Olmsted, John Hull (1825–1857) (brother), 4, 6, 8, 9, 10, 11, 13, 14, 15, 18, 20, 22, 46, 48, 68, 69, 71, 80, 81, 84, 87, 89, 91, 100, 110, 121, 122, 124, 125, 126, 127, 130, 140, 143, 153, 171, 172, 179, 180, 183, 184, 185, 192, 194, 195, 215, 216, 221, 227, 229, 239, 241, 244, 252, 254, 255, 256, 259, 261, 264, 265, 269, 273, 276, 277, 280, 282, 283, 284, 291, 297, 298, 312, 313, 319, 329, 331, 336, 337, 338, 339, 340, 341, 342, 354, 355, 358, 360, 362, 365, 367, 368, 372, 377, 385, 391, 392, 393, 394, 395; biography of, 86–88
Olmsted, Jonathan (1706–1770) (great-grandfather), 106, 112
Olmsted, Jonathan (b. 1740) (great-uncle), 112
Olmsted, Joseph (1654–1726), 200
Olmsted, Julia Mason (1832–1880), 324, 326
Olmsted, Lucius (1827–1862), 234, 235
Olmsted, Maria (1798–1859) (aunt), 129, 131, 139, 140, 143, 146, 169, 171, 172, 181, 183, 190, 319, 321, 324, 329, 331
Olmsted, Mary (1832–1875) (half-sister), 127, 129, 171, 172, 323, 324, 325
Olmsted, Mary Bull (Mrs. John Olmsted) (1801–1894) (stepmother), 4, 5, 84, 99, 100, 105, 110, 127, 128, 129, 198, 199, 225, 276, 277, 324, 325, 331, 391, 392
Olmsted, Mary Cleveland Bryant Perkins (Mrs. John Hull Olmsted) (sister-in-law and wife). See Perkins, Mary Cleveland Bryant
Olmsted, Owen Frederick (1857–1881) (son), 22, 88
Olmsted, Owen Pitkin (1794–1873) (uncle), 105, 110, 111, 260, 262, 271, 274, 391
Olmsted family, 398–99
Olmstede, Martin de, 356
Olmstede, Maurice de, 356
Olyphant, David W. C. (1789–1851), 135, 137, 138
Omer, Edward ("Old Davis"), 165, 166, 170
Opdyke, George (1805–1880), 28
Overbagh, Captain B., 240

Pacifico, Don David (1784–1854), 349
Page, Sophia Stevens Hitchcock (Mrs.

William Page). See Stevens, Sophia Candace
Page, William (1811–1885), 92, 93
Paredes y Arrillaga, 268, 270
Park, Trenor William (1823–1882), 28, 29, 30
Parker, Foxhall A. (d. 1857), 157
Parker, Harriet Colby Webster (1818–1896), 171, 173
Parker, Mary Ann Bissel (Mrs. Willard Parker) (1815–1896), 360, 362
Parker, Mary M., 274
Parker, Peter (1804–1888), 156, 157, 158, 171, 173
Parker, Theodore (1810–1860), 12, 16
Parker, Willard (1800–1884), 8, 362
Parker, Willard, Jr. (1850–1907), 362
Parkes, Josiah (1793–1871), 121, 341, 343, 354
Parsons, Samuel Bowne (1819–1906), 341, 343
Paul, Saint, 279, 281, 299, 300, 302, 367
Paxton, Sir Joseph (1801–1865), 9, 369
Pease, Lewis Morris (1818–1897), 386
Peel, Lady (Mrs. Robert Peel), 344
Peel, Sir Robert (1788–1850), 336, 343, 344, 347, 348, 349, 355
Peet, William (1822–1895), 130, 131, 166, 170
Penn, William, 298
Perkins, Cyrus (1779–1849), 7, 22
Perkins, Edgar, 392
Perkins, Emily Baldwin (Mrs. Edward Everett Hale) (1829–1914), 11, 22, 66, 67, 81, 83, 90, 229, 284, 323, 324, 325, 326, 327, 328, 329, 362, 394, 395; biography of, 89–91
Perkins, Francis (1808–1889), 338, 342
Perkins, Frederick (1828–1899), 89
Perkins, Mary Beecher (Mrs. Thomas Clap Perkins) (1805–1900), 11, 89, 227, 228, 229, 324, 326, 327, 329
Perkins, Mary Cleveland Bryant (Mrs. John Hull Olmsted; Mrs. Frederick Law Olmsted) (1830–1921), 11, 22, 86, 87, 88, 89, 90, 91, 342, 394, 395
Perkins, Thomas Clap (1798–1870), 11, 81, 89, 227, 229
Perkins family, 86
Peter, Saint, 300, 301, 302
Phillips, Stephen C. (1801–1857), 367, 371
Pierce, Benjamin, 375, 385
Pierce, James (1779–1846), 240–41
Pierce, Mary (1781–1863), 67, 240, 241, 263, 269

413

414

SUBJECT INDEX